GREENHOUSE
GARDENER'S COMPANION

GREENHOUSE
GARDENER'S COMPANION

REVISED AND EXPANDED EDITION

Growing Food and Flowers in Your Greenhouse or Sunspace

SHANE SMITH

Illustrations by Marjorie C. Leggitt

Fulcrum Publishing • Golden, Colorado

Dedicated to my wife and partner, Paige

Library of Congress Cataloging-in-Publication Data

Smith, Shane.
Greenhouse gardener's companion : growing food and flowers in your greenhouse or sunspace / Shane Smith ; illustrations by Marjorie C. Leggitt.—Rev. ed.
        p. cm.
Includes bibliographical references.
ISBN 1-55591-450-0 (pbk.)
1. Greenhouse gardening—Handbooks, manuals, etc. 2. Sunspaces—Handbooks, manuals, etc. I. Title.
SB415 .S663 1999   635 .0483—dc21
                                                                                              99-049512

Printed in the United States of America
0 9 8 7 6 5 4

Cover and interior design by Bill Spahr
Cover and interior illustrations by Marjorie C. Leggitt
Photographs by Shane Smith except where noted otherwise

Fulcrum Publishing
16100 Table Mountain Parkway, Suite 300
Golden, Colorado 80403
(800) 992-2908 • (303) 277-1623
www.fulcrum-books.com

CONTENTS

ACKNOWLEDGMENTS

Without the efforts of these people who gave the precious gift of their time, I could never have finished this book. I want to thank my mother who hand-typed the very first version of this book—back before computers; Sharon Gaus, who helped me to see from a different point of view and enabled me to say what I really meant to say (so many adverbs, so little time); Mary Tolan, who gave the original a voice; Claus Johnson, for his sharp eye that sees what others miss, his humor, and his wit; Don Mason, who could dissect a sentence like a surgeon while brightening up the day; and Jim Weis for his photographic assistance. Thanks also to Whitney Cranshaw for bug advice.

Thanks to the people of Cheyenne and the volunteers of the Cheyenne Botanic Gardens, who are the best at making greenhouse dreams come true. I appreciate the constant support of Mayor Leo Pando, executive assistant to the mayor, Joe Dougherty, and Cheyenne Parks and Recreation head Dave Romero.

I also want to thank Bob Baron, whose persistence allowed this book to become a reality. Also thanks to Jay Staten, Linda Stark, and David Nuss, who never gave up on this book; the many good friends I am blessed with, for their words of encouragement; and my parents, for their love, strength, support, trust, and advice through it all.

For this revised edition, thanks go to John Updike for his words of encouragement—may all great novelists take the time to listen to the whining of a how-to author in the midst of a revision. I appreciate the time of Carol Glenister of IPM Labs who assisted me with current trends in integrated pest management.

To my good friends Tom and Deborah Throgmorton, Jamie Emery, Rande Pouppirt, Rick Upham, Thom Wise, Gale Harms, Phyllis Atchison, Jane and Mike Sullivan, Tom Fox, Will Robinson, Steve Kline, Richard "Forrest" Henry, Dan White, and Aimee Reese, thanks for your moral support.

I want to thank Bob Baron and Jay Staten (once again) at Fulcrum for their undying patience. I also appreciate the attention to detail and creative enthusiasm provided by Marlene Blessing, and the hard work and great illustrations of Marjorie Leggitt. I am also indebted to Marykay Cicio, who spent many long hours improving the flow of the book where it had gotten tangled in webs of my own making. Also thanks to Bill Spahr for his excellent design and composition work.

I am also thankful to my two boys, Rio and Aiden, who put up with a dad who missed some ball games, reading time and wrestling matches during the many, many evening hours spent working on this book. And thanks, again, to my friend Jim Weis for providing photos and the calla lily quote in Chapter 8.

INTRODUCTION

"The best way to do something is to do it."
—JOSEPH STANDING EAGLE

BREATHE IN. THE AIR IS RICH—HUMID, FRAGRANT and full of life, warm on your face. It's comfortable. What is it about a greenhouse or sunspace that feels good to almost everyone? It's more than just stimulation of the senses. It goes deeper, further back. The tropics were the womb of human life, and the greenhouse is a connection to our origins. The tropics cradled our earliest developments; there we learned the basics of living on the planet. In returning the tropics to our temperate climates, perhaps we can remember some of those lessons.

It is interesting that the term "greenhouse effect" is used to describe the overheating of planet earth because of our mismanagement of the environment. There is another greenhouse effect with more positive connotations. It is the greenhouse effect that gives you a warm, sunny room beckoning you to stay and relax a while. The greenhouse effect is that of a fragrant plant in full bloom whose aroma fills the senses, that of a fresh-picked salad in winter. The greenhouse effect is a homegrown bouquet of colorful flowers to brighten up a cold, dreary, winter day.

I have always been intrigued by what goes through our minds when we garden or, perhaps more important, what doesn't go through our minds during that special time when we are working with our plants. When I'm working with plants in the greenhouse, the day's

The real "greenhouse effect" can enhance your yard and your life.

worries aren't nearly as important as they were earlier. Gardening is cleansing or, as a good friend says, like "mental floss." Another friend likes to say it is refreshing—like taking a nap. Whatever you want to call it, gardening is a therapeutic activity. It is also one of the most important leisure-time activities. It is one of the few activities that wonderfully meshes the body and the mind in meaningful work. I recently heard that average Americans spend 52 percent of their leisure time shopping. And who doesn't enjoy buying something new? But how would you really like to spend your limited leisure time: in a mall or discount store chasing a sale with the throngs of the crowds or in your own special garden? I sometimes

Gardening is a therapeutic activity; it helps make the worries of your life diminish in importance.

A greenhouse is like a tropical island—a warm and comfortable place surrounded by outside cold.

think about how few of the things we buy are actually made by another human. Almost everything we purchase comes from a machine—that's the reality of our economy and our system. Look at the label on your shirt or on the box of something you recently purchased. It was likely made very far away and mostly by a machine. When people make something by hand—with their own hands—it takes on a different level of value. So it is with the food and flowers that we grow with our own hands. This productivity is special to our psyche and our spirit. It is therapeutic to create things out of the earth.

Having a greenhouse enables you to enjoy this therapy on a daily basis in any season. With your greenhouse, you can simultaneously live in a temperate zone with the wonder of its changing seasons and reap the harvests of the tropics daily, only a few steps away from a snowbank and freezing temperatures.

Gardening to me, and perhaps to many of you, is important therapy. Usually therapy is not our reason for gardening per se; rather, it is the unexpected benefit of working with plants and the soil that attracts us. A growing greenhouse allows for this enjoyment on a year-round basis and can provide us with wonderful things such as fresh food, flowers, and exercise, but above all, with that unexpected gift of therapy.

Another benefit of gardening is that it teaches us much about the natural world. Nothing has given me a better lesson in ecology than using beneficial critters in controlling greenhouse pests (see Chapter 10 for more information on insects). As I have become more adept at using ecological controls, I have found as much enjoyment in dealing with bugs as I have working with plants. The greenhouse ecosystem can be a metaphor for the earth, teaching us much about how the planet works.

Gardening is said to be both a science and an art. The thing that makes gardening an art is that nobody knows exactly what will happen in a garden. Even the experts are often surprised. Long-held ways of gardening and specific methods of plant care are often tossed out when newer approaches are brought to light that work even better. This can make horticultural scientists appear to have egg on their face until they, too, adopt the new techniques. As a botany instructor once explained to me, "Plants don't read the books and sometimes do as they please." When injuries to the ego are put aside, I find this unpredictability is one of the things that makes gardening fun. Because gardening, and especially greenhouse gardening, is still as much of an art as it is a science, it makes you, the average gardener, a pioneer in your own gardening laboratory called the greenhouse. There will always be much that is new to share and learn about growing in a greenhouse (that is why I keep revising this book!). If you are like most gardeners, you will retain the pioneering spirit and try different things, while also growing the "tried and true."

My goal in writing this book is to produce a resource that any greenhouse gardener can use. The challenge is that every greenhouse is different. Throughout, I have tried to address the many types of greenhouses, among them: attached; freestanding; solar-heated and traditionally heated; large and small; and cool-running greenhouses and hot-running sunspaces. I have noticed that, as time goes by, the differences between solar-heated and conventional types of greenhouses have blurred as more energy-conserving glazings and heating systems have developed and have now become more commonplace.

Years ago, I believed that the only noble purpose for a greenhouse garden was to grow

A greenhouse garden provides the perfect place to enjoy creativity, light exercise, and a feeling of satisfaction from producing something of value.

food. I still believe that growing food crops in home greenhouses is very important, especially with the safety and quality of our food coming under increasing scrutiny. The older I get, the more I have also come to revere the "food for the spirit" that ornamental plants provide. When food and flowers are grown together, there is a wonderful, serendipitous effect of flavor, color, and fragrance. There are also some other benefits in reducing pests and diseases through companion planting!

Both the bouquets in a flower store and the food from the grocery have often traveled further than you will in twenty years. It is a sad fact that the United States now imports more fruits and vegetables than it exports. The majority of our cut flowers are grown overseas. Although the reality of the global economy is something we must all come to grips with, I really don't feel comfortable with the fact that we are becoming more dependent upon resources farther away. As a result, I derive great solace from the act of producing food and flowers year-round in my own greenhouse. Even

Growing your own food year-round in a greenhouse eliminates the worry that chemicals were used by commercial growers to produce your fruits and vegetables.

more important, it is fun. There is value in sustainability, even if it is the simple joy of a homegrown flower and a salad in winter.

As you read this book, the first thing you will find is that growing plants in a greenhouse is different from growing them outside. Yes, there are similarities, but sometimes there are just enough similarities to get a person in trouble.

A greenhouse or sunroom is a unique agricultural environment. It is not more difficult to grow plants in a greenhouse, just different.

In a greenhouse, space is limited, and light, humidity, temperature, and the atmosphere are all different from the outside climate. As a result, gardening techniques, pest controls, and timing are also different. A year-round greenhouse garden still has four seasons with which to be concerned, but as you might have guessed, these seasons are also different.

My goal in writing this book has been to give you the information you need whether you want to grow a few plants or turn your sunroom into a plant factory. I have spent a good portion of my life trying to give people good advice about their horticultural projects. I have been director of the Cheyenne Botanic Gardens since 1977, and I have gardened in a home greenhouse for what seems like forever. For decades, I have worked with hobbyists from all across the nation. I have been a consultant to commercial growers and community projects from coast to coast. I have been fortunate to gain much from these experiences, and it is my hope that the advice and experiences written here will shorten your learning curve. I hope the end result will be that the time you spend gardening in a greenhouse or sunroom will be rewarding and enjoyable.

There can be a whole world contained in a greenhouse if only you gather up some soil, water, and a seed.

CHAPTER 1

THE GREENHOUSE OR SUNSPACE ENVIRONMENT

EVERY GREENHOUSE OR SUNSPACE IS DIFFERENT. Take a close look at your unique sunroom. If you already have a greenhouse, take the time to notice the changes in the environment from season to season and day to day, from front to back and ceiling to floor. Pay attention to the climate where you live, because that also affects the environment within your greenhouse or sunspace. The first step in understanding how to garden in a sunspace is to get a good feel for its unique environment. Stop, see, and feel what is going on in there. Watch the shadows during the course of the day. Where do they rise and fall? Notice how they change through the seasons. If you do this, you'll observe how low the sun is at 12 noon in December versus how high it is at the same time in June. Feel the difference between being in the center of your greenhouse and standing against one of its walls. Feel the changes as the days get longer in spring and shorter in fall. Everything is changing, and every minute something is happening. A cloud maneuvers in front of the sun and the temperature drops. Water the plants, and it can quickly feel steamy and tropical ... or cool and clammy. Each cloud, storm, hot spell, or cold spell is part of this inside environment.

Walk up to a flower and look at it with a magnifying glass. Watch a bug go about its life for three whole minutes. Try to do this without feeling that this bug is the "enemy." Perhaps it isn't. Take a deep breath. Ready? Let's get into it.

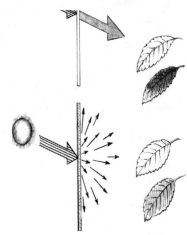

The outside environment affects the environment inside the greenhouse.

The basic principle of greenhouse gardening is as old and uncomplicated as the practice of placing a glass lantern over a plant to protect it from the elements. I can imagine the delight of some farmer, back in time, when the idea of protecting a plant with lantern glass came to him. How pleased he must have been when he came out after a frosty night to find the plant still alive! The glass created a totally new environment within its walls, extending the productive life of the plant. It's like creating an earth within an earth or an ecology within an ecology.

Working in a greenhouse is like being the conductor of a wonderful orchestra.

The simplicity of light and glass creates a wonderful micro-system of incredible possibilities. For instance, greenhouse gardeners in cold climates who utilize solar heat are elated by the simplicity of warming both their house and plants by using the same light that grows their plants. But these wonderful possibilities can't be realized without you—that would be like having an orchestra without a conductor.

A good growing greenhouse environment is determined by both the building's exterior structural design and the interior design. If this has been done right, then you are ready to become the conductor. The sun and plants know exactly what to do and just need a little coaxing and rhythm on your part to make your greenhouse an effective, productive place for year-round growing.

DESIGNING AND BUILDING A NEW GREENHOUSE

So what do you need to turn a sunspace into a tropical jungle full of blooms, fragrance, fruit, salad greens, herbs, and generally cool plants?

There is a lot you can put into a greenhouse besides just plants. In this chapter and the next, we will look at how to optimize the greenhouse environment's efficiency and productivity. These chapters address only the basics of interior and exterior greenhouse design and are meant to help steer you in the right direction. If you hunger for more information on the subject, refer to a specific greenhouse design and construction book in your bookstore or the library.

Before you get started with any greenhouse construction project, check into the local regulations in terms of permits, zoning, setbacks, potential underground plumbing and electrical lines, and more. Local regulations may also require a certain type of foundation. Greenhouses attached to a home may have even stricter requirements. In some jurisdictions, freestanding hobby greenhouses are considered storage sheds and fly under the radar of strict regulations. Size may also be an issue with local regulations, and some people have avoided the legal radar by keeping their greenhouse below a certain size requirement.

Another consideration is to decide whether you want to build the greenhouse from scratch or go with a kit greenhouse. Read on for more information on both.

BEGIN WITH A GOOD FOUNDATION

A foundation is what you set your greenhouse or greenhouse kit upon. It is usually built of wood timbers (such as four-by-fours or larger), concrete, or concrete block. The greenhouse is then anchored to the foundation. The easiest way to have an awful time building a greenhouse is to fail to make your foundation square. To make it truly square, you can cross-measure the foundation from far corner to far corner. To check whether you are building it square, measure the distance between the northeast and southwest corners. Then measure the northwest to the southeast corner. If your foundation is square, the two measurements should be exactly the same; if they are not, make some adjustments.

Except for walkways, I don't recommend pouring a whole concrete slab for the greenhouse floor because it inhibits your future growing options. If you already have a slab, don't worry—there are things you can do to make the best of it. (See a more thorough discussion about floors in the next chapter and about growing in containers throughout the book.) Having a direct soil connection, however, enables you to plant directly in a ground-connected bed. This is an advantage for growing larger plants. It may also solve many drainage problems. Often, you can build your greenhouse directly on the existing soil and garden on that soil (usually with some added amendments). But first, be sure to check the soil for poor drainage, nutrient deficiencies, or other soil problems at your location. If there are problems with the existing soil, you should consider removing at least 1 foot (0.3 m) of soil where the greenhouse will sit and replacing it with imported, well-drained rich topsoil. If drainage is extremely poor, consider adding some drainage tiles or other drainage system a few feet beneath the soil surface.

For those who are unclear about it, drainage is a function of how fast water percolates into the soil. If a small amount of water on the ground remains in a puddle for many hours then you may have a drainage problem. It is usually a result of heavy clay soil. You may want to consult some experts about how to improve the drainage and how to construct a drainage system. Your local county extension agent or other soils expert would be a good place to start if you have questions. Keep in mind that it is

(Top) *Don't overlook the importance of a square foundation! You should end up with the exact same measurement when you stretch a tape from the northwest to the southeast corner as you get measuring the northeast to the southwest corner.*
(Bottom) *A good foundation must be square as well as level all the way around.*

always easier to import soil and plan for drainage *before* you build your greenhouse. If your soil is in good shape and drains well, then you can proceed with construction.

Finally, consider insulating the perimeter of your foundation with 1- to 2-inch (2.5- to 8 cm)-thick rigid Styrofoam board placed vertically, 2 feet (0.3–0.6 m) deep, against the outside of the foundation. Doing so will help prevent the soil from cooling down in winter, thereby reducing your heating requirements. See the discussion later in this chapter on solar heating (pages 4, 50).

GLAZING

Glazing is the "skin" of the greenhouse, the feature that lets the light into the space. Glazing usually consists of glass or plastic sheets attached to the frame. Usually, the most expensive

A greenhouse is a relatively simple structure to build, especially when compared to the construction of a home or even a garage. Greenhouse framing options include wood, aluminum, steel, and plastic.

component of any greenhouse is its glazing material. The better the glazing, the more expensive the greenhouse. Most kit greenhouses use the double- or triple-thick polycarbonate plastic or glass glazings. I would suggest that you avoid single-pane or single-thick plastic glazing as it gets too hot in the summer and too cold in winter. Instead, go with double- or even triple-thick insulated glass or plastic. See more discussion about glazings later in this chapter. There are many cheap kits on the market that use plastic film glazings that usually won't last for more than a few years. I have seen these greenhouses ripped up in a strong wind. Sometimes you get what you pay for. Cheap can be expensive!

KIT FRAMES

A greenhouse kit offers a finished, workable design. It is also an easier solution for anyone who lacks building experience. That is not to say the experience won't have its frustrations. I have yet to see a kit that doesn't get even the better carpenters a bit frazzled. Still, most com-

panies offer good technical assistance to help you through the difficult parts of the process. Some also have helpful videos. Plan on spending as much time setting up a level and square foundation for the greenhouse structure as you will to set up the kit greenhouse itself. This is true even if you are setting your greenhouse on wood timbers.

Having a quality frame and door are also important. This is hard to determine from photos. If you are considering the purchase of a particular kit, ask the seller if you can find a similar kit already set up in your vicinity that you could visit. If this is not possible, check to see whether the company has references whom you could call about the kit.

You will find that the manufacturers offer many different size options. It is rare that a greenhouse gardener doesn't eventually wish for more space. Purchase the largest greenhouse you can afford and/or have space for.

Most kits are constructed with either wood or aluminum frames. Wood has an inherent appeal but often requires some basic regular maintenance. Aluminum greenhouses can be either fragile or sturdy, depending upon the model. Aluminum lasts virtually forever, but it is a conductor of cold outside temperatures unless an effort has been made by the manufacturer to create "thermal breaks" in the structure. With a thermal break, the outside metal is not directly connected to the inner metal structure, which keeps the inside a bit warmer.

Solar Heating for Kit Greenhouses

Speaking of warmth, many people wonder if their kit greenhouse is solar heated. I have yet to see one marketed as such. You can, however, retrofit the kit greenhouse to be more energy efficient even to the point of not requiring a heater! This requires that you insulate the north wall, insulate the foundation with Styrofoam at least 1 foot (0.3 m) deep; use double- or triple-thick insulated glazing; seal every nook and cranny to prevent air leaks; make sure the vents and doors are weather-stripped and caulked; add some thermal storage such as drums filled with water; have a proper orientation with the glazing facing south; and possibly even install a night curtain for extremely cold climates. See the section later in this chapter titled "Solar-Greenhouse Heating Checklist" for further details on these retrofits.

Kit Options

Some kits are designed for attaching to a structure such as a house or garage. If you can attach your greenhouse to the south side of a structure, you can take full advantage of possible solar heating for both the greenhouse and the attached structure. Also, having a greenhouse attached or even close to your home insures you'll enjoy and take better care of the greenhouse than if it is way out in the yard. Still, having a greenhouse out in the yard is better than not having a greenhouse at all.

You may also be presented with venting and paint options. I would usually recommend the most venting possible unless you live in a place with cool summers. Many manufacturers offer custom painting of the framing structure. Painting is a matter of personal preference, but keep in mind that white reflects the most light and seems to wear the longest.

The Company's Reputation

Finally, always check into the integrity of the company from which you are thinking about purchasing the kit. Here are some good questions to ask a potential kit seller. How long have they been in business? How many kits have they sold? What is their warranty? What technical help do they provide, and can you call them on weekends when you are liable to run into trouble setting it up? Most companies are rarely available on weekends. Ask if you can look at the manual to see if it is written in a simple manner. Does the company have a toll-free number? Does the kit require any special tools? Can you get a custom size? How is the greenhouse shipped and packaged? What if the kit arrives damaged? Do they provide any other free options? Many companies offer free growing books, thermometers, potting benches, fans, or other goodies as enticements to purchase their kit.

A greenhouse can be a big investment. You should feel comfortable with the company you choose to go with, so don't be afraid to ask questions!

GREENHOUSE CONSTRUCTION: GOING IT ALONE

Building a greenhouse from scratch may be a good option if you have some construction experience. Although building one yourself is usually cheaper than going with a kit-type greenhouse, it may not be that much cheaper. For some people, it might be worth spending a few extra dollars on a kit to avoid the added frustration of starting from scratch. For others, building things from scratch is a fun challenge and a joy that should never be denied.

First, you must come up with a design. Fortunately, a greenhouse is a relatively simple structure to build. The only things that distinguish a greenhouse from regular home construction are the glazing and the method of attaching this glass or plastic material properly. This is also a substantial part of the cost

Polycarbonate is an increasingly popular glazing. Here are three types of structured sheet polycarbonate (left to right): the triple wall (16mm thick—widest and most energy efficient of the three), the double wall (8mm thick), and the triple wall (8mm thick).

of building a greenhouse. Always shop around when considering a glazing purchase as you will find a wide variation in prices as well as shipping costs (be sure to read more about glazings later in this chapter).

Before you start your design process, be sure to read some books on the subject. Unfortunately, some of the best books on the subject of home greenhouse design are out of print. Two of my favorite out-of-print books are *The Food and Heat Producing Solar Greenhouse*, by Bill Yanda and Rick Fisher, and *The Homeowner's Complete Handbook for Add-On Solar Greenhouses and Sunspaces: Planning, Design, Construction*, by Andrew M. Shapiro. Still, these out-of-print books can be acquired if you check the library and used-book stores. There are also many on-line Internet services dedicated to searching for out-of-print books.

Sometimes you can find simple plans for constructing greenhouses in greenhouse supply catalogs, state energy conservation offices, or even through your local county agricultural extension office.

If you don't build it yourself or go with a kit, you can always hire out the design and construction of the greenhouse for your home at an increased price. For those who don't want the hassle of construction, this may be worth every penny. Look for someone who has some experience with a greenhouse. Still, you should do as much reading as possible so that you can be an active participant in the design process. It will be your greenhouse, and you need to have it fit your needs. Sometimes designers see themselves as creating a piece of art for you and have the disturbing attitude that you shouldn't be telling them what you want in *their* creation. Avoid these types of architects and designers. This is the time to be sure to assert and communicate exactly what you want in a greenhouse—both structurally and with the interior design.

When you design your structure, please try to keep your options open for solar heating in both the design and placement of the structure. Solar heating lessens the cost of operation and helps if you have a power outage or broken heater. Be sure to look at the section later in this chapter titled "Solar-Greenhouse Heating Checklist."

For a discussion about wood structures and rot, read the section "The Water Must Go

(A) *Clear glazings do not diffuse light well, so they create sharper, darker shadows. This is less than optimal for growing plants, but it is great if you want clear views to the outside.*

(B) *Diffuse glazing materials scatter light. Although these glazings are not perfectly clear, they allow in about as much total light as the clear materials do. With diffuse light conditions, shade is "lighter" and plants in the shade receive more total light. This creates better growing conditions for the whole plant canopy.*

Somewhere" later in this chapter. Also, before you pound the first nail, please read the next chapter to help you determine some of the interior spaces, which, in turn, will help you in designing the exterior structure.

GLAZING

Glazing is a critical element of the greenhouse, for it is the material that allows for the entry of light and heat into the structure—it is the greenhouse skin. Early glazings were made of thin sheets of mica, alabaster, or talc, laid over a hole in the earth. Before glass technology became well developed, small cold-frame season extenders were covered with oiled paper and even cloth, much in the same way we use flexible plastics today.

Today we have a wide array of choices for glazing, including glass, vinyl, fiberglass, polycarbonate, acrylic, and polyethylene. They vary in cost, ease of application, solar performance, and longevity.

Before you buy glazing material, be sure that it is sold specifically for use in the sun over many years without losing its clarity. Virtually all plastics eventually break down (they either turn yellow or white and/or become brittle) when exposed to the sun's ultraviolet light, limiting the amount and quality of light entering the greenhouse. Even so, that is no reason not to choose plastic. Many plastics are guaranteed for 20 years. Some plastics are many times stronger than glass. Where I live, it hails on the average of ten times a year, so glass is not an option. For our specific climate and budget, I choose polycarbonate. There are many pros and cons to consider in selecting the right glazing. Usually the number-one consideration is budget. One of the most important questions is the

warranty or guarantee; get a copy of it and read it before you buy. Let's look at some of the attributes of different glazings.

ACRYLIC

Acrylic is not as common as it used to be. It is available as a single- or double-walled material. It is very strong but is easy to cut. One drawback is that it may support an open flame (depending upon the manufacturer). It expands and contracts with temperature swings. Often, acrylic is a clear material. Although not as clear as glass, it can be clearer than polycarbonate. However, like most plastics it is easily scratched. It is moderately expensive as a single sheet. As you get into shopping for the multiple-layer, honeycomb types of sheets, the price rises rapidly. It is relatively easy to bend around large-diameter curves. Some acrylics readily crack when hit with a blunt object such as a large hailstone. The life span of most acrylics is usually from 10 to 30 years; check the warranty.

(Top) *This outer layer of corrugated fiberglass is being replaced. You can see the exposed, inner second layer of polyethylene, which provides a low-cost, double glazing.* **(Bottom)** *This fiberglass has seen better days. It has yellowed and the fibers are exposed, both of which reduce its ability to transmit light.*

FIBERGLASS

Fiberglass is commonly found in many brands and grades. Its life span can vary from 3 years to 20 years depending upon the grade. Some types turn yellow quicker than others. Be careful of what is sold in lumberyards; trust only the written warranty. Fiberglass is very combustible!

(Top) *Hail damage on a film glazing.*
(Bottom) *This is corrugated fiberglass. The white spots indicate hail damage.*

I would rate it as being moderately cheap. It is available in both corrugated and flat styles, with the corrugated being stronger for wind and snow loads. Unfortunately, the corrugated is slightly more difficult to weather-strip. Fiberglass glazing is only available in single-layer thickness. To get a second layer of glazing, fiberglass is often used as the outer layer with polyethylene placed as a low-cost, insulating interior layer. Fiberglass is easy to cut and easy to work with as long as you wear gloves and a breathing mask, as the fibers kicked up by a saw or knife can irritate. Fiberglass is relatively strong but can be bent around large-diameter curves. It has a low level of expansion and contraction with varying temperatures. Fiberglass is great for diffusing light, which increases photosynthesis in a greenhouse.

GLASS

Glass, the oldest type of glazing, is probably the most commonly available material. This is the only glazing I can think of that is recyclable. It varies in price from cheap (double strength) to expensive (if it has many energy-saving treatments). Glass is brittle and difficult to cut. It requires more precision and muscle in the installation process, as it can be heavy to work with. All of this may increase the installation price. Glass is available in single, double, and triple layers, with the third layer providing maximum energy efficiency. Tempered or laminated glass products provide increased strength.

The life span of glass can be indefinite (until a rock or hailstone attack). There have been and will continue to be many new, energy-conserving technological advances that make some brands of glass very energy efficient. These include low-e glass, which has a coating that reduces the amount of heat that escapes through the glass. Also available is the highly efficient Heat Mirror® product, with its thin, transparent film that reflects heat. The film is usually sealed between two panes of glass. The Heat Mirror® system improves insulation in a double-sealed unit and is available in different degrees of low-reflectance to high-light transmittance films (for most greenhouses you would want the highest transmittance available). Many of the Heat Mirror® products also have the ability to limit incoming heat as well as retain heat within the structure.

There are also special gases that can be inserted in the airspace between layers of most glass—including the low-e glass and Heat Mirror® products—that help improve the insulation of the airspace. These gases are usually krypton (not recommended for Superman) or argon gas.

The effects of these new innovations in glass technology on growing plants remain to be fully tested. In general, these surface treatments usually allow plants to grow with no problems except when they noticeably darken the glass, which reduces the amount of incoming light.

Some advantages to glass include its very low level of expansion and contraction with

The glass glazing on this greenhouse could last for decades. Glass has a very long functional life until it meets up with a rock or hailstone.

varying temperatures. Unlike many plastics, glass is not combustible, nor does it easily scratch like plastics do.

Clear glass creates sharp shadows and does not diffuse light much. This is less optimal for growing plants but is great if you want to look out of your greenhouse. You can also find glass that has been treated with a frostlike application that can diffuse light very well (see the related discussion on diffuse light and plant growth later in this chapter under "Light, Photosynthesis, Glazing, and Plant Growth").

POLYCARBONATE

This material is becoming more common, especially on kit greenhouses. I have even seen it in lumberyards. It is commonly available in single, double (usually 8 mm thick), and even triple layers (available in both 8 mm and 16 mm) for maximum energy efficiency. The more layers it has, the better the insulation and the higher the price. I would classify the price of single and double "polycarb" (as greenhouse enthusiasts call it) as moderate, given its life span, but triple-thick can get pricier. Even though polycarbonate is very strong, it is easy to cut with a saw. Its life span

is around 12 to 20 years, though you may see yellowing as soon as 12 years. Most warranties are for 10 years, and some even include replacement coverage against hail. Most brands of polycarbonate do not readily support a flame. Condensation (small water droplets on the glazing) can be a problem with the multiple-layer materials in the interior channels, or air spaces between the inner and outer surfaces. Some manufacturers are treating some of the surfaces with chemicals that minimize visible condensation. The double- and triple-thick materials are great for diffusing light, thus increasing photosynthesis.

(Top) *Notice the condensation on this polycarbonate glazing. Condensation can reduce the amount of incoming light on any glazing by as much as 15 percent. This can be substantial in areas with cloudy, cold winters.* **(Bottom)** *This is a sample of the woven polyethylene product.*

POLYETHYLENE FILMS

Films are the type of flexible plastic that is used in plastic bags or food wrap, only much thicker. There are numerous brands that have varying thickness, qualities, and life spans. In general, you get what you pay for. The biggest drawback to polyethylene (or "poly") is that the life span is only between 1 and 5 years (depending upon the manufacturer and a little luck). Only single-layer films are available, but commercial growers often set up a system with two layers of polyethylene and inflate an airspace in between (with a small squirrel-cage fan), providing an insulating quality. Some polyethylene films hold in long-wave (infrared) radiation better than others. This is important to some growers, because if the film can hold this radiation in, it allows the glazing to retain more solar heat.

There is a woven polyethylene available that is tougher for windy situations. I have heard some good reports on the woven poly from people who need a cheap glazing material with a life span of 3 to 4 years.

CHOOSING YOUR GLAZING MATERIAL

There are other more experimental and less commonly available materials that are sometimes available for glazing greenhouses. These may include ethylene vinyl acetate (EVA), which can last up to 7 years, tedlar, siliconized cloths, specially treated polyethylene, clear mylar, and so on. Before you use a lesser-known or experimental glazing material, consult others who have used them to see if they have had a positive, long-term experience with them.

No matter which glazing you choose, though, your glazing is only as good as the written guarantee or warranty. Always ask to see a copy of this prior to buying any glazing. Is the warranty prorated over the life? Is it based upon a decline of light transmission? Read it as if you were a Harvard-trained lawyer. I prefer to stick with a company that has been around awhile and that provides a written guarantee that covers important things like life span, impact resistance, yellowing, and hail damage.

Before you either reglaze or build a new greenhouse, have a long visit with a few different glazing salespeople at greenhouse supply houses and refer to as many books as you can dig up on the design and building of greenhouses. See the "Bibliography and Further Reading and Resources." Also, take a long look at the life expectancy. Of course, the longer-lasting glazings are going to cost you more

up front, but in the long run, they may be cheaper.

WHERE IS MY TAN? GLAZING AND UV RAYS

When I was in high school, I applied for my first job in a greenhouse. To my surprise, I was hired. I was surprised because it sounded like a piece-of-cake job being able to work in a tropical atmosphere in the middle of winter, surrounded by plants all day. What could be better than working around fragrant flowers, occasionally watering them and all the while getting a great tan? Well, was I wrong! Unlike a home greenhouse, this job was at a production enterprise, and that meant hard work. My job consisted mainly of hauling load upon load of hundreds of pounds of dirt (oops, I mean "soil") in a big wheelbarrow. It also included endless hours of boring transplanting of seedlings for spring bedding-plant production. Worse yet, I didn't even get a tan! I ended up hating that job.

Since then I have learned that there is nothing healthy about a tan. But why no tan in the greenhouse? The tanning rays just don't penetrate the glass or glazing materials on most greenhouses because most common greenhouse glazings filter out most of the ultraviolet (UV) light from the sun. So don't expect to get a glowing bronze tan while working in your greenhouse. It is ultraviolet light that produces the tanning effect, and those are the same rays that make plastic-based glazings become yellow and brittle over the years. In a way, ultraviolet does the same thing to our skin. It causes premature aging after repeated tannings and burnings. Don't despair. People who work in their home greenhouse appear to have more color in their face (though not a dark tan) and a healthier, happier look. Is it the glazing or the lifestyle?

GLAZING CONSIDERATIONS

When choosing a glazing, consider the following:

1. **Fire resistance.** Some plastics are incredibly inflammable, including some acrylics, polyethylene, and fiberglass. I have seen fiberglass burst into flame.

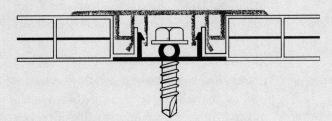

Side view of a polycarbonate mounting system.

2. **Hail / rock resistance.** If you live in an area with a high incidence of damaging hail, wind, or rock-throwing kids, check out the ability of the glazing to withstand an onslaught.

3. **Guaranteed life span.** Plastic glazings can last anywhere from 1 to 20 years. Glass can last indefinitely, at least until it breaks from a rock, a stray baseball, or a hailstone. Read the written guarantees. If it's not in writing, it's not guaranteed. Almost all plastic glazings eventually yellow and lose their light transmittance. Check for any stated guarantees against yellowing on any plastic-based glazing.

4. **Energy efficiency.** Some acrylics, polycarbonates, and glass are available in double and triple thicknesses, which greatly increase their energy efficiency. Also, there are new glass glazings available with added films and coatings that hold in radiant heat and even turn reflective to the sun on very hot days. It may pay over the long run to spend more on a more efficient material.

5. **Security.** Consider the level of crime where you live. If your greenhouse is attached to your home, you may not want to use a film-type glazing that can be easily broached or one that is easily broken into, thus giving an intruder easy access directly into your home.

6. **Ease of application.** If you are constructing the greenhouse yourself, you should check out any special considerations that apply to the glazing you use. Some plastics like polycarbonates may need a special mounting system that allows for expansion and contraction. Others may need special caulking. Glass, especially tempered and double- and triple-thick glass, can be extremely heavy to work with when applying it to your greenhouse. Also, if you live in an area where you receive a lot of snow, be sure your glazing can take the snow load.

7. **Light transmittance.** How much light can your glazing transmit? In sunny areas of the United States (see "Glazing R-Values for Energy Conservation," the lighting chart in Appendix 4), you can tolerate less transmission, whereas in the cloudier areas this is a big issue. The more layers of glazing, the less light that gets transmitted through. Glazing manufacturers usually state this in terms of percentage. Usually, you don't want to use glazings with less than 75 percent transmittance. In very cloudy areas, less than 75 percent may be a problem for plant growth.

Besides a lack of tanning rays without UV, people often wonder if there is any downside to growing plants in an environment where there is little ultraviolet light transmitted. After all, plants are used to unadulterated sunlight. Could there be a problem for plants if they don't receive a natural dose of ultraviolet light? There is very little research on this subject that applies to the home greenhouse gardener, and in fact this would make a great project for a budding young horticulturist in need of a research project. All in all, the jury is still out on this question.

Make no mistake, you can grow wonderful crops of great-tasting, nutritious food and beautiful flowers under glazings that inhibit UV rays. Still, I occasionally notice some interesting differences when the UV light is filtered out. For instance, certain rose varieties won't bloom in their normal color in some greenhouses. Sometimes these effects can be considered a plus: I recently found that morning glory flowers remain open all day when grown under polycarbonate glazing. For those of you wondering why this is so great, I should mention that morning glory flowers quickly close by late morning when grown outside, thus their name, "morning glory."

There are people who suspect that there may be a slight increase of plant disease incidence under UV-filtered glazings, but this is not enough to cause major problems for the home greenhouse gardener.

Among the most common greenhouse coverings, glass seems to block the least amount of ultraviolet light and polycarbonate blocks the most. There is a new acrylic, double-skinned extruded sheet called Exolite® UVT, developed recently by Ciba-Geigy, that allows the highest amount of ultraviolet light through, compared with most other greenhouse skins. It was developed for agricultural research and is not readily available to the home greenhouse gardener.

I never hesitate to grow plants under the common greenhouse skins that keep out most of the UV light. But if the day comes when we can readily acquire glazings that let ultraviolet light through, there are going to be a lot of sunburned and tanned greenhouse gardeners out there.

LIGHT, PHOTOSYNTHESIS, GLAZING, AND PLANT GROWTH

Now that we know what kind of glazings and glazing materials are available, it's important to understand how glazings affect plant growth. First, let's discuss the critical role light plays in a plant's life.

Let's begin with the basics. The basis for plant growth is the conversion of light into energy (sugar). This is called photosynthesis. Photosynthesis takes a lot more than simply a plant and some light. But let's keep it on the simple side. The major requirements for photosynthesis are: light, carbon dioxide (CO_2), temperature generally between 32°F (0°C) and 100°F (38°C), and water. If any one of these environmental elements is less than optimum, the whole growing process may be slowed.

Simply put, when light enters the chlorophyll of the leaf, there are special structures that combine the energy of the sunlight with carbon dioxide and water. By means of photosynthesis, these elements are converted into oxygen and sugar. The oxygen is both burned in chemical reactions and given off into the air as a component of water vapor. The sugar is fuel and is oxidized (burned) in the plant to provide all the energy the plant needs for growth. What do plants do at night? The major plant activity at night is the burning of these sugars in the plant, which is known as respiration. So think of photosynthesis as a way for plants to make plant energy and of respiration as a way for plants to use that energy. Photosynthesis and respiration are almost the opposite of each other—yet they fit so well together. Photosynthesis initially accounts for the source of all food and fuel for almost everything on this planet.

Let's look at how glazings affect plant growth. According to Colorado State University research, most glazings developed for greenhouses allow satisfactory growth. A marked difference, however, has been noted between crystal-clear glazings, such as clear glass, and those that are not clear, such as those that diffuse the light in a transparent way, like a bathroom window. Plants seem to grow better under glazing materials that are not visibly clear. Even though diffuse glazing materials are not clear to see through, they still allow in about as much total light as do the clear materials. The difference is that they scatter the light beams over a broader area, resulting in a more even distribution of light without sharp shadows. Under glazing that diffuses light, plant leaves located in "lighter" shade will receive more total light than under crystal-clear glazings; with clear glazings there are only sharp, dark shadows, where they receive substantially less light, and this results in less plant growth.

This diffused light is also helpful for solar greenhouses with thermal-mass components, such as rock, concrete, or passive solar-storage materials (water barrels) because it tends to moderate the temperatures of such structures. Fiberglass is one of the better diffusers of light; polyethylenes, polycarbonates, acrylics, and glass follow roughly in that order. This is not to say that fiberglass is the best glazing, because there are many other considerations listed earlier (such as heat loss, durability, fire resistance, aesthetics, strength, and cost) that may make other glazings much better choices. How much more will plants grow in diffused light? That's hard to say. It's not enough to alter a choice if the glazing meets most other considerations.

PHOTOPERIODISM

A photoperiod is not the art of teaching your plants to pose for glossy spreads in the garden tabloids. It describes the length of the day or night that influences plant growth. The plant's response to the length of the day or night is called photoperiodism. The length of light and dark periods can change how plants grow, when they flower and fruit, and whether seeds germinate or cuttings develop roots.

Usually the term photoperiod is applied to the flowering and fruiting response. In many garden books, plants are listed as long-day plants (which flower when days are long), short-day plants (which flower when days are short), or day-neutral plants (which aren't influenced by photoperiods). Day-neutral plants respond to other aspects, such as levels of maturity and cold or warm temperatures.

Scientists have found that photoperiodism is actually triggered by the length of the night. Uninterrupted darkness is the key. A long-night (or short-day) plant, for example, can be thrown off schedule if the night period is interrupted by light: This would simulate a short-night (long-day) situation. I know it sounds confusing, but fortunately, photoperiodism need only be taken into account when growing a few ornamental crops such as asters, chrysanthemums, poinsettias, snapdragons, and Christmas cactus (for more information, see these specific plants discussed in Chapter 8, "A Closer Look at the Plants"). There are a few vegetable crops that are affected by photoperiodism. Most onion varieties sold in temperate regions will bulb only with short nights (long days), though varieties have been developed for areas in the southern states, with its warmer winters, that bulb with longer nights (shorter days). Also, many strawberries are dependent on day length and won't produce during the winter, when they are naturally dormant. Day-neutral strawberries have been developed that aren't affected by the length of the night. Look in the catalogs that offer extensive lists of strawberry varieties that are called day-neutral types. These are generally the best types to attempt in a greenhouse.

Fortunately, the length of the night or day does not influence most vegetables and common flowers. Rather, it is a matter of maturity. For example, when a tomato plant grows for a period of time and reaches a certain level of maturity, it flowers and fruits regardless of the length of the day or night.

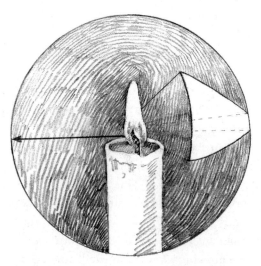

A footcandle is a unit of illuminance equal to the direct illumination on a square foot of surface one-foot from a standardized source called "an international candle." The international candle is a special candle only found at the United Nations gift shop in New York City (just kidding).

MEASURING LIGHT IN THE GREENHOUSE

Plants require certain minimal quantities and a certain quality of light for proper growth. These quantities are measured in a number of ways. The most commonly used term for measuring light striking a surface is "foot-candles" (fc). A foot-candle is a unit of illuminance equal to the direct illumination on a square foot of surface 1 foot (about 0.3 m) from a standardized source called an international candle (one might expect that to mean a special candle only found at the United Nations gift shop in New York City, but of course it isn't!). I know it's an odd definition, but it becomes easier to understand once you work with it. Almost all commercially available light meters that measure the amount of light use the foot-candle measurement.

Another commonly found term for measuring light is the word "lumen," which most commonly refers to the total amount of light energy given off by a lighting source. The term "lumen" usually rates the output of a given lamp and is often listed on the package that holds the lamp you buy. For example, a 60-watt incandescent lamp, the sort you might commonly use in your home, is usually rated at 890 lumens. A 100-watt incandescent bulb produces approximately 1,740 lumens at the bulb. As you move away from any bulb, the lumens striking a surface decrease with distance from the bulb.

A foot-candle generally refers to the amount of light that falls on a surface. It is equal to the number of lumens striking a surface divided by the area of the surface. For example, a foot-candle is equivalent to 1 lumen per square foot. Illumination intensity is measured as the number of foot-candles striking a surface (100 lumens striking a 1-square-foot area is equivalent to 100 foot-candles). The term "lux" is the metric equivalent of the foot-candle. One lux is equivalent to 1 lumen per square meter. As with lumens, the foot-candles or lux also decrease the farther you get from the light source. The main thing here is being sure your plants get enough light.

Bulbs use the lumen as the standard to measure light at the bulb, but most light-measuring meters use foot-candles as a standard of measurement for determining how much light is received by a given surface away from a lamp or light source. Light meters are available in greenhouse supply catalogs, and range in price from $20 to $120. The more expensive meters are usually more accurate and durable. For home use, the cheaper meters are fine.

Vegetables need between 700 and 1,000 foot-candles for proper growth, depending upon the plant species, the plant's age, the spacing of the plants, and the density of the leaves. Usually houseplants can get by with much less. For general greenhouse and sunspace gardening, I like to shoot for a minimum of 1,000 foot-candles on a good sunny day at around noon. If you are receiving less than that on a sunny day, you may need to replace the glazing. Is it getting old? If you are short on light, perhaps it is time to cut down that tree—or tear down that apartment building that is blocking your sun!

OK, you probably can't tear down any buildings, but take note that many states have established solar-rights laws that prohibit someone from blocking your "right to light," if you can prove that it is essential to the positive utilization of solar energy. In some states you must apply for this "property right" prior to anyone proposing to block your solar access. Check your local and state ordinances,

FOOT-CANDLE VALUES

Light Source	Foot-candles (approximate)
Starlight	.00011
Moonlight	.02
Overcast daylight	1,000.00
Direct sun	10,000.00

especially if there is potential for someone to block your light with a new building or tree growing in your light path.

To give you a feel for things, here are some approximate foot-candle values:

Every plant has its own preferred level of light, but for growing tall vegetables and cut flowers, the maximum photosynthesis occurs around 3,000 fc for tall plants to a minimum of 600 fc for short, bushy ones. The range for many ornamental blooming plants is slightly lower and varies much more. Houseplants generally prefer much lower levels.

If you want to get a close estimate of the foot-candles coming into the greenhouse without buying a light meter, you can try this method if you have a nonautomatic camera

Measuring light using a low-cost light meter.

with a built-in light meter. It helps if you understand a bit about cameras and taking pictures. This method is not 100 percent accurate, but it will give you a good ballpark figure:

1. Set the ASA (film type) at 200.
2. Set the shutter speed at 1/125 of a second.
3. Aim the camera at the light source (toward the sun).
4. Dial the F-stop to the proper photo exposure.

F-stop readings (below, left) roughly translate to these foot-candle values (below, right):

2.8	32
4	64
5.6	125
8	250
15	1,000
22	2,000

One interesting thing about plants is that sometimes you can increase one component of the basic requirements in the photosynthesis reaction to make up for a deficiency in another. For example, if you have a low-light situation, you can increase the CO_2 in the atmosphere; raise the temperature, as long as it's not past 85°F (29°C); or space the plants farther apart.

Fertilizer commercials and hydroponics enthusiasts will tell you that fertilizer is the most important need that plants have. Rarely is fertilization the main limiting factor. Rather, the limiting factors in most home-greenhouse situations are either inadequate light or improper temperature.

Crops compete for light if planted too closely, and nobody wants a fight in the green-house. Like people, plants can get unruly in a crowded situation. When plants are too close together, they will grow slower; the leaves will often become yellow, elongated, and spindly (they're always trying to get a head above their neighbors). As a result, the plants won't produce much in the way of quality leaves, flowers, or fruits. Even when plants are not crowded, they can be short on light. This is often a result of poor greenhouse design, but this will also happen in the winter if you live in very cloudy regions or northern Canada or Alaska.

Often, solar greenhouses or sunspaces are constructed with little or no glazing on the roof. In the late spring and summer this creates low-light problems that can be helped only by the addition of skylights in the roof or supplemental lighting, discussed later in this chapter.

A low-light situation can be helped substantially by painting interior surfaces white or in light colors. Dark interior surfaces can rob the plants of their light by absorbing it. In contrast, surfaces painted white or in light colors will reflect light to the plants (see "Increasing Reflective Surfaces," later in this chapter).

Shading can cause low-light problems and must be given some thought. For example, when you grow a bed of vining tomatoes, all 6 feet (1.8 m) high, you'll have a dense canopy of leaves 6 feet (1.8 m) deep. It would require much more than 1,000 fc to penetrate the canopy to maintain proper growth. The leaves at the center would be receiving far less than the original 1,000 fc. In this instance, these plants could likely use around 2,000 fc or more for optimum light penetration. So, as a general rule, taller plants with many leaves usually require higher light levels and shorter plants can get by with less than 1,000 fc.

SUN SUBSTITUTES: CHOOSING THE RIGHT LIGHTING SYSTEM

Nothing can take the place of that most precious star, our sun. But for those short winter days in the North Country or for greenhouses with poor light, there are ways to extend the light through the wonders of electricity (and money). I remember an old-time horticulturist who was fond of saying, "I can grow you a big crop of bananas above the Arctic Circle in winter ... if you give me enough money." With the input of heat and the wide assortment of grow lights available today, I'm sure he could grow those bananas, but they would cost at least fifty bucks a fruit.

The nice thing about sunlight is that it's made up of a rainbow of colors. Plants use only a portion of the spectrum of visible light. To put it simply, the most important colors in the spectrum of sunlight for plant growth are the red and blue spectrums. They don't use much of the green spectrum; in fact that is the color most plants reflect and that is why most plant leaves are green.

To greatly simplify, the red spectrum tends to trigger photoperiods and other growth regulation. In general, it doesn't take much red light to trigger a reaction in plants. The bluish spectrums tend to be the main light ingredient in most plant photosynthesis response. As a rule, it takes a pretty good intensity of this spectrum in order for photosynthesis to take place.

Years ago, most supplementary lighting was deficient in at least one of the colors that plants needed. Over the past decades, researchers have tinkered with the manufacturing process, resulting in specialized lights that cover the full spectrum of the rainbow and are designed with plants' needs in mind.

Supplementary grow lights are not a requirement for a home greenhouse or sunspace, and the more winter sun you receive, the less they are needed. However, there is no doubt that supplemental grow lights will increase the growth of your plants in the winter, especially if you live in the North Country where the days get very short.

Before you dive into using supplementary lighting, you need to think about the cost of such lights. Using a few cheap, small grow lights that use 100 watts is no big deal. But to install a couple of high-cost lights that pull 1,000 watts to grow ten bucks' worth of tomatoes may not be cost effective. As you can see, it is a question of economics, and perhaps your need for simplicity.

Elongation is a sure sign that the plant needs more light.

SYMPTOMS OF LOW-LIGHT CONDITIONS

1. Slow growth.
2. Spindly, slender growth and elongation of stems (this is the most important symptom to look for).
3. Yellowing of lower leaves (this could also be caused by a nitrogen deficiency).
4. Growth of softer, succulent, and sometimes larger leaves (this could also be caused by excess nitrogen).
5. Plants bend drastically toward the light source (this is called phototropism).

A number of important plants we like to grow in greenhouses are native to the tropics and subtropics. As you get closer to the equator, the day length evens out closer to 12-hour days and 12-hour nights. Crops native to more temperate regions are used to even longer summer days. This in part is why we see such a response to supplemental lighting in the winter when the days are shorter than 12 hours.

The three types of lights commonly used for growing plants are incandescent, fluorescent, and what is known in the industry as high-intensity discharge lamps (HIDs). Let's take a closer look at the attributes of each.

INCANDESCENT LIGHTS

Incandescent lights are the common old-fashioned lightbulb similar to what good old Thomas Edison created. They are hot to the touch and tend to give off light mostly in the red spectrum, which is good for triggering flowers but produces weak plant growth. They also have a relatively short life span. Producing enough light for a greenhouse using these bulbs would require a large number of fixtures that would result in a large amount of heat being generated.

As a result, incandescent lights are good for triggering photoperiodism-related flowering but are generally not a good choice for photosynthesis. So, incandescent lights are a poor choice when it comes to growing plants because it doesn't take much intensity to trigger a photoperiod in plants. By just flashing on an incandescent light in the middle of the night, you can confuse certain sensitive plants into thinking a night was short rather than long. This is because photoperiod-sensitive plants need a long period of uninterrupted darkness to trigger their reaction (usually flowering). For more information, see the discussion under "Lighting Duration and Photoperiods" on page 25; see also Chapter 8, "A Closer Look at the Plants," to find out if a photoperiod is important to your crop of interest.

As I said earlier, most incandescents primarily reflect the reddish spectrum, but there are always exceptions! There are special incandescent "grow lights" that have been altered to reflect both red and blue wavelengths. They do an acceptable job of growing plants but still generate a high level of heat given the amount of light they emit, and heat is usually a sign of inefficiency when it comes to electricity. This heat can also be a problem to a plant if the leaf is in close proximity to the bulb. There are better choices for photosynthesis. But if you just want to trigger photoperiods, these lights will work fine.

FLUORESCENT LIGHTS

We are all familiar with the long, white, tube-shaped fluorescent bulb, the light source used in most offices. The most common fluorescent is called the "cool white," which emits light mostly in the blue range. Lately, there has been a movement to make even the common cool-white bulbs radiate a more even spectrum (with more of the red spectrum).

If you go to a store that specializes in lighting, often you'll find three main choices in fluorescent lightbulbs: warm white (more of the red wavelengths), cool white (more of the blue wavelengths), and full-spectrum lights (a balance of the full spectrum). The full-spectrum bulbs are getting more popular, not just for their use as grow lights but because many people believe that they function better in an interior office if they are under a fuller spectrum of light (I think that they are right!). These full-spectrum fluorescent bulbs are also great for growing plants, though they have certain limitations.

The terms "warm" and "cool" fluorescent lights relate only to the wavelength spectrum, not the temperature of the bulbs, as all fluorescent lights tend to run cool to the touch. The cool-white fluorescent lights are more commonly available, but the other two can be found at lighting stores or greenhouse suppliers.

Wouldn't you know that the full-spectrum fluorescent grow lights are more expensive (usually twice as much) than the regular cool and warm white lights? I tell you this because you can do a bang-up job of growing plants if you use 3 cool-white lights to every 1 warm white light and save yourself a bit of cash. If you are just growing seedlings or leaves and don't need to trigger flowers, you can forget the warm-white light and go with 4 cool-white fluorescent bulbs.

Because of the low cost of both purchasing and operating fluorescent bulbs, they are a favorite choice of growers. But before you set out to install fluorescent bulbs all over the place, there is one important thing to consider.

Fluorescent lights grow plants well as long as they are situated close to the tops of the plant. Photo courtesy of Charley's Greenhouse Supply.

Fluorescent lights must be very, very close to the plant for the best growing effect. They are great for seedlings or plants that grow a foot or two high as long as you can get the light down to a few inches from the top of the leaf. Fluorescent lights are not appropriate for growing a 6-foot (1.8 m) tomato vine or a similar tall, light-loving plant. A general rule is to place fluorescent lights at least 3 to 4 inches (8 to 10 cm) from the top of the plant (especially those that need high-intensity light, such as vegetables and cut flowers). Only at this close range can these lights really make a difference in providing enough foot-candles of light intensity to do a good job. If the lights are too far from the leaves, you will notice the plants elongating and stretching toward the light.

I find the best use of fluorescent lighting is for germinating seedlings. A system can easily be set up in a basement or other area of your house, freeing up precious greenhouse space for growing the crops to maturity. I use about 2 tubes for every 10 inches (25 cm) of planting width. When you set up your germinating bench, it will be very helpful to hang the fluorescent lights from a pulley or chain so you can easily adjust them as your plants start to grow. Always maintain a distance of 3 to 4 inches (8 to 10 cm) above the tops of the plants.

A typical HID light with a ballast contained in the light box.

It's important to remember that fluorescent lights lose their intensity over time, so it's a good idea to replace them every 300–400 hours to maintain maximum brightness. Some of the full-spectrum fluorescent lights have been designed for longer life.

Please use extreme caution when you set up your electrical connections so you don't end up with the deadly combination of electricity and water. This is especially true with fluorescent lights because they are sitting so close to your plants and thus closer to the watering can.

There are ready-made fluorescent systems designed for growing (some types are for classrooms). These start at around $200 for a very small unit and range up to $850 for the most expensive three-tiered system of lights and shelves. You can also use shop lights, which are already outfitted to hold 3 or 4 bulbs. Most people set up a nice propagation area with 2 shop lights holding 4 tubes. Be sure to install the fixtures with the 40-watt bulbs, as opposed to the commonly available 25- or 30-watt bulbs.

HIGH-INTENSITY DISCHARGE LAMPS (HIDs)

If the term "high-intensity discharge lamps" sounds like the Defense Department's latest secret weapon, you're not too far off. This is some serious lighting. HIDs, as they are affectionately known to official lighting people, are the same type as the street lamps glowing faithfully every evening along your street. HIDs create light by passing electricity through a special vaporized gas that is usually under pressure.

These are the same lights that drug enforcement agents come across all the time. They call them "marijuana lights," due to their popularity among growers on the wrong side of the leaf law.

These lamps are usually either high-pressure sodium (HPS) or metal-halide (MH) lights. They give off by far the brightest light, and though they are relatively efficient in terms of electricity usage (in comparison to the amount of light they give off), they are also more expensive than the previously mentioned lights. The bulbs cost anywhere from $45 to $95, depending upon the wattage you need. But you need more than bulbs (read on): HID lighting systems usually start at a minimum of $250 to $300 and go up from there.

Shopping for these lights and lighting systems can be quite confusing. To make matters worse, there are always new types of bulbs coming out that don't follow some of the old rules of thumb. The first thing you should check into when purchasing a HID lighting system is getting the most bang for your buck. This comes down to getting the most foot-candles or lumens per watt of electricity. Each bulb sold usually lists its lumen output (which is basically the light output at the source) and the number of watts it uses. Simply divide the total lumens listed by the watts to get a number that you can use for comparison. The more lumens you get per watt the better. Let's look at the two main types of HID lights that are commonly available.

High-Pressure Sodium (HPS)

These lamps are identical to the yellowish street lights that have replaced the old bluish-colored mercury vapor lamps because they put out more light per watt and are thus cheaper to operate. The HPS lamps do an excellent job of growing plants, and they do a stellar job of triggering flowers (which also means you get fruit on fruiting crops). One of the downsides is that they give off a sickly yellow glow. This is not as noticeable in a greenhouse already receiving some natural sunlight. However, the yellow cast is unnerving at night.

HPS lights are highly efficient in terms of wattage per foot-candle or wattage per lumen. Also, the bulbs are very long-lived, up to 24,000 hours (which is equivalent to around 5 years of use). Because of the efficiency of the HPS lamps when compared to the metal-halide lights (see the following discussion on halide lights), HPS lights are a top choice for use by hobby greenhouse gardeners as well as commercial users. But many people don't like their sickly yellow light, so they go for metal halides. Also, in certain situations (such as starting seedlings), the MH lamps produce better-quality plants than the HPS lamps do with their limited spectrum.

Metal Halides (MH)

The metal halides emit a quality of light that is unlike most other artificial light, in that it appears to the human eye to be very similar to sunlight. They have a great balance of the spectrum that is both comfortable to the eye and good for photosynthetic activity. And like sunlight, MH bulbs also produce ultraviolet light, which could damage your eyes (if you stared at them for long periods) and possibly give you a bit of a tan or even a sunburn (or light burn?) if you're working under them for long periods

of time. It's not a bad idea to wear sunglasses and protective clothing when working under these lights.

The metal halides are not as energy efficient as the HPS lamps, but they are about equal in efficiency to a fluorescent (which still isn't bad). Working around MH lamps requires some caution, because if they are wired incorrectly or accidentally bumped hard or sprayed with cold water, they can explode. Because of this, many are sold with a protective glass covering in front of the light. Metal halides are the top choice for people who are growing crops in sunless enclosures or with little natural sunlight. They are also the choice of greenhouse gardeners who want their gardens and sunspaces to look pleasant to the eye when the lights are illuminating the space at night.

MH lamps are most often used commercially in propagation of seedlings, because they seem to grow young plants slightly better than HPS lamps. One of the drawbacks to MH lamps is that they usually have a shorter hours-of-life rating. Remember that the HPS lamp is rated at around 24,000 hours of life, whereas the MH lamps vary, ranging from 7,500 to a maximum of around 20,000 hours (depending upon brand). MH bulbs make up for their shorter life span by often being less expensive than the HPS lamps. There are also newer "super" MH lamps that can give off up to 10 percent more light than the older MH bulbs.

Life of the HID Bulb

Another important factor is the life of the bulb. You might get a good amount of light per watt, but the expensive bulb may not last as long. Fortunately, most bulbs have a stated "rated hours of life," listed as part of the specification. As the bulbs age, the amount of light they give off usually decreases. The life of the bulb is another

(Top) *The life of the bulb is an important factor with HID lighting systems.*
(Bottom) *This HID light has a remote ballast so the fixture is significantly lighter.* Photo courtesy of Charley's Greenhouse Supply.

important factor to consider prior to purchasing any HID lighting system.

Ballasts for an HID System

There is much more to an HID lighting system than simply the lightbulb. You'll also need what's known as a "ballast." A ballast gives the lamp its correct voltage. A ballast is usually a heavy metal box, and you need one ballast per bulb. Depending upon the system you choose, the light can either have the ballast attached as part of the bulb and reflector or be separate from the bulb so it can be located out of the way and not shade the crop from natural sunlight when the sun is out.

A ballast is usually specific as to the type of bulb it can handle. For instance, high-pressure sodium lamps can only work in ballasts designed specifically for them. The same is true for metal-halide lamps and their specific ballasts.

For people who wish they could operate a type of bulb not suitable for their particular ballast system, there is a possible solution.

There are special bulbs known as "conversion bulbs" to address this problem. For example, if you have a high-pressure sodium HID system and want to run a metal-halide HID type of light, there is a conversion bulb that will work. The same is true if you have a metal-halide ballast system and wish to run a high-pressure sodium-type bulb. In general, conversion bulbs are not as efficient in terms of watts consumed per lumen when compared to using the bulb for which the ballast was originally designed.

Electrical Needs for HID Systems

One HID light can consume between 400 and 1,000 watts. Many people opt for more than one light in a system. It can add up to a lot of wattage. Therefore, it is important to first check whether your house can handle that kind of additional drain on your circuit breakers or fuses. While you're at it, be sure your pocketbook can handle the increase in your monthly electric bills. It's always a good idea to consult an electrician in both the planning and installation of HIDs.

Running a few 1,000-watt lights can cause a noticeable bump in your electric bill. In the zeal to control drug use, authorities have been known to scan electric billing records for jumps in electric usage, assuming the cause is a new home-marijuana production operation. So if you add an array of HID lights to your greenhouse, don't be surprised if you have someone knocking at your door with a badge. Big Brother? Perhaps.

Other HID Lighting-System Considerations

There are some other things you should know before making an investment in HID lighting. First, some HID lights can be quite noisy and not the kind of thing you would want buzzing in an attached sunspace, especially if you like to spend time relaxing in or near there. This is something to check out before you buy.

HID lights can also become hot. This is both good and bad—good in that they will actually help heat your greenhouse in winter when you tend to need lighting the most. If your greenhouse is running too hot already, though, it could be a problem. Heat from HID lights can also burn the plants, so you must keep the lights an adequate distance away from the plants. The hot lamps could be dangerous to people as well if someone were to get too near them. Many lamps come with fans to provide cooling when they are on. Extreme heat will also shorten the life span of the ballast. One company even has a water-cooled HID light that needs (of course) extra plumbing.

Don't start flicking the on–off switch on HID lights because they won't restart immediately. They need to cool off for anywhere from 2 to 20 minutes before they will be able to glow properly again.

As with all lights, the amount of foot-candles a plant receives from the lamp decreases as you increase the distance between the light and the plant. This must be balanced with the need to illuminate the most plants per light, which requires that you move the light back away from the plants a bit. For example, a 1,000-watt high-pressure sodium lamp mounted at a 3-foot (0.9 m) height might provide around 1,000 foot-candles to plants in the vicinity closer to the bulb. However, a plant that is farther away from the lamp, say 7 to 12 feet (2 to 3.6 m) away, might only get half of that many foot-candles, or even less.

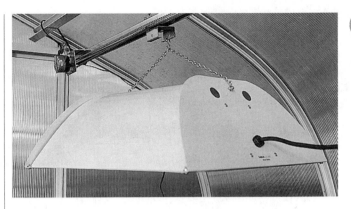

This HID lamp moves back and forth on a track that enables you to move the light back and forth in the greenhouse. This provides more uniform light to the plants as well as other advantages. Photo courtesy of Charley's Greenhouse Supply.

Increasing Lighting Efficiency

To use the lights most efficiently, manufacturers have found great ways to spread the light around the greenhouse, helping to illuminate more plants with less light. The most commonly used technique is to mount the lights on a track. The light has a built-in motor that moves the fixture back and forth over your plants. A moving light eliminates shading and allows more even growth and development, thus increasing your harvest. One such system takes twenty minutes to move 6 feet (1.8 m). There are other systems that move the light in a rotating circle. These light movers also minimize the possibility of light-caused plant burning. Some greenhouse gardeners take advantage of less burning with these light movers by moving the bulbs closer to the plants, to a foot or even less, which increases the amount of foot-candles the plant receives. Trying a closer position will likely require some monitored experimentation and perhaps the sacrifice of a plant or two.

Another common practice is to bounce the light around by reflecting it. By lining the perimeter of the growing area with a reflective material such as Mylar, over 98 percent of the light can be reflected back to the plant (see the discussion "Increasing Reflective Surfaces" later in this chapter). Bulbs also come with their own reflective hoods mounted directly over the bulb to focus more light downward. There are many variations on hood reflectors. The best hood-reflective surfaces tend to be the nonglossy white surfaces. By using the bulb movers and reflectors, you can get more foot-candles to your plants, which means you can get by with fewer watts or fewer bulbs.

HID lights are big compared with a regular incandescent lightbulbs, especially when you have a reflector as part of the apparatus (about the size of a large salad bowl). As mentioned earlier, many brands also contain the ballast as part of the lighting fixture, whereas others have the ballast separate. Because of their size, these lamps are usually mounted in the eaves of the home greenhouse.

Mixing HID Bulbs

Many gardeners have found that they can strike a good compromise and obtain the attributes of both types of HID lights by using a combination of high-pressure sodium and metal-halide bulbs in the same greenhouse. If you need more than one lighting fixture, this may provide a good solution.

Sizing HID Systems

What size HID light do you need for a greenhouse? Most lighting experts will tell you that the illumination is only slightly higher for high-pressure sodium lamps than for metal halides, therefore, they often use the same figures for both MH and HPS lighting. A common figure that many manufacturers use is 25 watts to 50 watts of HID light per square foot

of growing area. You can get by with less if you use rails or other light movers and other reflectors. This can also vary depending upon the height at which you mount the lighting system. For this, check with the manufacturers' recommended distance. Of course, check for plant burning before you let any lighting system go on its own.

Check with a retailer for more specific information. Also, lighting technology is rapidly changing, and these rules of thumb may not work over time. Here is a very rough sizing recommendation per watt for both HPS and MH: A 250-watt fixture will generally illuminate an area of 2 by 3 feet (0.6 by 0.9 m); a 400-watt fixture will light a 5 by 5 foot (1.5 by 1.5 m) area; a 1,000-watt fixture will illuminate an 8 by 8 foot (2.4 by 2.4 m) area for most growing needs. Again, for a more exact measurement please check with the lighting wholesaler or retailer.

The bigger the wattage, the bigger the lamp (and reflector). As a result, the 1,000-watt has a big reflector—sometimes as large as 25 by 30 inches (63.5 by 76.2 m)—which actually blocks out a fair amount of sunlight. Ironic, isn't it?

There is a lot to consider as you get more technical! You can see why I personally lean toward the simpler greenhouses for the home hobbyist. Figuring out which lights, which watts, which brand, and so on is like the math class you once dreaded and can become the "story problem" from hell. Still, if you live in an area with low winter-light potential, it may make a great deal of difference in whether you can grow successfully or not.

To pursue the idea of lighting your greenhouse further, try calling some of the many dealers offering lighting systems. You'll find them wherever you see hydroponics equipment sold. Also look for the magazine called the *Growing Edge,* often found at large bookstores (on the Internet, see www.growingedge.com). It is known for having many excellent greenhouse-oriented articles (usually with a hydroponic leaning). In *The Growing Edge* magazine, you will likely find advertising for lighting manufactures and retailers. Give some of these lighting retailers a call and you might find an "expert" to either enlighten you (pun intended) or further confuse you.

It will also help to buy your local electrician friend a beer or two before you get started. Perhaps you'll even decide to hire that friend to do the wiring job and save yourself from an "electrifrying" experience.

What does the future hold for supplemental lighting? New to the scene are lights that operate on microwaves. Currently, there is one bulb developed by FusionLighting and sold by BioLogic Technologies (website at www.biologictech.com) that utilizes microwave power to create light. The only one on the market at this writing is one called the Neutron 16. The beauty of using microwave energy to create light is that it is very energy efficient and doesn't require a filament. As a result, there is little to no degradation of the output of microwave-powered light over the life of the bulb. I am confident that in years to come we will see more innovations with lighting technology. Being an avid sci-fi reader, I predict we will someday mesh biotechnology with lighting physics and get biocellular lighting (glow-in-the-dark algae?). Ask your great-grandchildren about it someday.

By the way, how many lightbulbs does it take to blankety-blank? After dealing with greenhouse lighting you may need to lighten up. Check out the website at www.laughnet. net/archive/jokes/lightbul.htm, or just do a search on lightbulb jokes.

LIGHTING DURATION AND PHOTOPERIODS

Once you have a lighting system set up, the first question is: How long do you then leave lights shining each day? The simple answer is that you should turn them on for around 18 hours and leave them off the rest of the time. The off time should be during the night to insure proper photoperiod triggering (if needed). That leaves around 6 hours of having the lights off at night, if you do your math right. After all, plants need their rest, too! If you have decent daylight illumination, then save some money and turn off the lights when the sun is up and shining brightly into the greenhouse. Specific crops might require specialized schedules of lighting. If you are trying to trigger a plant to flower, then consider dropping back the hours to around 12 hours of light for a number of weeks.

Most commonly available timers work fine in turning on and off the lights. However, for optimum safety it is best to have a timer that has a three-pronged plug going into a three-pronged grounded outlet. Also, check the maximum watt capacity of the timer and don't exceed that capacity on any one timer or you could be asking for trouble in the form of an electrical fire.

INCREASING REFLECTIVE SURFACES

In the dark corners of your greenhouse, sufficient light may be lacking. Your plants will be telling you by the way they grow (elongating and bending toward the light). Shady areas are almost unavoidable in most greenhouses or sunspaces, but they are more common in

(Top) *White rock can function as a light reflector for a greenhouse.*
(Bottom) *Snow is a great light reflector for a greenhouse.*

those that are solar heated, which usually have glass or glazing only on one side. Shadows are also created by shelves and benches and around water drums in solar greenhouses. You can deal with these shady areas by placing shade-loving plants in these spots, or you can try bouncing light into these areas with reflective surfaces.

When we think of reflective surfaces, we usually envision metallic mirrored surfaces such as aluminum foil, Mylar, or the like. I like Mylar or aluminum foil for small spaces to increase reflective lighting as it is easy to set up. I often use it when I am propagating plants around a fluorescent light, wrapping it around to enclose the side areas and not allowing even one photon to escape.

To brighten up the whole greenhouse for better growing, I avoid these mirrored surfaces.

Although they do reflect a more accurate likeness of adjacent images, they are not the best overall light reflectors. They can focus light unevenly and even cause focused burning. Some aluminum reflectors are silver-gray in color. This color is halfway between the color white and black. Believe it or not, aluminum reflectors can and do absorb some light rather than reflecting as much as possible.

I have found that the best general wall reflector in a greenhouse is the color white. The more white surfaces in your greenhouse (except for glazing and thermal mass), the better your plants will grow. This means getting some high-quality gloss or semigloss white paint for the walls, the benches, and even the floor, if possible, to help reflect light. Check out the mildew-resistant paints designed for bathrooms. These paints last much longer in the greenhouse environment. There are also additives that provide additional mildew resistance. Epoxy paint lasts a long time, but it is expensive and has knock-you-on-your-rear fumes to contend with.

Paint the sides of your raised beds, trellising, potting bench, and anything else to bounce that precious sunlight around (don't get carried away and paint your seedlings or family pets!). You might also consider using a light-colored material for your floor, whether you settle on some type of waterproof flooring, gravel, or concrete walks.

Another solution to low-light greenhouses is to spread white rock on the outside of your greenhouse (south side), which will actually reflect more winter light into the structure (snow does this, too). This has been a successful practice with many greenhouses in areas that have cloudy winters and limited snow, such as the Pacific Northwest coast.

There are those of you with beautiful rock surfaces or exposed wood in your greenhouse saying to yourselves, "Paint this beautiful wood white, no way!" I can understand a reluctance to paint over a beautiful natural surface, so if this is your situation, you may want to look at installing more overhead glazing to increase light or perhaps consider the supplementary-light option mentioned previously in this chapter. Another option might be to hang a white curtain over your fancy wood or rock and then pull the curtain back to expose the pretty wood or rock when you want to show off the space to others.

For those of you who have solar greenhouses, paint everything white except for surfaces that you'll want to absorb solar heat (such as water barrels or rock walls).

If you have oil drums (or the like) along the north wall for thermal mass, you've probably noticed that area becoming a shady spot in the summer. Again, try the white-curtain solution here to cover the barrels in the summer to reflect more light. This will help keep the greenhouse cooler in the summer. When cool weather returns, pull the curtain back or, better yet, take the curtain down.

CARBON DIOXIDE (CO_2) IN THE GREENHOUSE

As I mentioned earlier, carbon dioxide in the air is essential to photosynthesis. The normal level of carbon dioxide in the air is about 300 parts per million (ppm), or .03 of 1 percent of the air we breathe. Because about 50 percent of a plant is made of carbon (and all that must come from the air), you can see that plants have quite an appetite for CO_2. Much of the CO_2 normally occurring in the air comes from animals (everything from bacteria to humans), the burning of fossil fuels, and the decomposition of organic matter. It is a component of what you are exhaling out of your lungs right now. Plants love you for your kind words and attention, but they also love you for your body—well, at least for your high-CO_2-laden breath.

When CO_2 is scarce, plant growth slows. But when the supply of CO_2 increases beyond the normal 300 ppm (up to a certain point), plant growth increases.

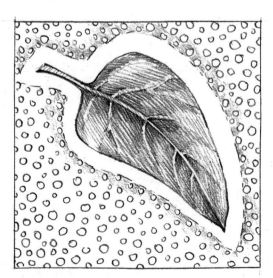 

*In still air (**left**), a leaf draws out most of the surrounding CO_2 above the cell surface, creating an envelope of CO_2 deficiency around the leaf. Turbulent air (**right**) prevents CO_2 deficiency, allowing plants to use the ambient CO_2 better.*

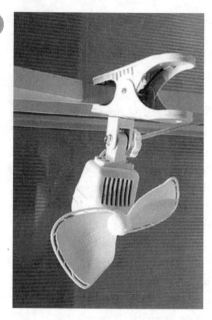

Use a fan to stir up the air to help plants make better use of CO_2 in the air. Photo courtesy of Charley's Greenhouse Supply.

When plants are in a sealed environment such as a greenhouse, they can actually deplete the supply of CO_2 in the air. This is exactly what happens in a greenhouse in winter when the doors are sealed tight. The level of CO_2 has been seen to drop from normal ambient level of 300 ppm down to 100 ppm by noon on an average winter day. This can slow plant growth by 68 percent—not a pleasant thought. This phenomenon occurs only in winter greenhouses when there is no outside ventilation and the structure is sealed to the outside. CO_2 depletion is much less in attached greenhouses where there are people, gas stoves, pets, and so on, all producing extra CO_2.

Depletion of CO_2 is also less in greenhouses with soils high in organic matter because of the billions of microbes breathing in that black, pulsing-with-life, humus-rich soil. But depletion may still occur because, by nature, our new sunspaces and solar greenhouses are tight structures.

What does a CO_2-deficient plant look like? Well, that's the big problem. It's almost impossible to see a CO_2 deficiency, because the only symptom is slower growth. You won't see any telltale signs in the crop you are growing. There is equipment available to measure CO_2 amounts in the air, but it's expensive and difficult to obtain.

CO_2 ENHANCEMENT

Early greenhouse operators in Europe quickly discovered that when they added a mulch composed of manure, peat moss, sawdust, and straw around plants, they saw an increase in crop production. Around the early 1900s, scientific experiments proved that CO_2 was created during the decomposition of organic materials in the soil. It was not until the late 1950s and early 1960s that researchers worked with levels higher than the normal ambient (300 ppm) amounts. Enhancing CO_2 levels from a depleted greenhouse atmosphere of 100 ppm all the way to 1,500 ppm resulted in significant yield increases. Since the 1960s, many commercial greenhouse growers have been enhancing the CO_2 levels in winter greenhouses to 1,200–1,500 ppm, with a yield increase of 10 to 30 percent. It's like fertilizing the plants through the air. However, there is such a thing as too much CO_2. It is thought that anything above 2,000 ppm is a wasted effort, and continuous exposure to levels of 5,000 ppm may be a problem to human health. What a way to go!

VENTILATION FOR MORE CO_2 FOR YOUR PLANTS

The amount of carbon dioxide supplied to the plant from the atmosphere depends upon the level of CO_2 at the leaf surface or, even more precisely, the CO_2 level at the cell surface on the leaf. In still air, a leaf can draw out most of the CO_2 at the cell surface, thus creating an envelope of CO_2 deficiency around the leaf. When there is no turbulence, CO_2 replenishment is slow. A lack of turbulence can be a common problem in the winter greenhouse, triggering carbon-dioxide deficiencies even though there is plenty of the gas in the air.

Turbulent air around a leaf disperses this envelope of low carbon-dioxide concentration, replenishing the air adjacent to the leaf with an ample supply of CO_2, so there is something good about wind. Research in the Netherlands by P. Gaastra in 1963 showed that the rate of photosynthesis can be increased by as much as 40 percent with no change in atmospheric CO_2 when the wind velocity increases from 4 to 40 inches (10 to 100 cm) per second.

The lesson here is to keep the air constantly moving around during the day, especially in winter when your windows are closed, and you will have better greenhouse plant growth. In winter, I set up a small fan to stir up the air. In larger greenhouses, a cheap Casablanca-style ceiling fan works well, especially if you can control the speed of the paddles. It seems to work best if you run the fans on days with good light (partly cloudy days or sunny days). When the day is dark, cool, and cloudy, it can be uncomfortable (for people, not plants) to have the fans on, and there is less photosynthesis. This is when I tend to turn the fans down or off.

One final note on greenhouse turbulence. There is no need to stir the air up for carbon dioxide during the night, because plants don't use CO_2 in the dark.

INCREASING CARBON DIOXIDE

Commercial growers are able to increase the level of CO_2 by burning propane or natural gas. It has also been increased by burning kerosene and less commonly by the release of CO_2 from pressurized tanks of liquid CO_2, which vaporize the gas in the air. The burning of fossil fuels for CO_2 requires special burners (called CO_2 generators) because the normal exhaust would contain carbon monoxide, sulfur, and fluorides, which are poisonous to plants and humans.

Because most of us can't afford a CO_2 generator or the fuel to run one, there are alternatives for the home grower, ranging from the use of decomposing organic matter in your soil as a mulch to even raising a few caged animals in the greenhouse (often chickens or rabbits). Unfortunately, raising animals in a greenhouse can cause offensive odors and added trouble. Manure from unclean cages and pens may emit ammonia gas, which in high concentration may cause some damage to plants.

So, perhaps adding and maintaining a high level of organic matter in your soil is the best solution, along with using some small fans. Of course, this is the simplest solution as well. Attached-greenhouse growers should probably not even worry about the addition of CO_2.

COMPOSTING, CO_2, AND THE HOME GREENHOUSE

Let's look at some specifics when it comes to organic matter, compost, and the level of CO_2 in your greenhouse air. When compost is mixed into the soil as an amendment or as mulch, it produces CO_2. Few people have the room to compost in their greenhouse, but let's look at this for a minute. Compost not only produces CO_2 but also gives off heat. As it breaks down, a compost pile can easily run above 100°F (38°C), which can even help to heat a greenhouse in winter. The former New Alchemy Institute of East Falmouth, Massachusetts, constructed an experimental composting greenhouse back in the 1980s in which half of the greenhouse was set aside for composting and was loaded from the outside. Inside, a significant increase in CO_2 (as high as 650 ppm) was noted, and, in addition, the compost contributed a major amount of heat to the greenhouse.

In other experiments, compost pioneers have been able to raise CO_2 levels in greenhouses to as high as 800 ppm to 2,000 ppm. Danish growers achieved CO_2 levels up to a whopping 5,000 ppm (possibly too high for humans with a long exposure). This was solely with the addition of a manure, peat, and straw mulch, applied at a rate of 200 tons (181.4 metric tons) per acre in their greenhouses. Well, it's unlikely any home greenhouse owner will import 200 tons of compost into a greenhouse. But if you have the situation of gardening in your greenhouse with raised beds (which I prefer over small containers), then you can actually increase the level of CO_2 substantially with a highly organic-based soil.

It is not all good news with CO_2 enhancement, however. *GM Pro Magazine* (a magazine for commercial greenhouse professionals) related research from the University of Guelph in Canada that demonstrated CO_2 may have some effects on insects. They found that CO_2 enhancement inhibits thrips in the initial stage of crop growth but enhances the growth of whiteflies and spider mites. Aphids also seem to grow more rapidly on young plants under higher CO_2 levels. Sometimes the increased growth of the plants as a result of the enrichment allowed plants to outgrow the effect of increasing pests. Someone once said this in a much more elegant way: When you mess with the environment, it is never simple.

You can't beat homemade compost for a home greenhouse, and it is so simple to make. For years I've had a compost pile in my backyard, and I'm always amazed at how much it returns to me in beautiful dark compost, for both my outside garden and my greenhouse, for such a small amount of work and effort. A friend recently bought his wife a garbage disposal as a birthday present. I realized for the first time that the thought of needing a garbage disposal had never occurred in our household. Our compost pile has served this same purpose so very well. Besides, garbage disposals break and get silverware stuck in them,

causing all kinds of trouble; a compost pile never breaks and won't eat your silverware.

SETTING UP FOR COMPOSTING

Some of you creative thinkers may be wondering right now: Why not put a compost pile in my greenhouse? The only major problem with that idea is the valuable space it can take up. That space might be better utilized by the growing plants, so unless you have a large greenhouse, I would suggest that you compost outside and then use the finished compost product inside your greenhouse.

Composting can be done in a dug-out trench, in fancy barrels sold by garden supply companies, or in homemade areas set aside with cinder blocks or fencing. Check out books on the composting subject, or better yet, find a simple brochure on composting. Often, cities have such a brochure on composting. After all, composting is really a simple thing to do. It doesn't matter how you compost. It is more important that you just get in the habit of composting, no matter how you pull it off.

The first step in getting into the practice of composting is to set a 1-gallon (3.8-liter) bucket with a lid next to your kitchen trash can and then get into the habit of filling it with appropriate kitchen scraps (soon to be greenhouse fertilizer). Then you set up your composting area outside. As your bucket fills, it gives you the perfect opportunity to go outside and take a deep breath of fresh air—perhaps you'll even catch a great sunset. If you have kids, this makes a great kid chore if you don't mind missing out on the fresh air.

I want to simplify the process of composting right now for those people who have had a history of bad luck with composting in the past or for you newcomers.

The first question is: What can go into a compost pile? Answer: Just about anything that was once growing or part of a living thing is fair game—virtually any kitchen scrap, from coffee grounds to potato skins.

What can't go into the pile? Avoid meat or meat by-products (they attract flies and dogs, and meat stinks up the neighborhood). Don't put any really salty food such as potato chips or pickles in the pile. Salt is tough on any garden soil. Watch out for anything that could be treated with herbicide. Grass clippings sprayed for dandelions are OK if they have been sitting in a separate pile for at least two months before adding to the compost. Compost starters have only a slight effect, so don't waste your money on them. You can readily inoculate your pile by adding a shovelful of manure or garden soil. Wood ash should be avoided in areas with alkaline soils. Wood or pieces of wood can also be a problem because wood takes forever to compost unless it is in sawdust form. Chipped wood is better used for paths in the garden to keep the weeds down.

CLASSIFY YOUR COMPOST

What I want you to do now is to set up a two-category classification system in your mind that labels everything you would commonly throw into a compost pile. Category one is what we will call the green list. The green list would include anything that is green and also includes all kitchen scraps (except meat, of course), coffee grounds, fresh garden waste, and manure. The term "green" basically means materials that are relatively high in nitrogen and low in carbon. But we can stretch the meaning of green a bit. Even brown human hair, being high in nitrogen, goes into the green category. Now you're wondering if I'm crazy. Hair is great for compost, which is good to know if you've just given the kid or the dog a haircut.

Compost is a great soil supplement! Setting up and using a compost pile is easy and rewarding.

The second category is what I call the "brown" list. This includes everything that is brown, meaning material such as straw, sawdust, and any plant refuse or organic matter that has turned brown (leaves, tan grass clippings, and so forth). These are things that are relatively low in nitrogen and high in carbon (compared to our green list of ingredients).

The key to this classification comes later in the compost recipe.

Before I give you the recipe, I must also give you the basic compost rules. These rules apply to the care and feeding of the microscopic critters that make compost happen (have you seen the bumper sticker "Compost Happens"?). It is the microbes that transform your refuse into rich humus for your garden. If you keep the microbes happy, the pile is a success. The mark of success is that the compost pile heats up and begins to break down into a material that looks more like good, rich dirt.

Compost Rules

1. **The smaller the size of the ingredients, the faster your compost breaks down.** The compost critters simply have less work

THE COMPOST TROUBLESHOOTER

Problem	Solution
Pile doesn't heat up	Check moisture; add more green material.
Pile smells bad	Add air holes or turn the pile; cut back on water if too wet.
Pile is slow to break down	The pieces you have added may be too large—chop them up or shred them. Or it may be too cold outside; be patient, things will speed up when the weather heats up.

to do if you start with smaller stuff. Make your ingredients smaller by just attacking them with a sharp-edged shovel on the ground before you throw them into the pile. Or you can go all out by obtaining a shredder/grinder. The basic goal is to get the ingredients no larger than 8 or 10 inches (20 or 25 cm) on any one side. I never chop up my kitchen scraps (they're usually small enough), but I do attack a cornstalk with a shovel before adding it to the compost pile.

2. **Compost needs to breathe oxygen to do the job well.** Actually, it's the microscopic organisms that need to breathe, and who doesn't need to breathe? If these critters can find adequate oxygen, they will happily eat up the raw materials, turning them into humus. You can get your compost pile to breathe in a couple of ways. One is by turning the pile every 2 weeks or so with a pitchfork or shovel. You can turn it less frequently

in winter, as the pile is usually more dormant then. For us lazy folks, there is another method to get air into the compost. Poke it full of holes! You can use an old broomstick, or if you want "poking perfection," there is a special tool developed to poke holes into the compost, which I have found to work well. It is known as a compost aerator and is a short metal pole with two wings that fold up as you poke down into your pile. When you pull it out of your pile, the metal wings open and fluff the pile as you withdraw it, adding air to your pile. It is readily available in many garden catalogs and is not very expensive.

3. **Compost piles need a drink.** Sometimes I need a drink, too, come Fridays! The microscopic critters who work the pile need occasional water to do the job of composting well. Now, don't get carried away and drown them. The pile needs to be moist—like a wrung-out towel, but not dripping wet! So an occasional watering is helpful to a good pile if it hasn't rained in a while. If it is raining too much, you might want to consider a tarp to protect the pile temporarily. Too much water and it will start to smell.

Now that we have our rules, let me give you a recipe for making some first-class compost.

The Compost Recipe

1. Combine by volume 1 part brown stuff to 1 part green stuff. Exceptions: Manures are twice as green as regular green stuff, so adjust accordingly and use $1/2$ part manure to 1 part brown stuff. Sawdust is twice as brown as regular brown stuff, so use only $1/2$ part sawdust to 1 part green stuff. These proportions can be added over time and don't even have to be added at the same

time. One day you can add green, the next day it can be brown. The main thing is that the final proportions should be close to this over time.

2. Occasionally mix the ingredients (there is no need to layer the pile) so that there is not a high concentration of either green or brown stuff in any one place in the pile.

3. Allow the pile to breathe and maintain moisture.

4. To get the pile to go through the winter, it needs to be at least a few square yards in size. If not, no big deal. It'll get going again come spring.

That's all!

POSITIVE RESULTS

When you compost you are greatly reducing your impact on the local landfill. You are also going to end up with an excellent fertilizer for your greenhouse. It is best to add about 2 to 3 inches (5 to 8 cm) of compost to your greenhouse soil about once or twice a year, depending upon how intensively you are growing plants in your beds. Do this prior to starting each new crop. You can also add compost to your potting mixes if you are growing primarily in containers and not using beds.

Compost has the added benefit of giving off a fair amount of CO_2 into your greenhouse air, which will help increase the rate of plant growth. For more information on fertilizers, potting mixes, and containers, see Chapter 9, "Getting to the Roots."

WATERING YOUR GREENHOUSE PLANTS

The problem is this: People generally think that they are good at watering. But this is where most people make the biggest mistakes in growing plants. Usually the problem lies in overwatering.

In the soil, there are small, open air pores that are important to roots. Roots not only take up water but also take in gases through these air pores. When you water, all those air spaces get filled up. Since roots can't come up for air like whales, overwatering the poor little roots causes suffocation. The odd thing is this: When roots suffocate, the most common symptom is wilting, which creates the almost irresistible urge among greenhouse gardeners to ... you guessed it! Greenhouse gardeners with the most frequent overwatering problems are people living in dry western climates because they are so used to watering their outside garden on a regular basis. When you come in the greenhouse, remember this rule for all greenhouse gardening: Even though it works outside, it may not work inside.

One reason a greenhouse uses less water is that it is a closed system. When you water in the winter and the windows are closed, there is nowhere for the water to go. You might even say greenhouses are quite water efficient. So what are the variables that we must look at when deciding how often and how much to water?

KNOWING WHEN TO WATER

Rule Number One: Don't water out of habit! Always check the soil before you water. When plants are wilting from drought, you are too late; some damage has been done. But few people realize that wilting can also be a symptom of overwatering. In cooler greenhouses, plants may also wilt because the air is cold. So, wilting is not a dependable indicator of when to water; however, it is a symptom that should not be ignored. If the soil is dry and the air is hot, then by all means, go ahead and water! But if you are only watering when you see wilt-

Sometimes the best way to prevent overwatering is to hand water only where needed with a watering can rather than blast everything with a hose nozzle.

ing plants, then you are using the too-late approach.

With the exception of seedlings, you should water very little or not at all on cloudy,

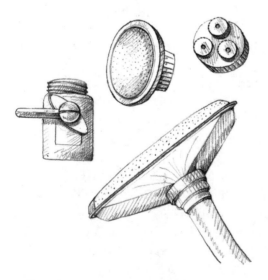

*Different hose-end nozzles are essential if you are to provide the right moisture levels to the wide array of plants in your greenhouse. The misting nozzle (**upper right**) is great for seedlings and winter watering. The fan (**bottom**) and round nozzles (**upper middle**) are fine for general watering. A heavy duty on-off valve (**left**) helps minimize excess water when watering between pots and beds.*

cool winter days. There is usually no need for it. Seedlings are different because they need constant moisture, especially if they are being given bottom heat. When you water, always try to do it in the morning to prevent evening condensation on the leaves, which can promote disease problems. Also, the greenhouse tends to need less water in the coldest winter months than during other times of the year. During periods of prolonged cold, cloudy weather, I have gone more than a week without a major watering. Except for seedlings, it is always better to do less frequent, heavier waterings than to get in the habit of frequent light waterings. Frequent light waterings also pose a problem because excess soil salts (that occur naturally and from fertilizers) accumulate and move with water. With frequent light waterings, these salts are never drained out of the soil. As these salts accumulate, they may reach toxic levels. The solution is to leach the salts out of the pot or drain them down below the root zone with an occasional heavy watering that moves the salts.

HAND WATERING

Irrigation systems, drip systems, misters, water sensors? Nah … old-fashioned hand watering is probably the most practical way for most home-greenhouse owners to water. By the term "hand watering," I mean using either a watering can or watering from a hose. Watering cans are helpful for watering small dry spots or an occasional water-hungry potted plant. It is important to obtain a quality watering can with a nozzle that lets the water out like a gentle rain. Whether you are using a watering can or a hose, be careful about the force of water coming out so hard that it knocks down seedlings or young plants. This can injure plants and expose them to disease or even snap their stems.

WATERING BASICS

Symptoms of Overwatering

1. Bluish-green mold growth appears on the soil surface.
2. There is an increase in seedling or plant diseases and seeds germinate poorly.
3. The number of slugs feeding on leaves increases (for "slugfests," see page 411, Chapter 10, "When Things Go Wrong").
4. Growth slows because there is less air in the soil and roots need to breathe.
5. Leaves may turn yellow or have numerous yellow splotches; they eventually fall off the plant. If several leaves turn yellow at the same time, the likely cause is overwatering, cold drafts, or air pollution from a heater vent or unvented burner.
6. The most cruel symptom—wilting—appears. Guess what most people do when they see wilting?

Variables Affecting Watering

1. The more sunshine plants receive, the more water they will need.
2. The more venting you do to cool the greenhouse, the more water your plants will need.
3. Different plants have different watering requirements. For example, cacti need less water than most plants (you knew that, right?). Seedlings and seeds trying to germinate need steady moisture and must never dry out. They should be constantly moist but not dripping wet or drowning in mud.
4. Clay soils and soils very high in organic matter (including most commercial potting soils) require less water than do sandy or well-drained soils. If you are growing in beds, it is always a good idea to get your soil tested to find out what type you have and what it might need. Check with your county agent for instructions.

Testing Soil for Watering

The first step in watering is to use your fingers instead of your eyes. You can feel the moisture level in a bed or a pot easily by just poking your finger into the soil surface an inch or so. With a little experience you'll be able to tell when a plant needs water. For larger growing beds, you may want to try the ball method of testing the soil for moisture. This is especially good for people new to greenhouse gardening. First dig 1 inch under the surface and grab a handful of soil. Form a small 3-inch (8-cm) diameter ball out of this soil with your hands. Then try to toss the ball from hand to hand.

If the ball …	is powdery dry and won't form a ball, then water your plants!
If the ball …	falls apart easily when tossed, then water your plants.
If the ball …	falls apart, but only after a few hard tosses, then don't water. Maybe tomorrow.
If the ball …	doesn't fall apart, then don't water. Wait a few days.

(Continued on next page)

If the ball …   doesn't fall apart and water can be squeezed out in droplets, then you got carried away and overwatered. Hold off a day or more and try to perfect your technique!

One note on the ball method: Be aware that soils high in sand tend to fall apart more easily than other soils, so also take into account how wet the soil feels to the touch. Experience is the best teacher and, over time, you will have a ball (pun intended) getting a real feel for it.

Watering-can nozzles should also be removable for cleaning, as they often get plugged up.

When you need to do a major watering, a watering can may be a tedious way to go about it. It is probably much better to use a hose. The first step is to purchase a high-quality rubber hose. Keeping it off the ground will help prevent the spread of disease from the ground. Consider getting a hose winder from your local hardware store, garden center, or greenhouse supply company to help keep the hose tidy and out of the way. Or you can also use an old tire rim to wind the hose on, but it takes a bit more effort than the real hose winder.

The type of hose nozzle you use on the end of the hose is all-important in greenhouse watering. A few quality nozzles are the most important equipment purchases for your greenhouse. Much of this is personal preference, but to head you in the right direction, I will suggest a couple of specific nozzles.

The two good nozzles to have on hand include a misting nozzle and a water-breaker nozzle. A misting nozzle produces a fine mist and is ideal for starting and growing small seedlings or light winter watering. One brand name that is commonly available is Fogg-it. This type of brass nozzle is used by professional growers and is available in different sizes, including "heavy mist," which puts out around 4 gallons (15 liters) of water per minute, and, on the other end of the spectrum, "super fine mist," which puts out only $\frac{1}{2}$ gallon (1.9 liters) of water per minute. There are also two sizes in between. You may want to have an assortment of these nozzles for different situations. These nozzles run around $5 each. If you have only one Fogg-it nozzle, I would suggest the "fine mist" nozzle. It puts out around 1 gallon (3.8 liters) per minute and is great for seedlings.

Another favorite is the water-breaker nozzle, which is commonly found in garden catalogs. These are good for watering pots or beds. They are nice because they put out a fair

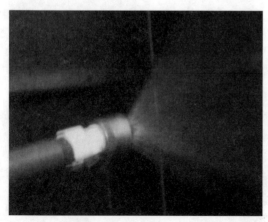

A misting nozzle is a great way to water fragile, young seedlings.

amount of water, but the stream is soft and won't knock down plants. "Dramm" is a good brand name for quality water-breaker nozzles.

When you water with a hose, it is helpful to have some type of hose extension handle, usually made of aluminum. This enables you to reach across beds or up high into hanging baskets. Extension handles are available in many different lengths, but I have found that a shorter length of around 16 to 24 inches (41 to 61 cm) works best in the small greenhouse.

A shut-off valve at the base of the extension handle is a favorite component of watering for me. Shut-off valves help prevent overwatering and enable you to put water only where you want it. In winter, the greenhouse is often too high in humidity because the water can't be vented out an open vent. This is where a shut-off valve really helps. You can turn off the flow of water between each pot or between each bed, keeping water off the floor and getting water only where it is needed. You will find both plastic and brass shut-off valves for hoses. Of course, the brass types are both better and more expensive.

When you have finished watering, be sure that you turn off the main hose valve at the faucet. If you use only your hose shut-off valve, leaving the main valve on for long periods of time, you can cause your hose to burst, creating leaks and other big wet problems that you don't need.

In general, when you are watering, try to keep the water off the leaves, with the following exceptions. Once a month or so it is good to water the leaves of your plants to wash off the accumulation of dust and debris. Sometimes it helps to water the leaves of plants prior to the introduction of beneficial insects if you opt for that type of pest control (see Chapter 10, "When Things Go Wrong," for more in-

formation). For the most part though, you should water the soil, not the plants. Try to avoid splashing mud, and be especially gentle with seedlings. A hard spray can bury seedlings forever and even knock down mature plants. Strive to have the water look like a gentle rain as it comes out of your nozzle. Water thoroughly and as infrequently as possible: When you do water, soak the beds well. Stop when puddles begin to form.

Never let the soil in your beds or pots completely dry out (except for cactus and other special plants). Besides the obvious stress that drought causes, you should also know that dry soil increases the concentration of fertilizer salts that naturally accumulate in the soil. This will cause the tips and margins of leaves to burn. To prevent this, try to occasionally water long enough so that the water penetrates deeply and flushes out the salts. These salts will move lower with the deeper watering, below the reach of roots. In pots, water will run out of the hole in the bottom, taking the salts with it.

When watering pots and containers, stop when the water comes out the drainage hole. If the soil in your container has dried out considerably, you may want to try the water-twice method. The first watering will immediately run out the bottom. However, it will cause the soil to expand and make contact with the sides of the pot. Still, the soil will have absorbed very little water. After a few minutes, do a second watering, which will soak into the center of the soil mass, finally getting water where the plant needs it. Sometimes this makes the saucer fill up and spill over, so be ready.

If you don't have the time or energy, there are systems you can set up to automatically water your greenhouse. These involve timers and extensive plumbing. These are usually

(Top) *A hygrometer will give you a good indication of humidity levels in the greenhouse.*
(Bottom) *This tank is designed to collect rainwater and is sold under the name "Water Butt."* Photos courtesy of Charley's Greenhouse Supply.

drip-irrigation or mini-mist systems. They're great if you're going to be away for awhile, but that is not all you need if you plan to be an absent greenhouse gardener. If it is a warm time of year, you may need an automatic ventilation system, too. When I leave town for a few days, I usually just hire a neighborhood youngster or ask a friend to watch things. Come on, now—get your friends and neighbors involved! Trade them some fresh flowers or produce from the greenhouse or sunspace harvest!

I generally don't advocate using automatic watering systems for day-to-day watering because it takes the fun out of greenhouse gardening. Watering is an important job, one that should not be left to a timer. If you are a gizmo nut, you can probably install an automatic system for $300 to $600, possibly even less if you are mechanically gifted in plumbing techniques. Check a greenhouse supply catalog for more information on automatic systems. Another alternative is to use the now commonly available black leaky-pipe drip system. It works like a soaker hose and can be easily laid under the plants.

WATER QUALITY

In some instances, people run into water-quality problems caused by pollutants or salts in the water. The quality of water varies greatly from region to region and is affected by both nature and people. It is the human factor that causes most problems because people often don't respect or maintain their water at a high-quality level.

Water is classified as either hard or soft. Hard water is high in minerals, usually calcium or magnesium carbonates. Dishwashing and laundry soaps work best in soft (low-mineral) water. People often soften hard water chemically for washing, but beware! Plants don't grow well in artificially softened water. Water softeners usually raise the sodium content in the soil, which causes poor soil structure and poor drainage. It is best to plumb your greenhouse with water that has not been run through a water-softener system.

Generally, chlorine is no problem, but if you suspect an unusually high level, just let some water sit in a bucket or in a plumbed 55-gallon (208-liter) drum overnight, and most of the chlorine will disappear. Usually, the amount of chlorine that it would take to harm plants would probably harm you first and the water wouldn't be suitable to swallow.

Highly fluoridated water can also be harmful to plants. Fluoride is added to many town water supplies to help prevent tooth decay. In many parts of the country, it occurs naturally in the water. Horticultural research has shown that fluoride may cause some leaf-tip burning, especially if your soil pH is below 6.5. Tip burn can also be caused by other factors, including a high soil pH, overfertilization, or a high level of salts. If you suspect the possibility of fluoride injury, be sure your water and soil are in the range between 6.7 and 7.3 pH. For more explanation of pH, see Chapter 9, "Getting to the Roots." For information on the additives to your drinking water, contact your local water board or local government.

Unless you live in an area where acid rain is a problem, rainwater may be a good alternative to tap water. But winter collection may pose a bit of a problem in cold areas. You'll have to be creative.

Droughts seem to occur somewhere in our country each year. Some droughts have been so severe that the growing of gardens has even been restricted by local governments. When water resources are scarce, people have often turned to gray water. "Gray water" is wastewater from sinks, clothes washers, bathtubs, and showers. As much as 80 gallons (303 liters) a day can be reused from a household of four. Please use extreme caution when using gray water and consider the following if you choose to use it in the greenhouse.

Gray water is commonly caught in buckets from disconnected sink traps, though more sophisticated systems are possible. Unfortunately, you may be breaking the law, as many areas have local ordinances against reusing water because of safety concerns. If you are concerned about usage, check with local authorities. I don't want you to break the law. If the quality of your water turns out to be a real problem, the only solution is locating another water source. Capturing rainwater at the drain spout is always a possibility to investigate before you get into using gray water.

WATER TEMPERATURE

No one likes to be splashed with cold water—and neither do plants. Cold water slows plant growth and lowers the soil temperature tremendously. Water is considered cold when it is below 43°F (6°C). The ideal water temperature for plants is between 65°F and 80°F (18°C and 27°C); above 80°F (27°C) is usually too hot.

TIPS FOR USING GRAY WATER

1. Avoid laundry water that contains bleaches, boron (borax), and high-sodium detergents. Because most detergents contain some sodium, it is usually best not to use laundry water; however, you can still use the rinse water.
2. Dilute gray water by 50 percent with tap water or rainwater when possible.
3. Devise a sand and gravel filter to remove lint, grease, and other impurities. Even a double-layer cloth bag around the end of a hose can help filter gray water.
4. Use mild, simple soaps. Castile soaps work well for gray water recycling.
5. Wash and rinse all your greenhouse produce before consuming it. For an extra measure of safety, soak vegetables and harvested fruits in a few drops of chlorine bleach per gallon of water, then rinse with tap water before you eat them. This is one way to help prevent the growth of harmful microorganisms that might occur with gray water.
6. Never drink this water.

HUMIDITY

Did you know that all plants have small openings in their leaves? Through these openings gases such as CO_2 and oxygen pass. Also, because plants don't use all the water they take up, a large amount of water vapor is emitted through these openings.

Vapor is also in the greenhouse atmosphere from water that has hit the soil or walkways and evaporated (use that shut-off valve to minimize this!). All this water vapor is called humidity.

SOME OPTIONS FOR RAISING WINTER WATER TEMPERATURES

1. Plumb in domestic hot water from your home hot-water heater. Be sure to have it run through a mixing valve with cold water.

2. Plumb a hose bib into the side of a black 30- or 55-gallon (113- or 208-liter) metal drum or even a plastic trash can. The drum must sit in the sun (to use solar heating) in a high location to use gravity flow for your pressure (see illustration on page 53). Then run your hose out of this valve after the water has warmed to room temperature or warmer.

3. Set a coil of black plastic tubing up against your north wall, which receives winter sun. Connect one end of the tubing to your house plumbing and put a valve on the other end for watering. Using solar energy, this will warm up the water a few degrees.

4. Look into commercially available solar water-heating systems. The company Zomeworks (**www.zomeworks.com**) carries the only one I've heard of for greenhouses. It's called Big Fin. See Appendix 7 for more information.

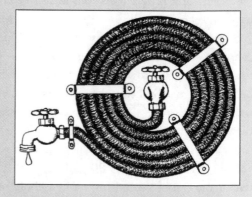

To warm up greenhouse water, try constructing a coil of black plastic tubing against your north wall, which receives winter sun. Connect one end of the tubing to your house plumbing and put a valve on the other end for watering. Using solar energy, this will warm up the water a few degrees.

Relative humidity is the term most often used to quantify the invisible water vapor in the air. More simply, it tells us how wet the air is based upon the air temperature. It is this relationship between water vapor and air temperature that gives us the term "relative." Relative humidity can be measured by a hygrometer, an inexpensive instrument. Hygrometers can be found in scientific instrument catalogs. With a hygrometer, humidity is often expressed as a percentage of the maximum moisture the air can hold at a given temperature and pressure.

Hot air can hold more moisture than cold air. When wet warm air comes in contact with a cold window, the air temperature rapidly cools. The resulting cool air can't hold onto the moisture, so it condenses (changes from vapor to liquid). This causes water droplets to form on your greenhouse glazing from the water vapor condensing. The colder the windows, the more condensation droplets form. This is why a single layer of glazing has more droplets forming on it than double or triple glazing. The more insulated the glazing, the warmer the interior surface of the glazing and the less condensation will form on the glazing.

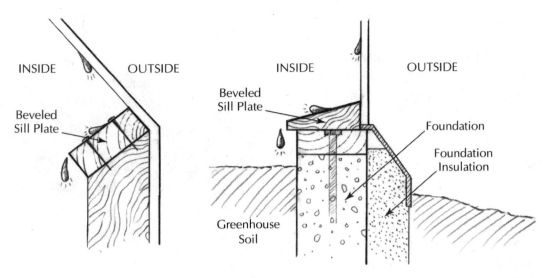

Condensation forms in every greenhouse, so it is important to use gravity effectively to allow the condensation to flow off of the structure. Try tilting or beveling structural areas that are normally flat, like the sills shown here. By avoiding a design with horizontal areas where water can collect, you will avoid rotting and premature structure failure.

THE WATER MUST GO SOMEWHERE

In the winter greenhouse, there is little air infiltration from the outside, so heat is retained and relative humidity is often high. Most plants grow best at a relative humidity between 45 and 60 percent. But the incidence of diseases also increases in higher humidity. Studies show that humidity over 80 percent fosters rapid development of various forms of leaf mold and fruit, flower, and stem diseases. Disease problems may become worse if the high humidity occurs at night. This is a good reason to avoid late-afternoon watering.

Another problem associated with high humidity is the aforementioned condensation. Condensation not only occurs on glazing but also on cold walls, doors, and even the roof, which sometimes drips as though it were raining, giving the illusion of a little weather system cruising through the greenhouse.

The problem with condensation on glazing is that it can block incoming light and solar heat. This can be a problem in solar-heated greenhouses or in greenhouses located in low-light areas.

Another problem with condensation is that it will drip onto your greenhouse's sills. If your greenhouse has sills made of wood, you may soon see some serious structural rot problems from the continual water contact. Some metal structures may also succumb to constant water contact. The solution to this structural damage lies in minimizing the humidity and condensation. It can also be dealt with by beveling any wood surface that could hold water. This alone can add years to the life of a wooden greenhouse. For metal structures, try to minimize any horizontal surfaces that could hold water from drips or condensation.

With double or triple glazings, always try to get a tight seal between the glazing and the frame to minimize condensation in this vulnerable place.

Many newer plastic glazings have been treated with a surface coating that helps to prevent droplets from forming. Some glazings are treated with compounds that provide a slickness on the interior glazing surface, causing the droplets to readily roll off. This allows more light to enter the glazing but could be a problem if the water were to land on a horizontal sill. There are also materials that you can spray on glazings to achieve similar results. These products help but do not cure the condensation problem.

Conventionally heated greenhouses have fewer problems with high humidity than solar-heated greenhouses. This is because the active heating burns off some of the humidity; however, they are not totally immune to condensation problems.

With high humidity, condensation is just a fact of life in winter greenhouses. Probably the one thing you can do is "water smart" and not out of habit, thus minimizing your watering. It's rare to see a home greenhouse that isn't overwatered to some extent. Overwatering is often the root of the problem, because all that water has to go somewhere and a good proportion of it ends up causing problems. Please read "Knowing When to Water" (page 33) in this chapter, and ask yourself before you grab for the hose, "Do I really need to water?"

WOOD IN THE HUMID GREENHOUSE

One thing you can do when you are in the process of building or rebuilding a greenhouse is to be sure any exposed wood surfaces in the greenhouse have been treated to prevent rot. Be careful here, because some materials that prevent wood rot also prevent the growth of plants and may be harmful to your health. You should avoid any wood preservatives that are made up of creosote, pentoxide, or pentachlorophenal (also known as "penta") because they are toxic to plants.

Even rot-resistant wood can eventually rot when constantly exposed to moisture.

I'll never forget a woman I met years ago who had built a beautiful freestanding greenhouse out in the country that was heated by an artesian hot spring. Sounds heavenly, doesn't it? She understood that the humidity would cause her wood to rot, so she applied the common wood preservative pentachlorophenal. After she was well into growing, winter came on. With the cold temperatures, condensation formed on the wood, causing the penta chemical to leach into the droplets that eventually found their way onto the plants, causing their death. It was a sad wipeout before winter was over.

One type of wood treatment that is commonly considered safe by most experts is the copper-naphthenate type of wood preservative, two of which are called Cuprinol and Copper 8 Quin Olinolate.

Up until the early 1990s, most people viewed pressure-treated landscape timbers as a safe material for constructing raised beds or for use in greenhouse construction. This wood is touted by the lumber industry as being safe for use in gardens and for landscaping. As a result, it was and in many situations still is commonly used for landscaping and raised-bed construction.

Landscape timbers and pressure-treated lumber for landscaping are generally treated with chromated copper arsenate (CCA). Even though the lumber industry has long extolled the safety of CCA, this compound has been brewing up a lot of controversy. The copper, chromium, and arsenate all have toxic properties, but many manufacturers claim that this stuff won't leach out of the wood in quantities that are harmful. Unfortunately, now there are new studies coming to light that do indeed show leaching of potentially harmful levels of copper, chromium, and arsenate into some soils. These materials could be taken up by a crop when used in landscape construction of raised beds or anywhere there is much exposure to moisture. Many studies have shown that plants tend to take up more of these elements where the soil is acidic. Where the soil is naturally alkaline, there is rarely a problem with these compounds being taken up by roots. Check with your local county extension agent to find out if your soil is naturally acidic or alkaline.

To make things even more confusing, all CCA-treated wood is not the same. Some manufacturers claim that their particular brand of lumber is safe but are quick to point out that certain other brands are not. I hope that in the future there will be even more research to clear up any controversy or questions. In the meantime, I would avoid using it around gardens, in landscaping, or in any new greenhouse construction if you live in an area where there are naturally occurring acidic soils.

If you have a raised bed, you might be able to slow or help prevent leaching from CCA-treated raised beds by lining your lumber on the soil side with plastic film (be sure not to line the bottom of the bed as this could create drainage problems).

To further confound those considering purchasing CCA-treated lumber, there is the long-term problem of disposal. If burned, it produces toxic fumes. Because leaching is a problem, the treated lumber is not a good choice for landfills.

If you do use CCA-treated lumber, take precautions. When sawing it, wear rubber gloves and a dust mask, doing all of your cutting outdoors and disposing of all sawdust in a bag in the trash. Also change your clothes when finished and wash them separately.

How do you know if you are buying pressure-treated CCA lumber? There is usually a label stapled to each piece of lumber stating "CCA-C" or "CCA oxides." If the treated lumber doesn't say anything, you have no assurance of what the lumber was treated with. You may even be purchasing something more hazardous than CCA. Avoid purchasing any pressure-treated lumber that is noticeably dusty or looks like it has sawdust on the surface, as this could be evidence of the powdered chemicals.

Some alternatives to CCA-treated lumber for raised beds include the rot-resistant heartwoods of cedar, black cherry, white oak, chestnut oak, redwood, and so on. You can even use the old standby, pine, if you don't mind replacing it in a few years. You might be able to find lumber treated with the above-mentioned copper naphthenate; but you should know that leaching has been observed with it, too, in some research studies, though the environmental impact is likely to be less than with CCA lumber. Plastic lumber is becoming a reality, thanks to recycling efforts. Although it is pricey, it will last virtually forever in a greenhouse. You might also consider building with concrete, rock, or cinder blocks in construction of raised beds. Galvanized steel could also be used for certain

HELP FOR HIGH-HUMIDITY PROBLEMS

Here are some things you can do to minimize problems (disease, structure rot, condensation) where there is a tendency for running a high relative humidity.

1. **Circulation.** Circulate the air even when the greenhouse is sealed to the outside in winter. This produces more uniform temperatures, reduces humidity, promotes better use of CO_2, and even helps keep the bugs and diseases down.

2. **Water early in the day.** This will help prevent evening humidity problems, which are the most severe as far as plant diseases are concerned.

3. **Water only when needed.** All too often, people overwater in greenhouses. Excess water increases humidity problems and is not good for roots (see "Knowing When to Water," page 33).

4. **Ventilate to the outside.** Whenever the outside temperature is warm enough, ventilate the moist air to the outside. This can also be done when the greenhouse is running hot, even if it is not warm outside. In a solar greenhouse, this practice is not recommended if you are heading into a long spell of cool and cloudy weather.

5. **Use air-to-air heat exchangers.** This is a fancy (and not cheap) piece of equipment that trades warm, moist air for cool, dry air. During the exchange process, the cool, dry air is heated by the exiting warm, moist air, thus minimizing heat loss while dumping out the wet air. Admittedly, this is probably a last resort unless you have a high level of disposable income (unlike myself). For more information, you should talk to an architect, engineer, or heating-and-cooling company.

greenhouse purposes, including posts, potting benches, and shelving.

There is a new wood preservative that is now available that could be a good alternative to CCA-treated wood. The wood is treated with a substance called "alkaline copper quaternary ammonium compound" (whew, what a mouthful!). Although this material is also likely to leach into the soil, it doesn't contain any highly toxic materials such as arsenic or chromium, which makes it a good alternative to CCA lumber. It reportedly lasts as long as CCA lumber but is slightly higher in price. This newer, less toxic material is distributed by a limited number of companies, but perhaps over time the product will become more ubiquitous. To locate distributors of this lumber, call the manufacturer, Chemical Specialties, Inc., at (800) 421-8661.

LOW HUMIDITY

Can the humidity be too low? Yes, especially in the summer, and this problem is more common if you live in the Intermountain West, where the humidity tends to run low anyway. Low humidity in a greenhouse with many plants is admittedly a rare occurrence. This is because people tend to overwater and because a greenhouse or sunspace is a relatively sealed environment from which it is hard for moisture to escape. Most greenhouses or sunspaces containing a number of plants will not have this problem because the plants will naturally increase the humidity.

However, low humidity can occur in summer months when a lot of outside venting is taking place. It can also be a problem when you are growing only a few plants in a sunspace.

High humidity is not good for plants, but neither is extremely low humidity. Fortunately, a low-humidity problem is easy to remedy. All you have to do is water the floor. Oops! Do you have one of those living-room-type sunspaces? If so, this is not a good idea for you.

There are also commercially available humidifiers that can provide a fine solution for the fancier living-room sunspaces with low humidity. The addition of a hot tub also works wonders with low humidity levels.

Humidity can also be increased if you are using a swamp-type air conditioner, discussed later in this chapter under "Cooling and Ventilating the Greenhouse and Sunspace." Besides helping to cool the greenhouse, swamp coolers (evaporative coolers) add moisture to the air. Swamp coolers do not work well in naturally humid locations. The drier your outside air is, the better a swamp cooler works. Drive out to the desert Southwest and you'll see one on every roof.

One place in the greenhouse where you should strive for higher levels of humidity is the area where you are germinating seeds and trying to root cuttings. Here you will see much benefit from regular misting with a special misting hose nozzle available from most greenhouse supply catalogs and gardening supply companies. This is discussed earlier in this chapter and in Chapter 5, "Plant Propagation."

AIR TEMPERATURE

The optimum high temperature that most greenhouse plants tolerate well is around 85°F (29°C), although there are always exceptions for certain plants. If the temperatures are running into the high nineties or higher, then you will usually see slower plant growth and even an inability of fruiting crops to set their fruit. It may also cause flowers to drop off the plant before they can set fruit. When it gets up above 85°F (29°C), it is also getting a bit uncomfortable for people. That's where proper ventilation comes in.

The optimum low-temperature range that most greenhouse plants tolerate well is between 50°F and 60°F (10°C and 15°C). When it gets cooler than that, you will also see problems similar to what happens when it's too hot (slow growth, poor fruit set, and blossom drop). It can also stress plants that are native to the tropics.

The optimum plant-growth temperature has a lot to do with a plant's native habitat. If a plant is used to the tropics, it can take warmer temperatures. If a plant is from a more temperate climate, then it can likely tolerate cooler temperatures. Although each plant has different optimum temperature requirements, it can also have different optimums for different stages of growth. Seedlings often benefit from warmer temperatures, whereas mature plants may not. For instance, many plants in the cabbage family require cool temperatures to mature properly.

One thing that all plants have in common is that their growth requires some level of heat. Temperature controls virtually everything in a plant: the rate of water and nutrient uptake, photosynthesis, and even the plant's cell division.

Some people use their greenhouse to extend the growing season and allow their greenhouse to freeze up when the extreme cold of winter sets in. Most people, however, have acquired a greenhouse specifically to grow plants in the dead of winter. The motivation to continue growing in winter is obvious and usually centers on the idea of harvesting food or flowers in defiance of winter and for the love of growing things year-round.

Others find themselves wanting a greenhouse simply to maintain their sanity in a northern climate. Sometimes a single sniff of an orange blossom in winter can change your whole day. No matter what, if you have a greenhouse, it is likely you will decide to keep your greenhouse warm come winter.

There are two main ways to maintain warm temperatures in the winter. One method is to design or retrofit your greenhouse design to be all or partly solar heated. This has been proven to work wonderfully well, even in areas with cloudy winters. After all, the light still comes through the clouds, and where there is light, there is heat. I have seen great solar-heated greenhouses in all sorts of climates, ranging from the upper peninsula of Michigan to cloudy northern Vermont. These places take the cake for winter clouds—but it still works!

Yes, the areas with sunnier winters run warmer winter greenhouses and can grow winter crops a bit faster, but a successful effort is still possible in the cloudy climes.

If you depend solely upon solar heating for your greenhouse, you will find that up to a certain point, you have little control over the minimum temperature. You can't turn up the heater if you don't have one. So you are at the mercy of the design of your solar greenhouse and the outside weather. The upside is that you are not at the mercy of the monthly energy bill, which can become substantial with nonsolar greenhouses. Nor are solar-heated sunspaces in jeopardy with every power outage. For these situations you will have to adjust the plants and growing schedule to the structure. This is

discussed further in Chapter 4, "Selecting the Right Plants," and in Chapter 7, "Scheduling."

If you have a heated greenhouse or a combination greenhouse using both solar and conventional heat, you benefit from a high level of temperature control. This will enable you to more easily adjust the climate to the type of plants you wish to grow with a simple turn of the thermostat. Later in this book, I discuss the temperature requirements of many plants, a handy guide for you to use when deciding at what temperature to set the thermostat.

CONVENTIONAL HEATING IN THE GREENHOUSE

I use the term "conventional heating" to describe the addition of supplemental heaters. They may be powered by electricity, natural gas, propane (LP) gas, heating oil, kerosene, or wood. One of the major concerns when burning gas, oil, kerosene, or wood is ventilation. You must exhaust the combusted gases to the outside. Why? Because combusted gases contain components harmful to plants. The only exception is certain gas heaters that have a high level of burning efficiency and exhaust mainly CO_2 gas, which is good for plants. These are sold as "nonventing" heaters. However, a word of caution is still in order for a product sold as a "nonventing" heater: Many building codes do not accept these types of heaters. Although they might be unharmful to people, they may still emit a very small level of gases harmful to susceptible plants. The common culprit with combustible gases is ethylene gas. In high quantities, it can cause a lot of plant damage, including leaf scorching and leaf drop. Orchids are especially sensitive to combusted gases. So in general, if you are going to have a heater that burns a fossil fuel, you need to have a safely installed venting system or stovepipe. Care must be taken with these to avoid any contact between glazing and heated surfaces, as many glazings can melt or can even explode into flames.

If you have any level of nervousness about the installation of a heater and the venting of gases, you can also install a carbon-monoxide detector. These can't tell you if you have plant-damaging gases, but often these are associated with elevated carbon monoxide levels. While you're at it, put one in your home, too. It's probably as important as a smoke detector.

If you are going to purchase a heater, the first question is: What size? Although this is a simple question, the answer can be incredibly complicated, especially if you ask an engineer. I prefer to ask people in the heating, venting, and air-conditioning (HVAC) industry. Or perhaps you have a brother-in-law or an engineer friend who'll do the calculations just for the challenge. Heaters are sold based upon their BTU (British thermal unit) output, the standard measurement for heating units. The next step is calculating how many BTUs your greenhouse or sunspace requires.

There are many formulas for calculating which size heater you need. Many greenhouse suppliers will often assist you in the calculation of your heating needs. I like the simplicity of the BTU-requirement calculation as presented in the catalog for Charley's Greenhouse Supply (see Appendix 7).

You also need to use a lot of caution with the installation and operation of heaters because plastic-skinned greenhouses are especially susceptible to burning! Heater installation is where you might want to consider hiring a professional; at the very least, read the directions thoroughly a few times before you do it yourself.

Many commercial greenhouses are turning to LP or natural-gas-powered infrared heaters. These radiant heaters, mounted on the upper eaves, are designed for use in larger greenhouses. Although they cost more than conventional heaters (two to three times as much!), they use from 30 to 50 percent less energy to heat the same space, so your savings will help justify the higher price. Unlike most gas heaters that blow hot air around, radiant heat is more like the sun and travels in a "line-of-sight." Check out some of the commercial greenhouse growers' trade magazines or commercial greenhouse suppliers for more on infrared systems.

(Top) *A vented 'conventional' greenhouse heater.*
(Bottom) *A small electric heater can prevent frost but your electric bill may reach record highs.* Photo courtesy of Charley's Greenhouse Supply.

One important tip when installing a heater is to locate the thermostat as far away from the heater as possible. This will allow the heater to accurately respond to the natural swings in the greenhouse temperature.

There are many heaters on the market designed for or adapted for use in a home greenhouse or sunspace. These tend to be either gas or electric units.

ELECTRIC HEAT

The downside to electric heating has two aspects. One is cost. Heating with electricity spins your electric meter at a rapid clip and up go your

(Left) *This automated temperature alarm, Sensaphone®, calls you on the phone when the temperature drops too low.* Photo courtesy Phonetics, Inc.

(Right) *Wood stoves must be watched closely in a greenhouse. Although they provide low-cost heat (if you have the wood to burn), they can cause some problems.*

electricity bills. If you have not installed any solar components (discussed later), you are also at risk of a freeze-up during a power outage. One outage could kill all your plants in an evening, unless you develop a backup plan. Power outages have destroyed many a person's romance with the greenhouse.

WHAT IF THE POWER GOES OUT?

So what can you do for a backup plan when the outage comes? The cornerstone of any backup plan is installing what is known as a "temperature alarm" developed expressly for greenhouses. The alarm can be set to go off when the temperature in the greenhouse drops to a predefined level. Most have backup battery power, so they work even when there is a power outage (the time when you really need to know whether your greenhouse is freezing). The number-one rule with temperature alarms is to be sure your backup batteries are always fresh and charged, or your alarm is useless. There are some alarm systems that can even phone you at a predefined number to warn you. But then what do you do if you're on a remote

beach in Mexico sipping a margarita? Perhaps you might not even (momentarily) care. Anyway, alarms start at around $30, and as you add battery backup systems and auto-dialers, the price skyrockets considerably.

After the power goes off, you need a quick and possibly portable backup heater that runs on an alternate power source. This heater could be fueled by LP gas, wood, oil, or kerosene, or you could even have a pellet stove. However, any option that burns fossil fuels requires a backup plan for ventilating the exhaust gas (as mentioned earlier) to prevent plant damage (from ethylene gas) and human injury (from carbon monoxide). Some people have permanently installed wood-burning stoves as a backup system. Others with hot tubs in their sunspace simply fire up the tub (as long as it is not powered by electricity).

Some people have even been known to squeak by in an emergency by carrying buckets of hot water into the greenhouse during the outage. And you thought only a baby could ruin a good night's sleep! Another problem could be that you have a gas-powered heater, but the fan that makes it all work is powered by electricity. Sometimes the flame of a heater is lit by a electrically generated spark. No electricity, no gas heat. The main thing is to at least give a power outage some thought.

On the subject of heaters, I am often asked about kerosene heaters. These are usually portable, nonventing heaters that people often use for emergency heating in times of extreme cold. As mentioned earlier, the downside is that most are nonventing, and this is not good.

If you are faced with the decision of either freezing the greenhouse or heating it with a nonventing portable kerosene heater, I would probably choose to heat with kerosene. To minimize the damage of using a kerosene heater in this situation, be sure that the kerosene heater is burning only fresh, moisture-free, high-quality kerosene and be sure that the flame cones are conical and blue, as opposed to yellow, which indicates less-efficient burning.

How do you know if you have done any damage to your plants with a nonventilating heater? It will usually show up within 24 hours. The tomato plant is one of the plants more susceptible to ethylene damage, so keep an eye on this "canary in the mine." I remember one winter when I heated a large greenhouse with a big wood-burning stove. I left the greenhouse with the fire stoked up enough to prevent frost. Unfortunately, the wind changed and the downdraft from the stove brought thick smoke into the greenhouse. The next morning, I opened the door and realized that I was lucky not only that the greenhouse hadn't frozen but that it hadn't burned down. It took about 3 hours for the first symptoms of plant burning to appear on a variety of plants. Tightly sealed greenhouses are notorious for not drafting heaters very well. The moral: Keep an eye on things and invest in a carbon-monoxide detector.

Styrofoam is placed on the exterior of this yet-to-be-poured concrete foundation. This prevents the cold from conducting into your greenhouse through the soil in winter. It also 'taps' your greenhouse into warmer earth temperatures, reducing your heating needs.

If you are in the sad situation where it seems you are about to face a lost cause with imminent freezing of your greenhouse, at the very least shut off the water line feeding the pipes to the greenhouse. If you can, drain the pipes before they burst. In any circumstance, this is an important task whenever you decide to shut your greenhouse down during the winter months in cold climates.

When you think about the headache of heating and power outages, the idea of a solar greenhouse starts to look pretty attractive, doesn't it? Read on.

Of course, the best solution is to have a primarily solar-heated greenhouse that in the worst-case scenario would get very cold but never freeze. Then you could always add extra conventional heating to enable you to grow more diverse and out-of-season or tropical crops. The best of both worlds is having a semisolar-heated sunspace that is attached to your home where you can introduce heat from your home as needed.

People with a well-designed attached greenhouse that faces south and is solar heated often allow it to pull small amounts of heat from their home. However, when the arctic front moves in, they shut the doors to the sunspace and let it go on its own. If designed well, it should never freeze. When the sun comes out, this same space can often contribute to the heating of your home. What a great deal! I have seen many attached solar greenhouses that can heat up to 2 square feet (0.19 sq. m) of house space for every 1 square foot (0.09 sq. m) of greenhouse space. Your results may vary (as they say in the ads).

SOLAR-GREENHOUSE HEATING CHECKLIST

If you are planning a solar-heated greenhouse or want to look into retrofitting your existing greenhouse, review this checklist. These are the basic requirements for benefiting from solar heat. Even if you have a conventionally heated greenhouse, you can still reduce the need for heat and reduce your heating bills by applying some of these solar-greenhouse basics for higher energy efficiency.

1. Insulated walls. If you have a free-standing greenhouse, can you insulate the north wall? If you live in a sunny area, you may also consider insulating the east and/or west walls. Start with the side receiving the winter prevailing winds. Some people retrofit an existing greenhouse for winter by using a foil-backed "bubble wrap" type of material on the north, east, and west walls and the north portion of the roof. This material is commonly sold as Reflectix insulation. It is found in lumberyards and hardware stores and is sold in greenhouse-supply catalogs. For even more insulating ability, you can double-up this material.

2. Insulated foundation. The foundation of your greenhouse should not be a heat sink. If the ground is freezing cold outside, then the cold will conduct directly through your foundation, making it cold inside. The solution is to insulate your foundation's outside perimeter with Styrofoam board, usually 1 to 2 inches (2.5 to 5 cm) thick. This insulation should be placed vertically and extend down to a minimum of 1 foot (0.3 m) in most temperate areas. If you live in gardening zone 4 or less (as determined by the U.S. Department of Agriculture [USDA] gardening zone map), consider even deeper foundation insulation. Set the foam-board insulation against the outside of your greenhouse foundation. What if your greenhouse has no foundation? Place the vertical insulation in a trench around your greenhouse perimeter.

3. Double or triple glazing. (Note: "Glazing" is the term for the greenhouse skin that the light shines through.) This is a must for an energy-efficient greenhouse and essential for any solar greenhouse. Of course, glazing should be tightly sealed, free of dust or dirt, and not yellowing (which is common to many older plastic glazings). If your existing greenhouse already has single glazing, you should pursue some type of retrofit. You could opt for an expensive solution: tearing out the old glazing and replacing it with a newer material. Other cheaper options include applying an inner film such as vinyl or other greenhouse polyethylene type of film.

Some greenhouse-supply companies carry clear bubble insulation. This is the very same stuff that is used for packing material that kids and some adults love to pop. To mount it, you

(Left) *Bubble wrap provides a good temporary winter insulation when placed on the interior of the glazing.* Photo courtesy of Charley's Greenhouse Supply.

(Right) *Whether you have a kit or a constructed greenhouse, weather-stripping vents and doors makes a gigantic difference in reducing heat loss. Weather-stripping needs to be replaced regularly—it rarely lasts more than a year.*

first need to spray a translucent adhesive in spots on the framework or glass. Then you press the bubble insulation in place. This stuff can be removed whenever the extra insulation is not needed. The spray adhesive, however, is not recommended for use on acrylic or polycarbonate glazings. For these glazings, you need to figure out some other way to get the bubble insulation to stay up against the glazing. I have used different types of tape with some success.

4. **Airtight sealing.** Seal every nook and cranny prior to winter's arrival. Vents and doors must be weather-stripped, and cracks must be caulked and checked for wear every year. I usually do an inspection for any potential air leaks in fall before the cold weather comes. I always find an area that needs some sealing up. A good way to search and destroy winter air leaks is to close up the greenhouse and light some incense. If you hold it near suspected leaking areas, you can visually note how the smoke responds to incoming air currents as you move the incense around. If the smoke streams in a new direction, there is your leak. Plug it up with caulk,

foam, weather-stripping, or whatever is appropriate for the spot. Improvise if you must. One small air leak can make the difference between above and below freezing!

5. **Thermal storage.** This is the use of rock, water, or other dense thermal-mass material to store the incoming solar heat. Water is by far the most efficient and easiest material to use (cheap, too!). Solar greenhouses are notorious for their accumulations of black 55-gallon (208-liter) oil drums filled with water and placed along the north wall to store the sun's heat. They are cheap and efficient. For smaller greenhouses, look for the 30-gallon (113-liter) metal drums. Many owners of heated greenhouses have also installed containers of water to increase heating efficiency. It's easy to use a water drum as a support for a plant or as a soil table. Read more about thermal mass in the next chapter.

6. **Air-lock entry.** If you have a freestanding greenhouse or if you use your attached greenhouse's exterior door with any frequency in wintertime, you should consider installing

a second door that creates an air-lock entry. This is a two-door setup with enough space between them so that when you open the outside door, you won't get a blast of freezing air sweeping over your poor little plants. Even if you heat your greenhouse conventionally, an air-lock entry will save an immense amount of energy. For freestanding solar greenhouses, an air-lock entry is essential equipment. Those of you with attached greenhouses can get away without one as long as you always go through the house! Never use the outside door when it's cold.

7. Site orientation. If you have a solar greenhouse, you had better hope it's oriented in the correct direction. If it's not, I guess there isn't much you can do about it now. A solar greenhouse should have its long side face within 20 degrees of either side of true south. For best results, the greenhouse should be two to three times as long as it is wide.

8. Night curtain. This is an option for people in very cold areas. It is not for everyone. A night curtain is usually an insulating cover you roll across the inside of the greenhouse glazing at night like a blanket to prevent excess heat loss. I often view night curtains with a bit of skepticism. One problem is that they are costly and often unreliable, nor are they easy to find if you want to buy one. Homemade ones are even less reliable. The farther north you live, the more they may make sense. But an alternative could instead be the addition of an extra layer of glazing. If you have single glazing, consider double. If you have double glazing, consider making it three layers thick. This can be achieved by reskinning your structure (but that's not what you want to hear, right?). A cheaper alternative is to apply a new inner layer of vinyl or of polyethylene film. Or there is the option suggested a few paragraphs ago about

using plastic bubble packing. By the way, a light evening snow on the glazing is a great nighttime insulator and is free. Always wait until morning to knock the snow off unless you have concerns about the weight of the snow on your greenhouse structure.

SOIL TEMPERATURE

Soil temperatures are more crucial than air temperatures, even though the latter usually has a lot to do with the temperature of your soil. The warmth of the soil is something we don't often think about because we live our days surrounded by air.

When soil temperatures are below 45°F (7°C), roots grow much slower and have a harder time taking up water and nutrients. When the sun comes out and air temperatures begin to heat up immediately after a cool period, you may see plants actually wilting, even though there is ample moisture in the cold soil. They wilt because of the slow water uptake by roots in the cool soil despite the fact that the air is rapidly warming. Don't be tricked into overwatering in the winter—the plants could just have cold feet. Stick your finger into the soil and check the soil moisture before you grab the watering can or hose.

Here is a cool fact: Research has shown that if soil temperatures are kept around 65°F (18°C), the winter air temperature can drop 10°F (6°C) without any loss in yield. This is especially true with fruiting crops. Many researchers believe that the positive results obtained by heating the soil are due not just to the effects of temperature but also to the effects of faster organic matter decomposition (warmer temperatures wake up the decomposition microbes, which creates more CO_2), increasing the rate of photosynthesis.

Soil temperature is almost as important as the air temperature. Check soil temperature by using a thermometer designed for the soil.

How do you tell the soil's temperature? There is a special thermometer with a 5-inch (13-cm) probe that is designed to measure soil temperatures (it looks just like a meat thermometer). These run around $8 to $10. Soil thermometers are a great help in discovering environmental differences and in just seeing the relationship between air temperature and the soil. You will soon get a feel for small microclimates located within your greenhouse that you can use to your advantage. It is also helpful to keep records of your soil and air temperatures to see the general trends and the relationship to the outside weather.

When people learn that warm soil helps to increase plant growth, they immediately start scheming about ways to heat up the soil. In earlier times, people invented the precursor to the hotbed. They used the heating qualities of decomposing manure to heat cold frames. They placed an 8-inch (20-cm) layer of raw manure about 1 foot (0.3 m) below the top of the soil. This manure would heat the soil that covered it for a few weeks until the manure cooled off. On top of the soil, above the ma-

nure, they started their seedlings in containers for later outside transplanting. Planting seeds directly in soil that has heating manure in it would eventually cause overfertilization, especially when the roots reached the raw manure. But containers sitting on top of this heated soil did fine.

Many people have set up soil beds with warm-water pipes plumbed through them, heating the water with solar or conventional hot-water heaters. This works fine, except when you accidentally hit the plumbing with your shovel.

For large growing beds, one of the easier methods to use to warm soil is to water the beds with warm (not hot) water. In areas with cold winters, water straight from the cold tap can be almost too cold to drink (brrr!). Plants love an occasional warm irrigation to offset the chill of winter. To do this, fill your watering can with warm water. Hot water can kill plants,

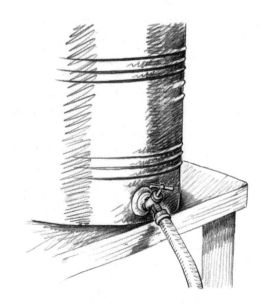

Plumb a hose bib into the side of a black 30- or 55-gallon metal drum, or even a plastic trash can. Set it up high (to utilize gravity's force) and use it for winter watering. If the sun is out, this water may also be warmer than wintertime tap water.

Small electric heating mats are great for keeping seedlings or small pots warm when the greenhouse air is cool. Photo courtesy of Charley's Greenhouse Supply.

so go for slightly warmer than lukewarm. You can even install a hot-water faucet and mixing valve right in your greenhouse plumbing to save a few steps.

Many industrious greenhouse gardeners often preheat water by irrigating from a black metal drum or trash can with a spigot on the bottom. Sometimes the drum is plumbed into the cold-water line. The drum should be placed in a warm sunny spot, where it will warm the water. Instead of having ultracold winter water coming out of the hose, you can gain a few precious degrees of warmth from the sun. Some people have had good luck using broken electric or gas hot-water heaters (with tanks that don't leak). These are usually free at any plumbing shop; tell them what you are looking for and they might set one aside for you. Strip the outer white metal and inner insulation completely off, and the tank can be found inside. It is usually already painted black. The advantage of these tanks is that they are already plumbed for a hose at the base.

There are also commercially available solar-heating panels designed to heat water. Or you can build one yourself. Check some old solar-energy books printed in the 1980s or look in a back-to-the-land type of periodical.

When it comes to starting seedlings and growing things in smaller pots, you can use electric heating mats or cables. These are thermostatically controlled mats or wires that heat up to a preset temperature. If your greenhouse is a solar-heated structure or if you are just running your greenhouse on the cold side, a heating mat can be a great way to create a microclimate for starting seedlings. Why heat the whole place if you can get away with heating a small area? Potted plants that require warmer temperatures can also be set on top of an electric heating mat.

Please don't jury-rig your own heating mat from old electric blankets or heating pads for arthritis unless you like the feeling of 110 volts jolting through your body. Instead, check a garden or greenhouse-supply catalog for a ready-made, waterproof heating mat or heating cables. I prefer the more expensive heating mats for their durability over the short-lived cable heaters. Mats cost anywhere from $70 to $100. You'll also need a thermostat for around $65 to $80. Cables run as cheap as $15 and go all the way up to $60, depending on the length and quality of cable. Overall, when it comes to bottom-heating systems, you get what you pay for. Opt for the cheap ones, and in the long run it may be expensive. An old friend once gave me this great advice: "Cheap is expensive."

COOLING AND VENTILATING THE GREENHOUSE AND SUNSPACE

I don't know why it is, but it seems like one of the most common problems home greenhouse gardeners have is summer overheating rather than winter heating. I see more problems with overheating than I do with greenhouses freezing or running too cool. When a greenhouse runs too hot, it can cause many problems with your plants' health. A hot greenhouse may reduce a plant's ability to flower or set fruit and even to resist bugs and disease.

Unfortunately, the origin of the overheating problem is rooted in the basic design of the greenhouse and a poor design for ventilation. Although this book is not a greenhouse-design book, the problem of overheating is so common that I need to spend some time discussing it. First, what is considered overheating? As I said earlier, it is different for different plants, but to generalize, I would say that a hot greenhouse is anything above a range of 85°F to 100°F (29°C to 38°C). To continue my generalization, if it is a plant that you grow for its fruit (yes, even tomatoes) or it is native to the tropics, then it can probably withstand temperatures on the high side. If it's a vegetable you are growing for leaf or root or if it is native to the more temperate regions, then it probably cannot tolerate the higher range of temperatures and prefers to grow on the cooler side of the high range. If your greenhouse runs hot, it may be at the expense of yields and/or plant health.

VENTILATION

One of the best ways to correct overheating is to be sure you have an optimal ventilation system. It's best to establish a natural cross-flow of air with both high and low vents. Where possible, the high vents should be placed on the side of your greenhouse that is opposite your prevailing summer winds. The high vents should be around 15 percent larger (in total square footage) than your low vents. A rule of thumb for sizing ventilation in solar or attached greenhouses is to have the total venting area (both high and low) equal to 25 to 30 percent

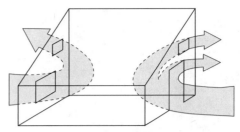

Low and high vents on each wall promote good ventilation. Exhaust fans placed in the higher vents greatly increase efficiency.

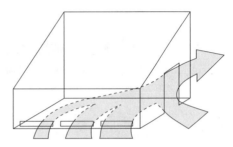

Summer ventilation in an attached solar greenhouse. Notice how the west side of the structure could use another exhaust area for more efficient ventilation.

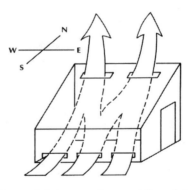

Ridge vents help promote a good flow of air.

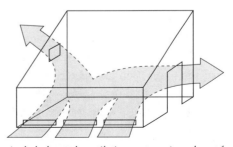

A nicely balanced ventilation system. An exhaust fan placed up high increases ventilation efficiency.

These vent openers are solar powered, require no electricity, and are quite reliable: Bayliss orchid vent (**left**) *and Solarlift* (**center**). Photos courtesy of Charley's Greenhouse Supply. *This high vent* (**right**) *opens automatically by a solar-powered vent opener.*

of the total area of glazing (yes, you can count your open door as a vent). For freestanding greenhouses, the calculation is different: around 20 percent of the total floor area for the upper vents and 10 percent of the floor area for lower fresh-air intakes. If you decide to add an exhaust fan, especially one that really moves the air, these numbers can be lowered substantially. Make adjustments in ventilation with a little experimentation (which is always more fun than doing math!).

If you have an attached greenhouse, *always* vent to your home on cooler days. This is free heat, so use it here first! Besides, if you vent outside instead of into your home in winter, you are contributing to global warming! Before it gets cold, be sure your exterior vents are built to shut tight and well insulated. However, you may still need to keep them operable. This means that your vents should be constructed so that you can open them any day of the year and then shut them up tight again, without air leaks (especially in regions where they say, "If you don't like the weather, just wait a few minutes and it'll change"). A lot of venting goes on in the spring and fall, when

the days can get warm but the nights are cold. When your vents to the outside are closed, you don't want to have them let cold night air leak in. The best vents must be able to be readily opened, insulated, weather-stripped, and sealed tight to the outside. Recheck your greenhouse every fall.

There is no such thing as weather-stripping that lasts forever, and most don't last for more than a couple of years. You will likely need to rip out some of last year's weather-stripping and replace it with fresh seals.

Opening and closing the vents may be automated by using commercially available electric openers or the wonderfully simple solar-powered openers. The heat of the sun powers the solar openers, causing a gas to expand in a cylinder. This pushes a piston out as the temperature rises, thus opening your vent. As the air cools, the piston retracts, pulling your vent closed just when you need it closed. Most of these openers can even be adjusted to work at a specified temperature, although they are not exact. These vent openers range in cost from $20 to $130. The more expensive ones are better made and can usually raise the heavier vents, weighing up to 35 pounds (15.9 kg). I have learned over the years that this is not a place to try to save money because the cheaper ones break quickly and the more expensive ones last. Remember, "Cheap is expensive!"

It is a rare greenhouse that can get by with just one of these vent openers, so open up your billfold: The average hobby greenhouse needs a few for the upper vents and maybe even one to open a lower vent. You can mount these vent openers in series to open a long or a heavy vent. Even with the higher-priced solar-powered vent openers, you will find that your piston wears out over time. The better manufacturers now sell replacement tubes or cylinders, which is cheaper than buying a whole new unit!

Electric vent openers are controlled by a thermostat to open and close vents automatically. These start at around $80. Often they are connected in such a way that they will open a vent (or a series of vents) just as your exhaust fan kicks on.

COOLING FANS

Some greenhouses can get by with just passive ventilation, where the cool air entering low and exiting high does the job of cooling your greenhouse. This is the ideal situation, but it usually happens only in areas with cooler summers. If this doesn't do the trick, then it's time to consider installing an electric cooling fan. The first rule for a greenhouse fan is to place it high: You get a much more efficient job of ventilation that way. The second rule is to set it so it exhausts the air out rather than blowing air in. Exhaust fans create a negative pressure that brings cool air in through the other, lower vents to replace the exhausted warm air. It is more efficient (in terms of the amount of air moved per electric bill) to exhaust the air

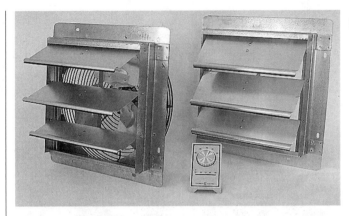

This is an automatic venting system that includes the fan box, intake vent box, and the cooling thermostat. Photo courtesy of Charley's Greenhouse Supply.

Electric shutter motors power greenhouse vents open; they are triggered by a thermostat. Shutter motor (**left**) *and H&C Thermostat* (**right**). Photo courtesy of Charley's Greenhouse Supply.

with the fan rather than to actively blow the air in with your fan.

Always try to get the air to travel across the full length of the greenhouse before being exhausted to the outside. This means you should place the exhaust fan as far as possible from wherever the air enters the greenhouse. If an intake vent (or open door) is located close to the exhaust fan, then you can short-circuit the ventilation, and the rest of your greenhouse not in the path of moving air will continue to run hot.

Good greenhouse fans are available in greenhouse-supply catalogs and run around

(**Above**) *Always place cooling fans in a high location that is on the opposite side of the greenhouse from a lower vent(s) or open door. Cooling fans should exhaust air out for maximum efficiency.*

(**Left**) *Aluminum shutters over a vent are fine in warmer areas, but where there are cold winters you may need an additional insulating cover to keep the cold out.* Photo courtesy of Charley's Greenhouse Supply.

$150 to $600, perhaps including a cooling thermostat. The price reflects not only quality but also how many cubic feet per minute (cfm) they move. For smaller greenhouses, I have had good results with simple box fans purchased at hardware or "mart" stores. The trick is rigging them up in a high vent to use them for exhaust purposes and then wiring them to a cooling thermostat. Perhaps it is time to talk to an electrician friend?

A cooling thermostat is different from the thermostat that keeps you warm in winter because it kicks on when the temperature rises. Many greenhouse-supply companies carry

these, or you might find one locally at a heating-and-cooling shop.

As mentioned earlier, fans are sold by size and by how many cfm of air they move. If you want to get scientific about your fan selection, you can do a little calculation to determine your fan size needs (based on cfm). A fan in a hot greenhouse needs to be able to move all the cubic feet of air in your structure around once every minute. To figure this out, you need to calculate the volume of your greenhouse. Multiply the length by the width by the average height. Then multiply this volume by 0.7, and you have the average cubic feet per minute needed by your greenhouse. For example, a typical 8 by 12 by 10 foot (2.4 by 3.6 by 3 m) greenhouse needs to have a fan that can move 670 cfm. Another simple way to calculate the needs of a solar greenhouse is to figure 5–8 cfm per square foot of south-facing glazing. (Use 5 cfm for areas with dry, cool nights; use up to 8 cfm for climates with humid, warm nights.)

Some greenhouse fans come complete with a shutter system to keep air out when they are not in use. Some shutters are simply sheet metal or rigid plastic and are powered by the fan draft. When the fan kicks on, the shutters open; when the fan shuts down, the shutters close. These are the cheapest and often leak air on cold nights. They also flap around noisily when there's a windstorm outside. This type of flap shutter is annoying but is better than nothing. The more expensive, motorized shutters are better when it comes to minimizing heat loss when the fan is off as they can stay shut tighter.

You will need to button up your greenhouse when winter arrives and close the fan and vent openings. I prefer to wait until the day before winter is finally here (good luck on that guess!). Then I go out and install an insulating cover over the fan opening and the vents, except for one small vent. The vent I leave is well weather-stripped and can be used for those occasional global-warming winter days. By insulating the fan and / or its opening in winter, I can maintain the tight structure needed for winter solar heating. A solar-heated structure needs more than thin shutters to keep the cold out. You need some insulation. You can craft an insulated shutter or vent cover out of 1-inch (2.5-cm) Styrofoam sheets glued to exterior plywood on one or both sides. Then hinge this in front of the shutters and be sure it is weather-stripped and tight for winter.

SCREENING VENTS

While we are on the subject of vents and venting, I want to mention a product that screens greenhouses against insects. This is a relatively new type of insect-barrier screen that is placed over all vents and fans. This screen allows air to move through freely, but, unlike traditional window screens, this type has very small openings that don't allow the smaller greenhouse insects through. This prevents the sucking of harmful insects into the greenhouse vents when you kick on your exhaust fans. For growers with an interest in utilizing good bugs to control the harmful ones, the screen has the equally important function of keeping your beneficial insects from escaping outside the greenhouse. The screen is available in small quantities from Charley's Greenhouse Supply (see Appendix 7).

These screens are not essential for all greenhouse owners, but they do gain importance for growers in certain locations. The further south you live, especially where it is humid, the more bugs you will have. This is where there is a high likelihood that you could get infestations of greenhouse critters directly from the outside. By

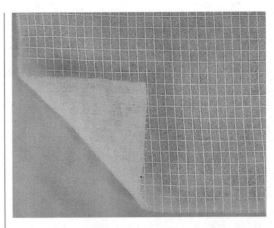

Insect-barrier screens can help keep bad bugs out and good bugs in without adversely affecting ventilation. Photo courtesy of Charley's Greenhouse Supply.

contrast, in the more northern states, many common greenhouse critters such as the whitefly can't survive through the winter. Therefore, they are less likely to get into your greenhouse from the outside. Notice how that last statement is couched in terms of "less likely"—as I never say "never" when it comes to bugs.

MISTING FOR COOLING

Another way to cool down your greenhouse is to use the cooling effect of evaporation. This is the same cooling effect that we feel when wind blows across sweaty skin. As water evaporates, it cools the air around it. Unfortunately, if you live in a humid part of the world, the air is already wet and evaporation just doesn't work very well, thus evaporative cooling is not as effective. But in many places, you can cool down a greenhouse considerably by just watering down the floors. The process can be as simple as air moving across a wet greenhouse floor; the water evaporates and thus causes a cooling effect.

A fine mist near an air-intake vent is also a way to increase evaporation (and cooling) in a greenhouse. Misting nozzles are commonly used in propagation areas and are available in

Some fogging systems can be permanently plumbed into a greenhouse but are quite expensive. There are cheaper, portable fogging systems such as this one that work well for home greenhouses. Photo courtesy of Charley's Greenhouse Supply.

greenhouse-supply catalogs. The downside to many misting nozzles is that the droplets of water are relatively large, and you end up with pools of water nearby, which can be messy. There is one misting system called Mist & Cool® that seems to create smaller droplets than most mist systems because of the use of a pressurized line. The manufacturer claims to be able to provide cooling of 15°F to 25°F (around 8°C to 12°C). This system is available from Charley's Greenhouse Supply (see Appendix 7).

FOG

A fog has even finer droplets than a mist and is able to stay suspended in the atmosphere longer. Mother Nature isn't the only one who can make fog. Commercial growers are turning more and more to sophisticated (and often very expensive) man-made fog units for propagation of seeds, rooting plant cuttings, and cooling. Fog has an advantage over misting in that it does not deposit nearly as much water yet has an even better ability to cool the atmosphere. It creates a less "wet" humidity ideal for plants that prefer a high-humidity environment. Most fog machines used to be out of the price range of home greenhouse owners, but that is changing. Now there are some small fogging systems coming on the market de-

signed for fogging a greenhouse 50 feet in length or smaller. One such unit is called the Husky-Fiber® Micro-Fogger. (Call Ann Mann's Supplies at 407-876-2625 or visit www.CFOG.com for more information; also see Appendix 7). Another fogger for smaller applications is the Humidifan® by Jaybird Manufacturing, Inc. (www.jaybird-mfg.com, 814-235-1807; also see Appendix 7). These types of units start at around $500. The overall effect of fog is a bit hypnotizing, like a dream. You can create your own little rain forest—an illusion that you are truly in a jungle where anything can happen. The only question is whether you can afford this type of Hollywood special effect.

Misting, fogging, or watering the floor is not possible in the living-room-type sunspace. For this environment, you might consider using either an evaporative swamp cooler or, if you live in a highly humid area, pay the energy bills for a traditional air conditioner.

SWAMP/EVAPORATIVE COOLERS

If you live in a relatively dry locale (usually below 50 percent relative humidity), you can effectively use a swamp cooler (also called an evaporative cooler). A swamp cooler is preferred over refrigerant types of air conditioners mainly because a swamp cooler uses much less energy, which is easier on the billfold. A swamp cooler operates by blowing air through a moist fibrous pad. As the dry outside air passes across the moist fibers, the water on the fibers evaporates. When water evaporates, it causes cooling (that is why we sweat on hot days!). The incoming air temperature can drop by as much as 20°F (11°C)!

Evaporation is a function of dry air. The drier the air, the more evaporation and the more cooling the effect. In humid air there is less evaporation, making swamp coolers less effective, especially when the relative humidity rises above 75 percent. At 90 percent outside relative humidity, evaporative cooling hardly works at all.

You can buy swamp coolers of varying sizes at a number of locations from hardware and discount stores to greenhouse-supply catalogs. I have seen small models go for as low as $300 and larger units for up to $700. You can often find used ones that are much cheaper, and spare parts are readily available in most hardware stores in the summer months. These are the exact same units used in homes.

The fiber pads maintain their moisture because they are plumbed directly to a live water source that lets in water as needed and pumps it to the top of the pad where it drips down. So you must be able to plumb a thin water tube over to the cooler. If you plumb it into a water source, you won't have to worry about keeping the cooler's reservoir full of water—it's automatic. You can even get a kit that allows you to plumb directly into a hose bib valve. Most swamp coolers have a cooling thermostat that kicks the cooler on and off as needed.

There are some small, cheap (around $80–$160), portable swamp coolers. Some require constant refilling of the water reservoir. They are a big headache because they require constant baby-sitting. If that doesn't talk you out of it, you should also know that they don't do a very good job of cooling. Also, if you forget to refill them, you might burn out the pump. Try to stick with the types that are plumbed into a water line.

The fibrous pads in swamp coolers require regular cleaning and/or replacement. If the pads aren't in good shape, they lose a lot of their effectiveness in cooling and they can get very slimy. The pads that are made out of

shredded aspen wood need to be tossed out at the end of each season. Some of the synthetic fiber pads may be cleaned with some effort. Try a dilution of chlorine bleach when cleaning them.

Don't automatically assume that you need a swamp/evaporative cooler. Before you commit to using one, try to solve your heating problems by just properly ventilating the greenhouse with an exhaust fan. If you're convinced you need a swamp cooler, you must begin by selecting the proper size. First, calculate the volume of air in your greenhouse. Do this by multiplying the width by the length by the average height. For example, if you have a 10 x 12 foot (3 to 3.6 m) greenhouse that has an average height of 7 feet (2 m), then you will have a volume of 840 cubic feet. The amount of air you need to move is based upon the cubic feet per min-

(Top) *The evaporative cooler uses much less electricity than a standard air conditioner but can be used effectively only in areas where humidity is low.* (Bottom) *Some smaller, portable evaporative coolers require you to hand-fill the water reservoir constantly and have a limited ability to cool.* Photos courtesy of Charley's Greenhouse Supply.

ute, as noted previously in the discussion on cooling fans. A good rule of thumb for how much air you need to move with either fans or swamp coolers is that a greenhouse needs to move between 1 and 2 air changes per minute (in hotter and more humid locations, use the higher figure). So you could then say we need to move 840 cubic feet (23.75 cubic meters) twice per minute for a final calculation of 1,680 cfm. The cfm rating is used for coolers and fans. Somewhere in the catalog, on the label, or on the box, you will see how many cubic feet per minute the swamp cooler moves. It is always better to err on the larger size rather than the smaller if you can't find one that meets your exact needs.

Try to mount the swamp cooler on the side of your greenhouse opposite a large vent or window. If you use your door as a vent to the outside, set the cooler on the opposite side of the greenhouse. Unlike a cooling ventilation fan, which should always exhaust air, a swamp/evaporative cooler should always blow air into the greenhouse. The cool air blowing out of the swamp cooler must exit somewhere and needs a minimum vent opening of at least 2 by 2 feet (0.6 by 0.6 m) that is as far away from the cooler as possible. This should be your vent, window, or door on the opposite side, where the cooled air finally exits to the outside. Again, your door will work as long as you prop it open. If there is no exhaust vent or if you have less than adequate exhaust openings either to the outside or into your home, the cooler won't function properly, if at all. As was mentioned earlier under the "ventilation" section, it would be best to have the cool air enter low and the hotter air exhaust outside at a higher point—the higher, the better. Set your cooler in such a way that you can disconnect it entirely from your greenhouse in winter so it is easier to seal up for the coming cold temperatures. If you can't remove your cooling unit, look into getting an insulating cover to place around it.

Commercial greenhouses commonly use an evaporative cooling system known as a pad-and-fan system, which works like a big swamp cooler. At one end of the greenhouse, water is dripped through a thin fibrous pad in front of an intake vent to the outside. An exhaust fan at the opposite end pulls outside air through the wet pad, cooling the air, and the cooled air flows across the length of the greenhouse where it's exhausted to the outside.

Misting, fogging, and swamp coolers will all increase the humidity while lowering the temperature. This will reduce the amount of water your plants need. In general, the humidity will be beneficial, but as the night temperatures start to cool considerably when the fall season approaches, you may see condensation beginning to form on cool surfaces. This can cause a wood structure to age prematurely and promote damaging growths of mold and algae on all surfaces. To avoid this, try to exhaust the humid air to the outside before the temperature starts to drop in the late afternoon.

REFRIGERANT AIR-CONDITIONING

If you live in a humid part of the world and money is no object, you may want to consider installing a refrigerant air conditioner. These work on the same principle as your refrigerator. Unfortunately, they are expensive to run. The price may not bother you when you are sitting inside your hot, humid greenhouse and sweating. Some of us will do (or pay) anything to keep our cool. You may also want to look at the newer heat-pump technology that many newer homes already have installed. This technology can provide both heating in the winter and cooling in the summer months.

Perhaps another option might be to tie your central cooling into your greenhouse. For this you need to talk to your local heating, ventilation and air conditioning (HVAC) experts.

SHADE TO COOL THE GREENHOUSE

When all else fails to cool off a hot greenhouse, you can always put something up between the greenhouse and the sun to create shade. There is commercially available shade cloth for hanging over the outside of the glazing or you can directly treat the glazing surface. Check out greenhouse supply catalogs for either shade cloth or glazing treatments.

A surface treatment can be made by applying a shading compound available from greenhouse suppliers. This is a paintlike material, usually white, that is sprayed or splattered onto the glazing. It is a temporary solution that typically lasts one summer. It can easily be removed and seems to come off quite readily after a few frosts. It decomposes on the ground. There are different shading compounds on the market, so check with a local commercial greenhouse supplier because these compounds can vary in life span and effect. Before you apply anything to your glazing surface, be sure to check the warranty (or talk to the manufacturer) on your particular type of glazing, as some plastic glazings may be permanently damaged by applications (including shading materials) to their surface.

A good, low-budget trick for cooling funky ragtag-type greenhouses is to just splatter some muddy water on the surface of the glazing. This works especially well for cold frames but may scratch plastic glazings.

A more handsome and less damaging way to shade your greenhouse is to use a shade cloth. These are cloths that are loosely woven to allow some sun in and are usually made out of some type of vinyl or polypropylene mesh. They can be found in varying degrees of density for heavier or lighter shading, depending on your needs. These can be placed on the outside or inside of your glazing, but they work best when placed on the outside. They can be installed on a roll shade so you can move them up and down, or you can tie them down to the surface. Like plastic glazings, commercially available shade cloth is often treated to resist

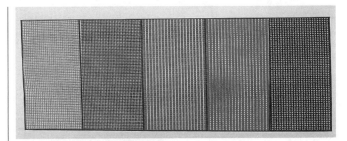

(Above) *Examples of different grades of fiberglass shade cloth.* Photo courtesy of Charley's Greenhouse Supply.
(Left) *Shade cloth can be tied down via grommets in the cloth and Tie Down clamps like this.* Photo courtesy of Charley's Greenhouse Supply.

the breakdown that occurs when plastic is exposed to the sun's ultraviolet light (to make it last a number of years instead of breaking down quickly). These are available in "attractive" colors—brown, green, white, and charcoal— or you can go with a reflective aluminized type.

It is always best to mount the shade cloth on the exterior. This keeps the solar heat absorbed by the cloth out of the greenhouse. In fact, it is best to not have the cloth touching the glazing in areas with warm summers in order to prevent conduction of heat through the glazing. It is for these reasons that the best types of shade cloth come with built-in grommets on a reinforced edging. This is to prevent that occasional heavy wind from blowing the cloth clean away.

If you are creative and short on dollars, you could also rig up some less permanent solutions by using cheesecloth, burlap, or an old sheet. Shading can also come from deciduous trees, sunflowers, pole beans, or grapevines planted outside of your greenhouse glazing.

Many people don't realize, however, that shading comes with a price. Although shading may help cool your greenhouse, it will also slow down the growth of many plants. This is especially true of most vegetables as well as many flowering plants. In defense of shade, there are also many other plants that might prefer the shadier space. You need to decide what kind of crops you want to grow before you put your whole greenhouse in the shadows.

All too often, shading is used as a way to solve a poor summer-ventilation system. The provision of shade is a great solution for shade-loving plants. This is best done in small areas, leaving the rest of your greenhouse for sun-loving plants. Since this book is primarily about growing food and flowers, you should know that the majority of food and flowering plants tend to prefer bright, unshaded growing conditions.

WEATHER AND THE GREENHOUSE

Even though your greenhouse is protected from the elements, the weather does have some impact. If you watch the weather, you can make some preemptive energy-saving decisions for your greenhouse. For instance, if you hear that you're in for a few days of cool, cloudy winter weather and it's still sunny out, then it might make sense to let your greenhouse heat up a bit, perhaps even going above the preferred high temperatures mentioned earlier. Solar greenhouses with thermal-mass storage such as water drums are excellent at holding heat. Even greenhouses without thermal mass will hold some heat.

When the weather is hot, I often look forward to a cool night when I might leave an exhaust fan on into the night. This can make the greenhouse run a bit cooler the following hot day. The cooling effect is even greater if you have quite a bit of thermal mass, such as water barrels in your greenhouse, as it takes longer to heat up again. Of course, the cooler the night, the better this works.

THERMOMETERS

The most important tool for measuring the greenhouse and sunspace climate is a good high–low thermometer. This will tell you what the low was last night and what the high temperature was for the day in your greenhouse. It's fun to have two high–low thermometers, one for outside and one for inside the greenhouse, to compare the difference. This is even more important for solar-heated greenhouses, where you can track the performance of the structure.

There are different types of high–low thermometers on the market. They run from $11 to $40 and are available in hardware stores and garden and greenhouse-supply catalogs. Starting with the cheapest, the three main types are:

Dial-type thermometers. These high–low thermometers run around $13 and are made of a cheap plastic. They are not known for their accuracy, but you can't beat the price.

Mercury thermometers. Two types are available through catalogs and even in some hardware stores. One type has a button you use to reset the highs and lows. I've found that these don't last very long. However, the mercury high-low thermometers that you reset with a small magnet have been dependable for me. Mercury high–low thermometers cost around $30. The magnet resetting can sometimes be a bit of trouble. It helps to use a stronger magnet than the one that comes with the unit.

Digital thermometers. These are rapidly becoming the new standard, replacing the

(A) *A low-cost, dial-type high–low thermometer.* Photo courtesy of Charley's Greenhouse Supply.
(B) *The mercury high–low thermometer works well but is not as convenient to read as the newer digital types. But, unlike the digital types, it never needs batteries.* Photo courtesy of Charley's Greenhouse Supply.
(C and D) *There are many different digital thermometers that measure high and low temperatures.*

above thermometers. They are now commonly available from discount stores, Radio Shack, and most greenhouse-supply catalogs. They give you a great digital readout to the nearest one-tenth degree. How's that for accuracy? The digitals run anywhere from $20 to $40. Some available types give you not only the high and low temperatures but also have a sensor on a wire that can give you a second high-low outdoor temperature. Lately, I have seen some that also give you a humidity reading (perhaps someday soon they'll even give you tomorrow's weather and pick out your wardrobe to match!). I've come to really like the digital thermometers because they are easy to read and reset. It may take a bit of time studying the operating instructions and practicing before you feel comfortable using them, but they are not as bad as programming your VCR. If the digital thermometer ever stops functioning, be sure to check the batteries.

Placement of the High-Low Thermometer

It is important that you not set your thermometer or the sensors of the digital thermometer in direct sunlight or you'll get some crazy read-ings. The best way to set a thermometer in your greenhouse is to build a little sun shelter that has plenty of air circulation around it and is painted white. With the digital thermometer, you need to set the sensor (which is a metal piece at the end of a plastic cord) out of the sun. If your thermometer receives any sunlight directly, it will give you an unusually high reading. Also place it where you won't accidentally water the sensor, as that too will set off crazy readings.

OTHER CLIMATE-MEASURING TOOLS

There are many instruments to measure the relative humidity. Most are not known for being particularly accurate, but they are adequate for giving you a ballpark figure that will help you determine how moist your air is. These range in price from $10 to $30. The most accurate humidity measurement is done with a sling psychrometer and a conversion chart to interpret what it reads. Generally, the simple, cheap, and less accurate ones work fine for the needs of a home greenhouse. Some digital thermometers may also give you a humidity readout.

There are thermometers that have been developed especially for measuring the soil temperature. These can be helpful in determining compost pile heat or soil temperatures, or in deciding if your climate is suitable in winter for warmth-loving plants.

There are meters on the market that will tell you how moist your soil is, but I have always found that my finger in a pot works even better.

Most carbon dioxide-measuring units are quite expensive. There are cheaper, expendable detectors that take a sample of air in a tube and indicate the level of your greenhouse carbon dioxide by turning colors. A kit with two tubes is around $20. Extra tubes are available for around $5 each. These are not readily available from hobby greenhouse suppliers. Check with commercial suppliers.

Most climate-measuring tools are available through good gardening or greenhouse-gardening catalogs (see "Mail-Order Supplies," in Appendix 7). Some may also be found in hardware stores or other supply stores.

PREDICTING THE WEATHER

If you have a solar-heated greenhouse or a greenhouse with little or no supplementary heat, the weather can have a real impact on the indoor climate. A good tool for these greenhouses is a weather radio. The federal government has set up a series of low-powered radio stations that play taped weather information 24 hours a day. Over 85 percent of the U.S. population lives within range of one of these stations. Radio Shack commonly sell radios that receive broadcasts on the weather band. This is not on AM or FM frequencies.

A weather radio can give you up-to-date weather forecasts as you work in your greenhouse.

The Internet has opened up more incredible options for accessing forecasts. You can now look at fresh weather radar and satellite photos taken within the hour right in the comfort of your home. There is also the Weather Channel on cable and satellite TV with predictions 24 hours a day.

All of these tools can help you make decisions about heating or ventilating solar greenhouses. For example, if it is a sunny winter day and the temperature inside the greenhouse has risen to 95°F (35°C) and is still climbing, you can access an up-to-date prediction for your area to decide what to do. If the weather is predicted to turn cold and cloudy, you might want to let your greenhouse run a little hot for a short while to store up some heat for the coming cool weather. If the weather is predicted to stay clear and sunny, you should probably go ahead and ventilate the greenhouse to help let in some cool, dry air while letting out the humid, wet air that winter greenhouses are notorious for. Of course, this approach assumes that the weather predictions are going to be correct. Remember the old saying, "Only fools predict the weather."

I have found that most five-day forecasts are only accurate about 60 percent of the time. This has not improved over the years, even with the addition of supercomputers, satellites, Doppler radar and other high-tech gadgets. I don't blame meteorologists for wanting these high-tech doohickeys, but it hasn't helped much. The truth is that the weather is very hard to model. Sixty-percent accuracy on an extended forecast is not much better than flipping a coin. You can flip a coin as well as a meteorologist. The moral of my rant is: If you haven't heard a forecast recently, don't rely on one you heard yesterday or earlier. Also, don't trust any forecast that is telling you what the weather will be like more than three days out.

Years ago, I was working in a greenhouse in Wyoming that needed a lot of buttoning up before it could survive the winter. Wyoming is a place where you can get fall weather ranging from a tornado to a blizzard to a heat wave. So far this particular fall, there had been crystal-clear warm days with cool nights, but no sign of winter. I had an 88-year-old friend named Howard who kept saying, "We're gonna have a rough, early winter." My weather radio kept saying, "Warm days ahead." So I kept putting off the task of caulking the vents and weatherstripping all the doors, vents, and windows for winter. One day Howard said, "It's gonna storm tomorrow!" I just smiled at Howard while I continued to work on other projects outside, shirtless, basking in the warm sun. The folks at the weather office kept saying, "Warm days ahead, partly cloudy."

That night it clouded up.

The next day we received 3 feet of "partly cloudy." Much of this snow was still on the ground in early spring. It was also cloudy for 12 straight days, which is unusual for Wyoming. Howard just smiled but never said, "I told you so." It was a rough winter, and I found that caulk just doesn't go on right when it's cold. Moral: Don't put all your eggs in just one weather forecaster. Sometimes the weather does what it wants to do, no matter what our satellite-aided, computer-modeled, scientific weather people say. To complement them I hope that you have a "Howard" living near you, too. If you do, listen to him.

GIZMOS FOR THE GREENHOUSE

I have always leaned toward simplicity in what is required to maintain a good growing environment (simple pleasures for simple minds). The trouble is, I love gadgets and there are some I can't resist. Still, when it comes to controlling the greenhouse environment, I have to temper myself, and when in doubt, I try to go the simple route. You will notice my love of gizmos dueling with my bias for simplicity throughout this book. There are an incredible number of gizmos and thingamabobs you can install in a greenhouse to feed, light, water, communicate, sense, and automate virtually everything. Let me count the ways: automatic watering systems, fogging systems, fertilizing systems, seeders, night curtains, pH meters, temperature alarms, misters, light meters, heaters, coolers, self-storing hoses, water guns, and much more. It can get to the point where you become more involved with the gadgets than with the plants. If this occurs, you'll lose touch with your plants (which makes for a poorly tended garden).

Fortunately, there is the self-limiting aspect of going gonzo over all these gadgets. Money. But if the cost of gardening gadgets doesn't slow you, think about the prospect of all these gadgets breaking. So I have devised this simple test: When tempted by greenhouse gizmos, I do a reality check and answer honestly if it makes life more simple or more complicated. There are some gizmos that pass this test but not the pocketbook test. As with all expenditures, keep a wry eye on the gizmos and remember the beauty in simplicity. I also like to run the gizmos through the "complicated test": the more complicated it is, the more likely that it will break or that you'll have trouble figuring out how to use it. If it fails "the complication" test, skip this gizmo.

YOU ARE THE MOST IMPORTANT GREENHOUSE GIZMO

Besides the things to buy for the inside environment, what is the most important thing required? Your powers of observation and expertise. No expertise? That's what this book is for. Not that I have included absolutely everything you need to know. But I hope to get you to a place where you can figure most of it out. Everyone who spends time gardening in a greenhouse can expect to become a bit of a biologist and ecologist. Over time you can also plan on becoming an olericulturist (vegetable grower), pomologist (fruit grower), floriculturist (flower grower), and horticulturist (general gardener). When things go wrong, you will quickly gain the skills of a entomologist (bug person) and plant pathologist (plant-disease person). A greenhouse will surely make a renaissance person out of you.

It is not hard to learn these things. Most of it will just soak in as you apply what you read, as long as you are observant and don't overdo things (gardeners have a great tendency to overdo everything from watering to fertilizing and on and on).

Now that you have an understanding of the elements that make up the greenhouse environment—such as structure, lighting, temperatures, humidity, and the rest—it is time

You are the most important gizmo in the growing greenhouse! (The author, 1983.)

to get ready to become the conductor of a biological symphony in this little microcosm of a planet called "greenhouse."

It all starts with the environment, but there's more. So grab your baton, maybe even put on some good music, and let's converse about what makes the plants grow well, producing wonderful things for you in your greenhouse.

CHAPTER 2

INTERIOR DESIGN

❧

WHEN PLANNING A NEW GREENHOUSE, people become preoccupied with the design of the exterior, leaving the inside design for an afterthought. Most don't realize until it is too late that the inside design is as crucial as the structure itself. Greenhouse space is always limited, making the interior design a most important consideration. No matter how the inside of your greenhouse ends up, it's a good idea to draw it out on paper first. It's much cheaper to make mistakes on paper than in bricks and mortar. After you read this chapter, get out a piece of graph paper and draw your dreams.

VISUALIZING AND PLANNING YOUR GREENHOUSE SPACE

Your first important decision is to determine how much space you want dedicated to growing versus how much will be used for living space. How important is it to keep your options open? Personally, I can't imagine any greenhouse without at least one or two chairs for enjoying the space and ambience. Some want every square inch devoted to plants, whereas others feel plants are there to provide a small touch of green in a glass-walled living room or hot-tub room that happens to be a sun-space. This decision is up to you.

The main idea is to create the ideal mix of living space and plant-growing space. No matter what, I feel that the goal is to have a comfortable greenhouse where both you and your plants will gain the most out of this area.

COMFORT

Comfort is the key word for both living-room greenhouses and the serious-grower greenhouse. The more comfortable it is to work in your greenhouse, the better kept your garden will be.

Every greenhouse should have a space to relax. At the very least, a chair or two is a must.

This attached greenhouse is being constructed as part of a barn-raising event. Attached greenhouses are always better tended. If it can't be attached, get it as close to the house as possible.

Ground beds (top) force gardeners to bend way over to reach them. A raised gardening bed (bottom) is much easier to tend.

Conversely, if getting to and working in your greenhouse or sunroom is an uncomfortable chore, your plants won't be very well tended.

I have noticed that the closer your greenhouse is to your kitchen, the better kept your greenhouse will be. Following this logic, gardeners tend to take better care of their plants if the greenhouse is attached to the house rather than freestanding in the yard. Why? Because it is more uncomfortable to first put on shoes and a jacket to go out to the greenhouse. Compare that with noticing the plants need tending while walking from the kitchen to the living room or while sipping your Sunday-morning coffee. I should talk—my current home greenhouse is freestanding and out in the backyard. The moral of this thinking is that if there is any way you can attach your greenhouse to your home,

do it! If you can't, try to get it close to the door while not sacrificing access to good natural sunlight. If neither of these suggestions works for you and you still want a greenhouse, do like me and put it where you have to. It is still better to have a greenhouse even way out in the backyard than to go without!

Comfort also comes into play when you design gardening beds. It is always more comfortable to have plants growing in raised beds or on a table rather than way down on the floor. This fact becomes more apparent as we get past middle age, a time of life when getting down to the ground level isn't hard at all but getting back up again poses a challenge. Greenhouse bed design is discussed later in this chapter.

SAFETY

A major concern in the greenhouse is safety. Electricity is often used in greenhouses: running fans, vent openers, automated watering systems, heat mats for seedlings and pots, and heaters. Unfortunately, electricity does not mix with water, and there is always water splashing around wherever you find plants. No one should have a shocking experience in a greenhouse or sunroom. Special care should be taken when using electricity in order to prevent any possible contact between water and electrical connections. Any electric outlets installed in your greenhouse should be of the ground-fault interrupter type, which can help prevent any possible electric shocks. These are also known by their initials: GFI outlets. They usually have little buttons on the outlet, one of which says "test." The beauty of GFI outlets is that they provide you with a line of defense if you receive a shock. When the GFI senses a short (you getting shocked), then it automatically turns the current off to the outlet, possibly saving your rear end (to put it bluntly). Be sure to have a licensed electrician install a GFI. Also, you should regularly press the "test" button to see if the current does indeed shut off. If it works, great; then press the "reset" button. If it doesn't work, call the electrician. If you need to press the reset button regularly to get power, it may indicate a problem.

As mentioned in the last chapter, gas heaters should be properly vented to prevent air pollution, which could harm both you and the plants. Any heater should be placed far enough away from the wall or any combustible material to prevent accidental fires. Fiberglass and many other plastic glazings are extremely flammable. Plastic flats and pots can literally explode into a blaze, so be careful with any flame in a greenhouse. (Another good reason to go with solar heat!) It is a good idea to have a smoke detector and a small fire-extinguisher in or near your greenhouse. Both are commonly available in hardware or department stores.

Any fans in a greenhouse that are within reach of children should have protective screens to keep out little fingers.

Pesticides, fertilizers, and sprayers should be placed in an area where children can't get to them, and they should never be left sitting out in a greenhouse. You should always be concerned with safety when handling pesticides and fertilizers. The best precaution is to follow the directions on the label. See Chapter 10, "When Things Go Wrong," for more information on the handling of chemicals.

A Ground Fault Interrupter (GFI) outlet. Note the 'test' and 'reset' buttons at its center. A GFI is safer for use in areas near and around water, such as a greenhouse.

I could go on and on about safety, but I don't want to sound like I'm from OSHA. I usually think in terms like this: If you sense any potential danger, deal with it and eliminate any dangerous possibility. Do this not only for yourself but also for any visitors (especially kids) who stop by to view your greenhouse. With that out of the way, let's get on with interior design.

DEFINING THE AREAS

Since this is a book about growing plants in the greenhouse, I am going to assume that you are interested in doing just that. However, in order to be a good greenhouse gardener, I would suggest that you consider creating a place to sit and enjoy this space. Watch the plants grow, notice what is happening, and soak up the greenhouse environment. As a result of having a place to stop and sit, you will find that you'll see something that you otherwise would have missed. Being observant is a prerequisite to being a good gardener: Perhaps you will see a flower about to bloom, a yellowing on a tomato plant indicating a potential problem, a fruit to harvest, or a beneficial wasp happily destroying your aphids. Sometimes you need to stop and look.

Besides, sitting in a greenhouse in winter is the perfect cure for cabin fever, which usually sets in sometime after Christmas. But where is the best place to locate that sitting place? Where is the best place to grow? Where does the potting bench go? Does it matter? Yes, it matters, and it matters all the more if your greenhouse depends upon solar heat to any extent.

Light and Shade

Because solar greenhouses have limited amounts of glass or glazing, the light is also limited. In temperate northern climates during winter months, the sun never gets very high in the southern sky (northern sky if you live south of the equator). When the winter sun is low, shading caused by interior objects may be a problem. Any tall object placed toward the southern half of a solar greenhouse in winter can cause shading. This will reduce the yields of vegetables and many flowering plants. So be sure that no furniture or any solar water storage, such as 55-gallon (208-liter) or 30-gallon (113-liter) drums, are placed to the south of growing beds holding plants that require high levels of light.

Interior Surfaces

Because of the constant problem of low light in solar greenhouses, it's important that all light entering the greenhouse be used either for plant growth or for heating dark-colored solar collectors or passive solar storage (usually water drums). The best way to utilize the rest of the light not directly striking these surfaces is to bounce (or reflect) it where plants or solar collectors can catch it. As mentioned in

Paint solid greenhouse walls white for the best reflection. This becomes more important in greenhouses that lack light or in areas that have cloudy winters.

the previous chapter, the best light reflector in a greenhouse is the color white. This includes painting walls, ceilings, floors, and even the sides of raised beds white. If you live in an area that experiences cloudy winters and you want to grow vegetables in your solar-heated greenhouse, then this can make a big difference (see "Increasing Reflective Surfaces," page 25 in Chapter 1).

THERMAL MASS

If you don't have a solar greenhouse, then you might be confused by the term "thermal mass." This is what is used to collect and store the sun's energy. Usually, it is water held in metal containers (either 30- or 55-gallon [113- or 208-liter] drums or 5-gallon [19-liter] oil tins), or it may be plastic tubes. There are other types of containers for storing water. Some people may be using rock as a thermal storage, but water is much more efficient. It is most efficient when placed in a metal container such as a drum, as opposed to a plastic (or fiberglass) container. This is because metal is quicker at transferring the sun's heat to the water, and it also radiates heat back out into the greenhouse faster than plastic or concrete water containers. Still, if it is a choice between plastic water containers or no water containers (as thermal mass), then use the plastic. Plastic tubes provide a much better-looking thermal mass container and are only 10 to 15 percent less effective than a comparable metal container. One of the better-looking plastic solar storage options are long fiberglass tubes. They are about $1\frac{1}{2}$ feet (30 cm) in diameter and come in many lengths. The only place I know that sells them direct is Solar Components Corporation, 121 Valley Street, Manchester, NH 03103, www.solar-components. com. Check out their catalog if you want some nice-looking thermal-mass tubes. They provide a unique look while storing a lot of water.

To best gather solar heat and moderate the greenhouse temperature, water storage in solar-heated greenhouses is usually located along the north wall. However, there is one exception: If your greenhouse is much wider than 18 feet (5.5 m), it may be wise to place some thermal mass (water drums) along the south wall, too. This will help create more even temperatures across the width of your greenhouse. If you do this, thermal mass along the south face of the greenhouse should be in small containers such as 30-gallon (113-liter) drums laid on their side to minimize winter shading. Any water drums placed on the south side of a solar greenhouse should be painted half black and half white, with the white half on the north side of the thermal mass container and the black half on the sunny side (toward the glazing).

In the summer in a solar greenhouse, the thermal mass storage along the north wall can be a very shady area. Light can be increased by hanging a white curtain over your mass containers to bounce and reflect more light to plants.

(Top) *Fifty-five- or 30-gallon drums painted black and filled with water provide a great thermal mass for storing heat.*
(Bottom) *Fiberglass tubes are more ornamental than metal drums.*

The effect of water as a thermal mass enables the greenhouse to collect the day's heat and then radiate it back into the greenhouse at night. If you've ever been in a solar greenhouse with water containers, then you probably noticed that even on a sunny day the containers did not feel all that warm to the touch. Remember, your fingers are quite warm, at around 80°F (26°C). Many people wonder how it can work if it is not warm. Actually, it works pretty well, and here's how. When using water as a thermal mass, you are not particularly trying to get the water extremely hot. Rather, you

(Top) *This greenhouse uses fiberglass tubes and old metal oil tins for storing water as a thermal mass.*
(Bottom) *For solar greenhouses wider than 18 feet (5.5m), drums painted black on the side facing out and white facing in provide thermal water storage and result in more heat gain when the sun is shining.*

A cloth can be hung across some black barrels to increase light to the northern half of a greenhouse in the summer.

are after gaining a difference between the day and night temperature. By having the water temperature rise just a few degrees (no matter how cool it feels to the touch), it can be translated into thousands of calories, or BTUs (a term for heat measurement), of heat for the interior greenhouse space.

Having water storage in your greenhouse will also help in another way. If for some reason your greenhouse space becomes incredibly cold and the temperature gets down to freezing, then there is an added benefit to having water containers. Near the freezing point

of water, there occurs what chemists call the "latent heat of water." This is a reaction in which water actually gives off heat as it starts to form ice crystals. I know it sounds odd that when water is about to freeze, it gives off heat. Ask your local chemistry teacher for verification if you don't believe me. I like to visualize the heat being chased out of the water by the cold. This is the same reason that fruit growers turn on a sprinkler system when their crop is threatened with frost. The droplets of water on the leaves give off enough heat to protect the plants until the sun rises. The same is true with water in a greenhouse threatened with frost. The water in drums or other containers will help prevent the temperature from going below the freezing point, thus protecting your plants. This can come in handy for people with 100 percent solar-heated greenhouses, and it can even be helpful for conventionally heated greenhouses, especially if your heater goes out or something else goes wrong that causes the temperature to drop to freezing.

I have worked in many a solar greenhouse that has been saved by its water mass. Once I had a recording thermometer that produced a graph of the temperature, which I set in a solar greenhouse on the high plains of Wyoming. This greenhouse had a lot of 30- and 55-gallon (113- and 208-liter) metal drums filled with water. It was winter, and the predicted low for the night was –30°F –34°C). The wind was blowing 15 to 20 miles an hour. I figured these conditions would be a challenge for any solar greenhouse to survive without frost. When I returned in the morning, the plants looked fine, with the exception of some slight frost damage to some plants sitting adjacent to the outer fiberglass-glazed wall. I was surprised to see on the thermometer graph that the temperature had been bouncing up and down slightly around 32°F (0°C) most of the night. It was evident to me that the water as thermal mass was giving off the "latent heat" as ice crystals were forming and that that was what had protected the greenhouse that night.

The question that everyone wants answered is how much water storage do you really need? The answer is as variable as your structure, location, type of greenhouse, and whether your greenhouse is attached or not. So take the following rule of thumb with a tablespoon of salt. The common rule of thumb is this: Provide 2 to 3 gallons (7.6 to 11.4 liters) of water for each square foot of glazing. Provide the higher amount or more for leaky greenhouses or for greenhouses in cold, cloudy climates.

Water as Thermal Mass for Nonsolar Greenhouses

Owners of conventionally heated greenhouses often investigate ways to conserve energy. Common sense usually steers people toward the obvious solutions, such as weather-stripping vents and doors; another common practice is to add some winter insulation to the north walls. An easy solution is to add a layer of glazing, usually a plastic film, on the inside of the outer glazing. But many gardeners ask whether they should use water drums.

The answer is yes, using water as thermal mass can help moderate both high and low temperatures in the greenhouse. I usually recommend that people try using water drums to hold up benches or tables for plants or as the base for a small potting bench. Although there is no hard research on this, I suggest that you try experimenting, and you'll find that it can help reduce heating costs. With every greenhouse being different, it would be hard to tell you how many to put in your greenhouse, but for an average greenhouse of 8 by 10 feet (2.4 by 3 m), I would try at least four 30-gallon (113-liter) drums or two to three 55-gallon

Tops of water barrels used for thermal mass can serve as shelves.

(208-liter) drums filled with water and sealed. It is best to place these drums in the north side of a greenhouse.

Where would you ever find drums for using as thermal mass? Check your local oil companies, junkyards, army-surplus stores, and construction contractors. New barrels are best, but old ones can work fine as long as they weren't used to store toxic waste. Drums are usually reasonable in cost. Always try to use drums with resealable lids to prevent evaporation. Fill the drums with plain water within 2 inches (5 cm) of the top (to allow for expansion).

There are chemicals you can put into the drums that will slow rusting, such as a small amount of antifreeze. It is important, however, not to set metal drums directly on dirt, as this will cause quick corrosion of the metal from the outside. In fact, most of the corrosion I see on water barrels starts from the outside, so it is a good idea not to allow water to sit on the drums for long periods. The drums should be set on concrete, wood, or brick for a long life. If you are interested in obtaining the much more ornamental (but less effective) plastic (or fiberglass) drums, check the Solar

Components Corporation listed earlier in this chapter. There may be other companies that carry the product, but this is the only one I can find that carries plastic water-storage units.

If you use the plastic storage tubes, you may need to occasionally add an algicide to the water to prevent the unsightly buildup of green scum. The algicide commonly used for spas, hot tubs, and swimming pools works fine in controlling algae. Many people wonder about increasing the solar-heating effectiveness of the clear fiberglass tubes by adding dyes to the water. I have not found an increase in efficiency high enough to warrant the addition of colorings, but it can provide a cool look for aesthetic reasons. Algicides may color the water in the tubes, usually adding a bluish cast. Without any addition, they usually take on a pleasant light bluish-green color anyway.

FANS AND VENTS

As mentioned in the previous chapter, fans and proper ventilation are important to the cooling of the greenhouse and to CO_2 absorption by the leaves. Unfortunately, overheating is an all-too-frequent problem affecting greenhouses and sunspaces. Usually, it is the result of an undersized cooling system. But fans are good not only for cooling. By stirring up the air, you can also help reduce the incidence of disease and pests, which love stagnant air.

When you are designing the placement of your cooling fans and winter fans, be sure they don't interfere with tall plants or the movement of people. Also, give some thought to safety, in terms of water mixing with the electrical parts and people (or kids) risking contact with the moving blades. The same kind

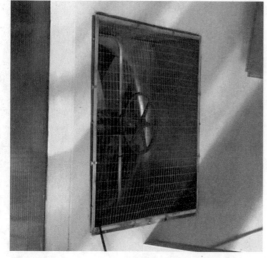

A screen should be installed in front of all exhaust fans to protect people and critters from the blades.

of consideration should be given to the windows and shutters that open for ventilation.

SCREENS

Screens can help in keeping a low, accessible fan or vent safe, and they can also keep critters out, like birds and the neighbor's dog or cat. Galvanized hardware cloth is a good material to maintain safety and keep most big things out. You may also want to keep out bugs. As mentioned in the previous chapter, researchers have produced a microfine insect screen for keeping little critters out, and this works to keep out even the smallest insect while letting a fair amount of air through. Check with a hobby- or greenhouse-supply company for more information.

AISLES AND FLOORS

There are a number of ways to deal with aisle and floor space. Each material has its special attributes: My favorite floor material is brick pavers, but let's look at how various choices stack up.

FLOOR SURFACING OPTIONS

Dirt. This surface gets muddy and may harbor disease and insects. It makes for dirty floors in your house if you forget to clean off your feet!

Wood boards. These may harbor slugs and insects, and wood floors are short-lived, rot readily, and are hard to clean. Barefooted? Watch out for splinters!

Brick. Brick is easy to clean and has a pleasing look. It is somewhat porous and drains excess water well. You can create some interesting patterns with the way you lay the brick. Also, it will store some solar heat. It can be expensive if you use real brick pavers. There are some concrete-based brick-like pavers that are cheaper and

work equally well but don't look quite as good as real brick. It's easy to install.

Gravel and rock. Use only pea-size gravel with some "fines" (a rock guy's term) to stabilize the rock so you don't sink down so much. These surfaces drain well and are great on hot days. Another advantage is that they can be watered down and the heat of the day will cause evaporative cooling. But they're not good for barefooted humans. The material is cheap to purchase and easy to install, but it's harder for wheelbarrows and wheelchairs to access, as they often sink into the gravel.

Concrete. If the whole floor is a concrete slab, water drainage may be a problem unless it is planned for. Concrete is a great material for greenhouse walkways, but I prefer not to have it under the beds. The grayish-white color is good for reflecting light. But don't paint the floor black for solar-heat storage as it will become too hot in summertime. For a brick-like look without the brick expense, consider mixing a terra-cotta dye into the concrete when you pour the floor.

(A) *Wood boards are less than ideal but are better than walking on dirt.*
(B) *Brick always makes a handsome-looking walkway and floor.*
(C) *Gravel provides a low-cost floor option.*
(D) *Concrete pavers are low-cost and easy to install.*

Those in wheelchairs can enjoy greenhouse gardening, too, if you design the space properly. It is especially helpful to build beds with adequate knee space so the gardener in a wheelchair can face the bed or growing table directly.

WHEELCHAIR ACCESS

People bound to a wheelchair can find as much joy in gardening as do people with working legs. Depending upon the severity of the handicap, there is much a person in a wheelchair can do in a greenhouse. Some people do just about everything required to grow great crops of food and flowers, whereas others reap great rewards from just dabbling with the soil and being among plants. The one requirement for a handicapped person to garden in a greenhouse is access for the wheelchair. Wheelchairs need to roll on a solid floor such as brick or concrete. Gravel and sand are tough to get through. Bed or bench spacing is also important. Wheelchairs vary between 2 and 3 feet (0.6 and 0.9 m) in width. They need a diameter of about 5$\frac{1}{2}$ feet (1.7 m) for a turnaround.

For complete access, replace any stairs leading into the greenhouse with ramps. Ramps should not rise faster than 1 foot per 10 feet (0.3 m per 3 m) in length. For wheelchair access to growing beds, it is nice to be able to position the chair so that it's facing a bed or growing table with an underneath clearance for the knees of 2 feet (0.6 m) rather than having to pull up alongside. The gardener's legs are then under the bed or table, which provides an easy front reach from the wheelchair rather than an uncomfortable twist to the side to reach plants.

Remember, being handicapped does not mean being "unable." That is why I hate the word "disabled," which sounds too much like "unable." Gardening is an art and adventure that can be enjoyed by many people with a variety of abilities. Even if you are not challenged by a handicap, please consider your options (either now or for the future) in making your greenhouse more accessible. You, yourself, could be only a moment away from being beset with a handicap. Wouldn't it be nice to continue to garden in your greenhouse?

PROPAGATION BENCH

Everything has to start somewhere, and having a special area in which to start seeds and cuttings is helpful to the overall scheme of a good growing greenhouse or sunspace.

This area is called the propagation area, or propagation bench (as the commercial greenhouse operators call it). The location of this area can be just about anywhere in your greenhouse. It doesn't even have to be in your greenhouse. In fact, it is a good idea to not take up good, well-lit growing areas for this purpose, unless you have a sizable greenhouse with space to spare. Through the wonders of grow lights, bottom heaters, and

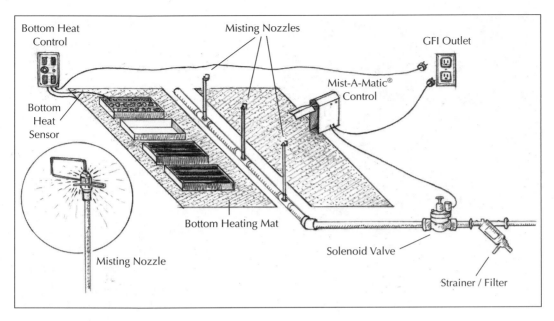

Labels in figure:
Bottom Heat Control
Misting Nozzles
GFI Outlet
Bottom Heat Sensor
Mist-A-Matic® Control
Bottom Heating Mat
Misting Nozzle
Solenoid Valve
Strainer / Filter

A well-equipped propagation area provides mist (humidity) and bottom heat as needed. This system includes the Mist-A-Matic misting® controller, a solenoid valve (to control water flow to the mister), a strainer / filter (to prevent nozzles from clogging), misting nozzles, and bottom heating mats to maintain a warm environment during cold spells.

automatic misting systems, you can have a great semiautomatic propagation bench setup anywhere. I must admit, however, that I prefer having a propagation bench right in my greenhouse. Although it can go anywhere, a good place to locate it is in a northwest or northeast area.

What do you need for a good propagation bench? Well, it depends on your pocketbook and how many plants you hope to start at any given time. Let's begin with the basics. One of the most important things needed to start seeds or cuttings is bottom heat. Seeds or cuttings benefit greatly from a steady source of heat from below; it makes germination and root growth take off at a phenomenal rate. Bottom heaters are set to maintain a temperature of around 70°F (21°C). All bottom heaters (that I know of) run on electricity, so first of all you must get electricity into your greenhouse.

A variety of electric bottom heaters for plant propagation are on the market and are available through garden centers and greenhouse-supply catalogs. As with many things in life, the more expensive ones are generally the better ones. I have had poor luck with the cable-type bottom heaters, which are just a plastic-lined wire that heats up. The cable heaters have never lasted for more than a year for me before they corrode or just quit working, although there are some new types of cable bottom heaters that claim to be more durable.

I find that the thicker the heating mat, the longer the bottom heater will last. There is a brand that comes in a terra-cotta color that is manufactured for commercial greenhouses called ProGro and it is the Cadillac of bottom heaters (and comes with a Cadillac price). I have some of these types that have been working for over 20 years. They start at around $90 for a 22 by 22 inch (55 by 55 cm) mat. You also need

A bottom-heater mat is very helpful in propagating seeds, cuttings, and other plants, especially in winter. Photo courtesy of Charley's Greenhouse Supply.

an adjustable thermostat, usually sold separately, starting at around $60. The thermostats come with a remote probe that tells the thermostat at what temperature it is running. For the most accurate results, it is important that you place the probe in a pot that has the same type of soil that you usually use in other pots on the mat. (Be sure to set the potted probe on the mat.)

Another brand, Heat-a-matic, is made of carbon and silver/copper conductors bonded to

This electric misting timer is one way to control the frequency and duration of turning misting nozzles on and off in a propagation bed. Photo courtesy of Charley's Greenhouse Supply.

aluminum, all of which is encapsulated in a thinner plastic mat. It runs a bit cheaper than the ProGro and uses less electricity per amount of heat generated. Some professional growers like this style of mat, though others believe that these don't have the life span of the ProGro brand. There are other small mats sold through greenhouse suppliers. It helps to check out the guarantee versus the price.

No matter what type of bottom-heating mat you end up using, it is important to monitor the temperature of your soil in some of the pots on the mat. All too often, I have found that the mats run hotter than the thermostat indicates, causing some damage to my plants and making them dry out too fast. If your mat runs hotter than the thermostat indicates, turn it down accordingly.

Any type of bottom heat should be set to keep your soil temperature at around 75°F (24°C) for faster germination or rooting. Keep an eye on things; if it gets too hot, your plants will dry out or burn up, and if it is too cool, germination will slow considerably. You will notice that the soil placed on a propagation mat will tend to dry out more rapidly, requiring regular monitoring.

Because the mats run on electricity and you need to water the plants on these mats, it is smart to only plug the mats into outlets equipped with a ground-fault interrupter (GFI), to avoid possible electric shocks.

Newer to the business of propagation are the little, self-contained plastic propagation units that have built-in bottom heaters. Some can water themselves with a capillary mat that feeds moisture to the plants from a reservoir. Others are just a plastic tray with a clear plastic top to maintain a high humidity. Some even come with built-in thermostatically controlled bottom heaters. These can be a good way to start and can

SETTING UP A PROPAGATION BENCH

Requirement	Comments
Location:	Locate it in a bright spot; don't take up precious growing space if you have limits on space. Propagation of cuttings requires less intense light but still must be in a bright spot.
Bottom heat:	Preferably, use thermostatically controlled heat mats. For cuttings or seedlings, maintain a temperature around 75°F (24°C).
Humidity:	Constant 80 percent or higher relative humidity is required, maintained best by a misting system set up with a timer or automatic, metal-leaf triggering device (see Mist-A-Matic®, above and below). Humidity can also be increased by placing propagated plants under a clear plastic cover and misting by hand frequently.
Lighting:	Fluorescent lights work great for seedlings when placed within 1 inch (2.5 cm) of the tips of the seedlings. The cheaper cool-white lights work fine for germinating seedlings. For propagating cuttings, light can be less intense. For seedling germination, light must be very bright.
Moisture:	If possible, locate a propagation light near a water spigot for easy access.

The Mist-a-Matic® is a simple control for an intermittent misting system.

take the mystery out of setting up the propagation environment. After a while, you may want to construct your own bigger versions of these.

Another important requirement for a successful propagation area is maintaining a high humidity. This can be done by hand if you are around often and can hand-mist your plants a number of times each day. An easier way is to set up an automated misting system. Although I try to avoid automation in the home greenhouse, I've loved having a good automated misting system. Check a good greenhouse-supply catalog for the many options. If you're not a plumber, you may want to get some help installing this type of system (although if you're a handy person, it's not too difficult to set up yourself). I have had good luck with a commonly available system called Mist-A-Matic®, which turns the mist on and off to match the rate of water evaporation from the propagation area. The last time I looked, the Mist-A-Matic system

This electrically controlled water valve (known as a solenoid valve) is required to control most misting or watering systems. It can be attached to a timer or other controller. Photo courtesy of Charley's Greenhouse Supply.

cost around $210. There are other acceptable misting systems, usually triggered by a timer, that produce an intermittent mist.

Most automated mist systems have a solenoid valve (which is an electric valve and switch that turns the water on and off), plastic plumbing pipe, and mist nozzles. A good greenhouse catalog usually does a fine job of explaining the options available for setting up an automated mist system.

A final option for a propagation area is lighting. This is especially required if you locate your propagation bench in a low-light area. If your propagation area is in the greenhouse, you are probably OK on lighting. If your plants are elongated and stretching toward the light, you probably need some supplementary lighting. Usually this can be accomplished with an array of common cool-white fluorescent lights (see the "Fluorescent Lights" section, page 18). Remember two things when using fluorescent lighting for growing or starting plants: (1) Safety. Be careful of mixing water with electricity. You might want to check with an electrician for help in installation. Be sure to use properly wired GFI outlets. (2) Distance. You must keep the lights close to the growing or germinating plant. A minimum of 3 inches (8 cm) is best. This means the lights must be adjustable (with chains or the like) to keep them close to the top of the growing plants. Fluorescent lights are a great addition to a propagation setup, if you do it right. If you have a lot of natural light, you probably don't need them.

In spring, I like to utilize a large percentage of the greenhouse for starting seedlings for my outside garden. This may require turning your whole greenhouse into a propagation area. No, I can't afford to put bottom-heating mats throughout the greenhouse. I just try to maintain a warmer and more humid environment. During seedling season, you need to use every square inch of space. I often set trays of seedlings on raised beds, tables, benches, floors, and solar-storage barrels. Then the only trick is keeping the environment warm and the seedlings moist (but not too moist).

A potting bench provides space to work. It can be in the greenhouse or in an adjacent area, freeing up greenhouse space for growing. Potting benches need a lip on the table (**top**) so the soil doesn't fall off onto the ground. Some benches (**bottom**) feature a tub to hold the soil and a place to work. Bottom photo courtesy of Charley's Greenhouse Supply.

POTTING AREA

A place to repot plants and transplant seedlings is always nice to have. But although a potting area is nice, it is not an essential component of a greenhouse. Like the propagation bench, it doesn't have to be in the greenhouse proper. Many people locate the potting area in their basement, toolshed, or garage. All you really need is a good tabletop where you can spread out the soil mixes and make a contained mess. This is where you pot up, transplant, or prune plants. It's basically a work area that will get dirty (what do you expect when you work with dirt?). A potting area is easy to build using plywood painted with a heavy-duty exterior deck paint or, better yet, covered with galvanized sheet metal. All you really need is a small area to work in, usually a minimum of 18 by 18 inch (46 by 46 cm) square (larger is even better), but the size is up to you and the space you have to work in. A most helpful component to any potting area are sides, which prevent the soil and mess from falling on the floor. Some people simply use a large, plastic, low-sided square tub.

You can also find premanufactured potting benches for sale in greenhouse catalogs. I like one sold by Charley's Greenhouse Supply called the Gro-Tub Bench, which runs around $170.

For true luxury, it is nice to have a sink adjacent to the potting area, but this is not a requirement. If you do have a sink for greenhouse use, be sure to install a dirt trap in the drain. With all the dirt "accidentally" going down the drain, a dirt trap will save hiring a plumber when you plug up the drain. A dirt trap is a small container under the sink that catches all of the stuff that shouldn't go down the drain. Every so often you must remove a small, pail-like container and clean it out. I must admit, this is a smelly job that I would rather avoid. Still, it is better to clean your dirt trap every once in a while than to have your sewer professionally cleaned out or, worse, to have your lawn dug up when your sewer plugs up beyond repair. A plumbing

shop usually sells these traps, and if you are good at plumbing, they are not too hard to install. If you are not an adept plumber, hire a real one. If you don't have a dirt trap, just be careful about what you let go down the drain. Try placing a screen in the drain to catch rocks and other debris.

If you locate the potting area in your greenhouse, as with the propagation area, don't put it in a prime growing area (with good light qualities). It is better to

The sink nearest your potting bench will likely have a lot of soil and debris going down the drain. The dirt trap shown here is helpful in preventing clogs in the sewer line.

put it in a darker area where plants wouldn't do well otherwise. Again, I prefer the northeast or northwest corner for nongrowing activities such as potting.

SHELVES

Shelving can help create extra growing space for potted or containerized plants. Shelves can be attached to the wall or, if space permits, they can be set up temporarily over a raised bed for extra room to start seedlings. They may also be hinged onto the side of raised beds to swing out into an area previously used for living or into an area where aisles are wide enough, as long as there is still enough room to walk (or waltz) through. When you are in need of every square inch for seedling season, shelves can come in handy.

For greenhouses short on natural light (including solar-heated structures), be sure

Shelves help create easy, extra space for potted plants. They can even be hinged to lie flush with the wall when they are not in use.

MIXING GARDEN AND LEISURE SPACE

Many people like to use their greenhouses or sunrooms primarily as a living space, with furniture, hot tubs, and just a few plants. Other people want the greenhouse for gardening and can't see wasting any space for just sitting around. I like a good mix in a greenhouse: a place to sit and a garden to enjoy. I like a greenhouse that is a mix of comfort—a place where I can relax and read the paper with a year-round garden close at hand, producing fruit, flowers, herbs, and spices. It sounds like heaven to me … and it is!

If you're like me and prefer a mix of leisure and garden, try not to use up the best growing areas of your greenhouse for leisure. Always locate the living or leisure areas in the shadier spots in a greenhouse. Overall, continue to follow the rule for nongrowing space: The best places for leisure tend to be the northwest and northeast areas. Sometimes the north wall is also a shady place, depending on your greenhouse or sunspace design.

to paint the shelves white. The shelves may create some shade below, possibly cutting out light for lower plants, but usually there is not a noticeable difference. Glazing materials that diffuse the light help to minimize shade problems (see page 7, on "Glazing," Chapter 1).

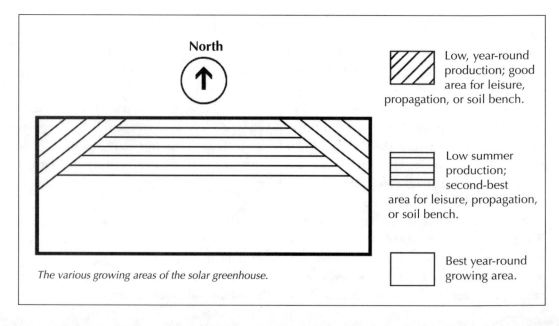

North

↑

Low, year-round production; good area for leisure, propagation, or soil bench.

Low summer production; second-best area for leisure, propagation, or soil bench.

Best year-round growing area.

The various growing areas of the solar greenhouse.

If you are going to use your greenhouse for leisure or socially in the evening, include overhead lights, not for growing but rather for seeing at night. Consider a dimmer switch for your light to create varying moods. If you go for real romantic lighting, please be careful with candles, because some glazings are quite inflammable. How about a stereo or extension speakers for music (botanists often say that plants like classical and jazz)? What a great place to visit with friends or just hang out with family!

PUTTING PLANTS TO SOIL

Once you have mapped out the space in your greenhouse and addressed all of the key aesthetic and practical design issues, you're ready to get down to the business of configuring how you will grow plants. You have various options and can mix and match many ways of putting plants to soil. It mainly comes down to two options when growing plants in a greenhouse: Grow them in soil beds or grow them in containers and pots. My preference is to do both.

RAISED BEDS

You have some options concerning where and how to grow plants. One of my favorite ways to grow plants is in raised beds. The number-one benefit of a raised bed is that of gardening comfort. But it is initially more uncomfortable to construct such a bed.

A raised bed is usually made out of wood and filled with soil or another appropriate growing medium. Raised beds may also be built of brick, concrete, or recycled material. I have found that growing in raised beds allows for excellent root production, and planting directly into a raised bed is especially well suited for food crops and cut flowers. Raised beds are also good for growing long-lived

Raised beds can be built to provide storage space underneath them.

To construct raised beds, bolt rot-resistant wood to support stakes. For extra protection from rot, line the inside of raised wood beds with plastic. You can also construct raised beds out of "plastic wood" cinder blocks and other materials.

Using raised beds does not eliminate opportunities to use potted plants. Simply use the top of the raised bed as a table for placing potted plants as needed.

tion of potted plants and plants growing in a raised bed or two. By having a raised bed, you do not eliminate the possibility of using the top of the raised bed as a tabletop and placing potted plants on it. This gives you the option later on of directly planting into the soil of the raised bed, which might be more appropriate for a 10-foot (25 cm) tomato plant that might have trouble growing in a 1-gallon (3.8 liter) pot.

As mentioned earlier, gardening with raised beds is by far more comfortable than reaching down to a ground-level planting. Ground beds also have the disadvantage of getting trampled as people walk through. Even a defining wooden two-by-four edge that lifts the soil a few inches off the ground can work wonders in keeping big feet off of your plants; of course, a low raised bed won't stop cats, dogs, or curious kids. Up to a point, the higher the raised bed, the less you have to stoop to garden. I have found that a 24-inch-high (61-cm-high) bed is about perfect for most people. Another advantage of a raised bed is that the

plants, such as perennial herbs, and tropical fruiting plants, such as citrus and figs. Of course, all of these plants will also grow satisfactorily in pots as long as they are suited to the size of the plant.

Many greenhouse growers like to mix both types of planting schemes, having a combina-

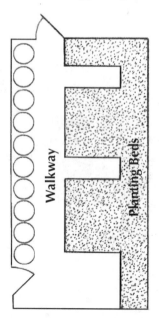

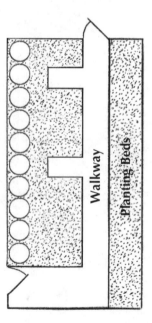

 = Thermal Mass Water Containers

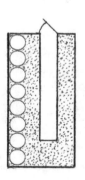

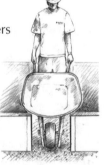

The old-fashioned, three-point–one-wheel wheelbarrow has its advantages. It can maneuver through aisles narrower than the width of the wheelbarrow, assuming of course that the sides of the beds are lower than the top of the wheelbarrow.

Peninsular Beds

soil also acts as thermal mass, complementing other thermal storage. If your greenhouse or sunspace is located in a place with poor soil, a raised bed enables you to create your own soil profile from the richest ingredients. However, don't overdo it, as most people get carried away with the addition of soil conditioners, peat moss, compost, and fertilizers (see Chapter 9, "Getting to the Roots").

There are a number of ways to lay out raised beds. The peninsular system uses space most efficiently, with the main aisle running north–south or east–west. The width of the raised bed should be comfortable for you to reach across, usually $3^1/_2$ feet (1 m), providing access from both sides. For one-sided access (such as a bed up against a wall), don't make the beds any wider than $2^1/_2$ feet (0.8 m). Again, bed and aisle width really depend on what is comfortable for you. Think about the size of your wheelbarrow and the route you must take to carry soil to the beds. The old-fashioned three-point, one-wheel wheelbarrow has the advantage of being able to roll down narrower aisles.

Another option for many greenhouse gardeners is to raise the beds by lowering the walkway. This leaves the top of your raised beds at grade level. This option is out for those of you who already have a greenhouse with a concrete slab for a floor—unless you're good with a jackhammer. This also requires that you have installed some type of floor drainage or you'll be walking in water. Also check into your particular groundwater conditions before you get going on this type of walkway.

Some growers prefer to raise their raised bed. This is like having a raised bed on stilts; there are usually built out of wood, but other materials may work as well. Usually, the bed is a minimum of 1 foot (0.3 m) deep. The main advantage here is creating storage space under the bed for things like pots, hoses, garage-sale accumulations, and other junk (just what you need, right?). If you attempt this kind of bed, be sure that this constructed bed has some drainage holes in the bottom.

Constructing Raised Beds

There is no single right way to construct raised beds. There are, however, methods and materials that make the bed last much longer. These are usually limited only by your budget and your imagination. For example, new lumber, landscape timbers, brick, cinder blocks, stone, concrete, and old tires can all be made into acceptable raised beds. Materials that are famous for being short-lived are plywood and scrap lumber, but you can't beat the price. To get a little longer life out of these materials, you can staple some plastic to the interior sides. Never put plastic sheets on the bottom of any bed, because they will cause drainage problems. As mentioned in the previous chapter, there is a lot of controversy brewing over landscape timbers and chemically treated wood. Before you get started using any wood in building a greenhouse bed, please see "Wood in the Humid Greenhouse" (page 42, Chapter 1), where treated lumber is discussed.

To prevent rust, use galvanized nails or, better yet, the brass-colored deck screws. In building wooden raised beds, you should sink vertical support timbers (treated or redwood four-by-fours are easiest to work with) or metal stakes on the side of the bed. Fasten your side lumber to these vertical supports. The supports will anchor the bed, keeping it from moving as you fill it with soil.

As mentioned earlier, if you want to maximize the light your plants receive, you can really help things along by painting the sides

It is easy to create a place to sit on the side of raised beds, for working convenience and for comfort.

of your raised beds white. A gloss or semi-gloss exterior paint will enhance the amount of photosynthetic light throughout the greenhouse or sunspace.

A 1-inch by 6-inch (2.5-cm by 15-cm) board laid on top of the perimeter of the bed makes a nice seat for people and a good place to set pots. If you don't do this, people will tend to sit on the edge of your beds anyway—unless you place some cactus there.

You can also make nice beds out of other materials besides wood, such as the new plastic wood made out of recycled milk jugs, reinforced concrete, or cinder blocks, although cinder blocks are a bit on the wide side and take up much growing space.

GROUND BEDS

Obviously, ground beds are easier to construct than raised beds. Basically, you just go in there and define the planting areas and walkways. Then just work the soil, add your amendments, and you are on your way. But do consider having some kind of barrier such as bricks or even a two-by-four staked into the ground to keep out wayward feet.

One advantage of a ground bed over a

It is helpful but not essential to have drainage for your floors.

raised bed is that there is more room between the floor and ceiling, which allows you to grow taller plants. This can be helpful when you let a greenhouse tomato, cucumber, or ornamental plant get extremely tall. It is not uncommon for a healthy greenhouse tomato variety to grow 10 feet (3 m) high, which is a major concern if you have a low-clearance roof. I love growing bananas in greenhouses, and even the dwarf varieties often need every inch of vertical space when they get going.

DRAINAGE IN SOIL BEDS

All water needs to go somewhere when you water a raised bed. Unless you are gardening on a space shuttle, all water eventually succumbs to gravity and goes downward. Drainage is a good thing and needs to occur for the soil and plants to become healthy. Good drainage is something that you can control by being sure that your fill material is well drained. This means if you must fill the bed with clay-based soil that you add sand to one-third of the total volume along with a good amount of well-decomposed compost.

If you are in the process of planning and designing a greenhouse or sunspace and want to have raised beds, I recommend that you *not* pour a solid slab of concrete over the whole floor. By leaving it dirt, you can take advantage of the natural drainage of the soil. Save the concrete for walkways and leisure areas, leaving dirt over which to build your raised beds (see "Aisles and Floors," page 77, for other options). This gives water a place to go downward into the soil.

Unfortunately, many greenhouses and sunspaces have already been built upon a concrete slab. No, you don't have to get out the jackhammer and start chopping away at the concrete. You do need to think a little more about the drainage of your raised bed. There should be small weep holes in the bottom of your beds where they touch the floor so water can escape. It is also important to fill the bottom 3 inches (8 cm) or so with 1 to 2 inches (2.5 to 5 cm) of gravel to help promote drainage (see "Filling Soil Beds" below).

Once you have established good bed drainage, you will need to think about floor drainage, which is often overlooked in sunspaces. If your greenhouse or sunspace does not already have floor drainage, that can cause problems, as it is hard to install after the fact. The best solution is to not overwater. As mentioned in Chapter 1, overwatering is a common mistake made by novice greenhouse gardeners. If floor drainage becomes a major problem, you may want to grow plants only in pots that have saucers to catch the water. If your floor starts to grow crops of slippery algae, you may want to consider applying an algicide, a product available through many greenhouse-supply catalogs.

FILLING SOIL BEDS

If you plan to do your gardening in a soil medium, here's how to fill your beds (for more about soil and plant nutrition, see Chapter 9, "Getting to the Roots"). First, determine the quality of the soil you plan to use (whether you're shipping it in or using what is on-site). This is best done with a professional soil test. You can find out how to get your soil tested by checking with your local county agricultural extension agent. There are also many home soil-test kits on the market that work well. In general, try to use rich topsoil. Avoid using soil found near heavily trafficked highways or streets, because it is often high in lead and other toxic substances.

Always strive for a well-drained soil in a greenhouse or sunspace. This is determined by finding out through your soil test if your soil is clayey or sandy. A less scientific way to make this determination is to use the "feel method" of testing. Wet a tablespoon of soil and rub it between your thumb and fingers. If it feels gritty, it's probably a sandy soil. If it feels only slightly gritty, it is probably a mix of sand and clay. And if it feels plasticlike and smooth, it probably leans more toward clay. (If it feels really, really slimy, you may have grabbed a slug.) A large number of hard dirt clods may indicate a clay soil.

Soils that are on the sandy side tend to drain best. Clay soils are notorious for slow drainage, causing problems that can lead to a salt buildup and waterlogging—and both can hurt the growing of plants. The ability to hold water isn't all bad, as any good-quality soil should have some ability to hold water. This is best achieved by relying on decomposed organic matter rather than on high clay content.

If you must deal with a soil high in clay for inclusion in a raised growing bed, you can reduce its impact by mixing in enough sand to provide for good drainage. You can add up to one-third sand to a heavy clay dirt for a good growing-bed soil. If you are building a greenhouse over soil extremely high in clay, you may want to consider drainage tiles under the greenhouse. Talk to a good contractor or engineer for more details. On second thought, forget the engineer. You can't afford that solution. Some of my best friends are engineers, but they tend to be expensive to hire and come up with expensive solutions.

If your soil test indicates that your soil is extremely high in salts, then this is bad news, as salts make it difficult to grow anything. You may want to find another soil source. Also, if the test indicates that the soil is low in certain nutrients, you may need to add specific materials to correct this.

Depth of Fill

For good plant growth, you should try to have a depth of workable soil of about $1^1/_2$ feet (0.5 m) or more. Less depth works, but it tends to produce some growing problems and plant stress. If your greenhouse bed sits on dirt rather than concrete, then by all means work the planting soil below the ground level to where you can get the required depth or better for healthy root growth.

Begin by filling the bottom with 3 inches (8 cm) or so of gravel, 1 to 2 inches (2.5 to 5 cm) in diameter, to help promote drainage. Then add 2 inches (5 cm) of coarse sand or pea gravel. Many gardeners place a fine-mesh nylon or plastic screening on top of the sand and gravel. This is not essential, but it does help maintain good drainage for many years. On top of the screen or gravel goes your soil mix (see Chapter 9, "Getting to the Roots," for details on how to make a good soil mix).

PLANTS IN CONTAINERS

There are lots of choices for containers, including plastic pots, clay pots, and a whole array of things that can be recycled to be pots for growing plants. When your greenhouse is set up with raised beds, you have your options wide open. You can grow in the beds themselves, or you can use the bed as a tabletop and set containers directly on the surface. When using the surface of a soil bed, be sure to set the pot in a saucer or the roots may grow out of the hole in the bottom of the pot and anchor into the raised bed. This has happened to me more than once. I find a walloping big plant growing in a little tiny pot sitting on a soil bed, and when I try to pick it up (to no avail), I quickly learn how it got so big. There are some major roots growing down into the soil, emanating from the drainage hole.

My personal preference is to use raised beds for growing the larger vegetables and cut-flower and herb plants and to use pots for smaller plants and for foliage, ornamental, and specialty plants such as cactus and orchids. The raised bed provides for more root development for the larger cut-flower plants and vegetables than will a container.

This does not mean that if you aren't set up with raised beds, you can't grow bigger plants. You just need to get a big pot or even a tub.

Special soil mixes and recipes are not as crucial when it comes to growing in a raised bed as long as the soil is rich, has a near-neutral pH (see page 318, Chapter 9, "Getting to the Roots," for more information on pH), contains a fair amount of organic matter, and is well drained. However, when you are growing plants in containers or starting seedlings, you need a more exacting soil mix. For instructions on buying or making your own potting mix, see Chapter 9, "Getting to the Roots."

Sizing Pots

The biggest mistake in selecting a pot is usually made not in the type of pot chosen but in using too large a pot. People think that they are doing the plant a favor by giving it a lot of room. But if the plant doesn't grow fast enough to use all of the space, trouble can result. An oversized pot can become waterlogged easily, and then the plant can suffer from lack of air (yes, roots need to breathe, too). The soil can also become sour, causing problems with the plant's health. When you are up-potting a root-bound plant, it is usually best not to jump to a size any more than 1 or 2 inches (2.5 or 5 cm) larger than the original pot.

Many houseplants do surprisingly well in a root-bound state for quite a while. It is the people who are bothered first by a pot-bound pot. Let it go for a while. Often, the problem is just one of needing repotting with some new soil. You do this by knocking off a fair amount of the old soil, pruning the roots as needed, adding some new, virgin potting soil to the void, and putting the plant back in the same pot. Be sure to fill in soil where there are gaps, and place the plant at exactly the same depth.

Vegetables in Pots

Vegetables can also be grown in pots quite well. Because this is not something ever shown on the cover of a garden magazine or a fancy gardening catalog, many people never consider this option. There are, however, some special things that you should do to make vegetables survive and thrive in pots. Be sure that the future size of the vegetable is in balance with the pot size. A vegetable plant that is too big for its pot will create a stress situation that can lead to bugs and disease. If you are growing a tomato variety that is known to get up to 5 feet (1.5 m) tall, you're asking for trouble if you plant it in a 6-inch (15-cm) pot. It would do much better in a 5-gallon (19-liter) pot.

Often you can choose to grow "bushy" or dwarf vegetable varieties instead of the larger vining types. For instance, bush beans do better in pots than pole beans; determinate (bushy) tomatoes do better than indeterminate (vining) types; try a bushy squash in a small tub, but don't try a vining pumpkin.

Why not break all the rules of convention and try mixing flowers, vegetables, and even herbs all in the same pot? Don't be afraid. It works fine, and it can create an interesting collection of food and flowers. Take care not to consume any inedible or poisonous flowers or plants.

When you are growing veggies in pots, watch for more-frequent wilting; as the root

It is better to move up in pot size incrementally than to take large jumps in size too quickly.

systems fill the pot, the plants have a need for more frequent irrigation. Also, you must make a better effort to supply the nutrient needs of the plants than you would with beds. All of the plant's needs are amplified when you are growing in pots. Excess nitrogen as well as nitrogen deficiencies are common in plants growing in pots. Get on a regular schedule of fertilizing (see Chapter 9, "Getting to the Roots," for more information).

Plastic Versus Clay

This reminds me of a boxing match in the 1960s—Clay won. There are two main types of plant containers on the market: plastic pots or clay pots. They both have advantages and disadvantages. Let's look at the advantages of both. Clay pots are heavier (won't easily tip over), drain better (because they are porous), and have that natural terra-cotta appearance. Plastic pots are lighter (easier to pick up or ship), hard to break (if dropped), easier to clean, need less watering (because they aren't porous), and come in many different colors and shapes.

Now let's look at the disadvantages of clay versus plastic. Clay pots are easily breakable, more expensive, and harder to clean. Clay pots

(Top) *Clay or plastic? Both have advantages and disadvantages but, in general, I prefer clay pots.*
(Bottom) *Every pot should have a hole in the bottom for drainage. This creates the need for saucers (which should never have holes in the bottom!).*

may create water stains on surfaces where they are placed, and plants in them need more watering than when in plastic. But with plastic pots, you risk overwatering problems; they are also easier to tip over because of their light weight and have a more artificial appearance.

Research has shown that plants growing in white or light-colored plastic pots have significantly slower growth when compared to those grown in dark-colored plastic pots. This is because the white or light-colored pots let light through to the roots, which confuses them, and thus you end up with an unhappy plant. Roots like it where the sun don't shine!

I use both clay and plastic, but to tell you the truth, I use plastic pots only because they are so abundant. If I had my way, I would use mostly clay pots. One reason clay is a good choice is because overwatering is more common than underwatering in greenhouses. I also like the way clay looks. Any interior decorator will tell you that terra-cotta and green go together naturally. There are times when I grab for a plastic pot. When I have a plant that needs constant moisture, I go for plastic pots. However, I always try to find terra-cotta-colored plastic pots. For some reason, most of the plastic pots in the world are green!

When it comes down to choosing between plastic or clay pots, I usually take the lazy way and use what I have available and close to me at the time.

One quick note on storing clay pots: I'll never forget one year when a friend gave me a great assortment of clay pots. I stacked the clay pots outside and went to great trouble to organize them by size and quality. Then winter came, and they were buried by snow. When spring came, I found that I no longer had a nice collection of clay pots. Instead, I had clay pot pieces. Clay pots don't hold up well if they are kept outside where they can absorb moisture. When stored outside, the moisture will cause the pot to crack when the temperature drops well below freezing. I have since had better luck storing clay pots out of the weather—even a unheated garage works fine.

Drainage in Containers: The Hole in the Bottom

A donut isn't a donut without its hole. The same premise is true for a plant pot. It must have the all-important drainage hole or it isn't worth using. The water, fertilizer, and salts that can accumulate in the soil need to drain out the bottom. It often helps to place a piece of broken clay pot or a large rock over the hole to prevent the dirt from spilling out. Another great way to keep soil from spilling out of the drainage hole is to use dryer lint. Of course, to prevent the water from coming out of the hole and spilling all over everything, some wise horticulturist invented the plant saucer.

RECYCLED MATERIALS OR POTS

Pots don't have to be of the store-bought variety. You can make pots out of all kinds of recycled materials. I have seen pots made out of everything from old tires to milk jugs, paper cups, plastic packaging, and more. All these recycled pots work just as well as the kind that you buy. Whatever you use, just be sure—you guessed it—be sure each pot has a hole in the bottom.

HANGING POTS

Hanging pots for growing either food or flowers are a good way to utilize the air space of your greenhouse. Hanging pots also add a nice design element to a greenhouse. Hanging pots don't have to be filled with just flowers or foliage plants. You can also hang vegetables, herbs, or other interesting combinations. My favorite is a pot of Alaska nasturtiums. They have a great variegated leaf. As I pass the pot each day, I eat one flower (yes, they are edible and tasty).

If you have a solar-heated greenhouse that tends toward the cold side, you can take advantage of the warmer climes of the upper reaches of the sunspace by putting a few hanging baskets up high, where it is considerably warmer. If a basket is in a position that is hard to water, try rigging it up on a pulley so that you can lower it for watering and grooming and then pull it back up to the warmer reaches of the greenhouse. Be careful, though. In summer it may be too hot up high, and you may want to keep the hanging pot lower until winter.

BE ADAPTABLE!

No design is permanent. After you have everything set up in your greenhouse, from aisles and flooring to potting benches to planting beds, be mindful of how it all works for you. Things change, and you may decide you need to create an area for orchids

(Top) This old cowboy boot makes a great pot and came complete with drainage holes on the bottom.
(Bottom) A crop of oak leaf lettuce growing happily in a hanging basket.

that have become a passion. Or perhaps you desire more space in which to simply sit and relax. Above all, your greenhouse needs to be both comfortable and functional. Remember, if it isn't exactly right, don't hesitate to make changes. After all, it's *your* greenhouse!

CHAPTER 3

GREENHOUSE SEASONS AND MICROCLIMATES:

MAKING THE MOST OF YOUR SUNSPACE

WHEN WINTER ARRIVES YOU WILL FIND YOUR greenhouse becomes a tropical island surrounded by cold. It is a world of its own, and over the course of the year, it undergoes changes in its ecology. The more you experience the interactions among the plants, the soil, the insects, and the sky throughout the seasons, the more complex and fascinating the relationships appear. Look closely, while focusing on some extra patience to see what's really happening. There are many microenvironments within the greenhouse. These are easy to identify and can help you in setting out plants in the optimal spot for healthy growth. The best way to learn about the differences is to be incredibly observant from season to season. Perhaps the learning curve will be shorter if I tell you what I have found.

GREENHOUSE SEASONS

The greenhouse environment changes through the seasons. These changes in the growing environment are mainly the result of changes in temperature and light intensities throughout the year. The seasonal changes are especially profound in solar-heated greenhouses or greenhouses that are run cool in winter. These changes

still hold true, though to a lesser extent, with conventionally heated greenhouses that maintain the same temperatures in winter and summer.

There are three distinct seasons in a greenhouse with respect to temperature and light. Two easily identifiable seasons are the summer season and the winter season. The third season is actually two seasons with very similar characteristics: fall and spring. Why call them one season? Because they are periods of time transition and they have very similar day lengths, light qualities, and heating characteristics.

THE SUMMER GREENHOUSE SEASON

The summer season is (of course) hotter than any other time of year. For solar greenhouses, the summer also has poor light penetration; contrary to what many people think, summer is not a bright, well-lit time of year. Although the days are longer and brighter, the light penetration is reduced because most solar greenhouses (or solar-heated sunspaces) have steep south angles to their glazing. Sun penetrates best when it comes through the glazing in a perpendicular or right angle to the glazing. The more perpendicular the light is, the better the penetration and the less reflection there is off

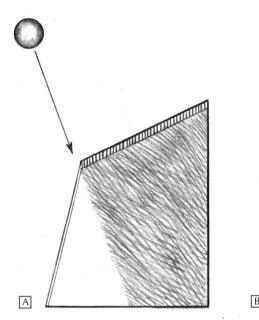
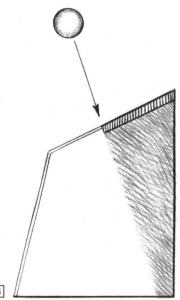

(A) *If you have a greenhouse without overhead glazing, it may not receive enough light during the summer months when the sun is higher in the sky. You can remedy this by adding some skylights.*

(B) *In some cases, providing just a portion of overhead glazing can help increase light penetration into the summer greenhouse.*

the glazing. Because solar greenhouses are designed to maximize winter-sun penetration at a perpendicular angle, this compromises the quality of light in the summer. This may work to advantage, though, because it can also lessen the amount of incoming heat in summer.

If your solar sunspace has little or no glazing on the roof, you will likely find yourself short on light in the summer, when the angle of the sun is higher in the sky. Vegetables, herbs, and flowering plants grow best in bright light. Because much of the greenhouse is engulfed in shadow as the sun moves to a steeper summer angle, you may find yourself having to move your plants to the first 2 feet (0.6 m) adjacent to the south glazing. If these plants are growing in ground beds, you will likely see the plants bending and stretching toward the glass because they are more shaded.

To avoid these low-light problems in this type of greenhouse, you might want to con-

sider installing three or four skylights in the roof of your sunspace. Of course, you can always switch to growing only shade-loving houseplants in the summer. You could also offset the effects of shade by painting surfaces of the interior white, as mentioned in the previous chapters, but there is no substitute for natural sunlight, unless you want to empty your billfold investing in fancy grow lights.

Watch your greenhouse day by day, and you will see the shadows change drastically in the greenhouse space. It's almost like a walk-in sundial or calendar. I know people who make marks on the floor signifying where the shadows hit on winter and summer solstices. With a little whimsy, your greenhouse could become a poor-boy's Stonehenge or Aztec calendar. The main thing is to watch and anticipate these changes in light.

Those of you with freestanding or nonsolar-heated greenhouses with glass on four

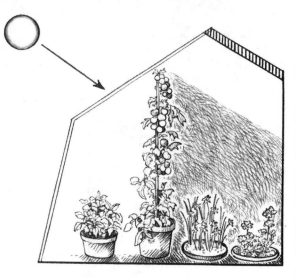

Mind the shading effects of taller plants. Locate taller plants toward the north wall, where shading will be minimized.

sides don't have to worry about the aforementioned lack of summer light. Because of the angles and quantity of glazing on your greenhouse, instead of worrying about a lack of light, you will likely have to cope with having too much light, which manifests itself as excess heat in the space. See Chapter 1, "The Greenhouse or Sunspace Environment," for more information on greenhouse cooling and ventilation.

Longer Summer Days

The most obvious thing that occurs in summer is that the sun stays up longer. This, combined with warmer temperatures, increases the rate of plant growth (as well as increasing the rate of bug infestations!). Summer is when your greenhouse will grow plants at full speed, so changes in plants (and bug populations) will happen at a rapid clip. As some old radio jingle used to say, "If you miss a day, you can miss a lot!" You can even hear the plants growing on a quiet summer evening, like corn farmers in the Midwest do. And someone said that there is nothing to do around here at night!

THE SPRING AND FALL SEASONS

The spring and fall seasons in a greenhouse are a compromise between the best attributes found in both summer and winter. It is a wonderful time to grow in a greenhouse because the environment is easier to adjust to what plants prefer—not too cold or too warm. Both spring and fall seasons have good light penetration that coincides with good temperatures. Ideally, this is a time of optimum plant health, and this is when I often see the plants in my greenhouse thriving at their peak of happiness.

THE WINTER SEASON

In winter, the angle of the sun is low in the southern sky (unless you live south of the equator). For solar greenhouses, this creates a situation for good light penetration. Unfortunately, it is also the time when the days are short and the temperatures are cold, both of which slow down the growth of plants. In many places, it is also the cloudiest time of year.

In winter, there are areas where the cold seems to concentrate in the greenhouse. These are known as temperature "microclimates" and are usually located up against windows. Near the cool windows, it can be much colder than your thermometer tells you. Be careful when placing plants adjacent to windows during cold spells.

Some plants may be more susceptible to the cold than others. I know many a greenhouse gardener (myself included) who has lost a favorite plant because it was sitting in a cold spot. In the winter, growth is slowed, especially on plants that are grown for their fruits and flowers. Many plants almost seem as if they are hibernating, though others prefer the cool temperatures. A friend of mine calls them the "antifreeze plants" in honor of their ability to weather the cold; check Chapter 8, "A Closer

Look at the Plants," to see if your favorite plant passes the antifreeze test. In general, plants grow slower in the winter, mainly because of the short days and cool temperatures.

Let's look at some other common winter microclimates: In solar greenhouses during the winter season, you'll notice that your north wall goes from being a very shady spot (as it was in summer) to being a very sunny and relatively warm spot.

Another change you'll notice is that when its very cold outside, you may sense that there is an increase in the relative humidity. This may be real, or it may be just psychological. Cold feels colder when it is humid. Because you are generally sealed off from the outside, the humidity can indeed increase over normal levels and your greenhouse can feel almost like a rain forest. This is the time when you need to ask yourself if you truly need to water the plants. As you get close to Christmas, "'tis the season of overwatering." In greenhouses that are seriously overwatered, the humidity almost rains on you, especially if the sun comes out. Then, evening causes the temperature to drop, and the condensation starts to drip incessantly from somewhere in the ceiling—so be careful of these highly humid situations in winter.

The best solution to high winter humidity, besides not overwatering in the first place, is to pick a warmer day when temperatures are above freezing and make an attempt to "dump" the water-laden air to the outside. Do this by simply opening an exterior door for a few minutes. For larger greenhouses, try kicking on a large exhaust fan for a few minutes during the warmest part of the day. Don't go opening the door on a cold day! It may be a real shocker to the plants and it may also take days for a solar-heated greenhouse to recover some decent warmth.

PLANTS IN THE GREENHOUSE ENVIRONMENT

The plants themselves also create change in the greenhouse environment. For instance, tall plants cause shading for adjacent shorter plants; overcrowding of plants causes competition for limited light, water, and nutrients. Research shows that plants growing adjacent to one another can have both positive and negative effects on each other. This can be as simple as competition for light, water, and nutrients, or one plant can actually give off substances that help or hurt other plants. Sometimes researchers don't know what is causing the effect, but they know there sometimes may be an effect.

The presence of plants also has a major impact on the humidity. The more plants you have, the more they will be transpiring moisture into the environment. Even more tangible are the changes in smells from the flowers, leaves, and herbs. There are other things you feel in a greenhouse, too—things that are hard to describe—but you know something special is going on.

In laying out crops within the greenhouse, it is important to use the differences in the environment to your advantage. This results in having healthier plants that grow faster, and you will harvest more from your fruit and vegetables.

Often when I am gardening in a greenhouse, I can almost hear plants speaking to me: "Help, I'm in the wrong place, and it has put me under incredible stress!" How can I hear a plant say such a thing? Is it that I have a good imagination? Now don't get worried, I really don't think plants can talk—at least not English. All I do is notice the plants that appear to be out of sorts. For instance, why would bugs or disease attack only one particular plant when

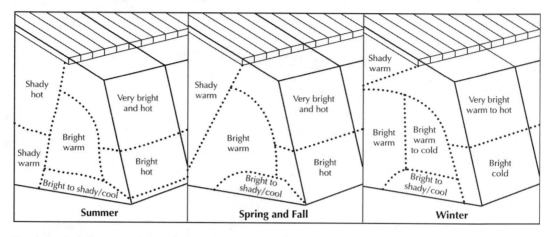

Daytime microclimates vary through the seasons in solar greenhouses.

other adjacent plants are doing just fine? This is what is happening: Think of yourself when you are under stress. That's when you are most susceptible to catching colds, your energy is low, your brain isn't working right, the words don't come out of the mouth correctly, and everything is harder than it should be. The same is true with plants.

For example, when you grow a plant that prefers warm night temperatures above 55°F (13°C) but your greenhouse consistently remains lower, you will likely see symptoms of its stress. It may be getting yellow leaves or leaves may be dropping. You may see increased disease and/or insect damage. In this case, by moving the plant to a warmer area, its health is easily restored, and the plant will forgive your innocent mistake.

The native environment for a plant (where it is originally from on the planet), usually determines the best environment for that plant. Where possible, I will try to help you by listing its preference when you look up specific crops in Chapter 8, "A Closer Look at the Plants." For example, most of our favorite houseplants are native to tropical forest floors—down where it is naturally shady, humid, and warm. These plants have learned to survive on low light and warm temperatures, conditions similar to the environment of our homes. Take a houseplant into the greenhouse, and it might suffer slightly from the higher light levels. If your greenhouse has widely fluctuating temperatures, even more stress may be induced.

A greenhouse can't provide a perfect environment for all your plants all the time. But hey, it is better than not having a greenhouse, and you can always make special adjustments by moving plants to different microclimates. With a little effort, you'll be surprised how much diversity you can have in the way of plants.

How would we classify the greenhouse in terms of its temperatures? A greenhouse is a subtropical or tropical type of environment. That's great, because the tropics are where many of our food crops are from. It is also the native environment of many of our favorite greenhouse flowering plants. This logic tells us that the plants (with some exceptions) that are the most difficult to grow are often those native to colder, more temperate climates, such as the ones that you see growing outside your window (I'm assuming that you live in a temperate climate). That is because these plants often need a winter to trigger proper growth.

Plants native to a temperate climate often require a winter season. It's almost impossible to grow apple trees in a greenhouse because they need the chilling of a winter in order to trigger flowers and produce fruit. Of course, you could grow a dwarf apple tree in a pot and carry it outside to give it a shot of winter or just leave the windows open in winter, but why bother? You can grow apples outside. Save your precious greenhouse space for something else— like a ripe November tomato or a winter-blooming orchid.

When people walk into my 80°F (27°C) greenhouse in the middle of a Wyoming winter storm, they can't believe that it feels so tropical. I tell people it's like having a few hundred square feet of Hawaii. In fact, why take a winter vacation to the tropical beaches when you have a greenhouse? Don't answer that. Just remember that a greenhouse can keep you saner than your cabin-fever-stricken brethren. But let's get back to crop layout.

LOOKING FOR MICROCLIMATES IN A GREENHOUSE

When you are trying to grow a plant out of its native place, you can always attempt to change the immediate environment to suit the needs of the plant. You can do this either by taking advantage of an existing microclimate or by creating one. Perhaps the word "microclimate" is new to you. Let me give you an example. If you are growing a plant that likes it warm, you can set it near the heater. If a plant likes it on the cool side, you can set it near a cold window. You create a microclimate when you withhold water from your cactus. Learn the microclimates in your greenhouse so you can

RULES FOR THE GREENHOUSE MICROCLIMATE

Here are some rules that apply to greenhouse microclimates. At first glance you will think that they sound simplistic, but stop and give this some serious thought as you look at the plants in your greenhouse. Think how you could use these rules to your advantage.

1. Hot air rises; cool air sinks.
2. Shade has less light intensity than sunny areas.
3. On sunny summer days, it is very hot near the glazing.
4. The closer the plant is to the glazing, the more light intensity it receives.
5. On cool winter nights, it is much cooler next to the glazing than in most other places in the greenhouse.
6. Plants near thermal mass (such as water drums in solar greenhouses) feel temperatures that are more even, with fewer night fluctuations.
7. In solar greenhouses, the area near a north wall is brighter and warmer in the winter and shadier and cooler in the summer.

use them to your advantage. Again, this requires you to be observant.

Different types of vegetables have different environmental requirements, so now it's a matter of plugging the plants' needs into the appropriate microenvironments. But remember, these microenvironments vary seasonally. (For more specific information on growing each plant, see Chapter 8, "A Closer Look at the Plants.") Your greenhouse may vary, depending on interior and exterior design and local climates.

CROP LIGHT AND TEMPERATURE REQUIREMENTS FOR EDIBLE PLANTS

CROP	LIGHT	TEMPERATURE	COMMENTS
Bananas	Bright	Warm to hot	Depending upon the variety, can grow 7 to 25 feet (2 to 7.6 m). Will cause a lot of shading. Grow fast when hot, very slowly when cold.
Beans	Bright to very bright	Warm to hot	Will tolerate some shade. Pole beans, when trellised, cause shading. Seeds need 65°F (18° C) soil temperature to germinate well. Fava or broad beans prefer the cool temperatures and also need trellising. Don't grow favas in summer—they hate the heat.
Beets	Bright to very bright	Cool to warm	May go to seed if temperature nears 32°F (0°C) and then rises again.
Broccoli	Shady to bright	Cold to warm	Will flower fast and produce small heads if temperature is consistently warm to hot.
Brussels sprouts	Shady to bright	Cold	Poor quality if temperature is consistently warm to hot. Get tall toward maturity and may cause shading.
Cabbage	Bright to very bright	Cold to warm	May go to seed if temperature is below freezing for a long period. Will not tolerate crowding.
Carrots	Shady to bright	Cool to warm	
Cauliflower	Shady to bright	Cold to warm	Will flower fast and produce small heads if temperatures are consistently warm to hot.
Celery	Shady to bright	Cool to warm	Likes many months of consistent cool temperatures. Will often go to seed before it matures in warm summer temperatures.
Cherimoya	Bright	Cool to warm	Grows 15 to 20 feet (4.6 to 6 m) tall and will cause shading. Will not tolerate temperatures below freezing.
Chicory	Shady to bright	Cold to warm	Not good in hot areas.
Chinese cabbage	Shady to bright	Cold to warm	Flowers rapidly in warm to hot conditions.
Citrus	Bright	Cool to warm	May get tall (depending on variety) and cause shading. Will not tolerate temperatures below freezing.
Coffee	Shady to bright	Cool to warm	Grows up to 10 feet (3 m). May cause shading after a few years of growth. Will not tolerate frost.
Collards	Shady to bright	Cold to hot	Can grow tall and cause shading. Well adapted to solar greenhouses, except in summer.

(Continued on next page)

CROP	LIGHT	TEMPERATURE	COMMENTS
Cucumber	Bright to very bright	Warm to hot	Needs nights above 50°F (10°C).
Eggplant	Bright to very bright	Warm to hot	Needs nights above 50°F (10°C).
Endive	Bright	Cold to cool	Poor quality with warm conditions.
Fig	Bright	Cold to warm	Grows 15 to 30 feet (4.6 to 9.2 m) tall. Will cause shading. Will tolerate light frost and some shade. May lose leaves in winter, allowing more winter sun underneath.
Garlic	Shady to very bright	Cool to warm	Will tolerate diverse greenhouse conditions.
Herbs	Shady to bright	Cold to warm	Most will tolerate diverse conditions. Basil prefers warm temperatures. Herbs native to temperate climates may require winter dormancy or chilling.
Kale	Shady to bright	Cold to warm	Poor quality with warm to hot temperatures.
Kohlrabi	Bright	Cool to warm	Enlarged stem (edible portion) cracks with hot temperatures.
Leeks	Bright	Cool to warm	Will go to seed if temperature goes below freezing and then returns to warm.
Lettuce	Shady to bright	Cool to warm	Will go to seed with consistent warm to hot temperatures.
Mustard greens	Shady to bright	Cool to warm	Will go to seed with consistent warm to hot temperatures.
Okra	Bright to very bright	Warm to hot	Will not grow in cool, shady spots. May get tall and cause shading. Needs warm temperature.
Onions	Bright	Cool to warm	Will not bulb in winter but good for greens year-round.
Parsley	Bright to shade	Cool to warm	Will often go to seed the following winter.
Parsnips	Bright	Cool	Plants that overwinter may go to seed.
Peas	Shady to bright	Cool to warm	Warm to hot temperatures will reduce yield.
Peppers	Bright to very bright	Warm to hot	Prefer warm temperatures when young. Will overwinter if temperatures remain above 40°F (5°C) but grow best above 50°F (10°C).
Radish	Shady to bright	Cool to warm	Consistent warm temperatures cause top growth and flowering. Poor flavor in warm to hot temperatures.
Rutabaga	Shady to bright	Cool	Poor quality with warm to hot temperatures.
Spinach	Shady to bright	Cool to warm	Consistent warm to hot temperatures cause rapid flowering and short production period.

(Continued on next page)

CROP LIGHT AND TEMPERATURE REQUIREMENTS FOR EDIBLE PLANTS (CONTINUED)

CROP	LIGHT	TEMPERATURE	COMMENTS
Squash	Bright to very bright	Warm to hot	Requires nights about 50°F (10°C). Winter squash varieties need trellising and cause shading. Summer squash generally stays bushy.
Sweet potato	Shady to bright	Warm to hot	Needs hot temperatures for a long period. May vine extensively, causing shading.
Swiss chard	Shady to bright	Cool to warm	May flower in spring if winter temperatures go below freezing.
Tomatoes	Bright to very bright	Hot	Will tolerate short periods of hot temperatures. Vining tomatoes cause shading. Little or no production below 50°F (10°C).
Turnips	Shady to bright	Cool	Warm to hot temperatures cause cracking and produce poor eating quality.
Watermelon	Bright to very bright	Warm to hot	Requires nights above 50°F (10°C). Needs trellising, which causes adjacent shading.

CROP LIGHT AND TEMPERATURE REQUIREMENTS FOR SELECTED CUT FLOWERS

CROP	LIGHT	TEMPERATURE	COMMENTS
Alstroemeria	Bright	Cool to warm	Needs trellising. Flowers at temperatures above 50°F (10°C).
Carnation	Bright	Cool to warm	Needs trellising.
Chrysanthemum	Bright	Cool to warm	May get tall and cause shading. Needs specific night length to flower. Flowers need temperatures above 50°F (10°C).
Rose	Bright	Warm to hot	Will not grow well if temperatures go below 40°F (5°C). Can get tall and cause shading. Will not tolerate shade well.
Snapdragon	Bright	Cool to warm	Tall varieties need trellising and may cause shading.
Stock	Bright	Cool to warm	A good winter–spring plant. Start between July 10 or after February 15 or plants may not flower. Some varieties are tall and will cause shade.
Sweet pea	Bright	Cool to warm	Usually needs trellising and may cause shading. Poor growth in hot temperatures.

If you don't see your favorite plant listed in the preceding charts, it is likely to be a plant that can be grown in a pot and thus can be easily moved to accommodate its needs. See Chapter 8, "A Closer Look at the Plants," for information on the above plants as well as on many plants not listed in these charts.

USING YOUR GREENHOUSE SPACE EFFECTIVELY

Spacing between plants is an important factor that can dictate the overall health of a crop. A lot of competition for light, water, and nutrients can occur when plants are too close. In a greenhouse, most competition between plants is for the available light.

PLANT SPACING

When plants are placed too close together, the results are not good. If it's food you're growing, you see decreased yields; if you're growing flowering plants, your chances for quality flowers are slim. The key to proper spacing for seedlings is not sowing the seed too closely. If seedlings do come up too thickly, then you have to be ruthless and get to the job of thinning. This is where new gardeners often fail. They can't bring themselves to pull up (and kill) baby plants. If this describes you, wait until you are in a bad mood—after paying the bills or having a domestic argument—and do your thinning then. It does wonders for your thinning abilities, and when you are done you'll find yourself to be in a much-improved mood. This is called "horticultural therapy" (a side benefit of growing in a greenhouse or sunspace). If you are doing some transplanting, then you need to be sure you are giving each plant enough room as you set out the new plants.

Normal spacing can change, depending on the light. For instance, if you are growing a plant that prefers bright light but you are trying to grow it in a spot with some shade, try to increase the space around the plant so that it can take advantage of as much indirect light as possible. How far apart should you space plants? Check in Chapter 8, "A Closer Look at the Plants," and if you are familiar with the plant, think about how big it usually gets. It really is just a matter of common sense. If a lot of the leaves of two plants overlap extensively, then there is probably some competition for both space and light.

Don't get greedy. There are only so many plants you can grow in a greenhouse. After that, if you are still interested in growing more plants, consider adding more greenhouse space to your structure or build another greenhouse. If all else fails, be patient and wait until spring—then you can go wild with more plants outside.

TRELLISING

And what about using your air space? It worked for Michael Jordan! You can use more of your limited space in a greenhouse by growing plants up a vertical trellis. Of course, you can't grow just any plant up a trellis, but a good number of plants may be grown in this manner for more efficient use of space.

Trellises can be made out of almost any material and are limited only by your imagina-

When put on a raised bed, a trellis is easier to reach and to train the plants.

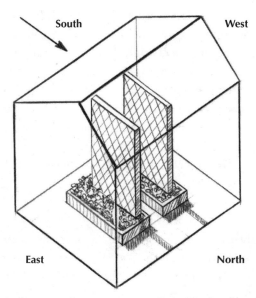

South   West

East   North

Trellises provide a great way to utilize space for plants that can grow vertically. For the most efficient use of space and light, run your trellises in a north–south direction.

tion. You can buy new materials for trellising: plastic netting (sold at garden centers), fencing materials such as chicken wire, other types of woven fencing, or redwood lattice.

Find creative options for using recycled materials for trellising. I once made a great trellis out of what remained of a sheet of plastic after driver's licenses had been punched out of it; I found it in an alley behind the motor-vehicle building. It was a perfect netted material for trellising. Old fencing or string is also easy to recycle into trellis material. A favorite material for both trellising and

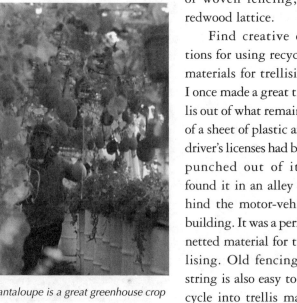

Cantaloupe is a great greenhouse crop and is grown best on a trellis. Notice the fruits suspended in recycled nylon stockings.

tying up plants is video and audio tape. It seems that there is always a tape around that has bitten the dust. Recycled magnetic tape is strong, and because it is a dark color, it is not unsightly.

To make a sturdy trellis, stick some support posts deep into the ground. Nail, staple, or wire the materials together. I always feel that the best trellises are those that can be set up and taken down readily as your needs dictate. One thing you shouldn't recycle is old twine, because it may harbor diseases or even some bugs that could reinfest the next plants.

I have found that it is best to run trellises on a north–south axis. This minimizes shading, because the sun will hit both sides of the trellis. An east–west axis is best used only in areas where adequate light is abundant and shading is not a problem. An east–west axis trellis can also be used without any problems if it is placed up against a solid wall or along the north wall, where shading is not an issue.

Trellises can be fun to put up and can become elaborate or creative if you wish. Trellises can be laid out in a serpentine form (who says they have to be straight?) or made into an arch or tunnel. You could almost call these trellises arbors. With these arbors, you can create great effects and new microclimates to work with. I often grow shade-loving plants under or behind these elaborate trellises.

The best trellis I ever made was a walk-under tunnel. Up the trellis, I grew several cantaloupe plants. On either side, as you walked through the tunnel, you saw a virtual wall of ripening cantaloupes, which are almost impossible to grow outside in my part of Wyoming because of the short, cool growing season. I had hand-pollinated each fruit's flower. As the cantaloupe fruits matured, each was slung into a recycled nylon stocking to support the weight of the fruits on the trellis. It was both beautiful and impressive. If you are growing a heavy-fruited plant, the technique of using nylon stockings and slinging the fruit will prevent the fruit from pulling the whole vine off the trellis. Tie a part of the stocking to the trellis and then slip the developing fruit into the stocking. The stocking will expand with the fruit (although watermelons cause the worst runs!). You, too, can recycle those old nylons into useful fruit supporters on a greenhouse trellis.

Some plants, such as cucumbers and vining (indeterminate) tomatoes, can be trained to grow up a single string. I prefer using rather thick string so that it doesn't cut into the stem of the plant. I have even used recycled videotape with great results. For this type of vertical training to work, you must prune off almost all the side suckers as the plant grows. You'll need to be knowledgeable about proper pruning of suckers, or you can do more harm than good (for pruning details, see tomatoes and cucumbers in Chapter 8, "A Closer Look at the Plants").

Begin by training the plants up a vertical string first: Tie the top of the string to a rafter or some other attachment in the ceiling. Then loosely tie the string at the bottom to a stake. Another alternative is to loosely tie the string to the base of the plant. Always be sure to leave ample slack in the string, as it will be taken up as the plant grows up this support. Then as the plant grows, you wind it carefully around the string, taking care to not strangle the stem. For further information on this type of trellising, refer to specific discussions of cucumbers and tomatoes in Chapter 8, "A Closer Look at the Plants."

Some plants, such as cucumbers take to trellising well because they have tendrils that grow out and physically grab onto the trellis to help them hold on. But many other plants

you may wish to grow up a trellis, such as tomatoes, do not have tendrils, so they will need your help to climb up the trellis. You'll have to weave the plant through or wind it around a trellis or string as it grows. When you are attaching a plant to a trellis, pole, string, or any other plant support, try to use a soft piece of cloth, string, or strap and tie it loosely to avoid cutting and injuring the plant.

Plants like the tomato can climb up a string if you take proper precautions to prevent strangling the plant.

Why are we going to all of this trouble? Because growing vegetables vertically enables you to get more yields out of less space. Most greenhouse gardeners always want to get the most out of their precious space. Trellising can be done with some unlikely candidates. New Zealand spinach and summer squash are never trellised in the outside garden, but in the greenhouse (with a little practice), trellising can stretch space like you never imagined. New Zealand spinach may be gently tied up to a trellis made of chicken wire or fencing. I've been able to get phenomenal yields from it on a 4-foot (1.2-meter) trellis when grown in this fashion.

I even surprised myself when I grew some summer squash up a string, in much the same manner as described for tomatoes. I must admit, however, that you need to be extremely careful not to break the stem when you attempt this. I killed a few plants getting my technique down. When I finally got the squash to grow up a string, I was able to grow some shade-

Greenhouse snapdragons in a horizontal trellis. Use the same type of horizontal trellising for any floppy plant, such as larkspur and taller carnations.

tolerating crops underneath, including spinach and lettuce. These techniques can often increase the productivity of a small space.

Horizontal Trellises

Most trellises are set up vertically, but many cut flowers benefit from a horizontal type of trellis. Some examples of plants that benefit from this type of trellising include carnations, snapdragons, larkspur, and freesias.

I usually make this kind of trellis using welded-wire "fencing." This is the same type often used by cement masons for concrete reinforcement. I also use regular woven fencing for this purpose. Any other type of fencing that has at least 3-inch-square (8-cm-square) openings will also work.

To set up a horizontal trellis, place four 4-foot-tall (1.2-meter-tall) stakes (or more, if needed) in the proposed flower bed, one in each corner. Then at a level of about 10 inches (25 cm), attach the fencing material horizontally to each post. You can attach the horizontal trellis to wooden stakes with wire or large staples. If the plants in the bed tend to get tall, such as greenhouse snapdragons, you will need to add another tier of horizontal fencing at 20 to 24 inches (51 to 61 cm) high. You can add more tiers as needed. This allows for a bed of cut-flower plants to grow straight and vertical, without unsightly bends in the stems. If you are growing just a few plants in a pot for cut flowers,

you don't need such elaborate trellising.

With plants grown in pots, you may use some small stakes placed around the edge of the pot with strings tied around the perimeter. I have also used small flower cages, which look like miniature tomato cages, placed in the pot to keep the plant growing straight. These are available from garden centers and greenhouse and gardening catalogs.

STAKING

You will often notice that plants growing inside a greenhouse or sunspace have noticeably softer and more succulent growth. This makes plants a bit more floppy, and you'll often find plants falling over or developing a lean. You can help these plants look and grow better by staking them. The stoutness of the stake is determined by the size of the plant that needs staking.

Stakes can be made out of all kinds of recycled materials, including old sticks, branches, and even pipe. Or you can buy stakes at your local garden center. My favorite store-bought stakes are made out of a green-colored plastic-coated metal rod made to resemble bamboo. These are less noticeable than other types and camouflage into the plant canopy.

Tomato cages or other cages can be used for ornamental plants; they help to keep floppy plants growing upright.

You can also use genuine bamboo stakes, which also look natural and work fine for staking smaller plants. If you have enough room, you can grow your own bamboo in the greenhouse. It provides excellent stakes, but be careful—it can become invasive, taking over any free space it can find in a very short time. Of course, pruning the fast-growing bamboo yields some wonderful stakes.

Be sure to bury the stake as deeply as possible to give your plant a good anchor. When you have your stake in place next to the plant, use soft string, old videotape, or a cloth strip to tie the plant to the stake. A tight string may strangle the plant over time as the diameter of the plant increases. When you drive any stake into the ground, avoid damaging any large fleshy roots that might be growing near the base of the plant.

PLANTING PATTERNS

Certain vegetable crops and some cut-flower plants grow more efficiently when laid out in a triangular pattern in the bed. With a triangular layout, there is usually less wasted space than with square layouts. Another efficient layout is to broadcast the seed much as you would grass seed when planting a lawn (although don't scatter as thickly as for a lawn). I find this works very well for leafy and root vegetable crops. This method leaves you with a solid bed of the plant with no wasted space. The broadcast method works best only when you avoid a thick sowing. Diligent thinning is also essential. If you skip the thinning job, you can forget about having decent vegetables to harvest.

CROP LAYOUT AND HARVESTING

Some crops are harvested only once, when they are mature. Examples include cabbage and car-

---

PLANTS SUITABLE FOR TRELLISING

Edible Crops	Flowering Plants
Cantaloupe	Bougainvillea
Cucumber	Golden-trumpet vine
Grape	some Jasmines
New Zealand spinach	Mandevillea
Peas	Mina lobata
Pole beans	Morning glory
Summer squash	some Nasturtiums
Tomato	Passionflower
Watermelon	Plumbago
Winter squash	Sweet pea
	Thunbergia

PLANTING OPTIONS FOR WIDE-BED LAYOUTS

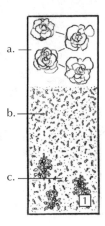 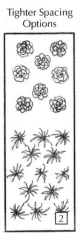 

Tighter Spacing Options

Rows

a.

b.

c.

[1] *This bed shows 3 planting options: a) zigzag spacing of larger plants, b) seedlings sprouting after a "broadcast" planting, and c) larger plants interplanted among the broadcast seeds of smaller- or quicker-growing plants.* [2] *This bed shows options for tighter and more efficient spacing. Plant in a triangular pattern to maximize the use of space.* [3] *Plant in rows if you wish to. You can also mix and match any pattern that suits you.*

APPROPRIATE LAYOUTS FOR WIDE-BED
VEGETABLE PLANTING IN THE GREENHOUSE

Crop	Distance Between Plants	Mature Height	Layout
Beans, bush	6 feet (1.8 m)	10 inches (25 cm)	△
Beans, fava	6 inches (15 cm)	4 feet (1.2 m)	⌗
Beans, pole	4 inches (10 cm)	5 to 12 feet (1.5 to 3.6 m)	⌗
Beets	4 inches (10 cm)	10 inches (25 cm)	⫶⫶
Broccoli	1.5 feet (0.45 m)	2 feet (0.6 m)	△
Brussels sprouts	1.5 feet (0.45 m)	3 to 4 feet (0.9 to 1.2 m)	△
Cabbage	1 foot (0.3 m)	2 feet (0.6 m)	△
Cantaloupe	3 feet (0.9 m)	10 feet (3 m)	⌗
Carrots	2 inches (5 cm)	10 inches (25 cm)	△
Cauliflower	1 foot (0.3 m)	15 inches (38 cm)	△
Celery	10 inches (25 cm)	1 foot (0.3 m)	△
Collards	1 foot (0.3 m)	3 to 4 feet (0.9 to 1.2 m)	△
Cucumber	2 feet (0.6 m)	10 to 15 feet+ (3 to 4.6 m+)	⌗ △ ↰
Eggplant	1.5 feet (0.45 m)	2.5 feet (0.8 m)	△
Garlic	4 inches (10 cm)	8 inches (20 cm)	△ ⫶⫶
Kale	1 foot (0.3 m)	1 foot (0.3 m)	△
Kohlrabi	8 inches (20 cm)	1 foot (0.3 m)	△
Lettuce	6 inches (15 cm)	10 inches (25 cm)	△ ⫶⫶
Onion, bulbs	6 inches (15 cm)	14 inches (36 cm)	△
Onion, greens	3 inches (8 cm)	1 foot (0.3 m)	⫶⫶
Parsley	1 foot (0.3 m)	1 foot (0.3 m)	△
Peas	5 inches (13 cm)	1 to 7 feet (0.3 to 2 m)	⌗
Peppers	1 foot (0.3 m)	2.5 feet (0.8 m)	△
Radish	2 inches (5 cm)	6 to 8 inches (15 to 20 cm)	⫶⫶
Spinach	8 inches (20 cm)	10 inches (25 cm)	△ ⫶⫶
Squash, summer	2 to 4 feet (0.6 to 1.2 m)	2.5 feet (0.8 m)	⌗ △
Squash, winter	4 to 5 feet (1.2 to 1.5 m)	10–15 feet+ (3 to 4.6 m+)	⌗
Swiss chard	1 foot (0.3 m)	1 foot (0.3 m)	△
Tomatoes, bush	2 feet (0.6 m)	2.5 feet (0.8 m)	△
Tomatoes, vining	2 to 3 feet (0.6 to .9 m)	6 to 12 feet (1.8 to 3.6 m)	⌗ △ ↰
Turnips	5 inches (13 cm)	10 inches (25 cm)	△ ⫶⫶
Watermelon	4 feet (1.2 m)	10 to 15 feet+ (3 to 4.6 m+)	⌗

(Continued on next page)

Symbol Key:

\#   Grow on trellis

△   Triangular planting. This plant may grow taller—the roof is the limit!

⁝⁝⁝   Broadcast planting

↟   This plant likely requires growing up a stake or string, especially when grown in a triangular layout

Note: Heavy fruits such as watermelon, cantaloupe, and winter squash will need a sling to support the developing fruit when grown vertically. Slip the developing fruit at baseball size into the end of a recycled nylon stocking. Tie the open end of the stocking to the trellis. Without a sling, the fruit may rip the whole vine off the trellis as it gets heavy. For more details see Chapter 8, "A Closer Look at the Plants."

rots. Once they're harvested, that's it. You need to start over again. Other crops, such as Swiss chard, spinach, or leaf lettuce, may be harvested many times, leaving the plant (and its roots) in the ground to continue growing between pickings. When planting vegetables in the greenhouse, always consider which category each food or flower crop fits into. Then (using logic) plant the crops that are harvested many times in the more easy-to-reach places. This would generally be on the edges of the beds. As you might have guessed, put those plants that are harvested only once in the harder-to-reach places. This would usually be in the center of the beds or other hard-to-reach areas.

This type of layout will prevent some likely trampling of crops and compacting of your soil as you reach (and step) into the bed for harvesting. It also makes for more comfortable harvesting.

MIXED PLANTING

Who says that each bed or area of bed has to be planted with all the same crop? With our seemingly logical minds and need for organization, this is often the way most of us plant. Besides, that is the way we see farmers do it,

isn't it? But there's no reason you can't mix it up. What does that mean? Well, if you are growing vegetables, you can cultivate a mixture of plants in one area, such as carrots with lettuce and an occasional broccoli plant (a good combination for winter growing).

It can even be a broader mix, including herbs, flowers, subtropical plants, and veg-

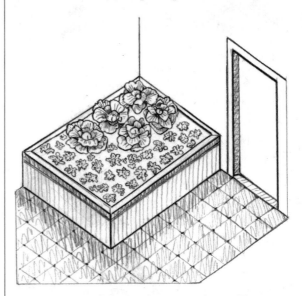

Locate crops you harvest only once (such as cabbage) toward the hard-to-reach areas. Plants that produce continuing yields (such as leaf lettuce) should be located along the easy-to-reach edges of the planting beds.

(Top) *Beds do not have to be mono-cropped. It's fine to grow many different plants in one bed as long as you take a few precautions.*
(Bottom) *Radishes are in and out before the squash in the middle starts to take up all the space.*

etables. Why mix things up like this? Here are some reasons: When two totally different plants grow next to each other, they compete less than two alike plants growing side by side. So you can plant more crops per square foot and have less competition. For example, try growing long-rooted carrots next to shallow-rooted lettuce for less competition for water and nutrients. The root systems are pulling and working in different places in the soil.

Another reason for mixed planting is to use space more efficiently by taking advantage of a slow-growing plant. Let's look at squash as an example. Try planting fast-growing radishes around a young squash plant. By the time the squash plants are vining up, the radishes will be gastronomic history. This adds up to higher total plant yields with closer spacing.

Mixed plantings have another benefit. They reduce disease and insect problems. Diseases are usually specific to plant families and often won't cross over to affect different plant families. A cabbage disease, for instance, usually won't affect the tomato family, but it could spread to a cousin of cabbage, broccoli (which is in the same family as cabbage—the cole crop family). When a bed is interplanted with different crop families, disease infestation spreads more slowly and an epidemic is prevented.

Insects prefer constant and similar stimuli from plant to plant. This means that they get used to the same taste and smell as they work their devastation. When a bed has many different plants growing in it, pests move much more slowly in their feeding because the stimulus is constantly changing as they jump from plant to plant. Also, some plants, such as garlic and other herbs and plants with strong-smelling leaves, may repel certain insects and frustrate pest attacks. This doesn't mean you can totally control bugs by mixing your plantings, but it helps!

The positive effect of mixed planting has been confirmed by research: Plants may secrete something that benefits adjacent and different plants. But secretions may also have negative effects. The research is still sketchy, so most of the information is still based on nonscientific observations or old tales.

Don't lose any sleep over coming up with the right mix of planting combinations. Just observe any positive trends when you mix up your plantings. Keeping records and notes on

BASIC CROP FAMILIES

This guide will help you plan integrated crop plantings and crop rotation season to season. Always try to cross-mix the groups wherever possible.

Bean (Legume) Family
Beans (soy, bush, garbanzo, broad, fava, wax, lima, pole), cowpeas, mimosa, peas, sweet peas.

Beet Family
Beets, spinach, Swiss chard.

Cabbage Family
(cole crop or crucifers)
Broccoli, Brussels sprouts, cabbage, cauliflower, Chinese cabbage, collards, cress, kale, kohlrabi, mustard, nasturtium, radish, rutabaga, stock, turnips.

Carrot Family
Anise, carrots, caraway, celery, coriander (cilantro), dill, fennel, parsley.

Cucumber Family
Cantaloupe, cucumber, melons, pumpkins, squash (summer and winter), watermelon.

Mint Family
Basil, coleus, mint, rosemary, sage (and many other herbs with square stems).

Onion Family
Chives, garlic, leeks, onions, scallions, shallots.

Tomato Family
Angel's trumpet (brugmansia), eggplant, datura, nicotiana, peppers, petunia, potato, salpiglossis, tobacco, tomatoes.

your greenhouse can help you learn some of these trends (see Appendix 8, "Keeping Records"). A basic rule that I follow is to try to mix plants from different plant families, but be sure they are all able to do well in the same microclimate and same season. Also, avoid mixing physically similar plants. For instance, you'll have better results mixing a root crop with a leafy crop, such as onions with lettuce, than mixing two leafy crops, such as lettuce with spinach. Try mixing crops recommended for a broadcast style with those plants that do best with a triangle layout. Try growing broadcast crops under a trellised crop (carrots grown under a tomato crop?).

Integrating different plants together is not all positive. Mixing up your plantings also has some disadvantages. You will often have to harvest each plant at a different time. This makes it harder to renew the soil and replant after a harvest without disturbing the other crop's root systems. Also, it's sometimes more difficult to see when a crop is ready to harvest, so you may have vegetables sneaking past their prime harvest time before you notice them.

If you are mixing flowers with vegetables, you should make a point of never mixing in any plant that could have poisonous parts. They could be inadvertently harvested (along with your vegetables) and be accidentally consumed. See specific flower crops in Chapter 8, "A Closer Look at the Plants," for a discussion on poisonous plants.

It is harder, though not impossible, to attempt mixed plantings in pots, tubs, and other containers. It does help, of course, to use a large container with room for more than one plant.

So with these negatives, should you mix up your plantings or not? You decide. It's a matter of what you want to grow, space considerations, and above all, personal preferences. Still, it is fun to try an integrated bed for the positive reasons. Some people have trouble getting used to the wilder look of an integrated (or mixed) bed, but others find it visually more interesting. Is your desk at work messy? If so, you might prefer the mixed-planting approach. Or is it clean? Then you may not like the mixed-bed look.

Me? I like to do it here and there, but not all the time. I especially like to mix flowers and herbs with vegetables in my growing beds. It adds to the overall beauty of the greenhouse. My attitude has changed about gardening as a result of some experiments with mixed plantings. I've decided that a garden doesn't have to be a picture of perfect order. I've even played around with some controlled chaos by taking a handful of selected seeds and randomly spreading them into a prepared bed. Later, I thin them out to the proper distances. This random pattern of different plants often becomes a very productive bed. On the whole, however, an organized style of integrated planting, combining triangles, trellises, and broad-

cast plantings, is easier to manage, especially when you are new to gardening.

By mixing flowers and herbs with your vegetables, you will not only add to the beauty of the greenhouse but the flowers will also provide a backup food source for beneficial insects and may repel harmful pests (see Chapter 10, "When Things Go Wrong"). Some flowers are edible and will be a great mix in a vegetable bed. Above all, be creative with mixing up your plantings; experiment and have fun.

CROP ROTATION

Crop rotation, an old practice, is still important when you are planting in the same bed season after season. You might think that you could remember what you have grown in each area as time goes on, but I can almost guarantee that you won't. This is where good record keeping is important so you can remember what has occurred in each area over time.

Whenever possible, try to wait a year or two before planting the same crop in the same place. It also helps to avoid vegetables of the same plant family in the same place year after year. Why? It is good preventative medi-

Rotating crops minimizes disease problems and makes for healthier soil.

cine against major diseases that can accumulate in soil over time. The less you can rotate the crops, the more you should work in well-decomposed compost and/or peat moss. These help reduce the buildup of disease organisms by adding healthy amounts of organic matter to the soil between crops; add some once a year, at a minimum (see Chapter 9, "Getting to the Roots").

CROP MATURITY

You'll find that crops will generally have different maturity times (often called "days to harvest") than what's specified on packets of seed or in catalogs. To better time your planting and harvesting, especially in winter, allow a 20 to 30 percent longer period than listed for crops to reach the harvest stage. For fall and spring greenhouse crops, add 10 to 15 percent more time to the days to harvest. Don't feel bad about the slower growth in fall, spring, and winter; it's not bad compared to zero growth outside.

USE THE SEASONS AND MICROCLIMATES TO YOUR ADVANTAGE!

Although your greenhouse is a relatively small space, always try to think about the small areas that have different attributes. In this small area, you indeed have many different microenvironments. Remember that it does matter what time of year it is. It does matter where you set your plants to grow and mature. Using these differences to your advantage, you can make a noticeable and positive effect in the overall health and yield of your greenhouse crops. It is not complicated, but it is different than an outside garden, where you can often put just about anything anywhere in the garden.

CHAPTER 4

SELECTING THE RIGHT PLANTS

IN EARLIER CHAPTERS, WE HAVE LOOKED extensively at the environment and even the microenvironments of the greenhouse. Selecting both the right plant and the right variety of plant can make a huge difference in your chance for success or failure in greenhouse growing. If you take a close look at what is available, you will find a lot of variety when shopping for even one type of crop. Let's use tomatoes as an example. You will find varieties that range from tall and vining to short to dwarf (for growing in little pots). Some can tolerate high temperatures and others can take lower

Sometimes you can find what you need from a seed rack, but you will find a larger selection in a good catalog.

temperatures. There are tomato varieties with in built-in disease resistance, which alone could greatly influence your possible success or failure. There are even tomato varieties that have been bred solely for greenhouse growing (Bingo!). There are also flavor, size, and even fruit color differences among them. So you can see that selecting the right variety for your greenhouse might require a little thought before you plant just any old tomato. This is true for a lot of plants besides the tomato.

MAIL-ORDER CATALOGS

The first question many people ask in the process of deciding what plants to select is: "Where do you get the best seeds?" You will find seed racks in almost every grocery and hardware store (especially in spring), along with the traditionally more extensive seed racks found at garden centers. I use seed racks only when I am pressed for time and can't wait the three or more weeks to order from a catalog. However, this only works in spring and summer when the seed racks are up. Seed racks are incredibly limited and rarely carry any varieties that are preferred for greenhouse growing. For the most part, I prefer ordering from catalogs for the following reasons:

ADVANTAGES OF ORDERING FROM CATALOGS

1. **Freshness.** The seed is usually fresher and comes directly to you after being in a proper storage situation, which results in better germination.

2. **Selection.** A good catalog will offer many more varieties to choose from than the selection available on a seed rack. For instance, a seed rack will have only three or four tomatoes to choose from. There are many catalogs that commonly offer more than twenty varieties! A better selection means you can have a better chance of finding a variety suited to your greenhouse growing conditions.

3. **Description.** Many catalogs do a good job of giving you a detailed description of the varieties they carry. This will often include the plant's physical and disease-resistant characteristics.

When you are filling out the catalog order, be sure to specify *when* you want your seeds or plants sent to you. Catalog companies will often assume that you are planning to grow them for the outside garden and will automatically send them in spring. Seeds seem to ship fine any time of the year. Plants are more of a problem in that regard.

ORDERING PLANTS

Winter shipping can provide you with some frozen plants. Many catalog companies refuse to ship in winter. Plants sent in the middle of summer may become wilted and heat shocked. When plants arrive by mail, don't hesitate to rescue them from the box and give them the care they need. Instructions will usually be included. It takes a few weeks for the plants to get over the shock of transcontinental travel.

You can find most any plant or seed if you get on enough catalog mailing lists.

Most plant catalogs advise you to resist the urge to immediately up-pot the plant and quickly drown them in "miracle" fertilizer. Usually, the best course is to be moderate in the type of care you give your newly arrived plants. This means moderate watering and moderate temperatures and light and withholding the fertilizer until the roots are more developed. Up-potting into the next-size pot should wait until a number of roots are pushing out of the hole in the bottom of the original pot.

ORDERING SEEDS

When you order vegetable seeds, you will often see a listing of the "number of days until harvest." Always take this stated number with a big grain of salt. If you do a little comparison for the same variety of seed, you will find that these figures are usually different in different catalogs. Still, the "number of days until harvest" is useful information. Think of the days-until-harvest numbers as you would the EPA mileage figures on new cars: Use them for comparison only. Never take these numbers literally. As Ronald Reagan used to say when negotiating with the Soviets, "Trust, but verify." The numbers are good for comparing things in the same catalog. Over time, you will figure out how long each crop will take. Read Chapter 7, "Scheduling," to help you along.

I prefer to use catalogs, but I have learned that they are not all created equal. I have found real discrepancies in price, service, and selection. It pays to do some cost and quality comparing. If you ever find that you are disappointed with a plant or seed received from a catalog, most of the time you can get a refund or credit toward something else. But this works only if you complain. My mom used to say "The squeaky wheel gets the grease." I have yet to find a catalog in the seed and plant business that hasn't gone to extremes to please.

Many garden catalogs can provide some useful information. To use a catalog most effectively, read the first few pages with a sharp eye. Here you will often find a shorthand guide (using a little symbol or letter) that is keyed to certain characteristics of the plant. Once you understand these notations, you can learn a lot more about a variety in question.

For a listing of catalogs providing essentials for the greenhouse, please refer to the "Mail-Order Supplies" list in Appendix 7. A few companies charge for a copy of their catalog (what nerve!), but most of the others will have you on their mailing list long after you are composted.

Reading a new seed and plant catalog is as entertaining as a good book, especially on a dreary winter day. Each one has its own personality. Some catalogs read like the *National Enquirer* or *Ripley's Believe It or Not*. Some are snooty; others are unabashedly aimed toward the upwardly mobile. I love the ones that make me drool over their beautiful color glossy photos of wonderful plant specimens. Over the years, gardening catalogs become like an odd collection of guests that invade your mailbox from December through spring.

It is easy to get the ailment my friend Sharon Gaus calls "seed-catalog burnout." The main symptoms include being overwhelmed by all of the choices in the catalog. Sometimes an uncontrollable desire can cause you to order everything and anything. The severity of seed-catalog burnout increases with the number of mailing lists you are on. The cure? First, get yourself off the mailing lists of the catalogs in which you have little interest. This will help you and will also reduce the solid waste in landfills that originates in your mailbox each day. When you request a catalog, ask that they not sell your name to any other catalog or mailing list.

Second, when you are looking at a catalog, try to keep in mind exactly what you need. If something strikes your fancy, ask yourself, "Where will it grow?" "Is there room for it in my greenhouse?" And if it is a food crop, ask yourself "Who will eat it?" A good rule to avoid seed-catalog burnout is this: When in doubt, don't order it.

HYBRIDS: ADVANTAGES AND DISADVANTAGES

When you are looking through seed catalogs, one of the first choices you will have to make is whether you want to grow hybrids or nonhybrids (sometimes called open-pollinated seeds). A hybrid is the result of the pairing of two genetically diverse parents. Agricultural scientists have developed what is called the "F1 hybrid." It is called F1 because it is the first generation of seed produced after the inbreeding and final cross with two parent lines of seed. When you see the word "hybrid" in a catalog or

MAIL-ORDER TIPS

Here are a few tips to keep in mind when ordering from a catalog:

1. **Substitutes.** Let the company know if you do or don't want substitutes. Often, you have your heart set on obtaining one particular variety, and if it's out of stock, you might not get what you want.

2. **Experiment.** Order a few different varieties of the same plant. In a short growing season, it's helpful to test different varieties until you are sure which one has the best performance. Be wary of a new variety on the market; it may not be as good as your old standby. Test the new variety next to the old one. Don't give up on the tried and true until the new is well proven.

3. **Carefully follow the ordering instructions.** Read the fine print for hidden items such as shipping and packing costs and possible sales tax. Some catalogs may even offer free growing information or free test seeds, if you mark the right box.

4. **Make a copy of the order.** Having a duplicate will tell you if you received the full order or if unauthorized substitutions were made. I like to make special notes on my copy, including the page that each variety is found and where I plan to grow the plant.

5. **Date the seed packets when they arrive.** Many companies already have a date on the packet, but if not, do it yourself immediately after your seeds arrive. This will help you in future years to determine if the seed is too old to plant. Seeds older than two or three years may have a lower germination rate and less growing vigor.

6. **Don't get mad, get even.** Or at least get your money back. If you are disappointed with a plant or seed you ordered from a catalog, most of the time you can get a refund or credit toward something else. I have yet to find a catalog company that hasn't gone to extremes for dissatisfied customers.

Be sure to check out the extensive mail-order appendixes at the end of the book.

---

on a seed packet, it really designates an F1 hybrid. For a description of the hybrid process, see page 128 in Chapter 5, "Plant Propagation."

Why do seed companies go to all this trouble? Mainly because hybrids yield better crops and have more vigor. They also have a few disadvantages. You should know about both.

They have one other trait that is important to understand. If you grow these F1 hybrids and then harvest seed from them, you are likely to see a significant decline in yield and quality. These varieties don't come true from seed, like unhybridized varieties do. This is good news for the seed companies because you are forced to purchase new seeds from them each season to maintain the high yield and vigor.

Because these hybrids take years to create, the F1 hybrids are more expensive. Farmers and professional greenhouse growers don't mind the higher-priced hybrid seed, because the extra yield of hybrids more than makes up for the increased cost of seed.

THE ADVANTAGES AND DISADVANTAGES OF USING HYBRID SEED

Advantages:

1. Hybrids can have up to 25 percent higher yield.
2. Hybrid plants are physically uniform. This is advantageous for farmers who harvest with machines, but it's usually not a big deal for small-greenhouse gardeners.
3. Hybrids often show greater vigor and faster growth.

Disadvantages:

1. Hybrids cost up to five times more because they take longer to develop and are more trouble to produce.
2. They often require a more exacting horticulture. When things aren't optimum, they may suffer more than plants grown from nonhybrid, open-pollinated seeds.
3. If you save and grow seeds from an F1 hybrid plant, don't expect a similar plant in the next generation. The resulting plants in the second generation are usually much lower yielding, have less vigor, and are quite variable in their physical characteristics. You don't know what you are going to get, and usually you'll lose all the advantages you had in growing the original hybrid.

Using hybrid seed is becoming more controversial among many people. Most of the controversy is associated with the need to depend upon seed companies and a worry about the lack of diversity as a result of less people saving varieties. There is also worry about resulting lack of use (and subsequent loss) of the old-fashioned varieties, whose genetic makeup is generally more diverse. Some seed companies and nonprofit organizations have made wonderful efforts to maintain availability of the older heirloom seeds. If you're looking for a hobby, I can't think of a better one than helping to preserve some of these interesting heirloom seeds. If you are interested in saving heirloom seeds, contact the Seed Savers Exchange, 3076 North Winn Road, Decorah, IA 52101. They have both a membership program and a wonderful seed catalog (free).

So if a plant is sold as a hybrid, is it bad? No, I don't see this is as a black-and-white issue; there is a lot of gray here. I have found a few hybrids that perform so well in the greenhouse that I routinely use them for various reasons. Sometimes I find a hybrid may have a needed disease resistance, or a hybrid may just have proved to be better yielding. You will have to decide whether hybrids are worth it for you. If you are discouraged because you can't produce seed from your hybrid plant, you can always try reproducing the plant from cuttings, as outlined in the next chapter. The best way to evaluate the worth of the hybrid is to compare it with nonhybrid varieties in your greenhouse. It is not uncommon to find a nonhybrid seed that can perform equally well. When this occurs, you can save money when you purchase the seed (nonhybrid seed is almost always cheaper) and have the added advantage of being able to save your own seed from these plants.

SELECTING VEGETABLE VARIETIES

Selecting the best plant variety or crop for greenhouse food production will help maximize yields in your greenhouse. This decision may seem easy and unimportant at first thought, but it is one of the most important factors in how much food you are going to grow. Let's say you wanted to grow some greens, such as spinach. Well, spinach is a fine plant to grow in the winter greenhouse, but if you instead made the decision to grow Swiss chard in the same place, you could quadruple your yields. The reason? Spinach bolts (goes to seed) with sunny days. I have had spinach bolt on me after only five weeks of growth. Bolting ends the productive life of the plant because it quits producing edible leaves. The best thing to do is pull it up and start over. Swiss chard rarely goes to seed (unless you give it a frost), so it produces abundantly for many seasons in the greenhouse. Swiss chard is a relative of spinach and has a similar taste. When cooked, some people can't tell them apart. Many people even prefer Swiss chard to spinach. But there are those of you who still won't eat chard over spinach. No problem. Grow spinach and put up with less of a harvest (but at least give chard a try first).

If you are really concerned with a productive food-producing greenhouse, then you need to think about every crop and how it grows before you decide to plant it. By their nature, some plants just produce more edible food than others. For example, compare cauliflower to cabbage. Virtually the whole cabbage plant is edible, every last leaf. Cauliflower produces many leaves that are tossed out, leaving a small edible head. Imagine two equal-sized plots of land, one growing cabbage and the other cauliflower. The total poundage of food in the cabbage plot will be much greater than that from the cauliflower plot.

Another example: Compare peas to beets. Peas require space to grow many leaves before you can harvest the small, round sweet pea. Beets, on the other hand, are almost 100 per-

If you want to grow the most food per square foot, grow crops that are mostly or completely edible, such as lettuce or cabbage. Compare the amount of food you get from cabbage versus broccoli. Virtually all of the cabbage is edible, whereas much of the broccoli will end up in the compost pile.

cent edible. The greens, or tops, are excellent when cooked like spinach. And, of course, the roots are edible. There is little waste. With a crop of peas, the vines, leaves, and roots are all thrown out (or composted). Hence, with peas, less food per growing space is produced than with beets. So if you are after high yields, you may want to give the crop some thought.

Don't get me wrong. I'm not trying to talk you out of growing peas or any other crop. Peas are one of my favorite things to grow and eat in a greenhouse (in fact, I really don't like beets). I only want to get you to think about these plants in a different light. If the price of fresh food were to skyrocket or if there were an emergency or survival situation, these considerations might become important.

Sometimes, it all comes down to the taste buds, old habits, and what people want to eat. What good is a bushel of fresh, greenhouse-grown radishes if nobody in your house likes to eat radishes? Plant only what you think will be consumed.

There are also economic considerations when it comes to selecting what to grow. I would suggest that you avoid growing foods in a greenhouse that can be stored easily and/or purchased cheaply. For instance, why grow potatoes when they can be purchased cheaply and keep very well in a root cellar? Instead, get the most value out of your greenhouse by growing the more expensive and perishable crops. When I see a small bag containing a few sprigs of fresh herbs selling for two bucks and 10 pounds (4.5 kg) of potatoes going for two bucks, it makes me want to go back into the commercial business of greenhouse gardening again.

I wish I could just give you a list of what will do best in your greenhouse and send you on your way. The trouble is, every greenhouse is different. It depends on where you live and the orientation and construction of your greenhouse or sunroom. No one variety will work for everyone's greenhouse. There are too many variables. Also, plant varieties change rapidly, with old varieties being dropped and replaced by new ones.

Whenever possible, I will list specific varieties of plants that I have found to perform the best over a wide variety of circumstances. Most of these plants are listed in Chapter 8, "A Closer Look at the Plants."

Since I can't give you a list of exactly what to grow, it is my hope that you will learn to understand the special qualities of your greenhouse. Discover the personality of your greenhouse. Then you can make your own informed decisions about which varieties will do best for you.

PLANTS FOR THE SOLAR-HEATED AND COOL-WINTER GREENHOUSE

The greenhouse that is solar heated or runs cool in winter has more exacting requirements when it comes to selecting plants. Conversely, a greenhouse that constantly runs a minimum of 60°F (15°C) at night can grow almost any crop year-round without much problem, as long as the light, soil, and water requirements are correct. But a greenhouse that gets down to the 40s or even the 30s (0°C to 9°C) requires some special consideration. It helps to start subscribing to the good seed catalogs. While you look through the many selections, keep the following considerations in mind.

HEAT TOLERANCE

Whenever your greenhouse is above 85°F (29°C) in the winter or above 90°F (32°C) in the summer, it's too hot for maximum plant growth. Above these temperatures, most plants slow their growth, and as the temperature rises, blossoms will not set fruit and many edible leafy plants and root crops will go to seed prematurely. This is a surprisingly common malady, especially in areas with sunny winters, where you can often have as much of a problem with high temperatures in the winter as you do in summer. The best way to deal with warm temperatures is proper ventilation, as described on page 54 in Chapter 1. In an attached greenhouse in winter, you should ventilate into your house. For an unattached greenhouse, you must ventilate to the outside. Occasional winter ventilation may be necessary. Also, you can select plant varieties that can tolerate warm temperatures.

For example, leafy crops are usually best grown in the cooler months of the year. A greenhouse in an area with sunny winters may get quite warm during the occasional sunny winter day. To minimize any problems, you can do a little research in the seed catalogs for leafy crop varieties that can thrive in a hotter situation. Just look for plant descriptions that say "heat tolerant," "heat resistant," or "slow to bolt." I can usually find a selection of lettuce and spinach (and occasionally radishes) with this type of notation. Another solution is to grow substitute crops, such as New Zealand spinach or Swiss chard, which are perennial in the greenhouse and will produce quality greens for many years regardless of the warm-day temperature, as long as it is above freezing.

Other plants may not bolt or go to seed but respond to overheating in other ways. For example, yields of peas drop drastically with hot daytime temperatures. However, certain pea varieties are tolerant of heat as well as being cold hardy. All it takes is some close investigation of the seed catalogs that have good descriptions.

VEGGIES IN THE COOL GREENHOUSE

Some people prefer not to heat their greenhouses in the winter. Those with solar greenhouses don't have to worry about heating, because they can let the sun do most of the work. Either way, if you have a greenhouse that consistently has cold night temperatures and you want to grow things, there are some great options.

When it comes to vegetables in the icebox greenhouse, it is best to stick to plants that are grown for their roots or leaves. The only exceptions are peas and plants in the cole/cabbage family, such as broccoli, cauliflower, and kohlrabi (see the plant family chart on page 111 in Chapter 4). Some of these plants can even tolerate temperatures below freezing.

For years, I had a greenhouse that would get down to 25°F (–4°C), when outside it would be –25°F (–31°C). I was still able to grow vegetables by sticking to plants that can tolerate some frost. In fall, before it got cold, I would start spinach, French sorrel, Swiss chard, lettuce, broccoli, chives, top-set onions, rad-

ishes, and carrots. I also grew some herbs, including rosemary, fennel, dill, and cilantro, which all grow well in the cold. In the dead of winter, I could still count on a fresh-picked, tasty salad spiced up with a few sprigs of herbs. These harvests occurred even with ice in the watering can every morning. For color, grow a few cold-tolerant flowers. Pansies, sweet peas, nasturtiums, and snapdragons are all quite cold tolerant.

Heat got to this lettuce crop, causing it to bolt.

If you plan to grow vegetables in a cold greenhouse, select varieties that have a relatively short number of days until harvest. This translates into a shorter wait for you. But don't expect your plants to be harvested in the number of days listed on the seed packet. It will take quite a few more days with the cold temperatures and short days of winter. Another thing you should know about plants that have a short number of days until harvest is that they may often be smaller or lower-yielding plants. This is especially true when compared to the longer-maturing varieties. But it is still worthwhile to grow quicker-maturing varieties in the cold greenhouse because it might be a choice of a smaller harvest compared to none at all. If the plants tend to grow smaller, simply space them closer together.

Nitrates in the Cool-Winter Greenhouse

Leafy vegetables such as spinach and lettuce, when grown in a cool-winter greenhouse, can

TIPS TO AVOID NITRATE ACCUMULATION IN EDIBLE PLANTS IN WINTER

1. Avoid the application of fertilizers containing nitrogen to greenhouse greens in the darker winter months.
2. Harvest later in the day on sunny afternoons, especially after a few consecutive clear days.
3. Harvest the older, more mature outer leaves first.
4. Set the harvested plants (roots and all) in water for 24–48 hours before eating.
5. Grow other edible crops in the winter besides just greens.

accumulate high levels of nitrate. The roots take up the nitrate from the soil. At high levels, nitrate can be dangerous to infants and pose potential health problems to both children and adults. When there is adequate light, the nitrate is a beneficial fertilizer that is quickly converted into plant proteins. When the light is low in duration and quality in winter and is accompanied by cool temperatures, the nitrate is not converted into protein and instead accumulates in the leaf. The nitrate accumulation increases in proportion to the amount of nitrogen in the soil.

The folks at the former New Alchemy Institute in East Falmouth, Massachusetts, did some research into this problem. They recommended some ways to minimize nitrate in greens grown in cool-winter greenhouses. First, select the right varieties. New Alchemy found

that certain varieties take up less nitrate than others. Green Ice lettuce (found in Burpee and Park seed catalogs) takes up 20 to 40 percent less nitrate than the greenhouse bibb variety Diamante. Researchers also found that the romaine lettuce variety Winter Density and bibb varieties Jeanette, Cantille, and Sabrina had around 12 to 15 percent less nitrate than other romaines and bibbs.

It also helps to plan your harvest according to the calendar. The researchers found that nitrate levels were highest near the winter solstice but much lower in crops harvested in the warmer, sunnier month of March.

Unfortunately, the old New Alchemy Institute folded up shop. In its day, New Alchemy sparked a new environmental awareness and demonstrated the importance of the home greenhouse. The organization helped people to do more with less and be aware that they should tread on this planet in a lighter, less destructive way. Fortunately, the institute produced and nurtured not only ideas but also many good people who have moved on to private and public projects. The work of this project continues to have a positive impact on how we treat our land and environment.

CHOOSING BUSHY VERSUS TALL PLANTS

When a plant grows vertically, it can make better use of unused air space. If you are growing vegetables or flowers, vertical growing might mean more of both for you to enjoy. Because the growing space in a greenhouse always seems limited, it is sometimes wise to grow vining or vertically growing varieties as opposed to bushy varieties. When it comes to vegetables, there are many types that grow both bushy and low or tall and vining. These include peas, beans, cucumbers, squash, melons, figs, and bananas. Tomatoes are also included in this list, but horticulturists have a special vocabulary for them that might pose some confusion. Bushy tomatoes are called "determinate" because they grow to a determined height and then the main leader on the plant quits growing. Tomatoes that grow tall and viney are called "indeterminate." That is because they can grow indeterminately, given the right growing conditions.

Bushy vegetable varieties can fit into special places in the greenhouse or sunroom—for instance, next to a knee wall with little headroom. But one of the best places to use bushy varieties is in pots. The tall vining varieties grown in a pot might quickly get out of balance, with too much top supported by a small, limited root system. This will cause the plant to wilt at the slightest provocation. It will also be under constant stress, which is an invitation to every bug and disease in the area. This type of plant stress can be avoided—just make sure that the pot or container corresponds to the size of the mature plant. Grow the big indeterminate tomatoes in tubs or beds.

I have had great luck growing bush beans in hanging baskets. I like to grow bushy determinate tomatoes in 1- to 5-gallon (3.8- to 19-liter) pots and have had decent yields. Play around with bushy vegetable varieties in pots, and you'll see that it works really well.

DISEASE RESISTANCE

The inherent high humidity of greenhouses and intensive plant production can bring conditions that promote plant diseases. As mentioned in Chapter 10, "When Things Go Wrong," diseases are rarely controlled with

Many common fruit and vegetable plants are available in bushy or tall (or vining) types. Bushy tomatoes are called "determinate" and the tall tomatoes are called "indeterminate." By growing the right type in the right place, you optimize your use of limited greenhouse space.

Low-growing bushy plants are perfect for places with little head space, such as a low knee wall.

chemicals and I therefore do not recommend them. The best defense against disease is to maintain healthy plant growth. But you can also help things out by selecting varieties that show some tolerance or resistance to a particular disease problem. Again, this is where you need to really study the seed catalogs and look for any listed as "resistant to disease." Before you start, it is important to make every effort to identify your disease problem. Begin by reading Chapter 10. There are many good books on plant diseases as well as good resources through your local university. Your county agricultural extension agent can also be helpful in identifying a particular disease problem.

Many plants show variability in their resistance to diseases. I had a problem with powdery mildew affecting squash and cucumbers. Powdery mildew is a white, powdery fungus growth that covers the leaves and slows growth. I went back to the catalog and found varieties that were listed as resistant to powdery mildew. By just changing varieties, I was able to see about an 80 percent decrease in the disease without doing anything else to control the mildew.

You should know, however, that the degree of resistance may vary a good deal, from totally resistant to only slightly more resistant than the norm. Don't be surprised if you are growing a variety that is listed as "resistant" to a certain disease and you still see evidence of the disease. The variety may be only more tolerant than other varieties. That is something that isn't explained very well in the catalogs. Usually, you have to find out for yourself.

You may discover that some varieties have some resistance to a disease, even though it is not listed as such in the catalogs. For this reason, don't put all your eggs in one basket. Try to grow more than one variety of a particular crop, and nature's genetic diversity will work

for you. Then with a little experience under your belt, you will have identified superior varieties. Good record keeping is helpful in determining what worked well and what was mediocre. Don't be lazy about being a good observer and making a few notes. It's not hard, and the reward is having healthy, productive plants. Sometimes you have to figure things out for yourself, as this valuable information may not be available anywhere.

PEST RESISTANCE

Plant varieties that exhibit resistance to insect pests are rarer than those that are resistant to disease. This seems to be a harder thing to breed plants for. The better catalogs will occasionally mention some resistance to bugs, but usually you have to learn on your own, as some plants are naturally more resistant to bug attacks.

A good example of selecting for pest resistance happened to me with lettuce. I used to grow a light-green Grand Rapids lettuce variety called Slo Bolt. It was a good producer in winter, spring, and fall, but it was readily attacked by both aphids and whitefly. Then I switched varieties to two newer, related lettuces: Green Ice and Royal Green M.I. The major difference was in the color of the leaf. Instead of having light green leaves, these were decidedly darker green in color. I found that the bugs were much less attracted to the darker-green lettuce varieties. For some reason, the insects just loved the color of the lighter-green plants. This simple change in varieties made a huge difference in my bug problem.

Don't expect that just by changing varieties you will totally eliminate a bug problem, but it can make a difference. Again, keep records. There may be other reasons for a crop's insect tolerance besides just the color of the leaf. Be observant. Watch the changes year to year among the varieties to be sure a change in bug infestation is truly because of a change in varieties and not because it might have been a bad year for bugs (yes, bugs can have good years and bad years).

GREENHOUSE VARIETIES

There have been many vegetable and flower varieties that have been developed especially for commercial greenhouses that sometimes are offered in regular retail seed catalogs. These greenhouse varieties were selected mostly with the commercial greenhouse grower in mind. They have been chosen for high productivity under ideal conditions of light and temperatures in a totally controlled energy-intensive environment. These varieties usually have the characteristics of disease resistance, high yields, vining growth, bolt resistance (lettuce), and resistance to physiological disorders (i.e., fruit cracking on tomatoes). In the case of cucumbers, some varieties are labor saving because they don't require any hand-pollination in order to set fruit.

In better seed catalogs, these varieties are usually flagged with a statement such as "For greenhouse production" or "For forcing." Forcing is a common European horticultural term used to describe the forced growing of the plant out of its normal season.

Two catalogs that commonly list greenhouse varieties are Stokes and Johnny's Selected Seeds (see "Mail-Order Seeds" in Appendix 6). When reading these catalogs, keep in mind that you might find the perfect home greenhouse cucumber (sometimes called a European forcing cucumber)—one that does well in cooler temperatures and is tolerant to powdery mildew. Here is where you apply what you

---

GREENHOUSE SEEDS AND PLANTS

Here is a list of seeds and plants that have been developed for greenhouse growing:

Vegetables: certain herbs, carrots, cucumber, lettuce, peppers, and tomatoes.

Flowers: alstroemeria, aster, calceolaria, carnation, chrysanthemum, cineraria, cyclamen, freesia, gerbera, ranunculus, rose, snapdragon, stock, and sweet peas.

---

know about your greenhouse environment and your greenhouse's specific problems with diseases in order to select the right variety.

Another way to find varieties bred for greenhouse conditions is through your local commercial greenhouse grower. These people might let you thumb through their wholesale catalogs, which only commercial growers use. See if you can buy some seed through a local commercial greenhouse grower. Greenhouse varieties are not available for everything, and you will find only a limited number of crops at any given time. I hope that in the future people will show the seed companies that there is a large demand for these varieties. Maybe then they'll start breeding a whole slew of crops specifically for the home greenhouse and even the solar-greenhouse environment.

PLANTS THAT NEED WINTER

Why not grow native wildflowers, asparagus, rhubarb, cherries, apples, peaches, pears, apricots, currants, or raspberries in your greenhouse? The main reason that these plants are difficult is that they are temperate-climate plants used to an environment where the cold of winter is not only expected but required for natural growth. Without the winter cold treatment, they do not produce properly. Also, these plants require an appreciable amount of greenhouse space, yet they produce for only a relatively short time. In addition, depending on where you live, these plants may do just fine outside but, unfortunately, won't do much better inside unless you live where summer frosts are common.

Still, there are those who would be in total heaven if only they could be eating fresh, homegrown rhubarb and peaches or even picking wildflower bouquets in the winter greenhouse. Well, with some effort there are ways to pull it off, although I'm not sure if it is worth the effort. All you have to do is fool Mother Nature (which is not always nice). You do this by faking a winter, or as horticulturists put it, you "force" a crop. Different crops and varieties have different chill requirements, and these can be imitated artificially. One way to provide the proper amount of winter cooling is to go outside in midwinter or early spring, carefully dig up the desired plants (you may need a pick for the frozen soil) and transplant them inside for late-winter harvests. I call this the "half-winter" treatment, which is usually enough to ensure proper production. Wintertime transplanting can be close to impossible with an 8-foot (2.4-meter) peach tree, but with dwarf varieties in movable containers on rollers, it could be done more easily.

Growing of these winter-loving temperate crops in a greenhouse warrants some further experimentation and development. There is some good potential for growing crops such as asparagus and rhubarb in winter greenhouses. In the South, plant breeders have actually developed varieties of temperate crops that require less chilling in order to produce yields. If you want to pursue this, begin looking through the many available regional, Southern U.S. plant catalogs and you will occasionally find a low-chill-requirement plant.

VIVE LA DIFFÉRENCE!

As you gain more experience in the greenhouse, you will find it is rare for the same fruit or vegetable variety that you grew successfully outside to do equally well inside. Gardening inside the greenhouse is different, and we need to approach it in that manner. The extra yields of vegetables and flowers make the reward well worth selecting plants especially suited to the greenhouse environment. The inside garden and the outside garden are two different and special worlds and for the most part should be treated as such.

CHAPTER 5

PLANT PROPAGATION

I ONCE ASKED A LITTLE GIRL WHERE SHE thought her French fries came from. She said, "France." Eggs? "The egg factory." Pineapple? "A pine tree." But she said bananas came from the store. When was the last time you wondered where your food came from? How about the origin of your water (before it got to the faucet)? How about the source for a gust of clean air? It's a healthy thing to wonder and discover where things originate. It is even healthier to be directly involved in the creation of things that are important to us. That is one of the inherent beauties of the greenhouse.

Plants use a variety of devices to reproduce, including seeds, and spores, and we help them along with cuttings, grafting, or even taking divisions from existing plants. They can also multiply from runners spreading from the mother plant from either above or below the ground. Your ability to start plants in the greenhouse is the heart of good gardening skills and provides some of the greatest of rewards. After all, what can be more satisfying than becoming involved in the process of creating new life?

If you never perfect the simple skills of plant propagation, you are stuck with buying

Work to master and enjoy the skills of plant propagation. Doing so will reduce your costs and dependence on others for plants.

other people's plants. This might not only become expensive but you will only be growing what they choose and will be unable to follow your particular passion.

There are simple, efficient tricks you can use in the greenhouse for starting and establishing plants. For example, rather than wasting precious bed space waiting for seeds to germinate, use another area for starting seedlings. Many greenhouse growers propagate seedlings in the basement under lights or on top of thermal-mass water drums in solar-heated greenhouses. Most seedlings are ready to plant in around 4 to 6 weeks. That is a long time to tie up a bed. Instead, you can grow your seedlings on in your propagation area, which allows you to save bed space. Then, all on the same day, you can replace an old planting with a new set of 6-week old seedlings. It is like hitting the ground running!

SEED PROPAGATION

Seeds come from the plant's flower. Pollination fertilizes an egg within the flower, and the results of this sexual reproduction are seeds. Seeds are truly amazing self-contained units. They are usually (not always) new genetic individuals. Within each seed is an embryonic plant and a food reserve to get the plant going until it can provide for itself: a nice little complete package.

The first step for the gardener is to obtain fresh, high-quality seeds. The older the seeds, the less vigor and quality they usually have. Old seeds are slower to germinate and proportionally fewer of them actually do germinate. How long do seeds stay viable? There is no hard-and-fast rule. Every species is different. It also depends upon how the seeds were stored. If seeds are kept cool and dry, you can count on 3 to 4 years for most vegetables, but onions and beets are usually good only for a couple of years. Tomatoes, peppers, watermelon, cucumber, and cantaloupe can stay viable for 5 years or more. Most flower seed can be stored for around 3 years under proper conditions. A good rule to remember is that every 10°F (3°C) decrease in the storage temperature (down to freezing) can double the storage life of your seed. However, once you get below freezing, you can have mixed results, depending on whether the seeds in question are more native to the tropics than the temperate zone. For that reason, I don't like to store seed in the freezer unless it is native to the temperate zone. As a general practice, I keep my seeds in the refrigerator and make sure they are in a moisture-proof container. Also, for every 1 percent decrease in seed moisture content, you can double the seed storage life.

The fresher the seed, the better the germination and plant vigor. It is important to avoid storing seeds for more than one season by ordering no more than you will use (easy for me to say). It is not easy to figure exactly how much to order. To help determine the proper amount to order, refer to the following list of the number of seeds per ounce. It is easy to see that a little amount of seed can go a long way.

A NOTE ON HYBRIDS

When you are looking through seed catalogs, one of the first decisions you will have to make is whether you want to grow hybrids or nonhybrids (sometimes called open-pollinated seeds). As I explain in the previous chapter, a hybrid is the offspring of two genetically diverse parents. Agricultural scientists have developed what is called the F1 hybrid. The F1 hybrid is created by pairing selected plants after a long process of inbreeding. I hate to put it this way, but inbreeding is best described as plant incest. Specific plant lines are inbred, and after many years, the resulting inbred offspring is allowed to pollinate the offspring of another plant line that was also put through many years of inbreeding. (Wait until the Society to Prevent Plant Cruelty finds out about this!) The seed resulting from these two inbred plant lines that are finally cross-pollinated is called the F1-hybrid seed. Where does the designation F1 come from? It is the first generation after the inbreeding. When you see the word "hybrid" in a catalog or on a seed packet, it usu-

NUMBER OF SEEDS PER OUNCE

Many seed catalogs allow you to order by quantity (reflected in ounces or a fraction of ounces). This will help you determine your needs.

Ornamentals and Herbs	Approx. Number of Seeds per Ounce	Ornamentals and Herbs	Approx. Number of Seeds per Ounce
Ageratum	130,000	Lavender	25,000
Alyssum	90,000	Marigold	10,000
Basil	20,000	Mimulus	700,000
Begonia	2,000,000	Nasturtium	175
Browallia	120,000	Nicotiana	400,000
Calceolaria	640,000	Pansy	20,000
Calendula	3,000	Parsley	19,000
Carnation	14,000	Phlox	14,000
Chives	22,000	Rosemary	24,000
Cineraria	100,000	Salpiglossis	125,000
Coleus	100,000	Snapdragon	180,000
Coriander	19,000	Stock	18,500
Cosmos	5,000	Sweet pea	300
Dahlia	2,800	Thyme	76,000
Dill	6,300	Verbena	10,000
Fennel	8,000	Viola	24,000
Geranium	6,200	Zinnia	2,500
Impatiens	44,000		

Vegetables	Approx. Number of Seeds per Ounce	Vegetables	Approx. Number of Seeds per Ounce
Beans	120	Kale	8,500
Broccoli	10,000	Kohlrabi	8,000
Brussels sprouts	8,500	Lettuce	20,000
Cabbage	7,500	Okra	550
Cantaloupe	1,000	Onions	9,500
Carrots	15,000	Peas	150
Cauliflower	10,000	Peppers	4,500
Celery	70,000	Radish	2,500
Chinese cabbage	16,000	Spinach	2,000
Collards	9,500	Squash	250
Cucumber	1,000	Tomatoes	10,000
Eggplant	6,000	Watermelon	250

ally means that it is really an F1 hybrid. There are certain advantages—and disadvantages—in using hybrid seed. Please refer to the discussion on hybrids on page 116 in Chapter 4 for further details.

STORING SEEDS

Seeds are best stored in an airtight container such as a glass jar. They keep best in a place that is dry, dark, and cool and that is close to freezing but not below 32°F (0°C). To maintain a dry atmosphere, I store seeds in glass jars with a teaspoon of dried milk, which helps absorb any possible moisture coming off the seeds. Always put a label on the jar that tells you what is inside and the year you put it there. Try to be as organized as possible when you store seeds because they have a natural tendency to become disorganized. Keep each type of seed separate in its own envelope or packet. Never mix this year's seed with last year's seed. Keeping track of the seed's age is important.

If you are interested in saving your own seed from mature plants, be sure to read the discussion in the previous chapter on hybrids. Hybrids do not come true from seed. If you have your heart set on propagating your own hybrid plants, you must either purchase the seed from a seed company or clone a hybrid plant, a procedure that is discussed later in this chapter. If you save seed from a hybrid plant, it will usually result in a plant that has less vigor and yields less than the mother plant.

GERMINATING AND PLANTING SEEDS

Starting plants from seed is by far the most common method of getting new plants. It is always amazing to see what can come from one

Thousands of seedlings can be started in a small amount of space.

little seed in a short time. Starting plants from seed is almost always cheaper than starting with plants. Sometimes it may be the only way to acquire a plant. In general, starting plants from seed is not hard to do. In fact, the problem is more often that people get carried away and start too many seeds.

Vegetables are usually easier to start than flowers, and this is partly because many flowering plants have such small seed. Native temperate-climate plants (many wildflowers) often require or, at the least, benefit from a chilling treatment to mimic winter in order to break the dormancy in a seed. Six weeks of temperatures below 40°F (5°C) usually does the trick. Many tropical plants have their own set of problems when it comes to growing them from seed. First, tropical plant seeds often have a short period of viability before the seed loses its ability to germinate, so getting fresh seed is important. If that isn't enough of a challenge, they sometimes take months to germinate or have other exacting requirements.

Unless the plant absolutely hates to be transplanted, it is usually best to start the seed in an ideal propagating environment for later transplanting. When planting seeds, keep in mind the discussion that follows.

GERMINATING SEEDS

To germinate seeds, you must create a specific environment that is conducive to helping seeds germinate. Think about setting aside a special area for starting seeds within the greenhouse. A seed and propagation area can even be located somewhere else in your house that has moderate temperatures and light. Good ventilation also helps. Here is a detailed list of what is needed for good germination.

1. Disease-free soil and pots. Many seedling diseases cause poor germination. Diseases can be borne on old, dirty pots. It's always a good idea to recycle, but if you are going to use an old pot, wash it well with some detergent and a little bleach. Old potting soil or garden soil can also harbor diseases. You can heat-sterilize the soil (discussed later in this chapter) to kill diseases before you use it. Even easier, you can start your seedlings in store-bought potting soil. See seedling diseases in Chapter 10, "When Things Go Wrong."

2. Moisture (for germination and seedlings). Seedlings that are germinating usually require constant moisture, so keep the soil moist but not dripping wet. If the soil dries out even once, it might kill germinating seedlings. If your tap water is extremely cold in winter, you can speed germination by using warm water on the seedlings. Be careful of water pressure or nozzles that create a force so powerful that it blasts the seeds out of the soil. Gently mist seedlings with a spray, much like a light, gentle rain. Misting nozzles available at good garden centers or in catalogs are ideal for watering seedlings. In general, seedlings need a bit less water than do seeds, so cut back slightly once they germinate.

3. Moisture (for seeds and cuttings). High humidity and moisture are also beneficial to starting both seeds and cuttings. Mist the plants with a squeeze bottle a few times a day or, better yet, set up a misting system. Many greenhouse catalogs offer misting systems. See the discussions of misting systems in both Chapters 1 and 2.

4. Aeration. Because seedlings need air to germinate, make sure the soil isn't constantly saturated. All containers in which you start seeds should have a drainage hole in the bottom.

5. Soil temperature. In the winter, many greenhouse gardeners have trouble germinating seedlings. This is often due to cold soil temperatures. Although plants vary in their temperature requirements, usually seeds have trouble germinating when the soil temperature is below 50°F (10°C). A temperature of 65°F to 75°F (18°C to 21°C) is optimum for germinating most seeds. Extreme high and low temperatures are harmful. During the cold season, you can create a microclimate of warmth by using heating cables or pads, as discussed in Chapter 1. I prefer the pad-type bottom heaters. Unfortunately, they are the most costly to install. I have found that you get what you pay for when it comes to electric bottom heaters for germinating seedlings. Try checking the temperature of your soil with a thermometer to see if you really need to do something about it. A 10-degree (3°C) variance can make a big difference in whether your seeds will germinate. An alternative to a bottom heater is to bring seedling trays inside your house to a warm, sunny window or place them under a proper lighting scheme. After the seeds germinate, you can either move them back into the greenhouse or continue to grow them to a good transplanting size before you return them to the sunspace.

6. Light. Some seeds, often the tiny ones, need light to germinate. Check your seed catalog or packet instructions. Those that need light should be planted shallow in a well-lit area. Lettuce is one common vegetable that requires some light through the soil to trigger germination. Seedlings also need light to get a good start on life. If light is lacking, the seedlings have a great way of telling you about it; they will become extremely leggy and elongated. Some garden catalogs offer light benches for growing plants and starting seedlings. They are usually made of an array of fluorescent lights on adjustable hangers to accommodate the growing plants. You can always build your own light table for germinating seedlings. Place it almost anywhere except in prime greenhouse growing space, which should be used for growing the big plants (see Chapter 2). For best results, always place the light 2 to 3 inches (5 to 8 cm) above the top of the plant or the soil, if you are germinating seeds. Please remember to be careful about mixing water and electricity. Read more about supplemental lighting in Chapter 1.

7. Depth. If seeds are planted too deeply, they may run out of energy before they reach the surface. A general rule on seed planting is to place seeds at a depth 2 to 3 times their width. Small seeds have less food-energy reserves to push through to the surface, so plant them at correspondingly shallower depths. For shallow-planted seeds (small seeds), be extra careful that the soil surface doesn't dry out.

8. Nutrients. Seed germination requires little, if any, added fertilizers or other nutrients. In fact, fertilizers such as nitrogen can cause major problems if used when the plants are too small. As seedlings grow, their needs for fertilizer increase, and they may initially benefit from a very diluted fertilizer, preferably one high in phosphorus and low in nitrogen.

When in doubt, don't do it—at least until the plant is starting to get 6 to 8 leaves, and even then go easy (see Chapter 9, "Getting to the Roots," for more information on fertilization).

STERILIZED SOIL FOR STARTING SEEDS

It's important that seeds get their start in soil that is free of diseases and weeds. The easiest way to eliminate these problems is to use soil that has been sterilized (also known as pasteurized) to kill any potential diseases or weeds that could cause problems to the germinating seeds. Luckily, sterile soil is easy to come by, as most commercial potting soil has been sterilized. Never reuse old potting soil for starting seeds unless you go to the trouble of resterilizing it first. See Chapter 9 (page 346) for more detail on sterilized soil and for a recipe for making your own.

CONTAINERS FOR STARTING SEEDS

You can start seeds in just about any container as long as it has holes in the bottom for drainage. In spring, many garden centers sell plastic flats (also called trays), that are ideal for starting seeds. Commercial plastic flats are usually 10 by 20 inches (25 by 51 cm). You can also use flowerpots or other recycled materials for pots. I like to use old milk cartons cut in half, with holes poked in the bottom. Containers previously used to grow plants may harbor seedling diseases. Be sure to clean any recycled or used seedling pot, tray, or flat with hot water and soap, and then dip it in bleach diluted in water (about 1 part bleach to 9 parts water) and rinse well with warm water. New containers that have never been filled with soil don't need cleaning.

Fill the container with soil and smooth out the surface. Where possible, sow seeds in rows rather than just scattering the seed. This slows

(**Top**) *The standard flat and plastic packs that fit into the flat. These are available at many garden centers or from garden supply catalogs.*
(**Bottom**) *This tray is designed for seedlings and features built-in plastic dividers for sowing in rows.*

diseases from spreading from plant to plant because it is harder for soil diseases to jump from row to row. It also enables you to plant more than one type of seed in one flat, but be sure to tag each row well. There are some plastic flats, or trays, that are designed for sowing seeds in rows. These work great as long as you keep the environment humid, warm, and never let the soil dry out. Use a small stick or board to make straight rows or minifurrows. I prefer to water the seedling soil prior to making rows and planting the seed. Watering before planting will help prevent washing out the seeds in the dry soil mix. It also improves the seed-to-soil contact, which is helpful.

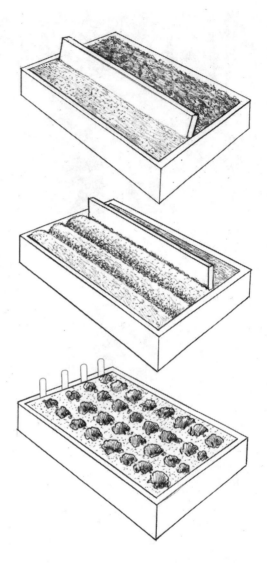

When sowing in flats, try to sow seeds in rows rather than just scattering the seed. This helps slow the spread of diseases. It also allows you to plant more than one type of seed in one flat in an organized manner, but be sure to tag each row well. Use a stick or small board to help define rows before planting.

Another pot option for growing seedlings is to use pots made of compressed peat moss, known as "peat pots." They have the advantage over plastic pots of being completely biodegradable. Besides the obvious environmental

(Top) *Peat pots are biodegradable but dry out much faster than other pots.*
(Right) *The soil block provides another option for a biodegradable pot. If you use the right soil mix in the block you can get good results.*
Photo courtesy of Charley's Greenhouse Supply.

advantage, there is the additional feature of avoiding transplant shock, because the plant in its pot may be set directly into the ground. This works best if you take care not to allow the edges of the pot to extend above the ground. If the edge of the peat pot extends above the soil surface, it can wick moisture away and dry out the whole underground part of the peat pot, damaging the root system. Also, peat pots tend to dry out more quickly than other pots, so keep a close eye on their watering needs. Peat pots are relatively low in cost but unlike plastic pots they can't be recycled.

Another environmentally sound approach is to use no pot at all. Instead, use "soil blocks." Making these requires a special tool that can turn your soil mix into a compressed block, a little less than 2 inches (5 cm) square, in which you directly plant the seed. By being compressed, the soil block stays together until it is time to transplant. Like the peat pot, soil blocks reduce transplant shock but also need more water than conventional pots. Many growers report problems with disintegration of the blocks, but others swear by them. The key to getting them to work seems to be in using the right soil mix, one that will stay together well. Soil blocks take some getting used to and some experimentation to make. Soil block tools run between $25 and $35.

While we are on the subject of environmentally sound seed pots, I also want to mention a simple wooden device that you use to make small pots out of strips of old newspaper. The process takes a little practice, but with a good technique, you can be churning out little paper pots for growing seedlings. This tool runs around $15 and is available from Gardener's Supply Company (800-863-1700; **www.gardeners.com**). Maybe it is just my poor technique, but my paper pots tend to fall apart before the plant is ready to go outside.

A number of plastic containers have been developed for transplanting seedlings. The most common are the multiple-pot containers that bedding plants are sold in at a garden center. They are usually made of a cheap, thin, molded plastic and have drainage holes. They come in twelve-packs, six-packs, and four-packs. Usually, they fit perfectly in the standard commercial plastic 10 by 20 inch (25 by 51 cm) flats mentioned earlier. If you have recently purchased spring bedding plants in these plastic pots, you may have some sitting around. They can be washed and reused for at least a few seasons before they start to split.

Similar to the "packs" are what are known as "plug" trays. These come in varying sizes and are formed sheets of pots. One sheet fits into a standard flat. These originally came from the commercial greenhouse industry, which uses plug trays in an automated seed-sowing system. If you can get ahold of the larger-celled trays, then you can use them to your advantage. Be sure to sow only one seed per plug hole in a plug tray.

There are also reusable Styrofoam trays with 24 to 40 cells per tray. These are good for starting seeds or for transplanting seedlings. Some come with a spongelike capillary mat that the container sits upon. The mat wicks water to the cells for self-watering as long as you keep it wet. Both Styrofoam and other types of plastic flats come with a clear plastic cover to help maintain humidity. If you use the cover, the seedlings will need little if any water. The Styrofoam setups usually run around $14 and work quite well.

SOWING THE SEEDS

There is no one right way to sow seeds. There are, however, lots of different ways to go about it. I prefer to sow a number of seeds initially into a small pot or flat or a milk carton cut sideways into a tray shape. As I mentioned earlier, I sow mine in rows. Then after they get about 3 to 4 true leaves (see the section "When to Transplant" later in this chapter), I transplant them into either cell packs or peat pots.

Everyone develops a personal sowing technique. The first mistake most people make is to drop the seeds too close together, creating overcrowding. This results in spindly seedlings that are fighting for light. It also makes a mess when it comes time to transplant these closely spaced seedlings and you find yourself trying to untangle this seedling riot. The distance

(Top) *The common "six-pack" is a great container to grow seedlings in until they are ready to transplant. Packs can be recycled for multiple uses if you wash them well between each use.*
(Middle) *These seedling-filled six-packs are sitting in the standard 10 inch by 20 inch flat.*
(Bottom) *The center tray is a plug tray or plug flat. Commercial growers commonly use these plugs for starting seeds.*

between seeds can vary greatly depending upon the size of the seed. I usually leave a minimum of $\frac{1}{3}$ of an inch (0.8 cm) between the seeds, but larger seeds need more room.

To sow seeds at the proper depth, you will often hear the rule that you should sow them twice as deep as they are wide. To make things a little more confusing, there are some seeds that prefer to not be buried under soil at all. To find out about each seed's special preferences, I either refer to a good propagation book or I often find helpful information right in the seed catalog (some are more informative than others).

The Super Seed Sower® is a great, low-cost tool to help you sow seeds precisely.

To plant a seed at the proper depth, some people sow the seeds on the surface and then poke the seed into the soil with a pencil or sharp object. Another, easier method is to not fill the pot, flat, or seedling tray all the way. Smooth the surface of the soil. Then sow the seeds. After that, carefully spread more soil mix over the seeds, adding enough soil to reach the desired depth (twice as deep as the seed is wide).

One tool I like to use, especially for small seed, is called the Super Seed Sower®, which looks like a small plastic trowel. It has a ratchet wheel that is turned with your thumb. This creates a vibration that bounces the seed out in an organized and controlled manner. It is sold in many gardening catalogs and usually goes for $6 to $10, which is money well spent.

There are also the more expensive electric vibrating seed-sowers that use a battery to power the tool. The vibration bounces the seeds out. I have found these imprecise and prefer the thumb-powered seeder. However, I know other greenhouse gardeners who love the electric seed-sowers.

For more precise sowing, I use a sharpened pencil with a slightly wetted tip. With the wet tip I can carefully pick up one seed at a time from a dry plate. The seed sticks to the pencil tip like a magnet. If everything works well, the seed drops off into the seedling soil when you ever so lightly brush the seed against the soil. You will need to clean the pencil tip and rewet it as needed. With a little practice, this can be a quick way to sow a small number of the smaller seeds right where you want them.

Seedlings flourish in high humidity. To maintain high humidity, many people slip the container into a clear plastic bag after planting. If you try this, your seeds will need much less water, so don't get carried away and overwater them.

Seedlings also need adequate light. When the seeds begin coming up, immediately remove the plastic bag and place them in a well-lit location. Keep a close watch: You don't want those seedlings short on light after they germinate, or they will become elongated and will bend toward the light. Then they are difficult to deal with.

AFTER GERMINATION

If the germinating plants begin to touch each other and look crowded, you may need to thin them out. It is best to thin by pinching or

HOW TO PLANT THE VERY TINY SEEDS

Some seeds of ornamental plants are so small that they are almost impossible to see with the naked eye. They might even resemble dust in the bottom of your seed packet. Don't despair. Here's how to deal with them:

1. Use a small clean pot for sowing. Be sure the pot has drainage holes in the bottom.
2. Fill the pot with virgin potting soil. Then firm the soil with your fingers.
3. Mix the seed in the packet with a teaspoon of granulated sugar, close the packet, and shake the mix of sugar and seeds.
4. Open the packet and hold it over the pot. Tap the packet lightly to release the sugar-seed mixture evenly over the top of the soil (or, better yet, use one of the seed sowers mentioned earlier).
5. Do not cover the seed with soil. Lightly press the seed into the surface of the soil with the bottom of a dry spoon.
6. Set the pot into a saucer filled with warm (not hot) water. The water will be absorbed automatically by the wicking action of the soil.
7. Cover the top of the pot with a piece of glass, plastic wrap, or a clear plastic bag to keep the soil moist and the air humid.
8. Keep the saucer full of water.
9. Place the pot in a very bright spot (but not direct sun), where the temperature is above 65°F (18°C).
10. As soon as the seeds have germinated, remove the cover and move the pot to a sunny spot.

A moistened pencil is a great way to pick up a small seed for sowing.

cutting out the excess seedlings with small, pointed-tip scissors. If you pull out the plants, it will disturb and injure the remaining plant roots. After the plants get 3 to 4 true leaves, it is time to transplant them into a small pot or directly into beds.

DIRECT SOWING AND THINNING

Some plants don't take to transplanting at all (see the above chart on planting requirements). When this is the case, it is better either to sow the seed directly into a peat pot, which limits the shock of transplanting, or to sow it directly into the pot or bed where the plant will be growing to maturity. The biggest problem gardeners have with direct sowing is sowing too thickly. This creates the extra chore of thinning. Failure to thin seedlings is an amazingly common problem. Some people just don't have the heart to kill a seedling. I admit it. I used to be guilty of not thinning my seedlings when they came up thickly. I would imagine the plants screaming and begging for another chance as I tossed them into the trash can. But without thinning, plants end up growing thick as a lawn and will never yield any harvest or flowers. So remember this rule: No thinning, no harvest. Over the years, I've learned that sometimes you have to be ruthless to be a good gardener. If you aren't, you soon end up with a garden that you don't particularly like. With a little ruthlessness, you'll be surprised how much more you enjoy gardening.

If you have trouble being ruthless with the thinning job, try gardening after a bad day at work or immediately after driving in heavy traffic. Be ruthless and take some of your daily frustrations out on a bed that needs thinning. You'll end up with a better-looking greenhouse garden, and you may find that the day's problems seem less troublesome. That's called horticultural therapy, and it is part of the magic of gardening.

Think about thinning if your plants are starting to become elongated or if each single plant is touching its neighboring plant. But rather than thinning, you may just need to do some transplanting.

TRANSPLANTING

Transplanting seedlings rather than planting seeds directly into a bed is an easy way to conserve on space. Think about it this way. If you plant directly into a bed or the final pot where the plant will be growing, it could tie up the bed or pot space for 6 to 14 weeks. Why waste precious bed space waiting for seed germination and initial growth? Use that space for mature, producing plants instead and grow small seedlings in a propagation area with an ideal environment until they are ready for transplanting.

Admittedly, some crops can't tolerate transplanting, but whenever possible, do it. It requires a bit of planning—at least a month or two in advance. See Chapter 7, "Scheduling," for help in planning. You must also be able to look at the space you are using to help predict when a bed or area will be freed up and readied for transplanting. It is ideal to have healthy-sized plants ready to place in a bed the same day old plants are removed. Before you put in new transplants, you'll probably want to renew the soil with some amendments. Refer to Chapter 9, "Getting to the Roots," for information on soil preparation.

Sometimes you will find that you have more seedlings ready to transplant than you have room. You must either throw them out (ruthlessly, remember?) or try giving them to friends with greenhouses or sunspaces. When I am growing edible greens for later transplanting and end up with too many plants, I often let them continue growing in the flat. Later, I harvest the small leaves for eating. These "gourmet greens" are good eating. Don't try this with all vegetables—for instance, you can't eat the leaf of the tomato plant—or with any ornamentals without first being sure the leaves are edible.

WHEN TO TRANSPLANT

The best time to transplant your seedlings is after the plants develop their second set of true leaves. You'll notice that the first set usually looks quite different than the rest of the plant leaves. These leaves, botanically known as cotyledons, were originally part of the seed and function only to provide food reserves to the developing plant. Don't be surprised when, after a few weeks, these cotyledon leaves turn yellow and drop off. The next set of leaves you see (after the cotyledon leaves) are called the first "true" leaves.

PLANTING REQUIREMENTS FOR VEGETABLES

Vegetable	Planting Method	Weeks to Transplanting	Soil Temperature for Germination
Beans	D	–	W
Beans, Fava	D	–	C
Beets	TPS	3 to 4	C
Cabbage	TP	4 to 6	C
Cantaloupe	TPS	3 to 4	W
Carrots	TPS	4 to 5	C
Celery	TP	7 to 10	M
Collards	TP	4 to 6	C
Eggplant	TP	6 to 10	W
Garlic	B	6 to 10	M
Kale	TP	4 to 6	C
Kohlrabi	TP	4 to 6	C
Lettuce*	TP	5 to 8	C
Okra	TP	5 to 9	W
Onions	B, TP	4 to 14	W
Parsley	TP	6 to 10	C
Peas	TPS	5 to 10	C
Peppers	TP	8 to 11	W
Radish	D	–	C
Spinach	TP	6 to 9	C
Swiss chard	TP	4 to 8	C
Tomatoes	TP	6 to 8	W
Turnips	TPS	4 to 8	C
Watermelon	TP	4 to 6	W

Planting Method Key

D =   Best if directly sown into bed and not transplanted.

TP =   Transplant to save time and space.

TPS = Can be transplanted with extreme care. If directly sown in a bed, it will probably need to be thinned.

B =   Started from bulb.

* =   Needs light to trigger germination.

Soil Temperature for Germination Key

C = Tolerates temperatures of 45 to 85°F (7 to 30°C).

M = Needs moderate temperature of 60 to 75°F (15 to 24°C).

W = Needs warm temperature of 70 to 75°F (21 to 24°C).

For information on flower propagation, look for your plant of interest in Chapter 8, "A Closer Look at the Plants."

If the roots of your seedlings are intertwined, place them in water to loosen their hold on each other and then gently pull apart.

Try not to let your seedlings remain too long in a small seedling flat or germinating pot. If a seedling is held too long in an increasingly crowded situation before it's transplanted, the stem might become hardened. On some plants, this may spell disaster when you

When transplanting, hold the seedling by the leaf. If you hold it by the stem you may damage the plant. Leaf damage may occur when you hold a seedling by its leaf, but a plant can withstand a damaged leaf more easily than a damaged stem.

grow the seedling to maturity. The hardened stem can cause poor growth characteristics. This is particularly true of plants in the cole crop family (cabbage, broccoli, cauliflower) and peppers. You might notice it on other plants, too. It is hard to tell you what amount of time is too long, but with practice and observation you will be able to tell. The stem becomes almost woody. The main concern is providing room for the plant to grow without a major interruption or competition. To avoid stem hardening, make an effort to give the growing plant plenty of room by up-potting before it becomes root bound and by occasionally fertilizing.

If you are a user of tobacco, be sure to wash your hands thoroughly with soap and warm water before transplanting petunias, nicotiana, datura, browallia, peppers, eggplant, and tomatoes. This will prevent your passing on the devastating disease called tobacco leaf mosaic, which can be spread from your fingers to these plants. See Chapter 10, "When Things Go Wrong," for more information.

Prior to transplanting the seedlings, water them in their original container. Dig deeply and gently adjacent to the seedling with a pencil or a dibble. A dibble is a transplanting tool, a round piece of wood with a sharpened point much like a pencil without the lead. Dibbles can be as fat as a finger or as skinny as a pencil. Make your own out of a dowel. Using this tool (or your pencil) remove one plant at a time while gently holding the leaf. Get as much root as possible as you pull up. Do not clean the soil off the roots, because this could cause damage to them. If you have a situation with many closely planted seedlings with their roots intertwined, place them in water, which will loosen the roots' hold on each other. To prevent their being damaged from drying out, place the plants on a moist newspaper or towel. Never pull out more than you can transplant in a few minutes, because dry air will permanently damage the roots. Don't hesitate to discard small or spindly plants or those with damaged or poorly developed roots.

You will be tempted to hold the seedling by the stem. Avoid this temptation, because you can damage the stem even with slight pressure while transplanting. Stem damage is hard for a plant to overcome. Yes, leaf damage will also likely occur when you hold the seedling by its leaf, but a plant can easily recover from a damaged leaf.

Using your dibble or pencil, make a hole in the soil of the new growing location (either another pot or a bed).

Tuck all of the roots into the hole with your dibble or pencil. Plant the seedling just slightly deeper than it was in the germinating container. Don't jam roots into a hole that is too shallow. Finally, use the dibble or pencil to collapse the soil around the hole and use your fingers or pencil to gently firm it around the stem and roots. Be careful not to compress the soil too hard around the new seedling. Is the plant sitting upright? Yes? Good.

After transplanting, gently water or mist the plants in their new spot. Avoid hard sprays that wash out or flatten the newly set seedlings. Protect the seedlings from drafts or cool or high temperatures.

Slugs love to munch on little seedlings. If you have a slug problem, you may want to put a slug trap near the seedlings for protection. Also check for aphids under the leaves and leaf tips; they love to congregate for feeding frenzies on new seedlings. (See Chapter 10, "When Things Go Wrong," for more information on dealing with these types of problems.)

(A) *Use a pencil, dibble (rounded piece of wood), or your finger to prepare a hole for the seedling large enough to accommodate its roots.*

(B) *Using the pencil or dibble, gently loosen the soil around the seedling (hold the plant by the leaf) and then carefully lift the roots and plant from the soil. Do not shake off excess soil.*

(C) *Set the seedling in the hole at approximately the same depth it was previously. Gently collapse soil from around the hole onto the roots, then firm the soil with your hands around the plant so that it stands upright. Don't pack the soil too hard around the plant. Lightly water the soil and maintain a high humidity (or occasionally mist) for the next few days.*

All of these plants originated from cuttings.

GIVING PLANTS THE SLIP WHILE CLONING AROUND

An alternative to starting plants from seed is to grow new plants from a cutting of the parent plant. Almost everyone has witnessed someone rooting a cutting from a plant. Who hasn't seen an ivy, a coleus, or a geranium in a glass of water happily growing roots? This practice is usually done with houseplants, but it also works fine for starting certain vegetables and subtropical greenhouse plants.

When you start a plant from a slip of another plant, you are basically cloning the parent plant, a common horticultural practice. And to think that people got so excited over cloning the sheep named Dolly. Wait until the press investigates the horticultural world!

Growing plants from cuttings is an easy way to get a new plant from an old plant. The resulting plant is an exact genetic duplicate of the original plant. It is usually faster than growing the plant from seed, and often it is much easier. It is also a cheap way to acquire more plants. I have propagated cuttings of a favorite tomato and European greenhouse cucumber with great success. Why propagate vegetables from cuttings when they are easy to start from seed? Well, it is a great way to create offspring from a hybrid vegetable that doesn't come true from seed. Also, it can save money. For example, European cucumber seed (also called forcing, or greenhouse, cucumbers) is incredibly expensive—sometimes more than a dollar per seed!

Some plants are so easy to root that all you have to do is set a piece of the stem and leaves into a glass of water. A good example is the multicolored leafy houseplant, coleus. Not all are easy to root, though, and some require a more exacting environment for rooting than simply water. By experimenting with different plants, you'll quickly find which are fast to root and which are more of a challenge.

The first step in taking a cutting is to select a healthy, disease-free, pest-free parent plant. If your prospective plant is showing any signs of disease, bugs, or poor health, don't use it for cuttings. You'll just pass on the problems!

The best place to take a cutting off a plant is from a tip. The tip doesn't have to be from the very top of the plant; it can also come from side branches.

To get started, you need to acquire one more thing to assist you in creating your clones: rooting powder. Rooting powder contains a synthetic plant hormone that is based upon naturally occurring plant substances. This hormone helps to stimulate the formation of roots. Rooting powder comes in different formulations for different types of plants. Addition-

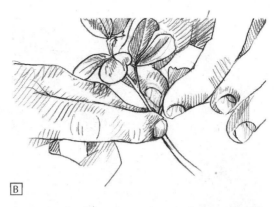

(A) *With a sharp knife, take a 3- to 5-inch- (8- to 13-cm-) long stem-cutting from the parent plant. If the cutting has any flowers or flower buds, pinch them off.*

(B) *Pinch off any large leaves from the lower end of the cutting; leave three or four smaller to medium-sized leaves toward the tip.*

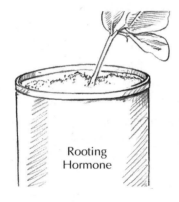

Rooting Hormone

(C) *Dip the bottom of the cut stem into rooting powder; shake off any excess.*

(D) *Using a pencil, poke holes about 3 inches (8 cm) deep into a half sand, half peat or pure perlite mix in a pot. Place each cutting in a hole and firm the mix around the cuttings so they stand upright. You can (and should) fit many cuttings; the minimum space between each can be as little as $^3/_4$ of an inch. Maintain a humid environment by misting cuttings regularly. You can place a plastic bag over the cuttings to keep humidity levels high (a good option if you don't have a automatic misting system). Place the pot in a warm, bright spot, but not in direct sun. An ideal spot is on a heating mat with a mist system (see "Propagation Bench," page 78).*

ally, rooting hormone usually comes mixed with a fungicide to prevent the cut portion of the stem from rotting, which is a common problem. You can often find rooting powder in catalogs or garden centers. A small aluminum envelope usually runs around $4. Rooting powder can really make all the difference between success and failure when it comes to rooting cuttings. One brand name that gives consistent good results is Hormodin I.

An alternative to rooting hormone is to brew up some willow tea. Willow extract has been shown to have great root-promoting properties. To make it, steep many fresh, small wil-

low twigs in hot water for 48 hours; then set your cuttings in this solution for 24 hours before placing them in the rooting soil. Water the cuttings daily with more of this willow tea. This willow method works much better

This rooted cutting is ready to be potted up!

than nothing, but not nearly as well as the rooting powder.

Along with your rooting powder (or willow tea), gather a clean or new flowerpot (or any other appropriate container with drainage holes), clean sand (or perlite or vermiculite), peat moss, a plastic bag, a sharp knife, and a pencil. Fill the pot to a depth of about 4 inches (10 cm) with the following 2-to-1 rooting mix: two parts sand, perlite, or vermiculite to one part peat moss. Water the mixture until the mix holds water. Place the pot on a saucer to catch the water that drains out of the bottom.

With a sharp knife, take a 3- to 5-inch-long (8- to 13-cm-long) stem cutting from the parent plant. If the cutting has any flowers or flower buds, remove them. Trim any large leaves off the lower end of the cutting; leave 3 or 4 smaller to medium-sized leaves toward the tip.

Dip the cut portion of the stem into your rooting powder and shake off any surplus. Next, using a pencil, poke a hole about 3 inches (8 cm) deep into the rooting mix in the container. Place the cutting in the hole and firm the mix around the cutting so it stands up-

right. In one pot, you can (and should) fit many cuttings; the minimum spacing can be as little as $^3/_4$ of an inch. For instance, one 4-inch (10-cm) pot could hold up to 10 cuttings. Always prepare more cuttings than you need, as not every cutting will grow roots.

Place the pot or container in a warm, bright spot, but not in direct sun. A perfect spot is on a heating mat with a mist system (see the "Propagation Bench," discussion in Chapter 2). Keep the rooting mix consistently moist; it should never dry out. High humidity is a key to greatly speeding up rooting and preventing the leaves on these rootless stems from wilting. You can help to increase the humidity by placing a clear plastic bag loosely over the pot. There are also clear plastic domes available through some greenhouse and gardening catalogs and stores. Humidity levels can also be maintained if you can mist the cuttings on a daily basis when you don't have a misting system.

Rooting can take anywhere from 4 weeks to 6 months, depending upon the plant. If the plant has no roots even after many months but is forming what looks like callus tissue, don't give up! Callus tissue is a fleshy, whitish growth on the cut end and can be the precursor of root formation. This is not uncommon to see when rooting plants.

After 3 weeks or more, check your cuttings by gently pulling up on them. If they seem to move easily up out of the hole when pulled, they have not rooted. Check again in a couple of weeks. If they seem anchored and won't budge when lightly pulled, they may have roots. If you suspect your cuttings have rooted, carefully dig the plant out of the mix to see for sure. If not rooted, carefully replace it. If you see callus tissue around the cut end, it often means roots will soon be forming, but some plants will never form roots even though they do a great job of forming callus tissue. Still, if you see this occurring, replace the plant and wait a few more weeks.

If your cuttings are wilting, try to increase the humidity with more misting. If the wilting continues, you may have left too many leaves on the cutting. Consider pruning another large leaf or two off of the cutting (usually toward the bottom of the stem). If the wilting remains severe after a day or more, it is probably best to start over by using new cuttings with fewer leaves. Also, try misting more often and keeping the temperature moderate. If the bottom of the cutting seems to have rotted, toss it out because it will never root. Rotting may be an indication of too much water in the rooting medium, or it can be an indication of not using rooting hormone or not covering the cut portion well enough with the powder.

If your cutting has a good set of roots, carefully transplant it into a small pot with new potting soil, taking care not to disturb the roots as you move it. Keep this newly rooted plant on the moist side for the first week or two and mist it often until the plant gets used to the real world.

Many (but not all) plants can be propagated from cuttings. Some easy plants to try include coleus, ivy, geranium, ficus, begonia, and even tomato. Don't be afraid to try almost any plant after you've succeeded with the easier plants. Next thing you know, you'll have a plant-production factory in full operation. When you really get good at rooting cuttings, you can even try your hand at propagating your favorite outside trees and shrubs in the same manner. The best time to take cuttings from

The trees in this 1979 photo were propagated in a home greenhouse, all from cuttings. Today, some of these trees are close to 25 feet tall.

outside plants is 5 to 6 weeks after the last frost. It is great to utilize your greenhouse to provide plants for your outside landscape. Who knows—you may want to go into the nursery business.

As you gain experience, you may want to try rooting plants from just the leaf stems (petioles) and from the leaves themselves (see instructions in many houseplant books under African violets).

There is more to plant propagation than I can cover in this one chapter. If you want to read more about propagating plants, there are many good books solely devoted to the subject (see the "Bibliography and Further Reading" at the end of this book).

There is an inherent joy in starting your own plants. This is also a good way to perpetuate and pass around a special plant as a gift or to keep a plant alive that may have been in the family for years. Plant propagation is a great family project for involving kids. Be careful, however, because it is addictive. Have fun!

CHAPTER 6

POLLINATION

In nature, insects, birds, wind, and even bats pollinate flowers. In the greenhouse, we usually lack these natural pollinators that otherwise ensure adequate fruit or seed production, so we must do the job of pollinating ourselves. Pollination is comparable to conception, the first step to creating a new individual. Why learn about pollination? In order to get plants to produce fruits, and occasionally, seeds, you must understand the critical role pollination plays in successful fruit and seed production. Since the main reason greenhouse gardeners need to know about pollination is for the production of fruits, most of this chapter concerns the growing of edible fruits rather than ornamental plants.

WHY PLANTS FLOWER

Pollination is a primary step in a plant's reproduction cycle, the result of which is the formation of a seed that grows into a new individual plant. But before any pollination can take place, the plant must flower. The flower is a plant's sexual reproductive part. The flowering response is usually triggered by maturity (unlike humans who often try to propagate without any matu-

rity). In the case of plants, maturity means a plant has reached a certain stage in its growth. This type of maturity-response flowering is most common for vegetables. There are, however, a number of plants that can also be triggered to flower by the length of the night (see the discussion on "photoperiodism" on page 13 in Chapter 1).

One interesting thing about the plant kingdom is that stress can also trigger flowering. This is hard-wired into many living things. In plants, it can be caused by the growing environment; low nutrient levels, too low or too high temperatures, wilting, and competition may sometimes induce premature flowering.

Conversely, luxuriant amounts of nitrogen and water can sometimes delay flowering; this is often true with tomatoes. A greenhouse gardener should be concerned about when flowering takes place because a plant that flowers too early or too late often produces lower harvests.

ENVIRONMENTAL CONDITIONS FOR POLLINATION

Pollination seems to work best in the greenhouse on the brighter days between 10 A.M.

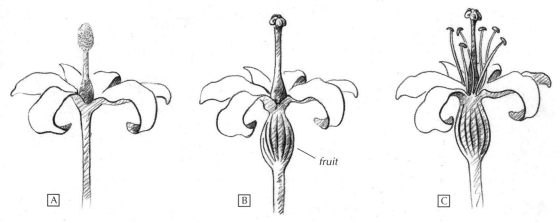

Male and Female Flowers
(A) *Male flower. The stalk in the center of the flower is tipped with yellow powder, which is the pollen.*
(B) *Female flower (typical for the cucumber family). Notice the bulbous, immature fruit sitting under the petals.*
(C) *A "complete" flower. It has both the male parts and female parts in the same flower.*

and 4 P.M. Optimally, it should take place at least once every other day. Unlike most things in life, it's impossible to overdo the pollination job.

Try to avoid pollinating flowers when the temperature drops below 55°F (13°C) in the greenhouse, because doing so may damage the pollen and greatly decrease the number of fruits produced. This is one reason it is more difficult to grow tomatoes in the middle of winter in a solar-heated greenhouse. Even though the plants may look fine, the poor little flowers just can't set fruit when the nights are consistently cold. Temperatures above 90°F (32°C) can have the same effect on the ability of flowers to produce fruit. At certain times of the year, your greenhouse may run above and below these temperatures. Scheduling can make a big difference in the ability of your plants to grow their best. Adequate ventilation and cooling in summer is helpful for good fruit set. In the cool-winter greenhouse, you may find it wise to grow fewer fruiting crops and more leafy and root types that don't need to produce fruit (see Chapter 7, "Scheduling").

WHAT AND HOW TO POLLINATE

In order to become a master pollinator in your greenhouse or sunspace, you need to learn some simple flower physiology first.

FLOWER PHYSIOLOGY

There are two major types of flowers. The first is the "complete flower," which contains both male and female parts. Some examples of plants of this type include tomatoes, peppers, and eggplant. These types of flowers are the easiest to pollinate because the male and female parts are often adjacent to each other in the same flower. This makes for easy pollination.

The other flower type is (you guessed it!) the "incomplete flower," in which the male and female parts are each in a different flower. Pollinating these flowers involves the physical transfer of the pollen from the male part in one flower to the female part in another (sometimes using a small paintbrush to transfer the pollen).

COMMON VEGETABLES WITH COMPLETE FLOWERS

Beans. Most common garden varieties will

Tomato flowers are "complete" flowers—they have both male and female parts in each flower. All you have to do to pollinate them is tap them with a stick every other morning.

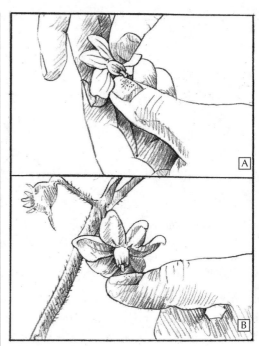

The best way to pollinate eggplant:
(A) Tap some pollen onto your thumbnail.
(B) Gently press your pollen-laden thumbnail against the center element of other eggplant flowers. This center part is the female flower part known as the "stigma."

produce a good crop without pollination. If you find your variety is not setting fruit, try changing to a more common variety. Runner beans are one exception; they seem to require pollination and are not a good choice for greenhouse growing because pollination is difficult.

Okra. Okra sets pods without being pollinated and produces a beautiful flower.

Peas. No pollination is required.

Tomatoes. An easy crop to pollinate. Use a long, thin stick about 1 foot (30.48 cm) long. A $\frac{1}{2}$-inch (1.3 cm) dowel will do fine. Tap the yellow blossoms gently, and fruit will generally set if the temperature conditions are correct. If you suspect that some of your tomato plants have a disease, always pollinate these plants last. Electric vibrating gadgets are available to commercial growers that work fine, but so does a stick—and at a much lower cost. A large greenhouse full of tomatoes can be pollinated in a short time. One or two light taps of your pollinating stick on each cluster of blossoms is sufficient.

Peppers. As with tomatoes, tapping flowers will help fruit set, but pollination will often occur by itself if the temperatures are right.

Eggplant. Eggplants are more variable than other plants when it comes to fruit set. Some varieties don't seem to need pollination, whereas others do well with a good tap, much like tomatoes. If you are having a problem with eggplants setting fruit, try this method: Find a flower that is shedding a large amount of pollen (a yellow dust will fall from the flower when touched). Put your thumbnail under this flower and knock some pollen onto your nail. Touch the pollen on your thumbnail to the tip of the female element on each blossom. The female element is the green stalk in the center of the flower surrounded by the yellow pollen parts. Apply more pollen to your nail after pollinating about four flowers, and repeat the process on other blossoms.

COMMON VEGETABLES WITH INCOMPLETE FLOWERS

Squash. First, let's do some sex I.D.: To locate the male flower, look for a thin stalk (or flower stem) leading up to the yellow petals at the base of the flower. Within the flower you will find a shorter stalk tipped with yellow powder (pollen). The female flower is easy to recognize. It always has a little immature squash fruit immediately below the flower petals at the point where the petals are attached to the stem. If pollen is not transferred to the tip of the female element on the female flower, the little fruit will not grow and will eventually begin to rot from the tip. To get the best fruit set, pollinate the flowers as soon as they first open.

There are a number of ways to transfer the pollen from the male to the female flower. Gardeners have long used a small paintbrush. Years ago, an old-time plant breeder in Cheyenne once saw me pollinating with a paintbrush, and he looked appalled. He said, "What the heck are you messing with that brush for? You don't need that to pollinate." I was fresh out of college and felt about two inches tall. But he showed me a wonderful technique for pollinating that has no need for brushes—especially when you are working with squash.

Here is what you do. Simply pluck from the squash a freshly opened male flower, stalk and all. Then, while holding the green stem, strip all the yellow petals off. In the center of where the petals used to be you will find a stalk (botanically called a "filament") tipped with yellow pollen (technically called an "anther"). Holding the green portion or bottom of the stalk like a wand, you can touch this pollen to

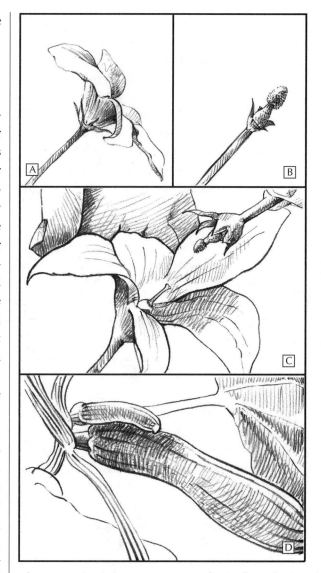

Try this easy method for pollinating squash:
(A) Distinguish the male from the female flower. Then, pluck a freshly opened male flower at the base of its stem.
(B) Peel the petals away from the stalk; leave the the yellow, powder-like pollen on the tip of the stalk (anther and filament).
(C) Locate a freshly opened female flower. Dab the pollen onto the tip of the female flower's center stalk (the stigma).
(D) Success will be confirmed by fruit enlarging over the next several days. If you have a small fruit that never enlarges, it was not pollinated successfully, especially if it develops a soft, brown tip.

the tip of the female element (technically called the "stigma," topped with what is called the "style" on the female flower).

With this method, there is usually enough pollen on one male flower to pollinate two or three female flowers with ease. It only takes a few seconds to do each flower. You can also sometimes use pollen from one type of squash to pollinate another type, for instance, by using a yellow squash to pollinate a green zucchini. I should point out that this is not a good idea if you are growing the fruit primarily to harvest the seeds resulting from this pollination.

Within days, you'll know if your pollination has worked. If it hasn't, you'll notice that the fruit will begin to rot from the blossom end inward. If this occurs, pick the rotting fruit and toss it out.

There is an occasional problem of having only one sex of flowers appearing at one time. This usually occurs with only the male flowers appearing, with no female flowers around to pollinate. All you can do when this happens is wait for the females, which often come as the plant matures. If all you have are male flowers, you can do what many do in Southwest cuisine: Eat them (check out a Southwestern cookbook for recipes that use squash blossoms).

If you want to see why flowers get pollinated, look closely into a male squash blossom. There you will find a bowl-like structure directly in the center of the flower, which contains a small amount of clear liquid. This is the nectar. If you taste it, you will see it has the flavor of sugar water (it's OK—squash nectar is edible). This is what the bees are after.

There is a new type of summer squash that does not require pollination. It is available from the Cook's Garden catalog, under the unromantic name "Type 1406." My experiments with this variety have not panned out with much

European forcing cucumbers produce high yields and need no pollination.

success as far as growing in a greenhouse is concerned. Keep your eyes out for future varieties that do not require pollination and thus need less of your time. At least Type 1406 was a start in the right direction. Perhaps in the future with more people gardening in greenhouses, there will be more demand for plants bred for greenhouse gardening.

Cucumbers. Europeans have developed a cucumber specifically for greenhouse growing known as the European forcing cucumber. It doesn't need to be pollinated at all and yields great crops. For more information, read about cucumbers in Chapter 8, "A Closer Look at the Plants." I recommend that you stick to these greenhouse forcing cucumbers. If you decide to grow the regular garden-variety cucumbers in your greenhouse, they will need pollination in order to set fruit. The process is identical to the pollination of squash except that everything is much smaller. Baby boomers get out your reading glasses! Some people may need tweezers. It is hard to pollinate cucumbers, but not impossible. The task requires some time and energy, so you might want to reconsider the benefits of the high-yielding European forcing cucumbers. The seed is expensive but worth the high yield that these plants provide.

Melons. Melons and cantaloupe are also pollinated like squash and, like the cucumber, they have much smaller flowers. To identify the female flower, look for the small, often fuzzy, immature melon or cantaloupe directly behind the female flower. The male flower will just have a stem up to the flower and will lack the small fuzzy fruit behind the petals. As with squash, transfer the pollen to the center of the female flower by either using a small paintbrush or by plucking the male flower stalk, as described earlier for squash.

Currently, there are no varieties of melons that do not need pollination; maybe someday that will change. If you want to grow melons or cantaloupe, then you must get good at this because the fruit will not set if the flowers are not pollinated.

Setting Fruit Artificially

Synthetic chemical hormones are available in a spray form that, when applied to blossoms, will often cause the fruit to grow even without pollination. These sprays work particularly well with tomatoes and not so well with melons and squash.

There have been reports of much-lower quality (soft, misshapen fruit with poor color and storage characteristics) when the fruits are triggered to grow artificially. In view of the quality risks and the always-present questions associated with using any synthetic chemicals on food, I don't recommend the use of these chemicals. Stick with good old-fashioned hand-pollination of blossoms.

Pollinating Tropical and Subtropical Fruiting Plants

The pollination of tropical and subtropical fruiting plants is a little trickier than for the more common fruits and vegetables. With these plants, you will find the terms "self-fruitful" and "self-unfruitful." A self-fruitful plant is one that can set its own fruit, either by providing its own pollen or by just automatically setting fruit without needing to be pollinated. Bananas are a good example of this. You simply grow a fruiting variety, and when it reaches a certain stage of maturity, it goes to flower and then sets fruit.

A self-unfruitful plant requires pollinating by another variety of the same plant, as is the case with avocados, for example. This means that you must grow two different varieties and cross-pollinate the flowers by hand in order to get the fruit to set. This can take up a lot of greenhouse space. However, you could attempt to graft a second variety onto one plant to accomplish this.

Often, you can choose whether the plant is self-fruitful or self-unfruitful by just growing the right variety. For instance, many fig tree varieties need insect pollination to set fruit. Some fig varieties, however, do not need pollination to set fruit. As you might have guessed, this is the type you want for a greenhouse. So, simply selecting the right subtropical or tropical variety will make all the difference in whether you will harvest fruit. Be sure to read the catalog descriptions well when you are purchasing any subtropical or tropical fruiting plants.

TROUBLESHOOTING POLLINATION PROBLEMS

Problem	Possible Causes
Poor fruit set	Temperature above 90°F (32°C). Sudden cold or cool temperatures. Very dry air.
Blossom drop	High temperatures. Cool temperatures. Low humidity and soil moisture. Nearby combustion fumes, generally from a heater. Plant stress.
Misshapen fruit	Incomplete pollination (not enough pollen transferred). Cool nights below 55°F (13°C).
Cracked fruit	Alternating high and low temperature. Usually not due to pollination.
Low numbers of blossoms	Too much nitrogen. Too cold.
Fruit rotting	No pollination. You used flowers that have been open too long and the pollen was not viable. Always use the freshest flowers when pollinating.
Immature, shriveled fruit	Usually with cucumbers; no pollination. Too many mature cucumbers on the vine may cause this, so keep the vines well-picked.

For more specific information on pollination of these plants, please refer to Chapter 8, "A Closer Look at the Plants."

FINAL THOUGHTS ON POLLINATION

Pollination is one of the necessities of growing under cover and is something that food-growing greenhouse gardeners quickly master. I don't know why, but whenever I am engrossed in morning pollination, it seems that a bit of pollen always lands on my nose. Perhaps my nose is a magnet. It takes a while before a good friend will tell me there's something on my nose (only good friends tell you when you look bad). Over time, I have decided that a bit of pollen on the end of the nose is an initiation rite for any serious greenhouse pollinator. So here's to some pollen on your nose, too!

CHAPTER 7

SCHEDULING

❧

IN SOME RESPECTS, SIMPLY HAVING A GREEN-house or a sunspace might mean that you could grow any plant, any time you wish. Most of us are motivated to have a greenhouse solely by the possibility of eating an off-season tomato or a picking a fragrant bouquet of flowers when it is snowing outside. The truth is, you can grow just about anything at any time of the year, but there are times when proper scheduling can make things work more efficiently, when plants respond best, or when your greenhouse could consume less energy by following a specific schedule.

SCHEDULING CONSIDERATIONS: BEFORE YOU BEGIN

Scheduling growing cycles for a greenhouse is far from an exact science. Much depends on your climate and the nature of your own greenhouse environment. But there are a few basic tenets you might consider before you begin planning and charting your growing schedules.

OPTIMIZING ENERGY AND YIELD EFFICIENCY

If you schedule the growing of fruiting crops such as tomatoes to coincide with the warmer temperatures of March through October, you will need very little supplementary heat to get a good crop. This is especially true for green-houses utilizing at least some concepts of solar heating.

Let's use tomatoes as an example. If you have your heart set on growing a tomato crop during the absolute coldest time of the year, usually November through February, then you will likely need to keep the temperatures above 50°F (10°C) to enable the flowers to set fruit. Even in the best-designed solar greenhouse this will most likely require the addition of supple-mentary heat. In addition, tomatoes like high light intensities, so this may also require you to consider supplemental lighting because of the shorter days of winter, especially if you live in an area with a cloudy winter. If you don't pursue adding extra heat (and light), then you are likely to see poor yields. Why fight it, when instead you can schedule an alternative edible plant that thrives in the cold winter months?

This is where scheduling comes in. It's all a matter of fitting the right plant into the right environment at the right time. Even in a cold greenhouse, every single month (including the coldest ones!) can be filled with the activity of sowing, growing, and enjoying plants that produce both food and flowers—but only if you schedule them right.

WATCH FOR THE PLANT'S BIOLOGICAL CLOCK

Some plants (usually certain ornamental flowering plants, but not limited only to them) require specific day and night lengths in order to flower or respond in some other way (see the discussion of photoperiodism on page 13 Chapter 1). In other words, a plant's response or its lack of response (such as flowering or growth habit) might be triggered by the length of darkness it is subjected to. This tends to be more noticeable in certain ornamental plants than edible plants. For instance, it is hard to get petunias to produce a lot of flowers in the wintertime unless they are given supplemental lighting. Garden-variety snapdragons grown in winter will often grow only leaves, with little or no sign of flowers developing (unless you grow special greenhouse varieties). This seasonal timing may have other effects. For example, figs often drop their leaves for a few months in winter and go dormant.

In time, you will start to notice that plants have their own schedules, no matter what you may want them to do. You will see that they continue to do certain things at specific times of the year. You learn to expect certain cycles in your plants after gardening in a greenhouse for a few years. In this chapter, I will try to shorten the learning curve and help you fit the right plant into nature's scheme of things. If everything goes right, you'll end up with a real orchestration of colorful flowers, herbs, and food that are in concert with each environment and each plant's own biological clock. A growing and planting schedule that works right will bring you new wonders to enjoy every month.

After you select the right plants (see Chapter 4), learning how to schedule planting and growing cycles will help you master the art of greenhouse gardening.

HEED THE SEASON

I have found that in most temperate zones of the United States there are two distinct seasons: the cool season, from mid-October through mid-March, and the warm season, from mid-March through mid-October. This is a good estimation for most places; however, you will want to adapt this to your own particular area over time. You will find that fruiting crops—those plants that produce an edible fruit (yes, tomato is a fruit)—usually do their best in the warm-season months. These months are characterized by longer days, more light, and warm to hot temperatures. Fruiting crops are not efficient producers in winter, but if you

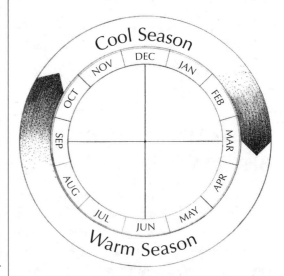

Understanding and planning for the two main greenhouse seasons will maximize your yields and productivity, especially if your greenhouse is primarily solar heated or runs cool in the winter. Begin planning for the changes in seasons at least one month before they actually occur.

want to grow them in the cool season, always put plants in the warmer areas of the greenhouse (see page 109 "Crop Layout and Harvesting" in Chapter 3). The warmer your greenhouse is—up to 85°F (29°C) in the day and no colder than 65°F (18°C) at night—the better your fruiting crops will grow. If you plan to provide supplemental heat to your greenhouse to grow fruiting crops in winter, think about the possibility that you may be spending $10 on heat to get $5 worth of tomatoes.

Conversely, cole crops (cabbage, broccoli, and the like), leafy vegetables, and root-producing vegetables all thrive in the cool-season greenhouse environment, when the night temperature might consistently drop below 50°F (10°C) but not below freezing. For instance, lettuce, grown in place of tomatoes during the cool season, might produce $10 worth of lettuce for $5 worth of heat. In the case of a solar-heated greenhouse, it would be $10 worth of lettuce for the cost of free heat.

I'm not saying, "Don't grow fruiting crops in the cool season." I'm only trying to point out which crops will do better and what kind of environment is needed, given the season. I usually rip out most of my fruiting crops in late September, but I often leave a few token tomatoes and peppers. They don't do much, but it's nice to have an occasional tomato from a plant that hardly produces more than four fruits all winter because of cool nights. Even if you don't start your tomato plants until February, you will still be eating fresh tomatoes about the time everyone else is just planting them outside.

Also, I'm not saying, "Never grow leafy and root crops in the warm season." You can still grow many of those crops in the warm season, even though it's a more optimum time to be growing fruits. I find the quality of cool-loving vegetables declines when they are grown

A bed (or part of a bed) that is declining in productivity can be ripped out and replaced with new plants or transplants. This allows for a succession of bountiful harvests.

warm to hot. Of course, growing cool-loving plants may likely be more efficient outside from March to October, depending upon where you live. Remember to think about efficient food production when you are growing in a greenhouse space.

For planning efficient planting and harvests, see the schedules beginning on page 163.

THE SECRET TO GOOD WINTER GROWING

In the heart of winter, when days are short and cold, I've noticed that seedlings grow in slow motion, as if they were in molasses. Plants often won't perk up until late February. I've learned that if I want my greenhouse to look good in the middle of winter, action should be taken in late August through September. Plants need to get their root systems established before the cool nights and short days set in, around mid-October into November; this is especially true for solar-heated greenhouses or greenhouses running cooler in winter.

Plan out and start your winter crops in late August into early September. Procrastinators

Summer is a great time to grow tropical plants in the greenhouse. An ornamental banana plant (left) sports beautiful red leaves; the banana plant on the right is producing fruit.

can even put it off until late September to early October, though with less success. After October, the window of opportunity is just about shut. The earlier you start your winter plants (no earlier than late August, however), the better. You may think this all sounds easy enough, but it isn't. Winter is the last thing you are thinking about in late August. It is hard to rip out some of your summer greenhouse plants that have been thriving. I don't mean to imply that you should rip everything out, but you have to make some hard decisions to make room for more appropriate crops for the coming cool growing season, and you must do it before the end of October. It is always best to start pulling the summer plants that show higher levels of insect infestation or disease. Try to leave some of the healthier summer

plants that are already growing in your warmer greenhouse microclimates. When you get an early start on plants for winter, they seem more able to tolerate the cold and continue to put on growth.

So, the secret to good winter growing is to get the cold-tolerant plants started in late August through early September and plan to make room for them as they grow.

SUMMER: WHAT TO DO WITH YOUR GREENHOUSE

Sometimes people aren't quite sure how to use their greenhouse in summer. This can be a time when the greenhouse suffers because the outside garden requires attention. For people who live in northern areas with a short growing season, the summer greenhouse provides a place to grow crops that might be difficult to produce outside. There are many places both in the North and in the high country where tomatoes, cantaloupes, melons, and long-season squashes have trouble reaching maturity in the outside garden before the first frost attacks. This presents a great opportunity when you have a greenhouse.

All too often, people abandon the greenhouse in summer because of hot interior temperatures. This is unfortunate and the result of faulty design. It can be corrected, however, with proper ventilation, cooling systems, and as a last resort, shading (see Chapter 1, "The Greenhouse or Sunspace Environment").

Besides using it to lengthen the growing season, then, how can you best utilize the summer greenhouse? The summer greenhouse allows you to go tropical! Consider growing some exotic tropical edible crops, such as figs, citrus, banana, and guava. This is the place to grow some of the more exotic perennial ornamental plants, such as angel's-trumpet, jasmine, bird-of-paradise, Amazon lily, croton, passionflower, chenille plant, and gardenia. The summer greenhouse allows you to grow and harvest vegetables and herbs much earlier and in greater abundance than outside (especially if you live in a short-season area).

Then again, there is no law that says you have to use your greenhouse in the summer. You might simply find it easier to let much of your greenhouse rest during the summer and use it as a living area with just a few plants inside. With some shade cloth strung over the outside or summer plants providing shade, you can keep the temperature comfortable for sitting and relaxing in a cool, quiet place, surrounded with shade-loving houseplants for a touch of green.

GROWING PLANTS FOR THE OUTSIDE GARDEN

Millions of people spend millions of dollars every spring at their local garden center buying bedding plants and vegetable transplants for the outside garden. Now that you have a greenhouse, you can grow your own for very little money. Giving plants a head start in your greenhouse will greatly increase the food and flowers that you can produce outside. And the farther north you live, the more important this becomes. Even a small greenhouse can produce hundreds of seedling transplants for outside, enough for you and your neighbors to enjoy.

Growing your own spring seedlings means you won't be buying them. Another plus is that homegrown plants are generally of better quality than store-bought transplants. I've come across many people with small greenhouses who sell their plants at local stores, swap meets, and food co-ops for some extra spending money.

GETTING STARTED

First, go back to Chapter 5, "Plant Propagation," for the basics on starting seeds. When it comes to containers, I have had the best transplants when I grow the plants in a pot $1\frac{1}{2}$ to 2 inches (3.8 to 5 cm) square. Growing seedlings in extremely small pots can often lead to stunted, root-bound plants. There are many types of pots on the market, and there are a number of homemade containers you can use for growing transplants. The main thing is that the pots all have drainage holes in the bottom.

If you end up using a peat pot and plan on setting the whole pot into the ground, be sure to slash a few cuts in the side of the pot to help the roots escape. Additionally, check that the whole pot is buried under the ground. If any portion is above the soil surface after transplanting, a wicking action can occur that draws moisture from the pot into the air. I've come across quite a few peat pots that never decomposed in the garden soil because all the gardener did was pop them in the ground.

No matter what pot you use, pay special attention to watering. It is amazing how fast a seedling can dry out on a warm, sunny day in your greenhouse. Peat pots, soil blocks, and clay pots will tend to dry out more readily than plastic containers. Soil for the seedlings can be a homemade mix (see the recipe on page 349 Chapter 9, for potting soil), or you can use commercially available potting soil.

As your seedling transplants grow, they will benefit from weekly feedings, beginning 4 weeks after the plants germinate. If you are transplanting from a germinating container, wait 2 weeks after the first transplanting. Houseplant fertilizer, the type mixed into water, works fine, but do not use full-strength fertilizer! Always dilute it by one-half the recommended rate. The best commercial fertilizers for seedlings are those that contain trace elements. The label should say that the plant food contains "minors," or it might list some ingredients such as iron or copper. You can also use diluted fish emulsion (stinky!). Take care if you use manure tea, as it is hard to tell how strong the stuff is from batch to batch. If you see any leaf or tip burning or yellowing of the leaves, stop fertilizing and check the symptoms out in Chapter 9, "Getting to the Roots." Please be careful here. Greenhouse gardeners have a natural tendency to love and overfertilize their plants to death. When in doubt, use less or none at all.

Warning: When growing transplants, keep your eyes open for aphids and other insect pests on the tips of plants and on the undersides of leaves. If you see them, follow the advice in Chapter 10, "When Things Go Wrong."

SPRING TRANSPLANTING

Scheduling is one of the biggest problems people have when growing seedlings for transplanting outside. It is easy to start a plant too early or too late. Most people opt for starting too early in their lust for spring. If a plant is started too early, it suffers more from transplant shock when set outside and may also be root bound and stunted.

Research has shown that when you compare the results from transplanting two different-sized tomatoes, the results are not what you would expect. When you add up the yields at the end of the garden season, a transplanted 1-gallon (3.8-liter) pot containing a big, blooming tomato plant will actually yield *less* than an 8-inch (20-cm) tomato transplant with a stem slightly wider than a pencil.

If a plant is started too late in spring, the transplant may not have developed enough roots to handle the stress of transplanting and may be late in producing food or flowers outside.

Garden centers tend to grow and sell ornamental plants that are in full bloom. This is because customers prefer them blooming. It is almost torture to see these plants in tiny pots, blooming their little hearts out before they have developed hardly any leaves. Getting plants to do this has become a fine art. Commercial growers know that transplanting plants with healthy leaves but with few or no blooms will result in healthier, faster-growing plants. But they also know that most consumers prefer the blooming plants to the nonblooming. When you schedule your plants, don't worry if your ornamental transplants are not blooming in the pots before transplanting to the outside—unless you're trying to sell them.

Growing your own spring transplants is easy, economical, and gives you freedom to choose more interesting and adaptable varieties for your region.

When it comes to vegetables, it may spell disaster if they are blooming before transplanting. This messes up their internal clock and damages the total yield. Pluck the blooms off if you see a tomato or pepper transplant trying to bloom while still a seedling. Consider giving it a bigger pot now, and plan for a slightly later starting date next year.

For the best results, refer to the Spring Transplant Schedule on page 160.

HARDENING OFF

When grown in a protective environment, young plants grow very rapidly. They also become tender, making them subject to substantial transplant shock, no matter how talented you are at transplanting. Some of this shock is just getting used to pure, unadulterated sunlight and wind. You can reduce this shock by putting your seedlings through an intermediate period to help them better withstand transplanting. This period is known as "hardening off."

To harden off a plant, set your calendar for a week before the date you will be transplanting it to the outside garden. During this week, cut back slightly on watering, but don't let your seedlings wilt. Set your plants outside during the day in direct sunlight. You can also leave them out at night if the temperature stays above 45°F (7°C). Take extreme care, however, as the plants will dry out much faster outside, and keep a very close eye on them!

Hardening off spring transplants is a helpful trick. Be aware that almost all the plants that you purchase from a garden center are rarely if ever hardened off. Many good gardeners don't do it either, but if you commonly experience transplant shock, then you might want to give this a try.

Whether or not you harden off the plants or not, shock can be reduced if you transplant to the outside garden on cloudy days or provide temporary protection from direct sun or wind with a piece of wood or cardboard. To reduce shock, the natural tendency for beginning gardeners is to water to the point of drowning the poor seedling. Yes, it needs water, but don't drown it! This is gardening, not mud wrestling. Too much water is stressful, especially if it is applied for several days running. Roots need oxygen, and if the soil is constantly muddy, no air gets under the soil surface. Remember, one symptom of overwatering is wilting (how ironic)!

BRINGING PLANTS IN FROM THE OUTSIDE GARDEN

When you see fall bearing down on your once beautiful and productive outside garden, it is a common temptation to dig it all up and bring it into your greenhouse. This is not always a good idea. For one thing, think about what kind of critters you'll also be protecting all winter. Check your plants over thoroughly for bugs; be sure to look on the underside of the leaves. If you find critters on your plants, it would be better not to bring them into your greenhouse.

Also remember, as pointed out in Chapter 4, "Selecting the Right Plants," that there may be varieties that are possibly better suited to your greenhouse—those that have been specially bred, for example. The plants from the outside garden may not be the best choice when it comes to the inside garden, anyway. For instance, a tomato variety that does well outside may not have the right disease resistance to be productive inside. Outside snapdragon varieties grow fewer flowers in the winter greenhouse than snapdragon varieties bred for greenhouse

ORNAMENTAL SPRING TRANSPLANT SCHEDULE

Ornamentals	Number of Days to Germinate in Proper Environment*	Weeks from Seed Sowing to Setting Outside**
Ageratum	4	12 to 15
Alyssum	5	12 to 15
Aster	15	7 to 11
Begonia, fibrous	17	13 to 16
Celosia	10	6 to 8
Cleome	10	10 to 12
Coleus	10	7 to 10
Dahlia	5	10 to 12
Dianthus	5	5 to 8
Foxglove	9	9 to 13
Geranium	7	18 to 22
Globe amaranth	10	11 to 13
Impatiens	17	9 to 12
Kale, flowering	5	7 to 8
Lobelia	18	10 to 12
Marigold	6	6 to 10
Nicotiana	11	9 to 10
Pansy	7	9 to 12
Perennials, outside	5 to 20	12 to 20
Petunia	7	10 to 13
Portulaca	3	6 to 8
Salpiglossis	7	10 to 14
Salvia	15	8 to 14
Snapdragon	10	12 to 13
Stock	7	5 to 7
Zinnia	5	5 to 8

(Continued on next page)

VEGETABLE SPRING TRANSPLANT SCHEDULE

Vegetables	Number of Days to Germinate in Proper Environment*	Weeks from Seed Sowing to Setting Outside**
Cucumber	4	3 to 4
Eggplant	7	7 to 9
Herbs	3 to 20	8 to 15
Lettuce	7	6 to 8
Melon	4	3 to 5
Onions	7	12 to 16
Peppers	7 to 20	11 to 13
Squash	4	3 to 4
Tomatoes	7	5 to 8

* These charts assume optimum germination conditions of constant temperatures around 65°F to 70°F (18°C to 21°C), consistent moisture levels, fresh seed, and proper planting depth.

** Plants are usually set out after the last average frost date for your area. For every week that the night temperature runs 52°F (11°C) or lower, add an extra week. For every week that the night temperature runs above 70°F (21°C), subtract a week.

culture. Conversely, European forcing cucumbers (bred for greenhouse growing) can be problematic when grown outside.

You may still find some plant(s) that take well to being brought into the greenhouse in fall. But as a general rule, avoid the big established plants such as a large, mature tomato plant, which will suffer a great setback when dug up outside for placement in the greenhouse. If you are going to bring a plant inside, go for the smaller plants, which usually do much better. Also, when it comes to flowers, in general stick to annual flowers, as most perennials require a winter and won't be happy if they don't get one in your greenhouse. Perennials will often refuse to bloom until they get a real taste of winter. Try a few experiments with bringing in plants for the winter. You might find some exceptions to what I have said here, and perhaps you will have some successes.

GROWING ORNAMENTAL FLOWERING PLANTS IN THE GREENHOUSE

Nothing is more frustrating than going to a lot of trouble trying to coax a plant to bloom, only to end up with a plant that never blooms or, even worse, gets sick and struggles to live. This often has much to do with the scheduling. By changing the time of year you plant, you could instead end up with a prolific bloomer.

It is also frustrating to have big peaks and valleys in the blooming periods of your plants, where one month the greenhouse looks and smells great, only to be followed by a few months without any real show of flowers. It is all a matter of scheduling. After much experimentation, I have found trends when things seem to do best. I have included the following schedule so that you don't have to make some of the same mistakes I've made. But this schedule is not perfect; you must still do some fine-tuning to adapt the schedule to your particular greenhouse environment. So be sure to keep your own records on how things do for you. Perhaps you should make some notes right in this book where you can refer to them easily; see "Record Keeping," Appendix 8.

Can't find a certain plant? It could be a perennial, as many ornamental plants are. Perennial ornamentals are not listed in the following schedule because their scheduling is not nearly as important. They generally always grow well in the greenhouse, regardless of the time of year or the schedule you create for them.

If you have jumped to this chapter without reading some earlier chapters, please know that even though scheduling is a very important component, there is more to successful greenhouse growing than simply having a good schedule. Besides proper scheduling, be sure you understand how to select the right plant (see Chapter 4, "Selecting the Right Plants") and be sure it is in the right location (see the section on page 109 "Crop Layout and Harvesting," in Chapter 3). And while you are at it, look up the plant that interests you in Chapter 8, "A Closer Look at the Plants," for more information in determining whether it will survive in your particular situation.

In the following charts, the term "grown warm" refers to a greenhouse that has night temperatures consistently above 50°F (10°C). When the chart refers to "grown cool," it is for a greenhouse with night temperatures that consistently run below 50°F (10°C). Keep in mind that the cooler the greenhouse, the slower your plant will grow and come into bloom.

GROWING VEGETABLES IN THE GREENHOUSE

A vegetable production schedule is not as critical if your greenhouse has supplementary heat and a good ventilation system and if you are able and willing to control the temperature to keep it at a consistent 70°F (21°C) during the day and 60°F (15°C) at night. If this is the case for your greenhouse, greenhouse climate can accommodate the vegetable crop and you can grow just about any vegetable at any time of the year.

Many people must run their greenhouse or sunspace at cooler temperatures in winter, usually to save energy costs, whereas those with solar-heated greenhouses are at the mercy of the natural temperatures that their structure creates. In these situations, you must fit the type of vegetable crop into the climate rather than fitting the climate to the plant. The following schedules can simplify the selection process for what will do best at what time of year, given these more challenging different night temperatures.

The following two schedules are designed for the timing of optimum growth and harvest of many different vegetable crops. I encourage you to fine-tune these schedules for your own particular circumstances. Of course, you don't have to follow this schedule, but chances are you may notice a drop in both the performance and yield if you vary too far, unless your greenhouse has supplementary heat. One schedule is for a warmer greenhouse, and one is for a cooler greenhouse.

SCHEDULE FOR YEAR-ROUND BLOOMS IN THE GREENHOUSE OR SUNSPACE

Note: All bloom dates are approximate. An asterisk (*) indicates that you should add up to 3 months or more if you propagate from seed. If you see the word "next," it means that the harvest will be 12 months past that month.

PLANTS STARTED IN DECEMBER AND JANUARY

Plant Name	Bloom Date Grown Warm	Bloom Date Grown Cool	Propagation
Begonia (tuberous)	April	May	Seed/tuber*
Calendula	March	April	Seed
Carnation	May	June	Seed/cutting*
Centaurea	April	May	Seed
Cyclamen	November	January (next)	Seed/corm
Geranium	June	June	Seed
Gloxinia	July	August	Seed/cutting*
Kalanchoe	December (next)	February (next)	Cutting
Larkspur	May	June	Seed
Marigold (African)	April	May	Seed
Mina lobata	April	May	Seed
Nemesia	May	June	Seed
Nicotiana	March	April	Seed
Pansy	March	April	Seed
Petunia	April	May	Seed
Poppy	April	May	Seed
Primrose	December (next)	February (next)	Seed
Ranunculus	April	May	Bulb
Salpiglossis	May	June	Seed
Snapdragon	April	May	Seed
Stock	April	May	Seed
Sweet pea	April	May	Seed

PLANTS STARTED IN FEBRUARY AND MARCH

Plant Name	Bloom Date Grown Warm	Bloom Date Grown Cool	Propagation
Bedding plants	April	May	Seed
Begonia (fibrous)	June	June	Seed/cutting*
Begonia (tuberous)	June	July	Seed/tuber*

(Continued on next page)

Plant Name	Bloom Date Grown Warm	Bloom Date Grown Cool	Propagation
Carnation	June	August	Seed/cutting*
Christmas cactus	December	December	Cutting
Dahlia	July	August	Seed/tuber*
Fuchsia	June	July	Cutting
Geranium	June	June	Cutting
Jasmine	December	February	Cutting
Kalanchoe	December	February	Cutting
Larkspur	May	June	Seed
Maple, flowering	August	September	Cutting
Marguerite daisy	July	August	Cutting
Marigold	April	May	Seed
Mina lobata	April	May	Seed
Morning glory	May	June	Seed
Nicotiana	May	June	Seed
Petunia	April	May	Seed
Pineapple sage	October	October	Cutting
Poppy	May	June	Seed
Primrose	December	March (next)	Seed
Salpiglossis	June	July	Seed
Schizanthus	March	May	Seed
Snapdragon	May	June	Seed
Statice	July	August	Seed
Stock	May	June	Seed
Swan River daisy	June	July	Seed
Sweet pea	May	June	Seed
Zinnia	May	June	Seed

PLANTS STARTED IN APRIL AND MAY

Plant Name	Bloom Date Grown Warm	Bloom Date Grown Cool	Propagation
Aster	August	September	Seed
Begonia (fibrous)	September	November	Seed
Bougainvillea	October	December	Cutting
Centaurea	July	September	Seed
Cleome	July	August	Seed
Felicia	March	April	Cutting
Gardenia	August	September	Cutting

(Continued on next page)

Plant Name	Bloom Date Grown Warm	Bloom Date Grown Cool	Propagation
Globe amaranth	June	July	Seed
Kalanchoe	January	February	Cutting
Marigold	June	July	Seed
Marmalade plant	September	October	Cutting
Mina lobata	July	August	Seed
Morning glory	July	August	Seed
Mullein	September	December	Seed
Nicotiana	June	July	Seed
Petunia	June	July	Seed
Primrose	February	March	Seed
Salpiglossis	July	August	Seed
Schizanthus	July	August	Seed
Snapdragon	July	August	Seed
Swan River daisy	July	August	Seed
Zinnia	June	July	Seed

PLANTS STARTED IN JUNE AND JULY

Plant Name	Bloom Date Grown Warm	Bloom Date Grown Cool	Propagation
Aster	December	January	Seed
Azalea	April	May	Cutting
Browallia	December	February	Seed
Calceolaria	March	April	Seed
Calendula	October	November	Seed
Geranium	October	November	Seed/cutting*
Globe amaranth	October	November	Seed
Gloxinia	February	March	Seed
Impatiens	September	October	Seed/cutting
Larkspur	September	October	Seed
Pansy	December	January	Seed
Poinsettia	December	January	Cutting
Polka-dot plant	October	November	Seed
Poppy	September	October	Seed
Salpiglossis	October	November	Seed
Snapdragon	October	November	Seed
Statice	September	October	Seed
Stock	December	January	Seed

(Continued on next page)

Plant Name	Bloom Date Grown Warm	Bloom Date Grown Cool	Propagation
Sweet pea	November	December	Seed
Thunbergia	October	December	Seed
Zinnia	October	November	Seed

PLANTS STARTED IN AUGUST AND SEPTEMBER

Plant Name	Bloom Date Grown Warm	Bloom Date Grown Cool	Propagation
Ageratum	January	February	Seed
Anemone	January	February	Bulb/seed*
Browallia	January	March	Seed
Calceolaria	March	April	Seed
Calendula	December	January	Seed
Chenille plant	August (next)	September (next)	Cutting
Cineraria	February	March	Seed
Freesia	February	March	Bulb
Geranium	May	June	Seed/cutting*
Gerbera	January	February	Seed
Hyacinth	January	February	Bulb
Kale (flowering)	January	February	Seed
Larkspur	February	March	Seed
Lisianthus	March	April	Seed
Lupine	April	May	Seed
Malope	April	May	Seed
Mimulus	November	December	Seed
Narcissus	December	January	Bulb
Nasturtium	January	February	Seed
Nemesia	December	January	Seed
Pansy	January	February	Seed
Polka-dot plant	January	February	Seed
Poppy	February	March	Seed
Primrose	February	March	Seed
Ranunculus	November	December	Bulb
Schizanthus	December	January	Seed
Snapdragon	December	January	Seed
Stock	December	February	Seed
Sweet pea	January	February	Seed
Tulip	January	February	Bulb

(Continued on next page)

PLANTS STARTED IN OCTOBER AND NOVEMBER

Plant Name	Bloom Date Grown Warm	Bloom Date Grown Cool	Propagation
Aster	April	May	Seed
Begonia (fibrous)	March	April	Seed
Browallia	March	April	Seed
Calceolaria	May	June	Seed
Calendula	February	March	Seed
Chrysanthemum	March	May	Seed/cutting*
Cineraria	April	May	Seed
Freesia	March	April	Corm
Fuchsia	May	June	Cutting
Gardenia	December (next)	January (next)	Cutting
Impatiens	February	March	Seed/cutting
Larkspur	April	May	Seed
Lisianthus	June	July	Seed
Nemesia	February	March	Seed
Pansy	March	April	Seed
Poppy	April	May	Seed
Ranunculus	January	February	Bulb
Schizanthus	February	March	Seed
Snapdragon	February	March	Seed
Stock	February	March	Seed
Sweet pea	April	May	Seed

ORNAMENTAL FLOWERS BEST SUITED FOR THE WINTER GREENHOUSE

Stick to plants on this list if your night greenhouse temperature runs below 45°F (7°C) in winter.

Ageratum	Cineraria	Kale (flowering)	Petunia
Alyssum	Cyclamen	Larkspur	Pineapple sage
Amaryllis	Freesia	Malope	Poppy
Anemone	Geranium	Mandevilla	Primrose
Angel's-trumpet	Gerbera	Maple (flowering)	Ranunculus
Azalea	Hibiscus	Marguerite daisy	Shrimp plant
Bird-of-paradise	Hyacinth	Mullein	Snapdragon
Bougainvillea	Impatiens	Nasturtium	Stock
Calendula	Jasmine	Nemesia	Sweet pea
Christmas cactus	Kalanchoe	Pansy	Thunbergia

PLANTING, GROWING, AND HARVESTING (P, G, H) SCHEDULE

The following schedules are coded like this: *P* designates a possible month to plant the crop; *G* indicates good months to be growing the crop toward maturity; *H* means the crop, if grown to maturity, could be harvested during these months. There are many variables involved in growing vegetables in a greenhouse that make it difficult to be totally accurate. But this general guide should help you in much of your planning.

WARM-GREENHOUSE VEGETABLE SCHEDULE

This chart applies to greenhouses that run winter night temperatures above 45°F (7°C) and to solar greenhouses that are in a climate that receives a winter monthly average of 45 percent or more of possible sunshine as listed by your closest National Weather Service office (see Appendix 2, "Average Percent Possible Sunshine").

Crop	Jan	Feb	Mar	Apr	May	June	July	Aug	Sept	Oct	Nov	Dec
Beans, bush	–	P	PG	PGH	PGH	PGH	PGH	PGH	PGH	GH	–	–
Beans, fava	PGH	PGH	PGH	PGH	H	H	–	–	P	P	PG	P
Beans, lima	–	–	–	P	PG	PG	PGH	PGH	GH	GH	H	–
Beans, pole	–	–	P	PG	PG	PGH	PGH	PGH	PG	GH	H	–
Beets	PGH	PGH	PGH	GH	GH	H	–	P	PGH	PGH	PGH	PGH
Broccoli	PGH	GH	H	–	–	–	–	–	P	PG	PGH	PGH
Brussels sprouts	GH	GH	H	–	–	–	–	–	PG	PG	PG	GH
Cabbage	PGH	GH	GH	GH	H	–	–	P	PG	PGH	PGH	PGH
Cantaloupe	–	–	–	P	PG	PG	GH	GH	H	H	–	–
Carrots	PGH	PGH	PGH	PGH	PGH	PGH	PGH	PGH	PGH	PGH	PGH	PGH
Cauliflower	GH	GH	H	–	–	–	–	–	P	PG	PGH	PGH
Collards	PGH	PGH	PGH	GH	GH	GH	–	P	PG	PGH	PGH	PGH
Cucumber	–	–	P	PG	PG	PGH	PGH	GH	GH	GH	H	–
Eggplant	–	–	P	PG	PG	PG	PGH	GH	GH	H	–	–
Garlic	PGH	PGH	PGH	PGH	PGH	PGH	PGH	PGH	PGH	PGH	PGH	PGH

MONTHS

(Continued on next page)

Crop	Jan	Feb	Mar	Apr	May	June	July	Aug	Sept	Oct	Nov	Dec
Kale	PGH	GH	GH	H	–	–	–	–	P	PGH	PGH	PGH
Kohlrabi	PGH	PGH	PGH	PGH	GH	GH	–	P	PG	PGH	PGH	PGH
Lettuce	PGH	PGH	PGH	GH	H	–	–	P	PGH	PGH	PGH	PGH
Okra	–	–	–	P	PG	PG	PGH	GH	GH	H	–	–
Onions, bulbs	–	P	PG	PG	PGH	GH	GH	GH	GH	H	H	–
Onions, greens	PGH	PGH	PGH	PGH	PGH	PGH	PGH	PGH	PGH	PGH	PGH	PGH
Parsley	PGH	PGH	PGH	PGH	PGH	PGH	PGH	PGH	PGH	PGH	PGH	PGH
Peas	GH	GH	GH	H	–	–	–	–	PG	PG	PGH	GH
Peppers	–	–	P	PG	PG	PGH	PGH	GH	GH	GH	GH	H
Radish	PGH	PGH	PGH	–	–	–	–	–	P	PGH	PGH	PGH
Spinach	PGH	PGH	GH	H	–	–	–	P	PGH	PGH	PGH	PGH
Spinach, NZ	PGH	PGH	PGH	PGH	PGH	PGH	PGH	PGH	PGH	PGH	PGH	PGH
Squash, summer	–	P	PG	PG	PGH	PGH	PGH	GH	GH	H	H	–
Squash, winter	–	P	PG	PG	PGH	GH	GH	GH	H	H	–	–
Swiss chard	PGH	PGH	PGH	PGH	PGH	PGH	PGH	PGH	PGH	PGH	PGH	PGH
Tomatoes	–	P	PG	PGH	PGH	PGH	PGH	PGH	GH	GH	GH	H
Turnips	PGH	PGH	GH	H	H	–	–	P	PGH	PGH	PGH	PGH
Watermelon	–	–	–	P	PG	PG	GH	GH	H	H	H	–

COOL-GREENHOUSE VEGETABLE SCHEDULE

This chart applies to greenhouses that run winter night temperatures below 45°F (7°C) and to solar greenhouses that are in a climate that receives a winter monthly average of less than 45 percent of possible sunshine as listed by your closest National Weather Service office (see Appendix 2, "Average Percent Possible Sunshine").

						MONTHS						
Crop	Jan	Feb	Mar	Apr	May	June	July	Aug	Sept	Oct	Nov	Dec
Beans, bush	–	P	PG	PGH	PGH	PGH	PGH	PGH	PGH	GH	–	–
Beans, fava	GH	GH	PGH	PGH	H	H	–	–	P	P	PG	GH
Beans, lima	–	–	–	P	PG	PG	GH	GH	GH	H	–	–

(Continued on next page)

Crop	Jan	Feb	Mar	Apr	May	June	July	Aug	Sept	Oct	Nov	Dec
Beans, pole	–	–	PGH	P	PG	PGH	PGH	GH	GH	H	–	–
Beets	PGH	PGH	PGH	GH	H	–	–	P	PG	PGH	PGH	PGH
Broccoli	GH	GH	GH	GH	H	–	–	P	PG	PG	GH	GH
Brussels sprouts	GH	GH	GH	H	–	–	–	P	PG	PG	GH	GH
Cabbage	GH	GH	PGH	GH	H	H	–	P	PG	PGH	GH	GH
Cantaloupe	–	–	–	P	PG	PG	GH	GH	GH	GH	H	–
Carrots	GH	PGH	PGH	PGH	PGH	PGH	PGH	PGH	PGH	PGH	GH	GH
Cauliflower	GH	GH	H	–	–	–	–	–	P	PG	GH	H
Celery	GH	PGH	GH	GH	H	–	–	P	PG	PG	GH	GH
Collards	GH	GH	PGH	GH	GH	GH	PGH	P	PG	PGH	GH	GH
Cucumber	–	P	P	PG	PG	PGH	PGH	GH	GH	H	H	–
Eggplant	–	–	–	P	PG	PG	PGH	GH	GH	H	–	–
Garlic	GH	PGH	PGH	PGH	PGH	PGH	–	PGH	PGH	PGH	GH	GH
Kale	GH	PGH	PGH	PGH	H	H	–	P	PG	PGH	PGH	GH
Kohlrabi	GH	GH	GH	PGH	GH	–	–	P	PG	PGH	PGH	GH
Lettuce	GH	PGH	PGH	GH	H	GH	PGH	PGH	PGH	PGH	PGH	GH
Okra	–	–	–	P	PG	PG	PGH	GH	GH	H	–	–
Onions, bulbs	–	P	PG	G	GH	GH	GH	GH	H	–	–	–
Onions, green	GH	PGH	PGH	PGH	PGH	PGH	PGH	PGH	PGH	PGH	GH	GH
Parsley	GH	PGH	PGH	PGH	PGH	PGH	PGH	PGH	PGH	PGH	PGH	GH
Peas	GH	PGH	GH	GH	H	–	–	P	PGH	PGH	PGH	GH
Peppers	–	–	P	PG	PGH	PGH	PGH	GH	GH	GH	H	–
Radish	GH	PGH	PGH	PGH	PGH	PGH	GH	–	P	PGH	H	GH
Spinach	GH	PGH	GH	GH	H	–	–	P	PGH	PGH	PGH	GH
Spinach, NZ	GH	PGH	PGH	PG	PG	H	PGH	PGH	PGH	PGH	PGH	GH
Squash, summer	–	–	P	PG	PGH	PGH	PGH	GH	GH	H	H	GH
Squash, winter	–	–	P	PG	PG	PGH	PGH	GH	GH	H	H	–
Swiss chard	GH	PGH	PGH	PGH	PGH	PGH	PGH	PGH	PGH	PGH	PGH	GH
Tomatoes	–	P	PG	PGH	PGH	PGH	GH	PGH	GH	GH	H	–
Turnips	GH	PGH	GH	H	H	–	GH	P	PGH	PGH	PGH	GH
Watermelon	–	–	–	P	PG	PG	GH	GH	GH	H	–	–

CREATE YOUR OWN SCHEDULE

Now that you have some schedules to refer to and an idea about where your greenhouse or sunspace fits into the scheme of things (as to temperature), it is time to figure out a potential schedule. Make a list of what plants you wish to grow, and then refer to the schedules to see where they would fit in best. It might also be helpful to read the specifics about each particular crop that you plan to grow in Chapter 8, "A Closer Look at the Plants." This is where each crop is discussed in depth, which could help you fine-tune your scheduling as well as provide you with other tricks to help grow them.

A Closer Look at the Plants

Now that we've covered how to arrange the interior of your greenhouse, select varieties, propagate plants, and schedule the growing of your crops, we need to look at the specific horticulture of each type of plant. This section is based on my experiences (and my mistakes) as well as on input from other growers with whom I am in touch. Even so, remember that there are always alternate methods that will also give you good results. That's why gardening remains as much of an art as a science. Some horticulturists like to get snooty about the "proper way" to grow something. The truth is that there is never one proper way to grow any one plant. Gardeners are individualistic and often like to try things their own way. By doing so, they discover new and different ways to get plants to grow well.

How to Use This Chapter

This chapter contains an alphabetical listing of selected plants—an encyclopedia of sorts. Divided into three sections, it covers ornamental flowering crops, fruits and vegetables, and herbs suited for the greenhouse or sunspace. I point out the common pitfalls of growing each particular plant and troubleshoot problems that may arise. When it comes to growing plants, I have already made most of the common mistakes—so you won't have to.

Some discussions about a plant are lengthier than others. This is because some plants require more attention, whereas others are just plain easier to grow and need few descriptors. The following are recommendations, not hard-and-fast requirements. In fact, I encourage you to break free of them occasionally to explore your own interests. If you do try something different, keep some records so you will learn from what you have done. It is all too easy to forget what you did many months ago. Record keeping shortens the learning curve and the level of frustration. See the Appendix 8, "Record Keeping," for some samples of forms you may wish to use.

Ornamental Flowering Crops

I have avoided some of the more difficult ornamental plants in the following list, opting instead to list those that are easier to grow or that produce spectacular results with a concerted effort in the greenhouse. A plant may also be listed here because of its interesting bloom or foliage or solely because it smells good. You should know my bias: Scent has a high priority when I grow plants. Although the following list of ornamentals is extensive, it is by no means complete. To cover every potential ornamental plant for the greenhouse or sunspace would fill many books, and this one is already too big! Besides, I had to leave some exploring up to you. With a little effort, you too can find some new incredible plants not listed here. That's the fun of being a horticultural pioneer.

The plants in this chapter are listed in alphabetical order, with their common name first, followed by the scientific (or Latin) name in parentheses. Exceptions occur when the plants' scientific names are commonly used; then I may have listed that name first.

Those of you nonbotanists should know that nothing identifies a plant more accurately than a Latin, or scientific, name. For example, there are many plants called black-eyed Susan and only a Latin identification will steer you in the right direction concerning a specific plant. But I believe that the Latin can be confusing to beginning gardeners. In the meantime, try to spend some time learning the scientific names of the plants you like most. Why? It will help you accurately tell the difference between the five or so plants known as black-eyed Susan, for starters.

Then there is the pronunciation of these oddly spelled Latin names. There are pronunciation guides available through many botanical gardens, but it is more fun to just spit it out as best you can; most people will think you are probably saying it better than they are. Besides, when you learn the scientific name, it will spice up your vocabulary and you can impress people with your new knowledge. The main thing is to have fun and not take yourself, the greenhouse, or the plants too seriously.

Ageratum
(Ageratum houstonianum)

Ageratum is sometimes known as **floss flower**. Although it is known for its dense, fluffy clusters of small blue flowers, it also comes in pink and white varieties. I still prefer the blue-flowered varieties. It tends to look best when the greenhouse runs to moderate temperatures in fall, spring, and early summer. If your greenhouse gets too hot, ageratum may suffer. If well established in August, it can often hold its own as temperatures get cool. It is an annual, and when it starts to look spent, it is usually best to just toss it out.

Ageratum is a common outside bedding plant and can be started in the greenhouse around late March for later transplanting to the outside garden. Ageratum looks best when planted in clusters. Most varieties only grow to about 10 inches (25 cm) high, but some varieties can get up to 20 inches (51 cm) in height. These tall ones are fun to mix into perennial borders in the outside garden. Most varieties of ageratum are not suitable as cut flowers in the greenhouse, unless you are growing the taller types. It is best grown as a border plant along greenhouse paths, set out at 6 inches (15 cm) apart, or you can plant 3 or more in pots 6 inches (15 cm) or larger. Ageratum is usually propagated from seed.

Aloe Vera
(Aloe vera)

Many people know of the succulent aloe vera plant as the "burn plant," because its sap is often used medicinally as treatment for minor skin burns and sunburns. Although it is not exceptionally ornamental, it is something many people like to have on hand (I know I do). Aloe vera occasionally blooms, but the flowers are not very striking. By simply dividing a mature plant that has developed smaller "pups" growing in a cluster, you can create many new plants. Try to separate the cluster so that you can get some root attached to each plant and set it in a mix of $\frac{1}{2}$ potting soil and $\frac{1}{2}$ sand. If the plant is getting a purplish hue to the leaves, it is telling you that you are giving it too much light. Only water it after the top of the soil has completely dried out. It benefits from occasional fertilization.

There are many cousins to aloe vera that are not used for burns but are grown for their ornamental foliage and flowers. Some put out blooming stalks in spring that are real showstoppers. If you have an interest in growing succulents (see "Succulents," later in this chapter), be sure to see what is available in the *Aloe* species in a good greenhouse or cactus specialty catalog (see "Mail-Order Plants" in Appendix 5). Diverse *Aloe* species may also be available in your local retail greenhouse or garden-center outlets.

Alstroemeria

(*Alstroemeria* spp.)

This plant is grown primarily for its cut flowers and is a relative of the amaryllis. It is also known as the **Peruvian lily**. The plant can grow up to 4 feet (1.2 m) in height and has showy flowers in shades of orange, yellow, pink, red, and white. Most are streaked or spotted in the throat of the flower. The cut flower keeps for many days.

Alstroemeria plants are started at the end of summer for blooming the following spring. They are often propagated from obtained rhizomes but can also be started from seed. Growing from seed can be tricky, however, as the timing may vary greatly. I have had some seed germinate in 2 weeks, but other times they have taken many months to emerge. It helps to soak the seed in warm water for 12 hours prior to sowing.

For best establishment, grow the plant around 65°F (18°C). Alstroemerias like to grow on the moist side with full sun and can be grown in either 1-gallon (3.8-liter) pots or ground beds. Optimal blooming is often best triggered by a 2-week cool period of around 40°F (5°C). The cool period is especially important if you are growing for red or orange blooms. The plants may need staking as they get taller.

Each plant will produce a fleshy, thickened, potatolike rhizome. Don't throw the plant away after it blooms. Often the plant will go dormant but will again come back to life, sprouting from the rhizome in a few months. The plant can live for many years but should be divided every 2 years.

Alstroemerias are heavy feeders, so periodic fertilization can be beneficial. Fortunately, they have few pest problems.

Alyssum

(*Lobularia maritima*)

Alyssum, also known as **sweet alyssum**, is another common annual plant seen in the outside garden, but it does very well in a greenhouse, too. Avoid the perennial alyssum, which is not suited to a greenhouse. Alyssum is a low-growing plant with dainty masses of flowers clustered like thimbles. Varieties are available with flowers in the colors white, pink, and purple. The flowers have a slightly sweet scent.

In the green-house, I use alyssum along walk paths as a colorful ground cover, or trailing over the sides of hanging baskets. The plant does fine in the greenhouse year-round but suffers some in hot weather. Alyssum may get slightly aggressive because it can readily reseed itself. If you overwater, you will often find that it provides a favorite habitat for slugs (see the "Common Greenhouse Pests," page 411, in Chapter 10). The slugs usually don't damage the plants, but they love to retreat in alyssum during daytime to plan their nighttime attacks.

Alyssum is easily started from seed. Just barely cover the seed; if it is planted too deeply, it may have trouble germinating. Germination should occur in about 10 to 15 days. If you have a plant older than 12 months, you should consider starting over or give the plant a good haircut-like pruning job.

Amaryllis

(*Hippeastrum* spp.)

I remember when I was a child and I grew my first mammoth sunflower. As it topped out at 8 feet (2.4 m), I felt like I was Jack with his beanstalk. The plant seemed to touch the sky and made me feel like a masterful gardener. I remember a similar feeling when I bought my first amaryllis bulb as a teenager. It flowered a month after I set it in a window—and what a show! It was by far the largest flower I had ever seen. To think that I had a hand in making it grow and flower was a wonderful realization!

The holidays are the season when you find amaryllis bulbs commonly for sale, but they may also be found in the nonholiday season in many catalogs and stores. The amaryllis is a native to Peru and is one of the easiest flowering plants to grow. Because of the huge 8- to 10-inch (20- to 25-cm) flower it creates, you will feel as if your brown thumb has instantly turned green.

Like the flowers it produces, the amaryllis bulb is also large, measuring up to 5 inches (13 cm) across. To get started with a new bulb, first select a nice-looking pot that is at least 2 inches (5 cm) wider than the diameter of the bulb; a 6-inch (15-cm) pot works well. A clay pot is better suited to amaryllis culture than a plastic one because its weight helps keep the top-heavy plant from tipping over. Set the bulb in potting soil and leave the top third exposed. If it comes prepotted, make sure it is not in pure peat moss, which is a cheap substitute for a good potting mix. If it is, repot it into higher-quality potting soil.

Amaryllis likes to be on the wet side. It usually takes 6 to 8 weeks after planting a new bulb before you see it start to flower. If the bulb seems to be taking longer to sprout and there are no signs of growth, try setting it in a very warm place (like on top of the hot-water heater) for 3 days to trigger growth. Once it starts growing, it greatly benefits from applications of a liquid or water-soluble fertilizer once every 3 weeks.

When you do get blooms, the top can become so big that you might want to consider using some small stakes to prevent it from tipping over. Because an amaryllis may bend toward the sun, it is helpful to give the pot a one-quarter turn every few days to keep the plant growing evenly.

Horticulturists have been debating for some time about the proper care after the amaryllis blooms. For years the common belief was that the plant needed a dormant, or rest, period. Now, many amaryllis enthusiasts claim that you can easily compel the plant to rebloom bigger and better without the dormant period. I am on the "no-rest" side of the fence, mainly because it is easier. After the flowers have faded, simply trim off the flower stalk. Then it will grow long, gangly, straplike leaves. It will do this until it decides to bloom again, usually in late winter. You can grow amaryllis in the same pot for 2 to 3 years before repotting it. Just wash away and replace the top inch of soil every summer.

Amaryllis are available in colors that range from bright scarlet through salmon, pink, and white. There are also some beautiful bicolored varieties. If you want to have many months of bloom, try buying 4 or 5 bulbs and pot one up every few weeks from October through December.

Unlike many showy flowering plants, the amaryllis requires no special conditions or treatment, and you will easily get incredible results. When people see the 9-inch (23-cm) blooms you have produced, they'll think you are a greenhouse-gardening genius. Also, the amaryllis is relatively pest free.

Anemone

(Anemone coronaria)

Anemones, sometimes known as **windflowers**, have a handsome, poppylike flower (some may look more like daisies) that comes in white, red, pink, and purple, measuring 2 to 3 inches (5 to 8 cm) across on 8-inch (20-cm) stems. The variety Mona Lisa is a good choice for large, showy flowers, and the flowers have a wider color range.

There are other species besides the *Anemone coronaria*, but *A. coronaria* is the best suited to growing under glass. They are usually started from small tubers, which are best planted in late summer in the greenhouse. Set the tubers a couple of inches deep and 2 to 3 inches (5 to 8 cm) apart in well-drained soil (soil that doesn't drain well can cause the tubers to rot). They may occasionally be plagued by rot (see the discussion on rots in Chapter 10, p. 425). If they are, be sure to go easy on the watering. Because they often bloom all at once and then stop blooming at the same time, you might want to stagger the planting over a month to spread out the period of bloom over a longer time.

Anemones can also be started from seeds, which germinate in 10 to 14 days. It is crucial when germinating anemone seeds to keep the temperatures below 60°F (15°C) because higher temperatures reduce the percentage of seeds that germinate. Seedlings are ready to transplant in about 10 weeks. When you transplant seedlings into larger pots or into beds, be sure not to set the plant any deeper into the new soil than it was before. If the crown gets buried, it may cause stem rot.

Anemones are best suited to a cooler greenhouse because they just love cool temperatures (50°–60°F, 10°–15°C). Warmer temperatures can cause problems with setting of blooms. Place the flowers in a spot that receives full sun. Wait a day or two after the blooms have opened before you cut them for bouquets. Cut anemones last 5 to 6 days. When the plant's flowers are finished blooming, you can dig up the bulbs and store them in a cool, dry spot. Next August or early September is the time to pot them up again for another winter's show. There is something about anemone blooms that can really brighten up a winter day.

Angel's-trumpet

(*Datura / Brugmansia* spp.)

Angel's-trumpet is a name given to many plants that are in the nightshade family (the family Solanaceae) or the genus *Datura.* They are found in both annual and in subtropical shrubby perennial flowering forms. Both the annual and the perennial plants are known for their large, fragrant, trumpet-shaped blooms. Flowers can be salmon, red, white, yellow, or purple. There is also a variegated-leaf variety that has white flowers and white leaf margins. All these species are also known for being very toxic if ingested, so take precautions with children.

The woody shrub types, usually sold under the name *Brugmansia,* are very showy greenhouse plants. The fragrance during the day is nonexistent—but come evening … Wow, is it intoxicating and sweet! Fragrance after the sun goes down is the best reason to have a brugmansia. I don't know exactly why the fragrance is only released in the evening, but I am sure it has something to do with attracting a night-flying pollinator. Still, even without a fragrance, this would be an interesting plant because of its large, nodding, trumpetlike flowers—real eye-catchers. A single flower can get up to 1 foot (0.3 m) in length. Angel's-trumpet can flower year-round, even with cooler winter temperatures (but not much below 48°F (9°C). Lower temperature may cause noticeable ebbs in the number of blooms. When it warms up, the blooms will be back.

The brugmansia angel's-trumpets are easy-to-grow, large plants that can reach heights of up to 12 feet (3.6 m) or more. Perhaps we should call it a tree? Be sure you have room for this plant, or be ready to control its fast growth with some regular pruning. This plant is one good reason to have a two-story greenhouse. It needs to grow in full sunlight and may need watering every day when temperatures get warm.

Brugmansias can be grown directly in ground beds or in large tubs. They will not do well in small pots, as they need some root space. They can be easily propagated from seed or cuttings; plants are also available from specialty greenhouse plant catalogs. Because the brugmansia is a subtropical perennial, it is long-lived in the greenhouse and may need occasional shaping to groom back leggy portions. To keep it happy and blooming, try fertilizing it regularly, as it is a heavy feeder.

Let's look at some specific varieties of brugmansias.

Brugmansia versicolor is a favorite of mine that has flowers that turn color in the first day or two. They start out creamy white, and after a day or so they turn a beautiful salmon color; they have a delightful fragrance, especially in the evening. There is also a double-flowered variety found in some catalogs (with double the number of petals in a flower) that is quite showy. ***Brugmansia suaveolens*** is a heavily scented white variety that is bushy and compact and might be a better choice for a tub.

The Glasshouse Works catalog (see "Mail-Order Plants" in Appendix 5) offers one called Dr. Seuss that has a fancier look, with a large, vibrant, yellow-orange coloration to the blooms. I find that a fitting name for any brugmansia, as the flowers seem to be the inspiration for many of the plants found in the books by Dr. Seuss.

The annual angel's-trumpet (often known as **datura,** or **moon lily**) has flowers similar to its shrubby, treelike cousin, brugmansia, but this plant grows much shorter (around 10 to 18 inches, 25 to 46 cm) and has smaller flowers. I have seen some of the datura grow ornamental fruit, but, like all other parts of the plant, it is quite poisonous. Keep it out of reach of toddlers! The annual angel's-trumpet is easy to start from seed. Because it is an annual, it can begin to look ragged after a couple of years and should be tossed out. It is an old-fashioned bedding plant used as a focal point and, like its name, "moon lily," shows up well on hot moonlit summer nights.

Aster
(Aster spp.)

Most annual and some perennial asters can be grown in a greenhouse. Annual asters (**Callistephus chinensis**), sometimes called **China aster**, are colorful flowers well suited to the greenhouse at certain times of the year. They make a great cut flower or a nice flowering potted plant. Because the flowering is triggered by the length of the night, the aster is genetically set to bloom in either May or in August and usually continues for a month or so. Commercial greenhouse operators have figured out ways to grow plants with special schedules and plant covers to simulate uninterrupted nights in order to trick them into blooming in any season. This is a lot of work for the home greenhouse gardener. It is much easier to just grow them during their natural time period, planting seeds around April or May for bloom in late summer. You can also get good results with a July sowing for December flowering.

There are many options to select from when you are growing annual asters. Asters can be found in almost any color and come in heights from short (6 to 12 inches, 15 to 30 cm) to tall (18 to 30 inches, 46 to 76 cm). The taller varieties may need staking in the greenhouse. The shape of the flower varies from daisylike to pompon, similar to mums. Annual asters also have many interesting petal shapes to choose from. The most interesting petal shape occurs in the cactus-flowered variety called Massagno Mix, which is a favorite of mine (available from Stokes Seeds; see "Mail-Order Seeds" in Appendix 6). Asters do not rebloom after the initial bud set, so after the plant is finished flowering it is best to discard the plant.

Annual asters are subject to many fungal diseases that are sometimes hard to deal with (see "Diseases," in Chapter 10). You can often select varieties listed in catalogs that exhibit varying levels of disease resistance. It also helps to use new potting soil if you are growing them in pots; or, when growing them in beds, rotate plantings around to new spots year to year. Annual asters are best propagated from seed.

I have found one perennial aster that blooms well in a greenhouse, botanically known as **Aster x frikartii.** It has masses of blue, daisylike flowers on a plant that gets around 2 feet (0.6 m) high. It is a fine plant, except that I've found that the whitefly insect likes it, too—so keep a close eye on the underside of the leaf. *Frikartii* are usually purchased as a plant. You can propagate them from cuttings in spring or by dividing thickly growing plants.

Azalea
(Rhododendron simsii)

Many people end up with an azalea as a gift plant around the holiday season. Unable to toss it out after it quits blooming, people look to their greenhouse or sunspace for azalea salvation in hopes of producing another bloom period in time. Unlike many gift-type plants, the azalea can be coaxed to bloom again.

Azaleas prefer growing in a cool and brightly lit spot. They suffer when the temperature hovers around 70° to 80°F (21° to 27°C). They also like to stay uniformly moist, but not dripping wet. Azaleas can be propagated from cuttings taken in the spring.

After your azalea is finished flowering, remove faded flowers. If your greenhouse is too hot in the summer, you might consider moving the plant outside to a lightly shaded, cool spot until fall, when it should be brought back inside. Buds seem to set best after a cool period, when temperatures are above 65°F (18°C) and below 75°F (24°C), ideally in late summer or early fall.

If you see your azalea getting shriveled, it is an indication of underwatering, too much heat, or too much sun. If the newer leaves turn yellow, it may be a sign that it lacks the acidic soil it requires. I have had good luck getting the soil more acid by using an acidifying houseplant fertilizer (check a good garden center) or by monthly watering with a mixture of $^1/_2$ teaspoon of vinegar to 1 quart (0.9 liter) water. Keep an eye out for spider mites (see Chapter 10) on the underside of the leaves, indicated by webbing and a stippling of small yellow spots on the leaves.

Begonia
(*Begonia* spp.)

The fibrous begonia (*Begonia semperflorens*) is so named because of its fibrous root system and is often known as the **wax begonia.** It is a common bedding plant used outside in shady locations. It can also make a nice greenhouse plant. It is a low-growing annual 3 to 5 inches (8 to 13 cm) high that has either green or bronze leaves with small pink, red, or white flowers. It is easy to care for and is best used in large hanging baskets and along walk paths. Fibrous begonia naturally gets bushy over time. It is easily started from either seeds or cuttings. It can tolerate some cool temperatures quite well. It suffers from too much moisture, so be sure to let it dry out between waterings.

Tuberous-rooted begonias (*Begonia* x *tuberhybrida*) are the show-offs of the begonia family and are grown mainly for their large, showy, double flowers 3 to 5 inches (8 to 13 cm) across. This flower is a real sight once its colorful blooms start opening. These begonias are propagated from large tubers set out in mid- to late winter and are best grown when eventually set into 8- to 10-inch (20- to 25-cm) pots. It is best to work your way up to such a big pot, starting with smaller pots and up-potting as the flowers need more room. Tuberous begonias need more warmth than the fibrous types, doing best between 55°F (13°C) and 75°F (24°C). They like bright spots but not necessarily direct sun and prefer the soil on the dry side. After flowering, the plants are often discarded. If you hate to throw them out, cut them back after flowering and grow them on the cool and dry side. They can be propagated from cuttings.

An interesting begonia is the *Begonia rex,* which has some of the most fascinating multicolored leaves I have ever seen. Each leaf looks like an incredible colorful painting. *Begonia rex* will surely hypnotize you with its artistic colors and dozens of named varieties to choose from. *Rex* needs warmth and should be allowed to dry out between waterings; overwatering will cause it to fade fast. These plants suffer when temperatures drop below 55°F (13°C). I have seen them occasionally lose their leaves and appear to be dead. Fortunately, they are sometimes just playing possum and going through a dormant period. If you suspect this, be sure to cut way back on the water and give your plant some warmth, and you may coax it to grow those beautifully painted leaves again.

Cane-stemmed begonias, sometimes known as **angel-wing begonia**, are also common but not quite as showy. They grow tall and usually have pink or reddish flowers that hang down in an interesting fashion. Some of the cane-stemmed begonias have whitish spots on the leaves. These are not as finicky as many other begonias and will put up with a variety of conditions.

Begonia feastii, usually known as **pancake** or **beefsteak begonia**, has interesting flowers and leaves. The leaf has a roundish, flat shape and is incredibly shiny. Rising straight above the leaves are beautiful dainty pink flowers on pink stems.

You may have noticed that almost all begonias benefit from the same general conditions of indirect bright light and the need to dry out a bit between waterings. All can be started from stem and leaf cuttings in spring or summer. The tuberous and fibrous begonias can be started from seed in early to late winter. Some of the begonias are not known for being long-lived, so if they start looking scraggly, think about propagating some new plants.

Bird-of-Paradise
(Strelitzia reginae)

The bird-of-paradise, native to South America, is one of the more exotic flowers you can grow in a greenhouse. As you can tell from its name, the flower looks like a bird head or beak and the leaves resemble its wings. It has the ability to make you feel your greenhouse or sunspace is truly a tropical paradise. Even the paddle-shaped leaves, which look a bit like a banana plant, create an exotic effect. The plant reaches heights of 3 to 5 feet (0.9 to 1.5 m). Being tropical, it prefers temperatures above 45°F (7°C). I've had good luck growing the bird-of-paradise both in ground beds and in large pots (15- to 20-gallon, 57- to 76-liter size).

The most common question is how to make the bird-of-paradise bloom. Fertilize it with chicken feed or birdseed? Nope. The main trick to get the bird-of-paradise to bloom is a large dose of patience. Flowering is mainly a matter of maturity. A new plant or even a good-sized transplant can take as long as 3 to 4 years to produce a good profusion of blooms. After that, it will seem to have regular periods of resting and blooming. I have a suspicion that the bird-of-paradise actually likes a period of cool temperatures to encourage it to bloom. Keep an eye out for some newer hybrids that are smaller and come into bloom a bit earlier. If you're really lucky, you may see an occasional bloom here and there in the first few years. Blooms can occur at almost any time of the year, but I tend to see the most in the fall.

After flowering, be sure to cut off the spent blooms and fertilize regularly. Water the plant freely in the summer and more sparingly in the winter.

The flower head can make an exotic cut flower for showy arrangements. The plants are for the most part trouble free, but they can get an occasional infestation of mealybugs, especially if you don't look them over once in a while. With some difficulty, the bird-of-paradise can be propagated from seed, which is readily available from greenhouse plant catalogs. The best way to propagate the bird-of-paradise is to divide a larger clump with a sharp shovel, taking care to get a good amount of roots.

There are other bird-of-paradise species that differ in coloring. One called *Strelitzia nicolai* is known as the **white bird-of-paradise**. It is a much larger plant than the *Strelitzia reginae*, especially if you give it a large tub or pot in which to grow. Still, it is an upright, narrow grower so it can fit into tight spaces—it can reach up to 8 feet (2.4 m). I like it because of its large, showy, banana-like leaves that lend a tropical feel to the greenhouse. Like the traditional bird-of-paradise, the white type is tough to get to flower but worth the try if you want a tropical background.

Bougainvillea

(*Bougainvillea* spp.)

The bougainvillea is one of my favorite greenhouse plants. This perennial native of Brazil requires little work or attention but puts on terrific displays of color at times when color is needed in winter and spring. Some even bloom a bit throughout summer and fall.

The colored blooms are not really flowers but bracts, which are a paperlike leaf positioned below an inconspicuous flower. The colors of the bougainvillea are bright and wonderfully diverse: white, pink, scarlet, orange, yellow, salmon, and lavender. The bracts (which I'll just call flowers to simplify things) are also available in varieties that have double the traditional number of "petals" per flower.

A dwarf variety of bougainvillea called Pink Pixie keeps a compact shape for a small pot. Also, there is a variegated type that has interesting patterns of white-and-green-colored foliage, but I have noticed that it doesn't grow as vigorously as the more common varieties.

Double-flowered bougainvilleas are available and have some different characteristics. They tend to have longer blooming seasons and are more compact growers. This makes them great for hanging baskets. The double-flowered varieties also differ from the single types in that they don't drop their flower petals. This is good in terms of being cleaner, but it means that you must occasionally cut the flowers off as they age and fade.

Bougainvilleas are woody vines that can rapidly cruise through a greenhouse if given free rein. Vines can reach up to 15 feet (4.6 m) and may need tying up or trellis support. But they take well to shaping. Prune the vines (if needed) only after they've finished a flush of flowering. The vines sometimes, but not always, have thorns, which can sneak up on you if you're not careful when working around them. When grown in a pot, they perform well but may need some tip pinching and fertilization to keep the plant bushy.

Aphids and mealybugs (see Chapter 10 for both) may make occasional visits to the bougainvillea vine, but if the vines are healthy, they seem to stay freer of pests. You might see some new growth yellowing occasionally, which indicates a micronutrient deficiency. Refer to Chapter 9, "Getting to the Roots," for help if this occurs. For best results, grow the bougainvillea on the dry side, letting the top of the soil dry out between waterings.

Bougainvilleas bloom best for me in the greenhouse anytime from fall through spring. Because the petals drop readily, they are not a good choice for bouquets, unless you don't mind a little cleanup under the vase each day. I have heard from dried-flower enthusiasts that bougainvilleas can be successfully dried for arrangements. For general bright color, the plant is a real treat for any greenhouse or sunspace and a good choice for the moderately cool greenhouse. Bougainvilleas prefer temperatures above 50°F (10°C) and can tolerate temperatures down to freezing.

I have had good luck propagating bougainvilleas from cuttings taken in late spring. They can also be purchased from greenhouse plant catalogs listed in the "Mail-Order Plants" appendix.

Bromeliads

(*Bromelia* spp.)

There are thousands of species of bromeliads. They are known for being easy to grow, unusual, and quite showy. The most familiar bromeliad is the pineapple (see discussion of how to grow the pineapple later in this chapter under "Fruits and Vegetables"). There are also some ornamental bromeliads that produce an ornamental fruit the size of a golf ball.

Many bromeliads (but not all) share a quality with many orchids, in that they are epiphytes. An epiphyte is a plant that in its native habitat grows lodged in the crotch of a tree or bush but is not parasitic and derives no nutrition

Notice how water sits in bromeliad's little cups.

from the host plant. Some people call epiphytes air plants.

The interesting thing about most bromeliads is that their structure is designed to get water not just from the roots but also from "cups" found at the base of the leaves. The leaves are often very tough, with some sharp serrated edges. Watch out—they can hurt if you rub up against them!

Bromeliads are slow-growing plants, but many have some of the most interesting flowers and leaves found in nature and interesting leaf variegations. This, combined with being trouble free in a variety of environments, makes them an ideal greenhouse ornamental. Most do fine in a variety of temperatures and light conditions.

Being epiphytic, they can be mounted in the crotches of trees, mounted on wood or bark, or grown in clay pots. When you mount them, you need to provide a bit of sphagnum moss in a little indentation where the plant can anchor itself. You may have to temporarily tie it with some wire or string until it gets established.

If grown in clay pots, bromeliads need very well-drained soil containing a high percentage of sand or a mixture of bark chips and peat moss.

Bromeliads are not difficult to grow, and many people develop a fascination for the many ornamental varieties. Although a few varieties require exacting care, most are easy to grow. The general recommendation for growing bromeliads is to apply the water directly into the vaselike cups (the British call them "cisterns") formed where the leaves attach to the main plant. It also doesn't hurt to allow the soil to run slightly moist, with occasional periods of drying out.

How do bromeliads fertilize themselves in a native habitat? After the cups fill with water, they will also catch an occasional insect, plus dust, twigs, and debris. As this material breaks down, it provides nutrients to the

plants. For the greenhouse, liquid feeding at only half strength can be watered-in during the summer months.

A few varieties, such as tillandsias, do not have the cups that can hold water. For these types, keep the soil on the moist side, but not muddy wet. I often just dunk the tillandsia bromeliads under water for a few seconds every week.

Bromeliads can survive cool temperatures but do best in warmer greenhouses. Over time, they often produce offshoot plants at the base of the mother plant, called "pups" by many people. These pups are easily split off and can be potted as newly propagated plants.

Some good choices for showy members of the family Bromeliaceae include the *Aechmea*, with its large gray-green leaves and a beautiful pink-and-purple bloom. After blooming, the main plant usually dies back but almost always creates some little "pup" plantlets around the base of the plant from which you can grow many new plants.

Tillandsia, also in the family Bromeliaceae, represents a large selection of plants, all of which are generally easy to grow. They are on the small side and can be placed in many small nooks and crannies. Tillandsias are often sold in seashells with a magnet glued onto the shell to be stuck on the refrigerator. This prac-

tice is a bit cruel, and I hope you would set them free of the refrigerator habitat and put them in the greenhouse. They look so much better in a greenhouse. I like to mount them in crotches of my fig tree. Every once in a while (usually in the summer), they will kick out an incredible flower that lasts for a month or more.

Billbergia nutans (also in the family Bromeliaceae and known commonly as **Queen's tears**) is among the easiest bromeliads to grow. Although this plant only flowers for a few weeks, it still has interesting grasslike foliage. When it does flower, it displays a rainbow of colors. I use the flowers in cut arrangements, and they always bring positive comments and interested inquiries.

The *Neoregelia* group of bromeliads is known for having interesting leaves with colors that often intensify prior to blooming.

Members of the *Cryptanthus* genus are called "earth stars," because of the star-shape rosettes the leaves form. They often have an array of stripes on their wavy leaves.

One last note on bromeliads: Copper can affect some bromeliads in a very negative way. If a bromeliad gets even a drop or splash of liquid containing a small amount of copper, it may cause disfigurement and may even kill the plant. Make sure your plants are not under any sweating copper pipes!

Browallia
(*Browallia speciosa*)

Browallia, also known as the **bush violet,** is a winter favorite of mine. I like to grow it in hanging baskets. This Columbia native has star-shaped flowers borne above glossy dark-green

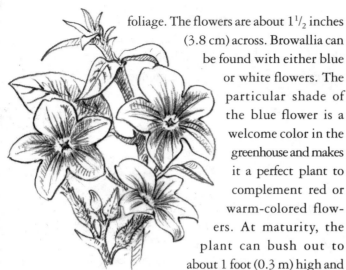

foliage. The flowers are about $1\frac{1}{2}$ inches (3.8 cm) across. Browallia can be found with either blue or white flowers. The particular shade of the blue flower is a welcome color in the greenhouse and makes it a perfect plant to complement red or warm-colored flowers. At maturity, the plant can bush out to about 1 foot (0.3 m) high and wide. It benefits from some slight tip pruning to maintain the shape. *Speciosa major* and those varieties in the Bell series and the Troll series are compact strains that branch out naturally and need little pinching.

Browallia is a tropical annual, and after it provides a show in its first year or so, it will often begin to decline. After that, it may be a good candidate for the compost pile. Then it is time to start new plants from seeds or cuttings. If you start it from seed, cover the seed and keep it moist. Provide a bright spot for best growth.

Although cold temperatures will slow its growth considerably, it can tolerate the brisk air well and will continue to flower. Beware of whiteflies (see Chapter 10)—they have a good appetite for browallia—fortunately, whiteflies often slow down more than the browallia does in winter. Even so, keep an eye on the underside of the leaf for any impending attacks.

Brunfelsia australis

This tomato relative from Brazil is sometimes known as "**Yesterday, today, and tomorrow.**" This name comes from the fact that the flowers are very short-lived but that the plant offers

new ones opening continually. The brunfelsia sets 1-inch (2.5 cm), slightly scented flowers that are usually purple, white, or yellow. It is generally grown as a pot plant in bright shade to slight shade. It likes to be kept on the moist side and responds well to ever so slightly warmed water in cool greenhouses. Cool temperatures between 50°F and 54°F (10°C and 12°C) will trigger the setting of flowers. It loves a location with high humidity. Yellowing can occur if your soil has a high pH. This can be corrected with the addition of iron chelate (follow the directions on the label exactly, as this can burn!).

BULBS—
Forcing Spring Bulbs for Winter Bloom

Many common outside bulbs that bloom in early spring can also be made to bloom in winter while the snow is still flying outside. Horticulturists use the term "forcing" when referring to getting plants to do things out of season. The word "forcing" has an unpleasant ring to it (violent plant slavery?), but the plants seem happy enough when forced, so don't feel bad.

SPRING BULB VARIETIES EASY TO FORCE

Crocus	Remembrance, purple; Blue Ribbon, blue; Giant Yellow, yellow; Jeanne d'Arc, white.
Hyacinth	Pink Pearl, Queen of the Pinks, pink; White Pearl, L'Innocence, white; Blue Jacket, Delft Blue, Blue Giant, blue.
Iris	One of the best irises to force is not the common bearded iris but rather the early-blooming dwarf *Iris reticulata,* which comes from a small crocuslike bulb. All types of *I. reticulata* work well and bloom in purple, blue, and yellow.
Narcissus or Daffodil	Almost all work well. Paperwhite narcissus do not need cooling treatment.
Tulip	Tulips are among the hardest to force because they need a longer cold treatment (13 weeks minimum). Some people simply aren't patient enough to do tulips. Usually it is best to force varieties listed as the early-flowering tulips, including: Brilliant Star, Couleur Cardinal, red; Christmas Marvel, pink; Diana, white.

The most common bulbs to force for winter greenhouse bloom include **crocus, hyacinth, iris, narcissus,** and **tulip.** (*Note*: Only the *bulb* types of iris work for forcing, such as *Iris reticulata* and Dutch iris. Don't try forcing with bearded iris!) To prepare bulbs for forcing, you must pot them up in the fall (preferably early fall) and provide them with a cold treatment to simulate winter. You do the cold treatment by storing the pots in a cold, dark place for 9 to 13 weeks. Then bring them out of the dark and into the warmth of your greenhouse or sunspace. The bulbs think it's spring, and this "forces" them into bloom, even though they wouldn't bloom for months outside. You can even time the bloom to occur for special events or parties. Finding a cold place for storing the potted-up bulbs is one of the harder challenges, as most people don't have a root cellar. I like to use the trench method explained later.

When it comes to selecting the bulbs for forcing, try to find a garden center or store that allows you to hand-pick each bulb out of a box. When you can do this, always go for the largest ones, which provide the better show when forced. In bulb catalogs, the larger bulbs are often called "exhibition" or "premium" size.

Some varieties of bulbs have proven to force better than others. The box above lists some of the easiest and most reliable. If you can't find these specific varieties, go ahead and use whatever varieties of spring bulbs you can find. Usually you'll still get a fine show right when you need it, just when cabin fever sets in.

The Process of Forcing

After you have purchased the bulbs, you will need to pot them up. Don't mix different bulbs in one pot, because the timing may be different for the varieties or types. You can use either plastic or clay pots, but they must have holes in the bottom for drainage. Smaller bulbs such as crocus and iris work well in 4- to 6-inch (10- to 15-cm) pots. For the larger bulbs, you can use pots that are anywhere from 6 to 10 inches (15 to 25 cm), depending upon how many bulbs you place in the pot.

Although some people often use small pebbles as the growing medium, I prefer to plant the bulbs in potting soil. Store-bought works fine. Fill the pots with soil so that when the bulbs are placed in the soil, it will be slightly below the rim of the pot. I put enough bulbs in each pot to be close but not touching each other. Be sure to put the bulbs in the pot

Forcing bulbs is a great way to have blooming plants from January to early spring.

right side up. This can be tricky. Look for indications of old roots at the bottom. Usually the flatter side goes down, and the pointed part of the bulb goes up.

Fill the soil in over and around the bulbs. It's ok to leave the top one-third of the bulb exposed, except for crocus and iris, which should be covered with about $1/2$ inch (1.3 cm) of soil. It helps to tag each pot so that you can later know what is in each. The final step is to water all the pots thoroughly and allow them to drain.

Next, you must fool the plants into thinking that they have gone through a winter. They need a cool treatment (without going much below freezing) for at least 12 weeks. This can be the trickiest part, and finding a cool spot is one of the drawbacks to central heating. Some of you may have an old root cellar or a very cool place in a basement. If so, great!

If you don't have a cool spot, don't despair. You can use the outdoors. Dig a trench in the garden or use a window well. If you use the trench method, you need to dig it about 2 feet (0.6 m) deep and wide enough to hold all the pots. Place the well-watered pots in the trench or window well and cover with sawdust or straw (available at most feed stores). Once it gets cold outside, mark your calendar for 12 weeks (leaving them in longer is usually ok). Tulips need 13 or more weeks. If it has been a very dry winter, then you should pull back the straw and water the pots once a month or so. The soil in the pots should never dry out completely.

After 12 weeks or more of cold treatment, you can bring the bulbs inside. When you are ready to start the forcing (usually after New Year's Day), simply push back the hay or insulation and grab a few pots every few days. Don't pull all the pots out at once. Instead, consider staggering the removal of the pots to prolong the bloom over many weeks.

When you bring in the pots, you'll notice the bulbs have sometimes started to sprout through the soil. Be careful of these delicate shoots emerging from the pots because they can break off easily.

I like to give the bulbs a few days of transition by placing them in a cooler, dimly lit room in the house, where it is around 60°F (15°C) or cooler. Then move them right into the greenhouse or sunspace. They will grow amazingly fast and the stalks will turn green right before your eyes. You may have to support the flower stalks with small stakes if they look as though they might flop over. I often place a few stakes around the outside edge and tie some green dental floss around the outside for support.

The blooming or almost-blooming plants make great gifts and will bloom prolifically for a week or more, often giving off an incredible fragrance. These bulbs can't be forced to bloom again next year, but you can plant them outside in spring, and if all goes well, they'll bloom in 2 years—if you have the space and the patience. Many people just toss them out when the blooming has finished.

You'll be surprised at how these plants will affect your mood and remind you that, yes, there is a spring coming one day soon. In the meantime, you have a little private spring going on in your greenhouse.

Cactus

(Cactaceae)

Many people turn to cacti thinking that they must be a good choice for anyone who has a hard time with plants. Perhaps this is because most cacti are forgiving plants when it comes to abuse. With a little special care, however, cacti can become some of your more treasured, exotic, and interesting plants. They can also

A cacti / succulent collage makes an attractive planter.

delight you with some of the beautiful flowers they grow.

What is the difference between cacti and succulents? All cacti are succulents, but not all succulents are cacti. Botanically, cacti are part of a very large group of plants known as succulents. The difference between cacti and other succulents shows in the area of the plant from which the cactus spines emerge. With the cactus family, the spines must arise from structures called "areoles," which are soft, cushionlike protuberances from which the spines, flowers, and new growth all emerge. Some succulents (such as euphorbias) have spines, but if you look closely the spines are not borne from areoles.

The idea that all cacti are happy desert dogs is not entirely true. There are some that live in trees located in tropical jungles. In general terms, cacti can be split into two groups: desert cacti and forest cacti. Knowing which kind you are growing makes a big difference in how you care for your cactus.

Desert cacti are native to sunny, arid climates and are usually characterized by having thick fleshy shapes, no leaves, and sharp spines or hairlike filaments. Desert cacti need water only once a month between mid-October and late March. Then increase watering to at least once every 2 weeks or more in spring and summer. Be sure to place desert cacti in a sunny, warm location. Cacti do best in shallow pots and like to be pot-bound, so don't give them too much room until they are really ready or rot may result.

Because desert cacti don't need as much water as other plants, people sometimes assume that they don't need fertilizer either. Not true! During the summer, give the plants a diluted water-soluble fertilizer about once a month. Almost any houseplant food will do. With a little feeding, you'll see amazing amounts of new growth. New growth often means you'll get a good shot at getting your cactus to flower. Flowering usually occurs in spring and early summer.

Contrary to popular belief, desert cacti usually don't do well in pure sand. Give them a one-to-one mix of sand and potting soil.

If treated like desert cacti, forest cacti will suffer unnecessarily. That's why it is important to know the difference. **Forest cacti** are native to the tropics and grow as epiphytes on trees (for more information on epiphytes, see "Bromeliads," earlier in this section). Because water is more abundant in their native locations, they do not have the fleshy attributes of their desert brethren. Forest cacti prefer darker, wetter conditions than the desert cacti do.

Forest cacti tend to have trailing growth, and many have flattened leaves. The most identifiable forest cactus is the Christmas cactus, which likes bright conditions but not direct sun. It needs a watering about once every 3

weeks in mid-winter and an increase in the frequency of water in the spring through the summer. If it is in budding or in bloom, give it a little extra water.

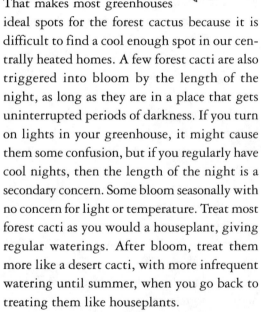

Christmas cactus

To bloom, many of the forest cacti need cool nights as close to 50°F (10°C) as possible. That makes most greenhouses ideal spots for the forest cactus because it is difficult to find a cool enough spot in our centrally heated homes. A few forest cacti are also triggered into bloom by the length of the night, as long as they are in a place that gets uninterrupted periods of darkness. If you turn on lights in your greenhouse, it might cause them some confusion, but if you regularly have cool nights, then the length of the night is a secondary concern. Some bloom seasonally with no concern for light or temperature. Treat most forest cacti as you would a houseplant, giving regular waterings. After bloom, treat them more like a desert cacti, with more infrequent watering until summer, when you go back to treating them like houseplants.

There is a lot of confusion surrounding the many different holiday cacti. There are **Christmas cactus, Thanksgiving cactus,** and **Easter cactus** (also known as **crab cactus** because of its crablike leaves). The easiest way to tell the difference is by looking closely at the leaves. Christmas cactus leaves have smooth, scalloped edges. The Thanksgiving cactus has teeth along the edges of the leaves that are more pointed. The Easter cactus has a thicker, slightly more upright leaf and often has a purple or maroon color along the leaf edge. The Easter cactus also has bristle-like hairs, often called cat whiskers, at the stem joints.

These sound like hard-and-fast rules, but to make things challenging, there are a lot of cross-hybrids that can make it tough to distinguish between many of the new hybrids.

Similar-looking to the holiday cacti is the orchid cactus, which also has very showy blooms.

Another favorite type of forest cactus is the **night-blooming cereus**, a large and thornless succulent. These produce huge, imposing blooms up to 9 inches (23 cm) across. The plants themselves can grow up to 8 feet (2.4 m) or more. There are many varieties of plants that go by the name "night-blooming cereus." Most bloom only at night, but some varieties are rebellious and disregard their name by blooming through the day. Blooms may be fragrant or odorless. I know of people who set up chairs around the cactus and invite their neighbors over when it gets dark, just to watch the grand opening of a night-blooming cereus. What a show!

Many people think that cacti are just slow-growing, boring plants with spines. With a closer look, that attitude usually changes. Given all the cactus varieties and all the unusual shapes, types, and blooms they have, it is easy to see how people can develop a real love for these plants.

Both forest and desert cacti can be propagated easily from cuttings. Take the cuttings in late winter and let them sit out overnight for the cut portion to dry out a bit. Insert the cut portion into a cactus potting mix. There is no need to place cactus cuttings in a humid or misty environment. If you get interested in making cactus a hobby, get a good cactus plant catalog (see "Mail-Order Plants"

in Appendix 5). There are also many good books written solely on cactus—you'll be an expert in no time.

Caladium
(Caladium bicolor)

The caladium is a plant grown for its unique colored leaf rather than for its flowers. The foot-long heart-shaped leaf has a display of color that is as beautiful as any flower. The color usually runs along the veins of the plant, creating stunning combinations of red, pink, green, and white. Caladiums dislike cool temperatures and prefer steady temperatures above 65°F (18°C). The temperature should never get below 60°F (15°C), so these are not a good choice for the cool greenhouse.

Caladiums also require a rest period. Usually around September, the foliage begins to look a little ragged and often begins to die back. This is the time to stop watering the plant and store the tubers in peat moss at around 50°F (10°C) until March. Then, replant the tubers and grow them on the moist side. Give them a humid, well-lit place with little direct sun. A good place for caladiums is under a table or bench. They grow well in pots or beds. If grown in pots, put only one bulb in an 8-inch (20-cm) pot. Yellowing leaves are a sign of cold air or overwatering.

Caladiums are generally purchased as tubers. Sometimes you will find small bulblets attached to the mother tuber that can be separated and potted individually as a way to propagate new plants.

Calendula
(*Calendula officinalis*)

Calendula, sometimes known as **pot marigold** (no relation to the marigold), is a short-lived annual with apricot, orange, cream, and yellow flowers. The 4-inch (10-cm) flowers bear a resemblance to the zinnia or daisy, depending upon the variety. Varieties can grow up to 36 inches (91 cm), but most reach 12 to 18 inches (30 to 46 cm). Some varieties have contrasting centers. There is one variety that even resembles a cactus dahlia with very thin petals, known as Radio Extra Selected, available from the Thompson & Morgan catalog (see "Mail-Order Seeds" in Appendix 6).

Calendulas prefer cooler temperatures and often suffer when the greenhouse is at its hottest. When temperatures start running warm, calendulas can go downhill and not flower very well. Even in cool temperatures, the plant may look good for only 2 to 4 months, but they are fast to come into flower and are well worth the effort. As with many annuals, they benefit from the removal of spent blossoms.

Grow calendulas in a sunny spot, either in pots or in beds spaced 8 to 10 inches (20 to 25 cm) apart. The stems are short, but with the right vase and a little creativity, they can make a fine cut flower. When the plant quits blooming, it will often decline in health, and this is usually a good time to toss it out and start over. Calendulas are easily propagated from seed and start blooming in about 6 to 9 weeks.

Calla Lily
(*Zantedeschia*)

I always think of how the actress Katharine Hepburn rolled the words "calla lily" off her tongue in the movie—wait, I'll see if any movie buffs can answer this trivia question. Time's up! Katharine Hepburn, playing the role of Terry Randall in *Stage Door* (1937), says, "The calla lilies are in bloom again. Such a strange flower, suitable to any occasion. I carried them on my wedding day, and now I place them here in memory of something that has died." Special thanks to my friend Jim Weis for providing the exact wording of the famous calla quote! *Stage Door* also stars Lucille Ball, among other young, soon-to-be-stars of the day.

And indeed, if there ever was an ultimate Art Deco flower, this is it. The flower has a perfect artistic swirl on a strong stalk. Did this flower actually inspire some of the lines of the Art Deco movement? Perhaps, but that interesting discussion more properly belongs in a book on art.

At any rate, the calla lily grows from a bulbous rhizome. Flowers are borne on stout stalks above shiny, arrow-shaped leaves. The unique blooms are most commonly found in pure white, but there are varieties of red, orange, and yellow. Some varieties have white spots on the leaf. The plant itself usually grows from 1 to 3 feet (0.3 to 0.9 m) in height.

Calla lilies are native to bogs. They like their feet wet most of the time, but especially when the temperatures are warm. They can tolerate some shade but bloom best when they get full sun. Although they don't generally flower much in the early winter, you can leave them growing in a bed without much care, and they'll surprise you in late winter or early spring with new blooms. Try to locate them where they get a little extra water, under or near a spigot, for instance. Callas can also be grown in 1-gallon (3.8-liter) pots with good success. They bloom in flushes from late winter through fall. During the hottest part of summer, they may go dormant for awhile.

The most common type grown is the *Zantedeschia aethiopica.* Most callas lack fragrance, but there is one exception, the compact, fragrant white type called *Zantedeschia childsiana.* I have found some good choices in the K. Van Bourgondien & Sons catalog (800-622-9997 or **www.dutchbulbs.com**).

If the leaf or flower tips turn brown, it is an indication of too much fertilizer or not enough water. Either can be remedied with the addition of water.

Callas can be started from either seed or bulbs. Bulbs are the most common way to start these plants, as seeds can take many years before you will enjoy a bloom. Older plants can be divided into many new plants with good success in late fall or early winter.

Camellia

(*Camellia* spp.)

People who live in the South often brag about their beautiful camellias. Now that you have a greenhouse, you can join in on the fun. Depending on the variety, they can bloom anytime between late fall and early spring. The camellia is an evergreen shrub that is related to the tea family of plants and is native to China and Japan.

Camellias have roselike flowers that vary in color from white to pink and red. They are found on shrubby plants with dark glossy leaves and are famous for their use in corsages and bouquets.

Camellias thrive in cool greenhouses in winter and not only tolerate but also prefer temperatures that regularly get down to the 40s (between 5°C and 9°C). As a result, this plant will do better in your cool greenhouse than it will in your home. Although camellias can tolerate hot summer temperatures well, they need the period of cold to get blooms to form and hold on. I find that they are best grown in large pots or tubs, but they can be grown in a bed. Place them in bright or filtered light. One problem with many camellias is bud drop. The only way to prevent this is to maintain temperatures below 60°F (15°C).

Camellias cannot stand to have wet feet. Therefore, add extra sand or perlite to the potting soil mix. Take care not to let the roots dry out, while not over- or underwatering. They also like an acidic soil and may benefit from fertilizing with an acidic plant food if your soil is alkaline. Camellias are famous for dropping unopened blossoms, which can drive gardeners crazy. Some drop is normal, but when it seems to be getting out of hand, consider checking possibilities that may be causing the plant some amount of stress, such as the amount of water, heat, or light.

There are two main types of camellias: *Camellia japonica* and *C. sasanqua*. **Camellia japonica** is more commonly used for greenhouse production. It can grow up to 20 feet (6 m) tall and has broad, nonserrated leaves. The japonicas bloom best in cooler temperatures and are a good choice for corsages. They tend to set buds and blossoms from January to early March.

Camellia sasanqua is probably the least troublesome type of camellia. It has smaller leaves than *C. japonica* and typically blooms from December to January. Being smaller than the japonicas, it can thrive in a slightly smaller pot. It can also tolerate cooler temperatures better than the japonicas.

Neither *C. sasanqua* nor *C. japonica* has any fragrance in the bloom. Luckily, there is a hybrid called **Camellia fragrans** that is (you guessed it!) fragrant. It is often sold as Fragrant Pink and has small leaves and a nice smaller flower. It grows to 3 or 4 feet (0.9 to 1.2 m).

Camellias are best propagated from cuttings that are most successfully taken in June. They are also readily available in greenhouse plant catalogs.

Campanula
(*Campanula* spp.)

Campanulas are generally considered as a hardy outside perennial or biennial used as a flowering ground cover or a tall showy plant. Some varieties, such as cup-and-saucer bells, can get taller. Campanulas are not often thought of as greenhouse plants, but certain varieties can be grown much like an annual.

Campanula isophylla (Stella or Stella Blue) can be grown much like an annual in a pot in the greenhouse. It has a spray of 1-inch (2.5-cm), star-shaped blue flowers on a smallish plant. Stella is well suited to a hanging basket.

Campanula carpatica (Bellissimo) is a new Thompson & Morgan hybrid with great potential as a greenhouse hanging-basket plant. It has 2-inch (5-cm) flowers that come in blue and white. It should be started in January for an early summer bloom but can be started anytime throughout spring.

Campanulas won't tolerate truly hot greenhouse temperatures, so blooms may slow or stop altogether in the middle of summer. Regular feeding with a high-phosphorus plant food can prolong flowering. They are best started from seed, or thick clumps can easily be divided. Cuttings can also be successfully propagated into new plants. Campanulas grow best in a potting mix that is well drained.

Canna
(*Canna* x *generalis*)

Cannas are generally thought of as a dramatic outside landscape plant, with tall stalks and broad, tropical-looking leaves topped with colorful flowers. When grown outside in the temperate zones, the canna must be treated like a dahlia, and the rhizome must be dug up and stored inside through the winter. In the greenhouse, I like to have at least one canna growing because the tall shape (up to 3 feet, 0.9 m) is complementary to other plants. The bloom is also interesting. They seem to do best in ground beds but would do fine in a pot that is at least 5 gallons (19 liters) in size. The colors of canna are generally red to yellow and orange. Most varieties of canna have green leaves. There are a few varieties in which the leaves themselves have a bronzelike coloring. One of my favorite is a canna with green-and-yellow striped leaves, which is botanically known as **Canna generalis striatus**. The common name is either Bengal Tiger or Pretoria Canna. It is showy all of the time. Although cannas have handsome flowers, they are generally grown for the effect of their bold upright shape rather than for masses of color.

Cannas are not good bloomers when temperatures get below 50°F (10°C), but they do well if given warm temperatures and full sun. They are relatively pest free.

Cannas are best propagated from a division of the rhizome taken in spring. Many people who like to grow cannas as an outside bedding plant find that digging them up and replanting them in the greenhouse is a good way to store the canna rhizome and get a greenhouse plant for the winter. I have seen other greenhouse gardeners who simply plant a few rhizomes under a potting or growing bench and let them grow with little care. In early spring, they divide and pot them up for the outside flower garden, leaving the stock population to grow in the greenhouse. This is a great way to have a wonderful outside canna show!

Carnation
(Dianthus caryophyllus)

The carnation is an old traditional greenhouse cut flower. The blooms are known for their long-lasting ability in bouquets. They come in the colors yellow, white, pink, and red. If you want any other color, grow white carnations and set the cut flower in a glass of water with a concentrated solution of food coloring (try any color or mix of colors). Over the next 24 hours, you can watch the flower take up the color of the solution.

There are many carnation varieties sold for outside growing that tend to bloom best in the warmer months. Most varieties sold in catalogs are the more dwarf types, which need no staking and are easy to grow. Some common varieties include the Knight hybrids, which reach 1 foot (0.3 meter) high; the Lilliput series, which are only 10 inches (25 cm) tall; and the Monarch series, which are the most compact. All can be grown in beds or in pots. Plants seem to go downhill after a year and should be tossed out at that point.

Commercial greenhouses grow much taller types of carnations, up to 3 feet (0.9 m), with large flowers borne on the long stems. These varieties are not readily available to home-greenhouse growers.

If you want to try these taller plants, you'll have to find a local commercial greenhouse that grows carnations as a cut flower and see if they will sell you a few plants or cuttings. If you grow the commercial types, you must set up a horizontal trellis system (see "Trellising" in Chapter 3 for more information) or they will flop around on the ground with poor blooms. The horizontal trellis may require at least three tiers, about 1 foot (0.3 m) apart. The commercial-type carnations make great cut flowers, but you'll have to prune the smaller buds that develop to the side of the main bud, which forms at the tip of the stalk.

Carnations need to grow in full sun and need a potting soil that drains well. Space three plants to 1 square foot (0.09 sq. m). They are slow growers, so you must be patient because it can take up to half a year before you get many blooms. Some varieties are quite fragrant, with a spicy clove scent, so look for fragrant varieties if that is a priority.

Carnations seem to do best in cool temperatures, and blooming seems to slow when the temperatures start reaching for the upper 80s and 90s (27°C to 37°C). Carnations can be started from both seed and cuttings.

Centaurea

(Centaurea cyanus)

Centaurea is also known as **bachelor button** or **cornflower**. It is a common reseeding annual often found in wildflower seed mixes. Centaurea is not usually thought of as a greenhouse plant, but I have had some good results growing it.

Centaureas have long-stemmed $1^1/_2$-inch (3.8-cm) flowers in the colors pink, white, blue, purple, and dark maroon. The thin leaves are gray-green. I like to grow them for cut-flower purposes, especially the blue variety because it is hard to find blue hues in greenhouse cut-flower plants. When grown in the greenhouse, they are not nearly as sturdy as when grown outside and tend to flop over unless provided some type of support, such as a stake or small cage. Even a tomato cage will work well. Most varieties reach up to 2 feet (0.6 m) or more, but there are some dwarf varieties growing only 1 foot (0.3 m) or so that are less likely to need much staking.

In the greenhouse, grow centaureas in a sunny spot in very well drained soil. The plants prefer to be grown on the dry side; if conditions are too wet,

they are susceptible to disease. If you don't cut the flowers for a bouquet, be sure to clean up faded flowers as soon as they appear. They can get almost weedy because of their ability to reseed themselves, but this is not nearly as much of a problem in the greenhouse as it is in the outside garden. As an annual, they will begin to look ragged after a major flush of blooms. After that, it is time to pull them and start over. They tend to bloom best in warmer temperatures of early fall and late spring and can suffer a bit if the temperatures start to get very hot in the middle of summer.

Another type of centaurea, which has an interesting flower with sharp pointed tips, is *Centaurea moschata*. It is also fragrant and will need staking like the other centaureas but usually doesn't bloom quite as prolifically.

Centaureas are easily propagated from seed but must be carefully transplanted. They can be grown in 1-gallon (3.8-liter) pots, 1 or 2 plants per pot. You can also grow them directly in a bed with 2 to 3 plants per square foot.

Chenille Plant

(Acalypha hispida)

The chenille plant is grown for the unusual fuzzy, bright-red cattail-like flowers that dangle downward from where the leaf attaches. There are also varieties with pink or cream flowers. This plant is best grown as an interesting potted plant and is not suitable as a cut flower. It tends to bloom from spring through early winter and does best in warm greenhouses but can tolerate an occasional cold night. The chenille plant prefers to grow in a spot with filtered light to full sun and needs a moderate amount of moisture. It is a perennial and can live for many years, getting as big as 4 to 5 feet (1.2 to 1.5 m) tall unless pruned. I have had good luck keeping the plant pruned and

bushy to maintain a moderate size. It can be propagated from cuttings taken in fall.

There is also the smaller form of the chenille plant, *Acalypha pendula*, that has flowers that hang down.

All parts of the Chenille plant are poisonous.

Chrysanthemum

(*Chrysanthemum* spp.)

Chrysanthemums, or mums, are a rewarding plant for greenhouse growing, but they require a specific schedule because they are genetically programmed to set buds only when the days are short and the nights are at least 11 hours long (the night period must not be interrupted with artificial light). Commercial growers do this by simulating day with artificial lights and then covering plants with a black sheet to simulate a longer night. That is a lot of trouble for home-greenhouse gardeners. Instead, you can just plan to grow mums when they will naturally bloom without the extra work of night simulations. If you time the chrysanthemum to bloom in fall or winter, the flowering will work out naturally. By starting plants any-

time from February through July, you should do fine.

Chrysanthemums come in most every color except blue. The flowers are also available in much diversity of form. Besides the traditional-shaped flower, there is also the more exotic "incurved" type of bloom, with narrow petals that curve inward. The spider type of chrysanthemum flower is very showy, with many long and narrow tubular petals. Check out the variety Spiders and Spoons in the Thompson & Morgan catalog for a wild-looking flower. Once you start looking, you will find many other interesting flower types.

There are mums available for outside planting and those that have been bred for greenhouse culture. Both can be grown in a greenhouse. Of the greenhouse types, some have been developed specifically for growing in pots, whereas others grow quite tall, up to 3 feet (0.9 m), and are mainly for cut-flower arrangements. These greenhouse varieties are hard to come by in most retail catalogs and are best obtained from a local commercial greenhouse, many of which commonly grow them. If you want to grow the greenhouse types, you'll probably have to talk a grower into allowing you to purchase some special mum cuttings or small plants.

Although you can use any chrysanthemum as a cut flower, the mums used for cut flowers by commercial growers tend to grow taller. These tall varieties need to be trellised with a horizontal trellising such as a tomato cage, or you can build your own for a bed of flowers (as described in "Trellising" in Chapter 3). You can also tie the plants to a series of bamboo stakes for support.

For mums grown in pots, it is helpful to grow a bushy plant. This can be done by regularly pinching off the tips of the plant as it is growing, which always promotes a fuller plant. If you are after bigger blooms, you may want to pinch the smaller flower buds that appear to the side of the terminal shoot, leaving only the big bud at the very tip to develop.

After chrysanthemums have flowered, consider a dramatic pruning. This is also a good time to repot and fertilize them to bring on new healthy growth and another flush of blooms.

Mums can be grown either directly in beds or in pots. Mums need full sun and room to grow. Different varieties need different spacing, so refer to the source where you acquired the plants for help in proper spacing. Chrysanthemums are best propagated by cuttings. Take a slip from a tip (before it develops any flower buds), and it will root readily with proper care (see Chapter 5, "Plant Propagation").

Cineraria
(*Senecio* spp.)

The cineraria is one of the more beautiful winter-blooming plants for the greenhouse. It produces colorful daisylike flowers in almost every color. This is a cool-loving plant that thrives even when the night temperature drops well below 50°F (10°C). Cinerarias do not like to grow in hot temperatures much above 75°F (24°C). For this reason they are best for the winter greenhouse. They are native to the cool, moist forests of the Canary Islands.

Cinerarias are always started from seed (just barely covered!) and when they are of decent size (4 to 6 leaves), they should be transplanted into a 6- to 10-inch (15- to 25-cm) pot, depending on the variety. Be sure to regularly up-pot them as needed because they wilt easily if root bound. Stick with growing them in pots, as they succumb to a variety of ailments when in beds. Place the pots in full sun to partial sun. Give each pot some breathing room because these plants will readily rot if the air is stagnant.

The best scheduling is to grow cinerarias for winter flowers. Start seed in June, July, or early August. As they grow, fertilize regularly. After flowering, the plants decline rapidly and should be discarded.

As long as the temperature is not too hot, cinerarias are happy. The biggest problem with cinerarias is aphids (see Chapter 10, "Getting to the Roots"). They will walk a mile to feast on this plant. Even so, you can grow a successful crop as long as you keep a sharp eye out for these invaders by regularly checking under the leaves. If you see aphids, immediately wash them off the undersides of the leaves or take some other appropriate control (see Chapter 10).

Cleome
(*Cleome hasslerlana*)

Cleome is also known as **spider flower** because it develops long, spiderlike seedpods. It is commonly grown as an outside bedding plant and used as a tall background flower but can also provide some interest for the greenhouse. Cleome are tall annuals growing up to 6 feet (1.8 m) tall. The flowers come in pink,

red, purple, and white. Grow cleome in clumps of at least three or more plants, as the flowers look best when they are grown en masse.

Cleome are best planted in a ground bed with some headroom and are not suitable in a pot unless it is a large tub. Set out seedlings in a ground bed at least 1 foot (0.3 m) apart. The flowers can be cut for large arrangements, but I like the way they look among other plants in the greenhouse better.

The stems get small thorns as they mature, so be careful working around them. Cleome prefers moderate to warm temperatures, doing best in full sun. Plants are easily started from seed. The only drawback is that they sometimes occasionally develop powdery mildew. Check in with—you guessed it—Chapter 10 for more information on controlling this disease.

Clivia, or Kaffir Lily
(Clivia miniata)

The clivia lily is similar to the amaryllis. This African native is not quite as showy, but it blooms for a longer period. The clivia is a plant with tuberous roots and sports dark-green straplike leaves. Clivias bloom during the cooler periods of October through February. Anytime during this period, expect to see a flower stalk that produces a collection of orange trumpet-shaped flowers. During budding and flowering, keep them on the moist side. The rest of the year let the soil dry out between waterings. After blooming, always cut the blossoms and flower stalk off.

Clivia should be grown in pots and seems to do best when left undisturbed for as long as possible. For this reason, it is fine to let it get pot-bound, sometimes for many years without any problems. When you do up-pot the plant, try not to disturb the fleshy roots. Place clivia in full to partial sun. Clivia does not need a rest period and grows year round. Clivia are propagated by dividing plantlets that develop in a pot over time. Each division should have a good set of tuberous roots attached to healthy leaves. In warm winter locations, you might keep an eye out for scale. In cool winter areas, keep an eye out for the mealybug. Both pests can be kept at bay by washing the leaves off on a regular basis.

Warning: Most parts of the clivia are poisonous.

Coleus
(Coleus blumei)

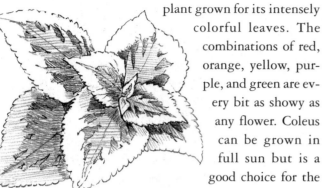

Coleus is a common, old-fashioned house-plant grown for its intensely colorful leaves. The combinations of red, orange, yellow, purple, and green are every bit as showy as any flower. Coleus can be grown in full sun but is a good choice for the darker areas of a greenhouse, where it is harder to grow colorful plants.

Notice that each coleus has perfectly square stems. This indicates that it is a member of the mint family, all of which have square stems. No, the leaves don't smell minty, but not all members of this family smell like mint.

Coleus is one of the easiest plants to propagate from a cutting, as it roots readily in water. Most people acquire plants as slips from friends. They are also easy to grow from seed. The seed is quite small, so just barely cover it. Growing from seed allows you more freedom to discover some of the more interesting varieties. They have an amazing diversity of leaf colors and shapes. *Coleus pumilus* is a low-growing species suited to a hanging basket. Often, coleus seed is sold as a mixture that combines complimentary colors and characteristics. The Wizard Mix is a dwarf variety that grows naturally bushy. There is a striped type called Striped Rainbow that has a splash of unsymmetrical colors. Old Lace Fringed has broad leaves that are deeply cut, serrated, and ruffled. Stokes Seeds offers both mixes as well as singled-out colors, which is great if you are after a particular color for a specific spot.

Coleuses tend to give the best show in the warm greenhouse but will survive cooler conditions if you go into winter with a good-sized plant. When it cools off, these plants seem to go into a state of suspended animation. They grow fine in either pots or ground beds. The flowers are usually a blue color but are not very significant when compared to the show of the leaves. To keep the leaves looking good, try to pinch off any flower stalks as they appear. Regular fertilization helps the plant continue to grow new, vibrant-colored leaves. Occasional pinching of the tips helps the plants look fuller and healthier.

Coleuses are prone to mealybugs (see Chapter 10, "When Things Go Wrong"), so look for the little cottony masses that might appear under the leaf or where the leaf attaches to the stem, and then take quick action. Less common pests occasionally visiting the coleus are whitefly and spider mites.

Columnea
(Columnea)

Columneas have glossy leaves and bright yellow, red, or orange tubular-shaped flowers that bloom almost all winter and sometimes well into summer. Some of the flowers are so vibrantly orange that one species of the plant has been named goldfish plant (*Columnea x banksii*).

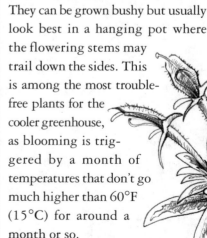

They can be grown bushy but usually look best in a hanging pot where the flowering stems may trail down the sides. This is among the most trouble-free plants for the cooler greenhouse, as blooming is triggered by a month of temperatures that don't go much higher than 60°F (15°C) for around a month or so.

Columneas do not require any special care except for occasional pruning and removal of the spent flowers. They like to stay on the wet side and can usually tolerate conditions from bright shade to semishade. Cuttings from most columneas will readily root into new plants.

Coral Bells
(Heuchera sanguinea)

Coral bells are a common outdoor perennial grown for their wispy scarlet sprays of small, reddish, bell-shaped flowers. The leaves stay low to the ground. As an experiment, I tried growing them in the greenhouse and have had great success. Except for a few months around January and February, this plant will flower on and off for much of the year. In the greenhouse, it tends to do best in full sun. The dainty flowers are perfect for small bouquets. It can be started from seed or easily divided from a mother plant. If you have an older clump of coral bells growing in your outside perennial bed, try dividing off a part of it for the greenhouse garden.

Crocus
(Crocus spp.)
See "Bulbs—Forcing Spring Bulbs for Winter Bloom" (page 184).

Croton
(Codiaeum variegatum)

Croton, also known as Joseph's Coat, is another plant treasured for its colorful leaves rather than for showy flowers. It has color combinations that run along the veins of a leathery, waxy leaf. The colors tend to be yellow and reddish-orange. The main variety is *Codiaeum variegatum pictum*, but there are many other named varieties.

This native to the tropics and subtropics is suited only for the warm greenhouse that never gets below 60°F (15°C). It also prefers a bright spot with some good sun exposure; without heat and good light, the leaves can lose some of their color. Most of the year, it prefers to stay constantly moist, except for winter, when you can cut back some on watering. It can be propagated from stem cuttings. Pests and diseases rarely occur on croton plants, with the exception of the mealybug.

With good care, it can eventually reach up to 4 feet (1.3 m) high and be filled with colorful leaves from top to bottom.

Cyclamen
(Cyclamen persicum)

Cyclamen is a common gift plant usually found in stores during the winter. People instantly fall in love with the interesting wind-swept, butterflylike flowers borne above heart-shaped, compact, patterned leaves. The flowers are available in shades of red, white, and rose. People often toss the plant out after it has bloomed, but with a little care it can be kept for many years. In the home, it is difficult to get it to flower again after the first bloom. In the greenhouse, however, you'll probably have an easier time of it because it needs cool nights of 50°F to 55°F (10°C to 13° C) to trigger the growth of flower buds. Cyclamens are best grown in a pot because they also need to be somewhat root bound before they will even think about setting flower buds.

Cyclamens need constant moisture and do best if watered from below by filling the saucer. If you must water from the top, try to keep the water off the leaves. After blooming, cut back on the water for a couple of months, and the plants may lose a few leaves. Then start watering them again and fertilize regularly, and you will be on your way to more blooms as long as you maintain cool nights. If your greenhouse consistently runs hot, cyclamens may suffer and get burned or yellow leaves, so try to find a cool spot for them. In the greenhouse, cyclamens will do best in full to partial sunlight but can tolerate shade as long as it is not too dark an area. Sometimes under a bench in the summer can be a good spot for them.

Cyclamens can be purchased as small round dormant tubers. Always plant the tubers concave side up. They can also be started from seed,

it may take up to a year before you see little tubers form and not long after that, flowering. Cover the seed with about $^1/_{16}$ inch (1.6 mm) of soil, and try to keep the temperature around 60°F (15°C). They rarely all come up at the same time, so be patient and wait awhile before you give up on all the seed you have sown.

If you repot an older plant, notice the little tubers just under the soil. When you set them in the new pot, be sure the top one-third of the tuber is above the soil surface. This will help them avoid rotting and they will establish faster.

The warmer you grow cyclamens, the more pests you will see, including aphids, mealybugs, and spider mites.

Dahlia
(*Dahlia pinnata* hybrid)

Dahlias are another plant commonly saved for the outside garden that can also be grown in the greenhouse with good success. You can grow both the large-flowered specimens and the dwarf varieties. The advantage of growing dahlias in the greenhouse is that you can benefit from a longer bloom period. Growing in the greenhouse is similar to growing outside. The larger varieties are usually started from tubers in March and will not begin to flower until early to mid-July. The dwarf varieties can easily be started from seed in February through April and will bloom from 7 weeks old through fall. There is much diversity in flower types to choose from.

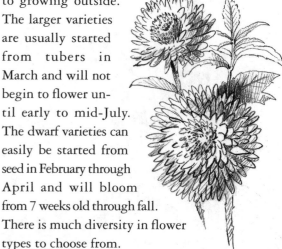

Plan on dahlias as a summer- and fall-flowering plant. The larger blossoms can be used in large bouquets. The dwarf varieties can be best grown in 6-inch (15-cm) pots or in beds along walkways. For some reason, dahlias can get floppy when grown in the greenhouse, especially the larger varieties. Try to gently tie them up to some slender stakes such as bamboo, or grow them in tomato cages to contain them.

Dianthus
(Dianthus chinensis)

These carnation relatives are also known as **pinks** and usually have single-petal flowers in white, red, pink, and combinations of all three. They are usually quite scented, often with a clovelike fragrance. Dianthus tends to stay compact, growing only to 6 to 12 inches (15 to 30 cm). Growing them is similar to growing carnations, only they need no staking. To promote longer bloom periods, be sure to make an effort to keep the spent blooms well picked. They are a long-lasting cut flower but are on short stems. They tend to bloom best in the moderate temperatures of fall and spring. Dianthus are easily propagated from seed but can also be started from cuttings.

Easter Lily
(Lilium longiflorum)

The Easter lily is a fun plant for the greenhouse. People commonly end up with one as a gift plant and wonder what to do with it after it is done blooming. The most common approach is to plant it in the outside garden, where it will often thrive and bloom in the summer every year. If you want to continue growing your Easter lily in the greenhouse, you will need to follow a specific schedule. After flowering, cut back on watering. The leaves will begin to turn yellow and die back. Water the plant when the top of the soil dries out. In late September, repot the plant in a 6-inch (15-cm) pot with new soil. Move the plant to a very dark, cool spot. Leave it there until 180 days before Easter. Then move the plant into a well-lit area with the temperature around 60°F (15°C). Keep the plant moist and fertilize every 2 weeks.

Another way to grow Easter lilies is to purchase precooled bulbs. This is how the commercial greenhouses do it. The trouble is, they are usually purchased only in large amounts on a wholesale basis, so where are you going to find a small number of precooled Easter lily bulbs for sale? Perhaps you could talk your local commercial greenhouse into selling you some. You could also try talking with some people at specialty bulb companies to see if they could sell you some. With precooled bulbs, you need to start storing the bulbs in a cool spot only 120 days before Easter.

With Easter coming at a different time every year, it is a task even for commercial growers to get the scheduling right. It is still more difficult for the home-greenhouse gardener to get the blooms to appear right at Easter because the climate control is often much less exacting. What I'm trying to say is, don't be surprised if your timing is a bit off. You will probably still enjoy the large white trumpet blooms even if they miss Easter by a few weeks one way or the other.

Felicia
(Felicia amelloides)
Felicia is grown for its profusion of 1-inch (2.5-cm) sky-blue daisies with yellow centers. It is also known as the **kingfisher daisy** and the **blue marguerite daisy**. It grows only about 1 foot (0.3 m) high and has rough-textured leaves that feel almost succulent. It blooms best when the nights are around 50°F (10°C). It seems to have blooms in every season except summer. Felicia can be propagated from seed. By starting it in spring, you will have bloom in the coming winter. It can be grown for many years before you will need to think about propagating replacements.

It can also be easily propagated from cuttings. The first felicia I ever grew was from one I saw outside an airport in California in winter. Being a trained horticulturist, I "accidentally" plucked a 5-inch (13-cm) piece of stem, put it in my pocket and smuggled it home to Wyoming, where the next day I placed it in my propagation flat. Within 6 months, I had a beautiful blooming twin sister to the felicia growing back in California.

There is also a variegated felicia, now becoming more popular for baskets and pots, that has marbled green-and-white leaves.

Foxglove
(Digitalis purpurea x 'Foxy')
Foxglove is a biennial commonly grown in the outside garden. When it finally blooms in the second year, it really makes a statement. Foxglove has 2-inch (5-cm) bell-shaped flowers in pastel colors with distinctive off-colored spots in the throat of each bloom. The flowers are borne on long spikes that can get 3 feet (0.9 m) or more tall.

Biennials are usually difficult to grow in a greenhouse because most need a good cold period that is hard to provide in a warm sunspace. Luckily, a few years back there was the introduction of the variety Foxy. Foxy has the unique ability to bloom in the first year of growth. If you grow foxglove for greenhouse flowers, it should only be the Foxy variety. Sow it from seed and it will bloom in around 5 to 6 months. Be careful not to disturb the roots when it is transplanted. Set the foxglove out in clumps of three or more plants, placed in full sun. In the greenhouse, they are best grown in beds or in pots at least 1 gallon (3.8 liters) in size with a well-drained soil. It is only worth growing for the first bloom unless you have the space to nurse the plant for 12 more months. At best, you should toss the plant out after the second set of blooms.

With warm temperatures, keep a keen eye out for whitefly.

Freesia
(Freesia refracta)

I am convinced that heaven has the scent of freesias. Their scent is not known for being powerfully strong, but the fragrance is most wonderfully unique. Freesias have become more and more popular as a gift plant and in bouquets. Freesia blooms are found in almost every color. The white varieties tend to be the most fragrant. There are also double-blossomed varieties. Freesia has 2-inch (5-cm) trumpet-like flowers and leaves that resemble thick-bladed grass. The plant itself reaches 8 to 12 inches (20 to 30 cm) high.

Freesias are best suited for growing in the winter and do well in a cool greenhouse. Although they can be started from seed, they are most often propagated from bulbs (corms) planted in late summer to early winter. A little cool treatment seems to make for healthier plants. I have the best luck if I simply place the bulbs in the refrigerator (not freezer) for 3 to 4 weeks before planting. They grow well in both pots and beds. Place the bulb in the soil, pointed end upward, 2 inches (5 cm) deep and about 4 to 6 inches (10 to 15 cm) apart. As freesias grow, they can get a little floppy. Support them with a small bamboo stake, and gently tie the leaves to it with a thin piece of soft cloth. They will bloom in 3 to 4 months. They are pest free for the most part.

After blooming, let the plant continue growing for at least another month. Then you'll notice the foliage begin to decline. At that point, remove the bulb and store it in peat moss in a cool, dark spot until it is time to plant it again, usually late summer or fall. If any of the leaves exhibit a reddish rusty color, it is a sign

of a fungus. These bulbs and/or plants should be discarded.

As I mentioned earlier, freesias can also be started from seed, but it adds an extra 6 months to the time before you'll see a bloom. I can never wait that long, so I always stock up on bulbs. They are readily available in garden centers in fall or in bulb catalogs. I can't imagine a winter greenhouse without a crop of freesias to brighten up the winter's gloomy days.

Fuchsia
(Fuchsia spp.)

Fuchsias are grown for their beautiful flowers, which hang like ornaments off the plant, often with a splash of two-toned color. The flowers can be found in many different color combinations, including red, pink, purple and white. The flower size varies from being as small as a thimble to as big as a medium-sized apple. The unique flower consists of showy colorful sepals, which are the part of the flower that flares back. Unfortunately, the flower has no fragrance, but it is so colorful you might be surprised what it can attract. In fact, one day I left my greenhouse door open, and as I walked by, I heard a strange vibration in the greenhouse. I looked and was surprised to see a little

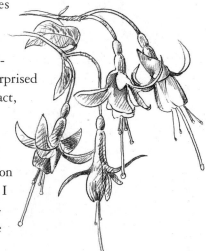

hardworking hummingbird (have you ever seen a lazy hummingbird?) working on the fuchsia flowers. The choices for different varieties are in the hundreds. Each has its own special name.

Fuchsias need a moderately cool environment to grow and flower. They can be gown in the greenhouse year-round, but when summer comes, you might try moving them to a cooler spot (perhaps a lightly shaded porch) to persuade your plants to continue the flower display. Although fuchsias like cool temperatures, they don't flower much if the temperature runs below 48°F (9°C). They need to grow on the moist side but also need a well-drained soil. Fertilize with a houseplant food every 3 weeks during blooming for good growth. If your plant isn't bushy enough for your liking, pinch the tips for good side-shoot development. Occasional pruning to shape the plant is helpful, especially in fall.

Fuchsias are easily propagated from cuttings taken from the tip. Be sure the cutting is at least 3 inches (8 cm) long. The biggest problem with fuchsias is that whiteflies love them (see Chapter 10). Always keep a keen eye on the underside of the leaf, as there is often a budding whitefly colony in need of eradication.

Gardenia
(Gardenia jasminoides)

The gardenia flower has perhaps one of the most hypnotizing scents in the plant kingdom. It has beautiful white to yellow blossoms on glossy dark green leaves. Some varieties can get large, up to 10 feet (3 m) tall. The smaller types are better suited for greenhouse potted-plant culture, and these are the types most greenhouse plant catalogs offer for sale.

Before you get excited about growing a gardenia, though, I should warn you that it is famous for being temperamental. Its require-

ments to set flower buds are exacting. The gardenia needs a night temperature of 60°F to 65°F (15°C to 18°C) and day temperatures only a bit warmer. It also needs ample water and should never dry out. Some people swear by the practice of always watering with slightly warm water in winter, as the plants get shocked if you use cold tap water in the dead of winter. It also needs a slightly acid soil. I have found that it responds better to growing in a clay rather than a plastic pot.

The gardenia is prone to iron deficiency and may need an acidifying plant food. If the temperature is not right or there is any stress on the plant, it may drop its buds or never form them. It is also a favorite of many greenhouse insects. If this all sounds discouraging, you may want to wait until you get some more growing experience before you grow gardenias. Don't despair—there are other ways to get a similar intoxicating fragrance. Instead try the many different fragrant jasmines, which are much easier and have a fragrance akin to the gardenia's.

Geranium
(Pelargonium)

Geraniums are one of the easiest and most trouble-free of all greenhouse flowering plants. They are perennial in the greenhouse, and many types provide year-round blooms and interest.

Most geraniums can be easily started from stem cuttings taken from the tip. Be sure to pinch off any flowers or flower buds from the slips that you are taking, in order to speed up the rooting. All geraniums benefit from a well-lit location and prefer some drying between waterings.

There are four main types of annual flowering geraniums you should know about. Let's look at each one.

Garden, or Zonal, Geraniums
(Pelargonium x hortorum)

The garden geranium is the most common type, the one you first think of when you envision geraniums. The leaves are usually velvety and soft with a unique geranium scent. Some of the garden geraniums have leaves that are totally green, but many others have what are called "zones." Zoned geraniums, or zonals, as they are often called, exhibit a zone of deeper color across the leaf. This color can be purple, brown, orange, white, or red. Some varieties have even been bred to make these zones more interesting and colorful. There are hundreds of different types of zonal garden geraniums. A good portion of them are great bloomers. The flowers are usually single or double and are found in a solid color (although spotted ones are gaining in popularity). Garden geraniums are commonly found with flower colors in white, red, pink, orange, and violet. With proper care and feeding, they can bloom nonstop for many years even in a relatively cool greenhouse.

These are shrubby plants that can reach heights of up to 4 feet (1.2 m) if given a chance and enough root room, but they look best if kept bushy and well shaped. How do you do that? Try regular tip pinching to promote bushiness. They also need to have spent flowers regularly picked to promote more flowering.

Unfortunately, geraniums don't make a very good cut flower, because most drop their petals quickly after being cut. Horticulturists call this quick petal dropping "shattering." There are a few exceptions to this trait of shattering. I have had luck with many of the cactus-flowered types, such as the variety Star of Persia. I have also been able to make good cut-flower arrangements with the variety Apple Blossom and many of the double-rosebud varieties. Every once in a while, I stumble upon a regular flowering geranium that doesn't shatter.

Garden geraniums, like most other geraniums, are among the easiest plants to propagate from cuttings. Unlike the other geraniums, the garden geraniums can also be easily propagated from seed. Don't set the small seedling in too large a pot until it has a well-developed root system.

By far the easiest way to bring color into any greenhouse is to grow a good selection of the many brightly flowered garden geraniums.

Ivy Geraniums
(Pelargonium peltatum)

As the name implies, the ivy geranium is known for its ivylike leaves, which are thick and almost succulent. Although it doesn't bloom as freely as the garden geranium, it is almost as trouble free. The ivy geraniums are best suited for hanging pots because the leaves need to trail off over the side of the pot. For the growth to look thick enough, try to plant at least three plants per pot. They seem to bloom best in the summer months, but the foliage is still attractive year-round. They bloom less than the garden geraniums but more consistently than the Martha Washington geraniums discussed below. There are a few varieties with some interesting variegated leaves that are even more attractive during the nonbloom periods. Some varieties are double flowered. The single-flowered types (sometimes known as cascade-ivy geraniums) are more heat tolerant. Don't let the soil dry out or it will cause some leaf burning.

Most geraniums are not prone to major bug infestations, but the ivy geraniums seem more predisposed to mealybugs (see Chapter 10) than any of the other geraniums. Keep an eye on the base of the leaves for these cottony critters.

Martha Washington Geraniums

(*Pelargonium domesticum*, or Grandiflorum hybrids) The Martha Washington geraniums (also known as regal geraniums) have the most impressive flowers of all. They are larger than any other geranium flower, growing 2 inches (5 cm) or more across. The flower often has other interesting, darker markings in its throat. The leaves may or may not be scented, and the blossom is rarely scented. Unfortunately, people see the blooms and fall in love, only to find that the bloom period of the Washington geranium is often very short, especially when compared to the garden geranium. Blooming is prolonged as long as the night temperature remains below 60°F (15°C). They bloom most commonly only in spring and early summer. These plants do best in a well-lit location.

After the blooms have stopped it helps to prune the tips back and fertilize to stimulate new growth. I have seen whitefly sometimes attracted to these plants, so keep an eye out for infestations on the undersides of the leaves.

Scented Geraniums

Many different species of geraniums have the most interesting scented leaves. A few of these also have showy blooms and some have unusual-shaped leaves, but most are grown solely for their scent. The scent is not very volatile, which means that you must first rub the leaf in order to get the air filled with their aroma. The most interesting thing about the scented geraniums is that they are incredible mimics. You can find scents that you would swear are almost identical to those of strawberries, mint, rose, lemon, lime, apple, and even chocolate mint (one of my favorites, as it perfectly mimics an after-dinner mint). You won't believe me until you grow some yourself. If you can't find some scented geraniums at your local greenhouse, check the "Mail-Order Plants" list in Appendix 5 for greenhouse plant catalogs. There are even one or two catalogs listed that specialize only in geraniums. Place the scented geraniums near walks and paths, where they can be easily touched or brushed against.

Gerbera Daisy

(*Gerbera jamesonii*)
The gerbera daisy, also known as **African** or **Transvaal daisy**, is a low-growing plant with striking daisylike flowers borne on thick stems. The flowers can be found in most warm colors. The plant reaches only to a height of 5 inches

(13 cm), with sturdy flowering stalks reaching up to 1 foot (0.3 m). The gerbera daisy is not too particular about temperature and is a good choice for cooler greenhouses. The main thing is to give it the sunniest spot possible.

The hardest part about growing gerbera daisies is getting the seeds to germinate. When you check your catalogs, you'll find that the seed is quite expensive in comparison with many other ornamental seeds, so it is important to get your investment to germinate.

One trick that I have found in germinating gerberas is to place each seed vertically with half of the seed poking above ground and the other half below ground. Don't worry, there is not a particular end that needs to face up or down. Doing this is easier said than done because they are small, though not too small to do this, especially if you use a pair of tweezers to assist. When you transplant them, take care not to bury the plants any deeper than they were originally. If the crown becomes buried, the plant may have some problems with rotting.

Gerberas do fine in both ground beds and 6-inch (15-cm) pots. I have found that the plants can easily get deficient in iron, exhibited by yellowing between the veins in the leaf. Treat with a plant food containing iron (follow the label exactly, as iron can easily burn plants).

You'll find that you get occasional blooms year-round, but you often get a good flush of blooms in both spring and fall. If you are growing them for cut flowers, let the bloom open fully before cutting. They make a long-lived cut flower in arrangements.

Keep an eye on the underside of the leaf because whiteflies like to hang around gerberas.

Globe Amaranth
(*Gomphrena globosa*)

Globe amaranth, also commonly known by its scientific name, **Gomphrena**, is a so-called everlasting flower. It has papery, thimble-shaped flowers that resemble a clover flower. Flower colors include white, orange, purple, red, and rose. For years it was a good plant for cooler greenhouses, but the flower always had a short stem. Woodcreek Nursery bred a wonderful selection called Strawberry Fields, also sold under the name Woodcreek Red. No matter what name it is sold under, you will find that this is the best variety to grow. Luckily, it is readily available in many seed catalogs. This is because of its longer stem, which reaches up to 20 inches (51 cm), making it showier and a great cut flower. Although gomphrenas come in other colors, they are not nearly as showy. The Woodcreek (or Strawberry Fields) red is best grown in ground beds.

The best way to grow them in the greenhouse is to start them in midsummer, allowing them to develop a root system before the cold of fall and winter sets in. With this schedule they can provide many blooms throughout the winter. Gomphrenas look best if planted in collections of five plants or more, spaced at around 6 inches (15 cm) apart. They prefer to be grown in full sun and on the dry side. Be sure to prune off spent flowers

and occasional brown leaves to keep the plant looking good.

Gomphrenas are known for having an erratic germination habit. It is common to get only around 50 percent of the seeds to germinate, so plant them thickly. Barely cover the seed, and try to keep the soil temperature around 70°F (21°C). Also when germinating and growing, go easier on the watering. Overwatering will cause poor germination and growth.

Gloxinia
(Sinningia speciosa)

The gloxinia has long been a popular blooming houseplant. It has dark, fuzzy, oblong leaves that sit under the 4-inch (10-cm) wide, bell-shaped flowers, available in shades of white, red, pink, purple, and blue, depending upon the variety. Some flowers have showy speckles in the throat; others have bands of contrasting colors toward the edge of the flower. They usually flower in the spring or summer.

Gloxinias are generally started from tubers or divisions taken from a larger tuber, but with a lot of patience they can be started from seed or propagated from leaf cuttings. Grow them in 6- to 8-inch (15- to 20-cm) pots. Gloxinias grow best in the warm greenhouse where the temperature rarely falls below 60°F (15°C). They like bright spots but not direct sunlight. Keep the plants moist at all times but not dripping wet, using lukewarm water. Try to keep water off the leaves.

Many people give gloxinias a rest period after flowering by stopping any watering

and setting the tuber in a dark, dry spot for a few months. There are many other growers who never give the plant a rest period with good success.

Most problems with gloxinias arise from growing either too cool or too wet. They must also have good humidity and be placed away from cool drafts. Getting the plant to survive for many years is not particularly easy, but it is always worth the challenge to see the beautiful display of flowers come again.

Golden-Trumpet Vine
(Allamanda cathartica)

As you can guess from the name, this plant is a vine with bright, trumpet-shaped golden flowers. It is native to South America and is best suited to larger greenhouses with enough room to roam because its vines can reach 15 feet (4.6 m) in length. Because of its size, it is best planted directly in a ground bed with a clear plan of where the vines are going to climb. Golden-trumpet vine blooms from spring to fall. The flowers are slightly scented, but the smell gets more heady at night. Plants can be obtained from greenhouse plant catalogs. It is best propagated from cuttings.

The golden-trumpet vine prefers an environment that offers high humidity and a temperature not lower than 55°F (13°C). This is a plant best suited for the warmer winter greenhouse. Pruning after blooming seems to encourage both new growth and new buds and blooms.

Logee's Greenhouses catalog (1-888-330-8038; see "Mail-Order Plants" in Appendix 5) has a smaller variety called *Allamanda compacta* that is easier to grow in smaller quarters or even in a pot.

Hibiscus
(*Hibiscus* spp.)

Why not grow the state flower of Hawaii in your greenhouse? This is an easy-to-grow plant for any sunny greenhouse that can tolerate both high and low temperatures. It is notorious for its large, hollyhocklike blooms, which can be up to 10 inches (25 cm) across with some varieties. Its colors include pink, red, yellow, orange, white, and multiple variations in one flower. The hibiscus can be grown successfully in ground beds or large pots. If allowed to have its own way, it can reach 10 feet (3 m) tall or more. In its native habitat, the hibiscus is a tropical evergreen shrub.

You'll have more blooms and a healthier plant if you occasionally prune it, which stimulates new growth. This is because most new flowering buds can be found primarily on the new growth. Some hibiscus can bloom year-round, though others tend to bloom mostly in late winter through spring.

Hibiscus is an easy plant to grow, especially if you can give it plenty of sun and maintain constant moisture. Feed with a general houseplant food once or twice a month. Plants can be obtained through plant catalogs or your local commercial greenhouse.

Logee's Greenhouses catalog (888-330-8038) offers a wonderful variety, sold as The Path, which has a sunset-colored flower that ranges from yellow on the edge to reddish-orange, complemented with a pink center. It gets more comments than any other hibiscus in my greenhouse. Hibiscus can be started from 6-inch (15-cm) stem cuttings taken from the tip.

Hibiscus may be bothered occasionally by aphids, whiteflies, and mites, so admire the flower but also occasionally look to the underside of the leaaves.

Hoya
(*Hoya carnosa*)

Also known as the **wax plant**, hoyas are popular houseplants. People often just let them go about their business, trailing all around the perimeter of a windowsill and even throughout the house. Some also let them trail out of a hanging pot with their thick waxy leaves looking quite orderly. Some have found a way to make the vines look thicker by spiraling them around and around on a wreathlike trellis stuck into a large pot.

Besides the leaf, the prized fragrant flower, which usually blooms in early summer, is also waxy looking and has pale pink petals. It is mesmerizing not only because of its fragrance and waxy appearance but also because of the fact that each flower looks like a five-pointed star and the cluster of flowers also arranges itself in a star shape.

Besides the *Hoya carnosa*, collectors have found many other types of hoya species that have different fragrances and leaf shapes. One species, the *Hoya longifolia,* has been described as smelling like chocolate cake. The fragrance this plant gives off is usually intensified at night.

The hoyas seem to thrive on neglect. As testimony to this, I had a friend grow one for 3 years in a glass filled with water. If the care you give it is too good, that is, if you provide ample water and fertilizer, the plant won't grow much and will likely not bloom. Instead, let it stay pot bound for many years and water sparingly (especially in winter), unless it is starting to grow flower buds, when it should not dry out. Fertilize the plant in the summer months. When it comes to light, hoyas do fine in the bright greenhouse but do equally well in a shady corner. They can tolerate a wide range of temperatures and can do fine even if the temperature occasionally drops down to 45°F (7°C). If you want to make more hoyas, they can be readily propagated from cuttings.

The main pest on the hoya is the mealybug. However, I have never seen a hoya die from a bug infestation of any kind.

Hyacinth

(*Hyacinthus* spp.)
See "Bulbs—Forcing Spring Bulbs for Winter Bloom" (p. 184).

Impatiens

(*Impatiens* spp.)
Also known as **Busy Lizzies,** this common garden-variety annual impatiens provides a good way to brighten up shadier areas in the greenhouse that are bright but don't receive full sunlight. Given medium temperatures that don't run below 45°F (7°C), they can provide almost continuous bloom in the greenhouse. Because they grow only low to the ground, with flowers on short stems, they won't do as a cut flower.

However, they are great in ground beds and hanging baskets. Impatiens are available in almost any color except blue. Because they can live for so long in the greenhouse environment, they will need occasional tip pruning to keep the plant bushy. I have great luck planting them under garden benches and in corners. For the most part, impatiens are relatively trouble free.

Impatiens are easy to start, both from seed and cuttings. When starting seed, just barely cover it, because they need to see a bit of light in order to trigger germination. Maintain a high humidity by misting the soil surface regularly, and keep the temperature around 70°F (21°C).

New Guinea impatiens are a type with variegated leaves along with an impatienslike flower. The New Guineas are more difficult to grow than the garden impatiens, needing more water and more stable warm temperatures. Still, they are interesting plants for the greenhouse.

There are also some more unusual impatiens, including a showy rosebud-type flower. More rarely available is the *Impatiens repens,* also known as Ceylon jewelweed, which is a trailing plant with rounded, bronze leaves and thick succulent stems. These have odd yellow flowers that look nothing like an impatiens.

Iris

(*Iris* spp.)
See "Bulbs—Forcing Spring Bulbs for Winter Bloom" (page 184).

Jasmine

(*Jasminum* spp., *Trachelospermum jasminoides*)
This is the plant to grow for fragrance. Most, but not all, jasmines have an incredible fragrance emanating from white or yellow flowers; however, some of the yellow-flowered jasmines are not fragrant. A single blooming plant can fill the air with a most intoxicating scent. Some jasmines are shrubby plants, but most have a vine-type growth. There are many species of jasmine worth growing. *Trachelospermum jasminoides*, commonly called the **star jasmine**, is not in the true jasmine family but has a jasminelike fragrance.

Jasminum humile is a yellow-flowered plant that, unlike many yellow-flowered varieties, has a nice fragrance and can bloom almost any time of year. It can tolerate a cool greenhouse nicely.

Jasminum nitidum is a good container plant, with bushy green leaves and star-shaped flowers. It can bloom in the cooler months as well as in the summer and can tolerate a very cool greenhouse as long as it doesn't get below freezing.

Jasminum officinale is the so-called **common jasmine,** or **poet's jasmine.** It is a slow-growing vining plant with fragrant white flowers that can appear almost anytime except late winter. This is a plant commonly used in the manufacture of perfume in France.

Jasminum polyanthum, also known as **winter jasmine,** is a relatively fast-growing plant that has finely divided leaves that like to vine around other nearby plants or structures. It is primarily a prolific winter bloomer, described by some as providing a "blizzard" of blooms. To get the best show, provide a well-lit spot and some warmth. The polyanthum can be trained up a small trellis and grows well either in pots or directly in beds. This is my favorite jasmine

because it is both showy and fragrant!

Jasminum sambac is used commercially both in making tea and perfume, and it is also important in some Buddhist ceremonies. It has a bushy habit that adapts well to potted culture. *J. sambac* prefers a minimum temperature of 60°F (15°C) and bright sunlight.

Jasminum x *stephanense* is good for summer blooms. It has fragrant whitish-pink blooms and likes to vine up adjacent plants and objects.

Jasminum tortuosum is a good choice for a year-round bloomer but blooms heaviest from spring through fall. It is a relatively fast grower and has a vining habit. It can tolerate a wide range of temperatures.

Trachelospermum jasminoides, not a true jasmine, is available in both white- and yellow-flowering varieties. Both have a rich fragrance. Although they can tolerate cool greenhouse temperatures, they tend to hold off blooming until things begin to warm up in spring.

Most jasmines are best suited to growing in pots. They usually have an open growth habit, which requires occasional pinching back and shaping. Over time, the plants can start to look a bit ragged and unkempt, especially if the foliage gets thick. Even though the plant may be healthy, sometimes certain leaves and stems may die back for no reason, lending an untidy look if not groomed. In general, jasmines need moderate moisture and light levels. Jasmines are generally propagated from cuttings taken from the more mature stems;

within a few months they immediately follow with a flush of blooms.

Kalanchoe

(*Kalanchoe* spp.)

Kalanchoe is a large genus of succulent plants that vary greatly in leaf types and flowers. Some have incredible blooms and / or unusual leaves. Others are known for their peculiar ways of easily propagating themselves with little plantlets that form on the leaves themselves and drop to the ground ready to grow. It would be hard to tell you about every kalanchoe that can be found, but I must pass on some of my favorites. With a little looking, you will likely stumble upon even more interesting kalanchoes in various catalogs and garden centers.

The first kalanchoe I mention here is probably the most common, often sold in stores as a blooming potted plant. It is known commonly as kalanchoe and scientifically as *Kalanchoe blossfeldiana*. It is more commonly known as **Flaming Katie**. It has wide, thick, waxy leaves and sprouts a profusion of red, rose, orange, or yellow flowers. It holds the blooms on for many weeks. After the blooms lose their luster, pinch off the faded flowers and continue to pinch the tips of the plants for a few more months to promote a bushy plant.

Some other kalanchoes that have caught my eye over the years include *Kalanchoe mortagei*, or more commonly, **Mother of Hundreds**. It is easy to see why it gets the name when you see that it produces hundreds of little plantlets along the leaf edge, which drop off onto the soil and almost immediately start to grow. The leaves of *K. mortagei* also are interest-

ing. The plant itself gets to 1 foot (0.3 m) or more in height. It also has a showy orange or reddish bloom.

Some similar plants that also produce an abundance of plantlets include *Kalanchoe pinnata* and *Kalanchoe daigremontiana*. These are fun plants for kids to have and experiment with and provide a good lesson in plant propagation.

Kalanchoe pumila is commonly called **flour-dust plant** because the silver-gray leaves look as if they were recently dusted. In the winter, it produces an abundance of beautiful pink flowers. It makes a real show in a hanging basket and, like all kalanchoes, is easy to grow.

Another silver-leaved succulent plant is *Kalanchoe tomentosa*, which is commonly sold as **Panda Plant** because of its furry leaves.

One of the best sources for dozens of varieties of kalanchoe is the mail-order catalog Glasshouse Works in Ohio (see "Mail-Order Plants" in Appendix 5), which has an incredible selection that could keep you busy experimenting with unusual-leaved and unusual-flowered kalanchoes for many years to come.

The general care for kalanchoes is to provide a very bright spot and let the soil dry out between waterings (see "Succulents," later in this chapter). They do fine in most store-bought potting soils. Kalanchoes tolerate both cool and warm temperatures quite admirably. However, prolonged high temperatures may cause a lack of buds and blooms. Kalanchoes are easy to start from cuttings of the leaf or stem. They root rapidly and grow quickly. They seem to do best in pots rather than in ground beds. Although some species, for example, *Kalanchoe blossfeldiana,* are occasionally beset with a mealybug infestation, in general they have few problems with pests.

Kale and Cabbage, Flowering
(Brassica oleracea)

Flowering kale and cabbage produce one of the most ornamental blossom-like shows that you will ever see—beautiful rosettes of pink, rose, red, or white against a mottled green background. They just need a few things to bring on the color: cool temperatures and a bright spot in which to grow. For that reason, they are a great plant for starting in the late summer to early fall and then enjoying from midwinter into spring.

Eventually, when the warm temperatures of late spring arrive, they will try to flower or just begin to look ragged. Neither is a pretty sight compared to the colorful show when they are at their peak. When this happens, it is time to toss them out.

What is the difference between flowering kale and cabbage? The kale has a frillier leaf, whereas the flowering cabbage has flatter leaves. I like both. When buying seed, I have found that it is best to select the hybrid varieties of either the flowering kale or cabbage because they seem to color up earlier and can tolerate warmer temperatures better than do the nonhybrids. There are also dwarf varieties for growing in smaller pots along with a variety called Peacock that has finely cut leaves.

Flowering cabbage and kale are only propagated from seed. They can be grown in pots, which need to be at least 1 gallon (3.8 liters) in size unless you are growing the dwarf varieties. If you grow them directly in ground beds, space them about 10 inches (25 cm) apart along walk paths where they can easily be seen.

Be sure to grow them in a cool, bright spot or they will never get the showy colorful leaves. On occasion, aphids may be a problem.

If you are wondering whether flowering kale or cabbage are edible, the answer is yes.

Not always tasty, but edible. Cooler weather produces the best-flavored flowering kale and cabbage. If it gets hot, the flavor might become highly bitter. For fresh eating, I prefer growing the regular varieties of edible cabbage or kale when taste and flavor are important. Many restaurants use the leaves of the ornamental kale and cabbage as a garnish. Although it is pretty, when it comes to a garnish I prefer the more functional and edible parsley.

King's Crown, Brazilian Plume
(Justicia carnea)

The common name, king's crown, is apt when you see the regal blooms that this plant produces. The tubular pink blooms resemble a most stately crown, made up of a cluster of flowers that are 5 to 7 inches (13 to 18 cm) in diameter. Usually a few weeks after the main flower has faded, some equally showy but smaller blooms will appear on side shoots.

I have the best luck growing it in a 1- to 5-gallon (3.8- to 19-liter) pot. King's crown benefits from regular feeding in the summer. It tends to bloom from May through August. When not in bloom, it still has handsome, dark-green leaves. After the flower show is over, pruning the spent blossoms is a good idea.

King's crown prefers a bright spot and a consistently moist (but not dripping wet) soil. Occasional pruning in early fall seems to stimulate a bushy and well-bloomed plant. Pests are rare. It is easily propagated by cuttings.

There is also a white-flowered variety, *Justicia carnea alba*, if you prefer a white crown. More rarely available are yellow- and red-flowering species. It is also a close cousin to the shrimp plant, *Justicia brandegeana*, listed later in this chapter.

Larkspur
(Consolida ambigua)

Larkspur is a tall-growing blooming annual that can grow anywhere from 1 to 3 feet (0.3 to 0.9 m) in height, depending upon the variety. Larkspur has flowers borne on spikes in the colors white, red, lavender, blue, purple, and pink. The blooms are not fragrant, but they make up for it in their dependable, colorful show and they make a fine cut flower. Take care to keep the plant away from toddlers as it is toxic if ingested.

In the greenhouse, larkspur does better if timed to bloom in winter through early summer. If not, warm weather may put them under stress, possibly causing bloom failure. They are best in the cooler greenhouse, where the nights are around 45°F to 50°F (7°C to 10°C). Even so, I have been experimenting with sowing the seeds during almost any month with decent results.

The seeds should be buried at least $^1/_8$ inch (0.3 cm) because they germinate best in a dark spot. It may take up to 25 days for germination, so be patient. Use your best technique when you transplant larkspur out of seed trays into pots or beds because it doesn't like its roots disturbed. Larkspur can be grown in 6- to 8-inch (15- to 20-cm) pots or planted directly in the ground, spacing them 8 to 10 inches (20 to 25 cm) apart. They like a well-drained soil with good fertility and often benefit from regular supplemental feeding. If you grow them in pots, don't let the soil run dry for any length of time, but be equally cautious of overwatering. A well-drained soil helps you create a good growing environment.

The taller varieties often need to be supported (staked or caged) to prevent them from flopping over. Because they are annuals, larkspurs should be tossed into the compost pile after blooming has finished.

Lisianthus, or "Prairie Gentian"
(Eustoma grandiflorum)

The lisianthus is grown primarily as a greenhouse cut flower. It is a native of the American prairie. The plant can reach up to 2 feet (0.6 cm) and bears roselike flowers with swirls of petals often in pastel colors but also found in blue, rose, and lilac, with different colorings on the edges of the petals. Flowers can last for up to 2 weeks after cutting. Although the flowers are not particularly fragrant, they are quite showy and great in a cut-flower arrangement.

Lisianthus is often slow to germinate and can be finicky about germinating. It germinates best when the soil temperature is warm, up around 70°F (20°C). I like to transplant seedlings directly into ground beds, but they also do fine in pots. Usually the stems are sturdy enough that they don't need support.

The best schedule I have found for the lisianthus is to sow seeds in late August through early October for blooms the following March through June. Most plants grow slightly over 2 feet (0.6 m), but there are some dwarf varieties that only reach 8 inches (20 cm) high. I think the taller varieties are best for the greenhouse because you get bigger flowers and more blossoms to add to a bouquet.

After 9 months to a year and a number of harvests of bouquets, the plants often decline, and then it is time to start over again. Pests are usually not a problem unless the plants are past their prime.

Lobelia

(Lobelia tenuior)

The best lobelias for the greenhouse are the low-growing annual flowers. I like to use them along walks or in hanging baskets, where they dangle attractively over the sides of the baskets. They have dainty little blooms that provide a mass of color: blue, white, purple, and reddish. They are easily started from seed and prefer to grow in a slightly moist environment. When grown in pots, try to not let the soil dry out completely. A favorite variety of mine is called Crystal Palace, which has bronze foliage. The darker foliage of Crystal Palace sets off the purple blooms, making them appear to glow. Unfortunately, I have found that in a greenhouse the foliage doesn't get nearly as bronze as it does outside. Still, it is a good-looker. As lobelias mature, they can benefit from an occasional haircut to help stimulate another flush of blooms; eventually however, they should be tossed out.

Keep lobelia out of reach of young toddlers, as the foliage is reputed to be poisonous if ingested.

Malope

(Malvaceae trifida)

I discovered malope by chance when I saw it mentioned in a Thompson & Morgan seed catalog. To my surprise, it ended up producing a grand display of blooms in my greenhouse. It has large, rich reddish-purple blooms on a shrubby plant that reaches around 3 feet (0.9 m) high and wide. Each bloom is about 3 inches (8 cm) across. The flowers have no real fragrance, but it is worth growing and works well in bouquets.

After my first success in growing malope, I had many failures. One of my problems turned out to be poor timing. It needs to be started (from seed) in late summer or early fall. Any other time of year when I started malope, the plant either grew poorly or succumbed to stress and disease. So, in the greenhouse, timing seems to be everything. Now that I have returned to fall sowing, things are back on track. With that kind of schedule, you can usually expect to see your first blooms in March or April, although you may have to wait as long as early June, but it is well worth the wait. Still, I should caution you that it is not the easiest plant to grow, because of its susceptibility to disease and moisture stress.

Malopes are best grown directly in a bed or eventually up-potted into a larger tub. As they mature they can sometimes get floppy, so before they get big, place a tomato cage over them for support. To promote bushiness and a fuller plant, pinch the tips of the stems when the plant is around 1 foot (0.3 m) high. Be sure to place your malope in a spot that receives full sun and regular moisture. As the plant gets larger, it wilts more easily and may need daily watering. After the bloom show, you'll have to toss the plants out, because they go downhill rapidly. If it was big, be ready to put something new in the big empty space that it occupied.

Mandevilla
(*Mandevilla* spp.)

Mandevilla is not a commonly known plant, but it should be. It produces a wealth of flowers, blooming mostly fall through spring, which hold on the vine for many weeks. They look like a cross between a morning glory and a petunia, usually having 3-inch-wide (8-cm-wide) blooms. The more common species is *Mandevilla* x *amabilis*, which grows in a vinelike fashion, with glossy, dark green leaves and pink flowers that often turn red as they open. It needs to be staked or set near some trellising because it vines. It can grow up to 10 feet (3 m) tall and can be grown in either a pot or a ground bed. I have had the best luck in pots. It can tolerate cooler temperatures well but seems to prefer more-moderate temperatures. It can bloom for up to 8 or 9 months. *Mandevilla sanderi*, sometimes known as **Red Riding Hood,** is a particularly beautiful plant with striking, lipstick-colored blooms that also requires trellising.

Mandevilla boliviensis produces a summer show of white flowers with golden throats.

Mandevillas are best propagated from cuttings. Grow them in rich, well-drained soil. They can look sickly when the soil is poorly drained. By mixing a little sand or perlite in the potting mix, you can prevent this. They like constant moisture in the summer but need to run a little dry between watering during the winter months. Yellowing of the new leaves might indicate a need for micronutrient fertilizing (see Chapter 9, "Getting to the Roots"). The main pest on mandevilla is the mealybug.

In general, these are easy-to-grow, dependable, long-lived plants that are suitable for larger pots with a trellis or support, or they may be grown directly in ground beds, again with trellising. With some pruning, I have seen mandevilla look good in larger hanging baskets. In pots or baskets, consider planting other complementary plants such as alyssum or lobelia.

Maple, Flowering, or Parlor Maple
(*Abutilon megapotamicum*)

These parlor, or flowering, maples are aptly named because of the resemblance the leaves have to maple trees, but they are not related. They are a nice plant for greenhouse culture because they bloom forever and are easy to grow. What makes them interesting are their bell-shaped, lantern-like flowers, which (usually) hang down as if casting a light below. The blooms are not fragrant but are showy and have the advantage of tolerating variable temperatures while blooming year-round in the greenhouse. The flowers can be found in pink, red, white, gold, and yellow.

Some of the varieties of flowering maple have interesting mottled foliage with white or orange variegation that complements the flowers. Plants can grow up to 3 feet (0.9 m) high but look best if kept pruned to a more compact shape. Instead, you can simply grow the more compact, dwarf varieties of flowering maples for easy maintenance.

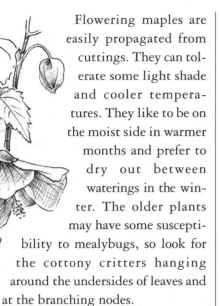

Flowering maples are easily propagated from cuttings. They can tolerate some light shade and cooler temperatures. They like to be on the moist side in warmer months and prefer to dry out between waterings in the winter. The older plants may have some susceptibility to mealybugs, so look for the cottony critters hanging around the undersides of leaves and at the branching nodes.

Marguerite Daisy
(*Chrysanthemum frutescens*)

The marguerite daisy can produce white or yellow daisylike flowers year-round in the greenhouse. The plants can grow up to 2 feet (0.6 m) tall but look better if kept pruned to a bushier shape. The leaves have a finely cut fernlike look and the flowers last well in bouquets. They can tolerate a wide range of temperatures. Unfortunately, the yellow variety is especially attractive to the whitefly and both the white and yellow are susceptible to aphid infestations.

In the greenhouse, the marguerite is a perennial, but it needs to be replaced every few years. Propagate new plants by taking stem cuttings. Marguerites like full sun and can tolerate most any soil. They do well in either pots or beds and need to have the soil dry out between waterings.

Similar to the *Chrysanthemum frutescens* is the yellow-flowered marguerite daisy, **Anthemis tinctoria.** It is sometimes called the golden marguerite and requires the same basic care as *Chrysanthemum frutescens,* discussed above.

Marigold
(*Tagetes* spp.)

This common outdoor annual can provide some easy greenhouse color, especially in summer. Marigolds are divided into two main groupings, but there are also many odd hybrids, which can confuse the lines of classification.

African marigolds are the ones that tend to grow tall. They have large double blooms in either yellow or gold. There are some shorter types that reach only 1 foot (0.3 m), but others can easily grow 3 feet (0.9 m) or more. There are also some rarer-colored varieties. Give the African marigolds at least 1 foot (0.3 m) spacing. Avoid getting water on the flowers, or they will quickly brown. Be sure to pluck faded flowers for continued bloom and a tidy look. The taller marigolds make long-lasting cut flowers.

French marigolds are the smaller types, usually growing only 1 foot (0.3 m) high or less. The flowers have either double or single petals, many of which are bicolored, with bands of brown or red on yellow or gold petals. The French marigolds are notorious for their ability to reseed.

Marigolds can be grown year-round in the greenhouse, but they tend to be at their best in the spring or fall. They are not demanding in culture, but they do have roots close to the soil surface, so take care when cultivating. They prefer full sun and moderate warmth and are readily propagated from seed. Being annuals, they reach a point where they begin to look unkempt and should be pulled. If you see a dusty-looking stippling of yellow on the leaves, use a hand lens or magnifying glass and look under the leaves for spider mites, which love to hang around marigolds. See Chapter 10, "When Things Go Wrong," for help.

Contrary to popular belief, the marigold does not prevent or repel insect pests, with one exception. They have been found to repel a soil-dwelling pest known as the nematode. Some of their reputation may come from the possibility that they might attract beneficial insects into a garden.

Marmalade Plant
(Streptosolen jamesonii)

Also known as **orange browallia**, the marmalade plant is so named for its floppy reddish-orange flowers that occur on the tips of the plant. If you are looking for a dependable winter and spring bloomer, try the marmalade plant.

The blooms of the marmalade plant are not fragrant, but being so floriferous in winter makes it a worthwhile choice. It is a floppy grower and therefore does best in a hanging basket. I have also had good results tying it upright with some small stakes.

The marmalade plant does best in regular potting soil kept on the moist side. It can tolerate temperatures down to the 40s (5°C to 9°C). Occasionally check the underside of the leaves for aphid gatherings.

Mimulus
(Mimulus x hybridus)

Mimulus is also known as **monkey flower** because some people can see a monkey's face in the flower. They are a delicate, short-lived plant, usually growing not more than 1 foot (0.3 m) tall, although some rare varieties can reach up to 3 feet (0.9 m) or more. The flowers somewhat resemble a large snapdragon, with interesting blotches of different colors, including mixtures of red, orange, yellow, and off-white. They are a good choice for the winter greenhouse and semishady spots in the summer.

Mimulus can be grown in ground beds, but I prefer them in hanging baskets so I can have the blooms at eye level in order to enjoy the interesting blotches of color in the flower. Occasional pruning can be helpful, as they tend to get leggy. They prefer rich soil (potting soil is fine) and elevated moisture levels. Mimulus is easily propagated from seed (barely cover the seed) and with some difficulty can also be propagated from cuttings.

Calypso Mimulus is a popular dwarf hybrid that is 6 to 8 inches (15 to 20 cm) tall and is quick to flower. Taller varieties are harder to find but can make a good cut flower with some staking. Thompson & Morgan carries one of the larger selections of mimulus.

Mimulus will suffer if you run very hot temperatures in your greenhouse, but you can always sow it in late summer for good production of winter blooms. After 3 to 4 seasons, the plant is best tossed out.

Mina

(Mina lobata)

The mina is also known as **quamoclit vine** or **Spanish flag** and produces clusters of unique 1-inch (2.5-cm) flowers. The interesting thing about the plant is that each flower begins as red and changes colors as it matures, going through a rainbow progression of colors from red to orange to yellow and white. All colors can be seen simultaneously in a cluster of flowers. Mina starts to bloom in the first 3 to 4 months and can be grown for up to a year. It is an easy plant to start from seed. The seed, however, is hard to find. At this writing, the only source I have found is Thompson & Morgan Seed Company (see "Mail-Order Seeds" in Appendix 6). This company also offers a yellow-flowered variety called Citronella, which doesn't have the interesting rainbow effect of the standard variety.

Mina needs full to part sun. Provide the plant a trellis to grow upon, as it can reach heights of up to 6 feet (1.8 m). Space 2 plants every foot (0.3 m) along the trellis.

Morning Glory

(Ipomoea)

There are many different types of morning glories that will compliment a greenhouse as long as you have some room for a good-sized vertical trellis. If you don't have room, there are bushy varieties that don't need to climb. Almost all grow best in the warmer months unless you have a well-heated greenhouse where they can do fine year-round. Let's look at the different choices for growing in a greenhouse or sunroom.

Moonflower, or *Ipomoea alba*, is a fragrant type of morning glory that can vine to 12 feet (3.6 m) or more. Be ready with your trellis because they are fast growing if you can provide some heat. If you like to sit in your greenhouse in the evening, the pure white flowers add a special touch of fragrance and will shine in the moonlight. Come morning, the 6-inch (15-cm) flower will neatly fold up. On occasions when the days are dark and cloudy, the flowers will remain open.

What most of us commonly think of as the morning glory is one of the annual species *Ipomoea tricolor*, *I. nil*, or *I. purpurea*, which have the heart-shaped leaves with blue, lavender, red, or pink flowers. After about 6 months of growth, it may come time to pull it up if it looks ragged. A few selections of *I. tricolor* do not vine and remain a low-growing bushy plant.

As most people know, the morning glory gets its name because the flowers only remain open in the morning and evening. They may also stay open on cloudy, foggy days. I have found that this must be triggered by ultraviolet light. I say this because ultraviolet light is severely reduced under many greenhouse glazings such as polycarbonate and glass. As a consequence, the traditional *Ipomea tricolor*, such as the Sky Blue morning glory, keeps its flowers wide open in the polycarbonate-clad greenhouses where I have been testing this phenomenon. Thus, it can be morning in America all day long! And that's another reason to have a greenhouse (if you like morning glories).

The *Ipomoea* genus also includes the ornamental sweet potato vines, or **Ipomoea batatas**. They come in other leaf colors such as dark purple, golden-green, and variegated types with pink and white edges. All of the batatas are grown for their foliage and rarely bloom. However, don't be surprised if you find a fleshy "tater" growing under the soil surface of these plants!

The general care for morning glories is to be sure to grow them in well-drained soil. For clay soils, add a good amount of sand or perlite to the mix. They also like to grow in full sun. Morning glories can easily be grown in larger pots or tubs and still put on a good bloom. If you are growing them in pots, you may have to either let them trail downward or trellis them up if they are the vining type. They also do fine in ground beds as long as they get a lot of light and have trellising available. With the exception of the batatas varieties, morning glories are most always started from seed; for quicker germination, try soaking the seed overnight before sowing. Contrary to the advice given in many books, morning glories can be transplanted, but use your best technique, taking care to minimize any root disturbance.

Mullein

(Verbascum bombyciferum)

This particular mullein is commonly known as both **Arctic Summer** and **Silver Lining**, depending upon the catalog source. It is not often thought of as a greenhouse ornamental and can be seen in more and more outside gardens. In fact, if you grow one it might well escape and taken on weedy characteristics! I have always loved its unusually large, fuzzy silver leaves, so I thought I'd give it a try in the greenhouse. It is a biennial outside, but when grown in the greenhouse, it gets a bit confused and may live for up to 3 years. The first year, Silver Lining grows large basal leaves up to 10 inches (25 cm) across and 1 foot (0.3 m) or more long. The silver color and the incredible fuzziness of the leaves always bring on a flurry of comments from friends. The leaves have more fuzz than the furriest lamb's ears *(Stachys lanata)* you've ever seen. If only they could make tissue paper this soft!

After about a year of growing the fat, fuzzy leaves, Silver Lining then sends up fuzzy 1-inch-thick (2.5-cm-thick) stalks that reach up to 6 feet (1.8 m) in height. Sometimes the stalks go straight up, but they occasionally take creative bends as they reach upward. Along the stalks are many 1-inch (2.5-cm) yellow blooms. Several people have remarked on how the flowered stalk looks like popcorn. There is a new variety out with reddish-pink blooms, but it is still hard to come by.

The mullein plant may continue growing these flower stalks for a couple of years in the greenhouse before it finally begins to go downhill as all biennials must, even though in the greenhouse you might call it a triennial or more. The flower stalks will add much drama to any bouquet and keep for a long time in a vase.

Silver Lining mullein is easily started from seed. The Thompson & Morgan seed catalog sells it listed as *Verbascum*. I have the best luck starting it in spring to trigger a good number of the early, low-growing large leaves. It does best in full sun and doesn't seem fussy about soil or watering. You don't need more than 1 or 2 plants growing in a small greenhouse at a time, because they can cover up to 5 square feet (0.46 sq. m) of space, and one plant provides enough of a show. Silver Lining is best grown in a ground bed or a pot that is at least 10 to 12 inches (25 to 30 cm) across. In spring, grow a few extra plants for planting outside, but be careful, as it will reseed prolifically.

Narcissus/Daffodil

(*Narcissus* spp.)
See "Bulbs—Forcing Spring Bulbs for Winter Bloom" (page 184).

Nasturtium

(*Tropaeolum majus*)
Nasturtium has recently become more popular as the trend of eating flowers has grown. Nasturtium is always at the top of the edible-flower culinary list. The flowers have a sweet, peppery flavor, and the leaves are also edible but are too hot for my liking. The sweetest part of the nasturtium flower is the tail that forms at the back of the flower. Unfortunately, there is one common variety with no tail, the Whirlybird. Nasturtium has very handsome rounded leaves that almost resemble little water lily pads. Its 1- to 2-inch (2.5- to 5-cm) flowers can be found in shades of warmer colors and cream. Some flowers have splotches of two colors.

There are two main types of nasturtium, the trailers and the dwarf varieties. The trailers can climb like a vine if given ample nearby plants or poles to coil up on, or they will just rapidly spread out over a hanging basket or along the ground, extending up to 8 feet (2.4 m). The dwarf varieties stay bushy and grow up to 2 feet (0.6 m), depending upon the age of the plant. There are many varieties in between the trailers and dwarf types.

A favorite bushy nasturtium variety of mine is called Alaska. Alaska has variegated leaves with marbled white blotches on the green. It looks handsome even without flowers. Jewel of Africa is also variegated but has a viney growth habit. I like to grow nasturtiums in hanging pots, but they do equally well in beds. They do seem to prefer soils that are well drained and not too rich. Nasturtium is generally a trouble-free plant and tolerates cool temperatures as well as warm. As a result, it can be a good plant to have growing almost any time of the year in the greenhouse or sunspace.

Besides using the sweet, peppery flowers to color up salads, you can use the flowers in arrangements, but they will last for only around 5 days. Nasturtium is easily propagated from seed. Plants that are in the ground for more than 9 months may benefit from some pruning. Nasturtiums will occasionally self-sow if they are grown for more than one year.

There are some wilder cousins to nasturtium. One is known as canary creeper or canary bird flower, which of course has open yellow flowers, shaped almost like open hands or bird wings.

There are some other interesting cousins in the genus of *Tropaeolum* native to

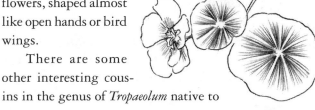

South America that have tuberous roots and exotic flowers. These plants are reputed to do very well in cooler greenhouses, but, unfortunately, the seeds and plants are difficult to acquire. I have yet to locate a source. If you find some of these plants, give them a try.

Nemesia
(Nemesia strumosa)

Nemesia is another good choice for the winter greenhouse, as it likes a cool environment. Flowers are usually less than 1 inch (2.5 cm) in size and come in almost any color imaginable, in a shape reminiscent of snapdragons. The plant is also small, usually around 1 foot (0.3 m) high. It can get lanky and benefits from some tip pruning as it grows to promote bushiness. It likes a moist, rich soil and can tolerate some light shade. For greenhouse color, sow the plants in late summer or early fall for winter and spring blooms. When the heat of summer comes, it is usually time to toss the plants into the compost pile.

With small flowers borne on short stems, nemesia is not a good choice for cut bouquets. However, it is a good plant for growing along walks, in beds, or in pots and hanging baskets. In my experience, the plants may often go downhill after only 3 to 5 months, but they are still a nice plant for brightening up the winter.

Nicotiana
(Nicotiana spp.)

Nicotiana is also known as **flowering tobacco**. This relative of petunias and tobacco produces masses of trumpetlike, star-shaped flowers about 1 inch (2.5 cm) across. The more common varieties are the Nicki series, which reach up to 18 inches (46 cm) in height, and the Domino series, which are dwarfs, only 1 foot (0.3 m) high. The flowers are available in red, pink, white, and lime green. I have never had an interest in growing a green flower, but it is out there for someone. There is also a variety called the Merlin series, which is a miniature that only gets 4 to 5 inches (10 to 15 cm) tall.

I first grew nicotiana because so many books talked about how fragrant the plants were. I never smelled a thing and later found that only some of the older varieties have a decent aroma. Even then, the fragrance doesn't seem to be released until evening. The older varieties are not hard to find with a little investigation. Some varieties of the more-fragrant types include Fragrant Cloud, Sensation, and Sylvestris. These tend to get much taller, growing up to 6 feet (1.8 m). They are not as colorful as the more common nicotianas but are good for their evening fragrance. The variety Sylvestris, also known as Peace Pipe, has showy flowers that look to me like a Fourth of July firecracker show.

Nicotianas need full sun and moderate temperatures. If it gets hot, you may see the flowers closing during the day. The dwarf varieties are good in pots, and the taller types do well in either large pots or ground beds.

Nicotianas are most easily started from seed but with some difficulty can also come from cuttings. They are somewhat susceptible to both aphids and whiteflies and tend to get more buggy in extreme cool or hot temperatures. For that reason, I usually plan to have them bloom during the moderate temperatures of spring and fall. This requires sowing them in the middle of summer or winter. Nicotianas can grow for many seasons but will need pruning and as they mature will gain more attention from the inevitable bugs. It is easier to enjoy them for one season or until they become trouble and then plan to start over again at an appropriate time.

For those who use tobacco products, yes, these are related, and you can also grow your own smoking tobacco leaf in the greenhouse. Check seed catalogs specializing in herbs, such as Richters, found in "Mail-Order Seeds" in Appendix 6. As for curing the tobacco leaf properly, you'll have to ask someone from the South.

Oleander
(Nerium oleander)

Oleander is an evergreen shrub that can easily be grown in a greenhouse but will need much pruning to keep it from reaching its natural height of more than 20 feet (6 m). It is best grown in a tub if you have the room. Those of you who readily grow it outside must think that I am crazy suggesting that you even grow this plant, but many who move to areas where it can't be grown have told me it is a "comfort plant," reminding them of home.

If you do grow it in the greenhouse, please take care, as the leaves are poisonous if ingested. It is not a good plant if you have curious toddlers on the move. It has 6-inch-long (15-cm-long), leathery, lance-shaped leaves. The flowers tend to bloom in the warmer part of the year. Oleander produces clusters of pink, white, or red flowers at the tips of branches. If you see suckers forming just below the buds of future flowering blossoms, then pinch them out. These suckers can sometimes inhibit the flowers from forming.

The oleander plant prefers to grow in full light for best flowering. Pruning is best done in late winter to control the rapid growth. It needs a soil mix that is well drained; be sure there are good-sized holes in the bottom of your tub. It can tolerate temperatures down to 40°F (5°C). During blooming, the plant needs a constant supply of water, but cut back on water during the winter. Most oleanders have a nice fragrance when in flower. They are easily propagated from cuttings.

ORCHIDS
(Orchidaceae)

I can't pretend to tell you everything you need to know about growing orchids. That's why there are so many books devoted solely to this subject. Rather, I would like to encourage you to not shy away from them. There is no doubt that some are difficult to grow, but many are quite simple to grow successfully and may even require less care than most houseplants. Why grow orchids, anyway? To begin with, they have incredible flowers with much color and diversity. Many species will hold one bloom open for more than a month, so you really get some mileage out of a flower.

Another good reason to grow orchids is to impress people with your gardening skills. Hey, just grow a few of the easiest orchids, and people will think you are an accomplished and certified green-thumbed gardener. Who knows, you might find that it is so easy that you'll venture into the exciting world of growing more of the unusual and select varieties. It won't be long until you truly become an accomplished orchid grower. After all, the most important person you need to impress with your ability to grow things is yourself.

Orchids are found growing native all over the planet, with the exception of the deserts. They are not limited to the tropics, and many live in the temperate zones as well as the Arctic. However, the majority of orchid species come from the tropics and subtropics.

Classifying orchids can become quite complex, so I would like to point out two major differences you should know. Most orchids are classified under one of the two major types: the **epiphytes** and the **terrestrials**. In their native habitat, epiphytes grow up in the air, living in crotches or nooks of trees or shrubs. Many of these plants often have what are called aerial roots that directly absorb moisture from the misty, humid air that occurs in the tropics. Most popular orchids tend to be epiphytic or semiepiphytic. Simply because epiphytes live on other plants does not mean they are parasitic; they do not take any nutrients from the host plants on which they may be attached. Rather, they derive their nutrition from the moisture and organic matter that collects around them. Thus, many of the epiphytic orchids will not grow in potting soil. It simply hems them in too much, and in the end, they suffer from overwatering and rot. Often, you will see epiphytic orchids sending roots straight up in the air because they sometimes don't take to pots.

Because orchids need air and a well-drained growing medium, they are grown in a number of odd materials. Fir bark and long-fiber sphagnum moss are the most common materials for the growing medium. Other materials include gravel, cork, hardened clay nuggets, perlite, and redwood bark. I have even seen some growers use the indestructible Styrofoam packing nuggets as an orchid growing medium. There are also some high-quality, prepared orchid mediums sold. These are a mix of specially selected, quick-draining materials. One brand, called Hoffman's Orchid Mix (800-725-9500), has a mixture of West Coast fir bark, charcoal, and redwood in appropriate particle sizes to provide adequate space for the roots while providing a good amount of air. Hoffman's Orchid Mix is available at many retail outlets. There are also a number of other good orchid mixes available. The main thing is to check these materials when you repot to be sure that they are not rotting over time, as indicated by the medium becoming wet and slimy. If so, the material needs to be tossed out (thrown in the compost pile) and replaced with new orchid medium.

Much of the success or failure of growing orchids has to do with the fine balance between how well drained the soil is and how often you water the plants. The more well drained the mix, the more frequently you can water. The less well drained the growing mix, the more you should skimp on water. In general, err on the side of less water and a ton of humidity. Remember that with epiphytic orchids, you will almost never see them perish from becoming too dry, but grow them too wet and they are gone.

Epiphytic orchids will not survive long in wet potting soil. This alone is a good reason to grow orchids only in clay pots that provide more breatheability.

Many orchids are able to store water for long periods and are easily killed by overwatering. Because epiphytes live in a growing medium that provides little in the way of nutrients, these orchids must be fertilized regularly. The easiest way to get nutrition to them is to use liquid fertilizers. To enable more frequent fertilizing, you can read the label of the material you plan to use, dilute the recommendation in half, and fertilize twice as often.

Terrestrial orchids in their native habitat live directly in the soil. Terrestrial orchids tend to be native to more temperate habitats.

There are also some orchids that fall between the terrestrial and the epiphytic, which might include some orchids that cling to the surface of rocks or that grow in decaying vegetation on the forest floor.

Most of the more popular orchids tend to be epiphytic. We'll cover some of the basics and let you discover the rarer and more complicated species on your own.

Orchids are also classified by their leaves: A **monopodial** plant is one that has new growth occurring only at the tip of the plant, growing taller each year. The leaves are generally in two rows on opposite sides of the stem. The flowers and roots originate at the point where the leaf meets the stem. Two common monopodial orchids are the *Phalaenopsis* and *Vanda* orchids (both discussed later). The monopodial types only grow from the tip of the plant. They will continue to grow up from the tip and may eventually get top heavy. At this point, you might need to do something to keep them from flopping over, as they can only get so tall. Dividing a monopodial orchid is one solution. Do this by cutting off the top of the plant. Try to make two plants out of one by cutting at a place where the top portion of the plant has both healthy leaves and some aerial roots. These roots will allow the plant to become reestablished. The remaining bottom portion of the plant will usually sprout new growing points, developing into a new, bushier plant.

A **sympodial** plant is typical of the majority of orchids. In these, the new growth begins at the base of the previous year's growth. The stem (called a rhizome) grows horizontally, and new shoots originate from buds on this stem. It is also from this point that each shoot will send out its own cluster of roots. They will bloom from the base of the plant or from between the leaves.

Monopodial plant

Many sympodial orchids grow what are called pseudobulbs, thickened areas at the base of the stem resembling bulbs. This is an adaptation that helps orchids survive periods of drought. These pseudobulbs store both water and food. Other epiphytic sympodial species grow thick-

Sympodial plant

ened leaves, which serve the dual function of both leaves and storage organs.

To divide a sympodial plant, simply cut it into sections that have a healthy amount of leaves (usually 3 or more) and some healthy roots. Trim off any rotted or shriveled roots. Each section can be repotted as a new plant.

Even if you don't need to divide a large plant, eventually every orchid will need to be repotted when the plant becomes too large for the space. Never repot orchids when they are in bloom or about to bloom. Try to size the pot (preferably clay) to the plant. Going too small may injure or inhibit root growth. Too big a pot increases the chance for overwatering. It is best to time your repotting for the end of flowering, as this is usually when new roots are initiated. Try to do this before new roots elongate more than $3/4$ of an inch (2 cm) in length to take advantage of this growth spurt

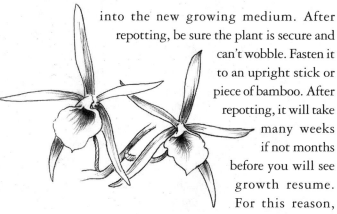

into the new growing medium. After repotting, be sure the plant is secure and can't wobble. Fasten it to an upright stick or piece of bamboo. After repotting, it will take many weeks if not months before you will see growth resume. For this reason, never disturb the roots if you can avoid it.

Unlike most houseplants, with which we carefully leave the soil around the roots, with orchids we must carefully remove the entire growing medium from around the roots. It sounds mean but is important to do this because you must remove any old rotting or slimy bark or other organic material that may promote later rotting.

Place the oldest growth against the rim of the pot, enabling newer growth to have the maximum amount of room for expansion. Don't bury the plant any deeper than it was originally growing. After repotting any orchid, avoid watering the plant for a couple of weeks to allow any injured tissue to heal over. If you water too soon, injured tissue may rot. Misting, however, is always a good idea after repotting.

Remember, even the best orchid aficionados started out as beginners, usually with the purchase of one plant. The American Orchid Society offers this good advice: Deal with a nursery staffed by knowledgeable growers who have some experience in growing orchids and can answer questions as they arise. The best plant for a beginner is a moderately priced mature plant, preferably in flower or about to flower. Expect to pay between $25 and $40, which will give you the best value for your money and will get you a plant that will flower more readily and reliably. The plant should be secure in the pot and weed free, with firm, succulent leaves and/or pseudobulbs (if it is a plant that has pseudo-bulbs). You want to see firm, fresh-looking roots. Beware of shriveled or splotchy leaves and roots.

Many orchids last well as a cut flower. Be sure the flowers are fully open before you cut them to get the maximum life in a vase. Many orchid flowers have a fragrance, but it often diminishes over time after the flower is cut for a bouquet or corsage.

Lets look a limited list of some selected orchid families and their general care.

Brassavola Orchid

The **Brassavola** are closely related to the cattleya discussed below. Many are known for having a wonderful night fragrance that disappears with the sunrise. In general, they need a very bright spot and a warm temperature. They can tolerate occasional dry spells. The best known of this family **Brassavola nodosa**, or **Lady of the Night**, gives off a wonderful evening fragrance. It produces 3-inch (8-cm) flowers that are usually white with some small colored spots. It can bloom almost anytime of the year and doesn't need a rest period. This *Brassavola* needs full sunlight and is well suited to the greenhouse environment as long as temperatures remain above 50°F (10°C).

Cattleya Orchid

Cattleya produce the large, corsagelike flowers. In general, they are easy to grow for the novice. They like a lot of light but not more than a few hours of direct sunlight. They are epiphytic and need to thoroughly dry out between waterings (usually a week or two between watering). A bonus with cattleyas is that many

are quite fragrant. Although they will bloom from 1 to 4 weeks, this is considered short when compared with many types of orchids. After they flower, they need a 2-month rest period in which you let them run even drier. Water no more than once every 2 to 3 weeks during this time. Whether it is flowering or not, never allow a cattleya's roots to remain wet for more than 6 days. Many Cattleyas produce pseudo-bulbs, the swollen bulbouslike structure at the base of the leaves. They should be pointing upright and be light green. The cattleya is sympodial in its growth pattern (see above for discussion on sympodial growth).

Cattleya labiata is among the easier cattleyas to grow. Many other cattleya and cattleya hybrids are worth trying in a greenhouse, as these are one of the more rewarding types of orchids to grow.

Cymbidium Orchid

Cymbidium orchids are among the most popular and widely sold of all flowering orchids. They tend to bloom in late winter through early spring. They have a narrow-leafed, grasslike foliage that can reach a height of up to 2 feet (0.6 m). The common cymbidiums that are commercially available can become large plants and need a large pot of at least a foot (0.3 m) in diameter. There are many cymbidium sold as "miniature" varieties, but the miniatures can vary in size from 8 inches (21 cm) to a foot (0.3 m) in height, not counting the flower stalk. Standard-sized cymbidiums are large and need a tub, but these orchids are rarely sold.

Instead of using bark or some other well-drained medium for the roots, most cymbidiums do fine in a very well drained potting soil. You can attain this by adding sand to a standard potting mix at about $1/4$ sand to $3/4$ potting mix.

Cymbidiums need to be moist most of the time if possible, except during a rest period after bloom when they should dry out considerably. As with many orchids, to induce flowering it is helpful to have a 10°F (6°C) drop in temperature at night. Its temperature requirements make it difficult to get to flower in most home windowsills but is quite easy to get to grow and flower in a greenhouse—especially if yours has cool nights in winter. Perhaps this is because many are native to the Himalayas. The cymbidium is sympodial in its growth pattern (see page 225 for discussion on sympodial growth).

Dendrobium Orchid

The many diverse and different *Dendrobium* types make it more difficult to generalize about their cultural needs. Many go through a growth phase followed by a rest phase during the course of one year. The flowers can last from one day to many weeks, depending upon the type. They produce small to medium flowers that can sometimes be found in twisted or curled shapes. Unlike most orchids that usually have a bloom period of only once a year, there are some dendrobiums that can bloom many times in one year.

In general, they require bright light, especially when they are growing rapidly. Their temperature needs vary widely, depending

upon the type you are growing, but most do well between 55°F and 80°F (13°C and 27°C). Watering needs are variable, depending upon the type of dendrobium, but they usually like to dry out a bit between watering. Most need a humidity of at least 40 to 60 percent.

Dendrobium aggregatum is a common favorite that has beautiful golden-yellow flowers on a compact plant. Another easy and common dendrobium is *Dendrobium nobile.* Because of the breadth of choices in dendrobiums, I don't want to generalize about their care, as nonspecific information might be more dangerous than helpful. There are good dendrobiums for beginners, but there are also some that are quite difficult. For more specific care, refer to the source where you obtained your dendrobium, as care can vary widely with dendrobiums. They are sympodial in their growth pattern (see above for discussion on sympodial growth).

Some new research suggests that the addition of peat moss to fir bark results in the best leaf and flower production in dendrobiums and many other orchids. Try to make it around 30 percent peat moss to 70 percent fir bark.

Oncidium Orchid

Oncidium orchids represent a large collection of many diverse species, most of which are epiphytic and need a very well-drained growing medium. In general, these are rugged orchids with a thick leaf. They thrive in bright light and prefer warm days up around 70°F (21°C) and nights down to 55°F (13°C). Although they like temperature swings, don't allow the temperature to go much below 50°F (10°C)

for very long. The water requirements can vary widely, depending upon the type you grow.

Oncidiums usually have flowers with warm colors, though there are some with white hues. Yellow and brown are commonly found in oncidiums. Many have small bumps occurring on the crest of the flower. You can get anywhere from 10 to 100 blooms per stem! The Dancing Lady oncidium has flowers that resemble tiny yellow figurines in long dresses.

As a general rule, oncidiums are forgiving and thus have a reputation for being easy to grow. They are often crossed with other related orchids, producing even more adaptable and easy-to-grow orchids. They grow in a sympodial fashion (see page 225).

Paphiopedilum Orchid

Often called the **Lady's-Slipper** orchid, *Paphiopedilum* are called "paphs" by enthusiasts. They are semiterrestrial and require a growing medium that is a bit more water retentive than the extremely well-drained type needed by purely epiphytic orchids. Try using a finer bark with some sand or perlite mixed in. Plants should be kept moist but not soggy wet; never let them completely dry out. When you do water, try to avoid getting it into the tips of the growing points where it can

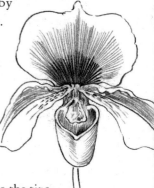

sit and eventually cause rot. If you mist these plants too much, you can also trigger leaf rot in the tips of plants. This is especially common in humid climates. They like bright light but no direct sun. If you see the leaf yellowing, it may be a sign of too much light. Limp foliage may indicate too little light and / or too little water. These orchids are free blooming and can set blossoms at any time. They have more decorative leaves than many orchids, with some having a mottled foliage. These plants are good choices in the greenhouse because many require a 15 to 20°F (7 to 11°C) difference between night and day, which is hard to do in a home but easy to attain in a greenhouse. Try not to allow the temperature to drop below 50°F (10°C). The paphs have a sympodial growth habit (see earlier discussion).

Phalaenopsis Orchid

Phalaenopsis, also called "moth orchids" for their interesting mothlike white flowers, are ideal houseplants under warm conditions. The blooming season can vary, depending upon the type of orchid you have. The phalaenopsis orchids are also good for warmer greenhouses that don't have an extreme nighttime temperature drop. Greatly fluctuating temperatures cause the flower buds to drop. They like to grow in a bright location but not direct sun. Don't allow your phalaenopsis to go dry for very long before the next watering. The smaller the plant, the more constant moisture it needs. Maintaining a high humidity is also helpful.

Many phalaenopsis flowers (such as the moth orchid), send out a long whip of a flower stalk, often reaching 2 to 3 feet (0.6 to 0.9 m) long with up to 40 blooms on one spike and can easily stay in bloom for 3 months or more. After the first flowers fade, avoid the temptation to cut the flowering stalk off. If you sim-

ply prune between the scar where the first flower was formed and the node that produced the last flower, you can sometimes encourage the plant to bloom again from that point. Look for a node to wake up again and initiate another round of flowers within 2 to 3 months. This doesn't always happen and is less likely to occur with younger and frailer plants.

Unlike many other orchids, the phalaenopsis produces new leaves at the top of the plant, as it has a monopodial form of growth. Over time, this can make the plant grow quite tall and even lanky, and it may need to be divided to create a more bushy plant (see earlier discussion on dividing monopodial plants).

I have efficiently killed my phalaenopsis by letting a small amount of water stand in the center of the plant for days on end. This causes rotting to occur in the main growth point. To prevent this, avoid getting water in the center tip of the plant. If you do, try to sop it up with a paper towel.

Vanda Orchid

Vanda orchids usually have a thick, upright stem. It is monopodial so all of its growth occurs at the tip of the plant. It has closely set, alternating, narrow leaves. They often have abundant aerial roots. These roots love to be misted. Because vanda orchids should be grown in very well-drained moss or bark, they need regular watering and frequent diluted fertilization. One caution, however: Don't let water sit on the plants overnight or rot may result.

Thin, cylindrical-leafed vandas, are called "**terete**" types. These terete types need a lot of light in order to flower; sometimes even full sun will be needed. You may have to experiment a bit. They also require temperatures above 50°F (10°C). The ones with wider, straplike leaves require less light, whereas hybrids of the two called "semi-terete" need full sun.

Vanda orchids can flower in almost any season but tend to put on the show in the summer months, sometimes continuing into the fall. But don't be surprised if, as with most orchids, they bloom almost anytime, because the newer hybrids have been known to bloom more than once in a year. They are often sold in full bloom. The color combinations of the petals are amazing, ranging from purple to yellow to orange, with even more available.

Vanilla *(Planifolia fragrans)* Orchid

There are so many different orchids to choose from—more than 20,000 named orchid species and five times that number of manmade hybrids! All are treasured for their beauty, but only one orchid has taken on any agricultural importance. Vanilla *(Planifolia fragrans)* is a climbing orchid vine native to the tropics, where it can grow up to 40 feet (12.2 m) tall, usually by climbing up trees. It produces orange to yellow flowers and forms a long, aromatic fruit pod. There are tens of thousands of very small vanilla seeds in each pod. The pure vanilla extract found in almost every kitchen is processed from these

small seeds (unless you use that awful fake vanilla flavoring). The vanilla plant is available from the Glasshouse Works catalog and is relatively easy to grow. I have yet to figure out how to get it to set fruit (vanilla beans), but others tell me that it simply needs maturity, size, and a bright growing location. Mine is potted in a mix of bark and potting soil.

One of the best ways to learn more about orchids is to hang out with the people who grow them. In many larger cities, there are local orchid clubs or societies whose members love to help new orchid enthusiasts. They might also have a regular orchid plant sale where you can pick up some real bargains. Check with your closest public botanical garden for more information on orchid clubs or societies near you. Also, you might want to contact the American Orchid Society at 6000 South Olive Avenue, West Palm Beach, FL 33405-4199 (561-585-8666). They have an informative and website at **www. orchidweb. org**. There they list some frequently asked questions, a list of good plants for beginners, and a thorough listing of books on orchids. The American Orchid Society is among the most informative and well-organized plant societies I have ever come across.

Orchid Troubleshooting Guide

Because orchids are such different plants, they also have different problems. I have created a chapter to assist with most of the generalized greenhouse plant problems, but because orchids are so different I want to provide you with a quick guide to some common problems with orchids in this section. I still encourage you to flip to Chapter 10, "When Things Go Wrong," for additional assistance in orchid troubleshooting, especially when it comes to bug problems.

ORCHID TROUBLESHOOTING

Failure to flower	Needs different day (night) length.
	Needs warmer or cooler temperatures.
	Hasn't reached maturity yet.
	Light—is either getting too much or not enough.
	Overwatering.
Mildew on leaves	Too much misting or humidity.
Brown spots on leaves	May be caused by sun scorch.
	Fungus disease.
	Bacterial disease.
	Be sure to provide a plant showing brown spots with the right conditions and prune off any dead or diseased areas. If it gets bad, it may become a toss-out candidate.
Limp plant	Overwatering or underwatering (underwatering more likely).
Streaks or patterns on leaves	Virus disease: a toss-out candidate.
Chewed leaves	Insect pest; see Chapter 10 for more information.
Mottled or disfigured foliage	Insect pest with a sucking mouth part such as scale, thrips, mealybug, or spider mite. See Chapter 10 for more information.
Root rot	Overwatering or old potting mix that is poorly drained.
Spots on petals of flowers	Your greenhouse is too humid. Can you dry it out? Perhaps they are supposed to be there, as orchids are known for their unusual flowers—many of which have spots.
Larger light brown spot on leaf	Brown rot. In the short term, be sure you are providing it with the right conditions and prune off any dead or diseased areas. If it gets bad it may become a toss-out candidate.

As I discuss in Chapter 10, there is little you can do to help a plant in the midst of disease, thus my statement in the above troubleshooting chart: "A toss-out candidate." However, you can prevent disease in a number of ways, including: watering early in the day; avoiding overwatering; pruning the diseased portion (but sterilize the pruners with alcohol between each cut you make to avoid spreading the disease); maintaining overall good plant health; and isolating a suspected diseased orchid from your healthy plants. Finally, consider disposing of the diseased plant. Ouch! What if it was expensive? Hey, it is better to lose one plant than to lose all of your orchids, which is even more expensive. Less scrupulous greenhouse gardeners simply give away their diseased and unhealthy plants. Shame on them!

Don't get too persnickety about your orchids' slight imperfections, as almost every orchid has at least one or two spots. Also, it is not uncommon for some orchids to take a year or more to flower (this is where the traditional "gardener's patience" comes in). When things really start to look bad, refer to the chart on page 231. It is designed to help you try to figure out what is going on and what you can do to help your orchid.

There is so much more to say about orchids that I could fill a book on it. Luckily, there are loads of good books out there devoted solely to orchids, so I don't need to. I hope I have whetted your appetite and interest in growing these plants. Now simply go out and buy a few orchids to start your collection and find a good book on the subject to help you along. You'll find that, yes, they are different to grow, but they are not necessarily difficult.

Oxalis

(Oxalis spp.)

These plants are also known as **tropical shamrocks** or **lucky clovers,** because they look like a shamrock but are not a true shamrock. Many of these cloverlike plants can be grown in a greenhouse. The oxalis has a lot of varying characteristics. Some fold up their leaves at night, and many are tuberous. The oxalis also has some interesting flower colors, with varieties displaying white, red, pink, and yellow flowers. Generally, they are small plants that do fine in a 6-inch (15-cm) pot.

The care for oxalis is relatively simple. Let the soil dry out between waterings. They can survive well in light shade to full sun. If the plant becomes ragged or buggy, try cutting all the leaves off down to the soil level and reducing the watering slightly. They will simply emerge again, usually more healthy than before.

Oxalis are easily propagated from division. Just split the mature plant into two or three parts and repot. Thrips and aphids occasionally bother them. Nonetheless, oxalis are easy to grow. Propagate a lot in late summer and you'll have a number of plants to give away for St. Patrick's Day gifts.

Palms

(Palmae)

Simply having a palm growing within your greenhouse can provide a real feeling of having a tropical paradise vacation. Put on the Jimmy Buffet CD and mix up a margarita! If nothing else, the view of a palm in winter can be a reminder of a recent vacation. There are a great variety of palms to choose from, with varying forms of growth habits. Here are some of my favorite palms.

The **sago palm** *(Cycas revoluta)* has stiff leaves on a short, round trunk. The leaves can reach 2 feet (0.6 m) or more and have sharp points. It is one of the oldest known plants on

earth, and archaeologists regularly find it as a fossil in rock formations. The sago is very slow growing but also very distinctive. It can tolerate more moisture than many palms and cooler temperatures.

Fan palms (*Chamaerops humilis* or *Livistona chinensis*) have broad, pointed fan-like leaves that can reach up to 2 feet (0.6 m) across. Each leaf has folds like an accordion. If you had enough leaves, you could roof a tropical house with them. The fan palm needs regular moisture but not soggy conditions. It also needs warmer temperatures or the leaves may yellow.

The *Roebelenii*, a type of **date palm**, is the dwarf or pygmy version of the taller date palm (**R. Phoenix**). It has very fine leaflets, the tips of which can be sharp. I often prune the sharp tips to a blunt end to prevent poking any eyes out. Although it is called "dwarf," it still grows up to about 4 feet (1.2 m) or more in height. The sky is the limit (or the top of your greenhouse) with the taller date palm. I have yet to get mine to produce any edible dates, but I still have high hopes. I grow the date solely because I love its silhouette against other plants and against the glass. It evokes such a tropical feeling when grown in a greenhouse or sunroom! Be careful, as the leaves can get very stiff; they could almost be described as sharp and could easily poke you in the eye when you are working near this plant. The pygmy date palm can tolerate cooler temperatures and more shade than others. This is among the most

drought tolerant of all the palms, so be sure to never overwater, as it prefers to grow on the dry side.

The **lady palm** (***Rhapis excelsa***) produces fan-shaped leaves, although not as perfect as the fan palm's. The plant is more sweeping and does best in light shade. It prefers to dry out between waterings. The lady palm prefers temperatures not higher than 65°F (18°C).

There are many more palms to choose from. Usually, plants must be acquired from large garden centers or catalog sources, and, unfortunately, they are often expensive.

The general care for palms is to avoid letting the roots sit in stagnant water. They do not like to have their roots disturbed; repot only when absolutely necessary. Most palms can be propagated with much difficulty from seed, so try to find plants to get a start with palms. Although palms can be grown in greenhouse beds, they are much easier to care for if you grow them in large pots or tubs, depending upon the size of the plant.

When it comes to critters, they seem to get occasional scale and mealybug infestations, neither of which is usually severe unless the plant is under stress.

Pansy
(*Viola* x *wittrockiana*)

The pansy is a great choice for the extremely cool winter greenhouse where you have trouble growing any other colorful flower in the winter. It is also a good plant for almost any greenhouse or sunspace from fall through spring. The unique flower can be found in just about every color, and many have the blotched markings in the center of the flower that resemble a face. For a long bloom period, you must start your pansies from seed in August or early September. If you want to use them in bouquets, try the Swiss Giant variety, which has larger blooms and longer stems. Unfortunately, the larger-bloom varieties are often less heat tolerant. Another favorite variety is Bingo, which comes in a variety of colors. There are also uniquely colored pansies to consider like the Joker Poker Face, with its interesting orange-and-purple coloring; Jolly Joker, which is also orange and purple; Brunig, which is black with a little yellow margin; and Rippling Waters, which is black with a white margin. Check out the intense orange of Padparadja Pansy, which can be mixed with some blue-colored pansies for a brilliant spring effect. Check Stokes Seeds and Thompson & Morgan catalogs for some good selections.

I like to grow pansies along walkways for entertaining color as people walk through. They can also be grown equally well in pots. I find they are not picky about care, but they will begin to go downhill when summer temperatures return. Pansies will benefit from occasional tip pruning and deadheading. Also lift the leaves up and clean out any dead leaves that may promote underneath rotting of the plants.

Try growing some pansies for beautifying the outside landscape. Sow them around early to late August for later planting in late September or early October. These will often look good into the winter (depending upon your local climate). Most will survive the winter and give you a wonderful spring and early summer show the next year.

Pansies can get occasional attacks of aphids, so get down close and look under the leaf to check for the little pear-shaped critters. If you see occasional holes in the leaf or flower, then you probably have slugs. In that case, clean dead leaf debris and cut back on watering a bit.

Passionflower
(*Passiflora* spp.)

The passionflower is grown for its intricate and beautiful flowers, which, depending upon the variety, are 2 to 3 inches (5 to 8 cm) across. The flower is often made up of two or three different colors, varying among blue, white, yellow, lavender, and red. These are the most intricate and ornate flowers I have ever seen.

There are many very different varieties to choose from. Some species (*Passiflora actinia* and *Passiflora* x *alatocaerulea*) are incredibly fragrant; the variety Incense is also highly fragrant. One species, *Passiflora edulis*, produces edible, egglike fruits that are purple or yellow. *P. edulis* is among the easiest to grow and very cold tolerant. This species and many other passionflowers grow a very vigorous vine, which may be either a blessing or a curse in the greenhouse. If you do not regularly prune the plant, it will quickly take over any area where it grows, especially if it is growing in a tub or ground bed where the roots can really roam. On occasion, I have used this quality to advantage, making arched arbors out of the plant, but this works only in larger greenhouses where you can spread out. If it does get out of hand, it can become very difficult to do a good pruning job. There are also more dwarf passionflowers available that are worth considering for growing in smaller containers. Two of my favorite catalog sources for the passionflower are the Logee's Greenhouse catalog (888-330-8038) and the Glasshouse Works catalog (800-837-2142). See "Mail-Order Plants" in Appendix 5 for more information.

The passionflower plant loves a cool winter environment and can tolerate temperatures down to freezing. It can be grown in a pot or bed, but the more space the roots have, the quicker it will try to rule the greenhouse. By simply growing it in a pot, you can control the overall size, but it is also less apt to bloom when the roots are limited. I try to grow them in a small tub about 1 foot (0.3 m) in diameter and then train the plant to grow in a wreathlike shape, using some wire or stakes to create a circle of growth. Passionflowers prefer a bright spot, humid air, and moderate moisture. New plants are readily propagated from cuttings. The main pest problem is the mealybug and the occasional whitefly.

Pentas
(Pentas lanceolata)
Pentas is a small winter-blooming plant that provides a splash of flowers in hues of red, rose, pink, and white. It produces a cluster of small tubular blooms. Unfortunately, the flowers have little fragrance, but they are full of nectar and are helpful if you are raising any beneficial insects that sometimes need to also feed on nectar. This is a popular plant in greenhouses where butterflies have been released.

The biggest problem for these winter bloomers is that they require warm night temperatures of around 60°F (15°C), so they are not a good choice for the greenhouse that runs cool in the winter. Water pentas sparingly in winter and keep them moist in the summer. Mealybugs occasionally infest these plants, especially if they are under stress.

Petunia
(Petunia x hybrida)
The petunia is a common outdoor bedding plant that does equally well in the greenhouse or sunspace. It does not flower as abundantly in winter as it does in summer. Still, it flowers enough to be desirable. Petunias can be found in almost every color except orange and true blue. The yellow varieties are almost always washed-out looking and should be avoided. There are some varieties called "blue" that are usually more on the purple side. If you like purple, they are fine varieties. The two-tone and dark-veined flowers are interesting. Petunias are also available in double-flowering varieties. One petunia I like to grow both inside and outside is the variety called Madness, which comes in many colors. This is a "multiflora," having abundant medium-sized flowers. There are also the old standby grandifloras, which have big showy flowers but are not as vigorous as the multifloras. New to the petunia family are the Wave petunias, which grow only 6 inches (15 cm) high but spread up to 2 feet (0.6m). They are great for hanging baskets.

Petunias are easy to care for in the greenhouse and always complement hanging pots or can add color to any beds, both inside or out.

They may benefit from occasional pruning to keep them from getting leggy. Petunias do best in bright spots, and the soil needs to dry out between watering. They are usually started from seed (just barely covered) but can also be propagated from cuttings. The plants should be discarded after a year of growth.

Pineapple Sage
(Salvia elegans)

This is really an herb that is in the mint family. It is so named because it has the distinct fragrance of pineapple. You must rub the leaf to release the aroma. It is listed here in the ornamental plant section rather than the herb section because of its striking scarlet blooms. The bright flowers are thin and tubular and about 1 inch (2.5 cm) long. The blooms are not a good choice for bouquets because they tend to drop, or shatter, as horticulturists say, after they are picked. Still, the flowers are quite showy in the greenhouse and can bloom for many months in winter through spring. Their scarlet blooms warm up a winter greenhouse. Don't confuse this plant with pineapple mint *(Mentha suaveolens)*, which is a fine herb with a pineapple scent but doesn't have the colorful bloom.

Pineapple sage can reach up to 2 feet (0.6 m) tall. You may see some of the leaves tipped with white edges. I have had good results growing it in pots or planted directly in beds. It does best in full sun and when allowed to dry between watering. Unlike many plants in the mint family, it is not aggressive.

The biggest drawback is that whiteflies and mealybugs often find this plant irresistible in the warmer months, so it may need some special care and attention to keep them at bay. The leaves can be used in teas and potpourris.

Plumbago
(Plumbago auriculata)

Plumbago is a perennial subtropical known for producing phloxlike powder-blue flowers. The blooms hold well in bouquets. It will wind up a trellis, if one is provided. Without a trellis, it grows shrubby. The light-green leaves and spent flowers like to stick to clothes, and I find them all over me after working around them. The plants, if given time, can vine up to 10 feet (3 m) or more in length, especially if there is a trellis adjacent to the plant. If you want to control the shape and growth, prune plumbago regularly. The unsightly old blossoms should be regularly removed.

Plumbago prefers bright light and drier soil conditions. It can tolerate moist soil as long as it is sandy or well drained. It is easily propagated from cuttings and is readily available in plant catalogs. Alba, a variety that has white blooms, is generally pest free and easy to grow.

Pocketbook Plant
(Calceolaria crenatiflora)

The pocketbook plant produces one of the more interesting flowers you will ever see. The flowers have a rounded, pouchlike shape. If the odd shape doesn't fascinate you, the contrasting blotches or spots on the flower surely will. The plant has broad leaves, and its flowers tend to be two contrasting warm colors. No matter

what, this plant, when in flower, will always garner comments from visitors.

There are outdoor perennial varieties that are not as suited to the greenhouse environment as the annual types. Look for the easy-to-grow Anytime hybrids, which produce a 9-inch (23-cm) plant in a 6-inch (15-cm) pot.

The pocketbook plant takes some planning to grow to maturity from seed. Because it likes to flower in the cooler temperatures of winter, the best timing is to plant seed in June for a good winter-flowering plant. For bloom around the Easter season, sow the seed in early August. Just barely cover the seed, and when it has grown four or five true leaves, transplant it into a 6-inch (15-cm) pot, using regular potting soil. It can tolerate cooler temperatures but prefers constant temperatures of 50°F to 60°F (10°C to 15°C), especially in its last 4 months of growth. It needs a bright spot to grow, but it requires sun for only a short time each day. It benefits from regular light feeding, especially when you see the flower buds appear. The pocketbook plant needs constant moisture. Try watering it from below by always keeping the saucer filled with water.

It is best grown as a potted plant, and, like many annual flowering plants, it is best donated to the compost pile after the blooms have faded. Maintain a lookout for aphids, which first appear on the underside of the leaf and on stems and tips.

Poinsettia

(Euphorbia pulcherrima)

The poinsettia has become the Christmas plant of choice. Everyone will want to give you their leftover plants when they find out you have a greenhouse or a sunspace. To avoid growing only poinsettias in the greenhouse, I eventually have to tell my friends, "Thanks, but two plants are enough, and I don't need any more." But no matter what, most greenhouse owners will eventually end up with at least one poinsettia. Perhaps an old ratty poinsettia kept far too long past Christmas gives us all a good reason to be ruthless and toss a few of them out. If you can't be ruthless, here is what to do. General care for the poinsettia is to provide a bright, cool spot and let the soil dry out between watering.

After blooming, or about late April, you may want to consider pruning it back to create a more bushy plant. They can get to be tall, lanky shrubs if left to their own devices. Spring is also a good time to repot poinsettia if it is root bound or if you believe it is in some exhausted soil. Continue watering it as before and occasionally give it some plant food. Because poinsettia likes a cooler environment, many people move the plant to a semishady spot outside in summer to avoid the hot greenhouse. This is a good idea if your greenhouse runs hot or if you live in a warm summer location.

When late September arrives, the work begins to trigger it to bloom for Christmas—are you up for this? First, you will need to control the light and the darkness that the poinsettia receives. It is the length of the night that triggers the formation of the colored bracts (most call them "flowers") that give the plant its bright show. The plant now needs 14 hours of uninterrupted darkness and 10 hours of light each day from late September for a period of 8 weeks (don't get lazy and skip a day!). Many people move the plant to a dark closet or slip it into a sealed

black bag (it takes three black trash bags to give you total darkness). Remember, you must do this every day. After the 8 weeks, you can finally rest and continue growing it as before. You need to be dedicated to this and never miss a day, which is admittedly a lot of work.

If all this work to get your poinsettia to look good again sounds like too much for you, there are two alternatives: (1) toss the plant out and buy a new one next Christmas like everyone else, or (2) just continue growing it without the light-control treatment and see what happens. Sometimes I get a poinsettia to do okay by placing it where no one turns on the electric light at night, such as a bright basement window. It is helpful if it does receive some natural light through a window. With this method, I have had some good results.

You can easily propagate poinsettia from tip cuttings at least 4 to 5 inches (10 to 13 cm) long. Both whiteflies and mealybugs can plague the poinsettia, and gift plants should be checked for unwanted "guests."

Polka-dot Plant

(Hypoestes phyllostachya)

This plant is also known as **freckle-face**. As the names imply, it has unmistakable spots on the leaves, which make the plant interesting and even colorful. The leaves are its main attraction, as the flower is insignificant. The plant usually grows to up to 1 or 2 feet (0.3 or 0.6 m) in height and has spots that are pink, red, or white against green leaves. Lately, there are varieties that have even more of the spots, to the point where the green seems to be spotted against pink, red, or white.

This is an easy plant to grow, although I usually find myself tossing it out after about a year of growth because it becomes lanky and too preoccupied with flowering and tends to go downhill. Don't be surprised if, after flowering, it reseeds itself as baby polka-dot plants coming up everywhere.

The polka-dot plant seems tolerant of almost any greenhouse condition and is relatively pest free. It is easily grown both in pots and in beds, usually propagated from seed. You can also get good results from cuttings. I prefer starting it from seed because it is easy to germinate and grows fast. It does seem to prefer brighter locations for the best leaf-color development.

Poppy

(Papaveraceae spp.)

Poppies are not often considered as a greenhouse plant, but I have had wonderful color shows from them. I haven't tried all the many species, but many are good for the greenhouse. I have had good luck with both shirley **(Papaver rhoeas)** and Iceland poppy **(Papaver nudicaule)**, shown here. The blue foliage and unusual flowers of **Papaver somniferum** includes a double-flowered variety that looks like a peony. I have found that the perennial Oriental poppy **(Papaver orientale)** is not a good choice for the greenhouse, because the period of bloom is so short and the plant has a difficult time in the greenhouse environment.

Poppies seem to do best in the greenhouse when planted in late summer or fall for a spring bloom. Don't get too carried away, because it may take the plants most of winter before they get ready to flower. But still a few plants are always good to have blooming.

Because poppy seed is so small, it is often sown too thickly, and if you do this it will need to be thinned. Contrary to what many say, the poppy can be transplanted, as long as you do it while the seedling is small and take care to limit the disturbance of the roots. Poppies need bright sun and may need staking if you have prolonged cloudy weather. I find that they do best if they can be planted in beds or larger pots of at least 8 inches (20 cm). The soil needs to dry out between waterings. Poppies should have the spent blossoms and seedpods that have developed picked off as soon as possible for continued bloom.

For bouquets, cut the stem as soon as the buds become upright and are just beginning to show some color. You should immediately sear the base of the cut flower stem over a flame for the bloom to last in a vase. With this method, you can get them to look good in a vase for up to 5 days. Without doing this, they won't last much longer than a day.

Primrose

(*Primula* spp.)

Primrose, also known as *primula*, is a lover of cool weather in the greenhouse. Primroses are low-growing plants that bear clusters of flowers in almost any color. They like cool, moist conditions to bloom and tend to suffer when the temperatures get warm. They also prefer only a few hours of bright sun, so pick your primrose location well. To best schedule your plants, start the seeds in February or March and just barely cover the seed, unless you are growing *Primula sinensis,* which should be buried a bit deeper as it needs dark to germinate. When plants are large enough, transplant them into 5-inch (13-cm) pots. Try to grow them in a cool spot.

The species *Primula obconica* is a good plant for the greenhouse, but you should know that the leaf can cause dermatitis in some people, so use gloves when handling this species. The **fairy primrose**, or *P. malacoides*, is known for its large flowers.

Although many people toss out the plants after the show of bloom, you can sometimes coax them into another year of bloom in the greenhouse. The main thing to remember when growing primroses is to think cool and moist rather than hot and dry. Plants also benefit from regular feeding in the summer months. Also, keep an eye out for mites.

Ranunculus

(*Ranunculus asiaticus*)

Ranunculus is also known as **buttercup**. It is usually started from small, hard tubers. The tubers look like a miniature petrified jellyfish the size of a penny. The flowers are delicate and found in most colors except for the blue shades. The flower shape can vary from a double that forms a small globe to a poppylike single-petaled blossom. A single tuber can produce a large number of blooms during a season. Each bloom can be 2 to 5 inches (5 to 13 cm) across. Ranunculus are best sown in the fall for late winter through spring bloom.

Before planting the tubers, try soaking them in water for a couple of hours. Don't forget them, because longer soaking may cause damage. Plant the tubers with the points down, about 1 inch (2.5 cm) or so deep in well-drained potting soil. Adding a bit of sand to the potting soil is helpful in giving them the good drainage that they need. Let the soil dry slightly between watering. Don't plant all of your tubers at the same time. Vary the planting through the fall and early winter to provide a longer period of enjoyment of these beautiful flowers. The plants do equally well in pots or in beds. Give yourself around 5 square inches (32 sq. cm) of pot per tuber. In beds, space the tubers about 4 inches (10 cm) apart. There are other species besides *Ranunculus asiaticus* worth experimenting with in the greenhouse.

Ranunculus is a great winter and spring bloomer. The flowers are useful in bouquets but also look great blooming in beds and pots. After bloom, most people discard the plants, but you can let the plant continue to grow until the leaves yellow. Set them in a cool spot with semimoist garden dirt (not potting soil) until it is time to plant them again. You should know that the tubers are not easy to store with great success, so buy a few new tubers next season just in case. On occasion, when growing ranunculus in beds, I have forgotten about the plants after they die back. The next season they often come up as a surprise.

Rondeletia
(*Rondeletia* spp.)
Rondeletia is not very well known, but if you like fragrance this is a "must have"! There are two types of rondeletia commonly available: **Rondeletia splendens** and **Rondeletia leucophylla**. Both are easy and relatively trouble free to grow in a small- to medium-sized pot. *R. splendens* grows to about 16 inches (41 cm) and can bloom most anytime of the year. *R. leucophylla* grows more shrublike, getting up to 2 or 3 feet (0.6 to 0.9 m) in height. It blooms from December to June. The flowers of both species tend to be red-hued. The treasure of this plant is the incredible fragrance it emits after twilight and into the evening. It is most pleasant and sweet, and quite impressive. When I first noticed my plant in bloom, it smelled more like I had 20 plants in bloom, the space was so filled with its sweet fragrance. The next day, the plant sat there innocently enough, giving no smell from the blooms. You would never imagine the exotic, fragrant party the rondeletia throws most every night from these modest blooms.

The only source I have come across for rondeletia is the wonderful dream book of a catalog from Logee's Greenhouses (1-888-330-8038; see "Mail-Order Plants" in Appendix 5 for more information).

Rose
(*Rosa* spp.)
No flowering greenhouse would be complete without a rose. You can grow almost any type of rose in a greenhouse, including the teas, floribundas, miniatures, climbers, and shrubs. I have enjoyed the different characteristics of the large-flowered tea roses and the many offerings in miniature roses, but

Tea rose

nothing seems to beat the profusion of blooms of the floribundas. They seem to put on more blooms than any other type and give you year-round flowers, often with incredible vigor, even in cool greenhouses. Yes, the stems aren't as long as the teas, but I like quantity, and no one has complained about the rose's shorter stems when I give a bloom to someone. In small greenhouses, the miniature roses are always a good fit in a few small pots and are easy to grow.

Unfortunately, plant breeders have developed a plethora of beautiful roses that have no fragrance. What a waste! These roses are only half as good as a rose that not only looks good but also smells good. No matter what rose you grow, always think about fragrance. Read the variety descriptions well, and look for those that say "strong fragrance" or "spicy scent." Whenever possible, go for a variety that has smell. There should be a law banning all roses that lack a decent fragrance. A fragrant rose can fill the greenhouse or sunspace with its wonderful aroma even better than it can perfume the outside air, and it is such a treat!

Another characteristic I look for are those described as "vigorous growers." This seems to help keep the blooms on the plant year-round.

Roses are very tolerant of varying temperatures; from hot to cold, they usually do fine. They need bright, full-sun location in well-drained soil. They can easily be overwatered, so be sure to let the soil dry out between waterings. Overwatering is indicated by yellowing leaves, often starting first with the veins. Another symptom of overwatering is a blotchy yellowing on the leaves and leaf drop.

As with outside blooms, if you want to cut some blossoms for a bouquet, wait until the flower is about $1/3$ to $1/2$ open. Be sure to cut just above a bud and down low enough so that you have at least five leaflets on the stem just below where you have cut.

Roses tend to benefit from occasional pruning, which will soon stimulate bushier and often healthier growth, especially if the plant is starting to get leggy.

Roses can be grown in pots as well as in beds. With the flori-

Miniature rose

bundas, I have the best luck planting either in large tubs or directly in beds. Roses have their fair share of problems and are subject to the same problems in the greenhouse as they are outside. Mites, whiteflies, and mealybugs all love to hang out on roses. If the blossoms are opening with some burned edges, you may have thrips. Like mites, thrips are also almost microscopic and can cause havoc with blossoms. Get out the hand lens, and you may see little cigar-shaped critters running around the buds. Try to spray the buds before they open with something like insecticidal soap. Cut back on the dosage if the soap causes burning. If soap doesn't do the job, you may have to go to something stronger. Also, roses are subject to powdery mildew. I have had good luck controlling the mildew by spraying an antitranspirant. See Chapter 10, "When Things Go Wrong," for more information.

The miniature roses fit nicely into any greenhouse, but most of these plants lack a decent fragrance. There is one variety called Sachet that has the most fragrance of all miniatures. If you want to embark into the area of miniature roses, call the catalog company that specializes in them, Nor'East Miniature Roses, at 800-662-9669.

Salpiglossis
(Salpiglossis sinuata)

Salpiglossis, also known as **painted tongue**, has one of the most beautiful blooms you'll ever see. It produces a 2- to 3-inch (5- to 8-cm) flower on 2-foot (0.6-meter) plants. Inside the bloom are some incredible markings that often remind me of an extraordinary sunset. The flowers are available in purple, yellow, red, gold, blue or pink, and each has a deeper color of patterned venation, often turning to a lighter gold background in the throat of the flower. You have to see it to believe it! The blooms work well in bouquets. The leaves have a sticky feel, and I often see bugs getting stuck to the foliage as if on flypaper. As good-looking as the flowers are, I think that the leaves are equally ugly, so be patient until you see the reward of the bloom.

Salpiglossis is related to the petunia but is a bit trickier to grow. It does not tolerate very hot or very cold temperatures. Additionally, it is an annual and often not long-lived. I usually start the seed in late January or February to take advantage of the moderate spring temperatures as it is blooming. You can also start it in late July or August for a late fall bloom before the cooler temperatures of winter. When cold or hot weather sets in or when the plants stop blooming, I find it easiest to toss them into the compost and plan to grow more next season. Salpiglossis does fine in pots and in ground beds. Occasionally, you may need to stake it up. Be sure to grow it in a well-lit, sunny location. It prefers drier soils and doesn't tolerate overwatering.

Some good selections for salpiglossis include Bolero and Casino, which each have short, bushy tendencies. There is also a taller variety called Splash. Grow just a few salpiglossis, and you will get a sigh from visitors when these plants are in bloom.

Salvia
(Salvia farinacea)

This type of salvia is not the common red-flowered variety most people are used to. The *S. farinacea* species has blue or white flowers and the leaves and bloom look very different, but it is a good plant for the greenhouse. The flowering stalk is less than $1/2$ inch (1.3 cm) wide but grows straight up 8 to 10 inches (20 to 25 cm) above the 15- to 20-inch-tall (38- to 51-cm-tall) plant. One plant will produce many vertical, flowering stalks. When you set many plants together spaced 6 to 8 inches (15 to 20 cm) apart, you get a beautiful effect. The blue variety, Victoria, is striking against other flowers in a bed or a bouquet. It is reminiscent of a lavender plant, with a more vertical nature to the blooms. A white variety, called White Bedder, grows 2 feet (0.6 m) or more in height. There is a mix of the white and blue in one plant, called Strata. Of all these choices, I tend to grow the Victoria because of its intense blue color, which is a rare color to find in a flower.

Salvia farinacea is best grown in sunny spots. It prefers warmer temperatures, though it can survive the cooler winter-greenhouse climate. In cool temperatures, I find the stress often brings on the bugs. In the greenhouse, it can live for many years but usually looks best for only one year or less. You may find the plant looks better when you remove the older flowering spikes as they finish blooming. *Salvia farinacea* is easily propagated from seed, taking a little more than 2 weeks to germinate, given the proper conditions.

Schizanthus
(*Schizanthus* x *wisetonensis*)

Schizanthus is also called the **butterfly flower** or the **poor man's orchid**, and when you see the bloom, you'll understand why. This is one of the shorter-lived plants for the greenhouse, but it has one of the most unusual and colorful blooms of any plant. The flowers come in almost every color except blue. Each flower is only 1 inch (2.5 cm) or less across but flowers are borne in profusion on a 12- to 24-inch (30- to 61-cm) plant, depending upon the variety. Like the salpiglossis, the schizanthus often has incredible markings in the throat. Sometimes they are set against a yellow center with another color around the outside of the flower. It is the unique markings that make people compare it to an orchid. The petals are irregularly shaped in a snapdragon manner, which reminds many people of butterflies. The beautiful blooms atop short branching stems are not fragrant. With a little creativity, schizanthus can be used as cut flowers for small vases.

Schizanthus will live at most only for a couple of seasons, blooming for a month or two before the foliage begins to die back, often with the flowers still in full bloom. Before flowering, it likes to be fed regularly. The plants may become lopsided, but a little tip pinching while they are 6 to 10 inches (15 to 25 cm) in height can make them much better shaped. It is not very tolerant of hot temperatures and grows slowly in cool temperatures. For these reasons, I tend to grow it through the fall, winter, and spring. Schizanthus can be grown in either pots or beds, but I have seen the best plants when grown in pots. It can tolerate varying soil moisture conditions.

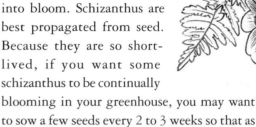

The taller varieties of schizanthus may need some small stakes for support as they come into bloom. Schizanthus are best propagated from seed. Because they are so short-lived, if you want some schizanthus to be continually blooming in your greenhouse, you may want to sow a few seeds every 2 to 3 weeks so that as they die back, new ones take their place.

Sensitive Plant
(*Mimosa pudica*)

The sensitive plant is revered for its sensitivity rather than its bloom. It has delicate, ferny leaves that fascinate almost everyone. These leaves move, folding up when lightly brushed or touched, almost as if they had a muscular response to your finger. If brushed a bit harder, the small branches supporting the leaflets may even fold downward. There is something magical about seeing a plant respond instantly to your touch.

This novelty plant delights children as well as adults. I have seen the sensitive plant foster a lifelong fascination with plants among some people (myself included). When evening arrives, the whole plant usually folds up as if it has been touched. Come morning, it will unfold until you touch it again.

Occasionally, you may see it put out a small pink flower that looks like a powder puff, but the flower is not nearly as important as the leaves moving with your touch. The sensitive plant likes warmth of at least 50°F (10°C) and constant moisture most of the year. In winter, you can let it run a little drier between waterings. It needs to grow in a bright spot but not necessarily in full sun. It is best grown in a pot and is generally started from seed.

Shrimp Plant
(*Justicia brandegeana* or *Beloperone guttata*)
The shrimp plant is a long-lived shrubby plant that blooms almost every day of the year. As its name implies, it has 3-inch (8-cm) salmon-colored, prawnlike flowers at the end of arcing stems. It is a good choice for the greenhouse because of its long bloom period and its ability to tolerate diverse temperature and soil conditions. Although the blooming stems may not be of great length, these flowers can add an interesting touch when used among other flowers in bouquets, and they are long-lasting.

Shrimp plants are best grown in pots. The bigger the pot, the shrubbier the plant will become. Occasional pruning can prevent the plant from becoming leggy and will help you to maintain a bushier plant. They have few pest problems and are easily propagated from cuttings. You may also like the solid yellow-flowering variety.

Snapdragon
(*Antirrhinum majus*)
Snapdragon is tops on my list for a winter-greenhouse cut flower. They are dependable and easy to grow, and they can provide you with long colorful spikes of flowers for many months. But if you dig up the outdoor snaps, you will likely be disappointed. There have been special snapdragon varieties developed to bloom in the greenhouse that are triggered by the short days of winter. Ordinary outdoor snaps bloom poorly in the winter greenhouse and pale in comparison to the specially bred greenhouse types. The greenhouse varieties (sometimes known as **forcing snaps**) produce beautiful blooms reaching up to 3 feet (0.9 m), topped by the longest flower spikes you have ever seen. They come in all the traditional snapdragon colors. I have also found that the greenhouse varieties have a stronger spicy scent than the outdoor types. Obtaining these special varieties for the greenhouse is not easy unless you can talk a commercial greenhouse operator into selling you some seed. At this writing, the only retail seed catalog selling greenhouse snapdragon seed (Stokes Seeds) has suddenly stopped offering it. Now the only way to get them is through a commercial source. Check with your local commercial greenhouse. This new unavailability is a real shame, because they produce one of the best winter bloom shows of all plants. If you can somehow prove that you are more of a commercial grower than a hobbyist (wink), you will often find them offered by the Colorlink Catalog (800-686-7380), which caters to small commercial-greenhouse operations.

If you are lucky enough to find seed, then you should know that timing is important in growing greenhouse snaps, and they are best sown September through December for winter through spring bloom. When you are growing greenhouse

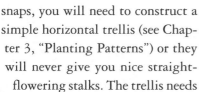

Horizontal trellis

snaps, you will need to construct a simple horizontal trellis (see Chapter 3, "Planting Patterns") or they will never give you nice straight-flowering stalks. The trellis needs to be at least 3 tiers high, reaching a level of at least 3 feet (0.9 m). I have had some luck using the smaller tomato cages as a support for these plants. Usually one cage can support 4 plants.

Snapdragons can easily tolerate most temperatures, including the very cold greenhouse, but they will have more problems with heat, including smaller flower spikes and wilting as the temperature starts to consistently reach above 80°F (27°C) during the day. They are a great winter plant because of their cold tolerance. They do best when grown in bright greenhouse areas.

Propagate your snapdragon seed by just barely covering it with soil. Snaps like to grow in full light, and I prefer to grow them in beds because of the horizontal trellis system, which is easier to set up in beds. If you want to try growing them in pots, you can place 3 or 4 pots in a 5-gallon (19-liter) pot (with drainage holes!) and put a standard tomato cage over the top of the plants when they reach 8 inches (20 cm) in height. The first bloom spikes are always the best and tallest. Each succeeding bloom will be smaller but still well worth growing. When you pick bloom spikes for a bouquet, always cut the stem at least 8 inches (20 cm) below the lowest bloom on the spike to give you sturdy subsequent flowering spikes. Try to maintain a good level of moisture in the soil, but don't create dripping wet mud. Wilting can set your blooms back and should be avoided, although with hot temperatures that

can become difficult. I usually rip the crop out when the bloom spikes the plant is putting on are only around 5 inches (13 cm) long. For prolonged winter bloom, try staggering your planting. Start a few different beds (or pots) of greenhouse-type snaps a month or so apart.

Occasionally, you may see aphids hanging around. Get suspicious if you see some sticky substance on the leaves and keep an eye on the underside of the leaves.

Staghorn Fern
(*Platycerium bifurcatum*)

The staghorn fern is a true fern, not a flowering plant, but an interesting plant to have in any greenhouse. It gets its name from its resemblance to mounted horns. It is best grown mounted on a slab of bark 8 by 10 inches (20 by 25 cm) or larger. Dig out a little pocket in the middle of a slab of bark and fill with some peat moss or compost. Place the plant there and secure it with thumbtacks and twine, and over time it will get a good hold on the bark. Lower fronds begin to grow around the bark and turn brown, which provides a good anchor.

About every 2 weeks, water the pocket; mist every 3 days if the humidity is low. Occasionally mist with a plant food (the type that is dissolved in water). It prefers the lower lighted areas of the greenhouse, and once it gets growing, it is relatively free of pests or problems. New plants must be obtained from commercial greenhouses or through the mail. You can propagate new plants from little "pups" that occasionally appear to the side of the mother plant. It is great to have some antlers hanging in the greenhouse that are alive and breathing without ever having to go hunting. The staghorn fern is always a good catch!

Statice
(Limonium sinuatum)

Statice, also known as **sea lavender**, is often grown as an outdoor everlasting because the cut flower can last for many years in dried-flower arrangements. I have had good luck growing *Limonium sinuatum*, the annual type, in the greenhouse, giving new meaning to the term "everlasting." You can even transplant outdoor statice into the greenhouse before frost, but you must get a lot of root to be successful; dig deep because these plants have a taproot. Good results can also come from sowing your own in midwinter that will bloom from summer through Christmas or longer. Although statice tolerates cool temperatures well, it grows very slowly in the winter. If the flower stalks fall over, try staking them. There are many varieties to choose from in *L. sinuatum*, which is available in most colors. It can grow to a height of 2 feet (0.6 m) or more. I prefer to grow the dwarf varieties, which are difficult to find in most catalogs (Stokes Seeds carries the Petite Bouquet dwarf). The dwarf variety only reaches 10 to 12 inches (25 to 30 cm) but has the advantage of blooming faster and needing little if any staking. I also like the mixed selections with a range of colors rather than growing just one color.

Statice likes to dry out between waterings and does best in well-lit areas. It does well in both beds and pots. When grown in pots, use a 1-gallon (3.8-liter) size to accommodate the long roots.

When the plant is in flower, you can use the blooms as you would any flower in a vase with water. If you want to dry the flower stalks, hang them upside down in a dark, dry room for 3 to 4 weeks. Then you can use them in dried-flower arrangements. You may have some grasses, dried wildflowers, or other everlastings to mix into the bouquets, but don't put any water in the vase of your dried-flower arrangement or it will quickly rot.

Stock
(Matthiola incana)

Stock is one of the most fragrant plants in the greenhouse, especially in the evening. The spicy aroma can easily fill any space, beginning about sundown. It can also be used as a cut flower but may drop some petals within a few days of being cut. Stock produces pink, red, apricot, purple, coral, and white blooms.

Plants can be found in both double- and single-flowered types. Whenever possible, try to grow varieties that have a high number of double flowers because they are much more showy than the single-flowered plants. In any seed packet, there will always be a few single-flowered plants that show up. You can identify the doubles from the singles when the plants are still seedlings. The doubles tend to be the seedlings that are the yellowish, pale green plants. The less desirable seedlings will be a darker green and can be tossed out before you transplant into any larger pots or beds. This leaf-color method of identification works best when the seedlings are grown at cooler temperatures of around 55°F to 60°F (13°C to 15°C).

Determining the doubles with warmer temperatures is less accurate but still worth trying. Another indication, which is not quite as reliable with all varieties, is to look at the very first leaves that emerge (the cotyledon leaves). If you see that one of the leaves has a little notch in it, that sometimes indicates a double-flowered plant. Because you may be throwing some of the nondouble seedlings out, sow more than you think you'll want to end up with.

Varieties of stock vary in height from 8 to 30 inches (20 to 76 cm). The smaller varieties are best for potted production, and the taller types are best in beds. However, with a large pot and a few stakes, you can grow the larger varieties in a pot.

Stock is mostly a winter- and spring-blooming greenhouse plant and can be unproductive in a hot greenhouse, so timing is important. Sow stock only when nights are cool (below 60°F). Sow between late July and early March for flowering plants from January through June (see Chapter 7, "Scheduling," page 153). If your timing is off, your stocks may just grow a lot of leaves with no sign of flowering, at least not until winter or spring. Once hot weather wrenches their internal clock, you never know when your greenhouse stocks may flower.

There are two varieties that don't need such specialized timing and can be grown and will bloom dependably almost any time. These varieties are Cheerful White and Cheerful Yellow. Unfortunately, they are difficult for retail purchasers to find. The Cheerful series used to be carried by the Twilley Seeds catalog but were recently dropped. Perhaps they will reappear again someday. If you can somehow prove that you are more of a commercial grower than a hobbyist (wink), you may find them offered in the Colorlink catalog (800-686-7380), which caters to small commercial greenhouse operations.

After the initial flower spike of the stock is played out, you can get secondary blooms on new stalks forming on the sides of the plant if you make a concerted effort to prune off the old blossoms and any forming seedpods.

There is another species of stock, commonly known as **evening-scented stock** (*Matthiola longipetala*), that is not nearly as showy as *Matthiola incana* but has a great smell. If fragrance is more important than looks, you should try it. This plant, as its name indicates, is mostly fragrant in the evening.

Stock does best in full sun and must dry somewhat between waterings. It is easily propagated from seed. It is occasionally bothered by aphids but in general is a trouble-free plant.

Streptocarpus

(*Streptocarpus* x *hybridus*)

Streptocarpus, also known as **cape primrose**, is a second cousin to the African violet. In the greenhouse, it is easier to grow and has less exacting requirements. It does, however, prefer cooler nights, which makes it a better choice for the greenhouse than for the house. Strepto-carpus has a larger leaf and flower than the average African violet, with some varieties having leaves up to 1¹/₂ feet (0.45 m) long. It has a showy, tubular, trumpet-shaped blossom that can be up to 2 inches (5 cm) wide. Often there are interesting markings in the throat of the flower. Flowers are found in red, purple, blue, white and pink. It is always a good choice for a long-blooming potted plant.

Streptocarpus can tolerate higher light levels than the African violet, but still it would prefer the shadier areas of the greenhouse or sunspace. I have had the best luck with streptocarpus when grown in pots. Use shallow pots, if you can find them, to prevent root rot. Let the top of the soil dry out between waterings and try to avoid getting water on the leaves by watering the plant from below or between the leaves. It does like a regular light misting. Be sure to remove faded flowers for prolonged bloom. Although it can tolerate cool temperatures, try not to let it grow in areas much below 45°F (7°C).

Streptocarpus can easily be propagated from divisions of large plants or, with more difficulty, from leaf cuttings. It is occasionally bothered by mealybugs, so look for the cottony critters hanging around.

Succulents

As explained earlier in the section on cactus, all cacti are succulents but not all succulents are cacti. Succulents are a general listing for a number of plant families, all of which have evolved with thick, succulent leaves, stems, or tubers (usually tubers above the ground). Some succulents have spines and some don't.

The wonderful thing about growing succulents is their often unusual, plump shapes. Because they are plump, they have evolved their own drought-survival water-storage system and thus must dry out between waterings and do not like to be overwatered.

There are many species of succulents worth growing in a sunroom or greenhouse, and you will always appreciate how easy they are to grow. Besides having interesting thick leaves, some have amazing flowers. Because succulents are not of one family or one type of plant, it is difficult to generalize as to their care but, what the heck, I'll do it anyway. For details about a particular plant not responding to my advice here, find a good book on cacti or succulents at the local library or bookstore.

Besides letting the soil run quite dry between waterings, especially in winter, succulents also need a porous, well-drained soil and will easily rot in wet soil conditions. They prefer plenty of bright light but can tolerate some light shade. Fertilize with a liquid houseplant food at half strength from April through September. Different succulents have their own requirements for optimum cool and warm temperatures. Check the plant tag or a book for more details.

I could fill pages with varieties of succulents to grow, but because their care is so easy, I'll let you decide what to try. If you provide them with their basic care, it is hard to go wrong with these plants. Walk into any com-

mercial retail greenhouse or garden center and you will likely find some interesting succulents "you can't live without." You should also check the plant catalogs that carry succulents for a great selection.

Some of my favorites include the many species of *Aloe vera* and *Kalanchoe* (see individual listings in this chapter). Some other neat types of succulents include **living stones**, **burro's tail**, **string** of beads, **pencil plants**, **pachypodiums**, the **Madagascar palm**, and one that is known only by its botanical name, *Cotyledon undulata*, which has unusual leaves. The Euphorbia family comprises many amazing succulents with diverse shapes. It would take up too much space to list all the interesting succulents, but once you start to see what is out there, you are sure to get hooked.

You simply won't find any other family of plants that has so many unusual and exotic plants that are so easy to grow. Consider setting aside a small area for a collection of both succulents and cacti. Mixing them with the other plants might cause you to accidentally overwater them.

Swan River Daisy
(Brachycome iberidifolia)

The Swan River daisy has 1-inch (2.5-cm) blue, purple, or white daisies borne on lacy foliage. One plant can bear a profusion of flowers. This Australian plant has finely cut, stringy leaves. The plants themselves are only 7 to 10 inches (18 to 25 cm) in height. I prefer to grow them in hanging pots. The Swan River daisy prefers warm temperatures and is best grown as a summer plant. I usually start it in April for all-summer bloom. The soil needs to dry slightly between waterings, and the plant must grow in full sun for the best

flowering response. When cool weather returns to the greenhouse, it tends to go downhill, so bid it farewell until next spring. Swan River daisy is easily propagated from seed.

Sweet Pea
(Lathyrus odoratus)

If you grow only one flower in your winter greenhouse, you should at the very least have one small row of sweet peas. They are a must for their winter and spring blooms, getting an A-plus rating for color, cut flowers, and fragrance. The sweet pea's fragrance and color have the ability to put even the worst winter day at bay. Sweet peas in the dreary winter will instantly brighten up even the toughest day you had at the office.

Because they like the cool weather to grow best, your sowing time is of the utmost importance. For best results, schedule the seeding as early as late August but no later than early October. The longer and colder your winter, the earlier you should sow them. You can grow almost any variety, but most give only a mediocre performance. Stokes Seeds catalog (see "Mail-Order Seeds" in Appendix 6) offers a few varieties that outperform almost all the others, and they were bred primarily for greenhouse growing. Look for the Cuthbertson floribunda mixture, which produces a wide array of colors on long stems. The Cuthbertson is also very heat tolerant for those occasional warm and sunny greenhouse winter days. It is also available in separate colors. Stokes also offers another equally good variety called Mammoth Series Mixed. I have tried a number of other varieties, and no others come close to the performance, fragrance, and long stems that these two varieties produce.

Be forewarned, however, because both of these varieties grow tall, up to 7 feet (2 m) or more in height. I have tested out pruning the tips to control the height and have had limited good results.

With just about any variety of sweet pea you grow (except for the dwarf varieties, which are not suited to the greenhouse), you will need some type of vertical trellising because they are fast climbers. It is best to build the trellis before you plant. I usually set the trellis on a north–south axis. You can use any number of materials for the trellis material, from recycled fence to new fence to store-bought trellising material. You can also use string and tall stakes.

Soak the peas overnight prior to planting. Don't let them soak any longer, as it may do some damage. Peas do best when directly sown in the location where you will be growing them. I have been able to transplant them with some luck and extreme care, but I didn't seem to gain anything in the effort when compared to those directly sown at a later date.

To prolong the bloom, it is important that you keep the vines well picked. If not, they will soon set nonedible pea pods, and this will send a message to the plant to slow down the setting of new buds and flowers. So the more you pick, the more you get, at least until spring starts to get really warm. I want to repeat that these pea pods formed on the sweet pea vine are *not* edible, so take precautions with toddlers.

I used to always cut the pea flowers with a good pair of scissors. Then one day my friend and avid sweet-pea grower, Lyman Spaulding, showed me another way to pick the flowers without scissors. What you do is this: With two fingers holding the flower at the base of the flower stalk try to bend the flower stem back towards the main stem of the growing sweet-pea plant. While you are doing this bending, gently pull the flower stem upward. If you do it right, it will make a clean break right at the node where the flower stem meets the main stem. This technique takes some practice, but after a while you can easily and quickly pick a full bouquet without scissors or knife.

However you harvest your sweet peas, be sure not to damage the plant by bending the main stem, ripping the flowers off at the expense of ripping stem tissue. This can set the whole plant back.

Sweet peas must be grown in a very bright spot but can tolerate a bit of partial shading during the day. I have found that they grow best in ground beds, but with some creativity, you could grow some in a 5-gallon (19-liter) or larger tub, as long as you can provide some type of trellising or string that is tall enough to accommodate a tall vine. Perhaps you can make a teepeelike trellis or suspend some string from the ceiling of the greenhouse.

Grow your sweet peas on the moist side, but not muddy wet. Sweet peas can become susceptible to both aphids and mites. This is often an indication that your greenhouse is running too hot for them, and you may want to adjust your schedule for growing during a cooler time or drop the temperature a bit if you can.

The sweet-pea bouquets you can grow make a great gift for friends in the winter. Once you get a crop, spread around the fragrance and flowers!

Thunbergia, or Black-eyed Susan
(*Thunbergia alata*)

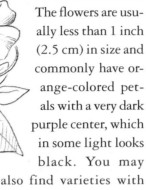

Of the many plants with the name black-eyed Susan, the thunbergia wins my support for the official dedication. The flowers are usually less than 1 inch (2.5 cm) in size and commonly have orange-colored petals with a very dark purple center, which in some light looks black. You may also find varieties with yellow or white petals. None of these flowers are particularly fragrant. The main reward is that they bloom year-round and can live for many years.

Thunbergia is a vine that can be grown in either pots or ground beds. These plants will often vine up the wires of a hanging basket or up a small trellis for a nice effect. They are slow growers, but over time they can reach 5 feet (1.5 m) or more, if given an opportunity and trellising.

Thunbergias are very tolerant of varying conditions and do well in both cool and warm greenhouses. They tolerate varying moisture, temperature, and light levels as long as it is not dark shade. The only problem thunbergia seems to have is an occasional mite infestation that is indicated by a yellow stippling of the leaves, making the leaves have the appearance of being dusty. They may also succumb to occasional visits from the whitefly. Because they are best grown in pots, you can simply take the plants to a large sink and give them a bath. That usually does a great job of washing off the critters.

Tulip
(*Tulipa* spp.)

See "Bulbs—Forcing Spring Bulbs for Winter Bloom" (p. 184).

Venus's Flytrap
(*Dionaea muscipula*)

There is always a fascination with any plant that has the ability to move on its own accord. When you combine that with a carnivorous habit, you really have a winner of a plant. The Venus's flytrap is especially entertaining to children and worth growing for that reason alone. At the end of the leaves is a twin-lobed blade edged with long hairs. When an insect touches these bristly hairs, the lobes close together in the blink of an eye, trapping the bug. A fluid contained in the lobes then dissolves the trapped insect, which turns the insect into a nutritious meal for the flytrap.

Plants may be obtained through catalog sources. Mature flytraps can sometimes be divided into two plants. They can also be started from seed.

The Venus's flytrap needs a constantly moist growing medium made up mostly of peat and sphagnum moss, along with a small amount of rich soil. Never let these plants dry out. They also need a bright location and consistently high humidity. I find that regular misting is helpful. The flytrap does best in a greenhouse with the winter-night low temperature on the cool side. Above all, the Venus's flytrap does best with a steady diet of living flies. That is where most gardeners come up short, especially in winter. Dead flies don't seem to work. However, injured living flies dropped into the open lobes work very well, if you have the constitution for this kind of care. I have had limited success with dropping cut pieces of fresh worm into the jaws of the plant, but that is only a short-term substitute for flies. For this reason, I have always had problems keeping the flytrap alive for more than a year or so. While they are alive, they are very entertaining.

Don't expect a Venus's flytrap to be much help in bug control for greenhouse pests. Unfortunately, I have never seen one eat common greenhouse pests such as the aphid or whitefly. They do best with the common black housefly.

There is a wonderful small catalog that specializes in carnivorous plants and supplies: Peter Pauls Nurseries, 4665 Chapin Road, Canandaigua, NY 14424-8713. You can find them on the World Wide Web at **www.peter pauls.com.**

Zinnia
(*Zinnia* spp.)
The zinnia is a common outdoor annual that can also be grown in the greenhouse with good results. It's a warmth-loving plant that provides good cut flowers. Zinnias have colorful rounded flower heads that vary from pomponlike to daisy-like. They range in height from 8 inches to 3 feet (20 cm to 0.9 m). Flowers come in almost every color except blue shades. In the greenhouse, they can be grown either in pots or ground beds. Because they like warmth, they are best grown in the warmer months of the year. You will probably have to discard this annual after a season of blooms. In the meantime, zinnias are nice as a colorful greenhouse plant and as a cut flower.

The most common problem in the greenhouse is powdery mildew disease, which turns the leaves powdery white. To avoid this mildew, try not to get water on the leaves; water below the leaf canopy. Find more details on how to avoid powdery mildew in Chapter 10.

A QUICK LOOK AT SELECTED CHARACTERISTICS OF ORNAMENTALS

Vining Ornamentals for the Greenhouse

Bougainvillea	Mandevilla	Passionflower
Golden-trumpet vine	Mina lobata	Plumbago
Jasminum polyanthum	Morning glory	Sweet pea
Jasminum x *stephanense*	Nasturtium (not all varieties)	Thunbergia

Good Choices for Greenhouse Bouquets and Cut Flowers

Alstroemeria	Bird-of-paradise	Carnation
Anemone	Calendula	Centaurea
Aster	Camellia	Chrysanthemum

(Continued on next page.)

Cleome
Coral bells
Dahlia
Dianthus
Gerbera
Gomphrena
Larkspur
Lisianthus
Malope

Marguerite daisy
Marigold
Mullein
Orchid
Pansy
Ranunculus
Rose
Salpiglossis

Salvia
Schizanthus
Shrimp plant
Snapdragon
Statice
Stock
Sweet pea
Zinnia

Fragrance Plants for the Greenhouse

Alyssum
Angel's-trumpet (mainly at night)
Carnation
Dianthus
Freesia
Morning glory *(Ipomoea alba)*
Gardenia

Geranium, scented
Hyacinth
Jasmine
Narcissus (not all varieties)
Nicotiana (not all varieties)
Oleander
Passionflower (not all varieties)

Pineapple sage
Rondeletia (mainly at night)
Rose (not all varieties)
Snapdragon
Stock
Sweet pea

Unusual or Colorful Leaves to Brighten Up the Greenhouse

Begonia rex
Bromeliads
Cabbage, ornamental
Cacti and succulents
Coleus

Croton
Geranium (not all varieties)
Kale, ornamental
Polka-dot plant

Sago palm
Sensitive plant
Staghorn fern
Venus's flytrap

Ornamentals for the Greenhouse That Runs Cool in Winter

Anemone
Bougainvillea
Cactus
Calendula
Camellia
Carnation
Cineraria
Cyclamen
Date palm
Felicia
Freesia
Narcissus
Geranium

Globe amaranth
Hyacinth
Jasminum nitidum
Kalanchoe
Kale and cabbage, flowering
Maple, flowering, or parlor
Nasturtium
Nemesia
Orchids (not all varieties)
Pansy
Passionflower
Pocketbook plant
Primrose

Ranunculus
Rose
Sago palm
Schizanthus
Shrimp plant
Snapdragon
Statice
Streptocarpus
Succulents
Sweet pea
Thunbergia
Tulip

Fruits and Vegetables

Besides using your greenhouse or sunspace for flowers, why not also mix in some fruits and vegetables? Nothing is more luxurious than eating a meal that includes some homegrown fresh food. That feeling is amplified tremendously on a cold winter day when you are eating fresh food from your greenhouse. Homegrown food, whether from your greenhouse or garden, provides you with the security of knowing where your food comes from and exactly how it was grown. By security, I mean that you know it probably doesn't have any deadly strains of *E. coli* living on the plants. You get to decide what it is sprayed with instead of wondering if it was sprayed by a toxic, illegal chemical, as often happens with imported food.

With the price of fruits and vegetables always on the rise (especially in winter), growing greenhouse food crops can also help save you money on your food bill. For that reason, I prefer to focus on growing the food crops in the greenhouse that are the more expensive ones in the grocery store. Why grow potatoes in the greenhouse when you can buy them so cheaply or store your own well into winter?

Greenhouses can become incredible food producers, although some crops are not as space efficient in terms of the amount of food they produce, and space is always at a premium when you are growing under glass (or plastic, too!). By following the recommendations in Chapter 7, "Scheduling," you can maximize your productivity. Growing plants at the right time will also reduce bugs and diseases.

In the following list, I occasionally mention specific varieties and their catalog source. Unfortunately, many companies often drop varieties in favor of new, improved varieties that come along. They may also drop a favorite variety of yours if they perceive a low demand for it. If you can't find a variety, you will have to see if you can locate it in another catalog or find a suitable substitute based on some of the characteristics that were important to you. You might also contact the catalog company for help in locating a variety that has been dropped. On a few occasions, I have been able to talk a company into restoring a dropped variety to the pages of their catalog.

Artichoke

Artichokes are relatively new to the American palate. They weren't widely available until the mid-1970s. As a result, some older people may not know what to do with them, as with the older volunteer who was interested in taking one home to eat that was produced in the Cheyenne Botanic Gardens. When we asked her if she knew how to cook and eat them, she said, "Sure, no problem." The next morning when we asked her how she'd liked that artichoke, she said, "Oh, it was pretty good, but I guess I didn't cook it long enough, because those leaf things were awfully tough to chew. I can't see why people like them so much." We kindly explained the finer points of eating an artichoke to her, and she later successfully ate one.

The globe artichoke resembles a large thistle. It is easily started from seed. You can also pro-pagate it from small plants and roots, which are commonly available through seed and nursery catalogs. Artichoke plants grow about 4 feet (1.2 m) high and up to 5 feet (1.5 m) wide. They do fine in a ground bed but may also be planted in a 5-gallon (19-liter) container. After about 6 to 8 months of growth, they will start to produce the globular buds. They tend to produce the majority of them in the spring and fall but can give you a globe most anytime. Artichokes will not ever win any awards for being great greenhouse producers, especially considering the amount of room they need, but greenhouse-grown artichokes are the sweetest you'll ever eat.

Be sure to harvest the globes while the bud still looks tight. If you wait too long, it will produce a large handsome blue or purple flower with a blue or purple center. If it does flower, it is equally valuable for its beauty and makes a great cut flower for a large vase or bouquet. Sometimes I purposely let the artichoke flower because I get in the mood to see its cool blue color in bloom. It is truly dazzling.

Artichokes benefit from regular fertilization. You may see the plant die back to the ground, but it often comes up again from a new side shoot, which easily grows into another full-sized productive plant.

Artichokes can be susceptible to aphids and mites, both of which are usually first noticed on the underside of the leaves (see Chapter 10 for help with controlling bugs).

You can also use your greenhouse to produce an outdoor garden artichoke. Those who live even in short-season areas can get a few good globes from an artichoke that received a head start in the greenhouse and was then transplanted to the outside. Try starting your plants between late January through February. Transplant them outside when you would normally set out tomatoes. They do best in rich soil in a spot with good sun penetration.

Avocado

Before you get too excited about homegrown guacamole fresh from your greenhouse, I need to tell you that avocados are extremely difficult to grow for fruit production in a greenhouse.

The plant itself is not hard to grow, as long as the soil is well drained. The avocado needs to dry out between waterings. Growing any old seed you find in a store-bought fruit is not a good idea if you want to shoot for actual fruit production. Normally, avocados reach 30 feet (9 m) in height. The tree size can be maintained to fit into a greenhouse by keeping the plant well pruned or by growing smaller, semidwarf varieties.

The tricky thing about avocados is their odd pollination requirements. Although one plant may produce both female and male plant parts, they often are not self-fruitful, meaning one plant can't pollinate itself. To make things more difficult, the flower may release viable pollen (the male part) only in the morning or afternoon, but not at both times. The female part of the flower may also be receptive only in the morning or afternoon, but not at both times. What to do? First, for best compatibility, you need to grow 2 varieties of trees, but not just any 2 trees. Contact a tropical plant mail-order source that sells avocado plants and ask which two they recommend. A mail-order source that I work with recommends growing the Haas and the Bacon varieties for good pollination. They are both full-sized trees, and in smaller greenhouses, they will need to be pruned as they grow toward maturity. Gardeners who are adept at grafting can eliminate the need for 2 trees by grafting one variety onto the other to save precious greenhouse space.

It can take between 3 and 5 years before

the plants will come into flower. Most varieties flower in the spring. To insure successful pollination, get a small artist's paintbrush and dab it gently into the flower to pick up some of the pollen. Move this way from flower to flower, leaving any pollen that may collect on the bristles as you go. You must go through this pollination ritual both in the morning and in the afternoon. Do not clean the pollen off of your bristles between morning and afternoon of the same day. Keep at it, and with a little luck, you will have fruit set. Then all that is required is patience, as it can take as long as 10 to 12 months before the fruits are ripe.

Now you can see why many people would rather buy their avocados in the store. But with a good-sized greenhouse and a fair amount of luck and patience, you just might find yourself in green guacamole heaven. If nothing else, the avocado makes a nice trouble-free tropical plant for the greenhouse.

Banana

Everyone should have a least one banana growing in the greenhouse, if only for the tropical look this plant brings to a sunspace. They are especially fun to grow when you finally get a flower and subsequent harvest from your plant. To start your own banana republic, you need to first find a source for the plants.

For one of the more extensive and well-written offerings of banana varieties, check out the catalog company Stokes Tropicals (800-624-9706). At this writing, the catalog costs $4. See more about them and other tropical plant catalogs in "Mail-Order Plants" Appendix 5. The Stokes Tropicals catalog has one of the better selections of banana plants, along with great descriptions. By the way, this company has no relation to the Stokes Nursery or Stokes Seed catalogs.

When considering which banana to grow, the number-one factor is the final height of the mature plant in relation to your greenhouse. Most home greenhouses have a roof at about 10 to 12 feet (3 to 3.6 m). That usually dictates that you grow the dwarf varieties, unless you want to cut a hole in the roof for a vertical room extension. The dwarf varieties reach up to 10 feet (3 m) in height. If you are one of the rare people with a 30-foot-tall (9-meter-tall) greenhouse ceiling, then you'll be glad to find many varieties that will fill your roof.

When looking through catalog descriptions of bananas, pay special attention to the heights of the different varieties. With the exception of the more dwarf varieties, it is a good idea to add 25 percent to the stated height for growing in the greenhouse. For some reason, they often grow taller under glazing.

There are many diverse banana varieties you can grow in a greenhouse. You will marvel at the options in leaf, flower, and fruit colors available in banana varieties. Some bananas are noted solely for their interesting flowers and grown simply for their ornamental value. Many banana varieties are of the plantain type, which produce a starchy fruit that is commonly fried or baked in many tropical recipes.

There are many different choices available in dessert-type sweet bananas. When you read a catalog description of what is available, you may decide you've led a sheltered life eating only the Chiquita-type varieties from the grocery. One variety even has aromatic creamy-sweet orange pulp. Unfortunately, you can't grow them all, as there is barely enough room for more than one or two plants in the average hobby greenhouse. It's too bad that many of the most interesting banana varieties grow too tall for hobby or home greenhouses, but they may be so enticing that you might be tempted to raise the roof! At least it makes for great reading and dreaming of a new greenhouse to accommodate a larger tropical paradise. The most common dwarf banana available is the dwarf Cavendish *(Musa acuminata)*, which only grows 7 feet (2.2 m) tall. It produces tasty 5-inch (8-cm) fruits.

Plants are usually sold as corms. A corm is technically an enlarged underground storage stem. If you purchase a mail-order banana, it will come either as a rooted plant or a corm. Corms are always much cheaper than rooted plants, but the corm option requires that you transform this hunk of flesh into a plant. If you opt for the corm, you will notice that the top is dark and may have a bit of decay. This is normal; if you see any mildew, remove it gently with a dry cloth. Plant the corm in a pot that is just large enough to hold the diameter of the corm. Use a well-drained soil or add a bit of extra sand or perlite to your regular potting soil to promote drainage. Set the corm in the soil so that the top sticks slightly above the soil surface. Water well after planting, but thereafter let the top 2 inches (5 cm) of the soil dry before watering to avoid rotting. Grow the corm in a bright (not direct sun) and warm (not hot) spot. Within a month or two, you should see roots taking hold and a leaf shoot forming. What you don't want to see is any sort of mushy rot. If this occurs, then you have likely buried it too deep and/or overwatered the poor thing. After a few leaves have formed, fertilize it with $\frac{1}{4}$ strength houseplant food, and apply half as often as recommended on the label. Up-pot the plant as it requires more

space. Eventually, set it in a large tub or, better yet, plant it directly in a ground bed.

Bananas prefer temperatures above 50°F (10°C), or the growth will slow and they may suffer. Bananas tend to grow very slowly in the winter, even with relatively warmer temperatures, partially because of the short days. When the warm temperatures of spring begin, watch out! The banana starts to grow incredibly fast. How fast? It is not uncommon to see plants grow one 5-foot (1.5-m) leaf every 10 days in summer.

When talking to banana enthusiasts or when reading about bananas, you may hear the term "pseudostem," which refers to the trunk of the banana tree. Bananas are not technically trees because they are not woody; rather, they are a fleshy stem called a raceme. For this reason, the trunk of the banana can't technically be called a stem, thus the word "pseudostem." The growth point for a banana is not at the tip as with most trees, but underground at the corm. Roots grow from the lower surface of the corm, and the pseudostem grows from the top of the plant. If you were to cut the top half of the pseudostem off completely, after a week or so you would likely see new leaves emerging through the middle that were growing from the corm, or you might see quick-growing side shoots develop, which will mature into full-sized plants. One night, a vandal cut the top half off a banana I was growing in a Cheyenne Botanic Gardens' outside flowerbed. Ten days later, you couldn't even tell, as the leaves kept on coming from the center of the plant's corm.

Bananas are easy to care for. They like soil that has constant moisture, and they benefit from regular feedings to accommodate their growth spurts, especially in the warmer months. In winter, go light on fertilization, especially if your greenhouse runs cool.

Even though the banana likes constant moisture, it is important that the soil be well drained, as it suffers in a stagnant situation. You will notice that bananas really thrive on heat, but when the greenhouse cools they may seem dormant.

Within 2 to 4 years, your banana plant (notice I didn't say banana tree) will reach maturity and will form one amazing flower cluster jutting out at the top of the plant. Take a long gander at the flower, as it is among nature's most interesting and unusual! This flower will then set fruit. The plant requires no work on your part as far as pollination is concerned in order for the flower to set fruit.

The ripening process can take up to 3 months or longer, depending upon temperature. If winter arrives while your fruit is developing, you may have to wait until the weather warms up. As the cluster of fruit ripens, it begins to curl upward. After it gets close to its proper size (check the size your variety is supposed to reach) and shows a definite upward curl (and sometimes even a slight yellowing on the tip of the fruit), you can consider cutting the fruit cluster off the plant for final ripening.

Final ripening is rarely done on the tree, as the fruit often cracks and rots when left on the plant too long. Instead, place the harvested cluster of fruit in a bag with three or four ripe apples. The apples will give off a naturally occurring gas that triggers ripening to perfection. Be sure to check your fruit daily.

After the fruit is harvested, it is time to get ruthless. Now you should cut the main stalk of the banana down to the ground. This is tough for most gardeners, who are usually quite proud of this plant and its harvest. But if you don't cut the plant back to the ground after the harvest, the main stem (pseudostem) of the banana will rapidly decline, become bug ridden, and die anyway. You need to realize that each main pseudostem will only produce one flower/fruit cluster. Leaving it will not result in another harvest.

If you want another harvest, you need to get a new plant up and growing. Look at the base of the mother plant. Usually there is already a new little banana plant or plants waiting in the wings or actually at the base of the mother plant. Choose the healthiest and tallest side-shoot for your next banana plant and prune all of the others to the ground. You can also dig up and pot other side shoots if you want to propagate more than one new banana plant either for yourself or as a gift to other greenhouse-gardening friends.

I often grow a potted ornamental banana in the greenhouse to later set out in an outside summer flower garden. You can't find a more dominant focal point in a garden.

When it comes to pests, bananas always seem to have a few, but they never seem to be bothered much by bugs in terms of hurting their growth or production. The main critter seems to be the mealybug, but it rarely sets the plant back in terms of its overall health.

Beans

Beans are a great and dependable greenhouse crop. Their main requirement is a bit of heat. For that reason, if your greenhouse runs cool they may be better grown between March and October. If you have a conventionally heated greenhouse, you can grow them any time of the year. There are two major types of beans: vines (such as pole beans) and bush or dwarf types. The pole beans utilize the vertical space well when trellised and can grow to 10 feet (3 m) or more if conditions are right. The problem is finding a tall enough basketball player to pick them. Pole beans yield over a longer period than bush beans but take 10 to 20 days longer to reach maturity. The bush beans need no trellising, as they reach only 1 foot (0.3 m) high. You will get more total yield and use greenhouse space more efficiently with pole beans, but the bush types grow better in containers. As long as the nights are above 45°F to 50°F (7°C to 10°C), you can always grow beans in some sunny spot.

Pole beans provide good shade when grown outside the south glass in the summer. This is a natural way to keep the greenhouse cooler, although it also cuts down on available light for plants growing in the greenhouse in summer. Inside the solar greenhouse, pole beans can be grown over the front of your thermal mass (water barrels or whatever you are using) to help keep it from absorbing summer solar heat, thus keeping your whole greenhouse cooler in the warm months. Whenever you grow pole beans, make a trellis for the plants to climb up that is at least 6 feet (1.8 m) in height. Plant one seed every 4 inches (10 cm) along the trellis. To prevent shading problems among plants, think about where your summer shadows fall before you plant the pole beans. Running a trellis along a north–south axis will help minimize problem shadows.

Most of the common beans can be grown with ease in a greenhouse, including yellow wax, French filet bush beans, purple podded beans, and even limas. For greenhouses in the North Country, you can even grow beans that are hard to produce in short-season areas, such as garbanzo beans. Garbanzos like sandy, drier soils, and their leaves look like locust tree leaves. For a novelty, you may want to try the asparagus bean, which can vine up to 15 feet (4.6 m) or more. It will get bean pods that are

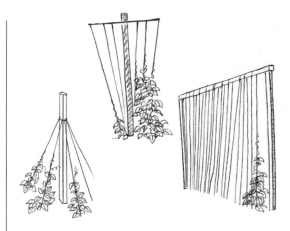

Types of vertical support for beans.

more than 1 foot (0.3 m) long and will do well in a greenhouse, if you have the room. A favorite of mine for both taste and ease of growing is the vining Meralda Spanish bean (available only from Shepherd's Seeds, 30 Irene Street, Torrington, CT 06790-6658, 860-482-3638, **www.shepherdseeds.com**).

For best germination, bean seeds need a soil temperature of at least 60°F (15°C). Lower temperatures often cause the seed to rot in the soil. A crusty soil surface can also cause problems for emerging seedlings, so you may need to amend this type of soil with compost or peat moss to prevent crusting before planting. Legume inoculants, which are available in many seed catalogs, when applied to the soil, will enable microorganisms to assist beans to get free nitrogen from the air in the soil and make for healthier plants.

Most bean flowers will set pods without needing to be pollinated. There are a few rare exceptions, including the scarlet runner bean. These should be avoided in the greenhouse.

Growing Precautions for Disease Prevention

Beans are susceptible to a number of diseases that can be minimized if you follow these precautions:

1. Use disease-free seed from a reputable seed company.
2. Don't work among your bean plants if the leaves are wet.
3. Rotate beans with other crops season to season when grown in beds (see Chapter 10, page 424, for more information about rotating crops in a greenhouse).

Prevention is always the best route, because curing a full-blown plant disease is very difficult. If you are having problems with bean diseases, consult your county agricultural extension agent for assistance in determining the problem and a possible cure. Also look through the seed catalog for a bean variety with some resistance to your particular bean-disease problem.

In the greenhouse, be sure not to let your temperatures get much above 95°F (35°C). Such high temperatures will cause beans to have lower yields because the plant may drop flower blossoms. Blossom drop will also occur when you over- or underwater the plants. When there are no blossoms, there are no beans.

With the correct temperatures and varied planting dates, you can have nonstop bean production. This is especially helpful with bush beans, which tend to provide you with one large flush of harvest and then begin to die.

All beans eventually reach the end of their productive life and rapidly decline. This is usually indicated by the leaves turning yellow after a good flush of harvests. This is normal and is a signal to pull up the plants and begin anew.

When it comes to bugs on beans, keep an eye out for whiteflies, mites, and thrips, all of which have a fondness for beans.

Beets

Each beet seed has up to 5 seeds inside of what appears to be just 1 seed. This can cause a problem for people who are lax about thinning, as they commonly end up with an overcrowding situation that hurts the yield if not dealt with. Always plan on thinning beets, and stick to your plan! Because both the leaves and the roots are edible, beets can be a good food producer.

In general, beets do best when the temperature is moderate to cool. I avoid growing them in a greenhouse during the summer months. Besides, that is when they do well in most outside gardens. Almost all beets do well in the greenhouse, as long as it isn't too hot.

There are some fun novelty types with diverse colors and shapes, such as Golden Beets, which are sweeter than most, or Chioggia, with white and pink rings inside. Check Johnny's Selected Seeds for a great selection of beets (207-437-4301, **www.johnnyseedscom**).

Beets like a slightly alkaline soil, so if your soil is acidic, you may want to add a small amount of wood ash or lime to correct the soil. If you are in doubt, don't do anything with the soil.

Beets resist many pest attacks. Beets can be grown in either large pots or beds. Sow beets directly into the area where they will be growing, as they don't take to transplanting well; they germinate rapidly, anyway, so you don't save any time by transplanting them.

Broccoli

Broccoli is another great greenhouse crop, but again, it is best grown in the cooler months of the year. When grown in the warmer months, it may "button," or produce small, bitter-tasting heads. I prefer to sow greenhouse broccoli in early September for winter through spring production. A new variety, bred in the heat of Taiwan, will soon be on the market. It is called Ching-long 45 and can yield good-sized heads under higher temperatures. It is said to be the first broccoli that can be grown in subtropical areas—which could include your greenhouse. This variety is not readily available as of this writing, but keep your eye out for it in catalogs in the coming years.

Depending upon temperature, most broccoli matures in 60 to 80 days. When starting seedlings of broccoli (and most other cole crops), it is important not to hold the plants in a small pot for too long. As soon as the seedlings are around 6 to 8 inches (15 to 20 cm), transplant them to their final bed or a larger pot. If you do hold them too long, they may suffer from terminal stunting and low yields.

When it comes to selecting a good greenhouse variety, I look for the those that produce side sprouts. Side sprouts are small heads produced after the main head is cut. None of the side sprouts are as big as the first main head. Still, they add up and are nice if you need a few small heads for stir-fry for dinner. Some varieties I like are Green Valiant, Saga (a Johnny's Selected Seeds exclusive, call 207-437-4301), or the readily available nonhybrid De Cicco.

Broccoli tolerates varying soil conditions and needs to be spaced $1\frac{1}{2}$ to 2 feet (0.45 to 0.6 m) apart. Broccoli transplants well about 2 weeks after germinating. When warmer temperatures of spring and summer return to your greenhouse, you'll need to pull up the broccoli and replant with a more warmth-loving crop. If you don't, the flavor and production will decline and the bugs will increase.

When growing broccoli, harvest the heads before they start to loosen up and flower. If a few heads get away from you and are flowering, prune them off and you'll encourage side sprouts to form (if it is a side-sprouting variety).

For a novelty, try growing the Romanesco broccoli that has interesting spiraled, peaked heads. Grow it as you would broccoli. It tastes similar to broccoli but has a "nuttier" taste to go with its nutty shape.

Recently there has been some amazing research that suggests broccoli is high in sulforaphane, which triggers enzymes that detoxify carcinogens in the body. It might be a good idea to eat some fresh greenhouse-grown broccoli every few days. Johnny's Selected Seeds catalog proudly tells us that their variety Saga placed among the highest in sulforaphane among all varieties of broccoli tested. If you really want to get serious, broccoli sprouts (grown like alfalfa sprouts) have the highest concentrations of this "wonder chemical."

High temperatures cause "buttoning," or small broccoli heads.

Brussels Sprouts

Brussels sprouts are slow growers, often taking more than 130 days to reach maturity. It is best to start them in late summer. If they mature in a warm greenhouse environment, such as that of late spring or summer, the taste may be bitter and the sprouts may form loose heads.

This crop is best suited for those living in a cool, cloudy area. Space the plants 2 feet (0.6 m) apart. Plan on their growing up to 3 feet (0.9 m) high, and be careful of shading. Brussels sprouts are easily transplanted while in the seedling stage.

When the plant has reached maturity and begins to form sprouts (small cabbagelike buds) up and down the stalk, pinch out the tip of the plant, the growing point. This encourages better sprout formation. Remove lower leaves and leaf stems as the plants mature to further encourage the development of sprouts. They take up a lot of space and are thus not a highly efficient food producer. But if you have a passion for Brussels sprouts, you can be eating fresh sprouts while others are just dreaming about planting them.

Cabbage

Cabbage falls into three main categories: early season, midseason, and late season. These categories relate to how long it takes until harvest. The earlier varieties are generally smaller but produce faster. Usually the early and midseason types provide better total yields in the greenhouse or sunspace. There are also choices as to the coloring of the leaf, which can be red, yellow, or green. All seem to do fine in the greenhouse. Leaf type can also vary. Savoy cabbage, for instance, is a handsome bubbly leafed variety, but it tends to harbor more bugs such as aphids and should be avoided in the greenhouse. When I am selecting a variety, I tend to look for resistance to splitting. Splitting is most common in the early varieties and is a result of rapid growth spurts and widely varying temperatures. Many varieties are listed as "split" or "crack" resistant. If you are still having problems, try twisting the plants a quarter-turn in the soil, which causes some of the roots to break and lessens the rapid uptake of water, which can cause splitting. Light cultivation adjacent to the plant will also have the same effect.

Cabbage transplants best in the seedling stage, 3 to 4 weeks after germination. If you hold it as a seedling in a small pot, it may have terminal stunting. Unless you are trying to prevent splitting, don't ever cultivate too deeply, because cabbage is shallow-rooted and you can slow the plants' growth.

If your greenhouse gets extremely cold (below freezing), cabbage may go to seed. Because cabbage is a biennial, the cold has fooled it into thinking it is 2 years old, and it is prematurely celebrating its birthday. Happy (last) birthday! Pull it up; it won't produce a head now.

Cabbage needs a rich soil and sun. It can grow in shadier areas, but growth will be slower. Like broccoli, cabbage does best in cooler weather but can tolerate growing in the summer as long as your greenhouse is not a very hot environment. Still, if you grow it warm the taste is not as sweet. Because you can eat all above-ground portions, cabbage is considered to be an efficient food producer.

Rotate areas where cabbage is planted if you grow in ground beds to prevent diseases.

Cabbage can be grown in pots or containers if they are a minimum of 1 gallon (3.8 liter) in size.

Cantaloupe and Muskmelon

Those who live in northern areas with short garden seasons will go wild over the new experience of abundant homegrown cantaloupes in the greenhouse. I have even seen some people build a greenhouse solely to grow cantaloupe and muskmelon.

Cantaloupes like a rich soil full of decomposed organic matter and need ample moisture. To use the precious limited space of a greenhouse most efficiently, try growing cantaloupe or muskmelon vertically, up a trellis. Construct the trellis (using old wire or any stout material) at least 5 feet (1.5 m) high and however long you wish. Set one melon plant every 3 feet (0.9 m) along the trellis. You can plant a few seeds in each spot and later thin to one hardy plant. To minimize shading problems, run the trellis north–south.

Unlike what happens when you grow melons outside, the flowers don't magically turn into fruits. They require that you pollinate them. When the flowers begin to appear, you must hand-pollinate as many as possible to ensure fruit set (see Chapter 6, "Pollination," for more information). Remember: No pollination, no fruit. While the flowers are small, it can be done quite successfully.

As the fruits begin to enlarge on the vines, they will need support. Without support, the fruits may get so heavy they will rip the vine off the trellis. When a fruit is about the size of a tennis ball, slip it into a (recycled) nylon stocking and tie it securely to the trellis. (What a great way to recycle stockings with runs!) If you can't come up with a stocking, you can also use cheesecloth, but nothing works better

than a stocking, which will stretch to accommodate the growing fruit. But guys, beware the innocent question that could be mistaken for a pickup line: "Hey lady, do you have any old nylon stockings that I can recycle for my greenhouse melon crop?" They'll never believe you are serious.

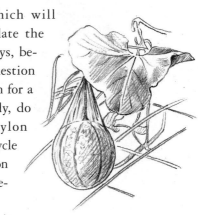

Recycled nylon stockings are great cantaloupe supports.

As you slip each fruit into the stocking, take care not to tie any knots around the stem itself, which will damage the plant and fruit. Instead, tie the stocking directly to the trellis, leaving the stem unhampered.

When it comes to guessing when to harvest, cantaloupe is among the easiest of the melons. It will tell you when it's ripe because the stem will easily slip off when the fruit is slightly twisted. Other melons are more of a challenge. But when in doubt, don't harvest—once you pick it, you can't get it to ripen much more.

Both muskmelon and cantaloupe are quite susceptible to the fungus disease called powdery mildew. It is indicated by a white powdery substance forming on the leaves. Search catalogs thoroughly for varieties with some resistance to this disease to minimize the problem. In general, I find the best selection and the highest potential for good greenhouse varieties by focusing on seed catalogs from the southern United States. A good source for southern-based seeds is the Southern Exposure Seed Exchange, 804-973-4703.

If you stray from the most common varieties, you will find some wonderful differences in flavor. I once grew a melon in my greenhouse that was bred in Israel and is, sadly, no longer available. It had overtones of sweet va-nilla and was ambrosial in flavor! But there are many unique, sweet varieties you can try that are unavailable in most grocery stores.

Expect to be halfway to heaven when you eat your greenhouse-grown cantaloupe or muskmelon. Be sure to invite me over to help you evaluate the quality of the fruit.

Carrots

Writing about carrots makes me remember when I worked in a large community solar-greenhouse project (the precursor to the Cheyenne Botanic Gardens). I was giving a tour to a class of 4-year-old Head Start students. They were all smiles, awed by the plants growing in the middle of the Wyoming winter. They were full of questions. As the tour progressed, a few kids became attached to me—I had two kids on my shoulders, a few on each arm, and even one sitting on my foot. I managed to drag myself, and the children, over to the carrot bed and hollered above the questions and giggles, "Does anybody know what this plant is?" "Onions!" one little girl shouted. "Dandelion," another said. A shy one, shaking her head no, quietly mumbled, "I don't know." "Everyone watch carefully," I said, as I shook a few kids off, moving toward a healthy carrot top. "I-i-i-ts a-a-a-a ..." They were all eyes as I exposed the orange root from the dirt. "CARROT!!!" they all screamed in unison. For that moment I was a magician ... presto: A carrot! I wondered how long it would have taken before they learned where carrots came from if they had never seen my greenhouse carrots.

A year-round supply of homegrown car-rots will add a spark to food that nothing else can provide. There is just no comparison be-tween homegrown and store-bought carrots.

Carrots will fit into any empty place in your growing beds and can be planted almost anytime of the year in a greenhouse. However, unusually hot weather can occasionally cause a strange flavor and/or fibrous texture. High amounts of manure in the soil have an even more profound effect, creating weirdly shaped carrots with lots of stringy, hairlike roots that are perfect for modern sculpture lovers.

Winter carrots in the greenhouse take longer to produce than outside carrots, but the harvest is well worth the wait. Some winter carrots may go to seed if you grow a winter-planted carrot into the summer, especially if your greenhouse ran very cool the previous winter.

Most gardening books will tell you that you should never transplant carrots and that they should always be directly seeded. How-ever, thanks to some proof provided by a Cheyenne Botanic Gardens senior volunteer, I am now a believer. They take to transplant-ing just fine. When you do sow the seeds, try not to drop too many seeds or you'll have a big thinning job ahead of you. Barely cover the seed and maintain moisture in the soil un-til you see them germinate. Each carrot needs about 2 square inches (13 sq. cm) of space to grow, so use that as a guide when you thin or transplant.

Carrots do best in well-drained soil. In heavy clay, you may have better luck with the shorter-rooted varieties. I've had good yields with the standard long varieties. I have also found some varieties that are super early or were developed specifically for greenhouse culture. These are good choices if you can get hold of them. They include: Coreless Amsterdam and Touchon from Stokes Seeds; and Kinko and Nelson from Johnny's Selected Seeds. The addresses for these seed catalogs are listed in "Mail-Order Seeds" in Appendix 6.

Carrots can be grown anywhere you have a bit of space, even in pots, as long as they are at least 8 inches (20 cm) or more in depth. The biggest problem most gardeners have is failing to thin out thickly sown seeds. Put on your "ruthless gardener" hat; get out there and thin!

Cauliflower

Cauliflower grows much the same as cabbage and broccoli. It needs around 70 to 90 days to mature and is best grown in the winter months from a late summer or fall sowing. If grown in prolonged warm weather, your plants may have very small heads and are not worth the space that they take up.

Cauliflower is easily transplanted in the seedling stage. As the plant begins to form the white curd, tie up the leaves around the head to prevent browning of the curd. Another method is to simply pluck a large lower leaf and set it over the forming white curd to provide protection.

Because cauliflower does not produce side sprouts, you should toss out the plant after it produces the head. For this reason, it is not an efficient user of greenhouse space for the amount of food that it produces. But for those who have a passion for cauliflower, it is easy to grow as a winter crop.

Celery

Celery is best grown where winters are long, as it likes a long, cool growing period. If grown in warm greenhouses, celery can become stringy and will flower prematurely, giving low yields. It is best started in late summer. Always grow it in rich soil with constant moisture available. Start plants in small pots. Then, about 3 weeks after the first leaves emerge and the plants look healthy and are growing well, you can transplant them into either beds or pots. Each plant needs a minimum of 6 to 8 inches (15 to 20 cm). Try growing just a few celery plants before you devote large areas to it to see if it is suited to your environment. A little practice is helpful when growing this finicky crop in the greenhouse.

Due to its exacting requirements and slow growth, it is neither an easy nor an efficient crop for greenhouses.

Chard, Swiss Chard

Chard is a close relative of beets and is a long-lived and productive spinach substitute for the greenhouse or sunspace. Everyone should have at least a couple plants growing at all times for some continued availability of fresh greens for the salad bowl. Swiss chard is very tolerant of both warm and low temperatures and can tolerate sun or shady spots well and grow rapidly.

Swiss chard comes in many colors to match any decor: red, orange, pink, and green-and-white-veined varieties. To get all three in one mix, look for the All America Selections winner called Bright Lights Chard, available in many catalogs. The white-veined seems to be the most productive in the greenhouse, but the others also do quite well. If family members like spinach but are uneasy about substitutes, grow the green-veined variety, often sold as "perpetual spinach," and just tell them that it is spinach. They may never know the difference. The green chard is a little harder to locate, but keep looking through your catalog and you'll eventually come across it. The red-veined chard, also known as rhubarb chard, is a handsome plant with brightly colored red veins in a dark green leaf. It looks like it is decked out in a Christmas motif. If you want to push the décor envelope, try adding a few colorful leaves to a Christmas bouquet (eat your heart out, Martha Stewart!).

As with beets, many seeds are contained within each seed, so be sure to thin out seedlings when they germinate thickly. Space plants about 6 to 8 inches (15 to 20 cm) apart. Harvest by breaking off the outer leaves when they are 8 to 10 inches (20 to 25 cm) in length. Don't leave the leaf stem (petiole) attached to the plant after harvesting, as it may rot on the plant and harbor disease. The leaf stem is edible, too, and may be cooked like asparagus. Chard can be eaten raw in salads or cooked like spinach. It's good both ways.

Swiss chard will only flower after being triggered by extreme cold. For this reason, it can grow for many years before flowering in the greenhouse. I have had some plants live for 5 years. After a few years, they get to look like a 3-foot (0.9-meter) palm tree and just keep getting taller and taller. Chard can be both sown and grown almost anytime during the year. Pests on chard are relatively rare, which is another reason to grow this plant.

All parts of the leaf and stem are edible. Please understand that rhubarb chard is totally unrelated to rhubarb, which has poisonous leaves. Be sure that your children understand the difference, as you don't want them thinking they can eat rhubarb leaves come spring.

Cherimoya

This subtropical South American native produces a tasty fruit. The tree grows to around 20 feet (6 m) but can be pruned to shorter, more manageable sizes. Because of its height, it is best suited to larger greenhouses. The tree may lose its leaves in winter and produce new leaves in spring.

The fruit is interesting in both appearance and flavor. It is about the size of an artichoke globe and even has a bit of resemblance to an artichoke. It almost appears to be an artichoke made out of Play-Doh™.

The cherimoya takes up to 5 years before it flowers and has a chance to produce fruit. Flowers tend to form on new wood, so on older trees, you may have to prune to trigger new growth and fruiting wood. Pollination must be done by hand on a daily basis. You will find that each flower has both the male and female parts. The female is reputed to be receptive before the pollen falls. To be sure you have pollinated the flower, you'll have to keep at it daily with a small paintbrush, moving beelike (make a buzzing sound to get yourself in the mood) from flower to flower, including the flowers that have just started to open. If all goes well, you'll soon see fruit forming.

The flavor of the cherimoya is hard to describe, but it is sweet (although some varieties are said to be more bland) and commonly compared to a cross between the banana and the pineapple. The flesh is creamy with black seeds. The fruit is ripe when it turns yellowish green.

Let the fruit sit until the skin it just begins to turn brown for best eating qualities. Serve chilled. There are many varieties to choose from. Some easier-to-pollinate types include Booth, Spain, Pierce, and White.

Chinese Cabbage

Chinese cabbage is a fast-growing crop for the greenhouse. It combines the texture of lettuce with the radishlike tang of cabbage. Unlike many leafy greens, it can tolerate warmer conditions quite well, so it can be grown just about any time of year as long as it is not too cold. Chinese cabbage goes to seed when seedlings are exposed to freezing temperatures or below, or when plants are grown at a temperature under 50°F (10°C) for long periods of time. Always select a "bolt-resistant" variety to minimize this problem if your greenhouse runs cool. You can also choose between two types of Chinese cabbage: The open-head types reach almost a foot (0.3 m) in height; or try the Napa, or closed-head type, which makes a tighter head. Both do well in the greenhouse.

Chinese cabbage transplants well in the seedling stage and matures in anywhere from 50 to 70 days. The biggest problem I have with Chinese cabbage is slugs. It amazes me how slugs come out of the woodwork to munch on the leaves, even in beds where there were no apparent slugs with any other crop. I honestly believe that a slug would walk (or slime) a mile to get an opportunity to eat Chinese cabbage. If slugs become a real problem, you'll have to set up a barrier for them or try other types of slug control (see Chapter 10 for more information about slugs and snails).

Chives

Chives are one of my favorite crops. I list it here rather than in the herb section because it makes such a great onion substitute. I guess I like chives so much that I consider it a vegetable rather than an herb. I prefer to use chives over onions, so whenever there are chive leaves available either outside or in the greenhouse, I'll skip the onions and go for chives. I love their fresh and unique onionlike flavor. Because you harvest only the green tops, the root system is never disturbed and the plant grows new leaves rapidly after each harvest. This makes it an efficient and trouble-free food producer.

Chives can be started from seed or easily divided from other existing plants. The common garden chives often grow very slowly in the winter. There are, however, a few varieties that are better suited to greenhouse production. Nichols Garden Nursery and many other catalogs carry Grolau chives. This is a Swiss strain developed for growing in greenhouses. The Richters catalog from Canada (905-640-6677 or **www. richters.com**) offers a special variety of chives called Profusion™, noted for its prolific production of flowers. The pink flowers of chives are quite edible when they first open and are great for soups and salads for those interested in a sweeter but also stronger onion flavor. Because many people (myself included) like to eat these sweet, colorful chive flowers, Richters has bred the Profusion™ variety to flower prolifically but not set seed. This enables the flowers to remain edible and sweet over a much longer time. It has also been shown to grow well in containers and in greenhouse situations. Perhaps it conserves energy by never having to produce viable seed.

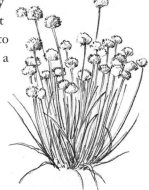

Besides being easily grown in beds, chives can also be grown in 1-gallon (3.8-liter) pots. Simply provide a rich, well-drained soil and occasionally feed them. Let the soil surface dry between waterings. Every greenhouse should have at least one clump of chives in production.

Garlic chives (not the same as garlic) have broader, flatter leaves than regular chives and have a strong garlic flavor. They are perennial producers like regular chives. I prefer the flavor of the regular chives to the garlic chives, but you may want to give the garlic type a try. You can find garlic chives with either green leaves or the more ornamental white-striped leaves, which are often grown solely for their ornamental value.

Chrysanthemum, Edible

I know it doesn't sound very tasty, but the leaves of the edible chrysanthemum have a sweet, mild, nutlike flavor. They are great when added fresh to salads along with other greens and can also be mixed into a stir-fry or cooked with spinach or chard. The edible chrysanthemum goes by a few different aliases, including **garland chrysanthemum, chop-suey greens,** and **shungiku**. All of the leaves are edible. It is a good winter producer and is best sown in late summer for harvest from winter through spring. Come warmer temperatures, it tends to get more buggy, especially on the tips of the plant. If it gets bad enough, it may be time to pull it out.

The plant grows to a height of about 3 feet (0.9 m). Each plant needs about 2 feet (0.6 m) of space when mature. After it reaches 6 to 10 inches (15 to 25 cm), you can harvest the older, lower leaves on the plant. In early spring, this chrysanthemum provides you with a beautiful crop of yellow, daisylike flowers that are a nice addition to a flower arrangement, a true dual-purpose plant.

Citrus

Citrus is a great greenhouse plant, if only for the wonderful fragrance of the flowers. Just one whiff and the smell will magically transform a dreary winter day into a bright hopeful one. Not many flowers have that power.

It is interesting to note that some of the earliest greenhouses were built to hold orange trees. In fact, they were called "orangeries." The first ones were built in Europe in the seventeenth century and had stoves to heat the room, with glass only on the south wall and no overhead glass at all. These were primarily brick buildings that were constructed to overwinter the treasured citrus trees. Over time, orangeries became more sophisticated and later evolved into the more traditional looking greenhouse. They were found all across Europe and were usually owned by royalty.

Now you can have your own royal orangerie. Almost any citrus plant can be grown in the greenhouse, but there are some tricks to it. Many people are tempted to start citrus from seeds found in supermarket fruit, but these will usually produce sour, poor-tasting fruit. Growing orange plants from seeds in the fruit you've eaten makes a nice educational project for kids, but this will not produce the best plants for a productive greenhouse. Instead, purchase plants from nurseries or by mail order that will be sure to produce good-flavored fruit as well as be more productive than your "homegrown" plants. It is usually best to grow semidwarf trees so that they fit nicely in your greenhouse.

I have found lemons and limes to be among the easiest and most rewarding citrus plants to grow. The Ponderosa lemon is a proven greenhouse plant and produces impressive large fruits, sometimes reaching the size of grapefruits. The Meyer lemon, first discovered near Peking, China, is a good choice for the greenhouse that runs cooler in winter. Imagine a gin and tonic with your own homegrown lemon! If you don't drink alcohol, try some fresh squeezed lemonade. The Persian (sometimes called Bearss) lime is a good choice for greenhouse growing if you need a lime for that margarita or key lime pie. For oranges, go for either the Washington navel or Valencia orange varieties. A few good catalog sources for citrus are: Logee's Greenhouses (888-330-8038, **www.logees. com**) or Mellinger's (800-321-7444, **www. mellingers.com**).

When it comes to harvesting, you will find that lemons and limes bear fruit almost any time of the year but fall seems to have a few more fruits setting on. You'll find that the oranges tend to bear from November through June.

With some simple care, you can produce high-quality citrus in your greenhouse or sunspace. Most citrus do best if grown above 45°F (7°C). They need to be grown in a rich but well-drained soil. Citrus needs to dry out occasionally between waterings, especially in the cooler months. However, never let it dry to the point of wilting. In summer, they need more constant moisture. Citrus can be grown in ground beds or in tubs that are 5 gallons (19 liters) or more in size.

Citrus also require the benefits of a well-lit location and regular feeding. I like to occasionally use fish emulsion to provide some micronutrients. A teaspoon of Epsom salts every few months also seems to help them produce. If the new leaves turn yellow, try a fertilizer that contains iron chelate (follow the application directions and don't add too much). It may take a few years before your citrus plant comes into flower, so be patient.

Almost all citrus are self-fruitful, meaning that they are easy to pollinate. They often set fruit without any extra effort on your part. If you want to be sure of a crop, simply take a small paintbrush and paint the pollen onto the female part (the short, sticky little stem protruding in the center of the flower). The fruit will start to grow noticeably in a few weeks.

The main pests of citrus are whitefly, scale, and the mealybug. Sometimes you can take care of these pests by hand picking (and squishing). You may have to keep a close eye out for these pests and be ready to take more serious action if you spot them in large numbers. Refer to Chapter 10 for assistance.

Coffee

Yes, you can even grow coffee plants in your greenhouse or sunspace! They are more suited to greenhouses that run moderate temperatures in the winter and don't do well when the temperature regularly drops below 45°F (7°C). They prefer slight shade but will put up with sun as long as it is only for short periods during the day.

In their native habitat in the tropics, they are an understory plant, growing in the shade of other taller plants. Coffee makes a great houseplant, with attractive glossy foliage, slightly fragrant white flowers, and showy berries. It is within these berries that you will find the revered coffee beans.

Coffee plants are sold by a number of catalogs specializing in tropical or novelty plants. They are best grown in tubs or planted directly in ground beds. Coffee seems to do slightly better in pots, as long as it doesn't become root bound. Grow it in well-drained soil. After the plant is 2 to 3 years old, you will finally see it produce a number of small, fragrant white flowers (the best fragrance is at night). Soon it will set a few small berries that are green turning to red. Inside each berry, you will find two coffee beans. When the plant is 5 to 8 years old, it can produce up to 2 pounds (0.9 kg) of beans with proper care. It is important to note that only the horizontal branches will produce flowers (and eventually beans). To encourage more horizontal branching, occasionally pinch the top of the plant, which will stimulate more side growth.

To help trigger a mature plant into flowering and thus setting on beans, try to mimic a dry season, as is often experienced by plants in their tropic native habitats. Let the plant run dry for up to 3 weeks and then return to a normal watering regime where you water as soon as the top of the soil dries out. When the flowers are triggered, you can get better production of beans with a bit of pollinating action. Pollinate when the flowers are freshly open. Using a small paintbrush, simply dab the tip of the brush in the very center of the flower where you see the pollen. Without cleaning the brush, proceed to every flower on the plant. Soon the berries (containing the beans) will form.

Here's how to get from berry to cup of java. When the berries have just begun to turn dark red or, better yet, when the berries begin to shrivel slightly, this will be your sign that the two beans inside the fruit are ripe. Pick the berries and remove the skin and any pulp you see. Let the beans soak overnight in water and then dry them in a warm dry spot for up to a week.

There are a number of ways to proceed in processing the bean, but for simplicity, just roast them in a shallow pan on the stove (don't use a nonstick pan—go with cast iron or stainless steel). Do not use any oil in the pan and set the burner on medium heat. Then roast a single layer of beans in the pan by constantly moving the beans around in the pan, taking care not to let them burn. They will darken and even pop a bit. Remove from the burner when they get a nice, rich, dark-brown color (like the kind you see at your local java joint). Finally, grind them and brew the freshest cup of coffee you've ever had!

The average plant is not a very prolific producer of beans. For this reason, don't plan on growing enough beans to be drinking home-grown coffee every day. But growing enough for an occasional cup is not difficult.

When it comes to pests, mealybugs get the prize for inflicting the most damage and plants should be monitored regularly to prevent them from getting a foothold.

Collards

Collards, for those of you who may be culturally deprived (or are from the North), are like a nonheading cabbage. They are generally eaten as a cooked green, much like spinach. Grow collards as you would cabbage, but be ready for it to grow a bit taller. Like many cabbage relatives, collards prefer cooler temperatures and are a good choice for the greenhouse that

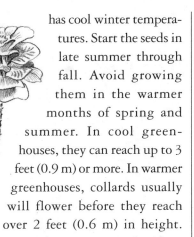

has cool winter temperatures. Start the seeds in late summer through fall. Avoid growing them in the warmer months of spring and summer. In cool greenhouses, they can reach up to 3 feet (0.9 m) or more. In warmer greenhouses, collards usually will flower before they reach over 2 feet (0.6 m) in height. They can be harvested over many weeks, if not months. When you harvest, start with the lower leaves, letting the new growth on top continue to produce. When the plant starts to flower, the flavor tends to go downhill and you need to think about a replacement for collards.

Collards are readily propagated from seed and suffer from few pests, unless the plants are under stress.

Cucumber

Cucumbers are one of the most productive summer crops you can grow as long as you grow what is known as the European seedless, or greenhouse forcing, cucumber. These have been bred solely for growing in the greenhouse. Their fruit resembles the burpless cucumber, with each fruit growing up to a whopping 20 inches (51 cm) long. They are thin-skinned, seedless, and very sweet. Best of all, the European greenhouse cucumbers are high yielding and need no pollinating.

Avoid the common garden types of cucumbers, unless you want to be diligent about pollinating on a daily basis; it is not easy, but it can be done (see Chapter 6, "Pollination").

The European cucumber is for fresh eating only and won't pickle very well because of the thin skin. There are a few American seed catalogs that carry the European cucumber seeds. Stokes Seeds (800-263-7233, www. stokeseeds. com) carries a great variety of greenhouse forcing cucumbers on their "Greenhouse Vegetables" page and probably has the best selection available to home greenhouse gardeners. Also, Thompson & Morgan (800-274-7333, www.thompson-morgan.com) often carries one or two greenhouse forcing varieties. The price of the seed is much higher than most other seeds (up to $2 per seed!), but given their high yield, the price is worth it. Grocery stores often sell the sweet fruits for a dollar apiece, and you will easily get up to 15 fruits per plant, if not many more than that. Besides, can you imagine how hard it must be to wrench a seed from a plant that produces a seedless fruit? It's a dirty job, but some rocket-scientist horticulturist somewhere has figured out how to do it, and it's probably a big corporate secret.

Don't despair over the seed price, as there is a back-door approach to getting more European cucumbers without having to pay for the seed; refer to Chapter 5, "Plant Propagation," and try your hand at making new plants from cuttings from a mother plant.

It is not a good idea to try growing both the regular, outside-garden variety and European cucumbers in the same greenhouse at the same time. If a stray bee were to infiltrate the greenhouse and do some cross-pollinating, you could find your cucumbers producing misshapen, bitter-tasting fruit.

When selecting a European cucumber variety, check out the characteristics of each, as each type has been bred with special characteristics. Select the one best suited to your particular environment. Some will tolerate higher temperatures better; others have more tolerance to lower night temperatures (a good characteristic for growing into the fall). I always like to grow those that have some resistance to powdery mildew. Probably one of the best all-around varieties is Carmen, which has good resistance to powdery mildew and is a good yielder. It is sensitive to day length (see "Photoperiodism" in Chapter 1) and should only be planted after March 1. You will also see some cucumbers that are sold as being good for both "indoor and outdoor" production. Although these will do better in a greenhouse than regular outside varieties, they will not yield as much, nor will they grow as well in a greenhouse environment as the greenhouse forcing types.

Most European cucumber varieties have primarily female flowers, but they might produce an occasional male flower. Male flowers don't produce fruit and aren't needed because these plants don't need pollination. If fact, if they are pollinated, it causes poor-quality fruit. Always prune off the male flowers on European cucumbers if they appear. The males are identified by their *lack* of small, immature fruit below the petals. In contrast, the female flowers have a small fruit directly behind the yellow petals.

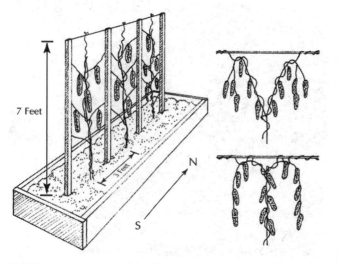

7 Feet

N

S

Trellising options for European forcing greenhouse cucumbers.

Because the seed is so costly, don't waste even one. Try planting one seed into a new peat pot or well-cleaned (or new) 2- or 3-inch (5- or 9-cm) pot filled with virgin potting soil. Set the seeds at a depth of about $1/4$ inch (0.6 cm). Maintain a soil temperature of around 70°F (21°C) and keep the pots in a well-lit location. Make sure the pots are moist at all times, but not soggy. Never allow them to get dry.

When the seedling has four to five leaves, it can be transplanted into its final location. They grow best in ground beds or in a minimum-sized pot of 5 gallons (19 liters). Always grow in rich, well-drained soil.

If you used a peat pot, poke a hole in the bottom of the pot to ensure quick root development. Transplant into moist soil. In ground beds, cucumbers do best when they have at least 2 feet (0.6 m) of soil depth and a spacing of 3 feet (0.9 m) apart. Only grow 1 plant per 5-gallon (19-liter) pot if you have no ground beds.

Cucumbers are very heavy feeders and need regular fertilization, but if the leaf edges turn brown, you are overdoing it. If this occurs, leach the excess fertilizer salts out of the pot with a few heavy applications of water. Cucumbers love warm temperatures and are best in the spring and summer. Wide temperature fluctuations can adversely affect flavor, and they won't tolerate much cool weather. High temperatures may also cause misshapen fruit. Cucumbers also require high levels of light, so growing in shade is not a good option. If your greenhouse is running cool, try watering the cucumbers with some slightly lukewarm water. As with most crops, morning watering is best. Avoid getting the plant leaves wet when watering to prevent disease. Also, try ventilating to remove excess humidity, which can also contribute to cucumber diseases.

The European cucumber needs to grow up

vertically and can be grown up a trellis with ease. Another option is to train them to grow up a suspended string or length of twine that hangs from the ceiling to the ground. Loosely tie the twine to the base of the cucumber. Do not tie any sort of slipknot, as it may strangle the plant. You can also anchor the twine to a stake in the soil. Leave a lot of slack in the twine, as it will eventually be taken up as the plant wraps itself around the string. You may occasionally need to wind the main stem around the twine to help it climb up. Avoid any bending or pinching of the stems. If needed, you can loosely tie the cucumber stem to the twine with soft strips of cloth, but don't tie too tightly and strangle the stem.

As the plant grows up the trellis or twine, you will notice that there are suckers coming off the main stem. For best production, it is a good idea to do some pruning of these suckers.

Cucumbers produce secondary side-shoots at almost every leaf axil. An axil is the spot where the leaf stem (or petiole) connects to the main stem. Because they grow rapidly, if you don't do any pruning, you may end up with one massive tangle of leaves and vines that are not very productive and don't use your space very well.

For maximum production, there are a number of ways to train greenhouse European cucumbers as they grow. As a rule of thumb, I usually go by spacing to determine how much pruning I am going to do. The wider the spacing, the more suckers I allow to grow to fill in a given trellis. If the cucumbers are tightly spaced (3 feet or 0.9 m apart), I allow fewer suckers to produce.

A generalized recommendation that commercial growers often adhere to is the following: Cut off any suckers (side shoots) that form at the first 4 leaf axils. You can allow the next 8 to 10 shoots to grow new suckers, but prune the tips of these suckers after they form 1 to 2 flowers (fruits). The remainder of the shoots should be trimmed to 2 leaves each, allowing fruits to form near each of these leaves. When the plant reaches around 7 feet (2 m), select 2 shoots at the top and allow these to head downward, back toward the ground, producing fruit and leaves all the way down. By this time, the plant will be toward the end of its productive life, and it will be time to start new plants in that place.

The cucumber harvest can be bountiful, even from just a few plants.

A simpler pruning method is to allow each plant to grow one side shoot and grow the plant in a V-shape, producing fruit all of the way up each vine. To do this, you will need to prune every shoot that forms up each of the two Vs. After the plant reaches the top of the trellis, let the vines continue back down toward the ground, producing fruit all the way.

If all this pruning sounds complicated, you can simply let forcing cucumbers go wild up a vertical, fence-like trellis (run the trellis north-south if possible and make it at least 6 feet [1.8 m] high). Be sure to keep the vines tied up to the trellis with some soft twine. Also, check under the leaves continually for mature fruit ready to harvest; it can hide easier in the jungle of cucumber leaves. Trellising does not yield the same fruit-per-space ratio that you get with the pruning methods, but you'll still get a great harvest.

The European cucumber is such an eager beaver concerning fruit production that it will often start setting cucumbers when it is only 1 to 2 feet (0.3 or 0.6 m) tall. This can damage future yields by stressing the plant, so do not allow these first small fruits to form. If you see the plant flowering too early, prune off the flowers and/or small fruits until it reaches a healthy size of at least 4 feet (1.2 m). Then it can start to support the fruit production.

With cucumbers, the more you pick, the more you get. If you leave a few fruits on the vine too long, it will slow the overall fruit production. Often you will see new fruits forming and then shriveling because they sense that there is an ample amount of other fruit on the vine. For this reason, it is very important to keep the vine well picked.

When growing cucumbers, keep a close eye out for marauding whiteflies, mites, and thrips. You may also need to take some measures against powdery mildew if it appears to be a problem.

After harvest, the European cucumbers should be stored in plastic bags in the refrigerator, as they do not keep well at room temperature.

European forcing cucumbers are so sweet you should always have at least one or two plants growing from spring through fall. Given their sweetness, it's no wonder that they are the most popular cucumber in Europe.

Eggplant

Eggplant is a cousin to tomatoes and peppers and, like them, it also prefers a warm greenhouse. It does best from March through October, unless your greenhouse or sunspace maintains good warmth in winter. Each plant needs about $1\frac{1}{2}$ square feet (0.1 sq. m) of growing space. They can be grown in pots—minimum 1 gallon (3.8 liters) in size—and ground beds. Eggplants like a rich soil, with a high level of moisture. To ensure good fruit formation, you will need to pollinate the plants every few days or so (see Chapter 6, "Pollination"). Some varieties need more hand-pollination than others. At the very least, you should gently tap the flowers with a stick every other morning. If your plants get big, try tying them up to a support stake or small tomato cage. Grow one plant for every two people you are feeding.

I get better and earlier yields when I stick to the earlier, more slender varieties rather than the traditional big, fat black varieties. As a novelty, you might want to try the golden-fruited eggplant, which looks like a golden egg—minus the goose. Also check out the new green-skinned variety, which are great producers, sometimes yielding up to an amazing 70 fruits per plant! You just need to get used to the idea of a green-skinned eggplant.

When it comes to harvest, try to do it before the fruits lose their glossy shine.

The eggplant is a relative of tobacco and is also susceptible to tobacco mosaic virus. If you are a user of tobacco, wash your hands before handling the plants in any way. There are some varieties resistant to this disease that may be of interest.

Because eggplants are relatives to tomatoes and peppers, they are also susceptible to many of the same diseases they get (see "Common Greenhouse Tomato Disorders," in this chapter, p. 298). Because of this, don't rotate eggplant with peppers or tomatoes in the same spot year after year.

Fava Bean, Broad Bean

These are the ultimate cold-hardy bean and probably the only one that will grow in a cool-winter greenhouse. Start them in late summer or early fall. You'll quickly notice that they look different from the common garden bean. They grow upright and have bluish green leaves that reach 3 feet (0.9 m) or more, depending upon the variety. They will benefit from some staking, as they may start to lean or fall over as they get taller. They are valuable because they are one of the best protein plants for the winter greenhouse. Because they are so cold-blooded, growing them in the warmer or summer greenhouse usually produces poor plants.

The beans are borne in fat pods. Inside the pods, the beans look much like soybeans. They have a lower oil content than soybeans but are similar in protein levels. To induce earlier and larger crops, you can pinch off the tops when the plants bloom. Some but not all varieties give off a wonderful evening scent that rivals any ornamental flower's fragrance.

A note of caution: Some people are genetically unable to properly digest favas. Within 24 hours of eating, symptoms including vomiting, diarrhea, and dizziness may occur. Fortunately, fatalities are rare and recovery is usually quick. The genetic groups most susceptible to this problem with favas include people (and their descendants) from the Mediterranean countries and from Egypt, Iraq, and Iran. More rarely, it can occur among people of Chinese and African descent. Check with an allergist for more information. Most people can enjoy fava beans to their heart's content. Check recipes that originate in Australia for the best ways to prepare fava beans, as they are a favorite down under.

Feijoa

The feijoa, also known as **pineapple guava**, is a small tree or shrub that produces beautiful red-and-white flowers and a tasty round fruit. Even though it is called a guava, it is not a true guava—but who really cares? Especially since it is easier to grow than a guava. The plant grows to 15 feet (4.6 m) or more and has thick grayish leaves, which it keeps year-round. It is a perfect plant for almost any greenhouse because it tolerates both cool winters and hot summers. Some varieties are not self-fruitful, meaning you need to grow more than one variety. You should avoid those varieties. Fortunately, there are varieties that readily set fruit solo, saving you precious space. Some self-fruitful varieties of feijoa include Apollo, Collidge, and Nazemetz.

When the feijoa flowers in spring, take a small paintbrush and dab the yellow pollen onto the female element in the center. The fruits begin to mature from midsummer into late summer and are about 2 to 3 inches (5 to 8 cm) across. It is easy to tell when to pick them because they fall to the ground when they are at their perfect state of ripeness (don't let them sit on the ground too long). The skin of the fruit is tough and not edible. Cut the fruit in half and scoop out the inner sweet meat. The small seeds inside are quite edible, too. There are only a few bites per fruit but they are among the best and easiest fruits you can grow in a greenhouse. The taste is akin to pineapple but hard to relate to anything else. I think it tastes delicious.

For adventuresome eaters, you may want to try eating the flower petals of the feijoa. They are entirely edible, with a succulent, marsh-mallowlike texture and are slightly sweet with no bitter aftertaste. My kids call it the marsh-mallow plant. The petals are thick and fleshy. They are two-toned, with white on one side and red on the other. Try slipping some into a salad. Luckily, you can harvest the flowers without hurting later fruit production. The plant tends to flower in the spring and to set fruit throughout the summer months.

Feijoa does fine in a tub of at least 10 gallons (38 liters), as well as in ground beds. It may take a few years before the plant is mature enough to produce fruit, but after that, it can be productive for many years. The plant is drought tolerant and actually needs to dry out between waterings. It takes well to pruning if you need to control the growth or height. You will probably have to purchase your first plant from a catalog that specializes in tropical plants. Once you have a plant, it is easy to propagate new ones from stem cuttings of new growth.

Although you may see an occasional pest on the plant, it is rare that they have any effect on the plant's health or its production. Every greenhouse should have at least one.

Fig

If you live in the North where winters are cold, you may never have had the opportunity to experience the pleasure of eating a fresh fig. Figs are an easy plant to grow in the greenhouse or sunspace. They can be grown either in large tubs or planted directly in the ground. In their native habitat, figs are trees reaching 15 to 30 feet (4.6 to 9 m) tall. When grown in tubs, they tend to stay a more manageable size, as the limited root space causes natural dwarfing.

When it comes to soil, all they need is something that drains well, and if they are in a pot, there must be some sizable drainage holes. If they sit in constantly wet soil, the stems may rot and die. Figs need to grow in a sunny location and need occasional feedings. They are fast summer growers, especially if they are growing in ground beds with more root room. If the branches start to cause too much shading, they take to pruning quite well. You'll notice that when you prune the stems, leaves, or branches, they will bleed white sap. No need to get out the Band-Aids, as this soon stops, and the plant will usually forgive you for the pruning (and bleeding).

Most of us call the fig itself a fruit, but what we actually eat is an assemblage of many inside-out flowers with all of the flower parts located inside the so-called fruit. The structure looks like a fruit, but when you cut it open, you can see what I mean: It is a collection of flowers (without petals), all facing inward. The edible crunchy seeds are not viable unless pollinated, which is done only by a specialized small wasp found only in certain geographical regions. For simplicity's sake, I will just refer to this unusual flower structure as a fruit.

After the plants are 2 years old or so, they will start bearing fruit. Fortunately, there are many varieties of fig which will develop edible fruits without the need for any pollination. In fact, most of the varieties sold for home growing do not need pollination. Just in case, check with your nursery or catalog source to be sure that you are getting the proper variety.

Most fig varieties bear fruit throughout the summer. It usually comes in two flushes. The first crop of fruit starts around June, and a larger second crop occurs around August into the fall. Depending upon the variety you grow, as the fig fruit approaches maturity, the outer skin becomes soft and darkens a bit, and the figs become easier to remove from the branch. They might even drop from the plant when mature. With a few taste tests, you'll figure out the best time to pick them. Sometimes they are most delicious when they are the ugliest. One variety I grew needed to have the fruits get almost black and wrinkled before they were truly ripe and sweet.

When the dead of winter comes around, some fig varieties have leaves that turn yellow and after a while will drop to the ground, leaving you with a leafless plant. Don't fret. This is a normal dormant period that they go through. It only lasts a month or two. Toward late winter or early spring, a new crop of healthy green leaves will start anew.

If you have a choice of fig varieties, besides being sure that the variety you choose needs no pollination, try to avoid the so-called hardy varieties. There seems to be less production of fruit on the hardy varieties in a greenhouse because they require more of a winter cooling period for good fruit production. In a greenhouse, you really can't provide a winter cooling treatment. That's why the less hardy types are a better choice. Some varieties to look for include Kadota, Celeste, and Brown Turkey. There are probably many more good choices out there. If you are good at grafting, you can try grafting more than one variety onto one tree.

If you have an established plant, you can easily propagate more plants from cuttings taken from stem tips in spring. Use cuttings that are around 8 to 10 inches (20 to 25 cm) long.

Kale

The cultivation of kale is similar to that for collards, and, like collards, kale is a member of the cabbage family. But it should be noted that kale is not nearly as heat tolerant as collards and many other members of the cabbage family. The flavor of kale improves as the weather gets colder, and it tastes best after going though a few frosts. Because frost in the greenhouse is usually rare, it is hard to get good quality. The only time to ever consider growing kale is through the cool months of winter. It would be a good choice for greenhouses that run quite cold. Better yet, it would do best in an outdoor cold frame during the winter if started in August.

Kale is very nutritious, and the older, lower leaves should be harvested first, as with many other leafy crops. If it begins to go to seed, as indicated by the formation of flowers, then the flavor may become bitter. Ornamental kale is a colorful plant that does very well in most winter greenhouses, as long as the temperatures aren't too hot. It can be eaten as you would any other kale, but the flavor may easily become hot and bitter. It is better used as an ornamental plant or as a garnish to the dinner plate. Read more about ornamental kale in "Kale and Cabbage, Flowering" in the previous section of this chapter on ornamentals for the greenhouse.

Kohlrabi

This relative of broccoli and cabbage is often described as an above-ground turnip. I think kohlrabi tastes better than a turnip. It sure is a lot more interesting looking. It grows relatively fast in the greenhouse and may be planted as close as 6 inches (15 cm) apart. There are both purple and green varieties. The hybrid variety Grand Duke is quicker maturing and more tolerant of the adverse warm and cold temperatures that can occur in solar greenhouses.

Occasionally, alternating hot and cold temperatures can cause the bulb of the kohlrabi to crack, but it is still edible. When it is a bit smaller than a baseball, it is ready for harvest. Peel the fibrous outer skin off, and then you can prepare it in any number of ways, including eating it fresh (great with dips) or cooking it as you would a turnip or carrot.

I like to grow kohlrabi in greenhouses because it can tolerate tight spacing, is pest tolerant, produces a crop relatively fast, and can take wider temperature extremes than its relatives in the cole crop family.

Lettuce

Lettuce, one of the oldest known greenhouse food crops, is also one of the most popular. It is the king (or queen—nobody knows for sure) of the salad greens and is very productive in the greenhouse. Lettuce is best grown from fall through spring, as it prefers cooler temperatures and can tolerate cloudy weather well. Warm temperatures and longer daylight hours of late spring and summer cause lettuce to prematurely go to seed and become bitter.

Lettuce prefers a rich, well-drained soil. When planting seeds, just barely cover them, as they need to see a little light shining through the soil in order to trigger germination. Keep the soil moist until the seedlings emerge. Lettuce also transplants well. The root system is shallow, so be careful if you are cultivating near it. Space the plants about 5 to 6 inches (13 to 15 cm) apart to give them enough room as mature. If you have sown seeds too thickly, be sure to thin them out. When you water, try not to splash soil up on the leaves to avoid sandy salads.

Lettuce is easy to oversow, which makes for some extra work thinning out the plants and is a waste of seeds. A few seed catalogs offer what is called "pelleted seed" to help with this problem and to make it easier for commercial operations to sow with machinery. Many greenhouse growers also like the pelleted option. The pellets are a coating of a clay material surrounding the seed that doesn't harm the seed or the soil. With pellets, you will see more uniform germination and sometimes faster establishment. Yes, pelleted seed does cost a bit more. But heck, you and your greenhouse are worth it! Splurge if you are in the mood.

You can grow lettuce with fine results in 4- to 5-inch (10- to 13-cm) pots, or you can use larger pots with more plants. I usually grow lettuce in a ground bed for simplicity. It can resemble a winter edible lawn and looks great when there are nearby winter flowers in bloom for contrast.

The key to good greenhouse lettuce production is not only understanding its growing requirements but also knowing the differences in types and varieties of lettuce. There are four basic types from which to choose: leaf lettuce; head, or iceberg; Boston, or bibb/butterhead (forming a loose head); and cos, or romaine. The leaf and loose-headed varieties are the earliest maturing varieties and the best choice for the greenhouse or sunspace. For example, if you are growing a leaf lettuce, you can expect a crop in 50 to 80 days. Head lettuce will take

Romaine Lettuce

Oak Leaf Lettuce

Leaf Lettuce

Bibb Lettuce

up to 150 days before you can harvest, a big difference if you are waiting to eat a fresh salad!

Even within one single lettuce type, there is a great difference in growing characteristics. These include the time it takes before the plant goes to seed (called bolting), resistance to an assortment of diseases, the likelihood of the tips burning, and even the color of the leaf (dark green, light green, yellowish, red). Many of these characteristics are listed in seed catalogs. It is these characteristics that greenhouse growers need to consider in order to get maximum lettuce production. Some varieties, usually leaf and bibb types, have even been developed for growing in a greenhouse.

One important characteristic to select for the greenhouse is heat tolerance, often indicated in catalogs as "slow to bolt." It takes only a few warm, sunny days in winter to make a greenhouse heat up tremendously, thus triggering the plant to go to seed and become bitter. When that happens, the plant ends its period of productivity as far as harvesting the leaf goes.

My absolute favorite types of lettuce, if you haven't guessed yet, are the leafy types of lettuce. Of the leaf lettuce varieties, I have a few favorites, including a variety called Green Ice available from Burpee (800-888-1447, **www.burpee.com**). Green Ice is everything you could want from a leaf lettuce—dark in color, slow to bolt, productive, and crispy. Another of my favorites—Royal Green M.I.—can be found in the Stokes Seeds catalog (800-396-9238, **www.stokeseeds.com**). It also has a dark-green leaf. Why do I keep saying that they should have a dark-green leaf? I have found that the lettuce varieties with lighter-colored green leaves are much more susceptible to both aphid and whitefly attacks. I think that as the leaf color tends more toward the yellow spectrum as it lightens, it becomes more attractive to many pests.

The Thompson & Morgan catalog also offers what the company claims to be a variety of lettuce resistant to "greenfly" (British for aphid), called Dynamite. I have not had a chance to see if their claim is for real, but I plan to test it in my next planting.

A couple of bolt-resistant red loose-leaf varieties include New Red Fire and Red Sails, both of which are commonly available. Try either if you are looking for both color in your salad and heat tolerance. One of the most heat-tolerant varieties available is the old standby, Oak Leaf, which has oak-shaped leaves. Unfortunately, it borders on limpness even when fresh, lacking the crispiness of the other leafy varieties mentioned. Always space the leafy lettuce about 8 inches (20 cm) apart. However, you can sow more thickly as long as you make sure to harvest the thinnings for your first salad.

"Bibb," "butterhead," and "Boston" all describe the type of lettuce that has large, thick, green outer leaves forming a loose head, with lighter green to yellow blanched leaves inside, where the texture is more refined and sweeter.

These are more popular in European greenhouses than in the United States, but their popularity is growing here. They are also a bit more perishable. You can grow common butterhead varieties in the greenhouse with limited success, but for more dependability, try growing the butterheads that were developed in Europe specifically for greenhouse culture. Stokes Seeds and Johnny's Selected Seeds catalogs offer a few good selections of greenhouse bibb lettuce. Stokes has a full page dedicated to greenhouse vegetables and offers three different types of butterheads that are all somewhat heat tolerant. Johnny's Selected Seeds catalog offers a variety known as Buttercrunch, which is a good choice for greenhouse production. Always space the butterheads about 8 inches (20 cm) apart.

Johnny's Selected Seeds and Thompson & Morgan also offer what is known as "continental looseleaf," "French," or "summer crisp lettuce." It has a loose head, much like a butterhead or bibb lettuce, but is crispy, like leaf or head lettuce. These crispy types are often heat tolerant and good for the greenhouse. Johnny's Selected Seeds catalog specializes in the summer crisp types and has one variety called Centennial that combines the characteristics of leaf and head lettuce along with some bolt resistance and is great for greenhouse production. Thompson & Morgan offer a similar type called Frisby.

Romaine (or cos) lettuce grows quite upright and has a sweet juicy flavor. Its long, dark-green leaf has a crisp white central spine. Always space each plant about 10 inches (25 cm) apart. If you have your heart set on growing romaine lettuce, always look for the romaines that are listed as being slower to bolt or go to seed. If not, you may find your production cut short. Romaine has a tendency to-ward what is called "bottom rotting," which can be prevented by not overwatering and by picking off any lower leaves that are yellowing before they start to rot.

Iceberg, or head, lettuce can be grown in the winter greenhouse or sunspace, but it will be the slowest producer and the lowest in nutritional value. This is because most of the leaves are inside the head and never turn very green. They are mostly water. Other types of lettuce have up to five times the vitamins that the iceberg has. If you still insist upon growing it, be sure to plan around 1 foot (0.3 m) of space for each plant. It is also hard to find varieties that are well suited to the greenhouse environment. Instead, grow the crispy leaf lettuces, such as Green Ice or Royal Green, mentioned earlier, or try some of the bibb types bred for greenhouse culture. Perhaps the "summer crisp" varieties mentioned above would also be a good alternative. Steering clear of the traditional head lettuce varieties will be not only more productive but also healthier. A few extra vitamins won't hurt anyone.

Harvesting lettuce can be done in one cut or pull (harvesting the whole plant). Instead, you can try to go for two, three, or more cuttings off the same plant before it goes to seed. To do this, harvest only the lower, larger, older leaves. Always leave the center young leaves to continue growing.

As you work with your lettuce, take the time to clean off old, dead, or broken leaves from the soil surface. If you don't, they'll begin to rot, which may spread to the underside of the healthy lettuce plant. This bottom rot can become very destructive.

In the wintertime, you can keep lettuce disease to a minimum by providing good ventilation. On a sunny day, if the greenhouse or sunspace is warm enough, open a vent to the outside for a few minutes for a breather. Use a small fan to prevent air stagnation during the day.

Lettuce is a heavy feeder and tolerates a high amount of fertilization. That can cause a fast growth rate but can also increase diseases. If the air temperature is cool, the leaves may accumulate increased levels of nitrates, which may not be good for the health (see discussion in Chapter 4, pages 121–122). For this reason, go easy on the fertilizer if the air temperature is on the cool side. To ensure continuous production during the winter greenhouse season, it's a good idea to always have a few lettuce seedlings started for later transplanting to fill in empty areas after harvesting other crops. Another option is to scatter a few seeds here and there every few weeks from late August through the spring.

Lettuce is very productive, and no wintertime greenhouse should be without it. Start studying the seed catalogs now. Seed catalogs are notorious for switching out old favorite varieties like a car company with a new model each year. If you don't find some of the lettuce varieties listed there, you will probably find something else with similar traits.

Nothing is better than to sit down to a winter dinner that includes a fresh-picked salad from your greenhouse. This alone is a good reason for having a greenhouse or sunspace—what an incredible luxury!

New Zealand Spinach

Also called "tetragonia," this thick-leafed spinach alternative has one great advantage over spinach: It's a perennial that doesn't die after it flowers. One plant can produce for many years. Also, the leaves still taste fine during flowering and in hot conditions. As it grows, it spreads out over a bed, and it grows slightly slower than traditional spinach, especially in cool temperatures. The beauty of this plant is that it grows well almost any month of the year, including summer, when it is hard to grow most of the more traditional greens such as spinach.

You can make efficient use of space by tying it to a north–south trellis. The vines are very delicate and break easily, so tie it up gently. By growing it vertically, you will gain much more yield per square foot. It can also be trained to hang off the edge of a raised bed, thereby making aisle space productive. I have also had good luck growing two or three plants in a 6-inch (15-cm) hanging basket for an ornamental foliagelike look that is quite edible.

New Zealand spinach likes a rich soil and has large seeds that germinate readily. For even faster germination, try soaking the seeds overnight prior to planting. Don't be surprised if you see new seedlings popping up under a mature plant, as it has a tendency to self-sow. New Zealand spinach can be easily transplanted when young. I have made efficient use of space by transplanting it under other taller plants such as tomatoes that are growing up a string or trellis. This provides for two-tiered production.

Okra

Growing okra in a greenhouse is a real treat for Southerners who have found themselves transplanted to the okra-scarce north. Okra can be grown in a greenhouse when the temperatures are on the warmer side. It loves heat, so try it from spring through fall.

Okra varieties differ considerably. Height can vary from 5 to 10 feet (1.5 to 3 m) tall. Pod size varies in length and width. Varieties also differ in color, leaf shape, and the look of the flower. For quicker maturity, I have grown mostly the shorter and quick-maturing types. The flower of the okra is extremely ornamental, and rightly so, because it is a close cousin to the hibiscus. It seems to do best in soils containing lower amounts of nitrogen, so go easy on the fertilizer. Heavy amounts of nitrogen may cause excess leaf production at the expense of the edible pods.

Okra prefers soil on the dry side and likes a sunny location. Seed germination is hastened if the seeds are soaked overnight prior to planting. Space plants 12 to 15 inches (30 to 38 cm) apart. Small plants can be started in small pots for later transplanting into beds. Try to minimize the disturbance of the roots.

The pods develop soon after the plants flower. Okra doesn't require pollination in order to produce the edible pods. The production can occur over a long period, as long as it is warm. If cooler temperatures of late fall begin, production will drop off. If your greenhouse tends to run cool in winter, fall may signal a good time to pull the okra up and switch to more cool-loving plants. I have found okra does best in ground beds or in small tubs that are well drained to prevent overwatering.

Onions

Onions are almost as old as civilization, originating in ancient Egypt. Onions can be grown for bunching (onion greens) or for their bulbs. Ever since I discovered storage onions, I have stopped trying to grow onions for bulb production in the greenhouse. Storage onions are special varieties that you can grow outside in the summer as easily as any onion. The beauty is that they keep all winter without any special treatment. I have eaten onions grown the previous summer as late as April, and they were stored in the kitchen drawer. Why don't we see them for sale in the grocery? Because it eliminates the planned obsolescence built into the traditional store-bought onion, which tends to rot after 3 weeks of storage, thus requiring you to return to the store for more.

A couple of good choices for storage onions include the Sweet Sandwich (which is getting increasingly harder to find) and Copra, both of which are yellow onions. There are also some red storage types available. If you are not convinced yet to try starting some storage onions, let me give you one last fact. Storage onions are more sweet and flavorful. They are said to have twice the sugar content of the mild varieties. They seem to get sweeter as they are stored. Also, when you cook with these onions, the pungency lessens, leaving only the sweet flavor. My preference is to grow the storage onions outside and stick to the easier-to-grow green onions in the greenhouse.

Although you can grow onions for bulbs in the greenhouse, you need to be sure to select the right onion for the right time of year. Varieties differ as to whether they require the longer summer days of the North or the shorter summer days of the South. If you are growing anytime other than the middle of summer, you will have better success with the shorter-day-adapted onions. Read the catalog descriptions well and stick to the catalogs that provide good descriptions.

Onions may suffer from being too hot in the

Green Onions

summer greenhouse, as they prefer slightly cooler temperatures. This often limits onions for bulb production, anyway. Again, you may find you get better-quality bulbs by growing them outside. Unfortunately you can't find the storage onions (touted earlier) for sale as seedlings, so you have to grow your own. That's another reason for having a greenhouse! Use your greenhouse as a nursery for starting your own seedling plants for later setting outside. Start them between February 15 and March 1. I grow mine in pretty close quarters, with spacing of about 1 inch (2.5 cm) between seedlings. If they get floppy simply prune them back by $\frac{1}{4}$ of their total length. Transplant these seedlings outside around a week or two before the last average frost date.

Growing onion greens is practical all year long and easy to do in the greenhouse or sunspace. They are easy to start either from commercially available onion sets or from your own seeds. When growing onions for greens, space the plants much closer than you would onion bulbs. A spacing of 2 to 3 inches (5 to 8 cm) works fine. The planting will soon resemble an onion lawn if sown in a block in a ground bed. The greens can also be easily grown in pots, and greens can be cut as needed or pulled up and consumed.

If you want to get serious about growing onion greens, you may want to try the varieties of onions that have actually been developed for this type of harvest. These are called "bunching onions" in the catalogs. Check out some catalogs, especially Stokes Seeds and Johnny's Selected Seeds catalogs, and you'll come across several excellent choices.

Another type of onion, called the multiplier or top-set, is very tolerant of cool temperatures and is quite productive in the greenhouse. During midsummer, the multiplier produces bulblets at the top of the flowering stalk. These can be planted like onion sets for more plants or even eaten as small pearl onions.

It is rare to have any pests on onions as long as you try to rotate each crop, being careful not to resow in the same place in a given year.

Because any type of green onion takes up relatively little space and can add so much flavor to winter food, I highly recommend them for your greenhouse. Another choice for onion flavor is chives.

Papaya

Up until recently, most papayas available required specialized pollination and grew too large. This meant that you had to grow two gigantic papayas, which is not easy to do in a greenhouse. Luckily, there is a type of papaya that doesn't need pollination, and it only grows about 6 to 8 feet (1.8 to 2.4 m) in height. This type is commonly known as the Babáco papaya. It can be found in many tropical plant catalogs. It grows well in a greenhouse and requires little special care. This papaya looks a bit like a palm tree with wide, smooth leaves.

The Babáco papaya needs to dry out between watering, and young plants are very sensitive to high levels of soil moisture. Also, go easy on watering in the wintertime. Always grow the plants where they will receive a good amount of light. They do best in ground beds or in a 10-gallon (37.8-liter) pot, moving up to a 15-gallon (56.8 liter) one as the plant matures. Within a year of growing the plant, you will likely be greeted by the formation of fruits. Healthy plants can produce up to 25 fruits per season. Each fruit is up to a foot long and about 5 inches (13 cm) in diameter. The fruits are seedless and the taste is great, like a cross between a banana and pineapple. The Babáco also has a slightly different flavor than the traditional store-bought papaya. Although the skin is edible, this papaya is not as sweet as many tropical fruits. However, it is great in smoothies, and you can always add a bit of honey to the flesh to bring out the flavor.

I have found that the plants decrease in productivity after 2 or 3 years. You can revitalize them somewhat by cutting the main stem down to about 2 feet (0.6 m) from the ground, and they will then sprout new leaves and get back to the business of growing fruit. You can take the part you cut and try to propagate it into new plants, making each cutting about 10 inches (25 cm) in length (see Chapter 5 for propagation help). If all this fails, you can always purchase a new plant.

When it comes to pests, keep an eye out for the occasional mealybug and scale.

By the way, papayas contain the valued digestive enzyme papain. In fact, the Babáco is higher in this enzyme than are the common Hawaiian papayas. They also are high in vitamins and minerals. Here's to papayas in the North Country! You just have to try at least one plant!

Peas

At the Cheyenne Botanic Gardens (see the Epilogue for more information on this project), we often try to get volunteers, who get to harvest and use the food grown in the greenhouse, to record the food yields by weight. I've noticed that it's rare to get any record of a pea harvest, even though peas are growing healthily, producing an abundance of pods. After a little closer investigation, I discovered the problem. The peas never make it to the scales!

The peas usually get eaten on the way. I have considered weighing the volunteers before and after they work around the peas for more accurate data.

Peas are one of the best wintertime treats a greenhouse can provide. They make good use of vertical space, as they grow up trellises, and are also a good source of protein. Pretty good for a vegetable that is as sweet as candy! In the summer when the temperatures are warmer, they are harder to grow, as they long for a cool environment. Besides, this is when you can grow them outside. When it comes to timing, I have the best luck planting them directly in ground beds in late August or September. You can also grow them in tubs, using tiered tomato cages wired on top of each other, depending on the height of the variety you plan to grow and its potential height.

Using a bacterial inoculant powder (available in many catalogs for peas and beans) to coat the seeds before planting will help enable the roots to capture free nitrogen from the air in the soil. It is not generally needed in soils where peas have been grown before.

There is a great choice of pea varieties, and I urge you to experiment with a few different ones each year. Pea varieties have been bred for many characteristics, including vining or bushiness, disease resistance, edible pods, earliness, and heat tolerance.

For the most efficient use of space, especially if you have the luxury of ground beds in the greenhouse, try to grow the pea varieties that vine, as opposed to the bush types. The bush types do have a place; they are good choices for growing peas in pots or tubs. Disease resistance is also important, especially against powdery mildew, which can be a common problem, so keep an eye out for any varieties listed with resistance to this. For people who live in sunny winter climates, heat tolerance is also an important characteristic to consider when perusing a catalog. Temperatures above 80°F (27°C) greatly slow the flower production and subsequent pod development.

I have had good luck growing the pea varieties Maestro and Green Arrow. Oregon Giant is a good choice for a snow pea if you are planning an Oriental dish or for simple snacking.

I would be remiss if I didn't mention the delicious snap peas like the Sugarsnap variety, which allows you to eat both the pod and pea at the usual "shelling" time, when the peas are full size. The pod is every bit as sweet as the pea! When growing the sugarsnap variety, be sure to set up a trellis that is at least 4 to 6 feet (1.2 to 1.8 m) in height because this plant loves to climb. Some other snap pea varieties are Sugar Ann, Cascadia, and Sugar Daddy, all of which do not grow as tall and need no trellis.

Sow the seeds a little over 1 inch apart and $\frac{1}{3}$-inch deep. If you are growing a tall, vining type of pea in a bed, run the trellis north–south to minimize shading. Chicken wire or other woven wire works fine when strung up on some stakes. Even a short trellis, 3 feet (0.9 m) long, can give you a good amount of peas to eat. In tubs, 5 gallons (19 liters) or more in size, you can grow peas with a tepee trellis. Pea vines are very fragile and frequently get damaged during harvesting. To prevent this, pick the peas with two hands instead of ripping them off with one hand. Keep the vines well picked to prolong harvest.

Keep your eye out for occasional green aphid infestations, especially if your soil is rich. You may also want to look for powdery-mildew-resistant varieties if that becomes a problem in your greenhouse.

Give peas a chance.

Peppers

Peppers are in the same family as eggplants, tomatoes, and tobacco. Like its cousins, the pepper also prefers warm temperatures and is best grown from spring through fall. It likes a moderately rich, well-drained soil. Each plant needs approximately 4 square feet (0.37 sq. m), unless the variety you have is a smaller dwarf type. Being a relative of the tomato, the pepper is susceptible to many of the same diseases (see "Common Greenhouse Tomato Disorders," page 298). A common problem is tobacco mosaic virus (TMV), which is easily transmitted by users of tobacco. If you use tobacco, wash your hands well before handling or working around pepper plants. Angular yellow splotches and lower yields are the symptoms of this problem. There are some pepper varieties that are "TMV resistant" or "TMV tolerant" that may be good choices for smokers.

Peppers can grow as high as 4 feet (1.2 m) and may need a small stake to keep them from toppling over. As with staking any plant, use a piece of soft cloth that is loosely tied to the plant to prevent stem strangulation.

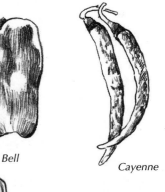
Bell

Cayenne

Pepper seeds are notorious for erratic and slow germination. They can take as long as 8 weeks to germinate. For best germination, use fresh seed and place the germinating seeds

Chili

Jalapeño

in a warm, sunny spot at least 65°F (18°C). Hot summer temperatures over 97°F (36°C) that occur when the plants are flowering can damage the pollen and reduce the fruit set. Temperatures below 60°F (15°C) will slow fruit production. High levels of nitrogen in the soil can cause luxuriant leaf growth at the expense of fruit production, so be alert if you suspect this problem and try to water heavily a few times to leach out excess nitrogen. Peppers benefit from high soil-moisture levels until the fruits begin to mature. This doesn't, however, give you permission to overwater them.

Try not to allow your pepper plants to set fruit when they are still on the small side (shorter than 10 inches [25 cm]) unless the variety is naturally small. Allowing early fruit set can stunt the plants and lower your total yield. If they do start blooming too early, simply pluck the little blossoms until the plants are big enough to go to town setting many flowers and the subsequent fruits. By doing this, you'll be trading some early peppers for a healthier plant and many more peppers in the long run.

There is an incredible variety of peppers to choose from, including **bell** peppers for sweet fruits; **cayennes** for hot, slender fruits; **chilis,** which are banana-shaped and range in hotness; and, of course, the **jalapeño,** which is a good choice if you can stand a red-hot tongue. Many varieties are worth trying, including the many "yuppie"-colored bell peppers, which are sweet and turn beautiful shades of red and yellow at maturity. One bell variety that I like for greenhouse production is Vidi, available from the Totally Tomatoes catalog (803-663-0016) and the Tomato Growers Supply Company (888-478-7333). The Vidi is tobacco-mosaic resistant, and the plants stay vigorous even through varying tough conditions while still setting on

a good crop. Look for more peppers bred for greenhouse gardening to become available in the future.

If you live in the South, your soil may be infested with a microscopic critter called the nematode. This makes it tough to grow peppers. If you suspect that this is a problem for you, first check with your local extension agent about the possibility. If it is a possibility, then try growing the new bell pepper variety Charleston Belle, which has some excellent resistance to the nematode.

Pineapple

Pineapples can easily be grown in a sunspace or greenhouse, but they are not known for being highly productive in that environment. Still, they are both fun and interesting to grow. You can start pineapples by using one from the store that you plan to eat. Select a pineapple with the greenest, healthiest-looking leaves. Twist—don't cut—off the leafy top of the pineapple (yes, you can still eat the fruit) and let the top dry in a shady place for about 1 week. This is to let the exposed tissue at the break dry out so that it will not rot.

After a week, take this leafy top and peel off the bottom half of the pineapple leaves completely from the stem. Examine the stem after you remove the leaves. In between where the leaves once grew, you may find some flattened little roots. If these roots are there, they will take hold quickly and your pineapple will be easier to start.

If you don't find these little roots, you can still get the pineapple to

grow new roots. Brush a small amount of rooting hormone on the bottom third of the plant (see Chapter 5 "Plant Propagation," for information on rooting hormone). Then place the plant 3 inches (8 cm) deep in a 6-inch (15-cm) clay pot that is filled with a mix of half potting soil and half sand. Keep it slightly moist, not wet (overwatering will cause bottom rot), and put it in a warm place with filtered light. Soon the pineapple will root and begin to grow anew.

Pineapples are bromeliads and like to be watered from the top, where water can rest in the leaves for a few hours before evaporating or being absorbed. After about a year and if the plant has been steadily growing lots of new leaves, you can trigger a fruit to set. The triggering is done with a treatment of ethylene, a naturally occurring gas given off by many fruits. Ethylene is commonly given off by ripe bananas, apples, and tomatoes. For our purposes, stick to either a banana or an apple, as they are less messy. To trigger fruit set, place a freshly peeled banana skin on the soil next to the pineapple, and cover both the banana skin and the pineapple with a clear plastic bag. Keep it out of direct sun. Leave the bag over the plant for about 2 weeks. You may need to replace the banana or apple with a fresh one if it starts to look withered. About a month or more after this treatment, with some luck, you'll soon see a shoot emerging out of the top of the plant. It is from this shoot that you will see the plant forming a new pineapple fruit! If triggering doesn't work, the plant needs to keep growing; try again in another 3 to 6 months.

You may need to stake the plant as it begins to set fruit, as it can become top-heavy. Before you start your greenhouse pineapple farm, you should know that the pineapple is a slow grower compared to many other food plants you can grow in the greenhouse. Start out with 1 or 2 and get a little experience first. A fruiting pineapple is a beautiful plant and a real conversation piece. It is a wonderfully trouble-free plant rarely bothered by low or high temperatures, pests, or disease.

Potato

The only reason I list potatoes here is to encourage you not to waste the precious space of a greenhouse or sunspace on growing them unless you really have your heart set on it. Why? Because they are so cheap at the store. Also, you can quite easily grow and store your own outside harvests. Why tie up precious space on this crop when you could be growing a more valuable plant in your greenhouse or sunspace? Besides, potatoes can be grown in almost any climate and keep quite well.

If you still want to try it, plant them in February and grow them as you would outside, giving them full sun and well-drained soil. If you don't have luck growing potatoes outside, don't try it inside. Wait until you have perfected the technique outdoors for a few seasons. Also, when planting tuber seed, be sure it is USDA-certified free of disease. Potatoes do best in ground beds or large tubs. Because they are relatives of the tomato, they are susceptible to many of the same problems as tomatoes.

Potato, Sweet

These potatoes are the orange-fleshed, sweet types. They are not related to the "Idaho" potato. Sweet potatoes grow in a vine fashion and need both full sun and a 3-foot (0.9-m) trellis. Run the trellis on a north–south axis to minimize shading. They also like rich soil. Although you can sometimes get away with it, you should avoid starting sweet potatoes from store-bought potatoes, because many are treated with a hormone that will not allow the plants to sprout or will slow the growth of sprouts. Rather, purchase plants from a catalog or garden center. I have had luck starting plants anytime from February through July in the greenhouse.

Fresh sweet potatoes are a luxury in northern climates, where the outside growing season is too cold and short for them. It will take them 4 months or more to reach maturity. Keep an eye out for whiteflies, which love to hang around them and cause problems.

Purslane

The more experienced gardeners among you are wondering why am I including this weed. Enthusiasts of wild edible plants have long eaten the succulent weed purslane. You can also grow a cultivated variety in your greenhouse. There are a number of purslane varieties available, including Golden Purslane, Large Leaf, and Goldberg. Purslane is similar to the weedy variety, except that it has a much larger leaf. It is available from Johnny's Selected Seeds and Seeds of Change (www.seedsofchange.com).

I include it here because in terms of flavor and texture it beats many of the other "newer" popular greens that are now on the market. The cultivated purslane is slightly sweet, with a wonderful succulent texture. It is great in any salad. On top of the great taste, it is high in vitamin C and omega-3 fatty acid, which helps to regulate the metabolism and serum cholesterol. It contains up to 10 times more omega-3 than any other leafy green.

Grow it as you would lettuce. Being a weedy relative, it is rarely bothered by pests. Be adventuresome and give some golden purslane a try.

Radish

Just as with growing radishes outside, in the greenhouse or sunspace they are fast producers, given the right environment. They like cool temperatures and moist, friable soil. Most varieties do best when sown in the fall and do well throughout the winter season, as long as your greenhouse is not too warm. A common problem with radishes is when they produce all tops and no edible radish. Prolonged warm temperatures generally cause this. The optimum night temperature is between 45°F and 50°F (7°C and 10°C). Be sure to thin the seedlings to at least 2 inches (5 cm) apart. The application of excess manure or nitrogen may also cause too much top growth.

Radishes are a great crop to interplant under or among other garden plants in ground beds. They can also be easily grown in pots. Be sure the radishes are growing in a bright spot. Because the seed germinates quickly, it is always best to seed them directly into the bed or pot rather than transplanting seedlings.

If all goes well, you will have radishes to complement your salad in 4 to 5 weeks. The closer they're grown to the winter solstice, the longer they will take to mature because of the shorter days. **Winter**, or **Daikon**, radishes are different from the common garden radish and will take 8 to 12 weeks or even longer. They grow carrotlike roots about 5 to 6 inches (12 to 15 cm) long. In contrast to the common garden radish, they are both larger and longer keeping. The winter radish is also more pungent. They do fine in the winter greenhouse and are generally used in Oriental cooking.

Sorrel

Sorrel, also known as **French sorrel**, is a real favorite of mine. It is a perennial green that almost always has some leaves to harvest. No matter what time of year, no matter whether your greenhouse runs hot or cool, you'll find that sorrel is a dependable producer. The flavor of the leaf is tart and lemony-pungent. Although you wouldn't want to make a whole salad out of this tart leaf, in small quantities it is a great addition, complementing other fresh greens and vegetables in a salad. When you add sorrel, it will flavor the salad as though you have put a bit of vinegar or squeezed some lemon into the bowl. It can also be cooked much like spinach or even added to spinach or chard in a cooked dish.

Sorrel is an almost effortless plant to grow. It regularly produces seed stalks, which should be immediately pruned to conserve its energy for producing leaves. Also, when the plant goes to seed, the leaf texture gets tougher and more bitter. Richters, the Canadian herb company with the extensive catalog (905-640-6677, www.richters.com), sells 5 different varieties of sorrel, which is more than any other catalog I have ever seen. One variety they offer called Profusion™ has been selected to never go to seed at all and thus remains more productive and tender.

Sorrel does well in either full sun or light shade and is not picky about soil or moisture. Harvest only the outside leaves, leaving the new ones to form in the center. Sorrel benefits from dividing every 3 or 4 years. If you don't need any more plants, you may have some friends who could use some. Sorrel has very few pests. Every greenhouse should have at least one sorrel plant.

Spinach

Spinach has one of the lowest tolerances to high temperature of any edible plant. When it experiences warm temperatures for a number of days, it quickly goes to seed and no longer produces edible leaves. For that reason, don't even attempt to grow it between late March and August. If you run your winter greenhouse on the warmer side, you may want to avoid spinach in favor of an alternative such as chard or New Zealand spinach. For greenhouses that run cold in winter and for people in cool, cloudy winter climates, spinach is a fine choice.

For the longest productivity, you must try to prevent or at least hold off the plant's urge to go to seed. This is best done by growing it at the right time of year, as just mentioned, but also by selecting the varieties that are slow to go to seed, or, as commonly labeled in catalogs, "slow to bolt." Some good varieties include Tyee, America, Bloomsdale Longstanding, Olympia, and Indian Summer.

If you have any disease problems occurring on spinach, try switching to the variety Melody, which has tolerance to many common diseases.

Spinach transplants fine in the seedling stage and likes a light soil that is somewhat on the moist side. Space plants 6 inches (15 cm) apart. It can be grown in pots as well as in beds. The best harvest and quality can be obtained when grown in temperatures below 70°F (21°C). When the climate isn't suitable for spinach, the best choice as an alternative is chard, as it will outlive and greatly outyield any spinach variety. It is also the easiest to sell to suspicious dinner guests.

Squash, Summer

Summer squash varieties include **zucchini, pattypan, gold,** and **yellow** squash. It is known as summer squash because the fruits are harvested at an immature stage (before the seeds mature within) in the summertime. When grown outside, it must also be eaten in the summer, as it will not keep. Winter squash, on the other hand, is allowed to mature and can be stored and eaten in the winter. Thus, we have the names "winter" and "summer" squash. Fortunately these seasonal rules can be broken in the greenhouse.

Almost every summer squash yields abundantly in the greenhouse (as it does in the outside garden), but only if the temperature remains warm, with night temperatures above 50°F (10°C). When the temperatures drop, so do the yields. For this reason, summer squash is best grown from late February through October in most greenhouses, unless your greenhouse runs warm in the winter.

Seed may either be directly sown or started in small pots and the seedlings transplanted (with care) into beds or large tubs, 5 to 10 gallons (19 to 38 liters) in size. If you are growing in tubs, put only one plant in each tub. They germinate and grow quickly, so you don't save that much time by transplanting. However, you can protect the little seedlings better from slugs and other critters if you grow them in pots for transplanting.

Most available summer squashes are bushy. There is a wide range of varieties: Some grow more compact, some are more open. I have found that the straight-neck and crookneck yellow squash are among the most prolific greenhouse producers.

Squash likes a rich soil with a lot of well-decomposed organic matter. Each plant will need at least 9 square feet (0.8 sq. m) by the time it's ready to produce. However, while the plant is small, you can often sneak a few quick-maturing crops into the surrounding area before the mature squash takes over its rightful territory. There is always room for some lettuce, kohlrabi, or radishes while the squash is young.

Always grow squash in a warm, sunny spot in the greenhouse or sunspace. After it starts producing fruits, you can help things along with an application of fish emulsion (hold your nose!) or another type of fertilizer watered into the soil, as they are heavy feeders.

After it grows five or more large leaves, the plant will start to flower. See Chapter 6, "Pollination," for instructions on how to get the flower to produce fruit, as it won't happen unless you do the pollinating!

There is a variety of zucchini that can potentially save you time and trouble because it has the reputed ability to set fruit without

Zucchini

Yellow   *Pattypan*

pollination. It is sold under the most boring name in squash varieties, Type 1406, and is available only from The Cook's Garden catalog (800-457-9703, **www.cooksgarden. com**). Early tests seem a bit disappointing, but the jury is still out. As a greenhouse squash, however, it does have a great flavor. I encourage you to give it a try. You'll find some other interesting squash, as well as other plants, while perusing the Cook's Garden catalog (try the Vining Trombocino squash if you have a lot of room). Whitaker is a new zucchini available from Territorial Seed Company (**www. territorial-seed.com**). It is purportedly resistant to a number of diseases, including powdery mildew and the viruses called yellow mosaic, papaya ring spot, and cucumber mosaic. I haven't had a chance to try it, but it looks promising for greenhouse culture. Whitaker was developed with some interbreeding of a wild squash species from South America. Like Type 1406 it is said to set fruit without the need of pollination.

On some varieties you may see small angular spots forming. This is characteristic of some summer squashes. If, however, you see more of a white powderlike material forming on the leaf surface, you may have the fungal disease powdery mildew, which can be a problem with some squash varieties. Fortunately, there are some varieties more resistant to powdery mildew. Stokes Seeds catalog offers a tolerant variety of zucchini called Select and Super Select. I have grown both with good results.

Harvest summer squash when they are relatively small, usually around 8 inches (20 cm) long for zucchini. Anyone can grow a large summer squash fruit, but large ones are not nearly as tasty and sweet. The large ones can also become fibrous and seedy. Also, the more you pick, the more the plant will go on to produce.

After a plant has yielded fruits for 2 to 3 months, it may begin to slow in its production. At this time, it may also be a large gangly plant, taking up a lot of space. This is usually a good time to be thinking about starting more new plants and pulling out the old ones.

Although most summer squash are classified as bushy, I've had luck making them grow up a thick string suspended from above. After the stem is 2 feet (0.6 m) long, I carefully lift the tip of the plant so the whole stem is vertical. Then I wind the string, with a little slack, down through the squash and loosely tie it to the base of the plant or to a ground anchor such as a wooden stake. As the plant grows, wind it around the string, and you have created a vertical bushy-growing squash. This process must be done with extreme care because it is easy to crack the stem and cause permanent damage to the plant. Unfortunately, you may have to sacrifice a couple of plants to get good at this technique. You may be wondering why I would want to grow squash vertically up a string. I do this to free up ground space to grow more plants underneath! With this vertical-growing technique, I have had two-tiered production, with the squash growing vertically, and under the its leaf canopy, I can grow other leafy crops such as chard or lettuce. This enables me to get some more productive square footage.

Squash, Winter

Winter squash includes many of the well-known storage squashes, such as **butternut, buttercup, hubbard, pumpkin, acorn,** and **spaghetti** squash. The fruits are considered mature when thumbnail pressure doesn't mark the skin. If stored properly, around 50°F (10°C), they can keep for many months. These squashes usually grow in a vinelike way, but there are a few good bushy varieties available.

Pumpkin

Butternut

Acorn

All nonbush varieties will need a trellis and can really sprawl. They may take up so much space that they are not a good choice for a small greenhouse or for gardeners not wanting to give up so much space to squash. In contrast, the bush varieties of winter squash are more restrained in their growth and may even be grown in a 5-gallon (19-liter) container. If you are looking for a bush winter squash, you are limited mostly to the acorn and a few bush pumpkin varieties, but I think in the near future there will be more types available.

Another interesting squash is the **Luffa squash**, is also known as the "vegetable sponge." That is because when you harvest mature squash and let the fruit dry, you can peel the skin to find a spongelike interior that can be used as a bath sponge and scrubber. It is a heat-loving plant that has long vines. Because it vines so much, it is best grown only in larger greenhouses with some surplus space.

Luffa grows best in ground beds and will use space more efficiently if you train it to climb up a vertical support. Luffa is best started in early spring and needs around 100 warm days to reach maturity. It will need to be hand-pollinated for fruit set. For the most part, you treat it as you would any other vining squash. According to the USDA, the immature squash is edible but not very tasty.

Winter squash is slower to produce edible fruits than summer

Luffa Squash

squash, so if you are looking for speed and efficiency, you may want to stick to summer squash. For the most part, cultural needs for growing winter squash are identical to those for summer squash, including the feeding and pollination.

Northern gardeners with short seasons may want to use the greenhouse to get a head start on growing winter squash inside for later outside transplanting. Some growers even start the squash near a window in the greenhouse in spring and when summer comes, they allow the vine to grow out the window and take off to other reaches of the outside garden. That is one way to avoid transplant shock! Whenever transplanting any squash, use your best transplanting technique, taking care to minimize the disturbance of the roots.

Strawberries

When people conceive of the idea of growing strawberries in the greenhouse, they imagine picking a quart of berries every day of the year. Unfortunately, it is not that easy and getting high, year-round yields is next to impossible. It is possible to pick a fair amount of berries in flushes from May through September, depending upon your setup and the varieties that you grow. For berries to be productive, they need relatively warm soil, but not too warm. The ideal is 70°F (20°C, but as you get into the 90s (32°C) or below the 60s (16°C), the yield can drop rapidly.

It is particularly important to grow the right variety when it comes to strawberry production. You should stay away from most of the common "June" and "everbearing" types. The best varieties are the types that have been bred for production in California, which are generally the day-neutral types. Some examples are Tristar, Chandler, Evita (which is a cross of Chandler), and Sweet Charlie. Some recent research done by the USDA Agricultural Research Service has shown that a variety called Camarosa proved to be the most productive variety when grown hydroponically. The plants were preconditioned for many weeks at a temperature below 45°F (7°C). (For information on this research see *Agricultural Research Magazine*, November 1998.)

Some catalogs for sources include Nourse Farms (413-665-2658, **www.noursefarms. com**), Hartmans Plantation (616-253-4281), and Jersey Asparagus Farms (800-499-0013, **www.jerseyasparagus.com**). You should also check out the company We Gro-Rite (1482 Fairview Road, Andrews, NC 28901, 828-321-4371, **www.wegrorite.com**), which specializes in plants and growing systems for strawberry production in greenhouses.

It is best to not grow the same plants for more than 8 months, as the yield begins to drop. You can start new plants from the runners by rooting them in your propagation area (see page 78).

The best timing for the plants is to set young plants out in October, not expecting much in the way of winter yields. However, when the days begin to get longer in March, you should increase regular fertilization and look for blooming to begin. The largest yields can begin in early spring and will last until your greenhouse gets too hot. Then it is time to allow your plants to produce runners for next year's plants. These can be grown in beds, hanging pots, or other containers.

Strawberries are primarily wind-pollinated but also benefit from an occasional bee. Neither are common options in the greenhouse. If you see blossoms forming, it is a good idea to manually tickle each fresh flower every other morning or so.

The main pest on greenhouse strawberries is the spider mite, but keep your eyes out for all of the regular greenhouse pests. Strawberries are not prolific greenhouse producers for amateurs but are always worth trying.

Tea

Tea is actually a type of camellia and is grown with much the same culture. It is a dense shrub with leathery, dark-green leaves. It has fragrant white flowers that are around 1 inch (2.5 cm) across. In its native habitat of China, it grows as a shrub and can attain a height of up to 25 feet (7.6 m). In the greenhouse, it rarely gets taller than 5 feet (1.5 m).

Tea plants are usually started from seed, but occasionally you may come across a nursery selling tea plants. Seeds are large and may take up to a year to germinate, so it will stretch even the best gardener's patience and skill. For this reason, it is easiest to try to locate plants with catalogs specializing in tropical plants.

Tea likes to grow in damp soil (but not muddy wet) and needs a bright location. It can be grown in large tubs or planted directly in a bed.

When the plant seems healthy and can spare some leaves, harvest some for a fresh cup, making sure to not overharvest so the plant can continue to grow. Here's how to process the leaves.

Black tea: Pick the leaves and let them wilt for a few days. Then roll and compress the leaves and place them in a sealed plastic bag for about 10 days, allowing some fermentation to occur. Then bake the tea at 190°F (88°C) until the leaves are completely crispy dry.

Oolong tea: Crush the leaves, place them in a sealed plastic bag for only 3 days, and then bake at 190°F (88°C) until dry.

Green tea: Crush the leaves and immediately bake at 190°F (88°C) until dry.

Now all you have to do is set aside some time in the midafternoon for teatime. The main problem I have had with growing tea is occasional infestations of mealybug. Aside from that, it is relatively simple to grow.

Tomatillo

Tomatillo is also known as the **husk tomato** and is often used in genuine Mexican salsas. It is a relative of the tomato but has smaller leaves and fruits that are only slightly bigger than a cherry tomato.

Each fruit is covered with a paperlike shell. The tomatillo needs warm temperatures and long days for best fruit production and is best grown from March through September. If your greenhouse runs warm, you may extend the period by a month or so on either side.

The plant needs soil low in nitrogen or it will favor production of leaves over flowering and producing fruits. You can grow the tomatillo in a tomato cage or just let it sprawl on a bed. It can also be grown in a pot. Each plant needs 2 to 5 square feet (0.2 to 0.46 sq. m) for good production. In smaller pots, the plants will be correspondingly smaller but will still produce. They need full sun and a warm spot to grow healthy.

Regularly tap or gently shake the blossoms that form to encourage the setting on of the fruit. You can tell that the fruits are ripe when the husk just begins to yellow, but if you are impatient you can harvest the little fruits at any stage you find something to pick. It is best, however, to let the fruit fill out the husk first. Blend the fruits with a bit of cilantro, chives, or onions and some chilis (fresh or dried), and you'll have a great salsa for dipping.

When it comes to pests and diseases, the tomatillo suffers from many of the same problems as its cousin, the tomato.

Tomatoes

Tomatoes are one of the most popular greenhouse crops, but they can also be among the more difficult to grow. This is primarily due to pests (see Chapter 10, "When Things Go Wrong"), diseases (see "Common Greenhouse Tomato Disorders," page 298), and their need for consistent warm temperatures. However, with some care and planning you can harvest abundant crops of tomatoes in your home greenhouse.

Like many annual fruiting crops, the tomato prefers to be grown at temperatures between 65°F and 85°F (18°C and 30°C). Growth slows and fruits stop setting when temperatures are below 50°F (10°C) and above 95°F (35°C). Tomatoes will live when the temperature gets near the freezing mark, but the plant won't grow and its developing fruits may look sickly because of stress. Tomatoes grow best when the days are longer and when placed in full sunlight or the brightest spot available. Given these constraints, you may find that growing greenhouse tomatoes in the middle of winter may not be as productive as in the other three seasons. So, if you live in a cloudy winter climate and have a cooler greenhouse, you may want to save yourself the trouble and wasted space of a winter-greenhouse tomato crop.

If you have your heart set on growing crops in the dead of winter, you need to be sure that your night temperature never drops below 50°F (10°C), so you'll probably need a good reliable heater. If you live where the winters are cloudy, you'll probably need some supplemental lighting (see Chapter 1). Most people who don't have the added winter heat or the light simply grow tomatoes from late February through October. Hey, three seasons are better than one and that's a big improvement over growing them solely in the summer months!

Homegrown tomatoes in the off-season are a great luxury, as much of the year the tomatoes sold in the grocery store are low in quality, poor in taste, and high in cost. One of the most common mistakes greenhouse growers make is trying to grow their favorite outside garden tomato variety in the greenhouse. Selecting for a greenhouse crop requires seeking out a variety that meets some special criteria. Unfortunately, the outside ones often don't fit the bill.

One of the main things to do when selecting a tomato variety for the greenhouse environment is to focus on varieties that are either highly disease resistant (because tomato diseases often prosper in a greenhouse) or that have been developed specifically for the greenhouse. These will give you better tomato yields and fewer problems with pests and diseases. In the end, you will have the most important result: vine-ripened high-quality tomatoes.

There is such a wide range of characteristics in the many tomato varieties that choosing the best ones can, at first glance, be confusing. Selecting the right variety is one of the most important decisions you can make, and only rarely will your favorite outside variety work, unless you test it against some other tomato varieties that have been selected with the greenhouse environment in mind. Let's look at what is out there. First, tomatoes are split into two major categories: bush and vining types. The bush varieties are commonly known as "determinate" and the vining types as "indeterminate."

The **indeterminate tomato** has a growing tip that's capable of growing indefinitely. The **determinate tomato**, on the other hand, will eventually produce a flower cluster that tops off the growing point, producing a low, bushy habit. The determinate tomato was developed mainly for use on large acreage with mechanical harvesting and for home gardeners who have limited space and want more manageable plants and early production. In the greenhouse, the bush tomato is best utilized for growing in pots or other containers that have a limited root space.

Vining or indeterminate tomatoes are best for growing in beds, where the roots have plenty of room to roam, as the plants can get very large. When you grow the vining/indeterminate tomatoes, you can train them up strings or stakes and get them to grow vertically. This enables you to get a high total yield as

Indeterminate tomato plants can be trained to grow up a string.

compared to bush tomatoes or vining tomatoes that must sprawl on the ground. You can grow the vining tomatoes in larger pots, meaning 5 gallons (19 liters) on up. For smaller pots, always try to stick to the bushy types. Almost all of the tomatoes bred and sold as "greenhouse tomatoes" are the vining indeterminate types.

Besides being able to select tomatoes that are vining or bushy, you can also find varieties that have been bred for tolerance to varying temperatures, resistance to cracking, specific fruit size, earliness, coloring, growing in small pots, and disease tolerance.

For a good selection of greenhouse and highly disease-resistant varieties, check these catalogs: Stokes Seeds (800-396-9238, www.stokeseeds.com), Totally Tomatoes (803-663-0016), and the Tomato Growers Supply Company (888-478-7333).

Some indeterminate greenhouse tomato varieties that I've had good luck with include Cabernet, from Tomato Growers Supply, and Trust, available from Stokes, as well as Caruso and Boa. There are many more worth investigating. Early Cascade (commonly available), though not developed for the greenhouse, is extra early, indeterminate, and somewhat disease resistant (it is also a good outside producer in short-season areas).

If you want to test the ability of your greenhouse or sunspace to produce winter tomatoes with less than ideal conditions, stick to varieties that are early, cold tolerant, and, where possible, disease resistant. Often they are sparse-growing, low-yielding bush types, but at least they'll kick out an occasional fruit. Some suggestions include Siberia, Polar Beauty, Glacier, Subarctic Maxi, and Oregon Spring.

If you want to grow small or cherry tomatoes in small pots, try Toy Boy, Totem, Florida Basket, Patio, Whippersnapper, and Red Robin. For larger tomatoes in 2- to 5-gallon (7.6- to 19-liter) pots, try the above-mentioned cold-tolerant types or Prairie Fire and Super Chief. For a tall, vining type of cherry tomato, try Sweet 100 or Sweet Million.

As you read the descriptions of available tomato varieties, you will notice many are listed with varying types of disease resistance or tolerance. In order to select a variety with resistance to a particular disease problem that you experience, first get a positive identification of the disease. You may need some help from a university that has a plant pathology department or from your local county agricultural agent.

When you go to the catalogs, you will often see abbreviations denoting various types of disease resistance, such as "V" for verticillium resistance or "T" for resistance to tobacco mosaic leaf virus. Be sure to read the catalog key so you understand the use of abbreviations on disease resistance.

After you have selected your variety and received your seed, you are ready to get growing. Before you even touch the seed, you should know that if you are a user of tobacco, you should be sure to wash your hands well before handling tomato leaves, stems, or seeds to prevent the spread of the tobacco mosaic leaf virus.

Tomato seed generally germinates quite easily, and it comes up in only a matter of days, as long as the temperature is 70°F to 75°F (21°C to 24°C). Cooler temperatures will slow the speed of germination. Be sure to move the seedlings to full light as soon as they emerge to prevent their elongating. Don't sow any thicker than 1 seed every inch. As soon as they get their fourth or fifth leaf (including the cotyledon leaves), they are ready for transplanting into larger containers or beds.

Some growers have found that tomato seedlings that were exposed to a cool treatment resulted in up to a 25 percent increase in yields. This, however, requires that you have excellent control over the temperature. Here is how it is done: Wait until the first true tomato leaves emerge. The first "leaves" are not considered true leaves, as they are the cotyledons that were part of the seed and nourish the plant. They don't look much like a real tomato leaf. The first real leaves appear after the cotyledon leaves and have veins. When you see these leaves emerge, reduce the air temperature to around 52 to 56°F (11° to 13°C) for 10 days (if sunny) or up to 3 weeks (if cloudy). This requires that you keep close tabs on your thermometer and that you have a perfect slightly cool spot to pull this off. If you can, the reward is worth it.

Whether you use the cold treatment or not, keep an eye on the seedlings because, as they become full-fledged plants, you can cut back on the amount of water you give them. Tomatoes like the soil to dry out somewhat between waterings but it should not be so dry as to cause wilting. Water at regular intervals, as irregular watering will promote the affliction called blossom-end rot, discussed later.

Space each tomato plant at least 2 feet (0.6 m) apart, unless it is a very small plant such as the more dwarf and patio varieties. Tight spacing can increase the incidence of disease. In areas of many cloudy days, it might help to space the plants even wider, to provide optimum light penetration. I've found that tomatoes receive the most light when rows are planted north–south.

Tomatoes do best in a well-drained soil with plenty of decomposed organic matter. It is important to keep phosphorus levels high, especially for fruit and flower formation. Try to use fertilizers that have a fair amount of phosphorus in comparison to the nitrogen content. Never use a fertilizer that has a higher percentage of nitrogen than phosphorous. Try adding a bit of commercially available bulb food. Bonemeal is slow to release its phosphorus but does contain calcium, which also helps prevent the tomato disorder called blossom-end rot, discussed below. Bonemeal is not a good choice if you have alkaline soil.

Rather than shooting in the dark (as most gardeners do), there is a way to determine exactly what your soil is lacking: Do a soil test. This is a great way to prevent overfertilization of your tomatoes (Note: I assume overfertilization because I rarely see a greenhouse plant that is underfertilized). This is important, because when they are overfertilized with nitrogen tomatoes produce big, luxuriant leafy plants but few fruits.

Tomatoes are also sensitive to a buildup of soluble salts, which occurs when there is too much fertilizer in the soil. Try to avoid chemical fertilizers that contain chlorine, and sodium, as well as high amounts of manure. Look for the tips of the leaves turning brown when this occurs.

When tomatoes start to flower, they will need to be pollinated. Fortunately, this is an easy chore and is done by lightly tapping the yellow blossoms in the morning with a pencil or length of $1/2$-inch (1.3-cm) dowel cut 1 to 3 feet (0.3 or 0.9 m) long for easy reaching. If you can't do it every morning, every other morning will work fine.

Pruning is always controversial. Let's try to clear up any questions here. Never prune bushy, determinate varieties of tomatoes in a greenhouse. They are not good candidates for training or pruning and are best grown in traditional tomato cages if they start to sprawl.

COMMON GREENHOUSE TOMATO DISORDERS

Blossom-End Rot

Description: First, water-soaked spots appear at the blossom end (bottom) of the fruit. Later, the spots increase in size and become sunken, flat, brown, and leathery round areas.

Cause: Environmental. Resulting from moisture stress, irregular watering, or low calcium levels in the soil. Vertical training intensifies the symptoms.

Control: Water regularly, never allow the plants to wilt, but take care not to overwater. Try mulching the soil. Use bonemeal or 1 cup milk for extra calcium in the soil. Spray a 1 percent solution of calcium chloride on the leaves for immediate results. Some varieties have some resistance. Noninfectious.

Catfacing

Description: Indicated by deformed marks or lines on the fruit. Also may cause odd-shaped fruit.

Cause: Insect damage, growth disturbances, and, most commonly, cold temperatures.

Control: Provide even growing conditions. Prevent temperatures near freezing. Some varieties have some resistance. Noninfectious.

Early Blight *(Alternaria)*

Description: Tan-colored spots appear on the leaves and sometimes occur on the stems. Spots enlarge to $\frac{1}{2}$ inch (1.3 cm) or more. Close inspection shows concentric rings inside of the spots. Whole leaves may yellow and defoliate. The fruit may also show dark brown spots. This disease is among the more common in a greenhouse.

Cause: Fungus.

Control: Try to reduce humidity and avoid water on the leaves. Rotate crop to new spot next time. Control insects, which may spread the problem. Use tolerant or resistant varieties.

Fruit Cracking

Description: Cracks in the skin of the tomato fruit.

Cause: Widely fluctuating temperatures.

Control: Maintain foliage covering fruits to avoid direct sun on the fruit's skin. Moderate temperatures. Many varieties are resistant. Noninfectious.

Fusarium Wilt *(Fusarium)*

Description: Usually, at first all leaves on one side of the stem become yellow and wilt. Later, all leaves wilt and die. There are two main races of the disease, fusarium 1 and fusarium 2.

Cause: Fungus.

Control: Best control is to plant resistant varieties and promote healthy soil with a good level of organic matter.

Gray Mold *(Botrytis)*

Description: Fruits rotting during and after harvest. Some rot may form on the stems.

Cause: Fungus.

Control: Promote good air circulation. Lower humidity, raise temperature slightly, remove all infected stems or fruits. Keep the area and soil surface around the base of the tomatoes free of debris.

(Continued on next page)

Gray Wall

Description: Gray-brown streaks on fruit; blotchy ripening. Look for light-green or clear blotches on green fruit. As the tomato ripens, these patches turn yellow and the fruit doesn't ripen evenly.

Cause: Low light intensities, low temperatures, high nitrogen levels, low potassium levels, and high soil-moisture levels. Sometimes caused by a mosaic virus.

Control: Keep soil potassium level high. Try to increase the light and raise the temperature above 60°F (15°C). Use resistant varieties. Usually noninfectious.

Leaf Mold *(Cladosporium)*

Description: Whitish spots on upper surface of older leaves. The spots may enlarge and turn yellow. The underside gets a velvet, olive-brown coating. Spores of this fungus are spread by air and water and more rarely may be carried on the seed.

Cause: Fungus.

Control: Improve air circulation. Lower humidity. Grow resistant varieties, including Floradel, Marion, Marglobe, Globelle, Vetamold, and Tuckcross.

Tobacco Mosaic Virus *(Marmor tabaci)*

Description: (1) If plants are infected when young: Stunted, with light-green and dark-green angular mottled leaves in a mosaic pattern. Few blossoms set. Yield is reduced. What few fruits do set are often of poor quality. (2) If plants are infected during or after blooming: Leaves have light-green and dark-green mottled areas. A yellow, nettinglike appearance may occur. Uneven fruit ripening, sometimes having yellow streaks appearing on the fruit.

Cause: Virus. Lives in leaves of plants of the family *Solanaceae,* including tobacco, tomato, pepper, eggplant, petunia, and salpiglossis.

Control: Avoid use of tobacco in any form while handling tomato plants. Don't allow any smoking in your greenhouse. Don't let strangers touch your tomato plants. Wash your hands before handling tomato plants or seeds. Wash after touching infected plants. Pull up badly infected plants. Control insects. Prune infected plants last. Clean your pruning knife with disinfectant between cuts on suspected plants. Pour milk into the soil of a suspected infection area (try to use milk that would otherwise be discarded, if possible). There are some reports that milk actually deactivates the virus. If this disease becomes a common problem, grow only those varieties listed as having resistance or tolerance. The disease is often mentioned in catalogs using its acronym "TMV" or simply "T."

Verticillium *(Verticillium)*

Description: Yellowing of older, lower leaves, which later turn brown and die. Wilting of the tips of plants during the day; may recover at night. Defoliation is common. Branches droop. Leaves are dull in appearance and fruits are small. Brownish, discolored look to the interior of the stem when cut in half.

Cause: Fungus.

Control: Best control is to plant resistant varieties, use healthy soil with a good level of organic matter, and to rotate crops.

Prune the "suckers" that form at the crotches of vining (indeterminate) tomatoes.

To best utilize greenhouse space, grow indeterminate/vining varieties in a vertical fashion by pruning and training the plants upward. To properly prune for this type of growing, you need to locate the tomato plant's side shoots (usually called suckers). They can be found growing immediately above where each leaf stem (petiole) is attached to the main stem. They grow at almost every crotch where a leaf emerges on the stem. If a sucker is not pruned early, it may quickly enlarge. Soon it will be hard to distinguish the sucker stem from the main stem. For this reason, begin pruning as soon as the first side shoots appear, and do it at least every 5 days.

After plants are 8 to 10 feet (2.4 to 3 m) tall, prune out the top 5 inches (13 cm) of the leader (the highest tip of the main stem) when it touches the ceiling or when it is getting too high to reach. Tip pruning will hasten the development of the existing fruits. If it seems that you have more than one leader, it is an indication that a sucker got away from you. As a result, it may be hard to determine

which is the main stem. It doesn't really matter—you can tipprune all of the tips. This is best done before the plants reach the ceiling or a month before you anticipate pulling up the plants.

You can decide to grow more than one main stem for production, as many people prefer to grow tomatoes into a V-shape by allowing one sucker to become a second "main stem." These two stems then will form the "V." To do this, follow the above procedure when it comes to growing and pruning indeterminate tomato plants, but let one sucker survive, pruning at about the 1-foot (0.3-meter) height. Let this sucker grow on to become the second main stem. As this second stem grows, keep it pruned as you did in the single-stem method. Space plants at about 3 feet (0.9 m) apart, using this two-stem V system. Always keep a keen eye out for any plants that are looking even slightly stunted or possibly contracting a disease. Always prune any plants suspected of disease last. You don't want to spread the disease with your fingers or knife to the healthy ones. If any plant starts to look severely stunted, be ruthless and pull the whole plant up.

If you are like me, you might (accidentally) let more than two main stems get growing and you won't be able to bear to prune them out, as they get big fast. What to do? The organized single-stem or V system starts to look a bit like an octopus system. Still, if you have the air space, it can work, especially if you do a good job of tying the plants up. But try to tie every stem up into the air. If you can't give each stem decent space, you just have to prune that shoot out.

As your vertical-growing, trained, pruned, indeterminate tomato plants grow, you will soon need to plan and install a support system. The easiest system is to simply suspend a long length of twine from the ceiling to the ground, directly above each plant. Use a length of twine for each stem you are allowing to grow. Tie one end of the twine to a well-anchored stake in the ground or to the base of the tomato. If you tie it to the tomato, don't use any sort of slipknot (or knot that slips tight when pulled), as it may strangle the stem. See a local boy scout, sailor, or knot book for help. Tie the other end to a part of the ceiling or a rafter or even attach it to a screw in the structure. Leave about 6 inches (15 cm) of slack on the twine. As the plants grow, gently spiral each stem around one length of string. As they get taller, they will eventually take up all of the slack. Although it may sound as though the plant doesn't have much to hold onto, this method holds the plant up remarkably well.

You can also support the vining plants on a tall stake pounded firmly into the ground or tub, such as a sturdy straight two-by-two timber that is at least 6 to 8 feet (1.8 to 2.4 m) tall. Don't use flimsy bamboo on tall plants; it is apt to fall over. As the plant grows, tie the stem to the pole with a soft strip of cloth. Tying it too tight may strangle the plant, so keep it on the loose side. I prefer using the earlier-described twine method, as it is simpler once it is set up and setting it up is easier than using stakes.

Some growers swear by the idea of pruning off leaves when growing tomatoes. In general, I don't recommend removing the leaves covering the fruits. They prevent the sun from heating the fruit, which may cause cracking. However, having good ventilation at the base of larger plants is important in preventing tomato diseases, and sometimes it may help to prune some of the lower leaves of tall tomato plants to get better air circulation under and through the plant.

Whenever you get the urge to prune, less is always better, and when in doubt, don't. I say this because it is easy to get carried away with pruning, and if you cut too much, you might be removing too many leaves, which are the food factory that helps to nurture fruit production. Sometimes when you have a hammer in your hand *everything* looks like a nail. Same with pruning shears.

Tomatoes are also very susceptible to insect attacks. The most notable suspect is the whitefly (see Chapter 10). Keep an eye out, especially on the undersides of the leaves, for early indications of critters to give yourself a head start in controlling them.

Because most people like to grow at least a few tomatoes in their sunspace or greenhouse, everyone is likely to experience at least one type of disease sooner or later (preferably later). For this reason, I have listed some common greenhouse tomato disorders to help you in trying to diagnose a particular problem. All diseases are infectious unless otherwise noted. For more discussion of plant diseases, see the "Diseases" section in Chapter 10.

Turnip

Turnips are an easy crop to grow in a greenhouse or sunspace. I have even seen them grown in a hanging basket. It was probably the ugliest hanging basket I've ever seen, but it did yield 3 large turnips in a 6-inch (15-cm) basket. They are also very easy to grow in the outside garden and keep nicely in a root cellar. Still, it is a treat to have a fresh turnip in the dead of winter. Being a root crop, turnips tend to grow best in the fall, winter, and early spring in the greenhouse or sunspace. You can even eat the turnip greens, cooked as you would cabbage or spinach. There are varieties of turnips that have been bred to just produce greens.

Grow turnips like radishes, only give them more space. They need a minimum of 4 to 6 inches (10 to 15 cm) per plant; however, I have seen them tolerate tighter spacing with good light intensity. The seed germinates fast, so it is best to seed directly into the bed or pot rather than transplanting. Because both the tops and roots are edible and it is a fast-growing plant, the turnip is an efficient food producer in terms of time and space in the greenhouse or sunspace.

Watermelon

Growing watermelons in the greenhouse uses many of the same techniques described for cantaloupe. In comparison, cantaloupes yield more and are easier to grow because of their smaller size. Watermelons need a night temperature well above 50°F (10°C). The two required ingredients for growing watermelons are plenty of room and a warm greenhouse. Watermelons will sprawl fast if given the hot temperatures they prefer. Like cantaloupes, watermelons can be trellised and require hand-pollination in order to get fruit development. With the weight and size of a watermelon, the large fruit can easily pull the vine off the trellis unless you have engineered a sturdy trellis and a sling to hold the developing fruit. One way to prevent the disaster posed by the development of a large fruit is to grow the smaller "icebox" varieties. Unfortunately, the vines of the icebox types still need a lot of room to roam.

If I haven't discouraged you from planting watermelon, here are more specifics for getting a good crop. If you plan to transplant them, use a peat pot because they don't transplant very well. Plan to provide each plant a minimum of 12 square feet (1 sq. m) or more. While plants are young, you can interplant with carrots, kohlrabi, lettuce, or chard. But as soon as watermelons start vining, they will need all of their allotted space. Watermelons like a well-drained, sandy soil, high in decomposed organic matter. They also need to grow in full sun.

One of the hardest things about growing watermelons is knowing when they're ripe, especially if you are not used to growing them. You can read all the garden books, talk to the old experts, thump the watermelon, look for when the tendrils turn brown near the fruit, count the days, and so forth, and you can still pick it too early or too late. I've concluded that knowing when a watermelon is ripe is a God-given gift reserved for a chosen few. If you grow the smaller icebox watermelons, they will produce more fruits per vine, which gives the unblessed grower a better chance in the ripening lottery.

HERBS

Although herbs are often considered exotic, don't be fooled. For the most part, herbs are among the easiest greenhouse plants you can grow. Herbs can provide teas, medicines, tonics for natural health, home remedies, and, best of all, fresh flavorings for cooking and salads. Herbs can be made into pest repellents and insecticides, and they have beneficial effects when interplanted with food crops. Most of us know that food tastes better when cooked with selected herbs. Growing herbs year-round is another luxury of having a greenhouse or sunspace. It will provide you with an opportunity to learn more about the many amazing properties of herbs.

Because there are already so many fine books on herbs, I won't go very deeply into every potential herb plant that you can grow. There are, however, some special considerations when growing herbs in a greenhouse.

For instance, because extremely cold winter temperatures are lacking inside the greenhouse, there will be some perennial herbs native to temperate zones that will never grow very well. This is because they need the cyclic cold treatment that winter provides. Without the winter, they lose their natural rhythm and flounder. Hey, the tropics aren't for every plant!

If you have a greenhouse that runs quite cool in winter, you may have the opposite problem when trying to grow some of the tender annual herbs, such as basil, that require consistent warm temperatures.

People, and especially children, are pleasantly impressed when you take them on a smell tour of your herb plants. I regularly give tours to young children and often get consistent answers to their impressions on the "odor" certain herbs give off. When they smell the mint, they often say it smells "like toothpaste"; when they smell the dill, they say it must be a pickle plant; fennel must be the black licorice plant!

One of the best uses of your greenhouse-grown herbs is to pick fresh herbs for special family dinners. You can even follow it with some fresh herbal tea. But when it comes to growing and using medicinal herbs, use extreme caution. They can and many do have very powerful properties. Consider consulting your doctor prior to using any medications, whether they are pills or plants you grow.

Besides the information in the many good books available, there is much to be learned from the many wonderful herb catalogs. My favorite ones is Richters Herb Catalogue of Canada (905-640-6677, or **www.richters. com**), which is by far one of the most extensive of all herb catalogs, and it also has great plant descriptions. Well Sweep Farm (908-852-5390) carries a wide variety of medicinal and culinary herb plants and seeds. Nichols Garden Nursery (541-928-9280, or **www. gardennursery.com**) carries a lesser but good selection of herb seeds and plants.

If you have ever purchased fresh-leaf herbs in the grocery, you know how very expensive they can be. With a greenhouse, you can produce all the herbs you need at a fraction of that cost. Many home growers have even found an added source of income by selling fresh herbs to local restaurants.

HERB CULTIVATION

If you plan to grow herbs through the winter, most of them are best started the previous spring. That will give the plants time to produce a well-developed root system, promoting more productivity during the winter months. Herbs that are started in the fall and winter grow slowly, taking a long time to produce any harvest. It is more difficult to get the seeds to germinate and get seedlings established in winter. When it comes to placement in ground beds, always try to locate them in an area that will not be disturbed during seasonal replantings, as most herbs will grow for many years in the greenhouse.

PROCESSING AND USING HERBS

Herbs may be processed in a number of ways, including drying and freezing. Many of the books on herbs explain this in depth. If you

Give your salad some real flavor by adding herbs!

decide to dry your herbs, avoid drying in the greenhouse, as the humidity levels are too high and may even cause the growth of dangerous molds on the leaves. Always dry herbs in a place with low humidity.

Using fresh herbs is a real treat. Many people have never had this opportunity and are familiar only with dried herbs. When using fresh herbs for cooking or making teas, bruise or crush them to bring out their full flavor. It takes 4 parts fresh herbs to equal 1 part dried herbs when cooking or making teas.

You will find that I list many herbs below as suitable for eating fresh in salads. Since my love affair with greenhouse gardening began, my salads have never been the same. A common dinner salad found at a restaurant (or on many dinner tables) has got to be the most boring dish ever devised. To spice things up, we often douse the salad with dressing. Instead, try some fresh herb leaves and edible herb flowers cut into a salad. It makes the salad much more exciting, colorful, and tasty. Now we're talking a real dish! It will also be more nutritious. You will probably find that the salad needs little, if any, salad dressing.

Try a salad with some French sorrel (listed in the "Fruits and Vegetables" section), orange mint, nasturtium flowers, chives, lemon balm, tarragon, root beer plant, fennel, basil, borage flowers, oregano, mint, dill greens, anise hyssop, sage flowers, or other herbs. This is a real salad—with real flavor!

The following is a list of herbs that do well in a greenhouse or a sunspace, along with tips and comments on their cultivation. There are thousands of herbs, and I list only the common ones or those that are particularly interesting. With so much potential for pioneering with herbs in a greenhouse, look in some catalogs specializing in herbs and you'll be sure to make some discoveries.

Anise

Anise is an annual herb with an aroma similar to that of licorice. Anise overwinters well in the greenhouse if started in spring. Transplant seedlings with care, as the plant does not like to be moved.

Avoid excess nitrogen fertilization, as it may inhibit or delay seed production. Each plant requires about 1 square foot (0.09 sq. m) of space. Anise can also be grown in 6-inch (15-cm) pots and may need to be up-potted after 9 months or so.

You can pick fresh leaves for flavoring anytime the plant can spare a few. For anise seeds, cut the flower heads when the seeds are hardened and well formed. Lay the seeds on a paper towel to dry in an airy, dark location. When well dried, rub the seeds off of the stalk by hand and sift the seeds from the stalk pieces. Store the seeds in an airtight jar.

Outside, anise needs a long season to mature; inside your greenhouse, it will thrive and mature year-round.

Anise Hyssop

This plant is in the mint family, as are many herbs. Although it is not aggressive like many mints, it can easily reseed itself. Anise hyssop, with its sweet and wonderfully unique flavor, is among my favorite culinary herbs. I love to add these leaves to salads, and they are great when made into a tea. It is also known as licorice mint; its scientific name is Agastache foeniculum.

It is easily started from seeds or cuttings and grows best in a bright spot. It produces blue flower stalks upon maturity that is also edible or can be used in bouquets. Depending upon the variety, anise hyssop grows from 1 to 4 feet (0.3 to 1.2 m) in height. I have found that the shorter varieties have a sweeter flavor than the taller ones. Anise hyssop needs a bright spot to grow but can tolerate a bit of shade.

Mites may frequent the plant, so keep an eye out for these invaders. I have yet to find someone who doesn't like the flavor of the raw leaf after they take that risky first bite. Give it a try!

Basil

Basil is a heat lover and for that reason is one plant that is hard to overwinter in cooler winter greenhouses, especially if your winter temperatures fall below 45°F (7°C). As the greenhouse warms up, basil is well worth planting, as it can produce leaves from spring through fall. Basil is always great with fresh tomatoes.

Always provide basil with a rich soil and a warm bright spot. It will want to flower after it has grown a couple of months, but the flowers rob the plant of its ability to produce the culinary leaves. When possible, keep the flowers pruned. Basil is easily propagated from seed. According to an old tradition, you should curse the seeds as you plant them. I've found it's best to do my planting and cursing after paying bills. It is great therapy.

For years I grew basil but noticed that it would consistently wilt just prior to my harvesting it. I couldn't figure out what was going on until I did a bit of research. The wilting problem was due to a fungus disease called *Fusarium oxysporum.* It causes sudden wilting of the leaves, and you will also see brown streaks that develop on the stems. The disease can live in basil-plant debris in the soil or can be spread through the seed. Some believe that much of the world's basil seed supplies are now contaminated with the *fusarium* disease. Once your plant starts to succumb to the disease, there is no cure. I have found that transplanted basil seems more susceptible than plants that arise from a direct sowing in a pot or ground bed. If you see these wilting symptoms, remove the infected plants immediately and avoid contact with any healthy plants when handling diseased foliage.

Fortunately, a few catalogs carry some seed free of *fusarium* disease. These include Richters Herb Catalogue, which has varieties called Special Select FT™ and Compattio FT™. Richters also carries a variety called Nufar that has built-in resistance to the *fusarium* wilt. Johnny's Selected Seeds catalog carries 4 varieties that are noted by having a "FTO" sign that

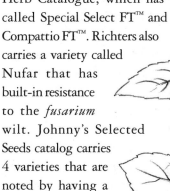

stands for "*fusarium* wilt-tested" seeds. Growing these will prevent any initial infection.

There are many other varieties to choose from. For culinary purposes, always grow the larger-leafed varieties rather than the globe or bush basils. There are also many other offbeat varieties of basil that sport different scents and flavors such as cinnamon, lemon, camphor, and more. There are also the opal-leaf or purple-leaf types. However, I prefer the more traditional "sweet" flavored basil.

If you have a greenhouse that runs cool in winter and want to have some fresh winter basil flavors, consider growing African basil. It is the most cold-tolerant of the basils. The only drawback is a slight camphor flavor that is mixed in with the more traditional basil aroma in the leaf. Still, it is not bad when used as a winter substitute.

Throw basil into Italian dishes or toss a bit into a fresh salad for a spicy, sweet taste. Look in a recipe book for instructions on how to make pesto, which is great on pasta or other foods for a quick and tasty meal. You don't even need a recipe to enjoy basil: Simply dice it up and serve with some chopped, vine-ripened tomatoes. Ahhh!

Bay Laurel

The bay leaf is a must for spaghetti sauces and soups and is an important herb in French cuisine. Having a fresh leaf is a real treat. Bay is an aromatic evergreen tree or shrub and is very slow growing in the greenhouse. One plant will live many years, and one plant is all you probably need. It can be easily grown in either pots or beds and requires no special care as long as you don't overfertilize it. Both scale and mealybugs can occasionally plague bay, so keep a close eye out for them. If after many years the plant gets too big, all you have to do is prune it to the size you want, as it takes well to shaping. Dry your pruned leaves for future meals. Generally, bay is acquired from catalogs but can easily be propagated from cuttings taken from the tips of the branches.

Borage

Borage grows larger than many herbs, so be sure to provide it with 2 to 3 square feet (0.2 to 0.3 sq. m) of space per plant. It will also get up to 3 feet (0.9 m) high, even in winter. If you grow it in a pot, make sure the pot is at least 1 gallon (3.8 liter) in size. Borage can tolerate some shading but grows best in well-lit areas. It has large, rough, hairy leaves and dainty blue flowers that can fade to pink. Many people like to grow it solely for the look of the flowers, as an ornamental. It is easily started from seed.

Borage grows well in the greenhouse year-round and can occasionally reseed itself in an adjacent area. Its flowers have a sweet cucumber flavor and, when eaten, are said to make you happier with life. The leaves are often made into teas to give a cooling effect and are reputed to provide some relief from congestion and coughing.

Catnip

Catnip is also known as **catmint** or by its scientific name, *Nepeta cataria*. It is in the mint family, as indicated by the square shape of the stems, and is a perennial. It can be propagated from divisions or cuttings or started from seed, and it can be grown with ease in either pots or beds. Keep an eye out for mites, which seem to like catnip as much as cats do.

Catnip gets its name because of the odd effect that it has on cats. Despite years of research in botany, neurophysiology, and chemistry, scientists still don't understand why cats are affected by catnip. Some speculate that chemicals in catnip cause cats to hallucinate, whereas others suspect that the chemicals in the plant mimic certain social odors to which cats respond. These odors, if this theory were true, would be triggering territorial or sexual behavior. Regardless of the deliberation by scientists as to why cats start licking, chewing, and rolling around in catnip, the phenomenon can pose a problem to greenhouse gardeners if they choose to grow catnip.

By the way, catnip is not alone in its ability to induce such symptoms in your cat. Other nonrelated plants, such as valerian, baby blue-eyes, and some species of viburnums, have been noted to cause the same symptoms.

There are also some species of catnip that don't seem to affect cats. If your cat is not affected by any type of catnip, then your puddy tat is part of the one-third of all domestic cats that don't react to catnip. Those pet owners who have a catnip-immune cat don't have to worry about a feline-made mess in the indoor herb garden. If you do have a catnip-sensitive feline, you may want to exclude catnip plants in your greenhouse. There are those humans who delight in watching a poor pussy have an out-of-body experience. Just don't get too cruel. Besides, your cat never spikes your breakfast cereal, so go easy. Most veterinarians I've talked to say that occasional exposure to catnip is not harmful to your cat. Just be sure to use a little moderation.

Catnip has been valued in history for its medicinal effects on humans. It is reputed to bring down fevers. Unlike its effect on cats, catnip tea is also said to relax and to decrease nervousness, unless you have a feline nature.

Chamomile

Chamomile is a low-growing plant treasured for the little yellow-centered, white-petaled, daisylike flowers it produces. It forms a ground cover that reaches only 3 to 4 inches (8 to 10 cm) high. It is easy to start from seed and needs to grow in a sunny spot in well-drained soil. The seeds are tiny, so lightly cover them with peat moss to ensure germination. Transplant the seedlings when they are 1 inch (2.5 cm) tall. A plant takes up about 1 square foot (0.09 sq. m) of space when it is mature. It can grow year-round in the greenhouse or sunspace.

To harvest, cut the flower heads and crush them for fresh tea, or you can dry them for later use. Watch out for aphids; they can easily camouflage themselves in the leaves. A cup of chamomile tea is said to help bring sound sleep and calm the stomach. Chamomile tea is quite tasty and worth drinking for absolutely no reason at all.

Chives

See listing under "Fruits and Vegetables."

Coriander / Cilantro

Coriander is also known as **cilantro** in the Hispanic culture. Coriander refers to the seed of the plant, and cilantro refers solely to the young leaves. Because I love Mexican food, you can usually find it in my greenhouse. I believe that a good hot salsa must contain some chopped cilantro. Cilantro is also common in Chinese cooking. I have found that most people new to the flavor of cilantro do not like the smell of the leaves. One Hispanic friend told me that he had never met an Anglo who liked the smell of cilantro the first time. But please, don't pass judgment on smell alone. Let your taste buds weigh in after you have tasted it in a dish or as a seasoning in salsa. Many minds have been changed after tasting cilantro.

Cilantro is easily grown from seed, but the plant is not productive for very long, especially in the summer, when it quickly goes to seed. If you are growing it for the leaf, you will notice that the young leaves start off without any serration, but become finely divided as the plant matures; that is a sign that the plant will soon flower.

Because cilantro/coriander goes to seed rapidly in warm conditions, you may want to plan to sow a few seeds every 5 or 6 weeks for a continual supply. Nichols Garden Nursery and Johnny's Selected Seeds offer slow-bolting (slow to go to seed) varieties, which will give you a longer period of producing lush tasty leaves. The leaves of cilantro lose most of their flavor when dried or heated. Freezing them does retain much of the flavor. That is why it is great to have fresh-picked cilantro leaves on hand.

There are some other plants that produce the cilantro/coriander flavors that are not true coriander/cilantro (*Coriandrum sativum*). One such substitute is Vietnamese coriander (*Polygonatum odoratum*). It is remarkably similar to true coriander/cilantro and is in the buckwheat family. It grows as a perennial in the greenhouse, saving you the trouble of constantly resowing the plant. Vietnamese coriander needs full sun and plenty of water. It is a hard plant to find but is available from Richters Herb Catalogue and Well Sweep Farm, both mentioned at the beginning of this section.

Another plant, called culantro (*Eryngium foetidum*), also has the flavor of true coriander. If you have a greenhouse that runs hot, this might be a good substitute, as it thrives in warm, steamy conditions. Culantro (note the spelling with a "u" rather than an "i") has tougher leaves and needs to be finely chopped when used as a culinary herb. Unlike cilantro, culantro can retain its flavor when dried.

Did you know that salsa now outsells the all-American catsup? The only trouble with even the best tasting store-bought salsa is that almost all of them lack any cilantro flavor even when it is an ingredient. This is because the flavor doesn't survive the heat of processing very well. Perhaps they should try some dried culantro in the recipe.

Dill

Dill is an annual that is ideal for the greenhouse or sunspace. It can be productive through both high and low temperatures and does fine in partial shade. Dill plants may reach heights of up to 6 feet (1.8 m) tall, but a shorter variety called Bouquet maintains a compact habit and would be a good choice for growing in pots.

Dill is easily started from seed and does fine in varying temperatures and conditions, but beware if you ever let a plant go to seed in the greenhouse! Because it is a prolific reseeder, you could end up with dill coming up everywhere in a very short time. Harvest the seed heads before they turn brown to save hours of weeding. Both the flowers and foliage are tasty and edible. I like to use fresh dill greens in salads, dips, and soups.

If you like more foliage than seeds, you might want to try the Dukat strain, available from both The Cook's Garden (800-457-9703, **www.cooksgarden.com**) and Shepherd's Garden Seeds (800-444-6910, or **www.shepherd seeds.com**). Dukat is known for producing abundant leaves and holding those leaves longer before going to seed. Chop up a few leaves and add to your salad!

Fennel

Except for its celerylike stalk, fennel greatly resembles dill. Upon close inspection, you'll also notice that it is a greener color than dill, which has a bluish tint to the leaves. This plant tastes like licorice. It's a perennial in the greenhouse and is easily started from seed. Fennel grows abundantly during all seasons in the greenhouse, and one plant can be productive for many years. It can tolerate partial shade and varying soil conditions. Because it can reach up to 6 feet (1.8 m) over time, it needs a large pot of at least 1 gallon (3.8 liter), unless you wish to grow it in a bed. The bronze variety has coppery-colored foliage and looks interesting against other ornamental plants.

The common Florence fennel produces a bulbous root that has a sweet flavor. Use it as you would use celery. The leaf of fennel is also edible and is good in salads or used as a garnish.

There are also some non-bulbing types of fennel for people whose main interest is the production of leaves and flowers. These are usually sold as sweet fennel.

My favorite part of the fennel plant is the small yellow flower, one of the tastiest edible flowers around. It has a sweet, candy-like licorice flavor and is great for munching fresh as you work in the greenhouse. It can also be used in salads, soups, and many other dishes. If you let the fennel plant go on to produce seeds, they are great in Italian dishes. Every greenhouse or sunspace should have at least one fennel plant.

Because fennel is a perennial in the greenhouse, it can live for many years. Still, it is a good idea to start new plants every 12 to 18 months. This is because older plants lose their vigor and become more susceptible to mealybugs and other problems. Older plants also grow more slowly.

Garlic

Garlic can be grown year-round and can tolerate a wide range of temperatures. It can be started from store-bought divided bulbs, but there are more interesting choices in catalogs that specialize in garlic. Plant the bulbs about 2 inches (5 cm) deep. Garlic does not take up much space, so if you like it, you can look forward to fresh garlic in the winter. It's a good natural food for

lowering blood pressure, not to mention its hundreds of other medicinal uses. One of the best sources for garlic is the catalog from Ronniger's Seed & Potato Company (800-846-6178).

Lavender

There are many types of lavender, but most can go under the classification of either English lavender *(Lavendula angustifolia)* or French lavender *(Lavendula dentata),* which is also called Spanish lavender. English lavender is an outdoor perennial in temperate climates and has narrow 1-inch (2.5-cm) leaves. English lavender has a problem growing in the greenhouse because it requires a winter cold treatment to grow properly. In the greenhouse, it seldom thrives, but it does survive.

A better choice for the greenhouse is French lavender. You'll know you have the French lavender because the leaf edge is scalloped, unlike the smooth edge found on the English lavender. The French lavender always outdoes the English and generally looks healthier. It blooms year-round and can grow to 2 feet (0.6 m) or more in height. It takes well to pruning if it gets too large. French lavender can be grown in pots or beds with equal success. It is hard to find a seed source, but I have found plants sold in catalogs regularly, especially if the catalog specializes in herbs.

The French lavender can grow for many years with little care, and you will find that it has a bloom almost every day of the year. It is also trouble-free when it comes to greenhouse pests.

If you get hold of an herb catalog with extensive listings, you will find many other types of lavender that you may wish to experiment with, as some will need winter cool temperatures more than others.

Lemon Balm

This hardy perennial is a relative of the mint family and is also known as **lemon mint**. It has wonderful lemon-flavored leaves. It can be started from seeds, cuttings, or division of a mature plant. Unlike mint, it is not aggressive and won't spread much. One plant will need about 1 square foot (0.09 sq. m) of space. Use lemon balm in iced tea or add a few sprigs to a salad.

Milk Thistle

What? Grow thistle in a greenhouse? Well, it does spur some conversation. This plant is a favorite of many herbal healers. The seeds of this plant have been reputed to greatly aid with problems of the liver. This is a striking plant with glossy leaves and angular white markings. It also has a handsome purple flower. It is easy to grow but is quite prickly. After flowering, the seeds can be removed from the dried flower and used either as food or as a medicinal herb. One plant can reach 3 feet (0.9 m) in height. One plant is probably all you need.

Mint

There are many varieties of mint. Some, but

not all, of these perennial plants can become aggressive and will appropriate large areas of ground if left to their own devices. For this reason, you should consider growing the more aggressive mints in a 1-gallon (3.8-liter) pot rather than in a bed. When potted, mint can easily get root bound and may need some root pruning and new soil every couple of years. Although mint can tolerate diverse soil, it seems to do best on the wet side, especially if you give it a well-drained soil. It can also tolerate diverse light and temperature conditions. It can be started from seeds, cuttings, and divisions from mature plants.

You will be amazed by all of the choices of different mints when you look in a catalog that carries a good selection. Let me list some of the choices: curly mint, with curly leaves; chocolate mint, reminiscent of the candy; spearmint, incredibly aromatic; chewing-gum mint, fragrance like bubble gum; and apple mint, a fuzzy leaf with a green-apple flavor. There is a mint called Corsican mint, which is not aggressive and is a delicate, low-growing plant. It forms a handsome carpet and thrives in moist, low-light conditions. The leaves look mosslike, very different from the traditional mint varieties.

Orange mint is also not overly aggressive. As you would guess, it has an orange flavor, but sometimes it even reminds me of basil. It is easy to grow in the greenhouse and needs the same culture as lemon balm or mint. Try it in teas or put a few sprigs in a salad.

Now you can have fresh mint for year-round mint juleps. Bring on the Kentucky Derby!

Oregano

There are many types of oregano, but it is easy to end up growing a variety that is disappointing if you expect a good pizza-flavoring spice. Many catalogs sell the less flavorful varieties of marjoram as oregano. To really get the good-flavored oregano, look for the scientific name *Origanum vulgare 'hirtum'* or in older nomenclature: *Origanum heracleoticum.* No matter what its scientific name, it is most commonly known as Greek oregano. This is the type that has the true oregano flavor most of us are used to on pizzas and in Italian cooking.

Oregano can be started from seed, and plants are often available from many catalogs. Oregano needs well-drained soil with a sunny location. It should be grown in 6- to 10-inch (15- to 25-cm) pots or in beds; one plant can grow for many years and is relatively easy to care for. The leaf can be used fresh or dried with good results.

A newcomer to the oregano family is one offered by Richters Herb Catalogue of Canada (905-640-6677, or **www.richters.com**). It is called Kaliteri, and it has a high oil content and correspondingly good flavor—wonderful for Italian dishes.

Parsley

Parsley is frequently put on plates to sweeten your breath at the end of a meal, but people seldom touch this nutritious leaf and often let it sit all lonesome on the plate. What a sin! Try eating it. It tastes good, really! It's great in salads and is chock-full of vitamins, especially A and C, and iron.

Parsley is a biennial and will often go to seed (ending its productive life) every spring or early summer. It is very productive, even in cooler greenhouses, during the winter if started before the end of September. Parsley can take up to 4 weeks to germinate. Soaking the seed overnight before planting will help it along. Warm soil temperatures in the middle of summer may slow the germination further. It does best in sunny locations but will tolerate a bit of shade. You can transplant parsley grown in the outside garden in fall, but you have to make a real effort to get the long, carrotlike taproot.

There are two primary types of parsley: the curled-leaf and the flat Italian parsley. Both do fine in the greenhouse, but I've found it easier to get people to try eating the curled-leaf parsley. If older leaves turn yellow, the plant may need some extra fertilizing.

Many people, including me, have a slight allergic reaction if they consume parsley that is in the process of elongating and going to seed (instead of growing in a more traditional mound). When you see it going to seed, it is time to pull it up and donate it to the compost pile, anyway.

Curled-leaf parsley has a bonsai-like globe shape after it gets a good collection of leaves and is quite ornamental anywhere in the greenhouse. Because of its taproot, it grows best in a ground bed or a pot that has some depth, as the root can get as long as a carrot!

On rare occasions, parsley can be hampered by spider mites and aphids.

Pineapple Sage

See listing under "Ornamental Flowering Crops."

Root Beer Plant

When I first grew this plant, I was surprised to find that it really does have the aroma of root beer. Scientifically, it is known as *Tagetes lucida,* but it also goes by sweet-scented marigold, Mexican tarragon, Mexican marigold, and winter tarragon. However, if you let any child smell it they will tell you that it is indeed the root beer plant. Kids especially delight in a plant that smells of root beer in the greenhouse. Like many herbs, the leaves must first be touched before the volatile aroma is released. The plant is often used as a substitute for tarragon, but I have decided the best use is to entertain children and adults alike, who love the fact that a plant really smells like root beer. It is not, however, actually used in flavoring root beer.

Root beer plant is also valuable for the nice orange flower it has in the winter. The plant is a cousin to the marigold, but you won't immediately recognize any resemblance. It is generally started from acquired plants and cuttings. You can find this plant in almost any extensive herb catalog, but because it has so many common names, be sure to look for it under the scientific name *Tagetes lucida.*

Rosemary

Rosemary is an evergreen perennial. It grows slowly, but after a few years you can have quite a specimen. I have often ended up with 6-foot-tall (1.8-meter-tall) rosemary "trees." They take well to pruning and can be easily poodled (made into a topiary) if you are interested in

creating plant sculptures. In late winter and spring, the plant will usually produce beautiful sprays of blue flowers.

Rosemary can be started from seed or cuttings. Cuttings are most successful if taken in spring or summer. Seed requires a constant temperature of around 65°F (18°C).

The big trick to growing it in a greenhouse is to grow it on the dry side. When it dies, it is usually from overwatering. Rosemary does equally well in pots or beds, but in pots you may need to increase the pot size regularly.

There are many different types of rosemary that have been selected for a variety of attributes, including stockier growth, trailing growth habits, pink flowers, and even one variety that develops golden streaks on the newest growth.

Because it's a perennial, one rosemary plant can live for years. Fresh leaves can be harvested anytime. Try it with fish or potato dishes. Besides culinary uses, rosemary is also reported to have medicinal and cosmetic qualities. It is traditionally believed that in the house where rosemary thrives, the woman is dominant. Watch for results. Also keep an eye out for mealybug. Rosemary tolerates bugs well, but it is always easier if they never get a foothold.

Sage

Sage is a hardy perennial that tolerates a wide variety of conditions. It is easily propagated from seed or cuttings, and it will do best with full sun and well-drained soil. It can grow to 1 foot (0.3 m) high or more. The flowers are a beautiful shade of blue and often bloom throughout the year. The flowers, as well as the leaves, can be used for culinary purposes.

Try golden sage, which has a handsome variegation on the edge of the leaf. There are also many other strains of sage worth trying.

Tarragon

Tarragon is another plant that I love to graze on while working in the greenhouse. It survives the winter and tolerates the greenhouse, but I have found it to be a plant that prefers to have a real winter. For this reason, greenhouse-grown tarragon never seems to thrive as well as tarragon grown outside. The best tarragon is known as French tarragon, which has the best flavor and is propagated only vegetatively (through cuttings or division). If you see tarragon seed for sale, it's the wrong stuff. The greenhouse is a great place to take cuttings of your outside plant for creating many new plants for gifts.

For best greenhouse-growing results, give tarragon full sun in well-drained soil. Locate the plant where it is cool in winter. I have had better luck growing it in clay pots, but it does reasonably well in beds, too.

For years, I had childhood memories come rolling back every time I tasted tarragon. Finally, a friend of mine clued me in to my reaction. He said, "It tastes like candy cigarettes." Every kid growing up in the sixties ate an abundance of candy cigarettes, which explained my memories triggered by tarragon. I'm not sure that tarragon is what the candy is flavored with, but my brain says it's close. If you eat too much fresh tarragon, your tongue may get tingly or numb—the "tarragon tingle." At the risk of getting the tingle, I love to munch on tarragon fresh. I also throw fresh sprigs into salads. Of course, there is always tarragon chicken and a plethora of other culinary uses for tarragon in a good recipe book.

Thyme

Thyme, a hardy perennial, is a handsome ground cover as well as an herb. There are a number of types of thyme, among them common thyme, which grows about 1 foot (0.3 m) tall; golden lemon thyme, with gold-and-green leaf variegation and a lemon scent; lemon thyme, which has a lemon scent and green leaves; Caraway thyme, which has red stems and caraway-scented leaves; and many others. Many of the thymes have ornamental flowers blooming in spring and fall. Thyme can be grown in a pot, but I like it as a ground cover along walkways. It can tolerate some traffic and gives off a nice scent when stepped on. Probably the best for use in walkways is Creeping Lemon thyme, which gives off a strong lemon scent when stepped on.

Most thymes can tolerate full to partial sun. It is helpful to occasionally divide plants and trim them back to maintain health. For harvesting, pick the leaves just prior to flowering. In years gone by, thyme plants were found in almost every garden and were thought to bring good spirits to the household.

OTHER HERBS

There are at least a hundred more fascinating herbs which I could talk about growing in a greenhouse—but that is what herb books are for. Since this is a greenhouse book, I hope that, at the very least, I have whetted your appetite to try growing them in your home greenhouse or sunspace!

CHAPTER 9

GETTING TO THE ROOTS

UNDERNEATH (ALMOST) EVERY HEALTHY PLANT IS a healthy root system. The root system provides nutrition for the plant as well as anchoring it into the ground. I could have titled this chapter something like "Greenhouse Soils and Fertilization," but all we are trying to do is to make the roots happy. When the soil is healthy, the plant is well.

Whenever I think about roots, I remember an experience I had running the Cheyenne Botanic Gardens. One primary purpose of the Botanic Gardens is to provide garden-oriented therapy to seniors, youth, and the handicapped. I was working with a fellow, aged 37, who was mentally handicapped. He functioned at the level of a 6-year-old, and he loved plants. There was a problem, however; he was afraid of plant roots. He often said, "I think roots are scary, don't you?" He always avoided any physical contact with a plant root. I searched my memories of childhood and remembered when there were parts of plants that scared me, too. I tried to reason with him, but to no avail. No logical explanation seemed to help.

One day, however, I had him adding some compost to the soil for an early-spring greenhouse planting. I left him to work by himself on a bed, preparing it for a new planting. Later, when I looked at the bed, I saw that he had done a great job except for leaving a curious-looking something rising out of the corner of the bed. I pointed to the big many-branched root system sticking out of the soil. "What's that?" I asked. He said it was an upside-down tomato plant that he had found in the compost pile. "You touched it?" He beamed with pride as I realized that he had actually handled a plant with—God forbid—ROOTS! I dug around the root sticking out of the ground, and sure enough, there was a whole tomato plant buried under the ground. "I just wanted to see how it would grow this way," he said. I thought about it for a few seconds and said, "Why not?" For many months, when giving public tours, I had a hard time explaining the upside-down tomato plant, but it was worth it. His fear was totally gone from that day on. He had found his own solution to his root phobia. Also from that day, he seemed to fit in better with all of the other people around the Botanic Gardens. I have always been convinced that gardening is the best therapy, whether you are handicapped or not. I think of this whenever I ponder the importance of roots, whether they are pointing up toward the sky or downward, where they prefer to be.

THE YEAR-ROUND SOIL

When you garden outside, your soil has all winter to recuperate and regenerate. In a greenhouse or sunspace, things are typically growing year-round. This means constant depletion of your soil and its nutrients, leaving no time for soil to rest and regenerate. When greenhouse plant growth slows as temperatures get cooler in the winter, the plant's use of soil nutrients also slows. Still, the roots may take up a substantial amount of nutrients over time. That is why greenhouse soil requires special attention between crop plantings when you are growing in beds. In pots, it means you need to pay attention to the health of the plant and repot as necessary. Plant nutrition and soil science are vastly complex. Numerous books can help you get a basic understanding of plant and soil nutrition, but they can be overly detailed and pretty dry reading for gardeners. This is a shame because it really is fascinating science.

In this chapter, then, I will try to give you the basic information you'll need to know in order to maintain soil and plant health. I hope you will learn how to deal with problems and, better yet, how to prevent them from happening.

As with the other information given in this book, I prefer using organic or biologically based fertilizers. But I am not against occasional use of chemical fertilizers in the greenhouse, especially when it is done with thought and understanding. Chemical fertilizers are especially handy when you are growing in pots or small containers, where you lack the ability to maintain well-rounded soil ecology.

Maintaining proper nutrition for your plants requires that you do some occasional testing for soil pH, salt content, organic matter, and specific elements such as nitrogen, phosphorus, and potassium. Besides the testing, it is also helpful if you can identify the plant symptoms indicating nutrient deficiencies or excesses. Read on, and we'll get to that!

When it comes to fertilizing, people generally overdo it. Keep this in mind when you are following a label or recommendation. As I mentioned before, people tend to love their plants to death—literally! If a little is good, people rationalize, then more must be better. When it comes to fertilizing, especially with chemical fertilizers, it is better to err on the side of discretion and frugality.

BASIC REQUIREMENTS FOR HEALTHY SOIL

Soil is a complex ecology. For good plant production, we need this ecology to be healthy. And for soil to be healthy, it requires certain ingredients, along with a cast of other characters, all of which must be operating properly. Let's look at the requirements for healthy soil.

AERATION

Aeration is a term that describes getting air into the soil. Roots need air as well as water; they'll suffocate from overwatering. The addition of sand, perlite (explained later in this chapter), and/or decomposed organic matter will help to provide the soil with aeration. Earthworms also greatly help aerate soil in greenhouse beds, but they are not usually present in the soil of smaller pots. Try adding some worms from your outside garden to the growing bed(s) in your greenhouse. You can even add worms to larger pots and tubs.

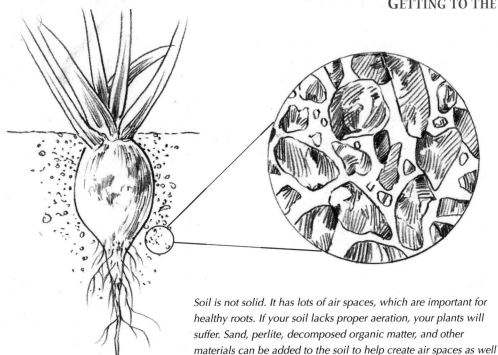

Soil is not solid. It has lots of air spaces, which are important for healthy roots. If your soil lacks proper aeration, your plants will suffer. Sand, perlite, decomposed organic matter, and other materials can be added to the soil to help create air spaces as well as to promote better drainage.

ORGANIC MATTER

Organic matter results from the decomposition of things that were once alive, including plants, food scraps, manure, and leaves. It provides these multiple beneficial effects to soils:

1. Adds nutrients.
2. Increases water-holding ability.
3. Holds mineral nutrients available for root uptake (much like a sponge or magnet).
4. Promotes beneficial microbial life that can keep diseases and soil-borne insects to a minimum.
5. Helps aerate soil.
6. Adds CO_2 to the air during decomposition, which increases plant growth (see Chapter 1, "The Greenhouse or Sunspace Environment").
7. Buffers the soil pH, that is, helps to neutralize the soil by helping to raise a low-pH soil and to lower high-pH soil.

MOISTURE-HOLDING ABILITY

Soil needs to be able to retain water for the roots. Two substances primarily hold water in the soil: clay and decomposed organic matter. Having a bit of both is helpful. Clay is usually already present in most soils. Getting organic matter into the soil requires some work on your part (see "Organic Soil Amendments," later in this chapter on page 332).

GOOD DRAINAGE

Greenhouse soils should drain well, unless you are growing a special ornamental plant that prefers to have wet feet. A well-drained soil is important because it is your main remedy if you have overfertilized a bed or pot. It also helps prevent the accumulation of soil salts. Salts move with the water, and if the soil moisture never moves on and out of the root zone, the salts add up. These salts can be damaging to many plants.

Aeration and drainage are very much related in what you need to provide. For a well-drained soil that provides sufficient aeration, you must provide some larger particles in a soil profile or mix. By large I mean materials such as sand, small pebbles, or a special growing medium known as perlite. Some soils are inherently well drained, as they contain a fair amount of sand naturally. Other soils, however, may be high in clay and need the addition of amendments that can remedy the poor drainage (see bed construction details in Chapter 2, "Interior Design").

When it comes to growing plants in a pot, drainage occurs when you have a good-draining soil mix and a hole in the bottom of the pot. Of course, the hole may necessitate the need for a saucer to catch the water that drains out.

A plant growing in a pot may at first enjoy the organic materials that are in the soil mix. Over time, however, microbes may actually consume that organic matter, making the soil denser, which in turn reduces the drainage. That is part of the reason we must repot potted plants.

PROPER PH

This is not the name of a shampoo or an acne medication. The pH describes the level of acidity—in this case, of your soil. It is based on a scale that ranges from 1 to 14. The halfway mark, 7, is the neutral point.

Try to keep your soil very close to neutral, or 7. A professional soil test or home soil-test kit (available in many catalogs or garden stores) will usually include a pH analysis. There are pH meters on the market, but you must purchase an expensive one (around $160) to get accurate results. The cheap ones that often cost $20 or less are usually not very accurate. Another alternative is to purchase what is known as pH litmus papers, which, when moistened with wet soil or soil in solution, will turn colors that correspond to certain levels of pH.

A professional soil test is by far the most accurate when it comes to determining the pH. Many county extension agents offer soil testing for a minimal fee.

The pH Scale

14	
13	
12	
11	Alkalinity
10	
9	
8	
7	
	Range of Good Growth
6	
5	
4	
3	Acidity
2	
1	

On the pH scale, 7 is neutral. Soil registering a pH from 7 down to 0 is acidic (the lower the number, the greater the acidity); soil pH from 7 to 14 is alkaline, or basic (the higher the number, the greater the alkalinity). Note that figures in the pH scale mark exponential increases. The best soil pH for most cultivated plants is roughly between 6.5 and 7.3. Most of the nutrients critical for plant health are available in this range.

What happens when the pH is not at the normal level? When pH is below 6.5 or above 7.3, it is more difficult for plant roots to take up and use existing minerals and nutrients in the soil. For instance, if the soil pH is quite high or low you could have a plant indicating a severe iron deficiency. This is because the roots can't process any iron when the pH is less than ideal, even when the soil is full of iron! The result is a sick-looking plant in poor health. This is why a plant grown at a poor pH level often resembles one with a nutrient deficiency.

A high pH can be corrected by adding well-decomposed organic matter, such as compost (avoid manures), gypsum, sulfur, or even commercially available acidifying plant foods. A low pH is generally corrected by adding wood ash or limestone. Read more about wood ash and limestone later in this chapter, or see some general gardening books. They usually go into this problem extensively.

HEALTHY MICROBIAL LIFE

Microbes (microscopic organisms) that live in the soil, such as bacteria and fungi, are beneficial to plant growth. They decompose the organic matter into more basic compounds. Microbes are important in controlling diseases caused by "bad" bacteria and fungi. The "good" microbes may actually feed on or parasitize the "bad" microbes. This is not unlike a tick on a dog or a coyote eating a rabbit in the nonmicroscopic world. It's amazing what goes on in the dirt, isn't it?

When microbes are in short supply, there is an increased likelihood of more diseases and/or nutrient problems. For growing in beds, the addition of decomposed organic matter will provide a healthy environment that stimulates microbial life. You should occasionally repot a containerized plant to help maintain a good environment and good level of soil microbial life.

Leaf margins and / or tips of leaves that are turning brown or black may indicate salt damage to the roots.

LOW SALT CONTENT

Salt is a broad term that doesn't refer just to table salt (sodium chloride) but describes the result of a chemical reaction occurring when acid compounds react with alkaline compounds. Certain fertilizers, both organic and inorganic, are noted for their potentially high salt content. Salt problems occur when high levels of fertilizers are used in soils, and often show up in soils with poor drainage. Salt problems can also be related to your source of water, as some people live in areas with a high level of salt compounds in the tap water.

Besides a plant's showing signs of salt damage, there is only one sure way to tell if you have a salt problem—with a soil test. It's almost impossible to escape some salt accumulation but, luckily, salts move with water. With heavy water applications, you can often leach the salts out to a level below the roots. This is why you hear the term "well-drained soil" so much. Salts tend to accumulate in the root zone of poorly drained soils, so there should always be drainage holes in the bottom of growing containers.

Salt concentration also rises as your soil dries out. If a lot of water has been evaporating from your soil, you may actually see white salt crystals on the soil surface.

SYMPTOMS OF SALT DAMAGE

1. Leaf tips or margins turn brown.
2. Leaves drop.
3. Soil surface gets a buildup of white powdery stuff (resembling ground table salt).
4. Growth is slowed.
5. Roots are damaged.
6. Micronutrient deficiencies may be apparent.
7. pH may be on the rise.
8. Accumulated white residue may appear on the sides of a pot, as the pot here shows.

Remove and re-pot plant in pots with salt residue. Soak and then scrub the residue off the pot if you plan to re-use

PREVENTING SALT DAMAGE

1. Go easy on fertilizing. Follow recommended rates; more is not better!
2. Avoid raw manures.
3. Soak old clay pots in water for a day and clean with a wire brush before replanting in them. Scrub salt deposits out of plastic pots in the same manner (but with less "elbow grease").
4. Be sure the soil drains well. A relatively high sand content helps if you have recurring problems with salt accumulation. Also be sure any potted plant has a drainage hole in the bottom.
5. Leach salt-affected soil by applying two to three heavier-than-usual waterings, then resume normal watering rhythm. If it is a potted plant, regularly dump the saucer water out into a sink drain.

NUTRIENTS FOR SOIL AND PLANTS

When asked, "Do plants grow?" a youngster once told me that he was sure they grew, but "they don't let you see it or hear it." When asked where plants get their food, he responded, "I think they eat the soil and the air, but I'm not sure how." The garden is a pretty good teacher of how our planet works.

Yes, plants do have to eat, and we have to help feed them. Feeding plants can become a complicated thing because it gets into the chemistry of the soil. Whenever you involve the word "chemistry," things tend to become confusing. But to keep it simple, the best thing to do when confused about feeding your plants is either to do nothing or to do less of what your natural urges tell you. This is because most of the problems with gardens and plants are not a result of underfeeding, but rather of overfeeding—that is, killing with kindness.

The time comes in every greenhouse grower's career when the plant talks to you with its symptoms, saying, "Things are not right, and you need to do something if you want me to thrive." Unfortunately, discovering symptoms of a nutrient deficiency usually means the problem started long before you spotted the symptom. By the time you see that the plant has a problem, you can be sure it has been suffering from this malady for some time. Yields from fruits or vegetables as well as blooms from flowering ornamentals could already have been lost. That is why prevention is better than cure when it comes to plant-nutrient problems. Still, plants do tell us, with some specific symptoms, what may be bothering them.

Nutrients needed by plants are generally divided into two groups: the major nutrients, and the micronutrients (sometimes called the "minors"). The major nutrients are those that are needed in larger quantities and are essential to growth, meaning that without them the plant will die. Plants also require the micronutrients for their survival every bit as much as the major nutrients, but with one difference. The micronutrients, or minors, are needed in much smaller quantities.

The three major nutrients are nitrogen, phosphorus, and potassium. Nitrogen promotes leafy growth. It is easily washed out of the soil because it moves with the water. It is also easy to overapply, which can trigger leaf burning and reduce flowers and fruit.

Phosphorus is generally associated with root growth. It also promotes flowering and is important for establishing seedlings. Unlike nitrogen, it moves slowly in the soil and does not move with water. Therefore, it is important to maintain a good supply in the root zone of the plants.

Potassium (also called potash) helps regulate water movement in the plant and contributes to its overall health.

Many micronutrients such as iron, zinc, and others are equally important. But because they are needed in such small quantities, people often overapply them, causing big problems. Micronutrient problems often occur not because the soil lacks nutrients, but because, even if they are present, the soil's pH is too high or low, making it more difficult for roots to utilize the micronutrients. The triggering of a micronutrient deficiency may also occur when another nutrient is overapplied, causing drastic changes in the soil chemistry. Usually, adequate amounts of micronutrients are contained in organic matter.

The following list describes important nutrients that plants require. I have included some general symptoms of deficiencies and excesses of the elements for plant troubleshooting. Keep in mind that plants don't read books like this and may not always follow the prescribed symptoms. Still, it is a start in helping you with your plants.

There are many other elements important to plant growth. Some may be essential, whereas others are not. One other element worth mentioning, though not essential in plant nutrition, is silicon. It has been found that after leaf infection, a greater deposit of silicon is found around the cells. The silicon has been shown to help form stronger, harder cell walls that may actually deter the powdery mildew fungus. There have been other research reports that seem to confirm the reduction of powdery mildew when silicon is added to the soil. The only commercial source of silicon fertilizer I have come across is a product called Pro-TeKt®, which contains 3.7 percent potassium and 7.8 percent soluble silicon. It is sold

(CONTINUED ON PAGE 325)

MAJOR SOIL NUTRIENTS—"THE BIG THREE"

Nitrogen (N)

Function: Required for leaf growth. Important for protein and amino acid production.

Contained in: Manure, fish, ocean plants, compost, and blood meal.

Excess: Luxuriant leafy growth, dark-green leaves, few flowers or fruit. Look for salt damage. Leaf tip and margin may brown. Aphids and other insects will delight in excess nitrogen.

Deficiency: Light-green to yellow leaves, mainly on the older, lower leaves. Yellow leaves may fall off. Stunted growth.

Applying N: If severe, try a foliar spray of fish emulsion or houseplant food. Mix at half the recommended rate and repeat weekly until the symptoms disappear. For a long-term solution, especially in pots, add a slow-release fertilizer, such as compost (preferably a rich compost if available), or if you don't mind using a synthetic fertilizer, try Osmocote®.

Phosphorus (P)

Function: Seedling hardiness; flower, fruit, and root production; helps in disease resistance.

Contained in: Bonemeal, ground rock phosphate, fish emulsion, compost, manure, superphosphate, and triple superphosphate.

Excess: Very rare. May cause micronutrient deficiencies.

Deficiency: Red- to purple-colored leaves. Dwarfed plants, small leaves, few fruits, leaves dropping early.

Applying P: For severe problems, water in a water-soluble houseplant food that has a higher middle number (phosphorus) than first number (nitrogen) on the label. Fish emulsion may stimulate the roots to utilize the available phosphorus in the soil. Bonemeal takes many months to work, especially in alkaline soils, but is good for soils that are acidic in nature. Be sure to strive for a neutral soil pH to enable phosphorus to be properly taken up by a plant.

Potassium (K)

Function: Regulates water movement within plants. Helps with stress and cold / heat tolerance, starch and sugar production. Increases the efficient use of other nutrients.

Contained in: Wood ash in small amounts (not good for alkaline soils), granite dust, compost, manure, kelp.

Excess: May create magnesium deficiency.

Deficiency: Lower leaves mottled, dead areas in leaf, yellowing begins at leaf edge and continues toward the center. Weak stems.

Applying K: Add compost to soil, fertilize with water-soluble fertilizer containing potassium. Add a kelp-based fertilizer to soil.

OTHER MAJOR SOIL NUTRIENTS

The following are not as commonly required as fertilizers because they often occur naturally in most soils in sufficient quantities. Still, deficiencies can and do occur.

Calcium (Ca)

Function: Cell-wall and enzyme production.

Contained in: Bonemeal, eggshells, limestone, milk, gypsum, ground oyster shells.

(Continued on next page)

Excess: Not very common, may affect pH or deficiencies of potassium, magnesium, and iron.

Deficiency: Yellow, hooked plant tips. Tips may die back; short roots. Blossom-end fruit rot on tomatoes. Centers of lettuce and celery may rot.

Applying Ca: Gypsum applied at manufacturer's recommended rate; bonemeal or ground oyster shells lightly dusted on the soil and then dug into the top inch will help; compost may also contain large amounts of calcium.

Magnesium (Mg)

Function: Chlorophyll production and respiration.

Contained in: Organic matter, Epsom salts, liquid kelp, seaweed extract.

Excess: Causes micronutrient imbalances.

Deficiency: Yellow between veins or yellow spots on older, lower leaves, which may eventually turn brown. More common in acid soils, especially where much dolomite limestone has been applied. Deficiency may trigger calcium deficiencies and higher levels of insect infestations.

Applying Mg: Add compost to soil mix. Mix 1 tablespoon of Epsom salts to 1 gallon (3.8 liters) of hot water; apply cooled mixture to plants once a week until symptoms disappear.

Sulfur (S)

Function: Protein production. Helps in maintaining soil pH.

Contained in: Ground sulfur, rain near coal-fired power plants, gypsum.

Excess: Causes soil to become acidic.

Deficiency: Light yellow on new leaves, including yellowing of the leaf veins.

Applying S: Add compost to soil. Add ½ pound (0.2 kg) ground sulfur to 100 square feet (9 sq. m) of soil. To use sulfur to lower an alkaline pH (common in Western arid soils), add 1 pound (0.45 kg) of ground sulfur to 100 square feet (9 sq. m) to lower pH by one number (i.e., to change a pH of 8 to a pH of 7). Sulfur is slow to react in many soils, so the results may take several months. The finer-ground sulfur works more quickly.

MICRONUTRIENTS (OR MINORS)

Boron (B)

Function: Cell-wall formation, carbohydrate transportation.

Contained in: Organic matter, seaweed.

Excess: Slight excess may kill plants. Excess is more common in acidic soils. Try to maintain a neutral soil to avoid excess.

Deficiency: Malformed leaf tips that may die back. Cabbage family plants develop hollow stems. Stunted heads of cauliflower and broccoli. Commonly found in soils low in organic matter.

Applying B: Correct soil pH, add organic matter (compost); apply foliar spray of liquid kelp or seaweed extract every 2 weeks.

Copper (Cu)

Function: Enzyme and photosynthesis regulation.

Contained in: Seaweed, kelp, manure, compost.

(Continued on next page)

Excess: Rarely found. May cause iron deficiency.

Deficiency: Often the result of too much nitrogen. Leaves look bleached. Light-colored leaf veins and margins. Stunting.

Applying Cu: Apply compost to soil. Water with seaweed or kelp fertilizer every 2 weeks until symptoms disappear.

Iron (Fe)

Iron deficiency is evident if there is yellowing inbetween green veins of new growth or on plant tips.

Function: Chlorophyll formation.

Contained in: Organic matter, bonemeal, iron chelate, iron sulfate.

Excess: Darker green foliage; then turns into magnesium or zinc deficiency.

Deficiency: Yellowing between veins on newly developing leaves. Old leaves remain green. Often due to a soil pH that is too high, poor drainage, or cold soils.

Applying Fe: The quickest solution is to apply a foliar application of iron chelate (take precautions to not overapply). Blood meal or compost will provide longer-term solutions.

Manganese (Mn)

Function: Helps in photosynthesis and respiration.

Contained in: Manganese sulphate, organic matter.

Excess: Similar to deficiency: dark spots, crinkling, and cupping of leaves.

Deficiency: Much like iron deficiency, but even the smallest veins remain green while all new growth turns yellow to white. Old growth remains green.

Applying Mn: Try correcting for an iron deficiency, using iron chelate; add organic matter to soil for long-term solution.

Molybdenum (Mo)

Function: Nitrogen fixation, enables plants' ability to metabolize nitrogen.

Contained in: Usually present in soil but often becomes deficient when soil has low pH or low organic-matter content.

Excess: Slight excess causes rapid death.

Deficiency: Stunting, similar to nitrogen deficiency; leaf may curl upward, some leaf-edge burn.

Applying Mo: Correct soil pH, common in acidic soils; add limestone or wood ash to correct deficiency.

Zinc (Zn)

Function: Chlorophyll formation, bud development.

Contained in: Zinc sulfate, organic matter.

Excess: May result in other micronutrient problems. Sometimes resembles an iron deficiency.

Deficiency: Top leaves remain very small; stunting, dwarfing. Mottled yellow leaves.

Applying Zn: Zinc deficiency is often caused by an alkaline pH. Try to correct the pH to a more normal level (near a pH of 7) and often the zinc deficiency will disappear. May also be corrected by the application of compost and zinc chelate.

by the Dyna-Grow Corporation (800-396-2476), a major producer of hydroponic solutions.

Silicon also occurs naturally in compost and other plant waste products. It is found in high amounts in the plant horsetail, or scouring rush. I have occasionally seen concentrates made from this plant for sale to enable the addition of silicon to a soil.

FERTILIZERS

When a plant problem occurs, we usually reach for some type of fertilizer to help bring back health to the soil and plant. But go easy here, because fertilizing is often the worst thing you can do to a plant under stress unless you recognize the problem as a specific nutrient deficiency.

There are so many fertilizers on the market that trying to decide what type to use can be mind-boggling. All fertilizers can be classified as either synthetic or organic. There are also mixtures of the two. Let's look at some of the attributes of organic and synthetic fertilizers.

Organic fertilizers are more forgiving if you apply too much because they are slower to release into the soil and are generally less concentrated. Organic fertilizers usually contain some if not most of the required micronutrients (minors). As organic fertilizers decompose, carbon dioxide is often produced. Increased carbon dioxide levels in your enclosed winter greenhouse increase plant growth. Also,

There are many different fertilizers to choose from. The more you understand about what makes them different, the easier it will be for you to choose the best one for your needs.

CROP NUTRITION NEEDS—A BASIC SUMMARY

Different crops have different needs. Because most of you can't (or won't) do a soil test every few months to keep abreast of what is going on with your soil, sometimes it is helpful to get a handle on what plants need. Here are some generalizations.

1. Crops grown in summer will need more nutrients. The warmer the temperatures, the faster your crop will grow and the more nutrients it will need.
2. Winter crops can get by with fewer total nutrients.
3. Squash, cucumber, and melon crops are heavy feeders and need about 20 percent more nitrogen than most other crops.
4. Tomato crops respond well to slightly lower nitrogen and higher phosphorus applications.
5. Peas, beans, and ornamental flower crops respond to lower amounts of nitrogen and steady levels of phosphorus.
6. Plants in small containers will benefit more from frequent but diluted feeding than will plants grown in larger containers.
7. Avoid fertilizing germinating seedlings. Very young plants should have only very diluted fertilization (cut the label recommendation in half or more until the plant is more mature).

organic fertilizers promote a healthy microbial life in the soil, which helps keep many diseases in check.

The downsides to organic fertilizer are few, but they do exist. First, *if* you must purchase them, they can be more costly than the synthetics. The alternative is to make your own (compost) or have access to a cheap local source (leaf mold, composted manure).

Organic fertilizers usually require more labor to get them into your soil, often requiring that you dig them in. However, don't let this stop you—exercise is good for you!

Organic fertilizers are also slower to work, which may be a disadvantage if you have a big problem that needs to be solved fast. In general, however, the slowness of the organic fertilizers is a good quality. All things considered, when time and ability permit, I prefer to use organic sources of fertilizer.

There are times, such as when I need a fast solution, that I find it is helpful to use a synthetic fertilizer. I particularly prefer using synthetic fertilizers with plantings in containers, where the root area is limited by the constraints of a small pot (i.e., growing bedding plants in small containers).

THE FERTILIZER NUMBERS GAME

Whether in a bag or a box, organic or not, almost all fertilizers have three analysis numbers listed somewhere on the package. It'll say something like "5-10-5" or "20-20-20". These are the percentages of nitrogen, phosphorus, and potassium, always in that order. This is often referred to as the "NPK ratio." The letters N and P are logical, but why the letter K? It is used because K signifies potassium in the periodic table. Remember that big poster in chemistry class?

When you are shopping for fertilizer, read the numbers and compare. To simplify things, the lower the numbers, the lower the percent of the element contained in the bag. Also, the lower the number, the less you get per dollar. Generally, it is a good idea to get the highest analysis for your money, as long as the analysis has a good balance. A good fertilizer number balance for growing most greenhouse crops is one where the numbers are even (or close to even) or where the middle number (phosphorus) is higher than the first number.

For instance, lawn food may be sold with a high percentage of nitrogen (i.e., "27-3-3") but contains very little phosphorus and potassium—not a good balance for greenhouse gardening.

Some plant foods are mixed for specific uses. Some try to encompass all uses, such as those known as "general" plant foods. A general plant food has all three numbers on the label either very close or identical in value, such as 20-20-20. A plant food chosen to promote leafy growth might have a higher percentage of nitrogen, the first number, compared to the middle and last numbers. A plant food chosen to promote flowers and fruit and help young plants get a good start would have the middle number, phosphorus, higher than the other two.

The standardization among most state laws and fertilizer manufacturers requires only the listing of the three major nutrients. To find out if your fertilizer contains micronutrients (minors) or other important ingredients besides the three major ones, you may have to read the label closely. Sometimes they are mentioned, sometimes not. If you call the fertilizer company (phone numbers are often on the label), someone there will likely tell you whether the product contains micronutrients or not and what the exact percentages are.

EQUIPMENT AND FEEDING: FERTILIZER SIPHONS, INJECTORS, AND FOLIAR FEEDING

Whether it is fish fertilizer or liquefied chemical fertilizer, people often wonder about other options for applying fertilizer besides simply mixing it in a watering can. There are some gizmos designed for just that. Commercial greenhouses have long used fertilizer injectors to apply fertilizers over a broad area. This eliminates the large amount of labor that would be used in mixing up fertilizers by the gallon and watering them in with a watering can. Injectors often use the water pressure or the siphon force of the water itself to provide a perfect dosing of fertilizers. Some even use flow meters powered by electricity.

One of my favorites and one of the simplest injectors to use is the Hozon Siphon, or the Miracle-Gro Siphonex. This is an ingenious little device that only costs around $15. For that reason, it is probably the best choice for a small greenhouse. All you have to do is mix up a solution of your fertilizer 15 times stronger than the normal rate. So, if you would normally apply 1 teaspoon per gallon, you would instead mix in a bucket a concentration of 15 teaspoons per gallon. Then you screw the siphon into the hose at the hose bib and stick the siphon's little tube into your concentrate. After that, you simply irrigate with the hose as you normally would—except you are getting a proper mix of fertilizer and water coming out of the nozzle. When you fertilize with a siphon or injector, you need to take special care to avoid overwatering (and thus overfertilizing) any one plant. Be sure you are watering and fertilizing your plants evenly.

There are many other more expensive and more appropriate injectors designed to dose out fertilizer for both larger greenhouses and for drip irrigation systems. These more *professional* types usually require that you also install a water filter to prevent the clogging of the injector and/or the drip emitters.

Is a siphon or injector something you really need? Probably not, unless the greenhouse bug bites you, and next thing you know you have expanded into something larger than a small home greenhouse. But if you have both a large outside garden and greenhouse in need of attention, you may find a low-cost siphon a real help in the application of fertilizers.

By the way, these siphons and injectors can apply more than just fertilizers. I have used them in the application of tiny beneficial nematodes for pest control of fungus gnats (see Chapter 10 for more information on beneficial nematodes and control of fungus gnats). Commercial operators have been known to use them for the application of certain chemicals.

The Siphonex allows you to apply a water-soluble organic or inorganic fertilizer directly through your hose rather than having to mix fertilizer in a watering can repeatedly. For larger greenhouses it can be a real time saver.

FOLIAR FEEDING

As mentioned earlier, one advantage to using chemical fertilizers is that they are quick acting. What many people don't know is that plants not only absorb nutrients through their roots but also absorb nutrients through their leaves. Foliar feeding is incredibly fast, and it is not limited to chemical, synthetic fertilizers. You can also use manure teas or fish emulsion, both of which are organic fertilizers. With foliar feeding, it is just a matter of getting the liquefied material on the leaves with a watering can, fertilizer siphon (found in many garden- and greenhouse-supply catalogs), or sprayer. When using synthetic chemicals or fish-emulsion fertilizer as a foliar spray, cut the label-recommended rate for dilution in half, then apply with a watering can or fertilizer siphon.

Do not use manure teas on leafy vegetables because you can get a buildup of nitrates in an edible leaf, which can make it slightly toxic, especially in cooler temperatures. It is a good idea to minimize the use of foliar feeding on all leafy vegetables (avoid it altogether in winter months). Thoroughly wash the leaves before consuming. All other plants are fair game for foliar feeding.

A WORD ABOUT HYDROPONICS

I always smile when people ask me about using hydroponics and mispronounce it as "hydrophonics." I'm not sure what hydrophonics is (water music?), but a lot of people are talking about it. Still, I know what people mean, and I give them my biased opinion of hydroponics, which I am about to give you. (Hydrophonics does sound like fun to me—grab the waterproof guitar!)

I have tried to make this book among the most complete on the subject of growing in greenhouses, but you should also know that this book is not going to teach you how to set up a hydroponic system. If you are thinking about using a hydroponic system, this book may help you with the many aspects of growing plants and understanding how to grow in a greenhouse. This book may also help you decide if hydroponics is right for you.

There are many good books and videos available on hydroponic growing. There are a number of regional retail outlets that can also provide assistance and sell all the equipment you need for a hydroponic system—but get your wallet ready.

Before we get too far, let me explain my bias about hydroponics. I see its place in commercial greenhouse production. I also have no problem with people who have a passion for it and want to pursue that passion in their home greenhouse. I would never fault anyone for advocating hydroponics or making a living associated with the industry. But I also want to use this book to inform you about an aspect that is not often mentioned concerning the appeal of hydroponics. My bias is this: In general, I believe that it is more complicated and expensive to go with hydroponics than to stay with a basic soil culture.

First, let's define hydroponics. With hydroponics, plants are grown without soil, using water-soluble nutrient solutions. Usually, the plant roots are grown in some sort of (usually inert) nonsoil material. This can include rooting material such as sand, gravel, rock wool, expanded clay, vermiculite, and even sawdust. The plants are constantly watered with special fertilizer solutions that supply all of their nutrient needs.

Hydroponics has a space-age, high-tech reputation, and as a result many people assume that it is the cutting edge and automatically creates phenomenal yields. Those that profit from selling hydroponic supplies help to perpetuate this belief. Although a hydroponic system can be set up in a simple manner, it lends itself to being capital intensive, meaning it requires a fair amount of money to get it up and running. Worse, there is no end to your need for supplies.

Despite the widespread belief that hydroponics is a new, modern technique, it has actually been practiced for more than ninety years. Only in recent history has it become more popular, as labor prices have increased and fertilizer prices have decreased.

The belief that hydroponics is a yield enhancer is based upon the premise that the limiting factor in yields is fertilizer—and that soil is inherently full of yield-robbing disease. In fact, fertilizer is rarely the limiting factor in controlling plant growth. Furthermore, people tend to overfertilize whether they are growing in soil or other mediums. But soil-borne diseases are not a major problem for home-greenhouse gardeners.

Usually, greenhouse yields are most commonly affected by a lack of light, temperatures that are too high or too low, low levels of carbon dioxide, and too much water. Fertilization is usually way down the list as an important factor.

Hydroponic enthusiasts can point to research that proves that hydroponics does indeed increase the yield of greenhouse crops, although I have my suspicions about some of this research and how it was funded. Assuming, however, that this is true, are the higher yields worth the extra cost that is required in a hydroponic system? I can't answer that for you, but it is a question you should be asking yourself before you commit to going into hydroponics.

Don't get me wrong, there are many advantages to hydroponics, but it probably won't solve the world's food problems or save us from ourselves.

ADVANTAGES OF HYDROPONIC GARDENING

So, why hydroponics? The absolute main advantage is that it can be easily automated, which saves labor. This is great if you are in the commercial greenhouse business, because labor is a major expense, if not the biggest expense. It takes a lot of money to set up a commercial system. However, in the long run, it can be a profitable way to go.

There are other advantages to hydroponics. Hydroponics enables more creative use of space. For example, imagine using a vertical plastic pipe with a number of holes drilled into the length and filled with perlite. In the holes, you can grow lettuce plants in a vertical manner up and down the pipe. That is hard to do with soil!

Aeroponics, or aerohydroponics, uses no pot or root medium. The nutrient solution is just misted onto the roots of the plants, which are anchored at the stem for support. This is the kind of thing you see at Disneyworld's EPCOT Center or in a NASA demonstration (see the Epilogue). However, I believe that we will probably end up taking our old-fashioned soil with us when we take our farms to the stars because of the need to establish whole ecosystems that support life. Aeroponics could enable all sorts of configurations in laying out plants efficiently within a space.

Hydroponic gardening eliminates the need to weed and cultivate. I should point out, however, that I spend probably only a few minutes a month at the most weeding in my soil-based greenhouse.

Hydroponics also eliminates the use of soil, either in pots or in beds. Instead, you have to mess with rooting mediums, extensive drip systems, pumps, pH testers, timers, and nutrient solutions. In many respects, soil may be less complicated.

DISADVANTAGES OF HYDROPONIC GARDENING

As long as I am giving you my biased view of the advantages, I might as well proceed to the

Hydroponics is not for everyone; it requires a long-term commitment.

disadvantages. First, hydroponics will make you inseparably tied to a fertilizer manufacturer or supplier because it is difficult to manufacture hydroponic plant fertilizer at home. You'll always end up having to return to the nutrient solution retailer for more. This takes away the feeling of self-sufficiency (a feeling that I treasure). What if there is a trucking strike or other interruption and you can't get the hydroponic supplies required? Personally, I don't like the idea of having to pay for every last nutrient your plant needs. It is reminiscent of an addiction.

Soil is a very forgiving medium. If you overapply something, such as a fertilizer, soil has the ability to absorb it and buffer the effect. Hydroponics, on the other hand, is an exacting practice. If you overapply your fertilizer, your plants will be immediately affected. Hydroponics doesn't tolerate mistakes as well as soil does.

Another drawback is that hydroponics is a nonsoil medium and lacks the many beneficial critters that live and breathe in soil. One thing that these soil organisms give off is carbon dioxide. This of course is good for plant growth. With hydroponics, there is little if any generation of carbon dioxide that could benefit plants.

It is difficult for a hydroponic system to adjust when you are growing a lot of different plants. For instance, many people like to grow many different plants in a greenhouse—tropicals, cut flowers, salad crops, fruits, succulents, ornamentals, and herbs. It is almost impossible for one type of fertilizer to supply the diverse needs of diverse plants. One plant needs higher nitrogen, but another needs more phosphorus. Hydroponics makes planting a diverse greenhouse that much more difficult.

One of the main problems that I have with hydroponics is that it requires so much equipment—at least that's what some manufacturers want you to believe. I know some people who have been told they need not only pumps, timers, soilless mediums, and special tubs, but also special enzymes, lights, reflectors, and, because there is no carbon dioxide generated (as in a soil system), a CO_2 generator. Of course, you still must purchase fertilizer regularly, too. This can really get expensive when you add it all up.

KEEP IT SIMPLE

In defense of hydroponics, you should know that you don't have to have an exotic, complicated, and extensive system. You can set up a relatively simple design, and many good hydroponic books discuss how to go about doing this. For instance, I have set up a simple ebb-and-flow system, with a simple pump. This is where you have a reservoir (for fertilizer), a timer, and an irrigation line with emitters feeding into growing containers. The timer will periodically trigger the pump to water the plants with the nutrient system, which sets below the plants. After the plants have been watered (with the solution), the fertilizer drains back down into the reservoir. You can eliminate the timer and the pump if you are willing to lift the reservoir filled with the solution to a height above the plants. This drains the solution into the pots or containers. The solution will need to fill the pots at least two to three times a day, and the nutrient solution should be changed once a week.

I have also used straw bales as a medium for growing plants hydroponically, a system in which the plant actually roots directly into the bale. The bale then generates carbon dioxide, solving one of the discussed problems associated with hydroponics.

Although I am not an extremist when it comes to the environment, I have learned that working with nature is usually the best course to pursue. I find myself getting a bit appalled at all of the chemicals there are in our environment and our food. I know they aren't all bad, but I get an uncomfortable feeling when we are dependent upon them. Perhaps that is where some of my bias is rooted when it comes to hydroponics.

As you can see, there are many variables in going about doing a hydroponic system. After you thoroughly understand what is involved—and that the advantages may not weigh out over the disadvantages—perhaps the less glamorous soil-based plant-growing methods may look more appealing. If you have an interest in hydroponics, I would encourage you to check out some books on the subject of hydroponics or talk to retailers selling hydroponic equipment to balance out the opinions I have expressed here.

Hydroponics lends itself well to automation; however, that can be done just as easily with a soil-based system, using automatic watering and venting. It is easy to set up a system that will allow you to leave your greenhouse unattended for a few days.

I will state emphatically that hydroponics is well suited for some commercial growers (especially greenhouse vegetable producers) who must contend with high labor costs.

In conclusion, a hydroponic system is good for people who are curious about automation or people with a passion for the other advantages of growing in a soilless culture. I always advocate following your passions. But it is my hope here in this discussion to get you to ask some hard questions before you take the hydroponic route. Question what you really want to do with greenhouse gardening. Also question the motivation of the person who may be trying to sell you on the hydroponic setup. In the final analysis, no matter what you choose, it is my hope that you enjoy a productive greenhouse to the maximum while having some fun!

SOIL AMENDMENTS

There is a wide choice of materials you can add to enhance your soil, but what would be best for your particular situation? It can get confusing. Different amendments have different effects upon a soil. It is important to know the characteristics of your soil as well as the effects of the many amendments available to gardeners. Some of the following are actual fertilizers containing specific nutrients, whereas other amendments have other beneficial effects. The idea is to try to plug in the right material to help address your soil's specific needs. For instance, do you need to promote drainage? Look for an amendment that does just that: perlite. Does your soil need some acidification and the benefits of organic matter? Perhaps sphagnum peat moss is a solution for you. Do you need nitrogen? Try fish emulsion. Although it is important to "feed the soil" regularly, be careful of overapplica-tion. Sometimes the old adage "If it ain't broke, don't fix it" is useful in helping you prevent more problems than you create as a gardener. There is such a thing as too much of a good thing. When in doubt about the application rates of any material, either look to the manufacturer or always err on the low side.

The following is a list of different common and not-so-common amendments, listed alphabetically, and categorized according to their organic and inorganic quality. This will give you some idea of the characteristics of each product you might want to use in your greenhouse soil or potting mixes.

ORGANIC SOIL AMENDMENTS

Organic means that these are products of nature and that they were once living. This often means that, over time, these materials are eventually broken down in the soil as they are consumed by other living things in the soil such as microbes and plants. Even though these are all in the same "organic" category, you will see that they have very different effects upon the soil.

Bark

Bark is getting more popular as an alternative to peat moss. It is generally derived from composted hardwoods, fir, redwood, or pine. It is gaining popularity because it is relatively cheap. If you come across bark that is not composted, it can cause a problem for your plants by taking up needed nitrogen (see the sawdust discussion later in this section). Also, uncomposted bark may contain other chemicals that can actually kill plants, so beware.

The benefits of composted bark in a soil include helping drainage and aeration and providing for increased nutrient retention. The composting also provides a natural disease resistance to many soil diseases. Many bark producers have even taken to inoculating the compost with special beneficial organisms that enhance the ability of the bark to suppress certain diseases.

Although the addition of bark can increase the water-holding capacity of a soil, it doesn't do this nearly as well as does peat moss or coir. The pH of composted bark can vary significantly, and you may want to check on your particular source. Bark does have the advantage of natural resistance to compaction. It is slow to break down and maintains porosity quite well over time.

Unlike many soil amendments, bark can vary greatly, and not all barks are alike. It is this variability that makes it hard for growers to generalize about the product. It is best to stick to one particular brand or mix that includes composted bark.

Blood Meal

Blood meal is basically a nitrogen fertilizer but also contains some small amounts of phosphorus. The NPK ratio is generally 10-0-0. I have also seen blood meal help with iron deficiencies. It is on the expensive side, compared to other fertilizers. It is generally added at a rate of $1/2$ pound (0.2 kg) per 10 square feet (0.9 sq. m) of soil, or follow label instructions.

Bonemeal

Bonemeal contains mostly phosphorus, with some calcium and a trace of nitrogen. It releases its nutrients in alkaline soils slowly but is a good choice in acidic or neutral soils. It contains 10 to 12 percent phosphorus. Add 1 pound (0.45 kg) per 10 square feet (0.9 sq. m) of soil. Bonemeal is sold in either steamed or raw forms. The steamed form is faster acting.

A note of caution: Some people suggest that there is a possibility (although remote) that people could contract mad cow disease by simply inhaling bonemeal dust. I think I'll put on a dust mask next time I use bonemeal just to be on the safe side.

Coir is often sold as a compressed brick **(left).** *When you set the brick in water, it expands as it absorbs the moisture. Coir* **(right)** *is made up of coconut fiber and is often used as a replacement for peat moss.* Coir brick photo courtesy of GreenFire Innovative Gardening Supplies.

Coir

Coir (sometimes known as coconut husk fiber) comes from (you guessed it) the fibers of coconuts. It is used both as a material for producing hanging-basket liners for ornamental plants and as an ingredient in potting mixes. It is getting more popular as a replacement for sphagnum peat moss and has some similar characteristics. Coir helps soils to hold nutrients as well as having water-holding ability much like sphagnum peat. It differs from peat in that it does not hold nutrients as well, but it does hold water better than sphagnum peat. Because it holds water better, I have seen people used to a peat-based mix change to a coir-based mix only to find that they are more prone to overwatering their plants. Unlike peat, coir readily absorbs water and is much easier to wet down when it is dry than peat is.

Because the pH of coir usually ranges from 5.7 to 6.4., this gives it an advantage over peat moss in that coir is not highly acidic. It also contains some small amounts of the nutrients potassium and phosphorus.

Coir is appearing more often in commercially available potting soils as an organic amendment for both its water- and nutrient-holding capacity. Many studies have shown that plants grown in coir-based mixes do as well as those grown in the old standby Canadian sphagnum peat moss.

Compost

Composting is a great way to deal with plant wastes. It can be an excellent soil conditioner because it is pure decomposed organic matter. There is enough written in most gardening books on composting procedures. You can find commercially available compost easily today, but nothing solves your home garbage problems like a home compost pile!

If you are having problems with diseases and use a lot of homemade compost, try to break any potential disease cycles that occur. Do this by using only greenhouse plant waste in the outside garden and outside plant wastes in the greenhouse. This may mean that you need two separate piles. Having parallel composting will help break up possible disease infestations.

Many people attempt to compost inside the greenhouse. I don't recommend this in small home or hobby greenhouses for the following reasons: If you don't know what you

Finished compost is an excellent soil amendment for greenhouse beds and soil mixes.

are doing, it may start to smell. It is a waste of precious greenhouse space. Greenhouses should be used either for growing things or for relaxation (often this is one and the same). Finally, you can always compost outside.

Yes, as mentioned in previous chapters, compost creates carbon dioxide, which helps plants grow, but you can get the same results from using compost in your greenhouse soil mix and as a mulch.

The recommendation for using compost in greenhouse or sunspace growing beds is to add 1 inch (2.5 cm) of compost and dig it into the top 6 to 8 inches (15 to 20 cm). Renew the beds with additional compost when you are planting new crops or every 6 months or so. It can also be used as mulch by laying a thin layer of compost on the soil surface. (See page 30 in Chapter 1, "The Greenhouse or Sunspace Environment," for more composting information.)

Fish Emulsion

Even though fish emulsion smells bad, I still like to use it regularly. Fish emulsion is high in nitrogen, with an NPK ratio of around 4-1-1. It is often treated with sulfur or phosphoric acid to inhibit bacterial growth. Fish emulsion has an incredibly strong smell. Most manufacturers claim that their fish emulsion is "deodorized." If that is true, I would hate to smell the nondeodorized product. "Deodorized" means that it smells only slightly better than if there were no deodorizer added at all. The good news is that the smell goes away within a day or two at the most. Try to apply it on a warmer day when you can ventilate a bit after the application.

What is intriguing about fish emulsion is the fact that many plant researchers feel that there is more than just nutrient value present in it. Recent research confirms that fish emulsion seems to have a positive effect on plant growth, vigor, and hardiness and increases the overall health of the plant. The only problem is that the researchers have a hard time explaining exactly why. They know it not strictly due to the nutrient value alone. Perhaps it contains special enzymes, micronutrients, or just plain old fish magic. Early ancestors long ago knew the value of placing a fish head or a whole fish in the soil for a good harvest.

Fish emulsion can be absorbed through both the root and the leaf. Generally, it is applied at a rate of 4 tablespoons per 1 gallon (3.8 liters) and either sprayed onto the crop or watered into the soil. See the label for more specifics, as the concentration may vary from brand to brand.

Leaf Mold

Leaf mold is simply composted leaves. It is very high in micronutrients and is a great soil conditioner. It is not very high in the major fertilizer elements, such as nitrogen, phosphorus, and potassium, but does contain enough to add some to the overall soil fertility. You can use well-rotted leaves as you would peat moss. As with peat moss, an excess of leaf mold may cause a high level of acidity, especially where your soil is already acidic.

I make leaf mold in a trench with a light sprinkling of manure and occasional watering to maintain moisture. You can also make it in a mound as you would a compost pile. Let it sit 12 months or more for it to properly age, like a good wine. Each fall you can turn over a new leaf or a pile of leaves.

Manure

Manure is both a soil conditioner and a fertilizer. Because of its high content of soluble salts, it can also cause plant burning. Manure should never be applied fresh. Always compost it for 1 year or more. Impatient? Check your local farm. Someone will have some well-aged manure.

Manures vary greatly in nutrient content. The age and the type of manure create many variables. This makes it almost impossible to know how strong it is. As a rule, the older the manure, the less nutrient value, but even old manure makes a good soil conditioner (for poor soils). Rabbit and poultry manures are about twice as rich in nutrients as those from horses, cows, and pigs. Sheep and goat manures sit somewhere between the two.

It's hard to give accurate recommendations for application, because even the same type of manure may vary a great deal. But I'll do it anyway.

Manure, unless very well composted, is not suitable for pots and containers, as it is too easy to cause burning. Generally, I use manure only in soil beds. First, do a soil test to be sure that your soil needs fertilizing. In soil beds that are at least 18 inches (46 cm) deep, I add no more than 1 inch (2.5 cm) of well-composted manure (half that amount for chicken or rabbit manure). Blend it thoroughly into the existing soil to prevent hot spots. If the manure is made up of large clods, try to break them up prior to applying it. There's nothing like the smell of manure (or a fresh application of fish emulsion) in the greenhouse to make everyone else wonder if you have truly lost your mind over this greenhouse gardening stuff.

Manure is usually higher in nitrogen than phosphorus or potassium, so be sure that that fits in with your goal and matches your soil needs. If you use it, you may need to also add some materials that are high in phosphorus and potassium.

Farm manure may also contain a high level of weed seeds. This is especially true of animals with only one stomach, such as horses. I have found that ruminants (cows, goats, and sheep) seem do a better job of digesting weed seeds with their extra "stomachs." As a result, I usually see fewer weed-seed problems with composted manure from ruminants.

Also, if you are good at composting or have found some commercially available composted manure, you may find that the heating that occurs with good composting practices will deactivate many of the weed seeds as well as pathogenic microorganisms.

Manure Tea

Manure tea is made by simply infusing water through manure. Prepare an old bucket to hold the manure. Take a nail and hammer, and poke hundreds of holes in the bottom and sides of the bucket and fill it with manure. Set the "holey" bucket full of manure into another bucket of water for a few hours. Remove the manure bucket, and your tea is ready. It is primarily a source of nitrogen and can be absorbed through the leaf as well as the root. Avoid getting it on the foliage of edible crops. If you do, be sure to wash and rinse any crop you might ingest. As you might have guessed, it doesn't smell great. If it's flavor you want, try Lipton's or Celestial Seasonings.

Microbial Enhancement and Biostimulants

Recently, commercial growers have had available some products that actually enable you to add specific beneficial fungi and bacteria to a soil mix, growing bed, or crop. These microorganisms help prevent disease, increase plants' tolerance to stress, and increase their vigor. Some have even found that these products even increase plants' cold tolerance. Many of these claims have been proven and such products are getting more and more acceptance among commercial growers. These products are often available as a powder you mix with water and add to soils or as a granular material that you mix into soil; other products are sold as liquid concentrates that you mix with water and add. Some products are mixed with nutrients that also increase the number of existing microorganisms.

One fungus that is being offered is known as a "mycorrhizal" fungus that coexists with roots and provides a natural defense against root diseases and other pest attacks. Although this type of fungus occurs in natural situations, it is often in short supply in soil mixes and artificial landscapes. It is also in lower quantities in soils low in organic matter or those suffering from chemical imbalances caused by pH or fertilizers.

Some companies market their fungi solely to prevent diseases. The fungus is applied to seedlings either through irrigation or as a granular application; the fungus then protects plants from the most problematic soil-borne diseases. It appears from some initial tests that even though these products sound like miracles, they do actually work. These fungi that act as disease protectants are not cures for a full-blown disease infestation, but if you start them with your seedlings, they can do as good a job as fungicides—or a better one. The big plus is that they are considered organic and nontoxic.

The bacteria-based products are cheaper than the fungal-based and mycorrhizal products. Both are designed to increase nutrient uptake, promote faster root development, and reduce heat, drought, and cold stress. These products also stimulate other beneficial soil microorganisms to thrive. In short, they can increase the overall health of a crop, especially one grown in "soilless" media or in soil that has become exhausted and overworked.

With the exception of some products sold by ROOTS, Inc. and BioWorks, Inc., most of the products are primarily aimed at commercial growers. But if you have an interest you may be able to get some in smaller quantities. Also, as they sense the demand, there will be more availability in smaller quantities by many manufacturers. Are they worth it for the home greenhouse grower? Perhaps, especially if you have problems with soil-borne diseases. They might also be of some benefit if you are growing primarily in containers with soilless media. If you are not having any soil-borne diseases, I am not sure if they would be worth the money to the hobbyist, but they can't really do any harm. However, these products may be perfect for a small home-based greenhouse business, especially if used to protect a small commercial crop of bedding plants from disease without the use of fungicides. And all the while, these products may stimulate some added growth and yields.

Here are some of the current major suppliers at this writing. There are and will continue to be more sources coming on the market. Perhaps an Internet search will show you who else is new out there selling these bioenhancers. For a more complete list, see: **www.barc. usda.gov/psi/bpdl/bioprod.htm.**

Sources:

AgBio Development, Inc., 9915 Raleigh Street, Westminster, CO 80030 (303-469-9221).

BioWorks, Inc., 122 N. Genesee Street, Geneva, NY 14456 (315-781-1703), **www. bio worksbiocontrol.com.**

The EKMA Co., P.O. Box 560186, Miami, FL 33256, (305-667-7175), **www.ekma. com.**

Plant Health Care, Inc., 14 Church Street, Hopkinton, MA 01748, (800-421-9051), **www.planthealthcare.com.**

ROOTS, Inc., 3120 Weatherford Road, Independence, MO 64055, (800-342-6173), **www.rootsinc.com.**

Miracle Products and Stimulants

For years, there have been products claiming to reduce transplant shock. One of the most common is a product that contains a synthetic hormone called indolebutyric acid and vitamin B1. I have seen this product help, but it wasn't a great help. It would be advisable to use this material only when you are worried about the transplanting of a very valuable plant. As with anything you put in the soil, more is not better. Follow the directions exactly.

There are always new so-called miracle products on the market that make incredible claims about boosting plant growth or soil fertility. Please view all of these products with a healthy amount of skepticism. Only a few actually do any good. A good indication of a scam is when there is no listing of active ingredients. The company that sells the so-called

miracle product should also be able to supply you with a list of independently generated research data validating its claim. When you see research from a university test, it is better, as they usually don't have the bias a private researcher might. Always use any miracle product in limited areas so you can compare the result with a nontreated area. Here is where I have to repeat the oft-quoted advice, "If it sounds too good to be true, then it probably is." Sorry, but I had to say that somewhere in this book!

Peat Moss

Peat moss is made of the remains of dead plants that have partially decayed and may be hundreds of years old. Because it is often quite low in nutrients, it is not considered a fertilizer, but it is a great soil conditioner. It increases soil aeration and water absorption and helps the soil hold other nutrients in an available state for plant roots to use. Some peat moss may have fertilizer added to it. The label should tell you if that is the case. Peat moss is the major ingredient of most commercially available potting soils for two reasons: (1) because it is compressible and lightweight (making it cheap to ship), and (2) because it holds water well.

There are a number of types of peat moss, each of which has significant attributes. The most common peat moss is sphagnum peat moss.

Sphagnum Peat Moss (aka Canadian peat)
Sphagnum peat gets its name because it is derived mostly from sphagnum moss that grows in the bogs of the North Country. This peat moss tends to have a very acidic pH (pH of 3.0 to 4.0), which is good for alkaline soils, but when you are using it in potting soils a liming agent is also required to bring the pH back up

In general, sphagnum or Canadian peat moss is a good soil amendment, particularly if your soil contains little organic matter.

to near neutral. You may want to check with the manufacturer or retailer as to the exact pH of your peat moss to assist you in determining its effect on your soil bed or potting mix.

Sphagnum peat is sold in different grades, depending on its degree of decomposition and how fine the particles are. Excess peat added to a pot or bed or a soil mix might cause an acidic reaction. This may require that you add wood ash or lime to bring the soil up to a neutral point if it has not already been done in the manufacturing process. If you have purchased a soil or potting mix that seems to be primarily "peat moss," it is probably sphagnum and has probably been treated to bring the pH closer to neutral.

In general, sphagnum moss, or Canadian peat moss, is a good soil amendment, particularly if your soil is low in organic matter. As much as 20 percent of your soil's total volume can be peat moss. Excess peat or organic matter can also cause your soil to become waterlogged.

Anyone who has worked with pure sphagnum peat moss will notice that dry peat moss is difficult to moisten and may need to be premoistened with warm water prior to mixing it into the soil. Once it is moist, it readily absorbs water. If it dries out again, it can be a problem getting it to absorb again. For this reason, most commercial peat and potting mixes that contain peat moss usually have an added "wetting agent" that enables the peat moss to better absorb moisture when applied.

Canadian, or sphagnum, peat moss is extracted much like a mineral is mined. It is a renewable resource. Some claim that the supplies of peat moss are being depleted. But the Canadian peat harvesters claim (this is their statistic) that more than 10 times as much peat moss forms each year than is harvested in their country. In some countries, peat is burned as a fuel for heat and cooking.

One of the advantages of Canadian sphagnum peat is that it can be easily compressed for low-cost shipping, and then, when opened, it returns to its normal density. I tell you this because if you buy a bale of compressed Canadian Peat, you will find that it will expand and go further than you might have imagined.

Because there remains some controversy over the environmental impact of using sphagnum peat as well as the rising price of peat, many researchers are testing promising alternatives. These alternatives include compost, decomposed wood, decomposed bark, and coconut fibers, or coir, discussed earlier in this chapter.

I have rarely come across live sphagnum moss, but if you do, please use it carefully. It can contain an infectious fungus organism known as *sporothrix* that can cause sporotrichosis. Although it is rare, it can cause a chronic disease in humans. If you must use it, be sure to wear gloves when handling it. It also helps to water the live sphagnum moss with a horticultural disinfectant such as Physan-20 prior to handling.

Peat Humus, or Mountain Peat

Peat humus is derived from reeds, sedges, and mosses that grow in moist bogs in undisturbed locations. It is highly decomposed and looks much like black to brown soil. The pH can vary widely, from 5.1 to 7.6. This type of peat can contain a fair amount of nitrogen. Because of this, it may also have an elevated salt level. This makes it unsuitable for starting seedlings or as a component of a seedling potting mix.

Commercial mining of peat humus has also come under much scrutiny by those concerned about the environment because it disturbs and endangers some special ecosystems. Once it is mined, the ecosystem is irreparably harmed. It is always a good idea to contact the manufacturer to ask whether they are using any of this precious resource in their potting soil. There are better alternatives.

Sawdust

Sawdust can work as a soil conditioner, but it can greatly inhibit the ability of plants to take up soil nitrogen, at least until the sawdust becomes well composted. In order for microbes to break down raw sawdust, they must first steal much of the soil's surplus nitrogen that would be used by plants. These organisms can steal nitrogen faster and more efficiently than roots, often leaving plants with a nitrogen deficiency. To prevent this, add an extra source of nitrogen such as compost, manure, or fish emulsion whenever you use sawdust. It is even better to wait and add sawdust only after it has been composted along with some other nitrogen sources. Avoid using sawdust from cedar, redwood, or walnut. They contain chemicals that inhibit the growth of other plants.

All in all, I don't usually recommend using sawdust as a soil amendment, as you must invariably add something else to make it work.

Sewage Sludge

Many cities sell their sludge in a dried and bagged form. One of the most famous is Milwaukee's Milorganite. Cities vary in their treatment of this sludge and its content of human waste. Some noncommercial sludge may need to be composted before using. Talk to your sewer-plant operators about the contents of their sludge. In general, sewage sludge is not recommended for use on vegetables, although China would never be able to feed itself if its public policy did not allow such use.

If you fear someone may have mixed sludge into your food-growing soil, don't worry too much. As should be a common practice with homegrown or store-bought fruits and veggies, you should always wash your produce before eating.

Sludges may contain an accumulation of toxic heavy metals. A common one is cadmium, which doesn't leach out of the soil and can be taken up by plants. This is a concern because it is not good for humans to consume it in measurable quantities. It has been found that plants take up heavy metals easiest when the soil's pH is acidic (usually below 6.8 pH). That is another reason to maintain a soil pH around 7, or neutral.

Wood Ash

Wood ash is added to soil to bring a low pH up toward neutral. It is also good for the addition of calcium, potassium, phosphorus, magnesium, and sulfur. Unfortunately, the exact amounts of these minerals are variable and difficult to determine.

Ash is used mainly to move an acid soil toward neutral because of its alkalizing effect. Wood ash is about two-thirds as effective as ground limestone in raising a low (acid) pH. If you live in arid areas where high pH soil (alkaline soil) is a common problem or have a soil pH above 7, you should avoid using ash altogether. If you have an acid soil below 7, then it might be worthwhile.

Wood ash is commonly added at a rate of 1 pound (0.45 kg) per 10 square feet (0.9 sq. m) of soil. Try to avoid using wood ash to adjust the pH more than once every 3 years, as it can cause an excess potassium level in the soil, which can cause other imbalances.

Another use for wood ash is to spread it around the base of plants to help keep slugs at bay. Coal ash is never good for soil or plants and should not be added to any soil.

INORGANIC SOIL AMENDMENTS

The term "inorganic" refers to materials that were originally a product of our earth's geology. Because the word "organic" is associated with chemical-free and fresh, you might think that you should avoid the following inorganic materials because they may be the opposite of that. In this case, that is not a correct assumption. These materials are often complementary to the organic materials listed above, and the fact that they are inorganic doesn't mean they are chemical products that are bad for you. For instance, sand is just sand and is classified as being inorganic. Sand is in almost every soil, and it doesn't mean you are not an organic gardener if you add it to your soil. In fact, with the exception of "superphosphate," the following products are often used beneficially in organic agriculture.

Epsom Salts

Epsom salts are not just for soaking your feet. They can also be used as a fertilizer, supplying magnesium and sulfur, because they basically contain magnesium sulfate. The sulfur can help alkaline soils become slightly more acidic. The usual application is at the rate of 1 pound (0.45 kg) per 100 square feet (9 sq. m) of soil. Do not just randomly apply Epsom salts, unless a soil test shows that you need to reduce the pH or your soil is low in magnesium. Overapplication can cause problems with other soil nutrients. I have found that Epsom salts seem to perk up roses when used at a rate of 1 cup (0.24 liters) per 10 square feet (0.9 m).

Gypsum

Gypsum is used to slightly lower a high pH and to improve drainage by enabling harmful levels of sodium to leach out of a root zone. It will also help improve heavy clay soils by loosening them. Gypsum contains calcium and sulfur and is usually applied at the rate of 4 pounds (1.8 kg) per 100 square feet (9 sq. m.) of soil.

Limestone

Ground limestone is commonly used to raise a low soil pH. There are two main types of limestone used in soils: calcitic and Dolomitic or dolomite limestone contains magnesium, which can be helpful if your soil test shows that you are low in magnesium.

The amount required to raise the pH one unit is approximately 1 pound (0.45 kg) per 20 square feet (1.8 sq. m) of soil. Sandy, well-drained soils need less limestone to alter the pH. Clay soils may need more. It can take a few weeks before the reaction that changes the pH has completely occurred, so wait at least 2 weeks before you recheck the pH. Take care not to overapply, because that can cause problems with other nutrients and can increase the pH too much.

If you overapply dolomite limestone, you may end up with an excess of magnesium, which can cause poor calcium uptake and injure the structure of the soil. Talk to an agricultural extension agent about the particular characteristics of your local soil if you are adding limestone to correct native soil used in a growing bed.

Perlite

Those white pieces of sand you often see in potting mixes are perlite. It is used for the same reason as sand: to promote drainage and help provide aeration. Perlite has been a popular amendment in potting mixes because is a very lightweight particle and makes soil mixes cheaper to ship. It is mined as an ore, then heated until it expands like popcorn. Perlite has no nutrient value and has a neutral pH. Either pure or mixed 50 percent with peat moss, it is a good material in which to root cuttings.

Precautions should be taken when pouring pure perlite into any mix because it generates much dust that can easily irritate the lungs. To avoid any problems, try moistening the perlite before you mix it. Also wear a protective dust mask over your nose and mouth.

When plants are heavily watered and are growing in a soil that contains perlite, you may see some of the small white particles floating up to the top of the pot.

Phosphate—Colloidal

This is a clay product that is high in phosphorus. It contains about 2 percent phosphorus, so it is not very concentrated but it is quicker in its availability to roots than rock phosphate or bonemeal. It is usually applied at 5 pounds (2 kg) per 100 square feet (9 sq. m) of soil. It also contains some small amounts of potassium and other minerals.

Phosphate—Rock

Rock phosphate is a ground mineral that is primarily calcium phosphate. It is roughly 30

Perlite is used for the same reason as sand: to promote drainage and help provide aeration.

percent phosphorus. It is a very slow-release material but is good for providing long-term phosphorus reserves in the soil. It is generally added at around 5 pounds (2 kg) per 100 square feet (9 sq. m) of soil. It is considered an organic source of phosphorus.

Phosphate—Super

Superphosphate is basically rock phosphate that has been treated with an acid to speed its reaction in the soil. As a result, superphosphate is indeed faster acting on plants. There is some worry that initially superphosphate can have a negative acidic reaction in the soil. It is recommended that superphosphate be mixed in evenly and thoroughly. Superphosphate is 20 percent phosphorus and should be added at the rate of 5 pounds (2 kg) per 100 square feet (9 sq. m) of soil. It also provides calcium and sulfur to the soil.

Because this fertilizer has been treated with an acid, it is often not acceptable for use in certified organic gardening. However, there are those soil scientists who take issue with this stance.

Rock Wool

Rock wool is derived by heating rock to a

molten state and then spinning it into fibers. I have never seen it being made but I am told that the process is similar to the making of cotton candy, only less sticky and very hot. It is available in fine, medium, and coarse densities. It is often available in slabs and cubes for propagation of seeds and cuttings; it is also a popular material for hydroponics. It can be processed to either retain water or to do the opposite by providing for drainage.

Sand
Sand is basically ground rock. It contains no real fertilizing ingredients, although it may help provide some minerals. Sand is usually added to the soil to help drainage and aeration and will greatly aid soils high in clay. Sands vary in pH, depending upon the parent material. Ocean sand should be avoided because of its high salt content. Planting beds in greenhouses should always be a bit on the sandy side to promote good drainage, which is needed for most crops.

Vermiculite
This mica-based mineral is similar to perlite as it, too, is mined, heated, and expanded. Each silver-colored piece looks like a miniature accordion. Unlike perlite, vermiculite can hold water (up to 300 percent by weight). Much like organic matter, it has the ability to hold some nutrients in the soil for plant roots. It also helps the soil resist changes in pH, and, like sand, it improves drainage. It is a common ingredient in commercially available potting mixes.

Vermiculite contains potassium, magnesium, and calcium, but they are in such small quantities that it is not considered a fertilizer. You should use only horticultural-grade vermiculite. It's available at greenhouse and garden supply stores and through catalogs.

Vermiculite helps with drainage but also holds in moisture and nutrients.

Construction-grade vermiculite, used for roof insulation, should not be used in soils because it may be coated with small amounts of oil, which is harmful to young roots.

Over time, vermiculite can wear out and collapse, losing many of its inherent benefits as a result.

OTHER SOIL AMENDMENTS
Chelated Micronutrients
Deficiencies of copper, iron, magnesium, manganese, and zinc are sometimes not deficiencies at all but just a problem of the soil pH not allowing the elements to be taken up. Chelation is a process that attaches these elements to other molecules, which allows the roots to take up the element, even in poor soil conditions. Chelated micronutrients can be absorbed directly through the foliage when the liquid is sprayed on the leaf. They can quickly correct a deficiency and will last longer in the plant than many other solutions. The most common use of a chelate is "iron chelate." As with any fertilizer, overapplication can cause big problems. This is especially true for micronutrients, so follow the label closely.

Cheated micronutrients are not the easiest material to find but are sometimes available at garden centers and can also be found through garden- and greenhouse-supply catalogs. They are more expensive than other fertilizers, but when they work, they are well worth it.

An alternative to using cheated micronutrients is to try a liquid kelp spray for supplying a good balance of micronutrients to the plant.

Water-Absorbing Polymers and Gels

New to the arena of soil amendments are water-absorbing polymers (sometimes called gels). They are irregular-shaped plasticlike granules that swell many times their dry size and hold up to 500 times their own weight in water (talk about thirsty!). Besides water, they can also absorb soluble minerals and nutrients. Roots readily grow into these jellylike blobs and can easily extract water and nutrients from the polymers. Polymers last up to 5 years, and manufacturers claim they eventually break down into harmless water, carbon dioxide, and traces of ammonia.

These polymers are chemically known as polyacrylamides and have the potential to replace the need for other water-absorbing materials in a soil mix, such as peat moss. The EPA has rated most of these polymers "nontoxic." They are gaining popularity among commercial growers, who often add them to soil mixes or soil for potted plants to help the plants survive dry periods better. They are available from many garden catalogs. Follow the label recommendation for application rates.

If you have a problem with getting a soil to hold water, these products may be of some help. One brand I like is called STA-Moist™ (www.digahole.com) because it is chemically based on potassium rather than sodium. Sodium is never good in soils, whereas potassium is a considered a fertilizer. It also has higher gel strength than many similar products, which means that it will last and perform a bit longer in the soil. For more information on this product, call 888-533-7764.

THE EFFECT OF SOIL TEMPERATURE ON FERTILIZER UPTAKE

Cool soil temperatures are common in winter greenhouses and sunrooms. Since this slows the uptake of nitrogen by plants, it can create a reservoir of nitrogen that might be released in excess amounts as the temperature warms up in spring. For this reason, it is important to not overapply fertilizers containing significant amounts of nitrogen during the cooler months of winter. Always fertilize in moderation, but be especially careful in the winter.

Leafy vegetables, such as spinach, chard, and lettuce, grown in a cool winter greenhouse can accumulate high levels of nitrate, which can be dangerous to infants and pose potential health problems to children and adults. The roots take up the nitrate from the soil. When there is adequate light and heat, the nitrate is a beneficial fertilizer that is quickly converted into plant proteins. But when there are low light levels in the greenhouse, accompanied by cool temperatures, the nitrate is not converted into protein and instead accumulates in the leaf. The nitrate accumulation increases when the soil is rich in nitrogen. Research shows nitrate levels are highest in crops harvested near the winter solstice; levels are much lower in crops harvested in the warmer, sunnier month of March. For more information on nitrate buildup, see the section "Nitrates in the Cool-Winter Greenhouse" in Chapter 4, page 121.

MAINTAINING HEALTHY, FERTILE SOIL

Now that we have some understanding of the many materials we can use to amend our greenhouse soils, as well as what healthy greenhouse soils require, let's get more specific. What exactly must we do to maintain healthy, fertile greenhouse soils in pots and beds?

FERTILIZING PLANTS IN CONTAINERS

It is hard to add compost to a large plant growing in a large container, but it can be done. It is far easier to deal with containerized plantings by adding liquid fertilizers as needed. Fertilizers such as fish emulsion, seaweed, or chemical houseplant foods that are mixed with water can help keep a potted plant happy as far as nutrients are concerned. When using chemical houseplant foods, try to find one that contains micronutrients if possible. Look for iron or zinc on the ingredient label. Peters, Rapidgro, Shultz, DynaGro, and Miracle-Gro have some fertilizer products that contain micronutrients, but they also may have some products that don't. I was talking to one company representative who said that they put micronutrients into all of their products but don't list them on the label. So, how are you going to know if a product contains micronutrients? Ask! Look for the company's 800 number or search out their website. If you are lucky, you'll find a knowledgeable person to talk to.

Follow the label on the product and resist the urge to overdo it. Try to use a nitrogen, phosphorus, and potassium (NPK) ratio that is compatible with the plant you are growing. Remember, a high first number (nitrogen) grows leaves. A high middle number (phosphorus) tends to promote flower and fruit

Enriching and turning the soil between crops helps maintain good soil fertility and quality.

growth. Three even numbers is good for general growing. Some manufacturers make this easy by offering plant foods specifically for certain potted plants, such as African violet plant food or fertilizers formulated for orchids. Repotting a plant occasionally with fresh soil mix can also be a good way to maintain fertility, and good soil structure and texture for a potted plant.

SLOW-RELEASE FERTILIZERS

A common characteristic of chemical fertilizers is that they are usually fast to work and fast to disappear. They often move with the water and, in the case of large farming and even commercial greenhouse operations, have been found responsible for polluting groundwater as they leach out of the soil. This is not only a waste of good fertilizer but also a preventable source of pollution.

Over the years, the makers of synthetic fertilizers have tried to emulate the slow-release quality that is inherent with organic fertilizers. Slow-release fertilizers are better because they work over a longer period of time and are less likely to pollute. Chemical companies have developed many products that are better for the environment and the plants. Most of these fertilizers have special "coatings" that allow a slower release of the fertilizer, based either on the temperature or the moisture content of the soil, or both. In general, the cooler the soil, the slower these products release the fertilizer.

Osmocote® is a popular, slow-release fertilizer. It supplies nutrients to plants for up to six months.

Most commercially available, slow-release fertilizers suitable for potted plants look like little BB-sized pellets or seeds. Each pellet contains fertilizer that leaks out over time, usually through the process of osmosis. This allows a slow, measured release. To apply, you simply put a measured amount of these pellets on the surface or top inch of the soil (based upon the manufacturer instructions). Read the instructions well as these slow release fertilizers can still be over-applied, causing such common overfertilizing symptoms as leaf burning.

One common slow-release fertilizer for potted plants is called Osmocote®. Of all the slow-release products available, Osmocote® has been around the longest. It is available in many different formulations and works from 2 to 6 months, depending on temperature and the product you select. Osmocote® seems to release nutrients better in cooler soils than many other slow-release fertilizer products, so it may be a good choice for a cool greenhouse. Some of the Osmocote® products contain micronutrients.

Nutricote®, which also goes by the name of "Dynamite Plant Food," lasts for about 6 months. It is sold in two main formulas: The red label, 13-13-13, is formulated for flowering plants, including fruits and vegetables; the green label, 18-6-8, is for foliage plants, including palms and shrubs. It also has some micronutrients.

Polyon®, also called Pursell's Sta-Green, can work for up to 9 months. Unlike many slow-release products, Polyon is not affected by soil moisture. This means that with excessive watering, you won't get the surge of growth common to some slow-release fertilizers.

There are other types of fertilizer sticks, plant food stakes, and tabs that can be inserted into the pots of plants. But because most of these are inserted into the soil I have found that they often burn the plant's roots.

The slow-release fertilizers work well for a potted plant that is in healthy shape and is not in need of a "quick fix." Whatever you end up using, please don't over-apply. (I know that I say that a lot in this chapter. That's because a lot of people routinely over-apply fertilizers. People are plants' best friends and worst enemies.)

The slow-release fertilizers can be used for plants growing in beds as well, but for these I prefer to use compost wherever possible.

SOIL IN POTS

When plants are growing in containers, maintaining soil fertility can be a bit trickier. Because of the nature of a container, there is a less dynamic soil ecology occurring. For this reason it is more difficult to keep the soil healthy. With potting soil, the health of the plant is directly tied to the health of the soil. Let's look at some of the issues and questions concerning soil fertility in pots.

Sterile Soil

Most commercial potting soils have been heat- or steam-sterilized. This is done to kill most potential disease organisms and/or weed seeds in the soil. People often ask if they should consider sterilizing their soil. As explained in Chapter 5, "Plant Propagation," the reason to sterilize soil is mainly to help seeds to germinate, and the process of heat sterilization kills most of the diseases that prey on young seedlings. After the seedlings are up and going, they can usually tolerate the real world, complete with soil diseases.

You can sterilize your own soil by putting it in an ovenproof container 3 inches (8 cm) deep. Put some aluminum foil over the top of the container. Then set your oven for 200°F (93°C), and bake the soil. When a meat thermometer reads 180°F (82°C), you will have killed off most of the harmful diseases that would be a problem for your germinating seedlings. Avoid letting the soil get much hotter. If overcooked, the soil may release some toxic compounds (toxic only to plants) from the nitrogen in the soil, so keep an eye on the thermometer. Be forewarned: Baking soil smells bad, especially compared to what you usually bake in the oven.

If you want to use the microwave to sterilize soil, place 2 pounds of moist potting soil (not dripping wet!) into a plastic turkey-roasting bag. Don't seal the bag, as it will likely explode! Set the microwave on high for 3 minutes. Let the soil cool before using.

If you don't want to stink up the oven, you can buy small soil sterilizers in many greenhouse supply catalogs, but at around $300, they are not cheap. There are also ways to chemically sterilize soil, but the chemicals are toxic, and it is a dangerous procedure. Avoid doing this.

If it is summertime, you can try this alternative to the oven. Go outside and find an area that receives sun most of the day. Spread out a 6-inch (15-cm) layer of well-watered soil on some clear plastic. Then fold the clear plastic over the top of the soil. Seal the edges with some heavy rocks. You thus let the sun do the work of sterilizing the soil by leaving the soil package sitting out for at least 3 to 6 weeks. This method works faster the more hot, sunny days you have. Leave it out longer for cooler weather. This does not work in the winter.

This method also works with small amounts of soil in a clear plastic bag. Turn the bag over every 5 days or so. Instead of sterilization, you are using what many call "solarization."

Never use soil found near heavily trafficked highways, streets, or industrial areas. It is may be high in toxic lead or other harmful chemicals.

You can see why greenhouse growers like to purchase commercial potting soil for starting seeds: It has already been presterilized and it provides consistent results. Luckily, after the plants have grown and go out into a pot or bed, it is not necessary to have them continue to grow in sterilized soil. These more mature plants can usually fend off most soil diseases. Besides, it is almost impossible to sterilize and maintain the sterility of whole beds or tubs of soil. So when it comes to growing more mature plants or when simply up-potting a healthy plant, sterilization is not necessary.

For starting seedlings or for any other time you might need to use sterilized soil, it is much easier to do what most commercial growers now do—simply purchase a bit of commercially available potting soil. Remember, this soil is only sterile the first time you use it. Although it is fine to recycle this potting soil for more mature plants and for growing in beds, don't use it again for starting seedlings unless it has been resterilized.

In beds, it is relatively easy to keep soil diseases to a minimum. Keep your soil healthy by regularly adding organic matter in the way of compost, peat moss, and the like. The good microbes that break down the organic materials in the soil also prey upon the bad soil organisms that cause trouble to your plants. It also helps to rotate your crops so that the same bed is not growing the same plants on a regular basis. Also, it helps to use disease-resistant varieties when possible. These suggestions are not foolproof in preventing soil diseases, but neither is sterilized soil.

Let's get back to growing in pots.

About Potting Soil

Back in the good old days (I always wanted to say that), most potting soils included three basic equal parts: (1) soil, to provide for any mineral needs, (2) organic material to act like a sponge, and (3) a material to help promote drainage. Today, most commercial mixes have eliminated the soil component and are simply a combination of the organic material and a drainage material. In the commercial greenhouse industry, these are called "soilless mixes."

More and more commercial potting soils are soilless mixes and contain absolutely no soil whatsoever. They are primarily made up of peat moss, vermiculite, and perlite. They may also contain some starter fertilizer to help the plants get established and a wetting agent that enables the mix to absorb water better. Some mixtures may also include some substitutes for or supplements to peat moss. These may include coconut fiber (known as coir) or composted bark. These substitutes usually work fine, but you may find that you need to adjust your watering frequency as you switch from peat-moss based potting soils to these alternatives.

These soilless mixes are lightweight but hold water like a sponge. Soilless mixes have the advantage of being sterile, which makes them good for starting seedlings. When used for growing plants for many months, the soilless mixes usually perform well. After a year or more, they can begin to get more acidic and compacted, and the plants may begin to show signs of stress.

For potted plants I often increase the life and viability of a soilless mix by adding (you guessed it) soil! I usually stir a mix containing rich soil and/or compost into the commercial potting soil mixes. How much you add depends upon what you are growing. I usually end up adding around $1/4$ to $1/3$ soil/compost to the potting mix. It may take a bit of experimentation. *Never* add soil or compost to store-bought potting mixes intended to be used for seed germination. If you add soil to a sterile mix, then the mix is no longer sterile.

The term "soilless" sounds like a gardener's blasphemy, but even without adding soil to these mixes you can get good results. Wait and see what happens before you try any additions to store-bought soil for plants growing in pots.

Besides the general potting soils that are commonly available, you can also find plant-specific potting mixes that have been developed for specific types of plants, including mixes for cacti, African violets, and orchids.

Homemade compost or potting soil often benefits from being filtered through a screen. This filters out rocks and other unwanted debris.

These generally work well but are more expensive. There are also mixes designed specifically for starting seedlings. These work well too, but are also more expensive than the generic potting soil. If you are going to start seeds in a commercial mix, it is imperative that the mix has been presterilized. If you go with a mix specifically designed for seedlings, you can generally be assured that it has been sterilized. Most but not all commonly available potting soils are sterilized, but you can never be totally sure unless it is stated on the package.

To further complicate your options when it comes to purchasing potting soil, you should also know that there are some other classifications such as "all-purpose," "premium," and "professional" mixes. The **all-purpose** mixes are designed for general use and work well for gardeners who are willing to add ingredients to customize their mix if need be. The **premium** soil mixes usually feature a wetting agent that helps provide quicker and more uniform water absorption by the mix. They also tend to include some perlite and vermiculite to increase aeration and improve drainage. Some premium mixes may also include a fertilizer that is sufficient to feed the plant for its first 6 months or so. **Professional** mixes are typically made up of peat moss, composted bark, vermiculite, perlite, wetting agents, and fertilizer. The main feature of a professional mix is in its great consistency, a factor that is essential to commercial growers who need to be able to get used to a particular mix and its inherent attributes. This allows them to better control the growth over time.

It is hard to generalize about the many different commercial potting soil mixes available. The best advice I can give you is this: If you find one you like, stick with it. If you keep switching, you will never get the feel and understand the needs of any one particular mix. One might need to be watered every two days, whereas another may hold water longer and not need irrigation for a week.

Like many things we buy, commercial potting soil is most expensive when purchased in small quantities. If you can purchase it by the larger bag or bale, you will save a lot of money.

Some people simply fill raised beds solely with commercial potting-soil mixes. This is not a good practice, as these mixes will likely hold too much water. It also will not last very long, losing the attributes of drainage, and the pH will likely go out of balance. In short order, it will need to be reworked with some other amendments and rich soil. Adding a small amount of potting soil to a bed is not a problem, just don't get carried away. Instead, use rich soil, compost, and sand as needed (see discussion on page 352).

Making Your Own Potting Mix

If you are determined to make your own potting soil, here are some tips.

One major ingredient in any homemade mix is rich outside garden soil. However, any rich soil can have problems with weed seeds and possibly even have plant diseases that could spread to your greenhouse crops. As mentioned earlier,

THE OLD-FASHIONED RECIPE FOR POTTING SOIL

A good potting soil must be well drained and at the same time be able to hold at least some water. Almost every commercial greenhouse has its own special recipe. Most potting soils include 3 equal parts: soil, an organic material to act like a sponge, and a material to help promote drainage. Here is a customizable recipe that has been around and used by greenhouse gardeners for decades:

Recipe for Potting Soil

RATIO	1 Part Soil	1 Part Organic Material	1 Part Drainage Material
OPTIONS	Rich topsoil	Peat moss or coir	Sand (*not* beach sand)
		Leaf mold	Vermiculite
		Screened compost	Perlite

Mix the 3 ingredients well, using a tub, soil bench, or wheelbarrow. Do not use ocean beach sand, as it is high in salts and hard on plants. If you live in an area with an acid soil (check with your local county extension agent), you may need to add limestone.

If you need to alkalinize the pH, add about 1 tablespoon (15 ml) of ground limestone per $1/2$ gallon (1.9 liters) of soil to adjust it toward a neutral pH. (A home or professional soil test will tell you the pH.) For more-tropical houseplants, you may want to add a bit more peat moss for more acidity and water-holding capacity. For cacti and succulents, add more sand for faster draining. If you want to increase the water-holding capacity, you can consider water-absorbing polymers, mentioned earlier. Sterilize any homemade soil mix to be used for germinating seeds (see Chapter 5, "Plant Propagation").

sterilizing the soil can neutralize diseases and weed seeds. For details, see Chapter 5, "Plant Propagation." Hold your nose, because this process can smell up the kitchen pretty badly, as the aroma of cooking soil is far from appetizing.

Customizing the Recipe

Over the years, I have played with this recipe and found that it is only as good as your base soil. If your soil is poor or has some troublesome idiosyncrasies, it can become a problem. I often end up tinkering with the recipe to compensate for a poor topsoil. If this is the case with you, try adding a higher proportion of the organic and drainage components at the expense of the soil in the recipe. If your base soil in the recipe is high in clay, it will tend to hold an excessive amount of water. If this is the case, increase the drainage component somewhat.

In cases where only very acidic soils are available, try to lessen the soil component, avoid the use of peat moss and leaf mold altogether, and increase the use of coir, vermiculite, sand, and compost. Where the soil is highly alkaline, try to increase the use of peat moss at the expense of both soil and the drainage component. If your topsoil is chunky, you may want to screen it to get a better blend.

For screening compost or any other components of the recipe, you might want to make a cheap screener. Simply stretch some "hardware cloth" (also known as "hail screen") across a square of pine two-by-twos. The screen should have approximately $1/3$- to $1/2$-inch openings between the wire.

As you have probably gathered, soil-mix recipes are not set in stone and require a bit of experimenting before you end up with the perfect mix for your particular soil and plants.

REPOTTING AND UP-POTTING

Whenever a potted plant takes on a sickly or weak look, we often wonder if it is time to embark on the chore of repotting or up-potting. What is the difference? Repotting is simply replacing as much soil as possible, using the same pot. Sometimes, you really don't want the plant to be in a larger pot. But the problem remains in that the potting soil often wears out and loses its positive attributes.

Also, a plant may have become root-bound, with the pot containing more roots than soil. To determine if being root bound is a problem for your plant, check the underside of the pot where the drainage holes are. Look for many emerging roots. Then you may want to remove the plant from the pot for further investigation. Even if your plant looks as though it is root bound, do a little research. Some plants actually prefer to be root bound! Check the plant out in Chapter 8 or another gardening book, or in a plant encyclopedia to be sure that it isn't one of the many plants that prefer tight quarters.

Repotting is done to control the size of the plant or at least maintain the current size while also maintaining the plant's health. Besides adding new soil, the process may also include some root pruning to stimulate new growth and to enable the plant to fit back into the same pot along with the new potting soil. The procedure is more difficult with larger plants. Before you get started, get ready for a mess. This is where a potting bench really is wonderful to have in a greenhouse or workroom (see Chapter 1 for more information on potting benches).

If you are using potting soil that is dusty dry, you may want to try premoistening it by watering it well in a bucket or on a potting bench. Sometimes new potting soil is hard to get wet—it just runs off, like water off a duck's back. This is why a wetting agent is added to the better mixes, which makes the water absorb quicker. If your potting soil is slow to absorb water, the solution may lie in patience; allow the water to be taken up overnight. You can also try using slightly warm water.

The first step in repotting is to remove the plant from the pot. This is best done with some sharp, blunt blows to the bottom of the pot as you support the plant in a close to horizontal angle. If you have a strong stem, you might try a gentle tug, grasping it while pulling away from the pot. After the plant is removed from the pot, you will need to shake out and physically remove as much soil as possible around the roots. If you determine a need to control the size of the plant, you may want to consider removing some of the roots. Never remove more than $1/4$ of the roots at any one time. If the plant is showing signs of stress, root pruning may not be a good idea. Finally, set the plant back in the pot at the same depth it was before, while adding the new potting soil to the pot and in between the roots. Water the plant thoroughly. Recheck the pot in a few days, as the soil may have settled and it may need a bit more filling.

Up-potting is done when a plant has become root bound. You must also be committed to the idea that it should be in a larger pot,

When plants become rootbound or the soil seems to be causing problems, it is time to repot. Never repot into a container more than 4 inches larger than the original pot.
1. Hold the plant upside down and tap the bottom of the pot with your hand.
2. Gently support the plant as it slides out of the pot.
3. If the plant is rootbound, pull some of the roots apart and consider pruning up to one-quarter of the total roots.
4. Add some potting soil to the bottom of the new pot to allow the plant to stay at the same level with the soil as it was in the old pot.
5. Add soil around the plant in the new pot. Gently press soil into the voids. Then water well.

triggering an even larger plant. The most common up-potting mistake occurs when gardeners put the plant into a pot that is too large. The result can be soil that holds too much water and starts to sour and degrade prematurely. Resist the urge to go big too fast. Only up-pot to the next-size available pot. This means going to a pot-size increase of only 2 to 3 inches (5 to 8 cm). Follow the previous instructions for repotting, taking care to add a little soil to the bottom of the pot so that the soil meets the stem at the same place it did in the smaller pot.

Some people worry about soil falling out of the drainage hole. The drainage hole also prompts people to fill the bottom of the pot with pebbles or crushed rock. Yes, soil will fall out of the hole for a short time, but after it has been well watered that usually ceases.

The pebbles that are commonly added to the bottom of the pot supposedly to help drainage are actually a waste of space. The soil will drain fine without the pebbles unless you used a poor potting soil. All the pebbles do is take up precious space that could be holding soil. The best solution to drainage is to use a quality potting soil or to customize your mix with more of the drainage components (perlite, vermiculite, and sand).

SOIL IN BEDS

When you are growing plants in beds year-round, you will need to put something back to make up for what you harvest and for what the plant itself takes from the soil. When you are growing perennial plants that stay in the same location for many years, such as a banana or citrus plant, it is almost impossible to remove or replace any of the soil with compost, amendments, or new, rich soil. What you can do is either top-dress with well-decomposed compost and/or water-in nutrients that may be needed as indicated by the plant. Better yet, using the information provided by a soil test, you could add a suitable fertilizer to the top of the soil to correct a possible problem.

In greenhouses beds, the addition of soil nutrients and/or soil conditioners is usually needed a minimum of twice a year, but many plants may be heavy feeders and need feeding every few weeks, depending upon the conditions.

Fertilizing beds can be done in many ways, including the application of a liquid form that is watered in, a granular form that is mixed into the top few inches of the soil, or through the addition of compost, which must also be mixed into the top 6 inches (15 cm) of the soil.

As mentioned earlier, I prefer the regular addition of organic components because they release their fertilizer elements more slowly over

Growing plants in beds year-round can deplete soil. Be sure to add organic and other amendments and rework the soil to maintain healthy plants and soil.

a longer period. They also have the added benefits of organic matter and of giving off carbon dioxide, which feeds the plants through the air.

It is very helpful to rework the soil prior to each planting in the beds. I usually apply 1 to 2 inches (2.5 to 5 cm) of compost to the soil surface and dig it into the first 6 inches (15 cm). This may require that you remove some of the soil in a bed to make room for the compost. As a general rule, I add a phosphorus fertilizer to the soil and regularly feed the plants with a foliar spray of fish emulsion. In the cold parts of winter, because of the slower growth and cooler greenhouse temperatures, it is best to stop using the fish emulsion or other nitrogen fertilizers to prevent a nitrate buildup, at least until your greenhouse warms up. In heated greenhouses, this is not as much of a concern.

USING MULCHES IN A GREENHOUSE

All good outside gardeners know the incredible benefits of applying mulch. It reduces weeds, conserves moisture, and helps the overall health of the plant. In a greenhouse, you get all of the above benefits as well as one other: It also helps increase the level of carbon dioxide in the winter air (when the greenhouse is more sealed to the outside).

After some extensive trials with mulches, I have found that mulches can pose a problem when used in growing beds. Mulching in greenhouse beds can increase soil-dwelling pests. This can include problems with fungus gnats, slugs, sow bugs, and pill bugs, all of which can increase tremendously when a mulch is present. These pests are difficult to control and create a new set of problems (for more information on these pests, see Chapter 10, "When Things Go Wrong").

A mulch makes it much easier to overwater. This, combined with creating a habitat for pests, sets the stage for a problem. For these reasons, I recommend that in greenhouse beds, and even in large pots, tubs, and containers, you go slow on using mulches.

THE WAY TO APPROACH WORKING WITH SOIL

Soil is forgiving, and I apologize if it sounds a bit too scientific or complicated. If you look at anything closely enough, it gains in complexity, and soil truly fills the bill when it comes to complexity. The study of soils is indeed a science—but it is not rocket science or brain surgery. Working with soil is more akin to baking a cake or making a casserole. If you're like me, you rarely follow a recipe to a "T." Besides, that is how all of the world's best dishes are made. When you approach working with the soil, don't be afraid to experiment.

Get your hands dirty! Soil is forgiving and alive—don't be afraid to experiment with it.

Get your hands dirty! You're not building a watch. Things just happen. And sometimes you should just let things happen. People get too serious about soil and view it as a win-or-lose chemistry experiment. Because soil is forgiving and alive, you rarely lose as long as you heed this final advice: When it comes to the soil, moderation is always the best course to follow.

CHAPTER 10

WHEN THINGS GO WRONG:

MANAGING PESTS AND DISEASES IN THE GREENHOUSE

WHEN YOUR FIRST PLANT DIES OR YOU DISCOVER the first bug infestation in a new greenhouse, you realize that the plants and the environment you have created won't always behave exactly as you wish.

Joan Loitz, a solar-greenhouse pioneer whom I met back in the 1980s, often said that new greenhouses go through a "honeymoon period." She is so right. If fact, you have probably turned to this chapter because your honeymoon is officially over. The first crop or two you grow in a new greenhouse are often amazingly pest free. It usually takes 2 to 8 months before the first pest or disease attacks occur. Just when you start to get cocky about how pest-free things are, watch out. From then on, it is an adventure, with a few new pests or diseases finding a way to your greenhouse regularly. But fear not, all this will prevent boredom and keep you on your horticultural toes. Some problems will be easy to manage, whereas others will be quite challenging. In any event, they are a fact of life in the greenhouse, as they are in any form of gardening. They will always be present on some level. Your task is to keep that level manageable.

Learning about how to get rid of pests and

diseases may seem like a grim subject, but the problem-solving aspect of controlling pests and diseases in your greenhouse can (and should be!) as much fun as growing the plants. Before you think I'm off my rocker in enjoying pest control, let me explain. For the most part, I use beneficial bugs and critters to control the pests in my greenhouse. I have found the culture of growing bugs to be much like the growing of plants. I actually get as thrilled when I see the good critters get a leg up on the ones doing the damage as I do when a special flower blooms. This type of holistic pest-control is both challenging and entertaining (ever heard of a flea circus?). No matter what type of pest control you opt for, the main goal is to keep the level of infestations down low enough to produce abundant food and flowers. It is not against the law to enjoy the pest-control part of greenhouse gardening as much as the other aspects of sunroom horticulture.

This chapter covers the pests and diseases that commonly afflict greenhouse plants and introduces a variety of methods and philosophies for controlling them. You will become acquainted with the pests and their natural enemies ("beneficials") and the environmental conditions that enable both good and bad critters found in a greenhouse to either thrive or perish. This chapter also covers the advantages and disadvantages of using sprays, fungicides, and other pest- or disease-control methods. The solutions I present throughout this chapter emphasize what I call "biologically sane" remedies for greenhouse problems, and put health and safety concerns first. But before we can get to solutions, we must first learn how to recognize and identify problems.

YOUR BEST DEFENSE: KNOW YOUR PLANTS!

Your best defense against pests and diseases is to know your plants. That way you will recognize symptoms when something goes wrong. This requires great powers of observation. I recently heard that we are barraged with over 300 advertisements per day in various forms. As a result, I believe we have learned to ignore and filter out much in our environment. In the greenhouse, you need to reawaken your ability to take notice when things change—especially when things are changing gradually and for the worse.

Learn to *observe* the plants growing in your greenhouse. Yes, I know you think you are looking at your plants, but I mean *really* look closely at them. It is surprisingly easy to look but not *see*. What is the tone and texture of the green in the leaf or the shine of the plants? Are they extra shiny today (that could mean bugs!)? Are they getting a slight yellow tinge to them that wasn't apparent yesterday? Are the tips of the leaves healthy and green? Look at the undersides of the leaves, the soil, the stems, and everything in all the nooks and crannies—this is where the action is! The trick is to notice the subtle changes as well as the in-your-face bug assaults. Make a point of looking around your greenhouse regularly. I like to do it before my day gets going, by just walking around the greenhouse with a cup of coffee in hand.

GET A LOOKING TOOL

There are some tools that will enable you to look even better. Every greenhouse gardener should own a small hand lens or magnifying glass. You can purchase a hand lens for very little money. They are commonly available at a power of 10x. I have found hand lenses in college bookstores (because they are often used in labs), scientific supply houses, and even some office-supply stores. If you like gizmos and have big pockets, there are a few Swiss army knives that have a built-in hand lens among the knife blades. These are perfect for looking at leaves and the knives come in handy if you need to do some plant pruning or tighten a screw on the greenhouse door. What other single tool could do all that and enable you to open a bottle of wine to share with your sweetheart while enjoying a greenhouse sunset?

There are a number of magnifying devices for viewing pests better, most of which work great. Even the one on a Swiss Army knife is acceptable.

CAUSES AND EFFECTS OF PROBLEMS: ANIMAL, MINERAL, OR YOU?

Greenhouse problems are caused by either an organism (disease, insect, or human) or the environment (heat, light, soiliter), or some combination of the two. Therefore, simply determining the cause of the problem can be quite challenging. The most important thing to understand is that pests and diseases don't "just happen." They exist because a certain chain of events has led to an environment that enables them to exist, or even thrive. Once you learn how to observe or identify the way one thing affects another, you will know how to deduce what the symptoms of the plant are telling you and how to take the right steps to remedy the problem.

For example, too much nitrogen in the soil causes soft, lush growth. This lush growth actually attracts aphids, a common greenhouse pest. Aphids can often spread a wilting fungus into a plant as they feed. Also, when aphids feed, they exude what is known as honeydew, a sticky-sweet substance that lands on lower leaves. The honeydew provides a nutrient that encourages a black fungus mold to grow on the surface of the leaf.

By simply adding too much nitrogen, we have encouraged aphids and a plant fungus, and

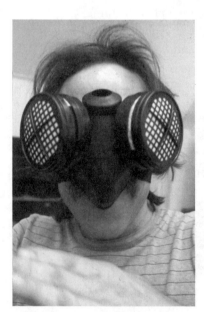

Sometimes the worst pest in the greenhouse is you! (Note: this is not the correct way to wear a spray respirator.)

Honeydew produced by pests drips onto leaves and provides a nutrient that encourages growth of a black fungus called "sooty mold."

on the surface of the leaf, we now have sooty mold forming. Whew! It is not my intention to scare you about nitrogen, which it is a required nutrient, but it makes a good example of how things can go wrong when there is excess. This example is not uncommon, as I have seen this exact chain of events many times in home and commercial greenhouses. It is a domino effect that can occur between the environment and plants. Much like any ecology, everything is connected to everything else in your greenhouse.

Let's look at some other examples where people are involved. Nutrient imbalance can mimic diseases by causing yellowing leaves or leaf splotches. Some sprays used to control pests can actually be toxic to the plants, even causing more damage than the original pest, and may produce an effect that looks like a disease. You've heard the old adage "The cure may be worse than the disease." The point is, when you see a new symptom, think about what you have recently done to the plants. Have you been fertilizing them, watering them, spraying them, or what? Think back. Did you do it the proper way, at the proper time, and in the proper dilution? Yes, sometimes you have already met the enemy. Look in the mirror. Quite often one of the worst culprits in the greenhouse is YOU!

The health of the plant is an important factor in preventing pests and diseases. When a plant is under stress, it becomes more susceptible to problems. The same is true with people; when we are tired or run-down, we are also more apt to catch a cold.

Many things can cause plant stress. The older a plant, the more likely it is to have problems. Stress is also caused by a number of environmental factors, including problems with temperature, light, nutrients, and water. When any of these factors is not at its optimum, the result is stress.

I once kept an eggplant bed alive long into the winter, even though my greenhouse temperature was far too cold for growing eggplants. The longer it lived into the cool winter, the more pests and diseases took their toll. It really shouldn't have been growing in such cool temperatures, and that was exactly what it was trying to tell me.

In another example, I once grew kohlrabi well into a hot summer. Kohlrabi is a cabbage-family crop that likes cool winter temperatures. Soon it had aphids all over it, whereas the more heat-loving crops such as tomatoes and cucumbers were pest free. I never saw aphids on my kohlrabi in the cooler winter months. Somehow, the pests knew which plant was under stress.

SYMPTOM I.D.

Identifying the symptoms of a plant problem is the beginning of developing effective controls. When you see a problem, you must determine whether the problem is caused by a pest or disease or by you! When there is a human-caused problem, look for this symptom: The trouble occurs on many different species of plants across a broad area.

When it is a disease causing the problem, the symptoms tend to be isolated to certain smaller areas or on specific plant families (see the box titled "Basic Crop Families" in Chapter 3, page 111). Pests often stick to plant families, but in high numbers they may spread more uniformly. Fortunately, with pest problems you can diagnose the problem by seeing the pest itself. Be sure to hold off on judgment until you have used your hand lens on the undersides of leaves. This is where the critters often hide.

Later in this chapter, there are specific descriptions of damage caused by pests and diseases. The following chart might help you get started in your mission to figure out what might be going on and eventually help you to determine the cause of your problems.

Now that you have some idea of how to identify symptoms, let's move on to explore pest problems and control strategies in particular. Then, later in the chapter, we'll get into the common greenhouse diseases.

PEST-CONTROL STRATEGIES

There are many options when it comes to controlling pests. Admittedly, it can be both confusing and overwhelming. It is my plan here to make the choices clearer. Above all, my primary concern is safety, both for the environment and for you and your family.

The way I see it, there are three main options for controlling pests in a greenhouse or sunspace:

1. **Prevention.** Do what you can to keep diseases and pests away from your greenhouse in the first place.
2. **Integrated control.** When problems surface, this involves the releasing and / or encouraging of beneficial insects and other critters in the greenhouse to help control the pests. This is done in conjunction (and only if needed) with the occasional use of

SYMPTOMS AND CAUSES OF PLANT PROBLEMS

	POSSIBLE CAUSES →	Air pollution: Faulty heat exhaust or appliance	Disease: Root or soil borne	Disease, leaf: Fungus, bacterial, viral	Fertilizer: Lacking	Fertilizer: Too much	Fungus gnats (insect that feeds on roots)	Pests that have sucking mouth parts: Aphids, whitefly, mealybugs, thrips, scale	Pests with chewing mouth parts: Beetles, weevils, grasshoppers, slugs, snails, caterpillars	Leaf miner (insect that lives within the leaf)	Light: Day length too long or short	Light: Excess	Light: Insufficient	Spider mites	Temperature: High	Temperature: Low	Water: Insufficient	Water: Overwatering and / or poor drainage
GROWTH	Slow or nonexistent		*	*	*		*				*	*	*	*	*	*	*	*
	Weak, soft, and thin				*	*							*					
	Elongated, skinny												*					
FLOWER	Brown tips and spots							*						*				*
	Blooms absent		*		*	*					*							
	Deformed							*										
	Bud drop	*			*	*		*				*	*		*	*		
LEAF	Sticky to tacky and shiny							*										
	Pieces of leaf missing: chewing / skeletonizing								*									
	Wilting		*	*			*								*	*	*	*
	Fine webbing and / or tiny yellow spots / dusty looking													*				
	Spots and blotches	*		*		*		*		*						*		*
	Dropping	*			*										*		*	*
	Yellowing	*	*	*	*	*		*		*		*	*	*				*
	Curling and/or bending down	*		*												*		
	Tips or margins brown					*											*	
	Purple cast				*							*	*			*		

safe sprays to assist in reducing pest numbers while not harming your beneficial critters. I say "critters" because the good guys are not always limited to just insects. They can also be spiders, bacteria, fungus, and, more rarely, even a frog, snake, bird, or lizard. This is "choice number 1" and is best known as "integrated pest management," or IPM, for short. IPM also utilizes prevention as the first line of defense. We'll get back to IPM in depth later in this chapter.

3. **Spraying.** This method of control depends solely upon spraying as needed (preferably spot spraying) with the least-toxic sprays, along with using occasional traps and other preventive measures to keep populations down.

AN OUNCE OF PREVENTION

The number-one strategy is to avoid ever letting the pest into your greenhouse. This would include being very careful when someone wants to give you a plant. This is one of the quickest ways to get a severe bug infestation. For this reason, your natural inclination should be to tactfully refuse any gift plants. Some people can't refuse a freebie, so whenever you bring a new plant into the greenhouse, always inspect it closely. It isn't even a bad idea to give the gift plant a bath first. This means washing the undersides of the leaves with water and insecticidal soap and then rinsing the plant well.

I hate to say it, but another way to get a pest in your greenhouse is through the purchase of a plant from a garden center or mail-order outlet. Again, inspect and bathe the plant before you let it into your greenhouse.

If you have recently visited another greenhouse with a moderate to severe infestation of bugs, you should avoid going directly into your greenhouse without first bathing and/or changing your clothes. Some bugs can easily hitch a ride in your hair or clothing.

Another way insects gain a foothold in your greenhouse is by coming through the door or vent. This is tough to prevent, but you can install a special microscreening material that has been developed to prevent the movement of small insects. It allows air to move through freely, but, unlike traditional screens, this special screen has very small openings that don't allow the very small insects to pass through. This prevents harmful insects from coming into the greenhouse and can help keep the beneficial insects from escaping to the outside. This screen is available in smaller quantities from Charley's Greenhouse Supplies (see "Mail-Order Supplies," in Appendix 7).

Prevention is something that should be a part of every greenhouse pest-control strategy. The rest of the strategy first requires a decision from you as to which avenue you would like to take in controlling pests. Let's look at the basic steps of prevention to minimize pests.

Preventive measures can only take you so far and do so much. Sometimes they can single-handedly solve a problem. Sometimes they can only lessen some inevitable damage. When prevention isn't enough, you have a number of options to consider and explore. Let's begin with pest management, starting with the method called "integrated pest management." We'll then cover disease control later in the chapter.

INTEGRATED PEST MANAGEMENT (IPM)

A greenhouse or sunroom garden is probably the closest garden you'll ever live with. Because of the many health concerns associated with chemical pesticides, it's especially important to

10 STEPS TO MINIMIZE PESTS

1. **Clean it up.** Keep dead leaves cleaned up and off the soil surface of beds or pots. Don't let any plant parts rot on the soil surface. Eliminate places where pests can thrive, or at least keep them away from the windows or vents of the greenhouse or sunroom. This includes weeds, poorly managed compost piles, and debris.

2. **Beware of gift plants.** This may be the best way to avoid having a new pest to romp in your indoor garden. Don't be a hospital for a friend's sick plant(s). If you must take on any new plants, including a store-bought one, inspect it closely. If you see anything suspicious, get rid of it. If you won't get rid of it, take it outside and spray it with the appropriate pest-control spray before bringing it into your greenhouse or sunspace.

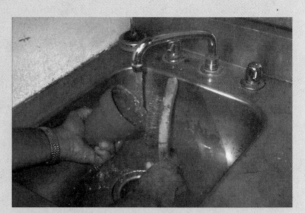

Old pots can harbor diseases and insects. Clean them thoroughly with a wire-bristle brush, hot water, soap, and diluted bleach. Rinse well.

3. **Pull up plants past their prime.** If a plant is starting to look sickly or infested, it quite possibly is past its prime. Unless it is a treasured plant, pull it up and toss it in the trash. Be very careful when removing a heavily bug-infested plant. If you are clumsy, you could easily sprinkle bugs all across many other plants, triggering a massive epidemic. The best thing to do is to sneak up on the plant with a plastic bag. Quickly and gently slip the bag over the plant, covering the total above-ground portion of the plant. Gather the bag together at the base of the plant and pull it up, keeping the bag sealed at the base as you take it to the garbage.

4. **Isolate plants in poor health.** If a plant is in poor health or under attack from a pest or disease, yet you can't bear to part with it, set it away from other plants. It is best to move it to another room out of your greenhouse or sunspace. With luck, you can move it to another suitable location (with the right light and temperatures for the plant). By isolating an unhealthy plant, you prevent the spread of bugs or diseases to healthy plants. I often take an unhealthy potted plant outdoors and spray it with an appropriate material, so as not to affect the good bugs living in the greenhouse with the spray.

5. **Before reusing pots, wash them.** Old pots can harbor diseases and insects. They also may have salt deposits that may cause soil problems later on for a new plant. Salt deposits are indicated by a crystalline or powdery white substance. Sometimes you'll need a wire bristle brush to clean a clay pot. When you wash any pot, use hot water, soap, and a diluted bleach. Rinse well.

(Continued on next page)

6. **Keep the air moving.** Both diseases and insects love stagnant air. So even in winter, run a fan during the day (a small fan set on low works well). Moving air also helps increase the level of beneficial carbon dioxide adjacent to the leaf surface (see Chapter 1, page 27). A fan exhausting warm greenhouse air into your home in winter is often enough air movement. It will also prevent air stratification, where the hot air stays at the ceiling and the floor remains cool.

7. **Integrate your plantings.** As described in "Crop Layout and Harvesting" in Chapter 3, planting beds with mixtures of crops (intercropping) rather than a single crop may help keep infestations of pests and diseases to a minimum. It confuses them. Also, vary your potted plants by mixing in some pots containing other types of plants.

8. **Rotate your crops.** When growing in beds, try not to plant the same crop in the same place in consecutive years. Keep records to help you remember what you have done (see the box called "Basic Crop Families" in Chapter 3, page 111).

9. **Grow varieties resistant to potential problems.** As explained in Chapter 4, "Selecting the Right Plants," some plant varieties may be resistant to insect or disease problems. Unfortunately, in real life the term "resistant," when listed in a catalog, may mean only "more tolerant." The plant still may succumb to the problem. Still, it is worth trying those particular varieties. It is also helpful to keep your own records (see "Record-Keeping" in Appendix 8 for help). You will soon find differences among varieties and their responses to pests and diseases. This is where record keeping really pays off.

10. **Maintain plant health.** When your plant is infested, it may be telling you something. Are you growing it at the right time of year or in the right location? Does it have the proper light intensity, nutrition, water levels, and temperature? Maybe a different plant would do better in that spot. Is the infested plant just getting too old? Perhaps it is time to kiss it good-bye. Give it some thought.

rethink traditional methods of pest control for the attached and / or enclosed garden. Integrated pest management (IPM) is probably the safest and most effective way to manage pests in a greenhouse, and employs a variety of strategies.

IPM involves three basic components: (1) prevention, (2) biological controls, and (3) if/when necessary, the use of safe and biologically compatible sprays, applied precisely and in a way that will not adversely affect any of the other controls involved in IPM.

Integrated pest management is, as the name implies, a strategy for managing pests, not annihilating them. The end result is a tolerable level of pests in balance with the environment. IPM uses a combination of beneficial critters, biological controls, crop rotation, integrated planting, constant pest monitoring, cultural controls, and also (but only when absolutely necessary—and rarely) some spot spraying of isolated plants with specially selected low-toxicity materials.

PEST CONTROL: GREENHOUSES VERSUS THE OUTDOOR GARDEN

Because greenhouses and sunrooms are often attached to the home and are enclosed environments, we must be especially careful how we go about controlling pests and diseases. Let's compare pest-control effects for the inside and the outside garden.

Controlling Pests in the Outside Garden
1. Repellents work well; the pests move out of your garden.
2. Pesticides rapidly break down in the presence of unfiltered sunlight.
3. Pesticides, if sprayed in the wind, cause unintended consequences.
4. The outside garden has a wealth of naturally occurring beneficial insects.
5. Purchased beneficial insects often fly away with the first wind.

Controlling Pests in the Attached Greenhouse or Sunspace
1. Repellents don't work well in an enclosed environment because there is nowhere else for the bugs to go.
2. Sprays can easily get into the household air if your greenhouse is attached.
3. Beneficial insects released into the greenhouse or sunspace will not escape and will stay in the environment.
4. Spraying pesticides in a greenhouse leaves little fresh air for the person spraying. Thus, filter masks are recommended.
5. The effect of a spray lasts longer due to the lack of unfiltered sunlight.
6. Greenhouse pests and diseases often differ from those in the outside environment because the environment is different.

Biological control is the cornerstone of IPM, for it involves managing pest populations through the use of natural enemies, also known as "beneficials." These beneficial critters are not limited to insects. Some biological controls are microbes such as fungi or small critters known as nematodes that attack pests. Even reptiles have shown excellent appetites for insects in certain greenhouse situations. I have a native salamander hiding in the corner of my greenhouse that I rarely see because he is nocturnal. At night, he takes a little feeding walk and then goes back into his hole. Some daring greenhouse gardeners allow snakes (nonpoisonous, of course), toads, chameleons, and other lizards to take up residence. They have excellent appetites for slugs, flying pests, and even a few (oops) beneficial insects, which all contribute to their balanced diet. They are also fun to watch.

I once had a small lizard that was the most patient character I have ever seen. He would perch on a stake and wait for the better part of a day for a fly or bug to come near. Some days he didn't catch anything, but other times he would strike gold. It was fun to be on hand when he actually caught something. I never had to provide any supplemental food for any reptile in my greenhouse. Of course, reptiles are definitely not for everyone!

Many people have had good luck with birds in the greenhouse. I know some folks with zebra finches flying around their greenhouse, feeding all day long as well as adding to the ambience of the place.

As you can see, beneficials can be many things, from spiders to reptiles, nematodes to birds and even fungi. However, the most common beneficials are insects.

IPM BACKGROUND

Biological control is not a new science. Mother Nature has been using it with good results since the beginning of time. It took a while for people to catch on to the idea of good bugs controlling the harmful ones. There was a flurry of researching and applying biological control techniques in the first half of the twentieth century. But with the advent of pesticides, especially DDT, followed by other effective chemicals developed during World War II, the use of biological control measures came to a virtual halt. A rediscovery of biological controls occurred in the seventies—and for good reason. As the expense and environmental hazards of pesticides came to light, along with the fact that insects developed quick resistance to them, there was a renewed interest in alternative pest controls.

In nature, biological control is a dynamic balance that is self-perpetuating. It is perhaps the single most important aspect of a healthy ecosystem. Of the approximately 1 million insects listed as plant feeders in the world, only about 1 percent are listed as pests of agriculture.

When using IPM and biological controls, you must ask yourself, "What level of pest or disease presence is personally tolerable?" Unfortunately, people have little, if any, tolerance for even one bug (good or bad). Our tolerance is usually lower than that of a plant. There are some estimates that a plant can sustain up to one-quarter of its leaves being destroyed by pests before there will be a decline in yield. If you can put up with a few bugs here and there, the rewards are great. You will be the beneficiary of a healthier environment, fewer overall costs, and less labor.

IPM IS NOT FOR EVERYONE

Before you undertake integrated pest-control management, understand that it requires you to be knowledgeable, involved, and tolerant. You'll have to know as much about particular insects as you do about how to grow a tomato. In using good bugs and other critters to control the pests, you must also tolerate always having some pests in your greenhouse. The good news is that the pests and beneficials are present at tolerable levels, meaning they should not be hurting your yield and overall plant health. Still, you have to put up with a low level of bad bugs in order to enable the good bugs to control them. For many people this is not an option.

When people are considering using biological control methods on an attached greenhouse or sunspace, there is a great worry about beneficial insects getting into the house and causing trouble. You can relax. A home is not their preferred environment. They prefer surviving in a sunny greenhouse full of plants over your bedroom or laundry room. They want to be where the plants and bugs are. Besides, most are so small that you wouldn't even see them even if they did get in.

Some people have a low tolerance to bugs or think that the only good bug is a dead bug.

Some people are simply revolted by bugs. If this sounds like you, then you might not be suited to this type of control. Some simply don't want to go to the trouble of working with beneficial insects. That is fine, as there are many safe alternatives in using low-toxicity sprays, traps, and other tricks also mentioned in this chapter. But if you're game, read on.

PREDATORS AND PARASITES

Beneficial bugs are classified as either predators or parasites. A predator simply eats the bad bug for its nutritional sustenance. Predators usually feed on more than one species of pest. They might have an aphid for breakfast and a spider mite for lunch. They are not picky and feed on almost anything. In contrast to the general nature of predators, parasites tend to be more species-specific, meaning that they are usually able to control only one target pest. Sometimes they are limited to one species of pest. For example, some wasps will only control one species of aphid. If you have another species in your greenhouse, they may not work.

The most common beneficial parasite in the greenhouse is a very small wasp. Many people have an innate fear of wasps, even small ones. Let me assure you—the ones we introduce in the greenhouse do not sting people. They will only help you control a pest population, and when they work for you, they do a great job!

The word "parasite" means the creature completes its life cycle in the host pest. How does this occur? The process is basically the same for most greenhouse pests, so let's use the aphid as an example pest to illustrate how this works.

First, the female wasp "stings" the aphid—but in this case she is actually depositing an egg through the stinger directly into the living aphid. Then, the egg hatches within the aphid and consumes it from the inside out, using the aphid as a shell and a food source for the new wasp's development. During this process, the aphid dies and (the now former aphid) turns into a copper- or tan-colored, bloated-looking aphid.

When the wasp has finally reached a certain stage of maturity growing inside of the former aphid, it is ready to "hatch." It does this by cutting a little opening or door in the copper- or tan-colored aphid shell. This process is reminiscent of much science fiction. Ever see the film *Alien*, starring Sigourney Weaver? Hey—where do you think Hollywood gets its ideas, anyway?

As part of a concerted program of IPM control, you must necessarily avoid many common pesticides. They will knock off the pests, but they will also kill your beneficial predators and parasites. There are, however some compatible pesticides that can be used successfully with an IPM pest-control program (see the chart later in the chapter on compatible pesticides).

THE BASICS OF A SUCCESSFUL IPM PROGRAM

It takes an incredible amount of time and labor to spray the top and bottom of every leaf in a greenhouse once a week with a pesticide. Then you will find yourself losing sleep wondering about the health effects of a particular chemical that you sprayed. It is much easier (and more fascinating) to plan out an IPM strategy by ordering a crop of good bugs, releasing them at the proper time and place, and then sitting back and letting them do much of the work. Although IPM is much easier, there are some chores you must do to insure success.

When an infestation occurs, identify the pest with certainty. After you "I.D." the pest, you need to decide which beneficial critter will be best to use to control the pest. Refer to the section later in this chapter titled "Common Greenhouse Pests" (page 397), which includes a listing of beneficials that will work with your bad bug. Preceding that section is a detailed discussion of beneficial predators and parasites (page 372), where you can learn the specifics about managing each particular good critter.

CREATE THE RIGHT ENVIRONMENT FOR THE GOOD GUYS

Creating biological balance with beneficials requires that you maintain certain environmental conditions in your greenhouse. First, you must be sure the environment is free from damaging pesticides (more on this below). Next, you need to provide proper temperatures in which they can thrive. In general, the beneficial insects prefer a moderate environment. If it is too hot or cold for you, then it probably is for them, too, and the beneficial insects' activity and effectiveness will slow. Usually, the best temperatures for establishment are between 55°F and 90°F (13°C and 32°C). For this reason, both good and bad bugs are always slow to establish in winter and spring. If you have a solar-heated greenhouse and have trouble controlling the cool night temperatures, don't despair. Most pests can't thrive in low night temperatures, either.

Third, as a general rule, the beneficial insects prefer a relative humidity of around 60 to 70 percent. Some require a specific day length in order to thrive, as is discussed later with the aphid predator midge (*Aphidoletes aphidimyza*).

You will need to prepare a proper environment for your good critters before releasing them in your greenhouse. Water the leaves of the plants prior to the release, as the beneficials arrive very thirsty.

LOCAL AND MAIL-ORDER BENEFICIAL CRITTERS

Usually, the beneficials (insects, spiders, or otherwise) are mostly purchased through mail-order suppliers (see "Mail-Order Pest Control," in Appendix 3 for sources). Sometimes, however, I have been able to collect them from the great outdoors. If you see the same pests on outside plants that you have inside your greenhouse, then you also might be able to find and collect these beneficial critters that are waging war in their native habitat. I have had good luck finding naturally occurring aphid infestations outside in the summertime. Among those happy aphids, I can often find a few parasitized aphids. I bring those parasitized aphids into the greenhouse and put them to work. Soon, wasps hatch out of the former aphids and I am on my way. I did this more often years ago, when finding commercially available sources for beneficial critters was next to impossible.

Acquiring beneficial bugs through mail-order catalogs has gotten easier in recent years. When I first started using biological pest control back in the seventies, it was difficult to find them at all. I used to beg for beneficial insects from local university research programs. I even had a special permit to directly import them from Canada and Europe. Things have finally changed, and now a number of commercial outlets in the United States sell beneficial insects. Even many of the common seed companies sell beneficial insects.

The selling of beneficials is a dynamic industry and such enterprises are constantly searching for and offering new critters and products to help control certain pests. Sometimes they offer great improvements. You will notice that the newer beneficial critters that come on the market are usually more expensive, due to basic supply and demand. Over time, you will usually see the price drop as the demand and production adjust.

Minimizing Costs of Mail-Order Beneficials

When you first peruse a bug catalog or price list, you might suffer from sticker shock. One order of bugs might run anywhere from $15 to $75. And to add insult to injury, they must usually be shipped "overnight" or "next day," which can run as much as $35 to $40. All that may not be so bad until you realize that it might take more than a few shipments to get a good establishment of critters in your greenhouse. If you go with only one shipment, you may find that the population of good guys goes down as their food supply (bad bugs) is depleted. When this happens, it can give the pests a chance to establish beyond the capability of your beneficial bugs to ever catch up with their numbers. By doing a few releases, you can even out these population swings and gain better control.

One way to minimize costs is to get together with other greenhouse enthusiasts and split an order. Many bugs are sold in commercial quantities, and by splitting an order two or three ways, you will still have plenty of beneficials for your greenhouse. When the order arrives, simply split it up.

Another way to minimize costs is to locate a good supplier that is the nearest one to you. Then you might be able to select a cheaper shipping method and still get the bugs within 1 or 2 days. This can provide substantial savings, because then you can conceivably go with second-day shipping versus next-day shipping.

You should know that there are many levels of bug suppliers. There are wholesalers, retailers, and companies that simply sell beneficials as a sideline to their larger gardening or greenhouse business. I always prefer dealing with companies whose main business is the selling of beneficial critters, especially those that specialize in beneficial critters for greenhouse control. With them, you tend to get the best price and informed advice and suggestions. Appendix 3 has a number of companies listed. It never hurts to ask them if this is their primary business or if they also sell wheelbarrows and trowels, too.

ESTABLISHING BENEFICIALS IN THE GREENHOUSE

When you order the bugs, agree on a definite shipping and arrival day with the seller. You can't dilly-dally when the bugs arrive. Unpack them immediately. Most often they must be released that day or evening, so you must be available that day to let them go. This is not something to put off until tomorrow or pass off to an uninterested spouse or friend. These guys can be quite perishable, and you paid good money for them! If your release doesn't go well, it can derail your whole IPM system.

When the beneficial critters arrive, put a few of them under a bright light and look at them closely through a magnifying glass or hand lens, even if you already know what they look like close up. Why? I have run into a few suppliers that were notorious for shipping dead or mostly dead bugs. You must make sure they are alive! If you have any questions, contact your supplier. Usually they will make it right. Unfortunately, a shipment of dead bugs can also derail your timing and screw up your whole plan to get beneficials established well enough to control the bad guys (more on timing the release of your critters below). Seeking out good suppliers and staying with them is essential.

It is hard to generalize about how to release all beneficial critters in a greenhouse. Sometimes you sprinkle them onto the leaves. With others, you simply pop off the top and they go flying out into the greenhouse air. Sometimes you hang cards containing the critters among your infested plants. Fortunately, most suppliers provide excellent instructions on releasing the beneficials. Some suppliers may even provide containers to aid in the release process. IPM Laboratories, Inc. (**www.ipmlabs.com**) offers a unique small cardboard container called a "Release Point™" which works very well.

As you might have guessed, you should release the beneficial critters on or near the plants that have the highest pest populations. Take special note of which plants or leaves you released them on so you can come back to check their performance with your hand lens. Look on the underside of leaves, and check adjacent plants for indications of the beneficial insects at work in new locations.

Upon the release of the beneficials, give them your best blessings.

TIMING AND MONITORING

Timing the release is everything to a successful program. You must get the good bugs in on the "ground floor." This means releasing the good guys when you *first see* the bad guys, not after they have turned into a big problem.

Timing is based upon good monitoring. To do good monitoring, you must have a hand lens and use it regularly. Monitor even if you don't think you have a bug problem. Get out there and look for the bad bugs. When you see

them, it is time to get ready to order and release the right critter to help control them.

After you release the good ones, you must monitor them, too. If you know you have a plant or area where your beneficial insect is in high numbers and well established, try plucking a few leaves and carefully relocate them to a heavier infested area of bad bugs. Try hanging or perching the plucked leaves containing good bugs in the upper portions of other infested plants that need more good guys.

It is important to spread your good bugs around. Although they can move fast on a particular plant, they often move slowly across a greenhouse. Physically moving the good bugs around also helps you reduce the number of beneficial insects you will need to buy over time.

If you already have a full-blown infestation, your good bugs will have a most difficult time getting control. The key to good control with beneficials is to allow both the good and bad bugs' populations to rise together simultaneously. Catching up is not a good option.

These tiny parasitic wasps have just arrived and are about to be released from these containers into a greenhouse to help control aphids.

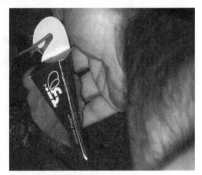

Some suppliers provide containers to aid in the release process, such as this cardboard container called a "Release Point™" offered by IPM Laboratories.

If you do have a large infestation and want to use good bugs, you can reduce the pests' population by spraying a few weeks prior to introducing the beneficials. Be sure to use a nontoxic or compatible spray (listed later) that has little toxic residual activity on your good bugs when they arrive. This makes it a fair fight between the good guys and the bad guys. See the following section called "Sprays with IPM" for more information.

WHAT TO EAT WHEN THE FOOD IS GONE?

A common question about biological control is: "What do the good bugs eat when they have eaten up all of the bad bugs?" This is a good question. The answer depends upon the type of predator or parasite that you introduce into your greenhouse. Some will never get rid of all the bad pests. This is the best scenario, as it indicates that a balance between the two has been established. It is good because then the population of the beneficials will stay high enough not to need as much restocking on your part.

If, however, the beneficials have devoured all the bad bugs, then they run the risk of also dying out because there is nothing to feed upon. They essentially become "extinct," at least in your greenhouse. Then you will have to reintroduce them when the pest population rises again (as it always will). This scenario is most common for the predator spider mite (the good mite that eats the bad ones), which does such a good job that there is nothing left for them to feed upon.

Luckily, many critters can get by in the absence of bugs by feeding on the nectar and pollen of the flowers. This can be helpful in keeping them alive to fight another battle. It also saves you money if you don't have to order more beneficials because they starved. For this reason, it is a good idea to have some specific flowering plants in your greenhouse at all times. Some good choices include fennel, anise, dill, the mints, and anise hyssop.

Some people wonder if a good bug can become a "bad" bug or pest. The answer is no. Most good bugs rarely go "bad" when life gets rough on them. The worst they can do is go off to feed on pollen or die of hunger. The ideal situation is one in which the population of the good and bad bugs is in an ongoing balance and there are always a few of each.

DON'T THROW OUT YOUR GOOD BUGS

Sometimes people throw away their best source of good bugs when they toss out a damaged or almost dead plant. Ugly-looking bug-infested plants sometimes are your best habitat for a beneficial predator or parasite. Look it over with a hand lens before you toss it out. If it does indeed host your next generation of good guys to save the day, consider leaving it for a few more weeks. To deal with my embarrassment of having an infested plant remaining in my greenhouse, I often post a sign next to it that says: "Bugs at work, beneficial insects are hard at work controlling the bad bugs on this plant!"

If you simply must throw out a plant (even into the compost) while using biological control, be sure to check the leaves on that plant for any good bugs. If you discover a population of good bugs, pluck some leaves containing good bugs and relocate them where they are needed. I have seen hundreds of beneficial critters thrown out on one plant that, if saved, could have made all the difference in a battle against a bad bug.

SPRAYS WITH IPM

With IPM you don't depend entirely upon the good critters, because they can't do it all. As mentioned earlier, you must also use complementary methods to supplement them. That is why it is called an "integrated" control. But this requires both care and understanding. For instance, if you try to assist them by spraying certain chemicals, you might also kill all of the good critters in your greenhouse.

With IPM, you should minimize the use of pesticides. When you must use them, you should only use the pesticides that don't kill the good guys. If your pesticide is not compatible with beneficial parasites or predators, then you must either wait for the pesticides' effects to dissipate or apply them in a limited and / or isolated manner, as discussed later.

I will never forget when I was first using beneficial insects to control whitefly and dutifully ordered and released the proper amount of the parasite *Encarsia formosa,* which is a tiny beneficial wasp that controls whitefly in the greenhouse. Unfortunately, I released too few, too late. (This is how I learned how important timing is when releasing good bugs. It is hard to play catch-up with good bugs.)

To help my *Encarsia* get a leg up on the whitefly, I sprayed "nontoxic" insecticidal soap around to assist with control. But instead of seeing my good guys get the upper hand on the whitefly, my *Encarsia* declined to the point where I couldn't find any left in the greenhouse. Guess what? My soap also did a good "nontoxic" job of killing the good insects, *Encarsia* included. I had spent $35 on an order of *Encarsia* to control my whitefly and then unwittingly set out to systematically destroy them. Live and learn.

Fortunately, there are some sprays that are compatible with beneficial critters, meaning they can be applied when beneficials are present or prior to their release without harming them. Some sprays require a wait period before you release or expose the beneficial bugs to them. The more common pesticides sold to gardeners, such as Orthene and Diazinon, require a 3-month wait before you release any beneficial insects. If you release before the suggested wait period, the residual toxicity of these sprays can remain high enough to kill the good guys. Even with "nontoxic" insecticidal soap, you should wait at least 1 day before you release beneficial insects into plants that have been sprayed. Never spray it directly on or in close proximity to your good guys, or you may end up like I did—with a lot of dead beneficial insects.

If an infestation is limited to just one plant, consider taking the plant outside (if it is a potted plant) and spraying it there, where it won't affect your population of good bugs. If you can't move it because it's in a ground bed, consider pulling it up and tossing it out. If it is not potted and is an incredibly special plant, try spraying with the most compatible material to try to gain a measure of control. Remember, even isolated spot spraying with incompatible insecticide sprays is risky when you have beneficial insects in the greenhouse. The good guys usually have even less resistance to most pesticides than the bad insects.

Another question you always need to ask when considering the use of a pesticide compatible with beneficials is whether it can be used on food crops. Each pesticide must be registered by the Environmental Protection Agency (EPA) as to whether it can be used on food crops. It costs more to register a pesticide for food crops than it does for ornamental crops. High costs will prohibit some companies from registering a low-toxicity pesticide for use on food crops, especially if they have a decent market for its use on ornamental crops. Of course, sometimes they don't go for food-crop

PESTICIDE COMPATIBILITY: BENEFICIALS / EDIBLE CROPS

Pesticide Name	Common Name	Registered for Edible Crops?	Wait Period Before Beneficials Can Be Released
Adept, Dimilin	diflubenzuron	No	0 days
Avid®	abamectin	No	21 days
Azatin® EC	azadirachtin	Yes, some	0 days
BotaniGuard™	Beauveria bassiana	Yes, some	0 days
Cinnamite®	cinnamaldehyde	Yes, some	7 days *
Conserve, Spintor, Success	spinosad	Yes, some	3–4 days *
Diazinon	diazinon	Yes, some	3 months
Enstar SE, Enstar II	kinoprene	No	0 days
Gnatrol®, BT	BT (Bacillus thuringiensis)	Yes, some	0 days
Horticultural oil	oil	Yes	1 day
Insecticidal soap	insecticidal soap	Yes	0 days
Mavrik	fluvalinate	No	3 months
Naturalis-O®	Beauveria bassiana	No	0 days
Neem oil	neem oil	Depends on brand—see label	0 days
Orthene®	acephate	No	3 months
Preclude, Precision, PT2100TR	fenoxycarb	No	0 days
Resmethrin	resmethrin	No	14 days
Talstar	bifenthrin	No	3 months

*New product; this is a best guess
This chart created with assistance from IPM Laboratories, Inc.

registration because the pesticide is too darn toxic to be used on food.

Whether a pesticide can be used on food crops is an important piece of information when you are trying to decide what to use to supplement your beneficial critters. A pesticide may well be safe for beneficials but not registered for food crops. This is something you shouldn't risk. *If the label does not say the product is registered for use on food crops, do not use it on food crops!* Besides the fact that improper use is illegal, it could also make you seriously ill, in the short and / or the long term.

It is unfortunate that many of the compatible pesticides are not readily available in the local garden centers. Instead, they are formulated more for the commercial market. For some odd reason, many environmentally dangerous pesticides are commonly available in garden centers, whereas many safer, more effective, and ecologically sound pesticides are only available at the wholesale level. Go figure! Sometimes you can persuade a supplier to send you some. Another option might be to work with a local commercial grower in obtaining some of the more compatible and safer chemicals.

IPM AND PATIENCE

Above all else, an IPM program requires patience. It can take many weeks for the beneficial bugs to get established. You just have to put up with this seemingly out-of-control period by using other compatible controls. Keep the faith by looking for slight increases in the good bug population and slight decreases in the harmful pests.

If you don't see even slight improvements, then you need to think about why and ask yourself these questions. Did you accidentally kill the good guys? Did they arrive alive? Did you order enough early enough? What about temperatures and humidity? It is important to learn from your mistakes, but I would prefer that you learn from mine, most of which I have discussed here in this book.

It takes a while for the population of the good bugs to get in gear. But once the balance is established, it works wonderfully, like a well-tuned piano that plays itself! After all, that is what an ecosystem is. If you are worried that things are not working, perhaps a call to a quality beneficial-bug supplier can help, as these companies can often shed some light on your situation and give you some free advice. It is in their best interest that you get their beneficial bugs to work in your greenhouse.

The experience of having a self-contained ecosystem within your greenhouse or sunroom is a source of continual amazement. The fun of having a room that produces food and flowers is doubled when you're growing not only plants but also these amazing critters that help to maintain a dynamic balance. It will become a self-contained biological island (or at least a peninsula!) to help bring your mind, body, and spirit into a better dynamic balance of their own. Now I'm sounding like a "doctor-reverend" extolling the virtues, but as you can see, I love using IPM!

BENEFICIAL CRITTERS THAT FEED ON MANY PESTS

In the "Know Your Pests" section found later in this chapter, you will find many potential beneficial predators and parasites listed that you can use as part of an integrated pest-management program for your greenhouse. Many of these beneficials are specific to one particular pest.

It is under that pest that the discussion of that specific critter or control mechanism is described in full.

There are, however, beneficials that are predators by their very nature and that tend not to be so specific. These predator beneficials can control a wide variety of pests. Rather than provide repeated in-depth information on these predators each time I describe a pest, I provide the in-depth information for you to refer to here.

BENEFICIAL PREDATORS OF MULTIPLE PESTS

Green Lacewings

Description
Adults are up to 1 inch (2.5 cm) long. They have a slender green body, large lacy wings, and long antennae. When you get close to them, you will notice that they have beautiful golden eyes.

The young lacewings are known as "aphid lions." They are $1/16$ to $1/8$ inch (1.6 mm to 0.3

cm) long, with large jaws and a body that tapers down to the tail. They look like a small centipede without all the legs. The lacewings' eggs are round and are about $1/16$ inch (1.6 mm) or less long. All the eggs are laid on the end of a $3/4$-inch-long (1.9 cm), thin hairlike stalk. This stalk has evolved to protect the eggs from other lacewing young. This is because the young are so voracious that they would eat all of their brethren if they could. Fortunately, they can't climb up this stalk, which holds and protects the other unhatched lacewing eggs.

Controls
Only the young lacewings are predaceous. The adults feed mainly on nectar from flowers. The young feed on a wide variety of greenhouse pests, including mites, and do a decent job on whitefly young. However, their favorite dish is succulent aphid sushi.

How to acquire
Usually through the mail; however, they may fly in from the outside on their own, if your vents are not screened. Lacewings can also be collected from the outside if you know how each stage of the critter looks. There are two different species of lacewings that are commonly available. *Chrysoperla carnea* is more commonly found outside and overwinters in most areas of the United States, but will work fine in the greenhouse. The more common choice for greenhouse situations is *Chrysoperla rufilabris,* which can tolerate higher humidities.

Comments
Green lacewings are usually very good predators but are subject to being eaten by other predators and each other. For this reason, try not to release them all in one spot—spread them around. Don't release any other predator

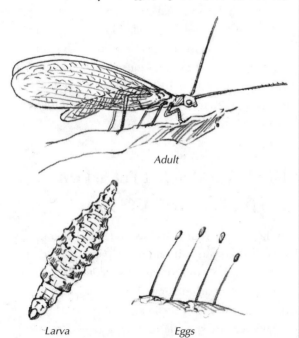

Adult

Larva   *Eggs*

in adjacent areas. If eggs have hatched when they arrive from the supplier, release them immediately, as the young will eat each other in close confines. To release, scatter the eggs or young on the leaves, in crotches of stems, and as near to pest infestations as possible. It is best to release them the moment they arrive in the mail.

Ladybug, or Ladybird Beetle

Description

Most people know what a ladybug looks like, but just in case you don't, here is a description. Adults are $^3/_{16}$-inch (0.5 cm) long and oval-shaped, with reddish-orange outer wings with dark polka dots. When they fly, their clear inner wings slide out from under the outer shell.

What you may not know about the ladybug is how it looks when it is in the young (larval) stage. The young are $^1/_{16}$-inch (1.6 mm) long. They are flat looking, and the body tapers from the head toward the rear end. They have the opposite coloring of the adults, with a dark-gray body and reddish-orange spots. The eggs of the ladybug are elongated, yellow, and football-shaped, $^1/_{16}$- to $^1/_8$-inch (1.6 mm to 0.3 cm) long. The eggs are laid in bunches, usually on the underside of a leaf.

Controls

Both the adult and the young ladybug feed on a wide variety of insects, including aphids, whiteflies (young), spider mites, mealybugs, and on rare occasions even scale. Usually, they are best for controlling aphids.

How to acquire

Usually through the mail. They may also come into the greenhouse naturally through windows. You can also hand-carry them in if you

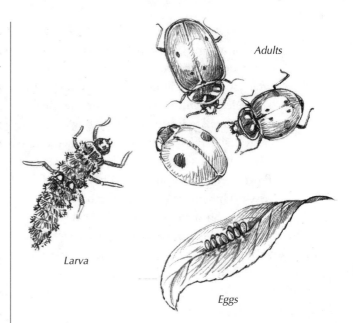

Adults

Larva

Eggs

can catch them. They are available from a variety of mail-order sources. Normally, they are purchased by the gallon, quart, or pint. One gallon (3.8 liters) is approximately 75,000 ladybugs. A pint is plenty for a small greenhouse.

Comments

Although ladybugs are helpful outside, they aren't all that they are stacked up to be for greenhouse pest control. I am not sure why, but I would guess that it is the higher temperatures and changes in light quality from natural sunlight. They also have variable feeding habits. I have seen them on occasion do a wonderful job on aphid populations. Still, I have often seen times when the aphids are almost dancing with reckless abandon in front of the ladybugs' noses while the ladybugs yawn (perhaps they're too preoccupied with mating, which they do often). To sum it up, they are sometimes good and sometimes not. I generally prefer to try lacewings before I use ladybugs.

Ladybugs will store in the refrigerator for up to 3 months, as long as you don't freeze them and a hungry teenager doesn't accidentally eat them. Use them as needed out of the refrigerator, releasing them only in the evening after a watering. The bugs are very thirsty when first released and must have some water droplets immediately available. Ladybugs may not be available during certain times in winter, so check with a supplier. Ladybugs will feed on flower nectar and pollen during times of few pests. They must often be periodically reintroduced into the greenhouse, as their numbers dwindle over time. Be sure to learn what an immature ladybug looks like so you don't mistake it for a pest!

Praying Mantis

Description

The adult is a walking-stick-like insect. The praying mantis is large, up to 5 inches (13 cm) long, with coloration varying from brown to green. It has a triangle-shaped head and large forearms it uses to catch its prey. The young insect resembles the adult, only it is much smaller, starting at $1/8$ inch (0.3 cm). When the young are first born, they almost look like a large mosquito. The young hatch from an egg case (up to 200 eggs per case) that resembles a wad of rigid brown Styrofoam about $1\frac{1}{2}$ inches (3.8 cm) in diameter.

Controls

While young, they feed on many soft-bodied insects. Unfortunately, the traditional greenhouse pests such as aphids and whitefly are low on their preferred list. As they grow, they feed on larger insects, including each other.

They are also more attracted to faster-moving, large-bodied critters such as bees or flies.

How to acquire

You can acquire the mantis through the mail, or, in warmer climates, the egg cases may be collected outside in their natural habitat. They are usually found in late fall and winter. Look for egg cases on branches of trees and shrubs.

Comments

Hang mantis egg cases from a branch in areas with pest problems. Egg cases do not change appearance appreciably after the young have hatched, so watch closely. Cases are generally available from suppliers from January through June. When they are young, mantises will work on many greenhouse pests but will never provide complete control. Unfortunately, because they are general feeders, a mantis can occasionally be found feeding upon other beneficial insects, such as ladybugs. Even though they are not the best greenhouse-pest eradicators, mantises are fun to have around, especially if you are not used to seeing them. I love the way they can turn their head to look you in the eye. Don't be surprised if you find yourself or your family treating them like pets, complete with pet names.

Spiders

Description

Spiders have four pairs of segmented legs (for a total of 8 legs). You will often find them near or in their webs. Their abdomens are strongly constricted at the base.

Controls

Spiders feed on many small insects, including winged aphids and whiteflies. They also feed on other crawling insects.

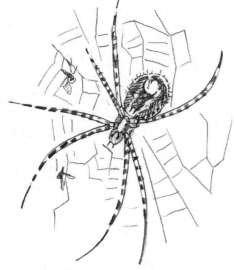

How to acquire

Spiders are not available commercially. Spiders can be found outside and brought in or will arise naturally. This is especially true if you minimize the spraying of pesticides. Smaller spiders seem more active and better at controlling greenhouse pests. Also, they're not as scary to people!

Comments

Spiders can be very helpful in controlling greenhouse pests and are an important general predator. For that reason, you should consider allowing them to coexist with your plants and the other beneficial critters in your greenhouse. I know some of you are thinking, "Are you kidding or crazy?" I am not kidding, although I have found a bit of craziness helpful in running greenhouses. The main point is that if you can get over your arachnophobia, spiders can become great helpers in controlling pests. Very few actually sting and poison people; most are quite harmless and very helpful (just don't make friends with black widows, or the brown recluse spider). A good book on spiders can help you identify those that are harmless to have around.

I have seen whole greenhouses cleaned of aphids in just a week by a healthy spider population. The best thing about most spiders is that they usually make every effort to stay out of your way by hiding under leaves and benches and in dark corners.

Syrphid Fly, or Hover Fly

Description

Adults are $^3/_8$ to $^1/_2$-inch (1 to 1.3 cm) in size. They look somewhat like a wasp in coloration but are actually more closely related to the housefly, which they resemble; they lack the very segmented body and narrow waist of a wasp. The hover fly has yellow or orange rings on a black body. It is so named because it has the ability to hover like a hummingbird or bee (usually around flowers). The young are $^1/_{16}$ to $^3/_8$ inch (1.6 mm to 1 cm) in length and look like a small gray or brown maggot. The eggs are laid singly and are oval, white, and $^1/_{32}$ inch (0.8 mm) in size.

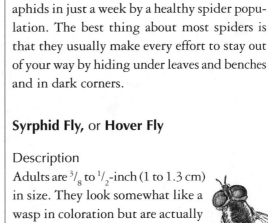

Controls

Usually only the young are predaceous and have a good appetite for aphids. The adults generally feed upon the pollen of flowers.

How to acquire

The hover fly is not commercially available. If you want some, you have to bring them in from the outside. Often, they will fly in on their own. If you are adept at identifying and catching flying bugs, you can hand-collect them (no, they don't sting). It is too bad this bug is not currently for sale.

Comments

If you happen to see the hover fly in your greenhouse or garden, consider yourself lucky. Flowers attract the adults into your yard and greenhouse. You can tell you have a hover, or syrphid, fly by its superb flying ability and the way it hovers in the air around flowers. Catch or coax one in for duty in your greenhouse.

Reptiles and Amphibians

Description
Toads, frogs, chameleons, lizards, salamanders, and snakes.

Controls
Slugs and assorted flying insects.

How to acquire
Pet shops or the outside.

Comments
Chameleons and toads often feed on flying insects. They position themselves on the tops of plants in search of food. Lizards, salamanders, and snakes will feed on many bugs,

as well as slugs. There is a lot of room for experimentation. Be sure to put away the mouse poison, because it may also kill the reptiles. If food gets low for these predators, you may have to supplement with food such as mealworms, available at pet stores. Reptile predators are not recommended for the squeamish or the commercial greenhouse, because these great little creatures often scare the heck out of people. If they do not bother you, give them a try—you may find a good friend under the scales.

SPRAYS AS PEST CONTROLS

Spraying is an important part of greenhouse gardening and pest control. It doesn't always mean using chemicals. Spraying is also the method used to apply safe, homemade botanical and microbial materials. On the other hand, there can also be problems when spraying is done incorrectly.

CHEMICAL SPRAYS AS PROBLEM SOLVERS AND PROBLEMS

Synthetic chemicals are often suspect in their effect on human health. Rarely does a year go by that another chemical isn't pulled off the shelves because of safety concerns. Home food and flower production may be our only form of independence from pesticides. Indeed, this is why many people initially start a vegetable garden and even move into greenhouse gardening.

The more we use synthetic chemicals, the more insects become resistant to the chemicals. Compared to 1965, twice as many insects (including many greenhouse pests) have developed resistance to sprays. Also, when massive spraying occurs, it kills many beneficial insects that often prevent harmful insect populations

Toad

Salamander   Lizard

from developing. With no good bugs to eat or parasitize them, the bad bugs will have an even faster-growing population.

Unfortunately, using chemicals is not a black-and-white issue. It is quite gray. Not every product you find in a spray bottle is totally harmful, nor should every chemical be considered evil. There are many new, biologically safe materials that are being released to control insects (see more discussion later in this chapter). On the other hand, there are some organic sprays that, by virtue of being "organic," may seem biologically safe but are potentially harmful to plants and people. I would generalize that synthetic chemical pesticides should be used only as a last resort. Selecting the proper chemical should be an informed decision, made with a commitment toward promoting biologically sane avenues of control.

BEFORE YOU SPRAY

If you have decided to control a pest by spraying, the first thing you must do is pick out the safest effective pesticide. This can include a homemade spray (listed later), or it might mean you are going to purchase something that controls the pest. If you are going to purchase a spray, don't assume it will work on the bug you want to control. First read the label; it should tell you what the material is registered to work on—and for what crops it is registered. If your crop or pest is not listed, this spray may not work. Even worse, it may not be safe to use if it is not labeled for the use you intend.

SPRAYING EQUIPMENT

You have a lot of options in spray equipment, everything from a recycled window-cleaner-type squeeze sprayer up to fancy expensive pressure sprayers. Because most home sunrooms

There are many different types of small sprayers you can use for a home greenhouse, including the well-made Polyspray 2.

and greenhouses are so small, you really don't need a big sprayer. A plastic squeeze sprayer that holds a quart or less will usually work fine. A favorite sprayer of mine, after trying many brands, is what is sold as the Polyspray 2. It runs about $20 in the catalogs and is well worth the price. It is a small pressure sprayer that you pump up a few times for an easy-to-control spray. It can give you a fine mist or a 30-foot (9-m) stream (for reaching the tops of the banana tree). It is durable and British-made. I have used other hand-held pressure sprayers, but none seem to have the quality of the Polyspray 2. (No, I don't own stock in the company; I just really like this little sprayer.) Still, the cheap squeeze sprayers or recycled sprayers can also do the job adequately.

If you use more than one pesticide, I strongly recommend you consider having a spray bottle for each type of pesticide you use. Spray bottles can also be used for applying foliar fertilizers. If you use the same container for spraying different types of pesticides, you risk contamination, even with good cleaning. Contamination can be a serious problem when two different pesticides mix, causing unforeseen negative results. Never use a sprayer that has held a herbicide or dandelion killer with an insecticide. The latent herbicide may be difficult to wash out of the sprayer and can cause big plant kills throughout the greenhouse.

I also highly recommend purchasing and using a respirator mask for spraying many commercial pesticides inside a greenhouse or sunspace. It can even come in handy if you are spraying a concentration of homemade hot pepper spray or other possibly caustic liquid. These masks are available through agriculture supply or feed stores and are occasionally found in some supply catalogs. Wear them over your nose and mouth when you are spraying, and be sure that they are sealed. You should never smell the stink of a pesticide through these masks. They run $35 to $60. A simple paint or dust mask will not do the job! The greenhouse is an enclosed environment, and you will likely need full protection. This holds true even for many botanically based sprays. The only exception might be insecticidal soap. The label of a spray will also indicate what type of protective equipment is needed.

Plastic or rubber gloves should always be worn when spraying, because many sprays can be easily and quickly absorbed directly through the skin. Even soap- or pepper-based sprays may irritate your skin.

Goggles are important equipment in preventing any spray from getting into your eyes. Your eyes can actually absorb some pesticides.

Also, have an old toothbrush around. Nozzles often get plugged and gummed up. An old toothbrush is the best way to clean them. After cleaning the nozzle, dispose of the toothbrush and do not reuse it. Never clean nozzles with metal pins or the like. It will damage the nozzles permanently.

SAFE SPRAYING

Before you use a spray, you need to know how to use it safely. And before you use any spray, you also need to have the answers to the questions in the following list:

1. What protective clothing should you wear when you spray?
2. Is this spray safe for use on food crops?
3. If it is sprayed on food, how long before I can safely consume the food?
4. Is this spray compatible for use with releases of beneficial predators and parasites? See the earlier chart titled "Pesticide Compatibility: Beneficials / Edible Crops" in the "Sprays with IPM" section.
5. Is it registered with the EPA to control my particular problem on my particular crop?
6. How long should I prevent anyone from entering the greenhouse after spraying? The EPA term for this is the "restricted entry interval," or REI. The REI is usually listed on the label in terms of number of hours after you have sprayed. For some commercial sprays such as soap, there is no REI. For more toxic chemicals, it can be up to 48 hours. Even with some botanically based sprays you may have to wait as long as 12 hours before you reenter your greenhouse safely (without protective equipment).
7. What is the correct dosage?

Where do you get the answers to these questions? Some can be found on the label. The manufacturer can also provide some assistance if you can locate the company. Also, don't hesitate to use your local county extension agent. Or you can call the EPA-sponsored National Pesticide Telecommunications Network at 800-858-7378. There they can refer to a large database to provide excellent assistance.

SPRAYING PROCEDURES

With the safe types of homemade pesticide sprays as well as with the soap-based sprays, many of the following safety concerns are not needed. For instance, you won't need to wear a respirator mask for most mild homemade or soap-based sprays. When in doubt, adhere to the following precautions when using over-the-counter pesticides. Also, the label requirements can change over time. Be sure to recheck each time you purchase a pesticide, even a so-called nontoxic type. Here are some tips:

1. Read the label at least twice. It can tell you much about the material: how to store it, how to apply it, what it controls, what plants it should be used on, what plants it should not be used on, and often how long before it is safe to consume food that has been sprayed with the material. Call a local county agent if you have any questions about the spray that are unanswered.

2. Seal off the greenhouse from the home until spray has dissipated (generally not necessary with insecticidal soap or BT [*Bacillus thuringiensis*]).

3. Wear protective clothing: gloves, goggles, and respirator mask as needed.

4. Use the recommended dosage listed on the label; more is not better.

5. Spray mostly the undersides of the leaves and tips of plants; that's where most pests hang out.

Be sure to aim your pest sprays to the underside as well as the tops of the leaves for best effectiveness. This gardener is spraying soap on the leaves of an artichoke plant.

6. Spraying is usually best done in the late afternoon or evening, with 70°F (21°C) being the temperature at which sprays are most effective.

7. Spot spray if possible. This means spray only the infested plants or even just the portions of a plant that are infested. However, don't miss any infestations. If the plant is growing in a pot and has an isolated problem, consider taking it outside or to a garage to do your spraying.

8. When spraying food crops, follow "days to harvest" guidelines on the label or advice from your county agricultural agent. Even with botanicals, it may be a few days before your food is safe to eat.

9. One spray application is rarely enough, especially for heavy infestations. This is because you never get every single pest. Even if you did a thorough job, the eggs (which are often resistant to insecticides) may soon hatch into a new problem. Mark your calendar for a repeat spray in somewhere between the next 5 to 10 days. It is often a good idea to plan on a series of sprays to gain good control.

10. Clean out your sprayer with hot water and soap after using it. Don't forget to run some soapy water through the nozzle, too.

11. Store the stuff as recommended on the label and in the original container. Always store away from children and pets and far from where food is prepared.

12. Wash your hands, have a shower, and change clothes immediately after spraying.

13. Don't open the doors to the greenhouse or return to the space until the sprays are dry.

14. Around 24 hours after spraying, I often try to wet down the leaves with water. This will clean any residue (and dust) off the leaves. When it comes to oils and soaps, both of which are notorious for burning the leaves, I like to water the leaves down sooner, usually about 2 hours after spraying.

15. Dispose of any old pesticides in a safe manner. Check to see if your community has a household hazardous-waste collection facility or holds any regular hazardous-waste collection days. Call your local government for more information. Also dispose of used pesticide containers properly. Usually you need to rinse them many times with water, but the label or your local waste officials may provide you with alternative instructions.

Another measure of safety of a pesticide is by using what is called the "LD-50 number." The EPA has set up a system that assigns a measure of toxicity to a pesticide. The LD stands for lethal dose. The LD-50 is a way to measure how much pesticide it takes to kill 50 percent of test animals, usually mice. The amount is expressed in milligrams per kilogram. There are LD-50 tests for each pesticide that reflect the amount it took to kill the animals dermally and orally (those poor mice!). Generally, it takes more dermally applied pesticide to kill the animals, so the dermal LD-50 numbers are higher. The higher the LD-50 number, the more pesticide it took to kill the test animals. So, the higher LD-50 numbers indicate a safer pesticide, at least if you're a mouse. The LD-50 test does not reflect the pesticide's long-term effects and effects on the environment. Still, like mileage figures for cars, you can use it for comparison.

If all this sounds both cumbersome and scary, you can see why I will constantly steer you away from chemical sprays and toward the safer methods of pest control using beneficial predators and parasites, along with other techniques. Still, there are important things to know about spraying even seemingly benign and low-toxic materials. Especially when it comes to equipment.

ALTERNATIVE SPRAYS AND CONCOCTIONS FOR PEST CONTROL

Many garden books have recipes for alternative and homemade pesticides. These can include ingredients such as garlic, nicotine, red peppers, onions, baking soda, potatoes, flour, oil, dead insects, and soap. One garden writer even uses mouthwash and birth control pills on plants.

Although some alternative insecticides are effective at killing pests, many act only as repellents (especially the homemade ones), which is not that helpful in the closed environment of a greenhouse. You will find many people who swear by homemade formulations, but you should realize that you are experimenting when it comes to these controls. Play around with dosages and notice the effects on the plants until you find something that works.

HOMEMADE INSECTICIDES AND SPRAYS

Some homemade materials can be as toxic as the most toxic synthetic chemical on the market. Nicotine tea for example, a spray made from cigarettes, is very effective on pests. If you get it on your skin, it can shoot your heart rate sky high and requires some precautions. People make this tea by steeping a cup of cigarettes (or butts) in water overnight until the water is dark-colored, and they spray it on plants the next morning. Treat it as you would a toxic chemical by wearing a respirator and protective equipment. Never let the liquid touch the skin, and don't inhale any vapors. They may be quite toxic.

Garlic is another popular home pesticide and has long been known to repel insects and to have some mild fungicidal effects. Many gardeners have reported being able to keep fungus diseases down by regularly spraying homemade garlic preparations. Usually, people just crush or blend 4 to 10 cloves in a quart (0.9 liter) of water and boil for 25 minutes. Strain out the solids, and spray when the solution cools. It works best on leaf-surface diseases such as powdery mildew. While you're at it, eat some garlic—it will keep colds at bay and friends at bay (then you won't catch their colds), and it might even reduce your blood pressure.

Whenever you make homemade pesticides, you need to filter these materials through cheesecloth or some other type of filter. This will prevent clogging at the nozzle of your sprayer.

Make only what you need each time and discard any leftovers. If you try storing these homemade materials, you might find that they begin to decompose and putrefy (stinky!). They can also harbor microbes harmful to you, and may not be good for spraying into your breathable air.

INSECTICIDAL SOAPS

Soaps have been used for killing insects throughout history, but in the past few decades we have seen the commercial development of soaps that have been formulated specifically to kill insects. Insecticidal soaps on the market work quite well on soft-bodied insects such as aphids, scale, whitefly, thrips, mealybugs, and spider mites. To control these pests, you must get direct contact with them when you spray. And when you do make contact, it does indeed work. In fact, one test at the University of California found that a soap spray was more effective on bush beans infested with whitefly than Malathion (a common synthetic chemical insecticide).

No one seems to know exactly how soap works in killing bugs. But most researchers believe that the soap dehydrates the insect. The nice thing about soap is that it is relatively nontoxic, unless you can't stand to have clean hands. Soap has no residual effect, which is good for people entering a recently sprayed greenhouse (or even eating a recently sprayed plant). But having no residual activity also means that if new bugs land on the plant after spraying, they won't be affected. Repeated applications are therefore very important and are usually necessary every 3 to 5 days for bad infestations, until the bugs seem to be under control.

It's not all a clean picture. Soap has its drawbacks. Soap can also kill the beneficial bugs that you might have introduced and can easily derail a biological-control program. When commercial insecticidal soaps first came out, I did not think they'd hurt my good bugs. I used soap extensively a few days after I had released the beneficial parasite *Encarsia formosa* (the small wasp that controls whitefly). The good news was that soap helped kill the whitefly, but it also killed all of my *Encarsia*. With soap as a control, I was then locked into regular spraying to stay on top of the whitefly problem all summer and well into fall. The moral is soap is not good for bugs, good or bad.

Soap can also readily burn plant leaves. This is especially true if you are making your own soap spray with common dish soaps. Dish soaps have many other ingredients that can be harmful to plant leaves. Still, with some experimentation you can make soaps that work. Even commercially available insecticidal soaps can burn sensitive plants. Testing any spray before you go spraying a whole crop or greenhouse is the only way to prevent damage.

Test soap sprays by spraying a small portion of a leaf from each crop. Then wait at least 24 to 48 hours to see if any burning occurs. If not, have at it. If burning does occur, try diluting the soap with more water. Test any plant you intend to spray.

Soap can be used on both ornamental and edible plants. Commercially produced soaps are becoming readily available. I even found some at the hardware store, which was unheard of a couple of years ago.

When making your own soap, avoid detergents and soaps for automatic dishwashers. Also avoid specially formulated soaps like the "antibacterial" or "softer hands" formulations. These have added ingredients that may likely cause problems with plants. Instead, use mild, regular dishwashing (not dishwasher) liquids, flakes, or soaps, such as the original Palmolive Green, Fels Naptha, or Dr. Bronner's soaps. Generally, you want to mix up a 1 to 2 percent solution, which is around 3 to 6 tablespoons (45 to 90 ml) per gallon (3.8 liters) of water. But again, always test and wait 24 hours to be sure you won't burn your plants. Plants most susceptible to serious burning are those with leaves having waxy or hairy coatings, but that is not always a hard-and-fast rule. Testing is the best way to predict injury. The only injury desired is that which occurs to the insects.

Soap seems to burn less if you make sure the plant is well hydrated, so water thoroughly a few hours prior to spraying. Also, there is less damage when soap is sprayed during a cloudy day rather than on a bright sunny day.

HORTICULTURAL OILS

Like soap, oils have long been used as a pest control, usually on outdoor plants such as trees and shrubs. The oils smother insect eggs, scale, and disease spores. Because many oils readily and severely burned the leaves, they were used only while plants were dormant and leafless. As a result, these were usually called "dormant oils."

Now we are lucky to have a new generation of what are called "horticultural oils."

These newer oils are highly refined and lighter weight, which helps to minimize the burning that occurs on leaves. The new oils are sold under a variety of names such as "summer," "supreme," and "superior" oils. There are also many brand names for these oils, including Sunspray Ultra-Fine® Spray Oil and Volk Supreme Oil. Note the fact that different brands often have different dilution rates and list different rates of application for leafy plants versus dormant plants.

The advantage of using oils as an insecticide is that they have a low toxicity to humans in comparison with many other pesticides. Oils work best on aphids, mites, leaf miners, mealybugs, caterpillars, thrips, and whiteflies. The oils kill bugs by coating the skin, plugging breathing holes and coating the wings of pests. It is difficult for insects to gain resistance to these oils. As with soap, in order to control these pests you must get direct contact with them when you spray. Also similar to soap sprays, oils have a high potential for burning plants. Before you spray, please read about "testing leaves" in the previous discussion under insecticidal soaps.

If you use oil, make sure that it is registered for use on green leafy plants as opposed to plants in a dormant stage. Avoid using any "dormant oils," as they will cause massive burning on most leaves.

Oil sprays, like soap, will also readily kill many beneficial critters working in your greenhouse. Always spray oil prior to releasing any good bugs, or only spray plants that don't harbor your good guys.

Burning of leaves can be minimized if you spray well-hydrated plants, so water a few hours prior to spraying. Never spray oils if the temperature has risen above 85°F (30°C).

Some gardeners have found that cooking

oil has attributes similar to horticultural oil. If you want to make your own oil spray, try using soybean oil diluted at a 1 to 2 percent solution, which is around 3 to 6 tablespoons (45 to 90 ml) per gallon (3.8 liters) of water. Add a few drops of a mild dish soap (see above discussion on soap spray) to help act as an emulsifier and shake this well after mixing and also prior to using. And again, test this on a few plants before you go spraying whole plants with it, as it may burn. If burning does occur, try reducing the amount of oil in the dilution by increasing the amount of water.

BOTANICALLY BASED INSECTICIDES

Derived from plants, these insecticides are designed to be easier on our environment. These commercially available insecticides usually (but not always) have a low toxicity to humans compared to many synthetic insecticides. These "botanicals," as they are called, tend to break down quickly into harmless substances. They also tend to be effective on critters for a shorter period of time. For this reason, you may have to spray more often.

When spraying commercially available botanical sprays, don't be any more lax than you would be with any other pesticide. Yes, botanicals are often better for the environment in the long run, but the immediate hazards still require great caution. Immediate harmful effects can include headaches, dizziness, and nausea; they poison just as readily as a synthetic spray. Always read and follow the label instructions on botanically based sprays, and reread the safety procedures that are outlined in this chapter. When using botanicals, always use the common precautions required for any spraying of insecticides. This includes wearing protective clothing and using a respirator filter mask. These sprays may also have a speci-fied restricted entry interval or REI (see earlier explanation on page 378).

Most commercially available botanically based pesticides also kill beneficial insects. With the exception of some products derived from neem oil (see below), they should not be used in conjunction with a biological control program involving releases of beneficial predators or parasites. When an infested plant is in a pot and you have beneficial insects in your greenhouse, consider taking the plant out of the greenhouse for spraying.

Here are some of the commonly available botanically based insecticides:

1. Pyrethrin. Also known as "pyrethrum," pyrethrin is derived from the flower heads of the pyrethrum chrysanthemum daisy native to West Africa. It is a contact insecticide, which means that the pyrethrum must physically touch the insect's body before it will kill it. The vapors have little effect. It is effective on most common greenhouse pests, including whiteflies, aphids, and mealybugs. It has a slight effect on some spider mites. Pyrethrin can be applied to edible plants up to 5 days before harvest. Commercial formulations are becoming more commonplace than they were even a few years ago. Some are mixed with other active ingredients, such as insecticidal soap or other botanically based chemicals. Pyrethrin is more effective when sprayed at sundown, as warmth and sunshine tend to lessen its ability to kill critters. Pyrethrin is not recommended for use when you have beneficial insects at work. It is toxic to fish, so take care to never let any get into a water supply. Pyrethrin is the active ingredient in many readily available houseplant sprays.

Don't confuse pyrethrins with *pyrethroids,* which is a term for a whole class of synthetic pesticides based upon the chemical makeup of the natural pesticide pyrethrin. Many pyrethroids are not registered for use on food crops, whereas pyrethrin is. Pyrethroids are not accepted by organic-producer regulations. These synthetic materials have the basic chemistry of pyrethrins but are modified to improve persistence, insecticidal activity, and so on. Pyrethroids are widely used in American agriculture under trade names such as Asana, Capture, Astro, Mavrik, Pounce, Resmethrin, and Sumithrin.

Interestingly enough, some synthetic pyrethroids are safer than the natural pyrethrins in terms of their LD-50 measurement (see earlier discussion on LD-50 on page 380). Pyrethroids are rarely registered for spraying on edible crops.

2. Rotenone. An extract of tropical legume plants, rotenone is a contact insecticide and stomach poison that acts on most common greenhouse pests. Amazonian natives used rotenone extracts to kill fish for large harvests. Commercial rotenone is toxic to fish and birds, so take care not to allow any material to get into water supplies or water drains. Always be sure that you use standard protective equipment. Rotenone used to be available in a dust formulation that is just shaken onto plant leaves and as a powder that is mixed with water and sprayed. Old rotenone can lose much of its punch, so purchase only what you will need in the immediate future. It is becoming rare in the marketplace.

3. Rayania. As with many botanicals, rayania is also derived from a tropical plant. In this case, it comes from the stem of a shrub. It is not a quick knockdown pesticide, but after a few days you'll notice the pest numbers have greatly dwindled. It is especially effective on aphids and thrips, as long as you can get a direct hit on them as you spray. It is available as both a spray and a dust, although the dust is more common.

4. Sabadilla. Derived from the seeds of a tropical plant resembling corn, sabadilla is a powerful stomach poison that kills many pests, with the exception of mites. It is generally sold as a dust and works as a broad-spectrum contact poison. Sabadilla has limited application in the greenhouse because it is hard to get dust on the underside of leaves (where many greenhouse pests like to hide). Rarely, you may find it as a wettable powder that can then be sprayed. Take caution, though, because there are some recorded instances of human poisonings with sabadilla.

5. Neem. This is one of the newer commercially available botanicals on the market, but it has been used for centuries in India, where the neem tree is native. The Sanskrit name for neem roughly translates as "village pharmacy" because it has so many beneficial uses. It is commonly used to heal wounds, as an ingredient in toothpaste, for pest control and more. Neem has also been used as a cure for diseases and disorders ranging from bad teeth and bed bugs to ulcers and malaria. The seeds, bark, and leaves contain compounds with proven antiseptic, antiviral, anti-inflammatory, anti-ulcer, and antifungal uses. It works well as a repellent, which doesn't help much in the closed environment of a greenhouse or sunroom. Fortunately, it offers some other benefits by acting as a growth regulator to many pests. It can interrupt their normal growth cycle, eventually causing death. It also curbs the appetite of many pests and may disrupt their ability to lay eggs. It works best on aphids, leaf miners, mealybugs, thrips, and whiteflies. Its toxicity is low for mammals.

Currently, there are more and more sprays coming out that contain neem or extracts of neem as the active ingredient, such as Azatin®, NeemGold, Neemazad®, and Bio-neem®. Some formulations are registered for use on ornamentals and food crops, whereas others are prohibited on vegetables or other edibles. Read the label for more information.

In general, neem-oil formulations can be used right up to the release of beneficial predators and parasites. However, it is a good idea to avoid spraying this material directly in an area where the beneficials have previously been released.

6. Nicotine. An age-old pesticide, nicotine has a high toxicity for both humans and insects. Even if you smoke cigarettes, you'd be surprised how sick you can get if you use this pesticide improperly. Its vapors are also quite toxic. Keep it off your skin, as it can be absorbed directly and cause an irregular heartbeat. Always use great caution with nicotine. It is very effective against almost all greenhouse pests. Although it is mainly a contact pesticide (requiring that the bugs come in direct contact with the spray), the vapors also seem to control insects in deeper hiding places. Nicotine is sold commercially as Blackleaf 40®, but it is becoming rare as health concerns about it are increasing. It is also sold as a dust under the name Tobacco Dust by the Biocontrol Network (see "Mail-Order Pest Control," in Appendix 3).

Some people successfully make their own nicotine tea by soaking tobacco in water. Be as careful of this as you would a commercial product. Also be aware that if they are not first sterilized by boiling, homemade nicotine sprays may harbor the tobacco mosaic virus that afflicts tomatoes.

Tobacco as an insecticide is not recommended for use with a biological control program or where you have released any beneficial critters.

7. Hot pepper. This has become more popular, thanks in part to the development of a commercial product called Hot Pepper Wax Insect Repellent. Its primary active ingredient is capsaicin, which is the "hot" component of hot peppers. This product is mainly sold as a repellent. However, repellents are not the greatest controls for the greenhouse and its closed environment, because there is nowhere you can repel pests to. But this product does more than just repel; it can actually help control pests, especially soft-bodied insects that feed on the leaves, flowers, fruit, and stems of plants. These include aphids, spider mites, thrips, leaf miners, slugs, whiteflies, and leafhoppers. Hot Pepper Wax Insect Repellent also has the potential to smother insect eggs that have been laid on your leaves, killing these insects before they hatch and begin to eat. It is registered for use on food crops but will probably have a negative effect on beneficial predators or parasites, so only spot spray in limited areas if you have released any good guys. It also has the effect of being an antitranspirant, which means that your plants will likely require less water (great for transplants). Go easier on watering if you use this product and be on the lookout for symptoms of overwatering.

It is sold in both concentrate and ready-to-use formulations. As usual, the concentrate is more cost-effective over the long run, but it means that you must take care to do the dilution correctly. For this reason, it is always a good idea to spray only a few leaves and wait 24 to 48 hours to check for leaf burning.

Like most pesticides, Hot Pepper Wax Insect Repellent works best when it makes contact with the insect, so spraying on the underside of the plant is important. You will usually need to repeat the spray every 3 to 7 days as needed for severe infestations. If things are under control, it can be used every 2 to 4 weeks to keep pests down. Also, when you use this spray follow all the label instructions about protective clothing and equipment, as well as the restricted entry interval. The beauty of this product is that it is relatively nontoxic as long as you take care to keep it off of your skin and out of your eyes. If you want more information on this product, you can call or check out their website (888-667-3785, **www.hot pepperwax.com**).

8. Cinnamon. This spice has had many important uses throughout time. Many gardeners have had success using cinnamon as a dust and spraying an extract of it to control insects, especially on orchids. It has also been shown to help in controlling diseases such as powdery mildew (see discussion later in this chapter under "Diseases"). The downside to the homemade preparations of cinnamon is that they also tend to burn many plants when applied at a high enough concentration to kill critters.

There is a new commercially available product for greenhouse ornamental and vegetable growers that utilizes the ability of cinnamon to control insects and spider mites and minimizes its plant toxicity. This product is called Cinnamite® and it has been proven to provide effective control of both mites and aphids. It is extremely fast acting, typically killing over 90 percent of mites and aphids within 6 hours of application. It also provides some control over powdery mildew.

Cinnamite® is formulated from cinnamon oil, a natural food additive. It has a 4-hour re-entry interval, as designated by the EPA. It is registered safe for vegetable crops and can be used right up to the day of harvest. Unfortunately, this product is intended for larger commercial-greenhouse operations and may be difficult for home gardeners to acquire.

MICROBIAL AND BIOLOGICAL INSECTICIDES

The term "biological warfare" conjures all sorts of negative images, but nature has maintained its delicate ecological balance for eons by using biology—or, more specifically, microbes—as "weapons." These microbes attack specific pests by causing a disease that kills them. Luckily, microbial insecticides won't affect humans or even most beneficial insects. They are famous for being incredibly safe and usually kill only the target population, leaving the people and other critters in the environment unaffected. Many microbial insecticides are safe enough to be used in conjunction with a biological pest-control program. This means that, generally, they don't harm the good predators and parasites that help control the bad bugs. Here are a few examples.

1. *Bacillus thuringiensis*. This bacteria is one of the most common microbial products for controlling bugs. Because its name is such a mouthful, many people refer to it as "BT." It is sold under a variety of names and is available in both dust and liquid forms. Some of the commercial products include Dipel, Thuricide, and Attack. These more common BT products work mainly on pests in the caterpillar family. Although caterpillar infestations are relatively rare in the greenhouse or sunroom, they can occur, and a little BT can easily control them.

There are a few strains of BT that have been isolated to provide control for some other pests. One such strain of interest to greenhouse gardeners is *Bacillus thuringiensis israeliensis*. It can help control fungus gnats, which are a common soil-borne pesky critter in the greenhouse.

The most common products containing BT for controlling gnats are commercially known as Gnatrol® and Vectobac™. By the way, this same strain of BT, *israeliensis*, can also control mosquitoes in certain situations. See a further discussion later under the pest "Thrips."

Unlike other pesticides, many BT products have a relatively short shelf life if stored in warm places. If a container is exposed to extreme heat, the product will lose its viability because it is actually a container full of microscopic creatures that suffer in extreme environments. The product is best kept in a dark, cool place (don't let it freeze). Also, when you mix up a spray from a concentrate or powder, the dilution will be viable for only a day or so. For this reason, never mix up more than you will need to use in a day. I prefer the dust formulations to sprays because they require no mixing or preparation. I just sprinkle a bit on the leaves after I have watered, when a caterpillar is sighted eating dinner regularly in my greenhouse.

2. Parasitic nematodes—Good nematodes. Nematodes are microscopic worms (not related to earthworms). There are so-called bad nematodes that can become plant pests, feeding on roots. For years, if someone mentioned the word "nematode," growers would think only of the nematode that is a plant pest. Fortunately, there are other species of nematodes, known as parasitic nematodes, that are in the good-guy category and are helpful in controlling soil-borne pests.

The way they control insects and other soil pests sounds like a scene from some horror movie. They seek out soil pests and insects and enter their natural body openings, such as the mouth. Once inside, the nematodes release a bacteria that kills the host. They then live, breed, and feed on this cadaver of a former insect or soil pest, from the inside out. When this food supply is exhausted, thousands of offspring leave the host in search for a suitable new host—which we hope will be another soil-dwelling pest.

Over time, their numbers decline, and then you need to consider rereleasing more of these beneficial nematodes. Usually, you get good results from one to two releases per year in the home greenhouse. They have proven to be fantastic in controlling fungus gnats and also help in controlling thrips and other soil pests. If you live where termites are a problem, these nematodes can even provide a possible solution!

They are one of the few safe biologically based controls for many soil-dwelling pests. It is surprising, however, that they don't seem to affect the beneficial earthworm. Nematodes often control pests better than highly toxic pesticides. Now that we have these good nematodes, we have an incredibly safe alternative. In fact, they are exempt from EPA registration, avoiding many of the regulations associated with the use of most pesticides. The nematodes are usually sold in a live, semidehydrated condition and may have a short shelf life at room temperature (a little longer if you can keep them in the refrigerator). There are many brands on the market, so check the label for more specifics.

There are a few types of nematodes on the market. They are lovingly known by their hard-to-pronounce scientific names. *Steinernema carpocapsae* and *Steinernema feltiae* are produced for controlling pests such as fungus gnats and thrips. *Heterorhabditis* is known for its ability to be more mobile and good for searching out soil-dwelling pests. They are sold by the names Exhibit™, EcoMask™, Savior™, ScanMask™, X-Gnat™, and others.

Most commonly, the nematodes arrive on clay particles that you simply add to water and then apply to the soil, much like you would a water-soluble fertilizer. The good nematodes are also available on sponges, in gels, and attached to peat moss and vermiculite. Follow each manufacturer's directions as to how to get them into the soil, as the method can vary among brands. It is important that you maintain a good level of soil moisture after you release them. The worst thing for these critters is to have the soil totally dry out.

Be sure to choose the right type of nematode for your problem. There are a number of commercial beneficial nematode products on the market, and the price can also vary greatly. Talk at length to your supplier to be sure you are getting the right nematode for your particular situation.

3. *Beauveria bassiana.* This fungus is relatively new to the list of pest-control options. It is relatively harmless to people, plants, and other animals but is deadly to the larval and nymph stages of certain soft-bodied insects. It is mainly effective on aphids, thrips, and whiteflies, and, depending upon the brand, it also works on mealybugs and spider mites (check the label for specifics on the pests it controls).

Currently, there are two brands on the market. *Beauveria bassiana* is sold under the names of BotaniGard™ and Naturalis-O®. Both have the same basic active ingredient, the fungus *Beauveria bassiana.* At this writing, only BotaniGard™ is rated for both food crops and ornamentals. The active ingredient is a formulation of fungal spores. These spores must have direct contact with the pest at the time of spraying or must be picked up by a mobile insect as it moves over treated leaves and flowers. For this reason, both repeated

and complete spray coverage is helpful, if not essential.

When the spores make contact with the insect, they will then germinate and pierce the insect's skin. The fungus multiplies inside the insect's body, causing it to die within a few days. Not all stages of insect growth are susceptible to this fungus, which is why repeated applications are important.

It is seems to work best when you time the spray to be applied when there are the most adult insect pests around. Repeated spraying is also important. The more spores that come into contact with the insect, the more rapid the kill. For thrips, it is best to apply 3 to 5 sprays at 3 to 5 day intervals. For whitefly control, it is better to go with 5 to 7 day intervals.

Although *Beauveria bassiana* is basically a chemical-free spray, it still is not something you want to inhale or get in your eyes. For that reason, it is important to wear protective clothing such as gloves, goggles, and a respirator mask. Each brand of *Beauveria bassiana* has its own specific "restricted entry interval," or REI, as dictated by the EPA. This tells you how many hours you must wait after spraying before you can reenter the greenhouse. See each label's instructions for more information or call the EPA sponsored National Pesticide Telecommunications Network at 800-858-7378 for more information.

Even though there are certain restrictions, this fungus-based material is many times safer than most synthetic chemical sprays and even botanically based sprays. It is also great if you are using beneficial predators and parasites in an IPM control scheme. This is because the *Beauveria bassiana* is highly selective and is safe to most beneficial predators and parasites. Soon there will likely be formulations of *Beauveria bassiana* that will be approved for use by organic growers.

It is unfortunate that, at this writing, all formulations of *Beauveria bassiana* are primarily sold in the commercial market to large growers. It is not readily available in small quantities to small home-greenhouse growers. Again, this is where you might need to get together with other greenhouse gardeners and share an order. Perhaps you can also look into working with a local commercial greenhouse or even regional greenhouse suppliers.

This is another example of a relatively safe product being difficult for home-greenhouse gardeners to acquire, even though they can readily obtain many highly toxic pesticides at the local hardware store.

OTHER NATURALLY BASED PEST SPRAYS

I use the term "naturally based" in reference to commercially available sprays that are derived from or work with nature. They are usually lower in toxicity than synthetic chemicals. Some, but not all, naturally based pest sprays are more specific in what they kill, meaning that some don't hurt the good bugs that control the bad ones. Even so, this does not mean you can go out and use them with reckless abandon. Even though these sprays are safer to the environment, it is still important to exercise the same care when applying them that you would use when applying synthetic chemicals. They may still pose a hazard. For this reason, always read the precautions on the label and follow the proper spraying procedures outlined on page 379.

Not all of these are registered for use on edible plants, even though they may be biologically more "sane" than many registered nerve poisons on the market. This could be because they are truly toxic when consumed, or it may be that the company can't afford the expensive process of registration with the EPA. Again, to be on the safe side, when a spray is not registered for application on edible crops, don't spray it on an edible crop. Read the label or call the manufacturer for more information on a particular product.

1. Avermectin B. Utilizing a product derived from the bacterial soil organism *Streptomyces avermitilis*, researchers have discovered a naturally occurring toxin that affects many insects. If the word *Streptomyces* sounds familiar, it's because it is the same family of bacteria in antibiotics used to cure human ailments, including the antibiotic streptomycin. The toxin derived from this bacteria is an insecticide known as Avermectin B. It is sold commercially as Avid® and is available only through wholesale outlets.

Avermectin B on some pests can be slow-acting, taking up to a month to kill, but usually it is quicker. Currently, Avermectin B is registered to control only spider mites and leaf miners on ornamental plants such as flowers and houseplants. Do not use it on ferns or poinsettias, as it will burn the leaves.

Avermectin B, or Avid®, is not currently registered for use on food crops, with one exception: In certain parts of the United States and in certain situations, it can be used on pears and strawberries. If you hope to use it on these food crops, please first talk directly to the manufacturer about this special use registration. Avermectin B has also been known to help control other pests, including whiteflies, fruit flies, and cabbage loopers. However, it is not registered for use on these pests and may be very slow-acting on them.

Both Avid® and Avermectin B will also negatively affect your good bugs, so limit any use with a biological control program. It is one of the few products that does a good job controlling spider mites and leaf miners and is lower in toxicity than many synthetic chemicals designed to control these same critters. If you can find it for sale, it will likely be through a wholesale outlet. The first thing you will notice is its high price. One 8-ounce (0.24-liter) bottle can cost well over $75. The reason it is so expensive is that it is recommended for commercial use and is available only in a highly concentrated form. For instance, 1 ounce (30 ml) of Avid® can make 25 gallons (95 liters) of spray for spider mite control. I put only four drops or so in a quart (0.9-liter) bottle. At that rate, one bottle will last for many years. When you figure out how much "control" one bottle contains, the price really isn't that out of line. Maybe you can go in on a small bottle of Avid® with a few other gardeners to make it more affordable.

Although Avid® is much safer than most any other spray registered for spider-mite control, it still is not something you want to inhale or get in your eyes. For that reason, it is important to wear protective clothing such as gloves, goggles, and a respirator mask. It also has a "restricted entry interval," or REI, as dictated by the EPA, meaning it is not safe to reenter the greenhouse for a certain number of hours. See the label instructions for more information, or call the EPA-sponsored National Pesticide Telecommunications Network at 800-858-7378 for more information.

For more options on spider-mite control see the specific discussion later in this chapter.

2. Kinoprene. Kinoprene is one of a newer type of insecticides known as "growth regulators." They interrupt the natural growth process of certain insects, resulting in death of the insect. In the case of kinoprene, it tends to affect those insects in the order Homoptera, which includes a number of favorite greenhouse enemies such as aphids and whiteflies. By killing only a specific family of bugs, it has little or no effect on other insects. It is one of the few commercial sprays that has a low toxicity to humans as well as to good bugs. I have tested it with great success in controlling whitefly while the parasite *Encarsia formosa* was present (see discussion under the following "Know Your Pests" section). There is some newer research that is now showing it may have a slight negative effect on wasp parasites that control whitefly (such as the *Encarsia*), more than we realize. Still, it is among the rare pesticides that is selective in its effect on certain pests.

Commercially, kinoprene is sold as Enstar 5E, Enstar II, or Enstar. It is registered for use only on ornamental plants growing in greenhouses and is not registered for edible crops. A pesticide developer who worked on the development of this chemical once told me that kinoprene could be registered for edible plants but the investment would not be worth it because kinoprene breaks down too rapidly in the ultraviolet light of direct sun. This would eliminate all potential sales to farmers and gardeners. It is useful only when used under the protection of a glazing where there is little ultraviolet light to cause the pesticide to break down, enabling it to stay active long enough to work on target pests.

Enstar is available from wholesale suppliers that deal with commercial greenhouses. It is hard to come by for average greenhouse gardeners. As with many of these safer pesticides, you'll be amazed at the high price for this stuff. A 1-pint (0.47-liter) bottle runs close to $150 or more. It's sold in a glass bottle, so don't be fumble-fingered when handling. Fortunately, it is also very concentrated; 1 ounce (30 ml) of Enstar, at the normal rate, can make up to 20 gallons (76 liters) of spray. At a few drops per spray bottle, one bottle could last for many years, or you could go in on a bottle with others. Perhaps there are other greenhouse gardeners you know who would be willing to share in a bottle to reduce the cost. As with most pesticides, it has special regulations concerning protective gear that you should wear while spraying and a restricted reentry interval, or REI. See the label for more information.

COPPER- AND SULFUR-BASED MINERALS AS PESTICIDES

These minerals can be used successfully to control certain types of leaf-based fungus diseases and spider mites. When applied at the recommended rate, they are generally considered quite safe. Copper is available as both a dust and a liquid spray. It is rare that you can cure a plant with a mineral-based spray, but you can help slow the spread and even reduce or prevent further infection. Copper is usually sold mixed with some sulfur (copper sulfate).

For centuries, European gardeners and grape growers have used what is known as a Bordeaux spray, which is a mixture of copper sulfate and hydrated lime. It is usually available as a powder that can be dusted or mixed with water and applied as a spray.

All copper- and sulfur-based mineral sprays are safe for both humans and the environment, as long as they are applied at the recommended rates. They do, however, have a great potential for burning the leaves. To prevent leaf burn, test the spray on some small portions of a leaf a couple of days before spray-

ing the whole plant. Also, it is better to apply these sprays in the morning hours after you have watered. The main thing is to apply these sprays as recommended on the label. Higher concentrations are famous for causing leaf burning.

Sometimes, applying a sulfur-based spray can trigger a spider mite population explosion a month or two later. This is because the sulfur will often kill both the bad spider mites, which feed on plants, and the naturally occurring good predator spider mites, which feed on the bad spider mites. When both are killed, the bad mite tends to return at a faster rate, causing a worse infestation. You may want to release predator mites a month after spraying to avoid problems. Look for more discussion on using sulfur-based sprays later in this chapter under Spraying for Disease (page 426).

WATER AS A DETERRENT

Not only is water good to drink and important in plant nutrition, it can also be used as a pest deterrent. On occasion, I have been able to control some infestations of spider mites and aphids by just giving the infested plant a good bath, taking care to rinse both the top and the bottom of the leaf surface. If a bath doesn't work or the plant is too big for this treatment, try a hard spray of water focused on the plant. Don't spray so hard as to damage the plant but do spray hard enough to knock the pests off the plant. Sometimes when an insect pest is knocked off its roost, it may never get back up to feed again. The water, when applied with a good amount of pressure, often permanently damages or even kills a good percentage of the bugs, as many of them are quite fragile. This prevents most from climbing back up a plant. If you knock a bug off the plant and down the drain, it is a goner for sure.

Using water to control pests is far from being a cure-all. It also has the drawback of causing overwatering stress on a plant. My editor uses water in this manner but reduces the amount of water that gets into the soil by covering the soil with aluminum foil from the plant stem out. Simply wrap foil around the stem and then down over the pot rim, sealing it with a fold before you give it the water treatment.

Water is all too often overlooked, perhaps because it is too simple. Always think about giving it a try before you go to the harder stuff.

SYNTHETIC INSECTICIDES

Synthetic insecticides should be considered a last resort and used only after you have tried all other control methods. Still, they warrant discussion. These are totally human-made preparations, famous for a quick knockdown of the target pest, and almost always taking along with them a knockdown of any beneficial insects that may be present. They tend to have longer-lasting activity, which is potentially harmful to the ecology of the greenhouse and possibly to you. Little is known about what these products break down into as they degrade in the environment over time, but some breakdown by-products of synthetic pesticides have been shown to be worse on the ecology than the original spray. Many of the synthetic pesticides that are on the market have a lower toxicity rating than natural sprays I have discussed earlier. These pesticides include but are not limited to Malathion, Methiocarb, Resmethrin, Sevin, and Sumithrin. However, even though these synthetics have low ratings of toxicity, researchers are uncertain as to what these synthetics transform into as they degrade and break down in the environment. Some wonder if the breakdown products may also pose a risk to human health. After all, these chemicals have not been on the planet very long, relatively speaking.

SYSTEMIC INSECTICIDES

Systemic insecticides are also synthetic chemicals but have the ability to be taken up by the plant's vascular system. When a bug takes a bite of the plant, it will also get a small amount of pesticide. If you use a little logic, you will quickly understand why you should never use a systemic pesticide on or near any edible food crop. If you do, you too will be ingesting the pesticide. Luckily, the labels of all systemic insecticides state that they should not be used on food. This is good as long as people read the label. *Please, make it a habit to read the label on any insecticide you plan to use.*

A systemic insecticide is not a good choice for plants that are heavily infested. Most systemics work better as preventive maintenance. If systemic types of insecticides are used at all, it should only be on ornamentals as a bug preventative. I usually try to steer people away from these chemicals entirely, because the danger they pose is far greater than their effectiveness.

SPRAY ADJUVANTS AND ADDITIVES

These are spray additives that make sprays work better, enhance the life of foliar-applied pesticides, and / or increase their toxicity. Some good examples are spreader-stickers and what are known as PBOs, or piperonyl butoxides.

SPREADER-STICKERS

Have you ever noticed how a sprayed liquid can bead up on some leaves after it is applied? This is especially true on plants with waxy leaves. A spreader-sticker added to the liquid enables the liquid to flatten out and spread over the leaf as it's sprayed. This helps the insecticide "reach out and touch" a bug (which is essential to enable most sprays to kill them). If it beads up too much, it is much less effective. Spreader-stickers are usually quite safe in terms of human and environmental effects. However, with so many brands of spreader-stickers on the market, you should thoroughly check each one out for the intended use (i.e., food crops, ornamentals, and so on). Insecticidal soap, by its very nature, is good at sticking to waxy leaves compared with many other types of insecticides. By adding a bit of insecticidal soap to a pesticide, you can often help it to stick to leaves better. To prevent unexpected leaf burning, be sure to test your mixture on a few leaves a day or two prior to using it on a whole plant.

Professional spreader-sticker formulations are not readily available to home gardeners, but they are in grower catalogs and wholesale catalogs. Follow the dilution rate closely, as too much spreader-sticker can also burn leaves.

PBOS

PBO is an acronym for piperonyl butoxide, which is added to many sprays to enhance the toxicity. It is a substance that has spurred many questions among experts as to its possible negative side effects on people and the environment. Unfortunately, you can often find botanical sprays mixed with PBO. It seems to me that this takes away the advantage of using a lower-toxicity spray in the first place. Make an effort to check the list of ingredients when purchasing pesticides. If you can buy the same product without PBOs, it might be worth considering until we know more about this compound.

OTHER NONSPRAY PEST CONTROLS

For those who harbor a particular aversion to bugs of any type and who also don't wish to use sprays, there are a number of alternative pest-control options. Some work better than others, and several work best when combined with other types of controls (especially in an IPM program). Here are some of the readily available options.

BAITS AND TRAPS

Rarely can baits and traps totally solve a pest problem, but they can still be excellent tools. Often, traps are used to simply monitor the pest, to enable you to determine if their numbers are rising or not. This can help you plan out your attack. For instance, many growers use sticky yellow cards to attract the whitefly, a common greenhouse pest. When they see the numbers rise, it may indicate that they need to release more parasites to help control the problem. Other gardeners set numerous sticky yellow traps to actually control the pest population. One common slimy pest, the slug, is susceptible to some very specific traps. Read more about those traps under the Slugs, Snails heading on page 411. Let's look at some of the general types of traps you can use.

Sticky Traps

It is well known that specific colors can attract certain insects. This can be used to your advantage when it comes to trying to control insects. For instance, the color yellow attracts many pests, including whiteflies and winged aphids. The colors blue and hot pink have been reputed to attract thrips.

You can find manufactured sticky yellow traps sold in many garden and greenhouse-

This trap was made from a piece of wood painted yellow with Tanglefoot™ spread over it.

oriented catalogs. I have found these to be expensive for what you get. One alternative is to make your own. Do this by painting a board or a wide stake the yellow color; then spread a thin layer of light-colored axle grease or the commercially available Tanglefoot™ or Tangle Trap™ on the board. Tanglefoot™ and Tangle Trap™ are commercially available sticky substances sold primarily for trapping insects. They are incredibly sticky and can be messy to deal with. Use these substances with care or you will get this stuff on everything. It is hard to clean off.

The exact size of your board(s) isn't important, but bigger means you'll be more likely to bump into it. One bump and you'll get grease or sticky stuff all over your clean shirt. Try making the boards

This yellow trap is simply a piece of cardboard with clear grease spread over it.

about the same size as letter paper, 8.5 by 11 inches (21.3 by 26.3 cm). Even half that size works well. I have also used yellow card stock stapled to a stake.

If you notice that your traps are losing their effectiveness, you probably need to re-apply the sticky substance or grease every week or so because it gets dusty and loses its ability to catch bugs. If you are using heavy card stock, you may need to start over after a few applications.

Some people have had luck with motor and cooking oil painted on yellow cardboard, plastic sheets, or heavy card stock. As you can see, it is not an exact science.

Place sticky traps where they won't stick to you or your visitors. One accidental brushing against them can ruin a shirt. Also, avoid using sticky yellow traps when you are releasing the beneficial insect *Encarsia formosa,* used to control whitefly (discussed later), because it, too, will stick to the yellow traps.

FREEZE-OUTS

A freeze-out occurs when you simply open up the greenhouse in the dead of winter. All the doors and windows are left open and the whole place freezes up. But it has its drawbacks, because it effectively freezes out the plants, too.

Yes, people can get desperate when they have a bad bug problem. Is it effective? On occasion. But unfortunately, there are often survivors. I know it is hard to believe, but insects are amazing. Sure enough, in some protected corner, one or two pest survivors are ready to populate the whole place. They will come back sooner or later on a neighbor's clothing, a gift plant, or a salad leaf from the kitchen. They'll fly or hitchhike, but no matter what, you can count on their return. You end up where you began, except without the plants you froze. This is a method that only postpones the problem.

For those rare people who don't use the greenhouse in the winter, a freeze-out might be a fine practice. Simply open the greenhouse doors and windows during some very cold weather to set back the residing pests. Before you even think about doing this, take precautions to prevent any freeze damage to faucets and water pipes.

DUSTS

Many common insecticides of all types are available in dust formulations. Because they move mainly with gravity, it is difficult to get coverage on the undersides of the leaves. There is also the problem of inhaling the dust when it is applied. A respirator mask is helpful here. With some exceptions, sprays are generally superior to dusts in the enclosed greenhouse or sunspace.

DIATOMACEOUS EARTH

One material that is found only as a dust is diatomaceous earth. It is composed of the fine silica remains of the skeletons of prehistoric one-celled organisms. To the untrained eye, it looks and feels like a fine baby-powder. But when it comes into contact with an insect, it is a potent insecticide. It kills by cutting into soft-bodied insects' skin and dehydrating the poor critters. It kills good and bad bugs alike, so avoid using it in a biological control program.

Diatomaceous earth is especially effective against slugs, pill bugs, and sow bugs when spread on the soil around the base of the plant. It is a good idea to wear a respirator mask or dust mask when applying it to avoid irritating your lungs.

Avoid pool-filter diatomaceous earth, as it is not suitable for the garden and is hazardous if inhaled. In fact, it is a good idea to avoid inhaling any type of dust, period. Use only diatomaceous earth formulated for controlling pests or diatomaceous-earth products sold as "natural grade." Some manufacturers are mixing diatomaceous earth with the botanical insecticide pyrethrin to give it more punch.

EAT THE BUGS?

I've eaten my fair share of raw aphids (usually by mistake). In fact, they taste sweet. I don't really suggest this as a real way to control bugs, but it does give rise to some interesting thoughts. Bugs are probably more nutritious than whatever you last ate. Roasted grasshoppers, a delicacy in certain cultures, have about 75 percent protein and 20 percent fat and are high in niacin and riboflavin. The idea may seem repulsive to modern sophisticates who dine on such delicacies as snails, frog's legs, chicken embryos (eggs), and Rocky Mountain oysters, not to mention BHA, BHT, sodium nitrate, artificial sweeteners, and yellow dye number 5!

The point is, if you happen to accidentally consume an aphid in the salad, don't worry; it isn't likely to harm you in the least. You would be surprised how many bugs (and bug parts) we regularly consume in processed food.

KNOW YOUR PESTS

This section is your pest identification guide. You must first determine what critter is bugging your plants before you can decide on the proper control strategy. This is important, as not all solutions to pest problems can be universally applied. Sometimes you even need to know what particular species of insect is causing the trouble in your greenhouse. This is especially true for aphid or whitefly infestations.

HOW TO USE THIS SECTION

The following is a list of the more common pests encountered in a greenhouse or sunspace. Following each description of the pest and the damage it causes is a list of many types of controls specific to each pest. Also under each pest is a list of control measures, including "beneficial critters," "sprays," and "other ideas". If the control measure is specific to that pest, then you will find it fully described under that pest's control section. To avoid repetition, if it is a control measure that works on more than one pest, you will find a more detailed description of that control listed earlier in this chapter.

The names of many pests and beneficial critters appear in italics, which denote the scientific name that describes the particular genus and species of that insect. In many cases, there is no common name, so we must use the scientific name. These are difficult enough to spell, let alone pronounce. As you get to know them, you can do as many entomologists (people who study insects) do—give them your own "pet" nicknames.

Under many of the greenhouse enemies listed, you will find a listing titled "sprays with beneficials." These are materials you *can* use in an IPM type of pest control, where good bugs have been released to help control the pests. These are selective sprays that will generally *not* hurt these beneficials you may have released.

Under many greenhouse enemies, you will also see a listing for "other sprays." These are sprays that are effective in controlling that particular greenhouse pest but are also toxic to any released beneficial predators or parasites. Materials that appear in the "other sprays" listing are not good choices for an IPM pest-management strategy and, if used, could decimate your population of beneficial critters.

IDENTIFYING PESTS IN YOUR GREENHOUSE

It is not good enough to know that you have a bug problem. It is important to also know the name of the bug. If not, the cure can sometimes be worse than the problem.

Although bugs have a tendency to give people the creeps, the bug you see may not be a bad bug but in fact might be a good bug that is eating the bad ones. For this reason, always assume innocence until proven guilty. How's that for bug rights in the greenhouse?

Before you go grabbing for a pesticide or other control, confirm that your suspect is a pest and is really doing the damage. More than once, I've come across greenhouse owners about to wipe out a bug that turned out to be a good one, such as a baby ladybug (it looks nothing like the adult, and the baby ladybugs are as important in controlling pests as the adults).

The best confirmation is to try to catch the suspect in the act of doing the damage. If you have damage but no bug to blame, you may have to try sneaking up on a plant in the middle of the night with a flashlight.

The best place to look for a bug is on the underside of the leaf. Another good place is the newer leaves of a plant, the ones toward the tip. Look for soil-dwelling pests under leaf litter, dirt clods, and anything else lying on the top of the soil.

What if you can't find any bugs doing damage? Get out your hand lens and dig deeper. Check around the plants in the back to see what's going on there. Sometimes the critter may have stopped feeding on your plant or is already under control due to some other beneficial bug or critter.

Please read the following descriptions of common greenhouse pests. If nothing seems to fit the bill, then you may need some outside help. Take a few pests as prisoners, put them in a plastic bag or into a small jar of alcohol (rubbing type, not drinking). Take them to your county agricultural agent (listed in the phone book) or local bug expert for positive identification. If they don't know the answer, usually they know where to get an answer.

Getting a positive I.D. is crucial to getting good, safe controls in place.

COMMON GREENHOUSE PESTS

Aphids

Description

Sometimes known as "greenfly," aphids are pear-shaped and quite small, with long legs and antennae. They have a pair of small "exhaust pipe" structures (aka cornicles) on their rear ends. They vary greatly in color, ranging from black and gray to red, yellow, and green, but by far the most common color is pale green. Adults may be winged or wingless. Females can give birth to live young without mating. Offspring can reproduce within 7 to 10 days.

Some species of aphids are actually born pregnant. They basically clone themselves in rapid succession. How's that for fast? Now you know why they seem to appear overnight.

Aphid

Colonies are usually found on new buds and plant tips and on the underside of leaves, especially near the main veins. They can also be abundant on seedlings that have the soft, succulent growth that they love. Also, ants may carry aphids to your plants.

Their feeding can be indicated by leaf distortion and even leaf curling. You may also see

Wingless aphid

white flecks on the leaf, which upon closer inspection are actually cast-off skins that aphids shed much like a snake. These cast-off skins are also a sign of a good-sized infestation.

There are many different species of aphids that can be found in a greenhouse. If you are going

Winged aphid

to be using beneficial parasitic insects to control aphids, then it pays to know a little about what species you are trying to control, as some beneficials may only control specific types of aphids. To identify these further, you will definitely need a hand lens, or magnifying glass. Let's look at some common species:

Cabbage Aphid. The cabbage aphid is among the most easily identifiable in that the body has a light-green, almost silvery, waxlike look. They are mainly found on plants in the cabbage family, especially in the winter greenhouse.

Chrysanthemum Aphid. This aphid is found mainly on the chrysanthemum. It is a small aphid that is red or brown to black. The exhaust pipes (aka cornicles) are usually short and black.

Green Peach Aphid. This is a common critter in the greenhouse. The color can vary from light green, light yellow, or gray-green to even reddish. Probably the most defining characteristic is a pronounced indentation between the base of the antennae of the head. The cornicles are the same color as the rest of the aphid, except for the very tips, which are darker in color.

Foxglove Aphid. This type is very similar to the green peach aphid but has a shiny, almost slimy look to the skin, along with darkened joints on the legs.

Melon, or Cotton, Aphid. The melon aphid is a smaller aphid. Its color runs from light yellow to very dark green. Sometimes these aphids are so dark green they may appear to be black. Unlike the green peach aphid, this one has no indentation between the antennae base. The big giveaway is that the cornicles are usually very dark, no matter what the body color.

Potato Aphid. This species is extremely variable. Although there is no way to generalize the appearance among them, I will try anyway. This aphid is among the largest aphid found in the greenhouse and often has a pronounced football shape. The color of the potato aphid varies from yellow to pink to green. The younger (nymph) aphids are paler and often have a dark stripe down the middle. They are restless and always seem to be in a feeding frenzy. One of my favorite identifiers is that when they are disturbed they readily drop off the plant. It's as if someone screamed, "Incoming human, everybody bail out!" and off they drop. The common, commercially available wasp parasite that works so well on many aphids, *Aphidius colemani,* is ineffective against the potato aphid. The only parasites that seem to work are *Aphelinus abdominalis* or *Aphidius ervi,* both of which are available commercially. It can also be controlled by the general predators listed below.

Rose Aphid. Rose aphids usually stick to plants in the rose family, and they are rarer in greenhouses than outdoors.

Damage

Aphids are sucking insects that cause spotty marks, wilting, yellowing, and deformation and curling of leaves and flowers. In high populations, they can greatly stunt growth or even kill plants.

Like other greenhouse pests, they secrete a sticky substance called honeydew, which drips onto lower leaves. A black mold often grows on the sticky honeydew, commonly known as "sooty mold." This mold also disfigures and damages the fruits and leaves. Aphids may transmit plant diseases that result in yellowing tissue and plant death. Aphids are also well-known for transmitting disease organisms.

Control

Beneficial critters:

There are a few parasitic wasps that provide excellent control of aphids. To further understand the biology of these wasps, see the preceding discussion, "Predators and Parasites."

Aphidius colemani. This is a wonderful little wasp that is about the size of a fungus gnat ($1/16$ inch, 1.6 mm) but has a more segmented, wasplike body. The *A. colemani* wasp is great for the "peach" and "melon" aphids mentioned above as well as for many other types of aphids. I have been able to attain long-term control using the *A. colemani* as the main control agent for aphids, saving me many hours of spraying soap, pesticides, and preventing nasty infestations. The *A. colemani* wasp is attracted to the color yellow, so remove any sticky yellow bug traps that you may have set.

The *A. colemani* wasp is readily available from most suppliers offering control critters for the greenhouse.

If the *A. colemani* wasp doesn't seem to work for you, then you may have the potato aphid, which the *A. colemani* wasp is unable to control.

Aphidius ervi* and *Aphelinus abdominalis. When it comes to critters that can control the potato aphid, these are your only hope. When they parasitize the potato aphid, the resulting aphid shell seems to be larger and lighter in color than the *Aphiduis colemani* parasitism. The *A. ervi* and *A. abdominalis* do not help much if your problem is the peach or melon aphid. The only downside to using the *A. ervi* or *A. abdominalis* is their higher price when purchased from suppliers.

Aphelinus abdominalis is more difficult to find than the *Aphiduis colemani* wasp, but I have obtained some from IPM Laboratories (315-497-2063, **www.ipmlabs.com**). *Aphidius ervi* is available from both IPM Laboratories and International Technology Services, Inc. (303-661-9546) as well as from other sources.

Aphidoletes aphidimyza. This aphid predator is also known as the "aphid midge" and works very well as a general feeder on aphids. The adult is $1/16$ inch in length and has long trailing legs and translucent wings that are larger than the body. Some would describe the adult as looking somewhat like a small, delicate mosquito. It is the orange-colored larvae that feed on the aphids. The wormlike larvae are slightly larger than the adults and taper to the head. The adults feed on flower nectar and pollen.

The adults usually lay eggs near aphid infestations, and larvae hatch out and feed on the aphid for 3 to 6 days before burrowing into the

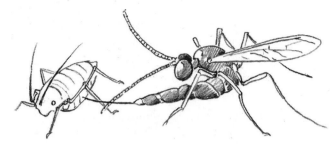

This wasp in laying its egg in, or parasitizing, its doomed aphid host.

soil to pupate into adults. The larvae kill the aphids by injecting a paralyzing toxin into them and then sucking out their body fluids.

During the winter months when the days begin to shorten, the aphid midge will often hibernate in the soil. Also, at temperatures below 55°F (12°C), the midge is not effective in controlling aphids.

For best control, release 3 to 5 aphid midges per infested plant, or 250 to 500 for an average-sized home greenhouse. The drawback to this predator is that it is dormant in winter when the day length shortens. You can, however, fool it into thinking the days are long by suspending an incandescent bulb or some other supplemental light to lengthen the appearance of day length to a total of 13 hours. Researchers are attempting to develop strains that need less hibernation.

A parasitized aphid turns tan, the body swells, and the parasite exits the aphid host through a hole in its abdomen.

The aphid midge is a good complement to the wasps, providing a one–two punch.

Green lacewings eat everything, but they are particularly fond of aphids.

Ladybugs do consume aphids, but for my money I'd rather use other controls first. I have found that wasp parasites and even green lacewings are more effective.

Aphid midge

Still, if one lands on your sleeve, by all means, bring it into the greenhouse.

Sprays with beneficials:
Beauveria bassiana, the fungus-based spray, works well on aphids and has a low toxicity rating. Check the differences between the available brands of *Beauveria* as to what crops and other pests it is effective on.

Enstar is a spray that is designed to work mainly on target pests such as aphids while being easier on beneficial parasites and predators. However, Enstar is not rated for use on food crops.

Neem oil is also easier on predators and parasites and can help reduce the numbers of aphids when you release some beneficials to help. Be sure to check the neem-oil label to be certain that it is safe for use on the crops you're growing.

Other sprays (not for use with beneficials):
Soap sprays and horticultural oils work well on aphids but must be used with care, as they can also cause burning on sensitive plants. Although they are nontoxic, they will also kill any beneficial bugs you might have released.

Hot Pepper Wax Insect Repellent (discussed earlier) will help to control aphids, but only if the material comes in contact with the aphid. It will also repel aphids from a susceptible plant, before they've had a chance to invade.

Pyrethrins are botanically based and kill both good and bad bugs alike.

New to the market is a cinnamon-based spray called Cinnamite®, which is formulated from cinnamon oil. It has been shown effective for rapid control of aphids. When used on vegetable crops, Cinnamite® can be used right up to the day of harvest. Unfortunately, this product is intended for larger commercial-greenhouse operations and will likely be difficult for home gardeners to acquire. Because it

is so new, there is little research available at this writing as to its effect upon beneficial insects associated with controlling aphids. Check with suppliers.

You may have luck with some of the home-made sprays mentioned earlier.

Other ideas:
Aphids love plants that have received excessive fertilizer, especially nitrogen. Although this isn't always the culprit, be sure you are not overfertilizing your plants. Control the ants sometimes associated with the aphids. Also, try growing darker colored lettuce—aphids tend to like the lighter-green shades of lettuce and other vegetables.

Cabbage Looper, Green Worm

Description
This is a green caterpillar up to $1/2$ inch (1.3 cm) long that moves with a looping gait. The adults are small gray moths. The eggs are very small, yellow, and bullet-shaped, and are usually standing on end.

Damage
Although this pest is not very common in the greenhouse, it can occur. Just one worm can do a lot of damage. These caterpillars cause small to large holes in leaves. In a short amount of time, they can actually defoliate plants. They are usually found on cabbage and cabbage relatives but may be found on other plants such as

Cabbage looper

peas, tomatoes, and potatoes. They are most likely to find their way into the greenhouse in mid- to late summer by flying in through a vent or window.

Control

Use the microbial insecticide **Bacillus thuringiensis** (BT), safe for use around beneficial insects. Handpicking and disposing of them also works well.

Cats and Dogs

Description

If unsure, refer to encyclopedia or look in every other backyard.

Damage

Crushed plants, uprooting of plants, leaves chewed on (common around catnip).

Control

Keep 'em out. Training. Positive and negative feedback. Squirt guns?

Fungus Gnat

Note: Much of this applies to the shore fly, too.

Description

These gnats are $^1/_8$ inch (0.3 cm) long, gray-black, with long legs. They are found near the soil surface, especially where there is decomposing organic matter, and are often seen flying around your nose or collecting near windows. The larvae are white and wormlike, about $^1/_8$ inch (0.3 cm) long or smaller.

If you are wondering if you have fungus gnats, simply set out some sliced raw potatoes on the soil surface (cut side down). After a week, look on the underside and you will see the larvae living on the potato.

The shore fly looks much like the fungus gnat except that it is larger and its head protrudes out farther than the head of the fungus gnat. They do not feed on plant roots or stems. Instead, they feed upon algae that forms on the soil and in moist spots. They

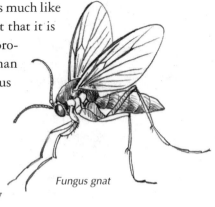

Fungus gnat

are often considered an annoyance to greenhouse gardeners but don't pose a threat to growing. The controls that work on the fungus gnat also apply to the shore fly.

Damage

These are as annoying to people as they are to plants. I have heard that they are attracted to the carbon dioxide in our breath, which might explain why they fly around our noses! Larvae may feed on roots and tunnel into stems. This damage in turn may promote invasion of root-rot organisms. Populations of fungus gnats tend to increase with more use of peat moss and the heavy watering needed for seedling germination. It is also believed that they carry fungal spores from plant to plant.

Control

Beneficial critters:

Beneficial nematodes: This is a wonderful long-term control against the fungus gnat. The nematode is so tiny you can't see it even with a hand lens. Usually, beneficial nematodes are sold in a mixture. The species may include one or more of the following: **Steinernema carpocapsae, Steinernema feltiae,** and/or **Heterorhabditis bacteriospora.** Nematodes are as cost-effective as pesticides and work really well! They are sold under various names, including ScanMask™,

EcoMask™, Savior™, Exhibit™, Guardian™, Lawn Patrol™, and X-Gnat™. Reapply as needed (see label or supplier for further information on reapplication frequency).

Hypoaspis miles is a predatory mite that feeds on the gnat larvae, along with a variety of other soil-inhabiting critters that include the shore fly, thrips, and others. Because it feeds on many things in the soil, it is good to introduce it at least once in a while, especially if you are growing in beds.

Bacillus thuringiensis israelensis (BTI) is a strain of a beneficial bacteria long used by gardeners for controlling caterpillar pests. This particular strain controls the fungus gnat when it ingests the bacteria. It is sold as Gnatrol® and Vectobac™. Although it does reduce fungus gnat numbers, I have not had nearly the success using this bacteria that I have had with the above-mentioned beneficial nematode.

Sprays:
Because this critter spends much of its life protected by soil, most general chemical sprays have only a temporary effect. Soon after you have sprayed, many more will hatch from the soil in a surprisingly short amount of time. For that reason, I recommend that you either try to minimize them by changing your watering habits or apply the beneficial nematode. For temporary control, you can knock down flying adults by using a pyrethrin-based spray, but you will also kill any beneficials you might have released. And adults will come right back in a matter of days after spraying.

Other controls:
Cultivate the soil surface; reduce watering slightly, as fungus gnats can be a sign of overwatering; remove any dead plant debris from the soil surface.

You can get limited results with a dusting of the soil with tobacco from cigarettes. The nicotine will do a good fast job of eradicating them.

It also helps to minimize moisture on the floor and to prevent any plant from being overwatered. Fungus gnats love extra water. However, if they are already present in large numbers and you then reduce the watering frequency, they will sometimes increase their attack on the roots and stems.

Some gardeners have reported that they have been able to reduce the numbers of fungus gnats by adding a small amount of Ivory liquid soap to water, at about 1 tablespoon (15 ml) per gallon (3.8 liters), and using it to water the a pot or pots suspected of harboring hatching gnats. But, for solid, long-term control you can't beat using the above-mentioned beneficial nematodes.

Leaf Miners

Description
These are very small flies—$^1/_{32}$ to $^1/_{16}$ inch (0.8 to 1.6 mm)— with black and yellow markings. Adults are seen flying when foliage is disturbed. Their eggs are white and laid in clusters on the underside of leaves.

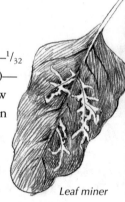

Leaf miner damage

Damage
Luckily, damage is rare in greenhouses, and unless damage is extensive it is usually more of an aesthetic problem than an actual one for most vegetable crops. Severe disfigurement of the leaves can occur. Look for serpentine tunnels in leaves.

Control
Control measures are required only in extreme cases. On ornamentals, you can spray with

Avermectin B, commercially known as Avid® (see earlier discussion on page 389).

Discard leaves with visible "mines."

If you see visible eggs in a cluster on the underside of leaves, brush your fingers across them, which usually destroys them.

Hot Pepper Wax Insect Repellent will help to provide control if contact with the bug is made. It will also repel pests from a susceptible plant.

Leafhopper

Description

This is a small light-colored (yellow or green) insect up to $\frac{1}{4}$ inch (0.6 cm) long. Look for leafhoppers jumping and flying when foliage is disturbed. They are fast.

Damage

The leafhopper is not a common greenhouse pest, but it occurs here and there. It causes spotting on leaves and is known for transmitting diseases. It also produces sucking effects similar to aphid damage.

Control

General predators give slight control. Try spot spraying with insecticidal soap or horticultural oils. Also try botanically based sprays such as neem or pyrethrin-based sprays.

Other Ideas:

Leafhoppers often come in with plants that were previously grown outside. Minimize the plants you bring into the greenhouse from the outside and this might help solve the problem.

Leafhopper

Mealybug

Description

The adults are white to tan, oval, and $\frac{1}{3}$ inch (0.8 cm) or less. They produce a waxlike cottony substance that covers their bodies. They are found near buds, leaf bases, along leaf veins, and even in the soil. When not covered in the cottony substance, they may appear to be pink in color. Mealybugs produce a mass of yellow eggs that are among a mass of white, waxy threads. Occasionally, the mealybug will go through a stage where it has a delicate yellowish body and a pair of wings. This enables it to move all over the place. It is very rare to see a winged mealybug.

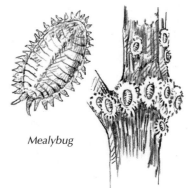

Mealybug

Damage

Mealybugs are sucking insects that cause problems similar to those brought on by aphids, including the sticky honeydew secretions on the plant leaf. They damage crops by removing plant sap. Unlike the common greenhouse aphid, the mealybug can attack all parts of the plant, including the root system. The most common mealybug in the greenhouse is the citrus mealybug, but there is also the root mealybug, which spends most of its life in the root zone of the plant, causing wilting.

Control

Beneficial critters:

Cryptolaemus montrouzieri, or "crypto," is a predator beetle that feeds on the mealybug. It is a cousin to the ladybug and is $\frac{1}{6}$ inch (0.4 cm) long, blackish, and hairy, with an orange head and orange wing tips. It also goes by the descriptive name of the "mealybug destroyer."

Larva

Adult

This beetle does a great job of going after the mealybug. The crypto has the distinction of having helped to save California's citrus industry in the early 1900s. It feeds mainly on mealybugs.

The hardest thing about using the *Cryptolaemus* against mealybugs is identifying it in the larva stage. The problem is that the "crypto" looks almost exactly like a mealybug! I wonder if this evolution allows it to sneak up on mealybugs unnoticed. Don't worry, it will soon turn into a beetle. Luckily, a trained eye can tell the difference between a crypto and a mealybug. The larval *Cryptolaemus* is distinguished from a mealybug by having a longer white body, several white leglike structures that are on the sides of the bug, and, unlike the mealybug, you can see it moving on the plant if the temperatures are warm. Don't derail your control by taking the *Cryptolaemus* larvae for mealybugs and accidentally spraying them! Both the larvae and adult (beetle-looking) crypto feed on the mealybug.

Releases should be on the order of 2 to 5 cryptos per square foot (0.09 sq. m). The *Cryptolaemus* does best in temperatures of 70°F to 80°F (21°C to 27°C). They also like a high humidity (up around 70 percent) but can tolerate lower humidity.

Recolonization is often necessary, because these beetles can work themselves out of a job by depressing the mealybug populations to such low levels that they themselves starve.

Although cryptos are not as expensive as the next wasp parasite mentioned, they are still pricey. The crypto is available from most pest-control suppliers. I recommend trying it even in small greenhouses. I have had luck getting several generations of cryptos to survive many years in a greenhouse. In the future, I expect the price to drop as the demand rises and production becomes more efficient.

Leptomastix dactylopii is a small parasitic wasp that helps to control mealybugs. Many growers have reported success with this wasp, but I have not personally had much luck with it. It is also expensive. Check with suppliers on prices and release rates. For the small greenhouse, I would suggest going to other controls to save money.

Green lacewings may feed on mealybugs.

Beneficial nematodes can be very effective on the root mealybug.

Sprays with beneficials:

Neem oil is also easier on predators and parasites and can help reduce the numbers of mealybugs when you release some beneficials to help. Check various brands for specifics on which crops it can be used on.

Beauveria bassiana, sold as Botaniguard™, is the only fungus-based spray that is rated for control of the mealybug. There are other fungus-based sprays with the same active ingredient that are not registered to control mealybugs. I have found that Botaniguard™ has limited positive effects and works best only if you get the mealybug soaked well with the spray.

Other sprays (not for use with beneficials):

Soap-based sprays and horticultural oils (superior or summer types) will eradicate mealybugs, but must be used with care as they can also cause burning on sensitive plants (see earlier discussion on horticultural oils and soaps). You must, however, make direct contact by spraying the undersides of the leaves.

Pyrethrins are a botanically based pesticide. They do negatively affect mealybugs, but they don't do a great job of total eradication.

Hot Pepper Wax Insect Repellent will help to provide control if contact is made with the bug. In the case of mealybugs, you need to drench the critters until their waxy covering is thoroughly soaked! It will also repel pests from a susceptible plant.

You may have luck with other homemade sprays mentioned earlier.

Sometimes you can severely set them back with a hard spray of water that knocks them off the plant.

Other ideas:

Rubbing alcohol is an effective agent against mealybug as well as many other pests. Before you go to the medicine cabinet to get the alcohol, use great caution. Alcohol always has a high possibility of burning leaf tissue. For this reason, never go whole hog on a plant without first testing it!

Use a mixture of 1 tablespoon (15 ml) of rubbing alcohol per pint (0.47 liter) of water. If that doesn't work, try up to a 50 percent solution, taking care to watch out for burning of the leaves. You can also dab undiluted rubbing alcohol on individual mealybugs, using a Q-tip or swab, but avoid getting it on the plant tissue, because the pure alcohol will burn many types of plant leaves.

In certain situations, I have been able to spray undiluted 70 percent isopropyl alcohol on a number of orchids, parlor palms, ivy (*Hedera*), cacti, succulents, and many ferns without any noticeable damage. *Caution*: Your results may vary, depending upon the specific species, temperature, and other variables, so test first!

How does alcohol work? It has the ability to penetrate an insect's waxy coat and is particularly effective on the mealybug, but it can also provide some help with aphids, thrips, scale, and the two-spotted mite. Remember, keep it away from heat and open flames.

You can also handpick and squash them, but this is neither for the squeamish nor the impatient gardener.

Mice

Description
You know.

Damage
They often creep into your greenhouse, especially when it gets cold outside. They can feed on a number of plants, causing damage by their chewing and consumption of your crops.

Control
There are a number of traps and baits. I prefer the traps. There are also many new live traps available. Trap them and take them out to a nearby field, where they will either live or become part of the natural food chain. Of course, the best beneficial critter is the house cat!

Millipedes

Description
These insects have long, slender, white to brown bodies with many legs and are up to 1 inch (2.5 cm) long. They are found on the soil surface, often under debris. They run for cover fast when disturbed.

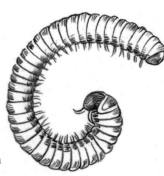

Millipede

Damage
They may occasionally feed on roots, causing stunting of plants. Most of the time, though,

they feed on decaying material, and therefore even if they are present in your greenhouse, they are not generally a concern.

Control

Practice good sanitation. Keep debris off the soil surface. Even when this pest is present, the need for spray is rare. Usually they are helping you out by consuming debris and turning it into organic matter.

Mites (Two-Spotted Mite), Spider Mites

Description

These are small critters—$^1/_{32}$ to $^1/_{16}$ inch (0.8 to 1.6 mm)—pale yellow to light brown to reddish. They may have red spots. Because mites have 8 legs, they are technically not an insect (which has 6 legs). Indeed, mites are a type of arachnid, more closely related to spiders. The first thing you will discover about mites is that they are tiny. It helps to get a hand lens, or magnifying glass, in order to see them. Upon closer inspection, you may see that the adults have 2 spots, one on either side of their body. Say hello to the two-spotted mite.

Damage

Mites feed on plants by puncturing the leaf surface and sucking the contents of the plant. This action of feeding causes leaves to look lighter colored, as if they are drying out or parched. Spider mite damage often makes the leaves look dusty or stippled with tiny dots. This appearance, associated with webs, which are found on the underside of leaves and growing tips, is a sure sign that you have spider mites. The webbing is not like that of a traditional spider but is of a finer material and can sometimes encase the whole leaf in webbing.

Mites feed on plants by puncturing the leaf and sucking the contents of the plant. The leaves become lighter colored, as if they are drying out, dusty, or parched. The mites' webbing is not like that of a traditional spider—it is a finer material and can sometimes encase the whole leaf.

High populations greatly reduce yield and may damage the appearance of plants or even kill them.

Control

Beneficial critters:
Leave it to Mother Nature to come up with both good and bad mites. Some of the most effective enemies of the two-spotted mite are predator mites, which eat the bad mites. There are a number of beneficial predatory mites that work well. The downside is that some species do not survive after they have consumed the target pest population. Each mite species has different advantages and disadvantages. The key is getting the right ones for your particular environment. In general, most beneficial mites perform best in moderate to warm temperatures and high humidity. To hedge your bets, you can often special order mixtures of species to enable a broader

range of control and to allow for their complementary characteristics to work for you.

As with many beneficial critters when they arrive, look at them closely (with a hand lens) so you can later recognize them in action on the leaf. One thing I first noticed was how fast the predator mites moved in comparison to the pesky two-spotted mite. Two-spotted mites are much like cows in a field of fresh green grass. They just stand there and feed. If they move, it is not very fast. The predator mites, on the other hand, are always in a hurry. They remind me of coyotes ready to enjoy a feeding frenzy on the fat cowlike mites!

Don't get too carried away looking at them, though. You should release the mites quickly after arrival! Of course, you want to set them out in areas of the heaviest mite infestation. Keep a close watch on their progress. Positive results are usually seen in 2 to 3 weeks.

One drawback to many mite predators is that after they kill all the harmful mites, they then starve and disappear. This requires more future releases if (or when) the two-spotted spider mite returns in high numbers.

Predatory mites are decimated by the use of sulfur-based sprays and most nonbeneficial compatible pesticides. Many also have a resting stage in winter and are not as effective. Fortunately, most two-spotted spider mites are also slower at infesting plants in winter when the temperatures are cooler.

In general, you need a minimum of 10 mites per square foot (0.09 sq. m) of infested area, or 300 predator mites per 20 to 30 lightly infested plants.

These mites are commonly available from a number of suppliers who specialize in beneficial critters for the greenhouse. One of the best and most knowledgeable wholesale suppliers of beneficial predatory spider mites is a company called Biotactics, Inc. They have an informative website (**www.biohaven.com/bus/biotactics**), and they supply many dealers with their mites.

Let's look at the commonly available mites and other beneficials for two-spotted mites:

Phytoseiulus persimilis. This good mite is small, $1/64$ inch (0.4 mm) long, and resembles the two-spotted mite, except that it has longer legs, is slightly larger, and can be reddish in color. Still, at these small sizes it is hard to distinguish them from other mites.

I have been releasing this mite for close to 20 years now. It is the most commonly used beneficial mite in the world. It has a healthy appetite for its pesky cousin, the two-spotted mite. It can eat up to 20 two-spots a day and multiplies fast. For these reasons, it is the fastest-acting beneficial predatory mite.

There are, however, some important environmental conditions that enable it to do its job. These are warm temperatures around 70°F (21°C). It can tolerate between 60°F and 80°F (15°C and 27°C). With these conditions maintained, the *P. persimilis* can reproduce faster than the two-spotted mite and thus provide relatively quick control.

Mesoseiulus longipes. This beneficial mite is a good choice for lower humidity levels (down to 40 percent) and temperatures that run between 70°F and 90°F (21°C and 32°C). To make them happy, the higher the temperature you run, the higher you should allow the humidity to go. This mite is also a good choice for a greenhouse that has a taller plant canopy. The *M. longipes* is similar in its feeding habits to the *P. persimilis* beneficial mite.

Noeseiulus californicus. Although the *N. californicus* survives lower humidity situations better than the many other beneficial mites, it is slower to provide control. A big plus for this mite is that it is better suited to survive the absence of prey. It provides a good supplement to the *Mesoseiulus longipes* or *Phytosieulus persimilis* beneficial mites.

Phytoseiulus macropilus. This is a good choice for greenhouses that are both consistently humid (above 60 percent) and consistently warm, never below 60°F (15°C). This is the Jimmy Buffet of beneficial spider mites, as this Florida native simply can't give up that Florida lifestyle and climate. It does a good job of keeping up with infestations as long as you provide the right environment. Perhaps some Buffet music would be appropriate when you release these critters into the greenhouse!

Feltiella acarisuga. This small midge is newly available to the list of beneficials for spider-mite control. It also feeds on the two-spotted mite. Early reports on this midge are positive, as it has the ability to forage for the two-spotted spider mites on both hairy and sticky leaf hairs, whereas the many other mite predators have a difficult time surviving. The main supplier (at this writing) of this midge is IPM Laboratories, Inc. (315-497-2063, **www.ipmlabs.com**).

Stethorus punctum. This is a predator ladybird beetle that has a voracious appetite for spider mites. Again, the main supplier is IPM Laboratories, Inc., mentioned just above.

Sprays with beneficials:
Water, when sprayed with some force onto the underside of the leaf, can often knock mites down off the plant and most don't get back up.

The fungus-based spray, Naturalis-O® (*Beauveria bassiana*), is registered for controlling mites. The other *Beauveria bassiana* product, BotaniGuard™, is not registered for mite control even though it has a similar ingredient. I have talked to some commercial greenhouse operators who have seen some positive results with the Naturalis-O® in controlling mites.

Other sprays (not for use with beneficials):
Soap-based sprays and horticultural oils (superior or summer types) eradicate mites (both the pest and beneficial types), but they must be used with care because they can also cause burning on sensitive plants (see earlier discussion on horticultural oils and soaps). You must, however, make direct contact by spraying the undersides of the leaves.

Pyrethrins are a botanically based pesticide that do negatively affect mites but don't do a great job of total eradication.

Hot Pepper Wax Insect Repellent will help to provide control if contact is made with the bug. It will also repel pests from a susceptible plant.

You may have luck with other homemade sprays mentioned earlier.

Avermectin B (Avid®) is particularly effective on mite populations but is not suitable for use on food crops. Avid® is not a compatible spray (see chart on page 370). This means that you should wait at least 21 days or more after the last spraying of Avid® before you release beneficial critters. If not, they may be adversely affected by the toxicity of the Avid® spray.

New to the arsenal of mite control agents is an extract made from cinnamon. It is commercially known as Cinnamite® and is an exciting new product for greenhouse ornamentals and vegetables. Unfortunately, this product is intended for larger commercial-greenhouse operations and will likely be difficult for home gardeners to acquire. If it is effective on harmful spider mites, I would guess that it may also be harmful to beneficial mites.

There are commercially available liquid-sulfur spray formulations that are effective on mites.

Follow the directions closely, as these can easily burn some leaves, especially if you overapply.

Other ideas:
Sulfur dusts can provide some control but can also cause some burning and may be detrimental to the beneficial critters.

The two-spotted mite generally doesn't like high-humidity situations and will sometimes succumb to naturally occurring fungi that are more present in humid greenhouses. Fortunately, the beneficial mites love humidity. Be cautious, because an extremely humid greenhouse can cause other disease problems.

Don't bother using the chemicals Orthene or Sevin on mites, as most are very resistant to these chemicals. In addition, they kill most of the pests' natural enemies.

Nematode

Description

Don't be confused. Yes, I mentioned nematodes earlier in a positive light under the fungus gnat, and other pests. There are both beneficial nematodes that are great in controlling some pests and, unfortunately, there are harmful nematodes. Both live in the soil and are so tiny they are not readily visible to the untrained eye. Although they are so small you will never see them, you can sometimes see their damage. Sometimes nematodes are called "eel worms," and they can be notorious root feeders in many outdoor agricultural crops. Harmful nematodes are most common in areas with a warm climate and sandy soil. This particularly describes the southern United States, where they are a constant threat. Plants that are originally grown in the South and then transplanted into northern greenhouses may also suffer from nematode problems.

Damage

Leaves may be an abnormal color. Plants become prone to wilting and have discolored roots and abnormal small bumps or bulges on their roots. Low productivity is another symptom. In general, nematode damage is hard to positively identify as being caused by nematodes. You may need an expert.

Nematode

Control

Unless common in your area, nematode damage is hard to confirm. Marigolds and compost made from marigolds have been shown to help reduce the existence of harmful nematodes. One of the easiest ways to control nematodes is through good soil management. Soils with high amounts of organic matter are rarely affected, as there is a beneficial fungus that lives in organic matter that preys on nematodes.

More recently, there has been some breeding of plants (especially tomatoes and peppers) that show some resistance to nematode attacks.

Scale

Description

There are a number of different types of scale, which appear in many different shades of brown and tan. Scale looks like a small, flattened, oval, brown-to-tan bump on the stem, leaf stem (petiole), or leaf. They are commonly present along the main leaf vein. Scale may have a small "nipple" in the center. Usually, scale insects are no more than $1/4$ inch (0.6 cm) in size or less. To distinguish

Scale

scale from a normally occurring bump on the stem, try lifting it with a small knife or fingernail. If it comes off easily, it is probably scale. You may sometimes see honeydew or a sticky substance associated with scale feeding on a plant.

Scale infestations are notorious for sneaking up on you because these critters hardly ever move and don't look like a living thing. They appear to simply be a small scab or unremarkable bump, until their numbers increase to millions of bumps! That is the point at which you suspect that something is afoot. They are mobile for only a short period of their life. For most of their life, they are permanently fixed to the plant like a turtle under its protective shell—only in this case the turtle can't move. It just feeds where it sits on the plant like a barnacle does on a ship.

Most scale insects are classified as either soft-scale or armored-scale types. Soft scales excrete honeydew that can make the plant sticky and promote the growth of sooty mold. Soft scales tend to be larger and more noticeable. They can jump around on a variety of plants and are easily spread. Armored scales are often smaller and harder to detect, as they do a great job of blending into the plant and its normal structures. They also tend to be more plant-host specific and not able to jump on just any plant.

Brown scale. Classified as a soft scale, this is among the more common scale pests found in the greenhouse. Brown scales are around $1/_{10}$ inch (2.5 mm) in length. They are pale yellow when young but later darken to a brown color. Upon close examination with a hand lens, you may see some mottling to the coloration.

Black scale and **long brown scale.** These are some other types of soft scales. Black scale has raised ridges. Long brown scale is similar to soft brown scale, except that the shell is noticeably elongated.

Cactus scale. Classified as an armored scale, this one looks almost like a pale fleck of flat sand. It is only about 1 millimeter in length (0.0393 of an inch). It can go undetected until the whole side of a plant takes on the ruddy pale tan color of the scale. It also makes occasional guest appearances on bird-of-paradise plants and on long-lived lilies.

Fern scale. This armored scale, depending upon its sex, is either pear shaped (female) or white and feltlike with three ridges (male). It can be found primarily on—you guessed it—ferns.

There are many more scales in the plant world that may find their way into your greenhouse, but the above are more common in greenhouses.

Damage

Scale weakens the plant by sucking the juices from the stem. In high populations, it can cause plant death.

Control

Beneficial critters:

I have yet to get good control using beneficial critters on scale, but others have had better luck. One problem is that there are many different species of scale that can show up in a greenhouse, and the parasites are selective about which species they attack. If you are lucky, you might find one that works. Check with a good supplier.

Metaphycus helvolus is the most notable scale parasite. It is a small black-and-yellow wasp that lays eggs inside the scale. Soon, out hatches another wasp, leaving a dead scale. It works mainly on the soft scales and has been used primarily on the brown soft scale, black scale, and a few others.

Lindorus lophanthae, both larvae and adults, consume armored scale.

Green lacewing predators will occasionally feed on scale but would rather eat aphids if they are around.

Sprays with beneficials:
There are few sprays that are compatible with beneficials while controlling the scale because of the scale insects' unique protective covering.

Other sprays (not for use with beneficials):
The horticultural oils (superior or summer) work with direct contact but must be used with care, as they can also cause burning on sensitive plants (see earlier discussion on horticultural oils). The oils help eradicate scales by suffocating them. Test a small area of leaf first and wait 48 hours to detect any unanticipated damage. If no damage occurs, have at it! You must, however make direct contact with the scale.

Other ideas:
If the infestation is not extreme, you can set about to scrape off the scales. Removing them basically kills them. You can scrape them with your fingernail as long as you are not damaging the surface of the leaf.

I have also used the plastic green pot scrubbers with good results, especially on more woody plant material. Although scraping works, like most bugs—and Arnold Schwarzenegger—they'll be baaack! But if you are vigilant—now that you know what those odd looking bumps are—you can keep the pressure on them. A few minutes of scraping every month or so can do wonders!

Breaking news: It has been mentioned to me by those in the know that some English gardeners have had luck controlling some scales by spraying them with the beneficial nematode *Steinernema feltiae*. One brand name that includes that particular species of nematode is ScanMask™. If this works, it will be great!

Slugs, Snails

Description
Slugs are slimy, dark-gray, soft-bodied creatures up to 1 to 4 inches (2.5 to 10.16 cm) long. They glide on the plants, leaving a telltale, wet-looking, shiny, and reflective trail. This is often called their "slime trail." They are usually nocturnal feeders but may feed on cool, cloudy days. They are often found hiding under debris. Snails are similar in habit and appearance to slugs, except they have a roundish shell that varies in color and markings. Both lay clear, round, sphere-shaped eggs in masses that can sometimes be seen around the base of plants or in organic material lodged in the soil. They love moist environments. Someone once wrote in the Hobby Greenhouse Internet listserv that, according to Jewish biblical law, slugs are one of the few things that can be killed on the Sabbath. Anyone with a bad slug problem will understand how that came about.

Slug

Damage
Slugs and snails eat irregularly shaped holes in the leaf about $1/2$ to 1 inch (1.3 to 2.5 cm) in diameter. They prefer tender leaves or new growth. Often, they kill seedlings and make foliage so full of holes that it is unmarketable or unpalatable.

Snail

Control

Beneficial critters:
The only critters that can consistently feed on slugs and snails are small animals such as frogs, snakes, and salamanders.

Other controls:
Avoid mulching and keep the top of the soil clean. Slugs and snails will increase their populations when you overwater; try cutting back on water if you feel this may be the case.

Slugs are famous for their love of beer. Actually, it is their love of anything that is fermenting. By pouring a bit in a shallow-sided container, you can make a great trap. But the trap is only effective for about a 10- to 15-square feet (0.93 to 1.39 square meter) area.

Try placing small flat boards or potatoes cut in half on the soil surface. The slugs will congregate there, looking for a place to hide at the end of their night feeding. In the morning, handpick the pests from the underside and destroy them (see below for more instructions on how to destroy them).

New to the snail and slug bait list is a blend of iron phosphate combined with luring bait. The iron phosphate is a low-toxicity, environmentally friendly alternative to other products that contain metaldehyde. The iron phosphate turns into a usable fertilizer in the soil. There are currently two products with this ingredient. One is sold by the company Gardens Alive!® and goes by the name Escar-Go!™ (812-537-8651). The other is called Sluggo™, produced by Monterey Lawn and Garden Products (559-499-2100).

There are also soap-based barriers and baits that the slimy critters refuse to slip across. Unfortunately, these products are tougher to find but will likely become more available in time

This bed was heavily infested with slugs until the beer bait was set.

and will likely be very environmentally friendly.

For the daring in need of a safari in your own tropical paradise, venture into the greenhouse at night (with a flashlight) or on a cloudy day and you will find them feeding on the plants. Then you can handpick them directly off the plant. Handpicking may sound futile, but it isn't; you can make a lot of difference by simply handpicking them. If you don't have the stomach, hire a kid. Remember that every slug you pick represents 30 slugs you won't have to deal with next year (say that to yourself each time they give you the willies). After you pick them, toss them into a can containing some rubbing alcohol. If you have a fishpond or aquarium, feed the caught slugs to the fish—they love 'em!

A 10 percent dilution of household ammonia (1 part ammonia to 9 parts water) kills slugs when applied directly, as will a 50 percent dilution of vinegar ($1/2$ water, $1/2$ vinegar). How to apply? How about a squirt gun? Remember, this will only work on cloudy days or at night when they are out and about.

Barriers such as diatomaceous earth, copper metal, soaps formulated for slug control (Slug-Out®), and ground red-hot peppers will protect young seedlings. The chemical baits containing metaldehyde should only be used as a last resort. See Baits and Traps (p. 393), earlier in this chapter.

Sow Bugs, Pill Bugs

Description

Sometimes called "wood louse," these pests have armadillolike, gray, slightly flattened to oval bodies with scalelike plates, and they are up to $1/3$ inch (0.8 cm) in size. Pill bugs (aka "roly-polys") are noted for their ability to roll into a perfect ball. Sow bugs have two tiny taillike appendages on the rear. Sow bugs can't roll into a ball and simply run away if disturbed. Sow bugs and pill bugs are classified as crustaceans and are more akin to lobsters and crayfish than to insects. They actually breathe through modified gills. This is one reason that they, like slugs, prefer moist conditions (you would, too, if you had to breathe through gills).

Damage

Usually, they prefer to feed on dead litter that is lying on the soil or near the soil surface. In fact, they are important in helping to decompose plant matter. However, they occasionally feed on roots, seedlings, and stems.

Control

Hypoaspis miles is a predatory soil-dwelling mite that feeds on other soil-dwelling critters. For more information on this insect, see the discussion on control under "Thrips" (page 414).

Some birds feed on these crustaceans, albeit rarely in most greenhouses. It helps to water early in the day so your plants and soil get a chance to dry out before the sun goes down and these little armadillos start crawling out.

Sow bug

Pill bug

Keep debris off the soil surface to eliminate their hiding places.

Diatomaceous earth makes a fine barrier that keeps them at bay.

Mulches are notorious for increasing the numbers of these critters. The greenhouse is one garden where mulching is often not a good idea unless it breaks down readily, such as a compost mulch.

Some have reported that beneficial nematodes (discussed under the fungus gnat and also later in this chapter) are helpful in reducing the numbers of sow and pill bugs.

You can simply trap them under boards or on potatoes cut in half and placed on the soil surface and then dispose of them in alcohol.

I know one greenhouse gardener who simply squishes them if he sees too many in one place or where they are doing damage to a crop.

Thrips

Description

Although it may sound odd, "thrips" is the word used for both plural and singular references to this critter. Thrips are very small, $1/50$ to $1/32$ inch (0.5 to 0.8 mm) in size, and yellow to brownish. They have a trademark tubular, cigarlike shape. The immature thrips are opaque and lack wings. The adults have narrow wings that are folded against their body. Although they are difficult to see with the naked eye, you can see them quite well with a hand lens.

They can be found mainly on the undersides of infested leaves and in flowers and flower buds. Thrips go through their pupae stage in the soil and then emerge to feed on the leaf.

Adult   Larva

Damage

Thrips suck on the leaves and flower buds, causing a stippling or small yellow brown or whitish areas on leaves and flowers. They can also cause misshapen fruit. They are notorious for causing brown streaks and spots on rose blooms. Sometimes their feeding can result in white streaks on the leaves and petals themselves. Look closely at the suspected spots and streaks on the leaves. Do you see smaller black spots in the larger light spots? If so, this is their fecal matter, to put it politely, which is one way to confirm that you indeed do have thrips. Sometimes the fecal matter spots are also found without any light streaks or spots present.

As if that weren't enough, thrips also transmit diseases. Among the most damaging disease they spread in a greenhouse is the "tomato spotted-wilt virus," or TSWV. Thrips are small and can populate and infest a plant very quickly. It is important to monitor the undersides of the leaves on a regular basis to be on the lookout for these cigar-shaped critters. Don't forget your hand lens.

Control

Beneficial critters:

None of the following beneficial critters alone is totally effective on thrips. To get the thrips population down to tolerable levels requires a concerted effort of releasing some or all of the following beneficials along with using other compatible controls. Because thrips pupate in the ground, they are much more difficult to control than other pests, but there is still much you can do. The main trick with thrips is to have the control in place early, before the noticeable damage begins.

Amblyseius cucumeris (aka *Neoseiulus cucumeris*) is a predatory mite that feeds on the young stages (larvae) of thrips. It goes into a resting stage in late fall and into winter, which is triggered by the shorter day length and cooler temperatures. There are some strains of *Amblyseius cucumeris* that don't go into this resting stage, but unfortunately they are not as effective as the strain that does. *Amblyseius cucumeris* are often sold in two ways. The first way is loose in a container suspended in empty hulls from grain. You simply shake the mites onto the leaves. Try to release at least 10 predators per square foot (0.09 sq. m) and do it at least 3 times, preferably every other week.

The other way *A. cucumeris* are sold is in "breeding bags," small paper bags that contain several thousand of these beneficial mites. The bags are suspended in a plant canopy, and they breed in the bags, multiplying the number of mites you get. This allows for a more stable release of overlapping beneficial mite populations for up to 6 weeks.

For best survival, *A. cucumeris* mites prefer a relative humidity up around 70 percent. They feed on pollen and other mites in the absence of thrips.

Amblyseius degenerans (aka *Neoseiulus degenerans*) is another predatory mite that also feeds on the young stages (larvae) of thrips. They feed a bit faster than *A. cucumeris* and can survive a drier environment. They can survive well on pollen in the absence of thrips. For this reason, they do best if you release them in areas where there are plenty of flowers. It is important to release them early in spring to allow them to spread throughout the greenhouse as the thrips population rises.

Hypoaspis miles is the only predatory mite that feeds on thrips during its pupae stage in the soil. Fortunately, they are good at getting around a greenhouse, so you don't have to orchestrate perfectly even releases. They live in the upper $1/2$-inch (1.3-cm) of soil and can feed on soil debris and other soil-dwelling critters (including fungus gnats) in the absence of thrips. The *Hypoaspis miles* mites are sold by the liter, and usually a small greenhouse can get by with $1/4$ liter (about $1/4$ quart) or less per year. Unfortunately, the smallest amount I have seen sold is $1/2$ liter (about $1/2$ quart). That is where the idea discussed earlier to share an order with a few other greenhouse enthusiasts comes in handy. As with all releases of beneficials, it is important to do it early in the growing season. That usually means a release in early to mid-spring in most greenhouses.

Minute pirate bug (*Orius insidiosus*) is a predator insect that can eat 5 to 20 thrips per day. They are unique in that they feed on all stages of thrips from the young larvae to the adults. They kill their prey by attacking with a piercing mouth (which looks like a needle-shaped nose) and then suck out the thrips' body contents. You can see how it got its name "insidious." Both the adults and young will feed on thrips. The pirate bug embeds its milky-white eggs in the plant, usually in the leaf stem or in the biggest vein on the underside of a leaf. As the young pirate bugs develop, they turn orange and have red eyes. As adults they run, fly, or fall away when disturbed. They will also feed on pollen and other critters if thrips are not present. Release 1 to 2 per square foot at least a few times during a season.

Sprays with beneficials:
The fungus-based spray *Beauveria bassiana* works well on thrips and has a low toxicity rating, especially on other beneficials.

Neem-oil sprays are often registered for use on thrips and are easier on predators and parasites. These sprays also help reduce other pest populations besides thrips.

Other sprays (not for use with beneficials):
Avid® and oils (superior or summer types) work with direct contact but must be used with care, as they can also cause burning on sensitive plants (see the discussion on "horticultural oils," page 382).

Hot Pepper Wax Insect Repellent will help to provide control if contact is made with the bug. It will also repel pests from a susceptible plant.

Pyrethrins are botanically based and kill both good and bad bugs alike.

You may have luck with other homemade sprays mentioned earlier.

Stronger pesticides will probably help but are not recommended in a home greenhouse.

Other ideas:
Some research has shown that you can trap some thrips on sticky traps. Although these traps might help assist with control, they are best used to monitor the rise and fall of a thrips population. You can make these traps by spreading Tanglefoot™ (see earlier description under "Sticky Traps") or clear grease on a piece of board or heavy card stock that is hot pink in color. If nothing else, it will make your greenhouse look festive!

Try some occasional overhead irrigation to control thrips. Thrips seem to thrive on plants with dry leaves and petals and go downhill when they must contend with free water. Be forewarned, the practice of regular overhead irrigation may stimulate other plant disease problems. Sometimes you walk a fine line to gain control of a pest.

Make an effort to pick and remove your spent blossoms (especially roses). This is where many thrips are hiding out, planning their next attack.

Whitefly, Greenhouse Whitefly

Note: There are two kinds of whitefly! See the description for the next listed pest, the silverleaf whitefly, to be sure you know which kind of whitefly you have. Controls may differ for each type of whitefly.

Description

These white flying insects are small, at $1/16$ to $1/8$ inch (1.6 mm to 0.3 cm). Their eggs, which usually go unseen, are very small, black, and slender, and look like flame-shaped specks. They might even look like very short black hairs, but you must look very closely in order to see them.

The greenhouse whitefly young are roundish and flat and are translucent to white. This is often called the "scale" or "crawler" stage. They are basically immobile during this stage, causing many people to erroneously assume that this is the egg. During this scale stage, the whiteflies are actually feeding on your plant. The eggs, scale, and adults are all found primarily on the underside of leaves, where you are less likely to notice their populations exploding! The sides of the whitefly scale are perpendicular to the leaf, making the scale look boxy or cakelike.

Greenhouse whitefly

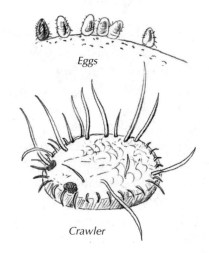

Eggs

Crawler

The greenhouse whitefly crawler has a more vertical sidewall, whereas the sweet potato whitefly crawler is more pillow-shaped (see page 421).

Damage

Greenhouse whiteflies are sucking insects that cause spotty marks, wilting, yellowing, and deformation and curling of leaves and flowers. In high populations, they can greatly stunt growth or even kill plants. Like aphids and certain other greenhouse pests, they can secrete a sticky substance called honeydew, which drips onto lower leaves. A black mold often grows on the sticky honeydew, commonly called "sooty mold." This mold disfigures and damages the fruits and leaves (the mold can be washed off and fruits can still be consumed). Whitefly may also transmit plant diseases that result in yellowing tissue and plant death.

Control

Beneficial critters:

Encarsia formosa is a small parasitic wasp that is usually the best beneficial critter for controlling greenhouse whitefly. It is small and harmless (it never stings anything but whiteflies) and is about $1/16$ inch (1.6 mm) in size (about half the size of a pinhead—not easy to see unless you use a hand lens). The most distinctive

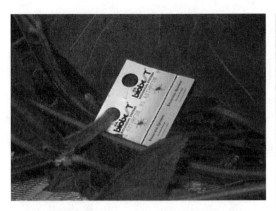

When purchased, the Encarsia usually arrive as black "eggs" on a small card. Actually, these are parasitized greenhouse whitefly scale. Hang these cards on the lower part of a plant that has an infestation of whitefly eggs.

characteristic of the *Encarsia* adult is that the head is black and the abdomen light yellow.

Encarsia eggs are laid into the living body of the whitefly during the scale stage. The whitefly scale, normally clear to white in color, turns black when parasitized. At first you will see a few scales turning black among the other healthy greenhouse whitefly scales on the undersides of leaves.

Encarsia are ordered through commercial suppliers of beneficial insects. You can also collect them from other greenhouse growers who may be using the wasp for whitefly control.

When purchased, the *Encarsia* will arrive as black "eggs" on a leaf or, more commonly, upon a small card. Actually, these are parasitized greenhouse whitefly scale. Hang these leaves or cards on the lower part of a plant that has an infestation of whitefly eggs and/or scales.

It is also important to control slugs in the area where you release the *Encarsia* because slugs love to eat these delicacies. I once had a bed with a minor slug infestation near where I had placed a number of the cards containing the *Encarsia*. I made the huge mistake of setting these cards on the plant too low to the ground.

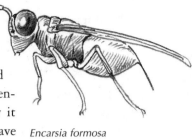

The next day, there weren't any *Encarsia* "eggs" left on the cards. The slugs had simply wolfed down my entire investment. I knew it was slugs because they leave a shiny slime trail wherever

Encarsia formosa

they go. This is why I urge people to first control the slugs when using *Encarsia*. Or at the least, make an effort to hang the *Encarsia* cards high enough to not become dessert for the slugs but not so high that they are exposed to full sun.

The *Encarsia* adults will soon begin laying eggs into more of the developing whiteflies by "stinging" an egg into each whitefly scale. The *Encarsia* young will then begin to grow within the formerly healthy whitefly scales. The wasp basically eats the scale from the inside out, eventually killing this developing whitefly. As it develops within the whitefly, the scale turns black, becoming the "egg and shell" for a new wasp.

As with all parasites, in completing their life cycle they control the greenhouse whitefly. They parasitize only the whitefly and affect no other insect. Successful establishment of *Encarsia formosa* is indicated by the blackening of many young developing whitefly scales 2 weeks after *Encarsia* have been introduced. If you have a good hand lens, you can look at the blackened scale under magnification to see if the *Encarsia* has hatched or not.

When a greenhouse whitefly crawler turns black, it has been parasitized by the wasp Encarsia formosa.

To determine if *Encarsia* has hatched, look for a slit or small hatch door, indicating that they have flown the coop. It is through this slit that the wasp escaped from its host. I encourage anyone using *Encarsia* to get good at identifying whether a wasp has hatched or not.

It is most helpful in determining if the leaves (with the black scale) have some viable *Encarsia* yet to hatch. It is also important in determining the viability of a recently arrived order. The untrained eye can easily be fooled, because the cards will seem to have black *Encarsia* scale that look viable. However, upon closer examination that may not be the case. When your order arrives, check to see if the *Encarsia* have hatched or not. An order of *Encarsia* will always have a few scales that have hatched. However, if you are seeing over 30 to 40 percent of the black scale that has hatched, call your supplier and complain. If this is the case, you are not getting your money's worth. On many occasions, I have received orders from suppliers where a majority of the wasps had already hatched and gone. Most suppliers will correct the problem by sending you more. However, your timing of releases may be thrown way off, making control of whitefly more difficult. That is why sticking with a good supplier of beneficials is important.

As with the release of most beneficials, it is a good idea to reduce the numbers of whitefly with compatible sprays prior to the first release.

For good establishment, begin releasing *Encarsia* when you first see whitefly. If your greenhouse often runs below 55°F (13°C) in the winter, then you will probably have reduced winter problems with whitefly. For these greenhouses, you should time your first release of *Encarsia* around the first few weeks of spring. Then, repeat releases at least 2 to 3 times, at 2- to 3-week intervals (1 week if you have a severe problem).

After you have established *Encarsia* in one area, make an effort to spread the *Encarsia* to other problem areas. This can greatly reduce potential hot spots and reduce the need to purchase more *Encarsia*. Do this by plucking off a leaf full of the black dots (developing *Encarsia*) and then hang the leaf in a new area of infestation. Use tape around the stem to attach it to another plant. Try to get a leaf that still has some unhatched black scales (see above discussion for identification of hatching).

While establishing the *Encarsia* wasp, do not prune the plants in the area of initial release until the wasp has begun some control of the whiteflies. Also, while using the *Encarsia* in your greenhouse, do not use any control methods for greenhouse whiteflies involving yellow sticky traps or boards, which are commonly touted as good for trapping whiteflies. I have found far too many *Encarsia* dead on these traps.

Essential to establishment of the *Encarsia* are warm temperatures averaging 65°F to 80°F (18°C to 27°C). Unfortunately, the whitefly can survive cooler temperatures better than the *Encarsia*, which may become sluggish during the short days of winter. During this time, you may need to look at using supplementary controls listed earlier. Establishment of *Encarsia* can take up to a month, so plan ahead and be patient.

Although most greenhouse gardeners need to rerelease *Encarsia* each spring and early summer, sometimes you can be successful in overwintering the *Encarsia* in a cool greenhouse. Do this by maintaining some old ugly poinsettias or scented geraniums or any plant that has a healthy population of both whitefly and *Encarsia*. Grow them near the warmest part of the greenhouse. With a little luck, the *Encarsia* will spend the winter here. As the temperatures warm up and the whiteflies start doing damage, repeat the spreading of *Encarsia* eggs (black scale) around the greenhouse, using leaves from the overwintered plant. Even with successful overwintering, you may still need to release newly purchased *Encarsia* if the whitefly seem to have the upper hand. Unfortunately, the *Encarsia* does not provide as effective control against the silverleaf (aka sweet potato) whitefly as it does against the greenhouse whitefly (see the next pest discussion).

You can get decent control using the *Encarsia* as long as your timing and temperatures are right. For many greenhouse gardeners, this can be a big "if." You may need a little practice to get the *Encarsia* culture down. Even with good practices, temperatures, and timing, you may always have a stressed-out plant or two in your greenhouse that seems to have a population of whitefly having a party at its expense. Also, remember that by using beneficials you seldom attain eradication of a pest. A few greenhouse whiteflies are all right, as long as a healthy population of *Encarsia* is chasing them everywhere they go. It never hurts to supplement the *Encarsia* with other compatible controls.

Delphastus pusillus is a very small, shiny black ladybird beetle (about 0.06 of an inch or 1.5 mm) that eats whitefly eggs, scales, and adults. The larvae are like little slender, narrow, fuzzy worms, and the pupae are fuzzy and round, often found near the main leaf veins. These beetles can complement the *Encarsia* because they do not feed on parasitized greenhouse whitefly. They must be released near heavy infestations in order to survive. IPM Laboratories recommends a release of $1/2$ to 1 per square ft. (0.09 sq. m) and always placing at least 25 per release site. They need a temperature of around 65°F to 90°F (18°C to 32°C). The main downside to using the *Delphastus* is the price (around $50 for 3,000), but you can offset this by going in on an order with other greenhouse gardeners.

Green lacewings eat everything, and will also feed on some of your whiteflies. Although they are a great help, it is rare that they will clean up a problem.

Sprays with beneficials:
Enstar is a spray that has been available since the 1970s. It is formulated to work mainly on target pests such as whitefly and is easier on beneficial parasites and predators than other sprays. However, there is some research that shows that though Enstar doesn't kill wasps, it may slow down the good parasitic wasp populations. Enstar is not rated for use on food crops.

Neem oil is also easier on predators and parasites than other sprays and can help reduce the numbers of whitefly. Be sure that the brand of neem oil you decide to use is registered for use (on the label) for your particular crop(s).

Beauveria bassiana, the fungus-based spray, works well on whiteflies and has a low toxicity rating. Check the differences between the available brands of *Beauveria* as to what crops and other pests it is effective on. Crawlers that are infected with the *Beauveria* often takes on a reddish-brown cast.

Other sprays:
Soap sprays and horticultural oils work well on whiteflies but must be used with care, as they can also cause burning on sensitive plants. Although they are nontoxic, they will also kill any beneficial bugs you might have released.

Hot Pepper Wax Insect Repellent will help to provide control if contact is made with the bug. It will also repel pests from a susceptible plant.

Pyrethrins are botanically based and can kill both good and bad bugs alike.

You may have luck with other homemade sprays mentioned earlier.

Other ideas:

Vacuum! Clean 'em up with a vacuum! There is something magic about a device that just sucks up the dirt in your life and takes it away forever. On certain occasions, you can do the same with vacuuming up the pest problems. It will not single-handedly solve a major infestation, and it is a lot of labor to go over each and every leaf. This is mainly a supplementary control and not for use with beneficials. Still, it can reduce the numbers substantially. Vacuuming works best on whitefly adults (the whiteflies that are flying around). I have experimented with plug-in vacuums and Dust Busters. Both work for sucking up a substantial number of critters, but you must take care to not injure the leaf of the plant. Sometimes suction too strong can actually suck the leaf right off the plant.

It is best to sneak up on the whiteflies and turn over a leaf to expose them all hiding on the underside. Then run the vacuum across the leaf, holding it just a fraction above the surface. Dispose of the vacuum bag or catcher carefully and far away from the greenhouse or sunroom. Happy cleaning!

Try yellow sticky traps. The color yellow attracts adult whiteflies. You will find yellow sticky traps sold in some garden catalogs, but I have found them to be quite expensive for what you get. One alternative is to make yellow-painted boards yourself.

Avoid using yellow sticky traps when you are releasing the beneficial insect *Encarsia formosa* (discussed earlier) to control whitefly because they, too, will stick to the yellow traps.

With a heavy whitefly infestation, I have found that I can reduce the numbers by making a hand-held yellow sticky trap. Just staple a prepared piece of yellow cardboard or painted board onto a handle such as a stake. On a good warm day, go into the heaviest infestation and shake the plants. Instantly, you will find yourself in a snow of whiteflies. Hold the yellow trap in a bright spot and move it around slowly. You will catch hundreds of adult whiteflies, which in a few more weeks would have translated into thousands.

Although this is another helpful tool in reducing whitefly numbers, it will not eradicate them. Quite often it is used as a method to monitor the pest populations.

Whitefly, Sweet Potato (Silverleaf)

Description

The sweet potato whitefly looks very similar to the greenhouse whitefly, so distinguishing between the two is very important. The sweet potato whitefly (also known as the silverleaf whitefly) adult is smaller than the regular whitefly. It tends to fly more rapidly. The sweet potato whitefly holds its wings close to the body at a 45 degree angle to the leaf, whereas the greenhouse whitefly holds its wings more parallel to the surface. The sweet potato (silverleaf) whitefly is best distinguished from the regular whitefly by looking for a yellow appearance of the body, as opposed to the solid white appearance of the

 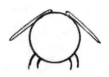

*The wings of the greenhouse whitefly (**left**) are only slightly angled to its body, whereas those of the sweet potato whitefly (**right**) are at a marked, downward angle.*

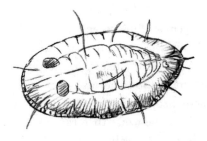

The sweet potato whitefly crawler has a more dome-shaped body than the greenhouse whitefly crawler (compare with the illustration on page 416).

greenhouse whitefly. Unlike the bright white wings of the greenhouse whitefly, the sweet potato whitefly has a more silvery or wax-paper-like appearance. The scale, or crawler, which is usually found on the underside of the leaf, is also more yellow than the generic whitefly scale. The scales also have a translucent color and a slight indentation at the center of the body. A hand lens or magnifying glass will help greatly.

Damage
The damage caused by the sweet potato whitefly is the same as that of the greenhouse whitefly, listed earlier.

Control
Beneficial critters:
Eretmocerus eremicus is a wasp parasite that feeds specifically on the silverleaf whitefly but has also been noted to feed upon the greenhouse whitefly. It is similar in size to the *Encarsia* but with an entirely yellow body.

Eretmocerus eremicus

Unlike the *Encarsia,* which inserts its egg directly into the whitefly scale, the *Eretmocerus* deposits its eggs underneath the scale of the sweet potato (silverleaf) whitefly. The egg then hatches and bores into the scale. When the silverleaf whitefly scale is parasitized by the *Eretmocerus,* the scale turns a dark gold-brown color. It functions best with a warm average temperature of 80°F (27°C).

Delphastus pusillus, discussed in the previous section on greenhouse whitefly, is also effective on the silver-leaf whitefly.

Green lacewings eat everything and will also feed on some of your silver-leaf whitefly. Although they are a great help, it is rare that they will clean up a problem.

Sprays with beneficials:
See the section "Sprays with beneficials" under "Greenhouse whitefly" (page 419), as the spraying options are the same for the sweet potato, or silverleaf, whitefly.

Other sprays:
Soap sprays and horticultural oils work well on whiteflies but must be used with care as they can also cause burning on sensitive plants. Although they are nontoxic, they will also kill any beneficial bugs you might have released.

Pyrethrins are botanically based and can kill both good and bad bugs alike.

Hot Pepper Wax Insect Repellent will help to provide control if contact is made with the bug. It will also repel pests from a susceptible plant.

You may have luck with other homemade sprays mentioned earlier.

Other ideas:
See the discussion on greenhouse whitefly about vacuuming the pest.

WEEDS

A weed is defined as a plant growing out of place. A greenhouse weed could even be a tomato that sprouted in the wrong spot from a fruit that fell on the soil last season. Weeds can also come from manure or compost that contains viable seeds or from mint plants or dill seeds that have the secret desire to proliferate over the earth. Sometimes a weed can even sneak through in a commercial soil mix. Small clovers are the most common in soil mixes.

The good news is that weeds rarely pose any serious problem in a greenhouse or sunspace that could not be easily controlled by a few minutes spent—you guessed it—weeding! Avoid any consideration of using herbicides, as it is overkill in such a small growing environment. Besides, there are too many things that can go wrong when using herbicides in the confined environment of a greenhouse.

DISEASES

A disease may cause the death of a whole plant, death to part of a plant, a cancerous overgrowth of plant tissue, and dwarfing or a slower growth response. Not all diseases are caused by organisms. From the plant's point of view, many are the result of an adverse environment. These nonorganism-caused troubles may resemble problems caused by an organism and can be just as destructive. Alternatively, some diseases may resemble a plant nutrient deficiency. Your plants may be afflicted with a combination of both. And all of this is aggravated by the fact that pests on the scene are avid disease spreaders.

The greenhouse environment is not a sterile place; it is full of life at all times, and sometimes it will seem as if insects and diseases appear out of thin air. But when it comes to disease, the reality is invariably that it has been present for some time. Upon the discovery of a disease problem, people often overreact and the "cure" turns out to be worse than the disease itself.

The hardest reality a greenhouse gardener must face is the fact that there is rarely an all-out cure for most plant diseases. In fact, most fungicides do not work well at all. This doesn't mean plants can't get well, but to get them well is usually a slow process. Curing a plant disease is not like treating a bug problem, where you kill the bug and are done with it. So where does that leave the gardener? Well, we have some good options. First, we have the ability to control the environment. By altering the environment, sometimes even slightly, we can often control a disease problem. For example, by just providing better ventilation we can reduce many diseases that afflict plants.

Second, we can take a number of preventive measures to keep diseases at bay. This can be as simple as keeping the plant at a level of optimum health by giving it the proper environment and preventing bug infestations. Any stress from the environment will promote the occurrence of a disease. Diseases can also be prevented by growing varieties that are resistant or tolerant to a given disease (as described in Chapter 4, "Selecting the Right Plants").

Third, we can go on the offensive with disease-controlling sprays. But I need to first give you some bad news. Most fungicides don't work that well. Those that do usually aren't worth the trouble. Also, it is rare that a fungicide is registered for use on food crops.

Fungicides come in official-looking bottles that are similar to those containing insecticides. Because we know that insecticides usually work, most of us assume that the fungicides also work.

This is a wrong assumption. To put it simply, it is rare that you can spray a diseased plant back into a state of health. The truth is, I can't remember ever seeing this happen.

In fact, if you read the label of most fungicides, you will find that they are not designed to cure a disease but rather to prevent further infection. Applying them can be a lot of work, requiring that you spray a plant many times throughout its life just so it won't ever get the disease. This requires quite a commitment to using a fungicide—before you even know if you need it or not! As a result, I regard preventive spraying with fungicides as a big headache. After all, most commercially available fungicides have some level of toxicity. Sometimes I would rather opt to let the plant succumb to the disease.

Without the ability to effectively cure diseases with sprays, you are only left with one main option: altering the environment. This includes changing the climate (temperature, light, humidity), changing the moisture level, changing the plant variety, altering the time of planting, or growing that plant in a new location. Any one of these changes might provide the key to gaining control of a disease. Sometimes you just have to experiment.

ORGANISM-CAUSED DISEASES AND CHARACTERISTICS

Microorganisms (also known as microbes) have a very complex biology. To even begin to understand the whole ecology involved is a grand task. Fortunately, identifying the disease symptom is easier. Identification is essential to proceeding with the proper steps of control.

Diseases are caused primarily by three organisms: bacteria, fungus, and virus. Depending upon the microbe, they survive by moving through air, water, soil, and plant debris. Insects can also transmit diseases. To complicate matters, disease-causing organisms rarely act—or exist—alone. For instance, there can be beneficial predators or parasitizing microbes that attack the disease-causing microbes (yeah!), coexisting around problem areas. This is why a sterile environment doesn't always offer the best control. In fact, the more we encourage high microbial populations in the soil, the less we see soil disease organisms taking hold. Much like beneficial insects, the harmful microbe populations can be controlled to some extent by beneficial microbes. Organic matter, when added to the soil, is the lifeblood of the microbes, which is one major reason why organic matter is so important. Let's take a look at some of the disease-causing microbes.

VIRUSES

Viruses are very small—ultramicroscopic—and very unusual life forms. They don't even have cell walls. Symptoms of virus infections include mosaics (yellow angular mottling or spotting), brown areas, and occasional leaf curling.

Insects commonly transmit viruses, but they can also be carried on seed and in the air with pollen. Even people can transmit a virus disease by simply touching a plant. This is the case with the disease known as tobacco mosaic virus that afflicts tomatoes and other plants in this family (see "Tomatoes" in Chapter 8). Tobacco smokers' fingers easily spread tobacco mosaic virus. Tobacco users should wash their hands thoroughly before entering or handling any plants in a greenhouse.

Controlling viruses is usually a difficult task. No sprays are available to do a good job preventing virus infections. Virus control usually

PREVENTION OF DISEASE

As you can see, it is much easier to prevent disease than it is to cure it. The old adage "An ounce of prevention is worth a pound of cure" also applies in the greenhouse. Here are some guidelines:

1. **Maintain plant health.** Avoid overcrowding, and provide a healthy growing environment with proper levels of ventilation, humidity, water, light, nutrition, and so forth. This also involves proper scheduling and maintaining soil health.

2. **Keep your greenhouse clean.** Remove diseased plants. Keep the hose nozzle off the soil. Before reusing old pots, clean with hot water, soap, and diluted bleach, and then rinse well. Keep dead leaves off the soil surface.

3. **Start seedlings in new potting soil** (usually sterile soil). See Chapter 5, "Plant Propagation," and Chapter 9, "Getting to the Roots."

4. **Use compost from greenhouse plants only in an outside garden.** Outside garden plants may be composted for greenhouse use. Running two parallel compost piles helps to break potential disease cycles because indoor and outdoor diseases are often different.

5. **Avoid taking on gift plants from friends, especially sickly looking ones.** These are the gift horse that one should look in the mouth very carefully before even considering acceptance. Also, try not to baby-sit or nurse other people's plants in your greenhouse. This is a great way to get new and different bugs and diseases.

6. **Keep the air moving.** Diseases, like insects, love stagnant air, especially during the day. Try to have a small fan moving the air during the day, even when the greenhouse needs no ventilation.

7. **Rotate the crops to break disease cycles.** Keep a map of your planting layout from season to season, and be sure you are rotating your crops. Avoid following crops with their relatives (this often occurs within the large cabbage family or tomato family of plants). See the box "Basic Crop Families" in Chapter 3 for family lists.

8. **Interplant by mixing up the plantings in an area or a bed.** Rather than growing a solid bed of radishes here and a bed of lettuce there, try mixing them both in a bed. See the section "Mixed Planting" in Chapter 3 for more information on interplanting.

involves growing resistant varieties, altering the environment, being careful when handling plants, eliminating insects that transmit the disease, and using disease-free cuttings for propagation.

BACTERIA

Many people think of bacteria when they think of disease, but only a small percentage of bacteria cause disease. Many, in fact, are beneficial and essential to the health of the soil and the overall health of people. Bacteria that cause plant diseases usually enter the plant through leaf or stem wounds or places damaged by insects. They can also enter a plant through microscopic openings in plant leaves. Bacteria need a relatively warm temperature to live and thrive. A bacterial infection is more rare in cooler greenhouses or in the winter.

Symptoms of a bacteria infection in a plant include both circular and angular leaf spots. At first, leaf spots often appear to be some shade of green in color, then gradually turn yellow, brown, or black. Other common symptoms include bacterial rots in which the plant tissue disintegrates and is often slimy and smelly.

Control of bacterial diseases in a greenhouse involves disposing of plants that are infected and practicing good greenhouse sanitation, such as keeping the soil surface clean and removing any dead leaves or stems from both the plant and the surface of the soil. Often, bacterial problems are associated with high humidity and overwatering in a warm greenhouse.

You can help prevent the spread of a bacterial infection by not touching or working among wet plants. If you suspect a bacterial infection on a plant and need to prune some dead parts off, try to disinfect your pruning shears or scissors by dipping them in a dilution of bleach or rubbing alcohol between every cut.

FUNGI

Fungi cause the great majority of plant diseases, but they are not all bad. There are beneficial species that help control some diseases and insects, and some of them are even commercially available (see *Beauveria bassiana,* discussed earlier in this chapter). Whether they are beneficial or harmful, fungi generally reproduce by spores, which spread in the air, soil, water, and plant debris. Fungi characteristically have complex life cycles with many different stages.

The symptoms of fungus disease include leaf spots, wilting, rots, mildews (usually a white or gray growth on the leaf surface), rusts (a rust-colored growth on the leaf), and blights (a rapid yellowing or withering and decay of tissue without rotting). Fungi are best controlled with good sanitation, resistant plant varieties, environmental management, and chemical- and mineral-based (usually copper and sulfur) fungicides.

In general, fungus diseases are difficult to identify unless you work with them on a daily basis. They are famous for mimicking each other and for deviating from the textbook symptoms. If you have a particularly bad problem and need a positive identification, get it diagnosed by a plant pathologist at your nearest agricultural university, agricultural experiment station, or county agricultural extension office. When you bring a sample of the diseased plant to an expert, be sure to pick it just before leaving for the office. Be sure the sample contains varying stages of the problem and contains leaves with slight to heavy infection. Place the sample in a plastic bag and put your name and phone number in the bag in case the experts need to get back to you about the problem.

DISEASE-CONTROL STRATEGIES

The symptoms of a troubled plant can tell you something about what is causing the trouble, your first step to controlling a disease. The second step is to choose the best means and method to solve the problem. As stated earlier, the most effective solution is prevention. If and when that fails, there are other options.

RESISTANT VARIETIES

Disease-resistant plant varieties are much more common than insect-resistant varieties. Don't be misled by the great sound of a plant actually being resistant to something. You should know that seed companies use the term "resistant" much too freely. Usually the plant will only be more tolerant than other varieties. A good rule of thumb to use whenever you see the word "resistant" is to replace it in your mind with "tolerant." Resistant varieties can still become infested with the disease to which they are supposedly resistant. But a variety with an increased tolerance to a disease is still worth growing. Sometimes a variety is truly resistant, and when that happens, it is a great discovery.

To find a resistant variety, read catalogs for descriptions of varieties with special characteristics, including resistance. If none are available, do your own variety testing. You will often discover more-tolerant varieties. See Chapter 4, "Selecting the Right Plants," for more information on selecting resistant varieties.

One of the wonderful things about most resistant varieties is that they are no different in flavor, vigor, or any other characteristic than you would find in a nonresistant variety, so there is no compromise or sacrifice involved in using them.

SPRAYING FOR DISEASE

As with spraying for insect control, spraying commercial fungicides for disease control should be used as a last resort. In fact, as I stated earlier, most fungicides don't work! They are primarily designed for disease prevention, not for getting rid of an existing problem. They need to be used regularly even if there is no disease present. For that reason, I don't generally recommend spraying chemical-based fungicides for control of existing diseases.

Although commercial fungicides have their problems, there are alternative "sprays" you can use that have fungicidal and disease-control qualities and that are, for the most part, nontoxic. You can mix up many of these at home, which means you are in control of what you put on your plants. Let's look at what can help.

Alternative (Nontoxic) Sprays

Milk. There is some evidence that milk can prevent tomato seedlings from picking up the tomato mosaic virus. How anyone ever stumbled upon this idea is beyond me, but you might consider giving it a try. Simply water the soil with a few cups of undiluted milk (the lower the fat content the better) once or twice per month.

Vinegar. Many growers have reported that vinegar can help prevent seedling diseases during germination. Water into soil a dilution of 1 part vinegar to 10 parts water. Let the soil sit for 5 days before sowing seeds. This is not needed when you use sterile or new potting soil to germinate seedlings.

Baking soda. When diluted in water, it can provide some help in controlling powdery mildew. You may want to experiment with the dilution rate. For starters, try mixing 4 tablespoons (60 ml) of baking soda in 1 gallon (3.8 liters) of water. Mix well and spray on the leaves. Repeat every week. This is not a cure-all for powdery mildew. Sometimes it works really well; other times the results are less than satisfactory.

Potato starch. When sprayed on the leaves, it has exhibited some control of powdery mildew. To prepare, try mixing 5 tablespoons (75 ml) of potato flour and 2 tablespoons (30 ml) of insecticidal soap in 1 gallon (3.8 liters) of water. Stir well. Let it sit overnight prior to spraying. Stir before using and spray every 5 to 7 days. Mix up a fresh batch each time you use this spray. There is some evidence that potato starch can control aphids to some degree. But go easy on this spray, as it will leave your leaves looking very white. They'll probably look worse than they did with the disease.

Cinnamon. This common table spice has been found by many to have antifungal and antibacterial properties. Since antiquity, it has been utilized for these special properties. Many hobby orchid growers have rediscovered its benefits and have found it is very helpful on problems with phalaenopsis diseases. It is generally used as a dust shaken on diseased spots or leaf damage. It helps if the damaged tissue is moist so that the cinnamon dust sticks. Do some tests with cinnamon before you apply it to every problem area, as it has been known to cause burning. Cinnamite® is a new product available to commercial growers (see earlier discussion under "Botanically Based Insecticides") that has been formulated to control spider mites and lessen any burning problems that raw cinnamon has.

Horsetail tea and **silicon.** Horsetail (*Equisetum arvense*) is a native plant found growing in many areas of the United States. It has been used for years by organic gardeners to control and prevent fungus diseases. To make your own solution, steep $1/4$ cup (60 ml) of chopped or ground stems in $1/2$ gallon (1.9 liters) of water overnight. Strain and spray. Horsetail leaves are typically found along creeks and in wetlands (never harvest more than 10 percent of the clump), but they may be much easier to get at a natural-food store that has a good collection of herbs.

The active ingredient in horsetail tea is silicon. After a leaf has become infected with a disease, a greater deposit of silicon is found around the cells surrounding the infection. This seems to be part of the plant's own natural immune-system response. Silicon has been shown to help form stronger, harder cell walls that may actually deter the powdery mildew fungus. Silicon is found naturally in soils but can easily become depleted, especially where there has been intensive agriculture and many harvests.

You can apply a more concentrated form of silicon to the soil as a component of a specialized commercial fertilizer. There have been other research reports that seem to confirm the reduction of powdery mildew when silicon is added to the soil. The only commercial source of silicon fertilizer I have come across is a product known as Pro-TeKt®, which contains 3.7 percent potassium and 7.8 percent soluble silicon. It is sold by the Dyna-Grow Corporation (800-396-2476), a well-known major producer of hydroponic solutions.

Sulfur. Sulfur spray was mentioned earlier in this chapter, to be used in conjunction with copper as a control for spider mites. It has the added effect of keeping leaf mildews down. One type of mixture containing sulfur is Bordeaux Mixture, which comes as a dust or wettable powder or as a prepared-liquid formulation. It works best as a preventative and must be applied to the leaf before it gets the fungus. Sulfur-based sprays work because they prevent the spore of the fungus from surviving on the leaf. If applied correctly, it can help prevent powdery mildew. It does little good when sprayed on leaf surfaces showing massive amounts of disease. Usually these types of mineral-based sprays are applied every 7 days (from well before you see the infection, until 20 days before harvest).

Do not use sulfur in any form if you anticipate temperatures above 90°F (32°C), as it will likely burn the leaves. Also, do not apply sulfur in conjunction with a summer oil spray, as the combination can cause massive leaf burning. If an oil spray has been applied in the last 10 days, hold off on the sulfur for a few more days to prevent leaf burning.

CHEMICAL FUNGICIDES

Chemical-based fungicides are also on the market for controlling diseases. As mentioned earlier, most fungicides do not control an existing disease but can work at preventing the infection. This requires an almost exhausting weekly schedule of spraying. Even so, fungicides are still not very effective with most greenhouse crops. With that in mind, why go to all the trouble of spraying these poisons in your greenhouse? I rarely recommend using a chemical fungicide. I usually have better luck altering the environment (i.e., reduce watering, alter scheduling, change varieties, and so on). Only on a very rare occasion, such as when

a special ornamental plant is in danger, would I consider using a fungicide. In this case, I might look to the chemical benomyl (aka Benlate). Benomyl has a systemic action and should be used only on ornamental plants, never on edible crops.

When using any chemical fungicide, always follow the directions before spraying on any plant. Never increase the concentration. Test the spray on one leaf and wait a day to see if there is any possibility for burning. Also, refer to the earlier discussion in this chapter on spraying procedures and safe spraying techniques.

BIOCONTROL OF DISEASES

More and more, we are seeing some very interesting products that actually enable you to add specific beneficial fungi and bacteria to a soil mix, growing bed, or crop. These microorganisms help prevent disease, increase a plant's tolerance to stress, and increase its vigor. Some have even found that these products even increase the cold tolerance of a plant. Many of these claims have been scientifically proven and are gaining acceptance among commercial growers. Now some of these products are becoming available to home gardeners. Many of these products provide control as effective as that of chemical-based fungicides. The advantage is that the fungi and bacteria are nontoxic, whereas most fungicides usually have some level of toxicity. Most of these biocontrols are effective on fungus-caused diseases. For more information, see the more complete discussion in Chapter 9, on page 336.

COMMON GREENHOUSE PLANT DISEASES

Leaf, Flower, Stem, and Fruit Rot

Description
Leaves have wet, brownish rot. This is often found on heading lettuce, cabbage, and Chinese cabbage. It is more serious in shady locations with lots of foliage where air circulation is lacking.

Cause
Usually bacteria, sometimes fungus.

Control
Try to minimize splashing the soil while watering or the problem may spread. Overwatering, high humidities, and poor air circulation aggravate this problem. Try different varieties and wider plant spacing. In the case of lettuce, try switching to leaf lettuce rather than heading types. Immediately dispose of any infected tissue.

Leaf Spots

Description
The leaf is covered with spots that range from pinpoints to quarters in size. Leaf spots are caused by a variety of insect pests, diseases, and environmental conditions. Get out a hand lens or magnifying glass to look for possible pests. If no pests are present, you may have a fungus. Consider getting some expert help in identifying the exact cause.

Cause
The most common cause is fungus, but it may also be caused by bacteria, insects, and environmental conditions.

Control
Control is usually based upon correct identification. Avoid splashing water on leaves when watering. Water in the morning only and avoid overwatering. Try resistant varieties.

Mildews, Powdery and Downy

Description
White to grayish leaf-surface growth with a powdery, dusty appearance. Downy mildew has a more gray appearance, whereas powdery mildew is white. Both severely stunt growth and reduce yield.

Cause
Fungus.

Control
Use resistant varieties; sulfur application prior to major infection works as a preventive (read earlier discussion); baking soda spray also works. I have had good luck with a spray commonly used to reduce transplant shock and leaf evaporation, known as an antitranspirant. It coats the leaves with a plasticlike coating that slows leaf evaporation and water loss and is commonly used on cut Christmas trees. I have found that it can be used to help control powdery mildew on ornamentals when sprayed at the first sign of the disease. Avoid using it on edible leafy plants. It can be found sold under such brand names as ForEverGreen and Wilt Pruf.

Also consider increasing silicon in the soil, as mentioned earlier under "Horsetail tea and silicon" (page 427).

Root Rot
Description
Plants wilt constantly, and roots rot.

Cause
Fungus and bacteria.

Control
This is often caused by overwatering, which is unfortunately the urge people get when they see a wilting plant. Try replanting in new soil with a higher percentage of sand, or use a soil with better drainage. Water only when the soil needs it. See Chapter 1, "The Greenhouse and Sunspace Environment," for more information on watering techniques.

Seedling Diseases (Damping-Off)

Description
Damping-off is a general term describing many different seedling diseases. They are very common but can easily be controlled. The symptoms may include:
1. The stem rots near the soil surface and the seedling falls over.
2. The seed decays in the soil before or after germination.

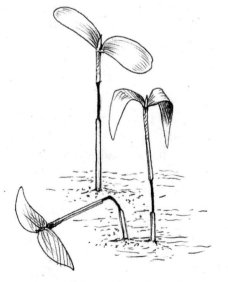

One of a number of signs of "damping off" on a seedling.

3. The root rots after the plant is germinated and growing. The plant first appears stunted and then dies; roots may turn a rust color at the rotted location.

Cause
Fungus and environmental causes.

Control
Control the environment. One of the best controls is to use sterile soil for seed germination. Most store-bought potting soil is sterile and suitable for seedlings. See Chapter 5, "Plant Propagation," for more information. In order to control seedling diseases, we must first understand the environment that fosters these problems.

Sooty Mold

Description
This appears as a black, sticky, dirty, dustylike growth, usually on lower leaves. You may first see a shiny cast to the leaf before it grows the mold.

Cause
Insect drippings (honeydew) from above the affected leaf trigger the growth of this black fungus.

Control
Control aphids, whiteflies, mealybug, scale, and other sucking insects.

Tomato Diseases
Tomatoes seem to have more than their fair share of disease problems, often very different from the more common diseases. Please refer to "Common Greenhouse Tomato Disorders" in Chapter 8 (page 298) for a listing of specific diseases affecting tomatoes.

ENVIRONMENTAL EFFECTS ON SEEDLING DISEASES (DAMPING-OFF)

1. **Overwatering.** Of course you should never let seedlings dry out, but overwatering and maintaining soggy soil will increase seedling diseases. Keep the soil moist, but not dripping wet.

2. **Fertilization.** The higher the level of nitrogen in the germination soil, the softer the plant growth will be. Soft growth is particularly susceptible to seedling diseases.

3. **Light.** Seedlings grown in ample light are more resistant to seedling diseases. If your seedlings are showing signs of a light deficiency (elongated, lanky growth; light-green leaves), they will also be more susceptible to seedling diseases.

4. **Soil salinity.** If your soil test shows a high concentration of salts in the soil or an unusually high pH (7.5 or more), you'll see more seedling diseases (damping-off).

5. **Temperature.** Seeds germinate best at temperatures between 65°F and 80°F (18°C and 27°C), depending on the specific requirements of each crop. When seeds are grown at higher or lower temperatures than optimum, they'll be more susceptible to diseases.

6. **Poorly aerated soil.** A great place for seedling diseases to grow is in poorly aerated soil. Add extra amounts of sand to your soil, or better yet, use a good commercially available potting soil.

7. **Old, infested soil.** Using soil that previously had seedlings or other plants growing in it will increase the incidence of seedling diseases. Such soil tends to be infested with the diseases that cause seedling death. Use either sterilized soil (see Chapter 5, "Plant Propagation," for more information) or virgin commercial potting soil, which is already sterilized.

8. **Depth of planting.** Planting seeds too deep delays emergence and allows for more seedling disease to occur (see Chapter 5, "Plant Propagation," for more information on planting depths).

9. **Age of seed.** Older seeds tend to be weaker and have less vigor. For this reason, they may also have more problems with seedling diseases. Use new seeds (no older than a year or two), especially if you are experiencing any problems with germination. Always store seeds in dark, cool, airtight containers (see Chapter 5, "Plant Propagation," for more information).

10. **Crowded seedlings.** Thickly planted seedlings compete for light, water, and nutrients. This creates a stress situation for the seedlings, which in turn makes it easier for them to be attacked by seedling diseases. Give each seed and seedling plenty of room to grow, so that adjacent seedling leaves don't touch each other. When starting seeds in flats or other containers, it is better to sow them in rows rather than just scattering them.

ENVIRONMENTALLY CAUSED DISEASES

A number of plant maladies common in greenhouses are solely the result of the environment. How can you identify an environmentally caused disease? Look for symptoms that occur on plants of many different species in a broad area of your greenhouse, rather than those that affect an individual plant. Disease organisms, in contrast, usually affect only one plant species or family of plants (see the box "Basic Crop Families" discussed in Chapter 3).

In contrast, it is rare that organism-caused diseases afflict different plants of different families. By looking at what is affected, you can discern the problem that caused the disease. For instance, if brown blotches are affecting flowers, herbs, tomatoes, orchids, and other plants, then you probably have an environmentally caused problem. If you see a problem on only one type of plant or a couple of related plants, such as yellowing of leaves on tomatoes and peppers (which are in the same plant family), then you probably have a problem with an organism-caused disease. Let's look at some of the common environmentally caused diseases.

Ammonia

How on earth does ammonia enter the air of a greenhouse? When it is attached to a barn. When high amounts of ammonia are in the air, leaves may have a cooked appearance, with brown to red splotches. Damage may also appear as tan and white spots on cabbage family plants, and leaves may drop off. Some people believe small amounts of ammonia may actually help plants, but there is debate on this. I once saw ammonia toxicity in a greenhouse attached to a large chicken coop. The ammonia came in from the coop's generous amount of chicken droppings.

Cold damage

Don't accidentally leave the vents open when it is cold. Cold damage can also occur in a unheated greenhouse during a cold snap or during a power outage that shuts off your heating system. Symptoms include dark green, wilted, or dry leaves occurring on plants nearest to glazing or to vents with air leaks. Also look for misshapen fruit, poor fruit set, and blossom drop.

Corky scab

This is indicated by a corky growth usually seen on the underside of the leaf. It is generally caused by overwatering. The leaves with these symptoms will not recover from the problem, so remove the badly affected leaves and cut back on watering. A low-light environment also contributes to the problem, so try to increase the light.

Ethylene

Ethylene is a by-product of the combustion of fossil fuels, or leaks of propane or natural gas. Look for growth reduction; leaf buds and flowers may fall off; also leaf deformities may occur. Be sure your heater is ventilated to the outside.

Finger blight

Dead green areas on the leaves may result from too much handling. This occurs most often on unusual plants, scented herbs, and other plants located at eye level. Also, smokers transmit tobacco mosaic virus to tomatoes and peppers by touching the leaves (see discussion under "Tomatoes" in Chapter 8).

Lack of light

Wherever there is shade, look for plants with elongated stems and spindly growth. This can be helped by the addition of more overhead windows or skylights and/or by painting the walls white to increase the reflective light that enters the greenhouse.

Nitrogen oxides

The symptoms are the same as for smoke damage, along with growth suppression. This is common in greenhouses located near manufacturing plants, refineries, sources of combustion of fossil fuels, or busy highways.

Nutrient problems

A little fertilizer is good; more is often a disaster. If you suspect you overfertilized, look for burned tips of leaves. Read Chapter 9, "Getting to the Roots," for more guidance. Also, see the discussion on blossom-end rot in tomatoes in Chapter 8, "A Closer Look at the Plants."

Pesticides

The use of pesticides can result in variable symptoms. The herbicide 2,4-D causes unusual leaf and stem curling. Many pesticides cause burn spots or burned leaves. Also look for leaf yellowing and/or stunting within 24 to 48 hours of applying a pesticide. When using pesticides, please read the label and follow all safety precautions. Even seemingly nontoxic sprays such as insecticidal soap can burn leaves when applied in a stronger formulation or on the wrong plants. Sprays drifting in from outside pesticide applications may enter the greenhouse through a vent in summer. Herbicides should never be used in the greenhouse. Accidental spills of herbicides in the soil can be helped somewhat by the addition of activated charcoal to absorb the chemical. Let's hope it never comes to that.

Smoke

Yellow, tan, or papery blotches appear between the leaf veins, while the veins usually stay green. All ages of leaves are affected. Smoke affects most crops, but lettuce is somewhat resistant. Check wood heaters or other types of heaters for down-drafting (which is not good for people, either).

Sunscald

Look for round or angular areas of browning. It is sometimes caused by water droplets acting as a magnifying glass. This is relatively rare in the greenhouse, but where there is clear, single-pane glass, it is more likely. This problem may also occur in greenhouses with aluminum foil on the walls or where light is reflected by a polished surface (including mirrors). It can also occur with the use of supplemental lighting when the lights are placed too close to the plants.

Water, too much

Too much water will actually trigger wilting. Wilting triggers people to water, and the fatal cycle begins. Check the moisture level in the soil before reaching for the hose or watering can. Overwatering can also promote whole leaves to turn yellow but can also be expressed by splotches of yellow developing on leaves. Too much water will also create an environmental condition ripe for diseases and rots.

Wind damage

In the greenhouse? Yes, particularly where plants are growing near fans, windows, or vents. Look for brown, papery leaf spots, wilting, and stunted growth.

MANAGEMENT OF THE ENVIRONMENT TO PREVENT DISEASES

The environment can often be slightly altered to help control your disease problems. The action you take depends upon the specific disease. Think about the environment when you are having a disease problem. Could one of these possibilities be creating the opportunity for disease?

1. **High humidity.** One of the most common environments that a disease needs in order to spread is high humidity. Always try to avoid overwatering, and use good ventilation practice. See more discussion on this in Chapter 1, "The Greenhouse or Sunspace Environment."

2. **Water management.** Old-time greenhouse operators have often told me that your watering habits will make or break you. Water in a manner that gets most of the water on the soil rather than on the leaf and walkways. Moisture on the leaf may help promote the spread of many diseases. See Chapter 1 for more about watering.

3. **Soil Stress.** Salty, alkaline soils or highly acidic soils will help weaken plants for disease infestation. Overfertilization, especially with nitrogen, is commonly the root of a disease problem because it encourages rich, succulent growth that diseases (and bugs) seem to love.

4. **Overcrowding.** If plants are not placed properly and are growing too close together, it can create stress and competition for light, which encourages diseases.

5. **Temperature.** Sometimes a disease can be controlled just by running the greenhouse a little bit cooler or warmer. If you have the ability to control the temperature, try experimenting with it. Run a few degrees warmer or cooler, and see what happens.

DISEASES: A FINAL WORD

Sometimes figuring out the cause and control of a disease can be very frustrating. To add to the frustration, the problem is often triggered by something you did to the growing environment that made the disease take off. When frustration sets in, the first thing to do is to get a positive identification of the disease from an expert, such as a master gardener or county agricultural extension agent. It may also be time to bite the bullet and consider tossing out the plant. Diseases are usually not as large a problem in a greenhouse as bugs. The learning curve for gardeners is quick, and you will find that a few preventive measures will handily take care of the problem.

EPILOGUE

A GLIMPSE AT THE FUTURE

GREENHOUSES ARE WONDERFUL THINGS THAT enrich our lives. But I am always curious about what the future holds for those of us who have an ongoing love affair with the greenhouse. For these reasons, each time I revise this book I take the opportunity to play the role of futurist and look into the crystal ball to see what the future holds for the greenhouse.

THE GREENHOUSE AS A HOME-PRODUCTION UNIT

I see a future in which people will become more concerned with the quality of their food supply as the production of our food moves farther and farther away from home in the evolving global economy. I will never forget the phone calls I received immediately after the Chernobyl nuclear disaster. Worries about radiation pollution abounded halfway around the planet and even concerned people in my own hometown: "Is food safer when grown under glass?" "Can I purchase some fresh greens from your greenhouse, please?"

Close to home, we all hold daily concerns about the safety of food found in supermarkets,

with worries of processing chemicals, harmful microbes, artificial additives, and pesticides. Concurrently, outside gardening is growing increasingly popular. People are more interested in producing their own food, even if it is simply for an occasional fresh, nutritious salad. Many people like you have discovered the luxury of growing their own year-round potted and cut flowers in their home greenhouses. The ability to grow both food and flowers in a home greenhouse will continue to give rise in the popularity of the home-based greenhouse.

The "energy crisis" in the late seventies helped provide the impetus for people to discover how effectively a simple, attached solar greenhouse can heat both itself and the home, even in parts of the country with cloudy winters. Solar-heated greenhouses spurred a rebirth of the home greenhouse and sunspace. Although interest in energy conservation has since waned a bit (it will likely rise again), the popularity of the home greenhouse has continued to rise consistently over the past 20 years.

The interest in a greenhouse that provides heat, food, and flowers right in the home will likely increase as our dependence on foreign

Rather than have greenhouses attached to homes, why not have homes attached to greenhouses?

goods continues to grow and people come to place a higher value on sustainability.

Here is one change that I foresee: Instead of greenhouses being attached to homes, we will have homes attached to greenhouses. The greenhouse would provide areas for living spaces that complement the house. Also, to minimize costs and maximize benefits, two or more homes or multifamily dwellings could be attached to one larger greenhouse. This especially makes sense using solar-heated greenhouses in cold-winter climates.

This would allow traditional living spaces to spill into the greenhouse. How about having two kitchens: an "outdoor" kitchen located in the greenhouse for warmer winter evenings and one in your home structure as well. After all, this is how many people use their patio grills in the summer. Imagine a kitchen where you could take a few steps to harvest your fresh herbs, greens, and fruits for the meal. Why not a bedroom that opens into a room fragrant with vining plants that create the walls? Nearby could be edible fruits always within reach. Think of the possibilities with bathrooms, family rooms, and dens. Play catch with the kids

on a green lawn area in January. You would be living in a tropical paradise while the cold and winds of winter raged outside the walls. It would be like a tropical island: Instead of being surrounded by water, you would be surrounded by winter outside. It sounds like Eden to me.

THE COMMUNITY GREENHOUSE CONCEPT

Ever notice how neighborhoods tend to become closer knit in summer months, when people are outside and interact more often? When winter hits, we rarely visit with neighbors until spring brings us back outside. Perhaps people interacting in a warm greenhouse space would extend the community connections among neighbors. Community gardens are sprouting up in most urban areas. These gardens have provided a positive effect by creating a new neighborhood ethic of cooperation and security. Urban community gardens have brought together whole neighborhoods that were being ripped apart by crime and drug use. Research conducted by the American Community Gardening Association (**www.community garden.org**) has shown that the effect of community gardens has often been to reduce neighborhood crime and promote positive interaction as well as beautification. Community gardens have also provided an increase in self-esteem among participants, who benefit from positive social interaction while they learn gardening and landscaping skills and feed themselves and their families.

But this is not the norm. All too often, people live in neighborhoods where they rarely communicate with one another. Lack of communication breeds fear and isolation and lessens neighborhood security. Although community gardens don't provide a total and instant solution to these problems, it is clear their overall effect is good.

However, there is one problem that most community gardens suffer from: winter. What if they could have a positive effect all year round? They might if they were in a greenhouse.

One example of taking a community garden concept and mixing it with a greenhouse is a unique botanical garden, like the one with which I have been intimately involved since 1977 in Cheyenne, Wyoming.

The Cheyenne Botanic Gardens.

THE COMMUNITY GREENHOUSE CONCEPT IN ACTION: THE CHEYENNE BOTANIC GARDENS

The Cheyenne Botanic Gardens (**www. botanic.org**) differs from traditional botanical gardens in that its primary purpose is social. It has one of the more unusual histories among public gardens. The project began in 1977 as part of a private, nonprofit, human-services agency with an antipoverty mission. Initial federal grants for construction and operating expenses resulted in building the first conservatory, a 5,000-square-foot (450-sq. m), 100 percent passively solar-heated building. It was the nation's first large-scale solar-heated greenhouse, designed to provide food and meaningful activity to senior citizens year-round, even through the cold, harsh winters of the High Plains. It was built primarily with volunteer labor, and to everyone's surprise the structure continued to stand and function for 9 years.

After having proved our worth to the community, we proposed and were awarded state block-grant funds for a new state-of-the-art conservatory. This enabled us to construct a new state-of-the-art conservatory in a local city park in 1986, and the project became a division under the Cheyenne Parks and Recreation Department. This helped to provide the project with welcome economic stability after struggling as a nonprofit for many years. Now, the project has both the stability and support of municipal government and a new nonprofit foundation that helps the project pursue many of its goals.

The current 6,800-square-foot (631.74-sq. m) conservatory includes a kitchen and gathering room for classes, meetings, and activities; a small library / conference room; offices; and a basement root cellar. The three greenhouse sections of the conservatory include demonstration gardens, herbs, cacti, orchids, tropical and subtropical plants, food crops, a water garden, and more. Surplus food is donated to programs for the low-income needy.

The project recently added another facet to the solar operation by adding a photovoltaic solar electricity system. The solar electricity provides the Cheyenne Botanic Gardens with 30 percent of its total electricity, and there are plans to eventually provide 100 percent of its electricity needs.

On the Cheyenne Botanic Gardens grounds, there are a variety of gardens, including annuals and perennials, a low-water-use plants display, a peace garden filled with inspirational quote stones, roses, a community garden, and a wheelchair-accessible orchard, among others.

The real success story is not in the beautiful display of plants or the solar greenhouse; rather, it is in the meshing of human services with a botanical garden. In the early days, as word of our project spread throughout the community, we were approached by other human-service agencies requesting that the physically and mentally challenged and youth at risk be involved in our project. These people were included with great success. Thus was formed the basis of our volunteer force: It is composed mostly of seniors, handicapped individuals, and youth (primarily "youth at risk"). These three groups are commonly isolated from the mainstream of society, hidden away in nursing homes and senior housing, sheltered workshops, and detention centers. There is a great separation and little communication among seniors, youth, and handicapped people in daily life. But at the Cheyenne Botanic Gardens, these three groups of people are integrated, often working side by side. This creates new understandings and friendships between generations and people of different backgrounds and life challenges.

On a winter day in the warm, humid conservatory, senior volunteer Adele Beedie recently explained: "Being here refreshes my soul. I can actually see the spirits of our volunteers rise once they start working with plants and enjoying the camaraderie of other volunteers."

Our volunteers provide 95 percent of all the physical work at the gardens, averaging more than 900 volunteer hours per month. In return, these same volunteers receive fresh food that they helped grow, feel a sense of worth and self-esteem from performing meaningful activities, and gain the feeling of being needed (which they are!).

The Cheyenne Botanic Gardens supports its human and social services by providing to the public the traditional services of a public garden. Included are demonstration gardens, community gardens, classes, and various educational plant displays, both inside and outside the conservatory. In addition, the Cheyenne Botanic Gardens serves as a municipal nursery, producing all the bedding plants for city park and parkway plantings.

The greatest cost of operating a public greenhouse is usually heating and labor. Because of the great dependence upon volunteers and the use of solar heating and electricity, the project has proved to be extremely cost-effective. The project stabilizes human services and enables a small city (Cheyenne has a population of approximately 60,000) to have a botanical garden, when previously the community did not have the resources to provide either. In fact, public botanical gardens are rare in communities of this small size.

The Cheyenne Botanic Gardens—a people-oriented botanical garden.

The most important crops grown at the Cheyenne Botanic Garden are pride and self-esteem—of the seniors, the youth, and the handicapped individuals who work there. Self-esteem is the best therapy ever developed. Their work is not the make-work type of activity common to many therapeutic programs. Rather, they do the real work that is so essential to this botanical garden. These people know that they are important to the project. In addition, these volunteers also receive more tangibles than just therapy; they also get to take home the fruits of their labors in the form of fresh vegetables, cut flowers, and plants grown in the conservatory.

The Cheyenne Botanic Gardens has not gone unnoticed, as it has been recognized by many prominent people and organizations. President Ronald Reagan awarded the project with a citation for exemplary voluntary achievements. President George Bush gave the Cheyenne Botanic Gardens his eighty-third Point-of-Light Award for volunteerism. President Bill Clinton, in association with the notable organization Partners for Livable Communities, awarded the gardens the American Entrepreneurial Leadership Award. Harvard University has also recognized the project. On a more local level, the gardens received the Community Hero Award from Wyoming governor Jim Geringer. The recognition was not given because the enterprise grows pretty plants but because of the innovation of community involvement. This success is the result of two things: a large base of ardent community supporters aiding the project through difficult political and financial times, and a highly devoted volunteer force and staff throughout its history.

Cheyenne Chamber of Commerce president Larry Atwell commented: "The Cheyenne

Senior volunteers at the Cheyenne Botanic Gardens.

Botanic Garden is a special piece of the city's puzzle which attracts both tourists and economic development to our area. The Botanic Gardens contributes to our high quality of life in a small town." During an average year, the project sees over 27,000 tourists from all 50 states and from 30 foreign countries.

Public conservatories and greenhouses always provide stimulation of the senses, but they can also be a vehicle for social progress. As many horticulturists throughout history have pointed out, gardening is not just the cultivation of plants, it is also the cultivation of human beings.

Community-oriented greenhouses such as the one in Cheyenne could easily be adapted to the needs of different neighborhoods, cultures, ages, and abilities. I sincerely believe that through projects of this type, and similar community-gardening programs, potentially positive effects can occur. The therapeutic benefits alone are worth the investment, but there are other social, educational, and nutritional rewards. Many universities even offer study programs and degrees in the field of horticultural therapy. For more information on horticultural therapy, contact the American Horticultural Therapy Association, 909 York, Denver, CO 80206 (800-634-1603, www.ahta.com).

For more information on community gardens, contact the American Community Gardening Association at 100 N. 20th Street, 5th Floor, Philadelphia, PA 19103-1495 (215-988-8785, www.communitygarden.org).

For more information on the Cheyenne Botanic Gardens, send a request, along with a suggested donation of $2 (cash or check) to help defray mailing costs, to the Cheyenne Botanic Gardens, 710 S. Lions Park Drive, Cheyenne, WY 82001. Also check out the Cheyenne Botanic Gardens website at www.botanic.org.

For consulting assistance, contact Seedpeople Associates. This is a consulting cooperative involved in the many related areas of community-based gardening and greenhouse project design, operation, and horticultural therapy. Write to Seedpeople, Attn. Shane Smith, c/o Fulcrum Publishing, 16100 Table Mountain Parkway, Suite 300, Golden, CO 80403, or go to www.greenhousegarden.com.

NEW PURPOSES FOR THE GREENHOUSE

In addition to having the role and function of growing plants and enhancing people's lives, the greenhouse is moving into new and sometimes surprising areas. Many people have successfully shown that greenhouses can be incredible fish producers, through the cultivation of edible fish in clear fiberglass tanks contained in the structure. Greenhouses are also being used as a more environmentally oriented alternative to processing sewage. For instance, in New England, Dr. John Todd (who founded the former New Alchemy Institute) and other researchers have been working on greenhouses that can imitate the recycling processes of a marsh in nature. They call it solar aquatics. Solar aquatics provides an efficient and economic means of purifying and restoring fresh water.

In a greenhouse, they have created an intensive man-made marsh. They run a stream of unprocessed sewage through a series of large fiberglass tanks filled with a diversity of bacteria, algae, microscopic plants and animals, snails, fish, and higher plants. After being filtered through the tanks, the once-polluted water is transformed into clean, clear water. An intensive environmental filter is created using the recycling and purifying powers of natural ecosystems created in a greenhouse. This concept might allow for a whole new way of processing our wastes and might even decentralize the processing of waste. Whenever we use biology to take care of our problems, things always seem to function better, thanks to the elegant simplicity of biological systems.

FUTURE PEST CONTROL

The reduction of spraying chemical pesticides is a trend that has and will continue in the future. Every year, a new good beneficial critter is introduced on the market to help control a greenhouse pest, making the future of biological pest-control seemingly secure. Perhaps someday, good bugs may obviate the need for pesticides, making the use of pesticides obsolete in the future home greenhouse.

The saddest thing about the current state of biological pest-control is that most of our beneficial critters come from Europe. For instance, almost all of the whitefly parasite, *Encarsia formosa,* comes from Europe. It is time to do more rearing of beneficial insects on our own continent, closer to home. This could only save us all more dollars. Even better, perhaps we can get into rearing the good critters ourselves in special setups in our own greenhouses.

As predicted in earlier versions of this book, new classes of less-toxic pesticides have been released that do not affect beneficial insects while knocking out target pests. More are on the way. Many of these pesticides will be made from naturally occurring by-products of microbial agents or plants, which will be easier on the environment.

One thing that I would like to see is the development of co-ops or purchasing clubs for smaller greenhouse growers that would make beneficial critters even more affordable to all.

THE FUTURE GREENHOUSE IN THE PRESENT

For those wishing to visit the future in the present, many people visit EPCOT center at Walt Disney World in Orlando, Florida. Among the many futuristic displays at EPCOT, you will find a complex of large futuristic hydroponic greenhouses that produce a variety of fruits, vegetables, and edible fish. The plants are grown in an "aeroponics" type of hydroponic system in which nutrient solutions are sprayed on the roots. Some plants are on conveyor systems that move them in and out of spray boxes. The plants always look incredibly healthy and the yields impressive. Visitors get to ride on a floating boat through the whole greenhouse system, and most of the riders are visibly impressed.

Once people have seen EPCOT's greenhouses, most become sold on the idea that hydroponics is the wave of the future. During a ride I once took through the EPCOT Center's greenhouse, the tour guide told me that "all the bugs were controlled by the introduction of beneficial insects that prey upon or parasitize the bad insects." We were also told that much of the food produced in the greenhouses was served at the restaurants in the same pavilion.

Besides a ride through the greenhouse, they offered a more in-depth walking tour of the EPCOT greenhouses. On that walking tour, I couldn't find any sign of beneficial insects or signs of any insects at all. This is highly unusual for biological pest-control systems in greenhouses. I immediately became suspicious. When I asked the tour guide about this, I was told that "certain crops were not working out for that type of bug control." "Well, then," I asked, "how do you control the bugs in these greenhouses?" The guide looked uncomfortable. "We spray them with Orthene," he reluctantly admitted. "But Orthene isn't rated for use on food crops!" I exclaimed. "That's right," he said. "We throw those crops out so they never get consumed." I was flabbergasted. This greenhouse was just a Disney fantasy.

I walked away from that EPCOT exhibit feeling that I had just witnessed an illusion—the future greenhouse as amusement park—an illusion that people so easily believed. Perhaps someday Disney and EPCOT will get a more accurate representation of what they are doing. I also wish that they would focus on a future greenhouse that would be a bit more sustainable (see the earlier discussion on hydroponics in Chapter 9, page 328).

I suppose it is nice to think that in the future no one will get dirty hands and everything will be so automated that we can spend all of our valuable time watching infomercials on cable. I will admit that EPCOT's greenhouses do a good job of getting people excited about plants and greenhouses. But what makes a home greenhouse gratifying is that you get your hands dirty while you work with the plants, all of which results in creating both beautiful and edible things. It can't be boiled down to a sterile recipe in which everything happens as we wish. Automation of growing plants, as is done in the EPCOT greenhouses, removes the fun parts of growing plants.

Automation is a fact of life for commercial growers, who must reduce labor costs. In contrast, doing a little physical work in a home greenhouse might feel good. To paraphrase the great poet and writer Wendell Berry, "Gardening restores usefulness to the body." Think about that: Gardening restores usefulness to the body. He goes on to say that the obsession with forms of exercise like jogging or aerobics makes us end up treating the body like a pet, taking it out for exercise. I am not against people staying healthy, but the beauty of gardening is that it meshes the mind and the body in a wholly creative pursuit in a way that few activities can accomplish.

Another view of the future greenhouse comes to us from Oracle, Arizona. There, a more down-to-earth but highly controversial project called Biosphere 2 evolved in the desert in the late eighties and early nineties. It was originally designed to house humans in a large, self-contained greenhouse environment for long periods with (supposedly) no outside necessities such as food, water, or oxygen. The goal was to have the greenhouse itself produce the required food and oxygen and recycle all of the water, nutrients, and wastes for the inhabitants living inside. It was hoped that the lessons learned there could apply to how we live on planet earth and might possibly live in future space explorations.

A view of Biosphere 2 from the outside. Copyright © by Biosphere 2 Center, Inc. Photograph by Karen Silva. Used by permission.

The results of this original Biosphere 2 project remain inconclusive. The oxygen ran low and the inhabitants looked hungry, but that is not to say that there weren't valuable lessons to be gained from the project. Many scientists question whether the calculations were correct in including all of the variables of the concrete foundation (which had an effect on the internal atmosphere) as well as the many diverse and complex biological systems within the greenhouse. The Biosphere experiment was a far cry from the assumption that in space we will be eating only dehydrated foods and washing it all down with Tang. Even with all the controversy, I would say that the Biosphere project took a more sensible and ecological view of the future than do the sterile, hydroponic-based, laboratorylike greenhouses of EPCOT.

Today, the Biosphere 2 project operates as a nonprofit education and research affiliate of Columbia University. Among other studies, the center investigates the earth and its many ecological systems and functions as a catalyst for interdisciplinary thinking and understanding about the earth and its future. For more information, contact the Biosphere 2 Center, 32540 South Biosphere Road, Oracle, AZ, 85623, (520-896-6400, or visit their website: **www. bio2.edu**.

GREENHOUSES AND WORLD HUNGER

Many have pursued the idea of promoting greenhouses for underdeveloped Third World countries as a solution to hunger. Unfortunately, hunger is usually more a matter of politics and distribution, which is not something that a greenhouse can solve. Also, much of the underdeveloped world is in the tropics, where greenhouses are not needed.

In the 1980s I was invited to help some high-altitude Mexican villages construct and operate food-producing greenhouses. After I assessed the situation, I realized it would be a mistake to build a grandiose greenhouse with imported materials. I instead worked with them in developing and constructing the simple miniature greenhouses called cold frames out of recycled and available materials such as old tires and clear-plastic feed bags. I also taught them simple methods for extending the growing season by utilizing available microclimates. Everything we made came from local sources and seemed much more appropriate. My greatest reward came when I visited this area again many years later and saw these ideas spreading from village to village, in part due to the simplicity of the technology.

I also found most of the gardeners in the Mexican villages to be hungry for basic, solid gardening information. But often the glamour of high-tech solutions takes precedence over simple knowledge and solutions, especially when the developed countries try to assist the underdeveloped.

As the world becomes more populated, it will become even more difficult to feed everyone. Simple small greenhouses, cold frames, and season-extenders may do more to feed the world than big, high-tech ideas greased with government grants.

HIGH TECHNOLOGY AND THE GREENHOUSE

High technology is affecting the future of greenhouses, especially in terms of glazing materials. The components of incredible change—computers, high-tech ideas, and glass and plastics—are already in place. And we are already seeing "smart" glazings, which change with the environment. By this I mean that the glazings themselves provide shading when the temperature becomes too hot. They can also become clearer in cloudy situations, thus increasing the incoming light. We may also soon be able to purchase glazings with amazing insulating abilities. There have been experimental glazings developed that let in more net heat than the amount of heat that is lost, even when placed on a shaded vertical north wall receiving absolutely no direct sun.

I have heard rumors of experiments with glazing that allow the material not only to let light through but also to produce electricity.

High altitude Mexican villagers construct simple cold frames out of readily available materials to help protect food crops from frosts.

In fact, we may be plugging our homes into the greenhouse for our electricity and other energy needs. The possibilities are awe-inspiring. Perhaps this means we all may soon be living in glass houses (should we outlaw rocks?). Purchasing a glazing might become similar to purchasing a computer. The day you purchase it is the day it is outmoded.

What else is in store for greenhouse glazings in the future? We will see glazings that actually store and reradiate heat. We will see glazings that can change in characteristics by simply applying an electrical current to them. Imagine a glass glazing that has special permeability characteristics and is able to pass certain gases, such as carbon dioxide or oxygen, and able to filter out pollutants. Perhaps greenhouses could become permeable to water while keeping the cold out. Lighter and stronger glazing materials will enable larger greenhouse areas to be covered with less supporting structure. With all of this potential technology applied to glazings, the design of greenhouses will change radically, while energy consumption will be almost nothing.

Right now, engineers and designers are working on glazings that will be used in space and on Mars. You can bet that a food-producing greenhouse will be among the first structures built when we first inhabit a place other than our Earth.

Closer to home, the most popular home greenhouse glazing is polycarbonate, with glass as a close second. Unfortunately, most of the production of the double- and triple-layer polycarbonate glazing material currently goes on overseas. In the future, it would be great if we could somehow encourage more of this production in our own continent. Then we would all benefit by having the price of a greenhouse drop substantially.

BIOTECHNOLOGY IN THE GREENHOUSE

As people tinker more and more with the genes of plants, who knows where this engineering will lead in all fields of agriculture (which includes greenhouse horticulture). They are even mixing animal genes with those of plants (can you imagine?). Working with plant genetics is nothing new, but breeding plants has always been slow work, taking years and sometimes decades to develop small incremental changes in a plant. Now, through biotechnology, a plant's characteristics can change very rapidly. This might enable us to develop a profusion of varieties specific to the greenhouse or sunspace that outyield anything we have available to us now.

For a more science-fiction-like scenario, biotechnology could produce some interesting things for the greenhouse. How about having them develop glow-in-the-dark algae for the greenhouse? You could culture it in clear greenhouse water tanks. Scientists could then breed the algae to glow bright enough to provide supplemental greenhouse lighting. Scientists are already doing their best to develop crops that are high-octane nutritional powerhouses that provide for all our nutritional needs and enhance our immune system. Our wildest imaginings may become reality.

But it's not all rosy. There are also some grave possibilities when we start tinkering with cellular genetics. What happens to the environment when we accidentally allow a breeding mistake to escape into the wild? Recently, it was found that the pollen of a genetically modified corn variety was toxic to the Monarch butterfly! What if some plants were developed to be highly adaptable and then escaped cultivation? They could end up displacing native species and derailing whole ecosystems! What if genetically modified characteristics were accidentally to cross with native plants and ended up negatively altering the natural environment? What if we couldn't save our own seed from our favorite plants because the characteristics allowing them to set seed were destroyed in its genetic expression? Can we be sure that the harvests from these new genetically modified plants are safe for human consumption? What happens to our indigenous plants and ecology if they are outcompeted by these superplants? There are lots of worrisome questions, and many of the experts in this field are not providing adequate answers.

We can only hope—and possibly become politically active—to foster positive effects as a result of this technology. The more one learns about these technologies, the more one realizes the many complex issues involved. However, I am convinced that it is not all negative, especially if more of us get involved. Besides, there may even be wonderful new varieties for our greenhouses as a result of biotechnology. I am concerned about the incredibly fast-paced speed with which these changes could occur with biotechnology. When changes occur slowly, we have a better chance to develop the wisdom required to deal with these changes. We can only hope and pray that the wisdom will come with the faster changes.

One thing is for sure—this high-tech breeding of plants is going to make people more suspicious about the safety and quality of the food they eat. As a result, I see people giving a higher value to food that is produced more locally. This may become one of the overriding factors motivating people to get or enlarge their own home greenhouse, in which they can grow more of what they eat on a year-round basis.

IN CONCLUSION

As the world becomes more technology dependent and our resources become more finite, I see the home greenhouse taking on a more important role in helping us achieve a more sustainable and healthy lifestyle. But it is not just in our homes that greenhouses can fill a niche. The greenhouse can play an important role in troubled (and even not-so-troubled) communities and neighborhoods. Greenhouses can even help us to become better neighbors, as evidenced with the Cheyenne Botanic Gardens and the many vibrant community-gardening projects across the nation. The greenhouse is not the total solution, but it can hold many important keys to the future. A greenhouse has the advantage of being based upon a simple and accessible technology that doesn't scare people away. In fact, it is both intriguing and inviting.

The greenhouse gets us closer to nature rather than just being tourists in the plant world, where we only occasionally visit plants in the park, the forest, or in the produce section of the grocery. A home-greenhouse garden allows plants to enrich our daily lives in ways that range from enjoying a fresh-picked salad to picking a bouquet of homegrown flowers to grace our home even in winter.

The term "greenhouse effect" has become a negative metaphor for our endangered planet, but there is this other effect of a growing greenhouse that is positive. In its positive meaning, the greenhouse can and will teach us many lessons. Like Dorothy says in the *Wizard of Oz*, "If you are searching for your heart's desire, you don't need to look any farther than your own backyard!"

HELPFUL ASSOCIATIONS AND ORGANIZATIONS

The following is a short list of associations that may be of help. If you are interested in a particular plant, chances are good that there is a society or association organized for that plant. For more information, check with your nearest botanical garden, garden club, or county agricultural extension agent. Those listed here have a broader appeal or are doing interesting things. Many may require fees for membership or information. Because addresses change, please check the website **www.greenhouse garden.com** for regular updates and additions.

American Community Gardening Association

100 N. 20th Street, 5th Floor, Philadelphia, PA 19103-1495, 215-988-8785, **www.community garden.org**. A national resource and member organization devoted to the promotion, creation, and maintenance of community gardens.

American Horticultural Therapy Association

909 York, Denver, CO 80206, 800-634-1603, **www.ahta.com**.

American Orchid Society

6000 S. Olive Avenue, West Palm Beach, FL 33405, 561-585-8666, **http://orchidweb.org**. Members receive a monthly bulletin great for beginners and experts alike.

Biosphere 2

Arizona 32540 S. Biosphere Road, Oracle, AZ 85623, 520-896-6200, **www.bio2.edu**. One of the more interesting ecological greenhouses used to study ecosystems and the atmosphere. Operated by Columbia University (see the Epilogue).

Cheyenne Botanic Gardens

710 S. Lions Park Drive, Cheyenne, WY 82001, **www.botanic.org**. A volunteer-based, solar-heated and powered community botanic garden and municipal nursery (see epilogue).

EPA-sponsored National Pesticide Telecommunications Network

Oregon State University, 333 Weniger Hall, Corvallis, OR 97331-6502, 800-858-7378, http://ace.ace.orst.edu/info/nptn. Free information about almost any pesticide, including safety information. A phone call is usually the best way to get information.

Hobby Greenhouse Association (The)

8 Glen Terra, Bedford, MA 01730-2048, www.orbitworld.net/hga. An excellent organization that produces a wonderful newsletter and quarterly magazine.

Hydroponic Society of America

P.O. Box 3075, San Ramon, CA 94583, http://hsa.hydroponics.org. A nonprofit organization dedicated to the exchange of information in the field of hydroponics; open to commercial growers and hobbyists alike.

International Geranium Society

P.O. Box 92734, Pasadena, CA 91109-2734, www.geocities.com/RainForest/2822/index.html. Produces a quarterly journal. Opportunity to order seeds and cuttings. A great source for unusual varieties.

SeedPeople

222 E. 1st Avenue, Cheyenne, WY 82001, www.greenhousegarden.com. Consulting services available in horticulture, horticultural therapy, greenhouse design, community greenhouse operation, and more.

Seed Savers Exchange

3076 N. Winn Road, Decorah, IA 52101, 319-382-5990. This organization works to preserve heirloom seeds and is responsible for saving many rare vegetable varieties from extinction. The exchange allows home gardeners to help in preserving heirloom seeds and facilitates the exchanging of seeds with others.

APPENDIX 2
AVERAGE PERCENT POSSIBLE SUNSHINE

This chart can help you determine how much sun you can count on for each month for selected locations across the United States. It shows the average monthly percentage of possible sunshine (data through 1998).

LOCATION	JAN	FEB	MAR	APR	MAY	JUN	JUL	AUG	SEP	OCT	NOV	DEC	ANNUAL
ALABAMA													
Birmingham	48	48	62	61	64	63	60	62	57	63	49	52	57
Montgomery	47	52	59	65	63	62	61	63	62	64	55	49	58
ALASKA													
Anchorage	34	42	50	50	50	46	43	39	38	36	32	27	41
Juneau	32	32	37	39	39	34	31	32	26	19	23	20	30
Nome	40	55	54	54	50	43	37	32	36	34	31	34	42
ARIZONA													
Flagstaff	77	73	76	82	88	86	75	76	81	79	75	73	78
Phoenix	78	80	84	89	93	94	85	85	89	88	83	77	85
Tucson	80	82	86	90	92	93	78	80	87	88	84	79	85
Yuma	84	87	90	94	95	97	91	91	93	92	87	82	90
ARKANSAS													
Fort Smith	50	55	56	60	62	69	73	72	66	65	54	50	61
Little Rock	46	54	57	62	68	73	71	73	68	69	56	48	62
CALIFORNIA													
Eureka	43	46	52	57	58	59	55	51	55	50	44	41	51
Fresno	47	65	77	85	90	95	97	96	94	88	66	46	79
Los Angeles	69	72	73	70	66	65	82	83	79	73	74	71	73
Redding	72	82	85	90	91	94	97	97	94	92	84	73	88
Sacramento	48	65	74	82	90	94	97	96	93	86	66	49	78
San Diego	72	71	70	68	59	58	68	70	69	68	75	73	68
San Francisco	56	62	69	73	72	73	66	65	72	70	62	53	66
COLORADO													
Denver	71	69	69	67	64	70	71	71	74	72	64	67	69
Grand Junction	61	65	65	70	73	81	79	77	79	74	63	61	71
Pueblo	75	74	74	74	73	78	79	78	80	79	72	71	76
CONNECTICUT													
Hartford	53	56	57	55	57	60	62	62	59	57	45	47	56
DISTRICT OF COLUMBIA (D.C.)													
Washington	46	50	55	57	58	64	62	62	61	59	51	46	56
FLORIDA													
Apalachicola	58	61	65	74	77	71	64	64	66	74	67	57	66
Jacksonville	58	62	68	73	70	66	65	64	58	60	59	54	63
Key West	74	77	82	84	82	76	77	76	72	71	71	70	76
Miami	66	68	74	76	72	68	72	71	70	70	67	63	70
Pensacola	48	53	61	63	67	67	57	58	60	71	64	49	60
Tampa	63	65	71	75	75	67	62	61	61	65	64	61	66
GEORGIA													
Atlanta	49	54	58	66	68	67	63	64	62	66	58	50	60
Macon	56	61	65	73	71	70	67	71	67	69	64	57	66
Savannah	54	57	62	71	68	65	64	62	58	63	61	55	62

LOCATION	JAN	FEB	MAR	APR	MAY	JUN	JUL	AUG	SEP	OCT	NOV	DEC	ANNUAL
HAWAII													
Hilo	46	46	42	37	37	44	41	42	43	39	33	37	41
Honolulu	65	68	72	70	72	74	76	77	77	70	65	63	71
Kahului	64	64	64	63	68	72	71	71	73	68	62	63	67
Lihue	55	57	55	54	60	63	62	65	67	59	49	49	58
IDAHO													
Boise	40	51	62	68	70	75	87	85	82	69	43	38	64
Pocatello	40	53	61	66	67	75	83	81	80	71	46	40	64
ILLINOIS													
Cairo	45	50	56	62	65	72	74	75	69	67	51	44	61
Chicago	44	49	51	50	58	67	66	62	59	55	38	43	54
Moline	48	50	50	53	57	63	68	66	62	58	42	40	55
Peoria	47	50	51	55	60	67	69	67	64	61	43	42	56
Springfield	48	52	51	56	63	68	71	70	68	63	48	44	58
INDIANA													
Evansville	42	48	55	60	64	71	73	73	69	65	48	42	59
Fort Wayne	46	51	55	60	68	74	75	74	68	62	42	38	59
Indianapolis	40	49	50	54	60	65	66	68	65	61	41	38	55
IOWA													
Des Moines	51	54	56	56	61	68	72	70	66	62	49	46	59
Sioux City	57	56	57	59	61	67	73	70	66	63	51	50	61
KANSAS													
Concordia	64	63	63	65	67	76	78	76	70	68	59	57	67
Dodge City	67	65	65	68	67	74	79	78	74	73	66	65	70
Topeka	56	55	57	58	61	66	71	70	66	64	53	52	61
Wichita	59	61	62	63	64	69	76	75	68	65	58	57	65
KENTUCKY													
Louisville	41	48	51	56	60	66	67	66	64	61	46	40	56
Paducah	44	47	54	63	64	60	69	70	61	64	48	42	57
LOUISIANA													
Lake Charles	59	63	72	69	70	76	82	80	77	74	66	59	71
New Orleans	46	50	56	62	62	63	58	61	61	64	54	48	57
Shreveport	49	55	58	60	63	71	75	74	70	70	59	53	63
MAINE													
Portland	56	59	56	54	54	59	63	63	62	58	48	53	57
MARYLAND													
Baltimore	51	55	56	56	56	62	64	62	60	58	51	49	57
MASSACHUSETTS													
Blue Hill	46	50	48	49	52	55	57	58	56	55	47	46	52
Boston	53	56	57	56	58	63	65	65	63	60	50	52	58
MICHIGAN													
Alpena	36	45	53	52	59	63	65	59	51	42	28	28	48

LOCATION	JAN	FEB	MAR	APR	MAY	JUN	JUL	AUG	SEP	OCT	NOV	DEC	ANNUAL
Detroit	40	46	52	54	61	66	68	67	61	51	35	31	53
Grand Rapids	28	39	46	51	56	62	64	61	54	44	27	23	46
Lansing	36	44	49	52	61	65	69	64	59	50	31	29	51
Marquette	32	39	46	49	57	60	62	60	51	42	30	29	46
Sault Ste. Marie	36	47	55	54	57	58	62	58	45	38	24	27	47
MINNESOTA													
Duluth	48	53	55	56	57	58	65	61	52	46	35	39	52
Minneapolis–St. Paul	53	59	57	58	61	66	72	69	62	55	39	42	58
MISSISSIPPI													
Jackson	49	54	60	66	63	70	66	67	65	70	57	49	61
Tupelo	53	53	61	73	72	74	75	73	72	62	51	46	64
MISSOURI													
Columbia	50	49	50	55	57	64	67	64	60	59	47	45	56
Kansas City	58	55	58	62	61	66	72	67	66	60	49	49	60
St. Louis	50	52	54	56	59	66	68	65	63	60	46	43	57
Springfield	50	52	56	59	60	65	71	71	67	64	52	48	60
MONTANA													
Billings	47	53	61	60	61	64	76	75	68	61	46	45	60
Great Falls	49	56	66	62	62	65	79	76	67	61	46	44	61
Helena	46	55	61	59	60	64	78	74	67	60	44	42	59
Missoula	33	44	54	57	59	63	81	77	69	55	34	29	55
NEBRASKA													
Lincoln	58	57	57	58	61	69	73	70	66	63	53	52	61
North Platte	63	61	62	64	65	71	77	75	72	70	60	61	67
Omaha	55	53	54	58	61	67	74	70	68	65	51	48	60
Valentine	63	62	59	59	62	69	76	76	71	68	60	60	65
NEVADA													
Ely	68	68	71	70	72	80	80	81	82	75	67	67	73
Las Vegas	77	81	83	87	88	93	88	88	91	87	81	78	85
Reno	65	68	75	80	81	85	92	92	91	83	70	64	79
Winnemucca	51	56	60	66	72	77	86	85	82	74	54	52	68
NEW HAMPSHIRE													
Concord	52	55	53	53	55	58	62	60	56	53	42	47	54
NEW JERSEY													
Atlantic City	50	53	55	56	56	60	61	65	61	59	51	47	56
NEW MEXICO													
Albuquerque	72	72	73	77	79	83	76	75	79	79	76	71	76
Roswell	60	68	75	77	80	83	77	73	72	77	73	71	74
NEW YORK													
Albany	46	52	54	54	56	60	64	61	57	52	37	39	53
Binghamton	37	42	46	50	56	62	64	61	55	49	32	29	49
Buffalo	31	38	46	51	56	65	67	64	57	50	29	27	48

LOCATION	JAN	FEB	MAR	APR	MAY	JUN	JUL	AUG	SEP	OCT	NOV	DEC	ANNUAL
New York City (Central Park)	51	55	57	58	61	64	65	64	62	61	52	49	58
Rochester	35	41	49	53	59	66	69	66	59	49	31	30	51
Syracuse	33	39	46	49	55	59	63	59	53	44	26	25	46
NORTH CAROLINA													
Asheville	55	59	61	66	61	62	60	54	56	61	58	55	59
Charlotte	54	58	61	68	67	67	67	65	64	65	58	55	62
Greensboro–Winston-Salem	51	56	60	63	63	64	62	61	62	64	57	53	60
Raleigh	52	56	60	63	59	60	60	58	58	60	57	53	58
Wilmington	56	59	64	71	67	66	64	62	61	64	63	59	63
NORTH DAKOTA													
Bismarck	53	53	58	58	61	64	73	72	65	58	43	47	59
Fargo	50	56	58	60	61	62	71	69	60	54	40	43	57
Williston	51	57	61	60	62	66	74	73	67	59	44	48	60
OHIO													
Cincinnati	33	40	48	56	57	61	61	61	61	54	36	31	50
Cleveland	30	37	45	52	58	65	67	63	60	52	31	25	49
Columbus	36	42	44	51	56	60	60	60	61	56	37	31	50
Dayton	40	44	48	52	58	66	66	67	65	59	40	36	53
Toledo	41	46	50	52	60	64	65	63	61	54	37	33	52
OKLAHOMA													
Oklahoma City	60	60	65	68	66	75	79	79	72	70	61	58	68
Tulsa	53	56	58	60	60	66	74	73	66	64	56	53	62
OREGON													
Portland	28	38	48	52	57	56	69	66	62	44	28	23	48
PENNSYLVANIA													
Allentown	43	48	53	46	53	62	57	61	58	57	49	45	53
Harrisburg	49	54	58	59	60	65	68	67	62	58	47	44	58
Middletown–Harrisburg	48	54	57	58	59	64	67	66	61	58	47	44	57
Philadelphia	49	53	55	56	57	62	61	62	59	60	52	49	56
Pittsburgh	32	36	43	46	50	55	57	56	55	51	36	28	45
Avoca	41	47	50	53	57	61	62	61	55	52	36	34	51
RHODE ISLAND													
Providence	56	58	58	57	58	61	63	62	62	61	50	52	58
SOUTH CAROLINA													
Charleston	56	59	66	72	68	66	67	64	61	63	59	56	63
Columbia	55	59	64	70	68	67	67	66	65	67	63	59	64
SOUTH DAKOTA													
Huron	57	59	59	61	65	70	76	74	69	63	50	49	63
Rapid City	57	60	63	62	60	65	73	74	70	66	55	55	63
TENNESSEE													

LOCATION	JAN	FEB	MAR	APR	MAY	JUN	JUL	AUG	SEP	OCT	NOV	DEC	ANNUAL
Chattanooga	43	49	53	61	65	65	62	63	64	63	53	44	57
Knoxville	40	47	53	63	64	65	64	63	61	61	49	40	56
Memphis	50	54	56	64	69	74	74	75	69	70	58	50	64
Nashville	41	47	52	59	60	65	63	63	62	62	50	42	56
TEXAS													
Abilene	62	64	70	72	70	78	80	78	71	72	67	62	70
Amarillo	69	68	72	74	71	78	79	77	73	75	72	67	73
Austin	49	51	55	54	56	69	75	74	66	64	54	49	60
Brownsville	41	48	53	58	63	73	80	76	68	65	51	42	60
Corpus Christi	44	49	54	56	59	72	80	76	68	67	54	43	60
Dallas–Fort Worth	52	54	58	61	57	67	75	73	67	63	57	52	61
El Paso	78	82	86	89	90	90	82	81	83	84	83	77	84
Galveston	48	51	56	61	67	75	73	71	68	71	59	48	62
Houston	45	50	54	58	62	68	70	68	66	64	52	51	59
Lubbock	65	66	73	74	71	76	77	76	71	75	69	65	72
Midland–Odessa	66	68	75	78	77	80	80	76	75	73	73	65	74
Port Arthur	42	52	52	52	64	69	65	63	62	67	57	47	58
San Antonio	47	50	57	56	56	67	74	74	67	64	54	48	60
UTAH													
Milford	58	64	63	69	73	82	77	79	80	76	62	60	70
Salt Lake City	45	54	64	69	72	80	83	82	82	72	53	42	66
VERMONT													
Burlington	41	48	51	49	55	59	64	60	54	47	31	33	49
VIRGINIA													
Lynchburg	52	56	58	62	62	65	62	62	61	62	56	53	59
Norfolk	53	56	60	63	62	67	62	62	61	59	56	54	60
Richmond	54	58	62	66	66	70	68	66	65	63	59	54	63
WASHINGTON													
Quillayute	22	30	34	35	37	35	43	44	47	34	21	19	33
Seattle	28	34	42	47	52	49	63	56	53	37	28	23	43
Spokane	28	41	55	61	65	67	80	78	72	55	29	23	54
PUERTO RICO													
San Juan	69	71	76	72	64	64	69	68	62	64	60	60	67
WEST VIRGINIA													
Elkins	29	32	39	46	44	48	44	44	45	46	37	28	40
WISCONSIN													
Green Bay	49	52	53	54	61	65	66	63	56	47	38	40	54
Madison	47	51	52	52	58	64	67	64	60	54	39	40	54
Milwaukee	44	47	50	53	60	65	69	66	59	54	39	38	54
WYOMING													
Cheyenne	64	67	67	63	61	67	69	68	70	69	61	60	66
Lander	65	68	70	66	64	72	75	75	72	67	58	61	68
Sheridan	57	60	63	60	60	65	75	75	68	62	53	55	63

MAIL-ORDER PEST CONTROL

Please note that some of these suppliers are producers of their product, whereas others are simply distributors. Those that do produce their own critters often charge less and have a fresher product. Do some shopping around, because prices and quality may vary greatly.

Also, if you want to purchase insects from foreign countries, you must first obtain an import permit. Write to the USDA PPQ/APHIS, Federal Center Building, Hyattsville, MD 20782. Ask for Permit Number 526.

Suppliers of Beneficial Organisms in North America is a web and print publication of the California Environmental Protection Agency's Department of Pesticide Regulation. It is one of the most comprehensive lists of suppliers of beneficial organisms used for biological control. Suppliers are located in Canada, Mexico, and the United States. You can find this list at **www.cdpr.ca.gov/docs/ipminov/bensuppl. htm**. For updates to this list of suppliers, check **www. greenhousegarden.com**.

Alternative Garden Supply, Inc.
P.O. Box 662, Cary, IL 60013, 800-444-2837, **www.alternativegarden.com**. Carries beneficial critters and other pest controls. Mostly carries hydroponic systems, CO_2 generators, lighting supplies, and other indoor-garden products.

Applied Bionomics
11074 W. Saanich Road, Sidney, BC, Canada V8L 3X9. If you are in Canada, this is a great source. If you are from the United States, you may need to get an importation permit to have bugs mailed across international borders.

Arbico
P.O. Box 4247 CRB, Tucson, AZ 85738, 800-827-2847, **www.arbico.com**. Also known as Arizona Biological Control. Has a good selection of beneficial insects, many for the greenhouse. Also other helpful products for growing plants.

Beneficial Insectary

14751 Oak Run Road, Oak Run, CA 96069, 800-477-3715, **www.insectary.com**. Carries beneficial critters for controlling aphid, whitefly, mites, and more.

Biocontrol Network

5116 Williamsburg Road, Brentwood, TN 37027, 615-370-4301, **www.bioconet.com**. Carries an extensive list of greenhouse pest-control critters and products. Informative catalog.

Charley's Greenhouses & Indoor Growing Supplies

17979 State Route 536, Mount Vernon, WA 98273, 800-322-4707, **www.charleys greenhouse.com**. Carries a wide variety of greenhouse-beneficial critters for the home greenhouse gardener as well as an extensive line of greenhouse supplies. Great catalog! Great folks!

Gardens Alive!®

5100 Schenley Place, Lawrenceburg, IN 47025, 812-537-8650, **www.gardens-alive.com**. Informative catalog with a wide selection of many biological-based pest controls, including beneficial predator parasites, beneficial nematodes, fertilizers, and much more.

Green Spot, Ltd. (The)

93 Priest Road, Nottingham, NH 03290-6204, 603-942-8925, **www.greenmethods.com**. Carries an extensive selection of beneficial critters for the greenhouse. Also carries natural sprays, Tangletrap™, books, and more. Very informative and educational catalog.

Greenfire

2527A Highway 32 West, Chico, CA 95973, 800-859-8307, **www.greenfire.net**. These folks carry a wide variety of pest-control materials as well as organic hydroponic supplies, lighting materials, and more.

Harmony Farm Supply and Nursery

3244 Gravenstein Highway, North Sebastopol, CA 95472, 707-823-9125, **www.harmony farm.com**. Carries a variety of growing supplies, pest controls, and beneficial insects.

Home Harvest®

3712 Eastern Avenue, Baltimore, MD 21224, 800-348-4769. An Internet-only catalog located at **http://homeharvest.com**. They sell beneficial critters, pest-control supplies, greenhouse growing and hydroponic supplies, and more.

Hot Pepper Wax

305 Third Street, Greenville, PA 16125, 888-NO-PEST-5, **www.hotpepperwax.com**. These folks carry a repellant and pesticide made of hot pepper and other herbs that is safe for most food and other crops.

Hydro-Gardens, Inc.

P.O. Box 9707, Colorado Springs, CO 80932, 800-634-6362, **www.hydro-gardens.com**. Offers a wide variety of biological and other pest-control supplies and sprays for the commercial grower but also sells to the hobbyist.

International Technology Services, Inc.

P.O. Box 19227, Boulder, CO 80308, 303-661-9546, **www.intertechserv.com**. Carries a full line of beneficial critters and many biologically based sprays for the greenhouse. Carries the hard-to-find *Aphelinus abdominalis* and *Aphidius ervi*. Caters to large and small growers. Knowledgeable staff, quality products.

IPM Laboratories, Inc.

Main Street, Locke, NY 13092-0099, 315-497-2063, **www.ipmlabs.com**. This company produces a very informative catalog and newsletter with helpful information on using its many beneficial insects for greenhouses. Carries whitefly egg parasites and predators, as well as a number of wasp parasites for aphid control, including the difficult to find *Aphelinus abdominalis* and *Aphidius ervi*. They always carry a quality product.

Kunafin

Rt. 1 Box 39, Quemado, TX 78877, 800-832-1113, **www.kunafin.com**. Carries ladybugs, lacewings, and controls for house and barn flies.

Ladies in Red

P.O. Box 2639, La Pine, OR 97739, 541-536-6212, **www.ladiesinred.com**. Carries ladybugs (now I get the great name!), praying mantis, beneficial nematodes, and more.

M&R Durango, Inc.

P.O. Box 886, Bayfield, CO 81122 (aka The Goodbug Company), 970-259-3521, **www.good bug.com**. Carries *Encarsia formosa*, thrips predator, spider-mite predator, green lacewing, and more.

Mellinger's Nursery

2310 W. South Range Road, North Lima, OH 44452-9731, 800-321-7444, **www.mellingers. com**. Carries ladybugs, beneficial nematodes, Tanglefoot™ and Tangle Trap™, sprays, equipment, and more.

Natural Pest Controls

8864 Little Creek Drive, Orangevale, CA 95662, 800-873-1252, **www.natural-pest-controls.com**. Carries a wide variety of beneficial pest-control critters. Informative website.

Nature's Control

P.O. Box 35, Medford, OR 97501, 541-899-8318, email: **bugsnc@teleport.com**. Carries a wide variety of beneficial critters for the greenhouse, and hydroponic supplies. Informative catalog.

Peaceful Valley Farm Supply

P.O. Box 2209, Grass Valley, CA 95945, 888-784-1722, **www.groworganic.com**. This is an extensive catalog of seeds, supplies, beneficial insects, pest-control products, and more.

Planet Natural

1612 Gold Avenue, Bozeman, MT 59715, 800-289-6656, **www.planetnatural.com**. Carries beneficial critters and a wide variety of natural-based gardening products.

Rincon-Vitova Insectaries, Inc.

P.O. Box 1555, Ventura, CA 93002-1555, 800-248-2847, **www.rinconvitova.com**. Carries a wide variety of pest-control supplies and beneficial critters. Has a large selection and has been in the business longer than most.

We Gro-Rite

1482 Fairview Road, Andrews, NC 28901, **http://WeGroRite.com**. These folks specialize in plants and growing systems for strawberry production in greenhouses, but they also carry some beneficial insects and provide consulting services on pest control. Especially helpful for greenhouse strawberry growers.

Worm's Way–Urban Farming Source Book™

7850 North Highway 37, Bloomington, IN 47404, 800-274-9676, **http://wormsway.com**. Carries beneficial critters for the home-greenhouse gardener, as well as hydroponic and lighting supplies, books, and other greenhouse / indoor gardening materials.

MATERIAL PROPERTIES

GLAZING, THERMAL STORAGE, AND WATER FOR SOLAR HEATING

Many of the materials you'll use in a greenhouse have different, noteworthy characteristics. This section might come in handy when you are working with, retrofitting, or constructing greenhouses.

R-VALUES FOR ENERGY CONSERVATION

The "R-value" of a material refers to its energy conserving (or insulating) properties. The R-value rates the resistance a material has to heat penetration. Or, in other words, how well the material conserves, or "contains," heat in a structure through its insulating abilities, which is critical to a properly functioning greenhouse. The higher the R-value of the material, the more energy-conserving it is, or the better able it is to contain heat in a structure. The R-values in the following table correspond to "real world" outdoor situations. R-values of specific brand name products may vary from these figures. Check a product's R-value rating when you are evaluating glazing material, along with the other important attributes of glazing and insulating materials that are discussed in Chapter 1, "The Greenhouse or Sunspace Environment."

Note: Some products are sold with a "U-value" rating, versus an R-value rating. Where the R-value is a rating of a material's insulating abilities, the U-value rating measures a material's ability to conduct heat *through* the material. The higher the U-value, the poorer a material is at conserving heat in a structure.

To convert the U-value to R-value: 1 divided by the U-value equals the R-value. For example: Fiberglass has a U-value rating of 1.20. To find the R-value, divide one by 1.20, which is 0.83. The R-value is thus 0.83.

R-VALUES FOR ENERGY CONSERVATION

Polycarbonate 16 mm triple wall	R = 2.5
Polycarbonate 8 mm triple wall	R = 2.0–2.1
Polycarbonate 8 mm double wall	R = 1.6
Acrylic double wall	R = 1.82
Glass double layer	R = 1.5–2.0
Glass double layer low-e	R = 2.5
Glass triple layer $1/4$-inch (0.6 cm) space	R = 2.13
Fiberglass glazing-panel, single layer	R = 0.83
Polyethylene Double 5 mil film	R = 1.5
Polyethylene Double 6 mil film	R = 1.7
Polyethylene single film	R = 0.87
6 inches (15 cm) of fiberglass bat insulation in the wall	R = 19.0
Polystyrene (styrofoam) 1 inch (2.5 cm) thick	R = 4.0

THERMAL STORAGE VALUES

These values illustrate why water is a preferred storage medium for retaining the heat in greenhouses, and especially in solar greenhouses. The higher the number, the better the material will store heat. Heat storage is also a function of how much of the material you have in the greenhouse.

Material	Value BTU/Sq. Ft./Degrees F
Adobe	20
Brick	24
Concrete	35
Earth	20
Sand	22
Steel	59
Stone	35
Water	**63**
Wood	10.6

SUGGESTED GALLONS OF WATER (THERMAL-MASS)
TO ASSIST WITH SOLAR HEATING OF GREENHOUSES

Attached greenhouse:

2.5 gallons (9.46 liters) per square ft. (0.093 sq. m) glazing area for cool climates
(4-month winters)

2 gallons (7.57 liters) per square ft. (0.093 sq. m) glazing area for temperate climates
(3-month winters)

1 gallon (3.78 liters) per square ft. (0.093 sq. m) glazing area for warmer climates
(2-month winters)

Freestanding greenhouse:

3 gallons (11.35 liters) per square ft. (0.093 sq. m) glazing area for cool climates
(4-month winters)

2.5 gallons (9.46 liters) per square ft. (0.093 sq. m) glazing area for temperate climates
(3-month winters)

2 gallons (7.57 liters) per square ft. (0.093 sq. m) glazing area for warmer climates
(2-month winters)

Note: The "winters" designated here mean that most nights during the span of months
will dip well below freezing—24°F (-5°C) or lower.

MAIL-ORDER PLANTS

I have listed catalogs of note either because they carry a particular variety listed in the book or because they are just good catalogs to have. I am sure many other catalogs offer quality plants suitable for greenhouses, but to list them all would fill many pages. This list is a good start. Mailing and website addresses are subject to changes over time. Some companies may charge for their catalog. For updates of these addresses, check **www.greenhousegarden.com.**

Abbey Garden
P.O. Box 2249, La Habra, CA 90632-2249, 562-905-3520, **http://vvv.com/~amdigest/ abbeygdn.htm.** Carries many cacti and succulents, living stones, forest cacti, air plants *(Tillandsia)*, and more.

Aloha Tropicals
1247 Browning Court, Vista, CA 92083, 760-941-0920, **http://alohatropicals.com.** Carries a wide assortment of banana corms and other tropical and subtropical plants.

Ann Mann's
Aroids, Bromeliads, Hoyas, Orchids, and Supplies, 9045 Ron-den Lane, Windermere, FL 34786-8328, 407-876-2625, **www.cfog.com.** As the name implies, this company carries a selection of aroids, bromeliads, hoyas, orchids, baskets, foggers for small greenhouses (Husky-fiber® microfogger), fertilizers, organic potting mediums, and more.

Cactus King Nursery
1534 Crest Drive, Encinitas, CA 92024-5209, 760-753-6939, **http://cactusking.com.** Carries a wide selection of cacti and succulents.

Dixondale Farms
P.O. 127, Carrizo Springs, TX 78834, **www.dixondalefarms.com.** Carries onion plants and onion-growing supplies and information.

Edible Landscaping

P.O. Box 77, Afton, VA 22920, 800-524-4156, **www.eat-it.com**. Carries citrus, figs, strawberries, and more.

Exotica

P.O. Box 160, Vista, CA 92083, 760-724-9093, **www.bonusweb.com/exotica**. Carries a wide selection of plants and rare tropical fruit trees from around the world, including mango, lychee, guava, cherimoya, sapote, papaya, banana, persimmon, jujube, star fruit, bamboo, palm, and others.

Fig Tree Nursery (The)

Box 124, Gulf Hammock, FL 32639, 904-486-2930. Specializes in fig trees but also carries some other plants.

Forestfarm

990 Tetherow Road, Williams, OR 97544-9599, 541-846-7269, **www.forestfarm.com**. Offers a wide variety of seeds and plants.

Garden of Delights

14560 S.W. 14th Street, Davie, FL 33325, 954-370-9004 (800-741-3103 for automated orders), **www.gardenofdelights.com**. Specializes in palms, rare tropical and subtropical fruit trees, and more.

Garden.com

www.garden.com, carries a wide variety of tools, fertilizer, books, and other supplies, along with seeds, plants, and more. This is solely an Internet site.

Glasshouse Works

P.O. Box 97, Stewart, OH 45778, 800-837-2142, **www.glasshouseworks.com**. Contains one of the largest listings of ornamental greenhouse plants. You will also find a large selection of herbs, bonsai, coleus, begonias, cacti, succulents, ferns, and many other foliage and flowering houseplants. They also carry interesting collections.

Hartmann's Plantation, Inc.

P.O. Box E, 310 60th Street, Grand Junction, MI 49063-0100, 616-253-4281, **www.hartmanns plantcompany.com**. Carries unique, intriguing, and unusual plants, along with more common fruiting plants.

Jersey Asparagus Farms

105 Porchtown Road, Pittsgrove, NJ 08318, 800-499-0013, **www.jerseyasparagus.com**. Carries day-neutral strawberries.

K & L Cactus and Succulent Nursery

9500 Brook Ranch Road East, Ione, CA 95640-9417, 209-274-0364. Carries a wide selection of cacti and succulents.

Kartuz Greenhouses

P.O. Box 790, 1408 Sunset Drive, Vista, CA 92085-0790, 760-941-3613. Carries a great selection of begonias as well as numerous other flowering plants for the greenhouse.

Logee's Greenhouses

141 North Street, Danielson, CT 06239, 888-330-8038, www.logees.com. Offers a wide selection of greenhouse ornamentals and herbs; beautiful color photos in their catalog.

Lychee Woods

721 S.E. Ninth Street, Fort Lauderdale, FL 33316-1209, 954-728-8089, www.safari.net/~lychee. Carries a wide selection of tropical and subtropical edible trees and plants.

Mellinger's Nursery

2310 W. South Range Road, North Lima, OH 44452-9731, 800-321-7444, www.mellingers.com. Carries a wide assortment of plants, seeds, and supplies.

Nichol's Garden Nursery

1190 North Pacific Highway, Albany, OR 97321-4580, 541-928-9280, www.gardennursery.com. Carries a wide variety of herb plants. Also carries vegetables, home-brewing supplies, everlastings, dried flower supplies, and more.

Nor'East Miniature Roses

P.O. Box 307, Rowley, MA 01960, 800-662-9669, www.noreast-miniroses.com. Sells a wide variety of miniature roses.

Nourse Farms

41 River Road, South Deerfield, MA 01373, 413-665-2658, www.noursefarms.com. Carries a good selection of strawberries, including day-neutral types.

Pacific Tree Farms

4301 Lynwood Drive, Chula Vista, CA 91910, 619-422-2400, www.kyburg.com/ptf/Default/htm. Carries a nice variety of tropical and subtropical plants and trees.

Peaceful Valley Farm Supply

P.O. Box 2209, Grass Valley, CA 95945, 888-784-1722, www.groworganic.com. This is an extensive catalog of seeds, supplies, beneficial insects, pest-control products, and more.

Peter Pauls Nurseries

4665 Chapin Road, Canandaigua, NY 14424-8713, 716-394-7397, **www.peterpauls.com**. This is one of the best sources for carnivorous plants and seeds as well as supplies for growing them.

Pineapple Place

Bromeliad Specialists, 3961 Markham Woods Road, Longwood, FL 32779, 407-333-0445. Carries a wide variety of bromeliads and supplies for growing them.

Plumeria People

910 Leander Drive, Leander, TX 78641, 512-259-0807, email: **leuzinger@jumpnet.com**. Large selection of named plumeria. Specializes in greenhouse plumeria and other tropical and subtropical plants.

Raintree Nursery

391 Butts Road, Morton, WA 98356, 360-496-6400, **www.raintreenursery.com**. Carries berries, fruits, nut trees, citrus, figs, and more.

Richters Herb Catalogue

Goodwood, Ontario, Canada L0C 1A0, 905-640-6677, **www.richters.com**. Among the most extensive listings of herb plants and seeds anywhere. The description is incredible. Carries both medicinal and culinary plants. The company adjusts for the difference in value of currency between Canada and the United States.

Shady Hill Gardens

821 Walnut Street, Batavia, IL 60510-2999, 630-879-5665, **www.shadyhill.com**. Carries one of the most extensive selections of geranium plants.

Stokes Tropicals

P.O. Box 9868, New Iberia, LA 70562-9868, 800-624-9706, **www.stokestropicals.com**. Not to be confused with Stokes Seeds, these folks stick to tropicals, including a great banana selection, plumerias, gingers, heliconias, and more. Colorful catalog.

Teas Nursery Co., Inc.

P.O. Box 1603, Bellaire, TX 77402-1603, 800-446-7723, **www.teasnursery.com**. Carries many tropical plants, including orchids, tillandsias, and hibiscus, along with growing supplies and more.

Tropiflora

3530 Tallevast Road, Sarasota, FL 34243, 800-613-7520, **www.tropiflora.com**. Carries an extensive list of bromeliads, tillandsias, orchids, and succulents. Excellent catalog with great enthusiasm. There is also a great catalog supplement called the "Cargo Report," which describes the company's latest adventures in collecting exotic species.

Van Bourgondien, K., & Sons

245 Route 145, P.O. Box 1000, Babylon, NY 11702-9004, 800-622-9997, www.dutch bulbs.com.

We Gro-Rite

1482 Fairview Road, Andrews, NC 28901, 828-321-4371, http://www.wegrorite.com. These folks specialize in plants and growing systems for strawberry production in greenhouses. They also carry some beneficial insects. Consulting services are available for pest control and larger strawberries.

Well-Sweep Herb Farm, Inc.

205 Mt. Bethel Road, Port Murray, NJ 07865, 908-852-5390. Has a very large selection of herb seeds, plants, and some supplies.

MAIL-ORDER SEEDS

There are hundreds of wonderful seed catalogs out there. I have listed just a few of note either because they carry a particular variety listed in the book or because they are just good catalogs to have. I'm sure many other catalogs offer quality seeds suitable for greenhouses but listing them all would fill many pages. This list is a good start. Mailing and website addresses are subject to changes over time. Some companies may charge for their catalog. For updates and additions to this list, check **www.greenhousegarden.com**.

Burpee Seed Company

300 Park Avenue, Warminster, PA 18991, 800-888-1447, **www.burpee.com**. Carries a wide variety of seeds, plants, and supplies.

Colorlink

622 Town Road, West Chicago, IL 60185-2698, 800-686-7380. This is operated by the Ball Seed Company, which usually services only big growers. The Colorlink catalog's motto is "serving small growers nationwide." This is a good source of varieties that generally are available only in large quantities. They are still commercial-greenhouse oriented (mainly servicing small commercial operations) but could be a good source for a small bedding plant operation or even a serious hobbyist.

Cook's Garden (The)

P.O. Box 5010, Hodges, SC 29653, 800-457-9703, **www.cooksgarden.com**. Sells a variety of seeds, herbs, flowers, and supplies.

Fragrant Path (The)

P.O. Box 328, Ft. Calhoun, NE 68023 (no phone listing). Carries seeds of fragrant and old-fashioned plants of many types.

Garden City Seeds

778 Highway 93 North, Hamilton, MT 59840, 406-961-4837, www.gardencityseeds.com. Carries a wide variety of vegetable and herb seeds as well as supplies. Catalog is very instructional and informative.

Garden.com

www.garden.com. Carries a wide variety of tools, fertilizer, books, and supplies, along with seeds, plants, and more. This is solely an Internet site.

Gourmet Gardener (The)

8650 College Boulevard, Overland Park, KS 66210, 913-345-0490, www.gourmet gardener.com. Carries a good selection of herb, vegetable, and edible-flower seeds, and more, from around the world.

Harris Seeds

60 Saginaw Drive, P.O. Box 22960, Rochester, NY 14692-2960, 800-514-4441, www.harrisseeds.com. Carries a wide variety of flower and vegetable seeds and some plants. Also sells greenhouses and growing supplies.

Johnny's Selected Seeds

Foss Hill Road, Albion, ME 04910, 207-437-4301, www.johnnyseeds.com. Carries a wide variety of vegetable, herb, and flower seeds as well as supplies. Lists some varieties adapted to greenhouse culture. Informative catalog.

Mountain Valley Growers

38325 Pepperweed Road, Squaw Valley, CA 93675, 209-338-2775, www.mountain valleygrowers.com. Organic herb and perennial seeds.

Nichol's Garden Nursery

1190 North Pacific Highway, Albany, OR 97321-4580, 541-928-9280, www.garden nursery.com. Carries a wide variety of herb, vegetable, and flower seeds. Also carries plants, home-brewing supplies, everlastings, dried flower supplies, and more.

Park Seed

1 Parkton Avenue, Greenwood, SC 29647-0001, 800-845-3369, www.parkseed.com. Carries an extensive listing of seeds, plants, and supplies.

Peaceful Valley Farm Supply

P.O. Box 2209, Grass Valley, CA 95945, 888-784-1722, www.groworganic.com. Sells a variety of fertilizers, gardening equipment, natural pest controls, seeds, and more.

Pepper Gal (The)

P.O. Box 23006, Ft. Lauderdale, FL 33307-3006, 954-537-5540. A small operation offering many, many pepper varieties.

Pinetree Garden Seeds

Box 300, New Gloucester, ME 04260, 207-926-3400, www.superseeds.com. Carries a wide selection of flower, vegetable, and herb seeds and plants. Also carries many supplies. Very informative catalog.

Redwood Seed Company

P.O. Box 361, Redwood City, CA 94064, 650-325-7333, **www.ecoseeds.com**. Carries "traditional," unique, and unusual seeds. Very interesting selection.

Richters Herb Catalog

Goodwood, Ontario, Canada L0C 1A0, 905-640-6677, **www.richters.com**. This is among the most extensive listings of herb plants and seeds anywhere. The description is incredible. Carries both medicinal and culinary plants. The company adjusts for the difference in value of currency between Canada and the United States.

Ronniger's Seed & Potato Company

Star Route, Moyie Springs, ID 83485, 208-267-7938. A good source for garlic.

SBE Seeds

3421 Bream Street, Gautier, MS 39553, 800-336-2064, **www.seedman.com**. Primarily an Internet catalog, featuring rare, exotic seeds from around the world, and more.

Seed Savers Exchange

3076 North Winn Road, Decorah, IA 52101, 319-382-5990. This organization works to preserve heirloom seeds and is responsible for saving many rare vegetable varieties from extinction. Great catalog and exchange program. This is a fine source, especially if you have an interest in heirloom varieties.

Seeds of Change

P.O. Box 15700, Santa Fe, NM 87506-5700, 888-762-7333, **www.seedsofchange.com**. Carries many unique and heirloom vegetables, flowers, and herbs, and also supplies. It is a fun and colorful catalog to peruse.

Seeds of Distinction

P.O. Box 86, Station A, Etobicoke (Toronto), Ontario, Canada, M9C 4V2, 416-255-3060, **www.seedsofdistinction.com**. Carries a wide variety of perennial and annual ornamental seeds. Has special pricing for U.S. purchasers.

Shepherd's Garden Seeds

30 Irene Street, Torrington, CT 06790-6658, 800-444-6910, www.shepherdseeds.com. Carries a wide variety of flower, vegetable, and herb seeds. Also some supplies.

Southern Exposure Seed Exchange

P.O. Box 170, Earlysville, VA 22936, 804-973-4703, www.southernexposure.com. Carries a wide selection of varieties with heritage, flavor, disease resistance, or other qualities of interest to gardeners. Also carries many supplies. I have found many varieties that are good for greenhouse growing.

Stokes Seeds, Inc.

Box 548, Buffalo, NY 14240-0548, 800-396-9238, www.stokeseeds.com. One of my favorite seed sources because their listing is extensive and their descriptions are excellent. Carries vegetable and flower seeds as well as some supplies. Look for the page dedicated to greenhouse tomatoes, cucumbers, and lettuce.

Territorial Seed Company

P.O. Box 157, 20 Palmer Avenue, Cottage Grove, OR 97424, 541-942-9547, www.territorial-seed. com. Carries a wide variety of seeds, plants, and supplies. Informative catalog. Among the few companies that carry greenhouse forcing cucumbers. Geared toward the Northwestern vegetable gardener but carries many things of interest to greenhouse gardeners as well. Has a wide selection of lettuce and greens, flowers, and more.

Thompson & Morgan

P.O. Box 1308, Jackson, NJ 08527, 800-274-7333, www.thompson-morgan.com. Carries a wide variety of vegetable and flower seeds (many are from Europe) and supplies.

Tomato Growers Supply Company

P.O. Box 2237, Fort Myers, FL 33902, 888-478-7333, www.tomatogrowers.com. More than 300 tomato varieties and 100 peppers, many of which are well-suited to greenhouse culture.

Totally Tomatoes

P.O. Box 1626, Augusta, GA 30903-1626, 803-663-0016. Comprehensive offering of both tomatoes and peppers.

Twilley Seed Company

121 Gary Road, Hodges, SC 29653, 800-622-7333, www.twilleyseed.com. Carries a wide selection of vegetables and flowers for small growers and homeowners.

Vermont Bean Seed Company

Garden Lane, Fair Haven, VT 05743, 802-265-4212. Carries an extensive listing of beans, along with many other vegetables, flowers, and supplies.

Veseys Seeds Ltd.

York, Prince Edward Island, Canada C0A 1P0, 800-363-7333, www.veseys.com. Carries a wide variety of vegetable and flower seeds and supplies. Specializes in short-season varieties.

Well-Sweep Herb Farm, Inc.

205 Mt. Bethel Road, Port Murray, NJ 07865, 908-852-5390. Has a very large selection of herb seeds and plants and carries some supplies.

Mail-Order Supplies

Almost every seed or plant catalog carries a few supplies, but these catalogs specialize in a good selection of things you may need in a greenhouse. Some companies may charge for their catalog. For updates and additions to this list, check **www.greenhousegarden.com.**

A Gardener's Resource

P.O. Box 85072, Tucson, AZ 85754, 520-792-8023, **www.greenhousesupplies.com.** Greenhouse supplies, greenhouses, and more.

A. M. Leonard, Inc.

6665 Spiker Road, Piqua, OH 45456, 800-543-8955. Specializes in tools; also carries grafting supplies, shade cloth, and glazing materials. Has a good price for the small Polyspray II sprayer.

Aarons Creek Farms

380 Greenhouse Drive, Buffalo Junction, VA 24529, 800-487-8502, **www.acfpl.com.** Sells hobby greenhouses and strawberry plants for greenhouse production.

Alsto Company (The)

P.O. Box 1267, Galesburg, IL 61401, 800-447-0048. Carries furniture, potting benches, tools, plant supports, watering supplies, pots, and composters.

Alternative Garden Supply, Inc.

P.O. Box 662, Cary IL 60013, 800-444-2837, **www.alternativegarden.com.** Carries hydroponic and lighting supplies, pest controls, and more.

Ann Mann's

Aroids, Bromeliads, Hoyas, Orchids, and Supplies, 9045 Ron-den Lane, Windermere, FL 34786-8328, 407-876-2625, **www.cfog.com.** As the name implies, this company carries a selection of aroids, bromeliads, hoyas, orchids, baskets, foggers for small greenhouses, fertilizers, and specialized potting mediums.

Arbico

P.O. Box 4247 CRB, Tucson, AZ 85738, 800-827-2847, **www.arbico.com**. Known mostly for beneficial insects but also has a selection of fertilizers, pest traps, and sustainable agricultural supplies.

Biologic Technologies

P.O. Box 700909, San Jose, CA 95170-0909, 408-873-1619, **www.biologictech.com**. Sells a variety of grow lights, including a unique microwave-powered light.

Cascade Greenhouse Supply

214 21st S.E., Auburn, WA 98002, 800-647-0606. **www.cascadegreenhouse.com**. Sells greenhouses and growing supplies. Nice catalog.

Charley's Greenhouses & Indoor Supplies

17979 State Route 536, Mt. Vernon, WA 98273, 800-322-4707, **www.charleysgreen house.com**. One of the most complete sources of supplies and accessories. Large selection of quality greenhouses and other products specifically for the home greenhouse. Great informative and colorful catalog. Great folks!

Co-Ex Corporation

41 Hammer Mill Road, Rocky Hill, CT 06067, 800-888-5364, **www.horticulture.com/coex**. Manufactures polycarbonate glazings. A wholesaler, but they are informative and helpful when shopping for glazing.

CropKing, Inc.

5050 Greenwich Road, Seville, OH 44273, 330-769-2002, **www.cropking.com**. Carries indoor hydroponic kits, lights, growing mediums, books, and more for large and small growers.

Dyna-Gro Corporation

1065 S. Broadway, San Pablo, CA 94806, 800-396-2476. Carries a number of general fertilizers, specialty fertilizers, and growth stimulants, as well as hydroponic fertilizer and supplies. Also carries the silicon fertilizer mentioned in Chapter 10 to reduce powdery mildew.

E. C. Geiger, Inc.

Box 285, Rt. 63, Harleysville, PA 19438-0332, 800-4GEIGER. Carries greenhouse supplies primarily for larger growers.

Florist Products, Inc.

P.O. Box 3190, Barrington, IL 60011, 800-828-2242 (800-777-2242 in Illinois). Carries a wide variety of greenhouse supplies.

Four Seasons Sunrooms

5005 Veteran Memorial Highway, Holbrook, NY 11741, 800-368-7732, **www.four-seasons-sunrooms.com**. Sells greenhouse kits. Has many local dealerships.

Garden Under Glass

40 Huron Road, Bellerose, NY 11001, 516-775-0866, **www.gardenunderglass.com**. Sells greenhouse kits and supplies.

Garden.com

www.garden.com. Carries a wide variety of tools, fertilizers, books, and other supplies, along with seeds, plants and more. This is solely an Internet site.

Gardener's Supply Company

128 Intervale Road, Burlington, VT 05401-2850, 800-863-1700, **www.gardeners.com**. Carries greenhouses, tools, growing supplies, and more.

Gempler's

100 Countryside Drive, P.O. Box 270, Belleville, WI 53508, 800-382-8473, **www.gemplers.com**. Carries gardening tools, clothing, protective equipment, pest management supplies, and more

Glass Structures Limited

P.O. Box 3222, 296 Irving Street, Framingham MA 01705-3222, 508-877-6457, **http://glass structures.com**. Sells greenhouse kits and Lord & Burnham greenhouse parts, supplies, and more.

Gothic Arch Greenhouses

P.O. Box 1564 (ZN), Mobile, AL 36633-1564, 334-432-7529, **www.zebra.net/~gothic**. Sells greenhouse kits and supplies.

Greenfire

2527A Highway 32 West, Chico CA 95973, 800-859-8307, **www.greenfire.net**. These folks carry quality organic hydroponic fertilizer supplies, lighting materials, a variety of pest-control materials, growing mediums, and more.

Harmony Farm Supply

3244 Gravenstein Highway, North Sebastol, CA 95472, 707-823-9125, **www.harmonyfarm.com**. Carries a wide variety of growing supplies, pest controls, and beneficial insects.

Hobby Gardens

P.O. Box 83, Grand Isle, VT 05458, 802-372-4041, **www.hobbygardens.com**. Sells greenhouse kits and supplies.

Home Harvest®

3712 Eastern Avenue, Baltimore, MD 21224, 800-348-4769. An Internet-only catalog located at **www.homeharvest.com**. They sell books, fertilizers, pest controls, beneficial insects, lighting systems, hydroponic systems, greenhouse accessories, and more.

Hoop House Sructures

1358 Route 28, South Yarmouth, MA 02664, 800-760-5192, **www.hoophouse.com**. Sells greenhouse kits and more.

Hummerts Seed Co.

4510 Earth City Expressway, Earth City, MO 63045, 800-325-3055, **www.hummert.com**. Carries a wide variety of seeds, growing supplies, and more. Has a wholesale division for larger growers and a division for smaller, hobby-greenhouse gardeners.

Hydrofarm

755 Southpoint Boulevard, Petaluma, CA 94954, 800-634-9990, **www.hydrofarm.com**. Specializes in hydroponic supplies and equipment.

Hydro-Gardens, Inc.

P.O. Box 9707, Colorado Springs, CO 80932, 800-634-6362, **www.hydro-gardens.com**. Carries a complete collection of supplies for growing; specializes in hydroponic vegetable production and sells to commercial growers as well as hobbyists. Also carries seeds and pest-control supplies.

Jacobs Greenhouse Mfg. Ltd.

371 Talbot Road, Delhi, Ontario, Canada N4B 2A1, **www.jacobsgreenhouse.com**. Sells greenhouse kits and more.

Janco Greenhouses

93990 Davis Avenue, Laurel, MD 20723, 800-323-6933, **www.jancoinc.com**. Sells greenhouse kits, supplies, and more.

Jaybird Manufacturing, Inc.

2595-B Clyde Avenue, State College, PA 18601, 814-235-1807, **www.jaybird-mfg.com**. Carries a variety of foggers for creating humidity.

Let's Get Growing

1900 Commercial Way, Santa Cruz, CA 95065, 800-408-1868, **www.letsgetgrowing.com**. Catalog is oriented toward children and gardening curriculum and supplies.

Mellinger's

2310 W. South Range Road, North Lima, OH 44452-9731, 800-321-7444, **www. mellingers.com**. Carries a wide variety of seeds, plants, herbs, tools, supplies, fertilizers, pots, and more.

North Country Creative Structures

Route 197, RD# 1 Box 1060B, Argyle, NY 12809, 800-833-2300, **www.sunroomliving.com**. Sells greenhouse kits, supplies, and more.

Northern Greenhouse Sales

Box 42, Neche, ND 58265, 204-327-5540. These folks specialize in woven polyethylene glazing and also carry greenhouse building supplies and more.

Peaceful Valley Farm Supply

P.O. Box 2209, Grass Valley, CA 95945, 888-784-1722, **www.groworganic.com**. Sells a variety of fertilizers, gardening equipment, natural pest controls, seeds, and more.

Planet Natural

1612 Gold Avenue, Bozeman, MT 59715, 800-289-6656, **www.planetnatural.com**. Carries a variety of gardening and naturally based products.

Polygal

P.O. Box 1567, Janesville, WI 53547, 800-537-0095, **www.polygal.com**. Manufactures polycarbonate glazings. They are a wholesaler, but they are informative and helpful when shopping for a glazing.

Solar Components Corp.

121 Valley Street, Manchester, NH 03103, 603-668-8186, **www.solar-components.com**. Specialize in glazing, greenhouse kits, and environmental control systems for greenhouses and sunrooms. Also one of the few companies (if not the only one) to carry fiberglass water containers (tubes) for thermal mass and aquaculture.

SPS Corporation

P.O. Box 20909, San Jose, CA 95160, 800-994-5626, **http://spscorp.com**. Manufacturer of polycarbonate glazing materials. They are a wholesaler, but they are informative and helpful when shopping for glazings.

Standup Gardens

1630 Route 33, Greenland, NH 03840, 603-427-6000, **www.standupgardens.com**. Sells specialized portable gardening beds, some including built-in lighting and irrigation systems.

Sturdi-built Greenhouses

11304 S.W. Boones Ferry Road, Portland OR 97219, 800-334-4115, **www.sturdi-built.com**. Sells greenhouse kits and supplies.

Sundance Supply

800-776-2534, at www.sundancesupply.com. Sells polycarbonate, fans, shade cloth, heating equipment, and misting equipment for build-it-yourself greenhouses, sunrooms, and solariums. Extensive how-to information on their website. An informative, Internet-only catalog with great, built-in, online glazing needs' calculators.

Sunglo

214 21st S.E., Auburn, WA 98002, 800-647-0606, **www.sunglogreenhouses.com**. Hobby greenhouse manufacturer.

Sunglo East Greenhouses

12763 Bradwell Road, Herndon, VA 20171, 800-941-5166, **www.sungloeast.com**. Sells greenhouse kits, supplies and more.

Sunshine GardenHouse

P.O. Box 2068, Longview, WA 98632-8190, 888-272-9333, **www.gardenhouse.com**. Sells greenhouse kits, growing supplies and more.

Teas Nursery Co., Inc.

Orchid and Supply Catalog, P.O. Box 1603, Bellaire, TX 77402-1603, 800-446-7723, **www.teasnursery.com**. Offers tropical plants, growing supplies, equipment, and more.

Texas Greenhouse Company

2524 White Settlement Road, Fort Worth, TX 76107, 800-227-5447, **www.texas greenhouse.com**. Sells greenhouse kits, accessories, and more.

Turner Greenhouses

P.O. Box 1260, Highway 117 South, Goldsboro, NC 27533-1260, 800-672-4770, **www.turnergreenhouses.com**. Sells greenhouse kits, growing supplies, and more.

Ventura Sunrooms

8274 Quincy Street, Ventura, CA 93004, 800-747-3324, **www.sunroom.com**. Sells greenhouse kits and supplies.

We Gro Rite

1482 Fairview Road, Andrews, NC, 28901, 828-321-4371, **www.wegrorite.com**. These folks specialize in plants and growing systems for strawberry production in greenhouses, but they also carry some beneficial insects and provide consulting services for pest control. Especially helpful for greenhouse strawberry growers.

Worm's Way

Urban Farming Source Book™, 7850 North Highway 37, Bloomington, IN 47404, 800-274-9676, **http://wormsway.com**. Carries hydroponic supplies, lighting, books, and other greenhouse and indoor gardening supplies.

Zomeworks

P.O. Box 25805, Albuquerque, NM 87125, 800-279-6342 or 505-242-5354, **www.zome works.com**. This company carries the only solar water-heating system that I know of designed for greenhouses. It's called Big Fin.

APPENDIX 8

RECORD KEEPING

To help make record-keeping easier, it's useful to know when and where each plant is growing. To achieve this, number each bed, part of bed, or growing area. It may help to make a map of the greenhouse and then determine a logical way to number each area. These sample forms may be a helpful guide or good place to start.

GENERIC RECORD

This is one way to track general plant progress.

Plant Name or Variety	~~Date Sown~~ *Clone*	Date Transplanted	Date Harvested	Comments
Clamitas Purple -17	6-24-05			
Bleeding heart ~10	6-24-05			
Rose ~18	6-24 05			
Rose of sharon ~8	6-27-05			

Plant Name or Variety	Date Sown	Date Transplanted	Date Harvested	Comments

PLANTING RECORD

Use this record for keeping track of planting and harvest dates, schedules, and plant varieties.

Date Planted / Sown	Maturity / Date Harvested	Location	Plant	Genus / Species	Variety	Comments

Date Planted/Sown	Maturity/Date Harvested	Location	Plant	Genus / Species	Variety	Comments

MONITORING PESTS AND DISEASES

Keeping track of pests and diseases in your greenhouse is the first and most important step to controlling them. Survey plants in all areas of your greenhouse for bugs and disease regularly, but randomly. A hand lens or magnifying glass comes in handy for spotting microscopic critters, such as spider mites, which are virtually impossible to spot with the naked eye. Pay special attention to the tips and undersides of plant leaves. Note conditions every few days and watch for trends or progressions in them. Refer to Chapter 10, "When Things Go Wrong," for more information on pest control.

Date	Location	Plant	Pest / Disease Observed	Level of Infestation	Control Method(s)	Effects of Control	Comments

Date	Location	Plant	Pest / Disease Observed	Level of Infestation	Control Method(s)	Effects of Control	Comments

BIBLIOGRAPHY AND FURTHER READING AND RESOURCES

Barash, Cathy Wilkinson, *Edible Flowers: From Garden to Palate*, Golden, CO: Fulcrum Publishing, 1999.

Barton, Barbara J., *Gardening by Mail: A Source Book*, Boston: Mariner Books / Houghton-Mifflin, Co., 1997.

Berry, Wendell, *Gift of Good Land*, San Francisco: North Point Press, 1981.

Greenhouse Grower Magazine, 37841 Euclid Avenue, Willoughby, OH 44094, 216-942-2000. Trade magazine for commercial greenhouse operators.

Grower Talks Magazine, P.O. Box 532, Geneva, IL 60134, 630-208-9080. Trade magazine for commercial greenhouse operators.

The Growing Edge Magazine, 215 S.W. 2nd, Corvallis, OR 97333, 800-888-6785, **www.growingedge.com**. A magazine devoted to greenhouse growers (primarily hydroponic-based), and other articles of interest to hobbyists.

Harris, Linda D., *Growing Seeds! Starting From Scratch*, Golden, CO: Fulcrum Publishing, 1999.

Jaworski, Henry, *Orchids Simplified,* Boston: Houghton-Mifflin,1998.

Martin, Tovah, *The Essence of Paradise: Fragrant Plants for Indoor Gardens,* Boston: Little Brown & Company, 1991.

Overy, Angela, *Sex in Your Garden*, Golden, CO: Fulcrum Publishing, 1999.

Schoser, Gustav, *Orchid Growing Basics*, New York: Sterling Publishing Co., 1993.

Shapiro, Andrew M., *The Homeowner's Complete Handbook for Add-On Solar Greenhouses and Sunspaces: Planning, Design, Construction*, Emmaus, PA: Rodale Press, 1985 (out of print).

Yanda, Bill, and Rick Fisher, *The Food and Heat-Producing Solar Greenhouse: Design, Construction, Operation*, Santa Fe, NM: John Muir Press, 1976 (out of print).

INDEX

Boldface numbers indicate pages with illustrations.

ABOUT THE AUTHOR

SHANE SMITH is a founder and the director of the Cheyenne Botanic Gardens in Cheyenne, Wyoming. There he has developed a "people-oriented" solar greenhouse and public garden that employs seniors, at-risk youths, and disabled individuals, and that serves the larger community in many ways. The Garden has received national acclaim, including awards from Presidents Reagan, Bush, and Clinton. Smith has a degree in horticultural sciences, has served as a Loeb Fellow in Advanced Environmental Studies at the Harvard Graduate School of Design, and is a registered horticultural therapist. Amidst numerous lecture tours, a weekly garden radio program, and writing, Smith still finds time to operate and enjoy his greenhouses at work and at home.